COLLINS
POCKET GUIDE

CORAL REEF FISHES

CARIBBEAN, INDIAN OCEAN AND PACIFIC OCEAN

INCLUDING THE RED SEA

EWALD LIESKE • ROBERT MYERS

HarperCollins*Publishers*

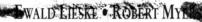

ACKNOWLEDGEMENTS

This book would not have been possible without the generous assistance of colleagues, friends, and our families as well as numerous taxonomists who have labored over the years to bring stability to the field of ichthyology.

Our friend Dieter Eichler provided generous logistic support and services to enable us to observe and photograph fishes in remote places.

Special thanks are due Terry J. Donadson and Gustav Paulay for reviewing much of the manuscript and providing considerable advice and encouragement.

We would also like to thank:

We would also like to thank: Gerald R. Allen (Perth), Myles Archibald (Collins *NaturalHistory*, London), Hans Bath (Pirmasens), David R. Bellwood (Townsville), Eugenie Böhlke (USA), Peter F. Bollen (Jakarta), Yolande Bouchon-Navarro (Guadeloupe), Urs Büchli (Palawan), Bruce Carlson (Hawaii), Kent E. Carpenter (USA), Kendall Clements (Sydney), Patric L. Colin (USA), Bernd Condé (Nancy), Charles E. Dawson (USA), Helmut Debelius (Frankfurt), Alisdair J. Edwards (UK), William N. Eschmeyer (USA), Klaus E. Fiedler (Lübeck), Pierre Fourmanoir (Paris), Malcolm Francis (New Zealand), Edie Frommenwiler (Mollucas), Ronald Fricke (Stuttgart), Michelle Gardette (Praslin), Anthony C. Gill (Australia), Philipp H. Heemstra (South Africa), Walter Heyne (Flensburg), Loky Herlambang (Sulawesi), Axel Horn (Maldives), Tony Hughes (England), Susan L. Jewett (USA), Patricia Kailola (Australia), Jörg Keller (*tauchen*, Hamburg), Helga Kopp (La Digue), Randall Kosaki (USA), Rudie Kuiter (Australia), Helen K. Larson (Australia), Keichi Matsuura (Japan), John E. McCosker (USA), Jack T. Moyer (Japan), Tetsuji Nakabo (Japan), Daniel Pelicier (Mauritius), Theodore W. Pietsch (USA), Richard Pyle (Hawaii), Norman Quinn (Lizard Island, Queensland), Helen R. Randall (Hawaii), Barry C. Russell (Australia), Rolf Schmidt (Sharm El Sheik), Hiroshi Senou (Japan), William F. Smith-Vaniz (USA), Ranjit Sondhi (Kenya), Victor G. Springer (USA), Jürg Straub (Basel), Arnold Suzumoto (USA), Pierre Szalay (Mauritius), James C. Tyler (USA), Michel van Gessel (Holland), Robin S. Waples (USA), Jeffrey T. Williams (USA), Richard C. Winterbottom (Canada), Hans Wirth (Germany).

John E. Randall deserves very special thanks for his assistance over the years with inumerable taxonomic problems, for sharing indispensable unpublished information, and providing reprints and advice.

Finally, without the love, encouragement, and patience of our wives, Christa Lieske and Kathleen J. Dummitt, we would not have been able to complete this task.

HarperCollins*Publishers*
77–85 Fulham Palace Road, London W6 8JB

First published in 1994. Reprinted with correction 1996

02 01 00 99 98 97

10 9 8 7 6 5 4 3

ISBN 0 00 219974 2

Printed and bound in Italy

CONTENTS

Introduction

The Colour Plates

Indo-Pacific

Caribbean Species

Glossary

For further definition of terms used in the species descriptions please also see the Introduction, especially the diagrams of fish anatomy (p. 24) and Coral Reef structure (p. 10)

adipose fin: small fleshy fin between dorsal and tail fins that lacks spines or rays
axil: inner base of pectoral fin
barbel: fleshy sensory appendage on the head, usually on the chin or near mouth
basal: portion (as in fins) closest to the body
benthic: occurs on the sea floor
cryptic: pertaining to concealment by colour or behaviour
demersal: living on the seafloor
detritus: organic matter, primarily plant material and faeces
distal: portion (as in fins) furthest from the body
diurnal: active during the day
ectoparasite: parasite occurring on outer surface of body or within mouth or gill chamber
endemic: found only in a given limited region
epipelagic: the upper 200 m of the open ocean
intertidal: portion of the shoreline or reef that is between the lowest and highest tides
marginal: along the outer edge (e.g. of fins)
nocturnal: active during the night
ocellus: round spot surrounded by a ring of contrasting shade or colour
pelagic: in the open water, well above the bottom
submarginal: immediately basal (q.v.) to the margin (q.v.)
thermocline: zone of rapidly dropping temperature with increased depth

Abbreviations

A = anal fin
Ad. = adult
C = caudal fin
D = dorsal fin
♀ = female
juv. = juvenile
♂ = male
sp. = species
spp. = species (plural)
ssp = subspecies
subad. = subadult
V = ventral fin
var. = variety

Conversions

0.01 m = 1 cm = 10 mm = 0.39 inches
1 kg = 1000 g = 2.205 lbs

INTRODUCTION

Scope of the Book

There are at least 4,000 species of fishes that inhabit coral reefs. Although it would be impossible to include all of them in a useful field guide, the number becomes manageable by excluding most small (under 3 cm) cryptic species, species that spend most of their adult lives buried in sand or deep within the infrastructure of the reef, and species that inhabit primarily non-reef habitats. This guide attempts to include all fishes that are likely to be observed by the non-specialist diving on coral reefs of the Indo-Pacific and western Atlantic oceans to a depth of 60 m. The species accounts are in two parts, the first covering 1,700 Indo-Pacific species, the second covering 350 western Atlantic species. The few species common to both regions are typically included in one section and cross-referenced in the other.

The term "coral reef" is used broadly to include areas adjacent to reefs where corals may occur such as harbors, bays, and rocky tidepools as well as reef-associated habitats such as seagrass beds, sandy expanses, and open rocky bottoms. The term "shorefish" refers to a species that typically inhabits coastal marine waters to a depth of about 200 m. The term "coral reef fish" refers to a species found on coral reefs to a depth of 100 m although it may also occur in other habitats, and "shallow water reef fishes" refers to those found to a depth of 60 m. The metric system is used throughout. The following conversions can be used to obtain the English equivalents: 1 cm = 0.394 in; 1 m = 3.281 ft or 39.37 in; 1 km = 0.6214 miles; 1 kg = 2.205 lbs; °C = 5/9[°F-32]).

Evolution and Zoogeography

Why are there no anemonefishes in the Caribbean? Why do some species of fishes range from the Red Sea to Mexico while others occur only in Hawaii? Why are there more species of reef fishes on the Great Barrier Reef than in the Hawaiian Islands? The answers to these kinds of questions may be found in the field of zoogeography. A direct comparison of the numbers of shorefishes between localities is difficult. In general, diversity decreases as one moves away from continents and large continental shelf islands; decreases with decreasing island size; and decreases as one moves further from the tropics. The distribution of coral reef fishes and other organisms and the resulting species composition and diversity of a given coral reef may be explained by a combination of factors including 1) the evolutionary history of its flora and fauna, 2) the prehistoric distributions and movements of the world's crustal plates, 3) the ability of species to disperse and colonize new areas, 4) the availability of suitable habitats, and 5) the affects of changes in the worlds climate and sea level. The end result is a tropical marine fauna consisting of four zoogeographic regions, each with a distinct assemblage of species. Well developed coral reefs are widespread in only two of these regions: the Indo-Pacific and Western Atlantic. Conditions for coral reef development in the tropical eastern Pacific and tropical eastern Atlantic are generally poor, and were even worse during the ice ages. Consequently there is only one coral atoll and a few isolated areas with true coral reefs in the eastern Pacific and no coral reefs in the eastern Atlantic. These areas are therefore not considered further.

Western Atlantic Region: Well-developed Atlantic coral reefs occur only from the Caribbean north to the Florida keys, Bahamas, and Bermuda (inside back cover). Along the continental shelf of North America, the northernmost coral reefs are the Flower Garden Banks and Florida Middle Grounds at 28°N. A few coral communities exist where there is hard bottom along the Atlantic coast as far north as North Carolina; the northernmost of these are well offshore due to the effects of cold winter coastal currents. To the south, coral reefs occur only along the coast of eastern Brazil. These poorly developed reefs are isolated from the Caribbean by 2,500 km of coastline subject to sedimentation and freshwater intrusion from the Orinoco and Amazon drainage systems.

There are perhaps 1,500 species of tropical western Atlantic shorefishes, about half of which inhabit coral reefs. The reef fish fauna is rather uniformly distributed with the highest diversity in the western Caribbean and the lowest along the North American shelf north of southern Florida, at Bermuda, and in Brazil. The number of endemics, that is species that occur nowhere else, is low in any given area, with the highest rates of endemism in eastern Brazil. About 50 species of shorefishes are trans-Atlantic and a further 21 have their eastern limits at Ascension or St. Helena. During the late summer and early fall, juveniles of many tropical species may occur as far north as Rhode Island, transported by the warm Gulf Stream.

Indo-Pacific Region: The vast Indo-Pacific region stretches from the Red Sea and South Africa to the islands of Polynesia, fully ⅔ of the way around the world (inside front cover). It contains the world's richest shorefish fauna, estimated at over 4,000 species in approximately 179 families. The bulk of these, perhaps 3,000 species, inhabit coral reefs. Most of the families and about 25% of the species have broad distributions that extend from the western Indian Ocean to the central Pacific. The Indo-Pacific can be divided into subregions characterized by a number of broadly distributed endemic taxa. The three primary subregions of the Indo-Pacific are the Indian Ocean, West Pacific, and Pacific Plate. Each of these may contain smaller areas of high endemism such as the Red Sea and Hawaiian Islands. The West Pacific subregion is the richest, closely followed by the Indian Ocean. Each contains nearly all the families (175 and 162, respectively) and over half of the species of Indo-Pacific shorefishes. The term Indo-west Pacific is applied to both subregions collectively which contain all of the families and at least 3,700 species.

The Western Pacific subregion extends from Sumatra to the Mariana, Caroline, and Samoan Islands where it overlaps the Pacific Plate subregion. At least 3,200 species of shorefishes occur here including perhaps 1,000 found nowhere else. The Indo-Australian Archipelago is known as the "center" of diversity with at least 3,000 species of shorefishes. The Philippines, Indonesia, and perhaps Papua-New Guinea each have at least 2,500 species. A dynamic and complex geotectonic history as well as fluctuating sea levels during the Pleistocene glacial periods have caused repeated isolation and remixing of faunas throughout the region. This has promoted speciation and allowed the mixing of Indian Ocean and Pacific faunas. Diversity drops off as one moves away from the center, but remains above 1,000 in all continental areas. Peripheral areas with distinct endemic elements include the Andaman Sea, Taiwan to s. Japan and satellite islands, northwestern Australia, northeastern Australia, the Coral Sea, and Fiji. Where warm currents move poleward coral reefs occur as far north as Miyake-Jima (34°N) and as far south as Lord Howe Island (31.5°S). There are broad zones of mixed tropical and temperate species along the coasts of southern China and southwestern and southeastern Australia and seasonal influxes of juveniles of tropical species well into temperate regions.

As one moves west into the Indian Ocean there is an abrupt decrease in diversity due to the absence of reefs along most of the Burma-India coast. Soft bottoms and massive seasonal intrusions of sediment-laden fresh water inhibit reef development westward to Pakistan, where low winter temperatures prevail. To the south, shorefish diversity is high, above 900 species where reefs are present at Sri Lanka and in the Maldives, higher along the continental shelves of Madagascar and East Africa, but lower at the Chagos and Mascarene Islands (Mauritius and Réunion). The latter is characterized by a significant endemic element. Along the African coast, coral reefs occur as far south as Durban (30°S), and juveniles of many tropical shorefishes are transported seasonally as far as the Cape of Good Hope. To the north, upwelling and soft bottoms inhibit reef development along the Somalia Coast. This as well as lower sea levels during periods of glaciation isolated the Gulf of Aden and Red Sea, allowing many endemics to evolve. The Red Sea has a rich shorefish fauna of about 1,000 species; about 15% are endemic. Endemism is also high from the southeastern Arabian Peninsula to the Arabian Gulf, but diversity is lower. Sandy bottoms, upwelling, and in the Arabian Gulf, extreme winter and summer temperatures inhibit reef development. The Indian Ocean shorefish fauna contains perhaps 2,400 species including several hundred endemics.

The diversity of the western Pacific subregion drops off rather abruptly as one moves out onto the Pacific Plate with only 111 families (62%), containing some 1,312 species, occurring there nonmarginally. Approximately 1,000 of these are wide-ranging species leaving 10 genera and less than 300 species endemic to the Pacific Plate or some portion thereof. The Caroline Islands is the only Pacific Plate archipelago containing more than 1,000 species of shorefishes. The Marshall Islands (817 spp.), and Samoa (915 spp.), are comparable in diversity and there is a gradual decrease as one moves east, or north and south of an axis running from Samoa to the Tuamotus. Most Pacific Plate islands are atolls. The only high islands occur along the western margin of the plate and in eastern Polynesia. The absence of estuarine and other coastal habitats hinders many species from inhabiting the plate or dispersing across the large gaps between high island groups. At the present time there is active dispersal of western Pacific species on to the plate. However, during recent glacial periods, lower sea levels reduced the shallow water habitats of all atolls to a narrow exposed margin while increasing that of most high islands. This reduction in habitat must have adversely affected the ability of many species to disperse in either direction across the plate and further isolated the Polynesian high islands. Nearly all of the single island group endemics occur in archipelagos with high islands and all of the widespread plate endemics are characteristic of exposed seaward reefs. The highest rate of endemism among coral reef animals in the world, about 25% for fishes, is at the extremely isolated Hawaiian Islands, followed by Easter Island (23%), the Marquesas (10%), Lord Howe /Norfolk Islands (7%) and Rapa (6%).

The Coral Reef Environment

The term "coral" as used here refers to reef-building corals of the Order Scleractinia, all of which have limestone skeletons. Coral reefs are the massive structures built by these corals. Reef-building or hermatypic corals require ample sunlight, warm temperatures, fully marine salinity (over 20 ppt), relatively sediment-free water, and a stable hard bottom for attachment. Coral reefs are best developed in shallow tropical seas. In the clearest seas, hermatypic corals become sparse below 60 m, and reach their lower limit at 100 to 120 m. Many stretches of tropical coastline and shallow continental shelves are devoid of coral reefs due to the influences of freshwater and sediment from rivers or cold upwelling currents. Most corals cease growing at temperatures below 20°C, and die at temperatures below 16°C. Where warm prevailing currents flow poleward, coral reefs occur in temperate regions, as far north as Miyake-Jima off southern Japan (34°N) or Bermuda (32°N) in the Atlantic, and as far south as Lord Howe Island off southeast Australia (31.5°S).

Water clarity depends to a large extent on coastal influences and degree of circulation with the open sea. Inner coastal bays influenced by rivers are typically murky with visibility ranging from three to 10 m, but dropping to near zero when rivers flood. Visibility is highest on seaward reef slopes, typically ranging from 25 to 40 m, occasionally reaching 60 m. Visibility in lagoons and channels can be quite variable and depends largely on tidal influences. Areas of atoll lagoons with poor circulation can be quite murky with visibilities of as little as 6 to 20 m whereas areas adjacent to deep channels can experience visibilities of 40 to 60 m at the peak of incoming tides. Time of day also influences visibility with the early morning often the clearest. As the day progresses, tradewinds increase in strength, creating a chop that stirs shallow lagoon waters, and particulate matter from the foraging activities and feces of fishes begins to cloud the water.

Types of Reefs

Coral reefs have traditionally been divided into three basic types: fringing reefs, barrier reefs, and atolls. These correspond with stages of development, with fringing reefs representing the earliest stage and barrier reefs and atolls representing the mature stage. Fringing reefs are relatively young, generally narrow platforms that extend a short distance from shore and do not contain a substantial lagoon. As the reef grows outward, or upward if the seafloor sinks or the sea level rises, the innermost corals cannot keep pace and a lagoon may develop. The reef has now become a barrier reef. Atolls start from fringing reefs surrounding volcanic islands. Erosion and subsidence of the surrounding seafloor cause the island to shrink and sink. The seaward margin of the fringing reef keeps pace with the sea surface, leaving a lagoon along the shore. An atoll results when the island has completely disappeared beneath the surface. Other factors that affect reef development such as changing sea levels, uplift, subsidence, temperature, and freshwater intrusion shape reefs into a wide variety of forms. In sheltered seas, steep-sided flat-topped platform reefs may occur far offshore. At all stages of development the seaward slope is steep, often reaching depths of 200 m or more within 1.5 km of shore.

Habitats and Zonation

The terms habitat and zone have rather broad and often overlapping definitions. For the purposes of this book, the term habitat describes the kind of place where an animal lives in either physical or biological terms. Generally the name of the dominant or most easily recognizable character of a given place is used as the name of a habitat. Terms like tide pool, seagrass bed, or sand flat describe habitats. Habitats can be further subdivided into specific microhabitats such as a Pocillopora coral head. A zone describes a place in terms of its overall physiographic structure and location. A reef zone refers to a part of a reef in relation to the physical parameters of land, sea surface, and depth. A variety of habitats characterize a zone. Some habitats may be present in several zones while others are restricted to one or two. Characteristic reef zones are shown in figure 4.

The coastlines of continents and high islands contain the greatest number of reef zones and habitats. They often have significant fresh and brackish water habitats. Nutient-rich rivers may carry large quantities of silt as well as fresh water which result in highly productive, but turbid, muddy habitats where coral growth is inhibited. Mangrove forests thrive along the intertidal shorelines of estuaries and river mouths and seagrasses thrive on silty inner reef flats and shallow lagoon floors. Mangrove and seagrass habitats are required by the young of a large variety of marine fishes, some of which migrate to coral reefs as adults. Consequently continental shelf and high island reefs tend to support a greater diversity of inshore fishes than atolls. Coastal areas or high islands consisting of highly porous limestone lack rivers and are often characterized by steep cliffs plunging directly into the sea, sometimes fringed by benches or reef flats. These areas often have the clearest water but may lack species associated with mangroves or river mouths.

Atolls lack rocky cliffs and benches as well as rivers and well-developed mangrove communities and thus lack many of the species associated with these habitats. However, the sheer size of the lagoons of large atolls may provide better opportunities for colonization by dispersing fishes, so that the number of species on large atolls may exceed that on nearby poorly developed coastal reefs or smaller high islands.

Coastal bays: often have sheltered, somewhat turbid waters and silty bottoms, sometimes with a river emptying at the head. Mangroves often line the shore, particularly where the slope is gentle, and along the banks of rivers to the upper limits of tidal influence. By extending roots laterally beneath the mud, mangroves consolidate sediments, spread seaward, and may eventu-

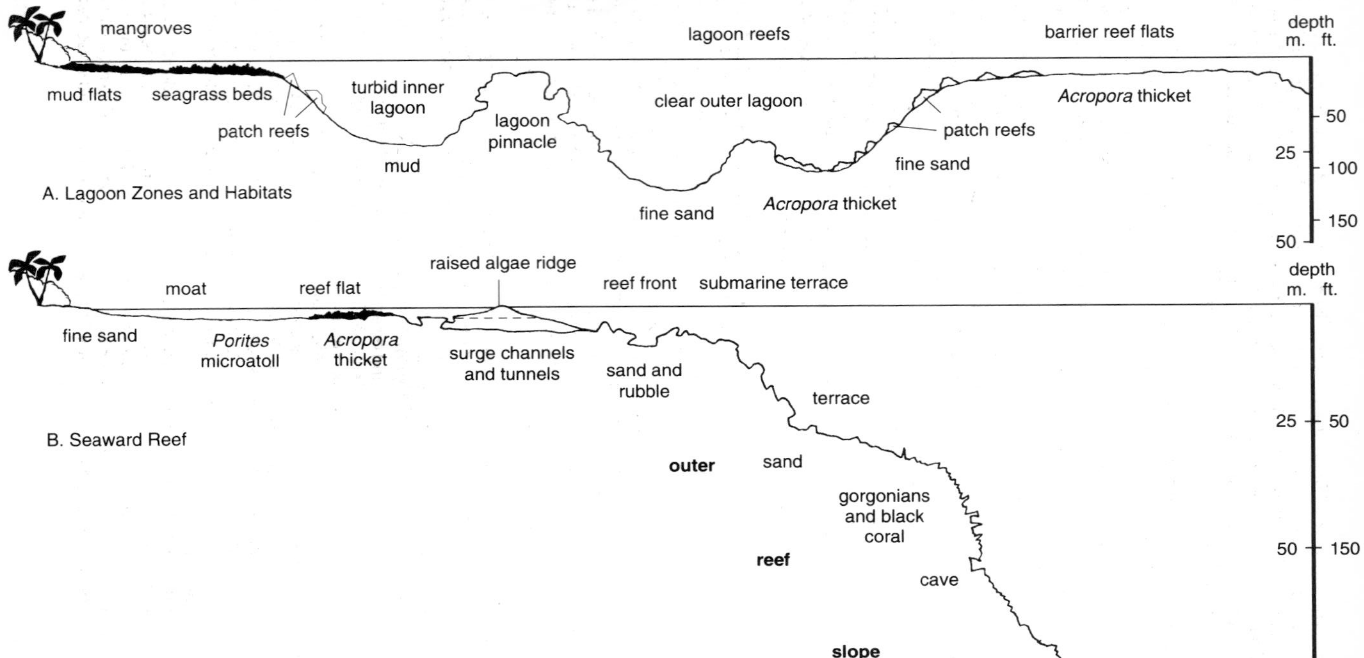

mangroves
lagoon reefs
barrier reef flats
depth
m. ft.
mud flats
seagrass beds
patch reefs
turbid inner lagoon
mud
lagoon pinnacle
clear outer lagoon
fine sand
Acropora thicket
patch reefs
fine sand
Acropora thicket
50
25
100
150
50
A. Lagoon Zones and Habitats
raised algae ridge
moat
reef flat
reef front
submarine terrace
depth
m. ft.
fine sand
Porites microatoll
Acropora thicket
surge channels and tunnels
sand and rubble
terrace
B. Seaward Reef
outer
sand
gorgonians and black coral
reef
cave
slope
25 50
50 150
75 225

REEF MORPHOLOGY

ally transform mud flats into dry land. The shelter provided by their extensive root systems and nutrient-laden waters make them rich nursery grounds for a wide variety of marine life including many species of coral reef fishes. Coastal bays may be bordered by narrow reef flats which drop off steeply and are often riddled with caves and holes along their seaward edges. Several species of fishes not commonly found on offshore reefs occur here.

Lagoons: subtidal waters enclosed by barrier reefs or an atoll reef flat. Depths may vary from < 1m at low tide to 90 m. Lagoons often contain numerous patch reefs ranging in size from a few small pieces of coral to massive pinnacles which may be topped with reef flats and islands. Some lagoons contain a maze of elongate or interconnected reefs that may enclose isolated pools. Water clarity depends on the degree of water circulation, input of terrestrial runoff, and proximity to channels. High island lagoons are often relatively turbid with muddy bottoms. Deep channels often lie opposite river mouths and follow the river's prehistoric course that was formed during periods of lowered sea level. Atoll lagoons may be clear in some areas and turbid in others. Incoming tides, particularly in the vicinity of major channels, flood the lagoon with clear oceanic waters, and outgoing tides dump turbid lagoon waters out to sea. Surf generates currents that flow over the reef crest and into the lagoon, carrying the sand that accumulates on the lagoon slope. The finer sediments accumulate on the lagoon floor. Protected from wave action, delicate branching corals thrive where they can find a stable surface to settle and grow. Meadows of seagrass may grow on shallow sand or mud flats and may be particularly well developed in coastal or high island lagoons. Many species of fishes are characteristic of lagoons and various lagoon habitats.

Channels: deep cuts connecting the lagoon to the outer reef slope. Tidal currents provide ideal conditions for plankton-feeding animals. Filter-feeding invertebrates thrive wherever they can maintain a foothold. Channel walls are frequently densely overgrown with both soft and hard corals and gorgonians. Deep channels entering large lagoons may have such strong tidal currents that the channel floor is a barren wasteland of shifting sand and rubble. In channels with less severe currents, hard-bottomed portions of the channel floor may be as overgrown with corals as are the walls. Here one may find a diversity of fishes rivalling the richest areas of outer lagoons and outer reef slopes. Sharks and other large predators such as groupers, snappers, and sweetlips are often abundant.

Reef flats: the intertidal and extreme upper subtidal portion of the reef. Reef flats can range in width from a few meters to a few kilometers. The surface can range from a featureless, pavement-smooth platform to a complex maze of sand patches and coral-choked tidepools. Coral growth is limited to the areas low enough to avoid desiccation during the lowest tides. Coral growth is relatively poor in areas regularly subjected to overheated stagnant water during low tide and is luxuriant in areas nearly constantly washed by clear water. Reef flats can often be subdivided into several zones.

The inner reef flat frequently retains some water during the lowest tides. Flat-topped heads of massive corals called microatolls, are common. Subtidal areas of inner fringing reefs not quite deep enough to qualify as lagoons (0.5-1 m at the lowest tides) are known as moats. Seagrass meadows are a common feature of inner reef flats of high islands. Luxuriant growths of branching and massive *Porites* corals and thickets of branching *Acropora* corals may be present.

The outer reef flat is often a barren, pavement-smooth expanse dotted with blocks of dead coral rock wrenched from the reef margin during storms. This "barren" zone is generally covered with a thin film or thick mat of filamentous algae which is grazed by roving schools of herbivorous fishes during high tides.

The seaward margin of reef flats are frequently quite porous and dissected by deep undercut channels running perpendicular to the reef edge and extending well down the outer reef slope. Low profile corals are common here. Where the seaward margin of a reef flat is subject to a nearly constant surf, a raised ridge of encrusting coralline algae, the "algal ridge", may form.

Reef front and spur and groove zone: the area from the seaward edge of the reef flat to the submarine terrace. Where there is frequent wave assault, the reef front is dissected by the deep channels originating beneath the reef margin. This zone of alternating ridges and vertical sided sand, rubble, or boulder-floored channels is known as the "spur and groove zone." The lower channel walls are kept smoothed by the constant abrasion of sand and even boulders during storms. The tops of the ridges are typically covered with corals. Where wave assault is severe, the corals tend to be stout-branched or low and stubby, and the channel floors consist of boulders; where wave assault is moderate, the corals may be more delicate, and the channel floors sandy. In sheltered areas, the reef front may lack deep channels and instead consist of a gentle slope covered with large stands of branching and tabular corals. Here other species of fishes less characteristic of the surge zone dominate.

Submarine terrace: a gently sloping shelf at the base of the reef front. Here the channels become shallower and have sand rather than rubble floors. On reefs exposed to constant surge, the corals are mostly low-profile encrusting, croymbose, or massive species. Scattered pinnacles, often topped with fire corals, *Millepora* spp., may be present. In sheltered areas, large branching and tabular *Acropora* corals are generally common. Many species characteristic of the reef front also occur on shallow exposed reef terraces and roving mixed-species schools of scarids and acanthurids are common.

Outer reef slope: the portion of the seaward reef that slopes into deep water. It is generally fairly steep (30° or more) with moderate to high coral cover. The slope may be dissected by sand- and rubble-bottomed channels. Branching and tabular species of corals are more common where there is less frequent exposure to storm swells. The diversity and abundance of corals as well as fishes is greatest along promontories and other areas exposed to tidal currents. In clear mid-oceanic waters coral cover and diversity often remain high to depths of 40 to 60 m. Below these depths, coral cover decreases rapidly and branching corals are replaced by platelike forms which have been observed as deep as 112 m. The dominant calcareous algae, *Halimeda*, occurs to beyond 100 m, and some small macroalgae and algal films have been observed as deep as 140 m. Gorgonians and soft corals are the dominant growth forms below 100 m. Many of the species found in the deepest lagoons also occur here. As one goes further down the slope, a number of common shallow water fish species are replaced by deeper water equivalents.

Dropoffs (often known as "walls"): outer reef slopes that are nearly vertical ($\geqslant 70°$) to slightly undercut. Sand and rubble occur only where there is sufficient shelving or in less steeply sloping channels or chutes that may dissect the reef face. Since heavy surge inhibits the development of vertical reef faces, dropoffs tend to occur in shallower water on leeward or sheltered exposures. The diversity and abundance of corals and fishes is highest in areas exposed to current. Small planktivorous fishes typically swarm within a few meters of the wall and deep-dwelling organisms tend to occur in shallower water here. Gorgonians and black corals compete for space with stony corals to within a few meters of the surface, and some species of fishes normally found below 30 m may occur in 10 m or less.

Benches: narrow reef flat-like structures occurring at the bases of steep high-island slopes. They are best developed where there is constant wave action and are formed primarily by the outward growth of coralline red algae. Where there is enough wave action to keep the surface awash, benches may be raised a few meters above sea level. The top may consist of a series of shallow terraced pools. The surface is generally covered with a thick mat of fleshy and filamentous algae. Small corals may be present in the deeper pools. Blenniids, tripterygiids, and juveniles of many surge zone fishes are common.

Cliffs: a near vertical terrestrial slope extending into the sea. There may be a certain degree of shelving at depths of 12 to 20 m. Boulders fallen from the cliff face may be piled on this shelf. Coral cover is often low, but where there is enough shelter in the form of corals, holes, or boulders, there is an abundance of fishes. Roving schools of scarids and acanthurids roam the shelf grazing on algae. Planktivores are abundant where there are moderate to strong currents.

Ecology

Coral reefs provide a wide variety of habitats, each with its own set of characteristic species. Differences in the degree of exposure to wave action, currents, light levels, the amount of algae, plankton and other food, and the abundance, shape, and varieties of coral and other shelter combine to create a large variety of possible niches. Not only is each conceivable niche occupied by a species of fish, but some niches appear to be occupied by a random assemblage of a number of species of fishes. Differential recruitment of juveniles, occasional disturbances such as storms that wipe out whole groups of fishes from a coral head, and heavy predation may keep any one species from realizing an advantage over another.

Animals may be classified by their place in the food chain. In the simplest form, a food chain consists of producers (plants), consumers (animals), and decomposers (bacteria). Each tier from the producer to the terminal carnivore is called a trophic level. Most food chains are complex with numerous levels, subdivisions, and alternate pathways, so the term food web is also used. Among consumers, there are three basic trophic levels: herbivores for those that feed on plants, omnivores for those that feed on plants and animals, and carnivores for those that feed on animals. For fishes, the term planktivore is used to identify the carnivores that feed on zooplankton. (Very few fishes, primarily mullet, feed on phytoplankton). The term corallivore is used for the omnivores that feed on corals, since corals contain both plant and animal tissue. The term detritivore is used for those omnivores that feed on decomposing plant and animal particles. The term piscivore refers to carnivores that feed primarily on fishes.

At the base of the reef's food web are marine plants, including diatoms (benthic unicellular algae with a silica exoskeleton), dinoflagellates (unicellular benthic or floating algae), phytoplankton (unicellular floating algae), zooxanthellae (unicellular algae that live within the tissue of corals and certain invertebrates), benthic algae (seaweeds), and seagrasses. There are fishes that feed on each of these. Few fishes feed on phytoplankton; mullets and milkfish feed on the algal diatomaceous and detrital scum of soft bottoms; a number of butterflyfishes and other corallivores feed on zooxanthellae contained within the tissue of corals; a few species of parrotfishes and surgeonfishes feed on seagrasses; and a very large number of herbivorous fishes feed on filamentous and fleshy benthic algae. Grazers scrape the thin filamentous algal film that grows on all bare surfaces, while browsers nip fronds of leafy algae. Parrotfishes, surgeonfishes, and rabbitfishes are the primary roving grazers, the marine equivalent of cattle. Smaller grazers such as blennies and many damselfishes are generally territorial around small areas affording sufficient shelter. Some parrotfishes, surgeonfishes, rabbitfishes, and rudderfishes browse on the fronds of leafy macroalgae.

Butterflyfishes as well as triggerfishes and puffers and their allies are the primary omnivores. Many species of butterflyfishes feed on a variety of small invertebrates and coral polyps, taking a little of each over a large home range.

Some butterflyfishes and the filefish *Oxymonacanthus longirostris* feed exclusively on coral polyps which are snipped from the coral skeleton by specialized snouts and teeth. The large humphead parrotfish, *Bolbometapon muricatum*, and several triggerfishes, filefishes, and puffers feed on pieces of corals, skeleton and all. A number of triggerfishes, filefishes, and puffers feed on a variety of well-armored invertebrates such as sea urchins, crustaceans, and star-fishes as well as hard calcareous algae. Detritus enters the fish food chain primarily through benthic invertebrates that are preyed upon by carnivores. Only a few fishes such as mullet and some gobies feed directly on detritus.

A large number of reef fishes feed on zooplankton. The largest of all fishes, the pelagic whaleshark and manta rays, feed on zooplankton strained from the water, as do anchovies, herrings, and silversides. Damselfishes and fairy basslets feed on individual zooplankters, chiefly copepods, picked from the water one by one. Some triggerfishes and snappers, particularly deep-dwelling species, feed on large, gelatinous zooplankton such as salps and ctenophores. Nocturnal planktivores such as squirrelfishes, cardinalfishes, and bigeyes feed primarily on large zooplankton such as crustacean larvae.

Most species of reef fishes are carnivores, ranging from tiny gobies that feed upon minute benthic crustaceans to large sharks that feed on large fishes, turtles, and other sharks. A variety of strategies are used to capture prey. Eels are specialized for slithering through narrow crevices, or through sand and rubble, locating prey through the sense of smell, and seizing prey with long, needle-like or stout, crushing teeth. Well camouflaged scorpionfishes, lizardfishes, and flatheads sit on the reef's surface, or partially buried in the sand, waiting to ambush unwary fishes or crustaceans. Groupers and snappers cruise about the reef in a nonthreatening manner, all the time prepared for an unwary fish to drop its guard, then lunge, more often than not unsuccessfully. Jacks rush into a school of small fusiliers or silversides, attempting to separate an individual from the safety of the school so it can be captured with relative ease. Many of the piscivores become more active at dusk and dawn during the day-night changeover when they become less visible to potential prey. Goatfishes probe the sand or crevices of the reef with long barbels to detect buried crustaceans or small fishes. They may be accompanied by opportunistic wrasses or small jacks that grab prey that are flushed out. Emperors scan the surface of the sand for any sign of movement that betrays the presence of buried prey. Rays excavate craters in the sand for buried molluscs which they crush with their pavement-like teeth. Some species such as the cleaner wrasses are specialized feeders of parasites and damaged tissue of other fishes while others pose as cleaners in order to aggressively tear out scales or pieces of fins.

On a typical coral reef, more than 75% of the fishes are diurnal species that spend the daylight hours on the surface of the reef or a short distance above it. Most of these are the colorful and conspicuous fishes most often associated with coral reefs, including most wrasses, damselfishes, fairy basslets, groupers, butterflyfishes, surgeonfishes, parrotfishes, snappers, angelfishes, triggerfishes, hawkfishes, and some goatfishes. Approximately 30% of reef fishes are cryptic reef species seldom noticed by the casual observer. Most are generally small and well camouflaged or spend most of their time hidden within the structure of the reef. Moray eels, most gobies, blennies, pipefishes, and most scorpionfishes fit this category. These include diurnal as well as nocturnal species and some that may be active around the clock. Many morays and scorpionfishes as well as some goatfishes become more active and spend more time in the open at night. Approximately 10% of reef fishes are primarily nocturnal species that remain hidden in caves and in crevices during the day but emerge to feed on the surface of the reef or in the water close above it during the night. Squirrelfishes, soldier-fishes, many cardinalfishes, and bigeyes typically feed on larger elements of the zooplankton in the water above the reef, while soldierfishes and many cardinalfishes feed on motile invertebrates on the reef's surface. A surprising number of reef fish species, perhaps 10%, live on or beneath sand, mud, or rubble. Snake eels, lizardfishes, flatfishes, sandperches, flatheads, and many gobies live on or just beneath the surface, while sandivers, wormfishes, and certain wrasses spend a good portion of their waking hours in the water immediately above the sand. Most of these are carnivores of small invertebrates. Many fishes that shelter on the reef venture well out over large expanses of sand or rubble. These include some of the larger herbivorous surgeonfishes and several species of carnivorous groupers, snappers, emperors, and breams. A large variety of smaller reef fishes tied more closely to the shelter of the reef may forage on small sand patches. A relatively small portion of the shorefish fauna, 8%, is composed of mid-water species that roam large areas. This group includes the fusiliers, jacks, barracudas, and most sharks. Most are carnivores, but a few, primarily the fusiliers, are planktivores. The largest reef-associated species of all, the manta ray, feeds on zooplankton. Carnivorous needlefishes and omnivorous halfbeaks typically occur immediately beneath the water's surface. Occasionally pelagic species - those adapted for life in the open ocean such as tunas and flying fishes - visit seaward reef dropoffs or enter deep lagoons. Most are carnivores. Although they rarely feed on adults of reef fishes, many of them feed on the late larval and early juvenile stages of reef fishes.

Social Interactions

Fishes exhibit a diverse array of life styles to cope with living together in the crowded and competitive world of the reef. Some species are always found in groups while others occur in pairs or are solitary. Schooling is a strategy adopted by many species that live or travel in open water away from the protection of the reef. The sheer numbers of fishes in many schools insure that all but an unlucky few survive each attack by a predator. An individual among large numbers of closely spaced, constantly moving, and identical looking fishes is much more difficult for a predator to single out than if that individual were alone. If the predator blindly lunges at the school it will usually come up empty. Some aggregating as well as schooling species rely on disruptive coloration, such as a pattern of contrasting vertical bars, to make it even more difficult for a predator to single out an individual. Many roving herbivores occur in large mixed-species schools. Not only does this increase an individual's safety in numbers but it also enables the schooling fishes to overwhelm the defences of territorial species guarding an algal food source. Many species of parrotfishes, surgeonfishes, and some rabbitfishes adopt this strategy. Species that depend on a small isolated area, such as a single coral patch for shelter tend to occur together in groups or colonies. This is particularly true for small planktivores that must feed in a vulnerable position above their shelter. By occurring in groups they eliminate the need for leaving the vicinity of their "home" coral for reproduction. When danger threatens they quickly retreat to the safety of the coral. Fairy basslets, many damselfishes, and some wrasses are common examples.

A large number of reef fishes are territorial. Territorial species typically guard an area enclosing one or more resources of food, shelter, or potential mates or nesting sites. They are typically most aggressive towards outsiders of their own kind. The dominant territory holder will generally drive away rivals such as another adult of the same sex but share the territory with smaller subordinates of the opposite sex. Some species are aggressive towards almost any intruder while others are aggressive primarily towards their closest competitors - similar species with similar needs. Some species may have quite large territories or separate feeding and sleeping territories. Species that roam the same large area of reef on a routine basis are known as home-ranging species. They may carry with them a "portable" territory within which competitors are not allowed. Many home-ranging species may be relatively sociable during times of abundant resources, but become aggressive during lean times. Most medium to large species are home-ranging. They frequently have a favorite sleeping site to which they return and aggressively defend at the end of each day. Many species maintain a territory for reproduction. It may have the same boundary as a feeding territory or be a small portion of a home range (see reproduction).

Many small herbivores maintain a territory enclosing a patch of rock coated with a thin veneer of algae. Several damselfishes, blennies, and some surgeonfishes are common examples. Some species share territories with others. The aggressive surgeonfish *Acanthurus lineatus* may share its feeding territory with a much smaller damselfish *Stegastes fasciolatus*. The value of the pugnacious damselfish at driving away other competitors outweigh its cost as a competitor or the cost that would be required to drive it away, so its presence is tolerated. One or more species of blennies may also occupy the territory as parasitic freeloaders since they do not contribute to the territory's defence. Their small size, speed, and ability to hide in very small holes enable them to remain in the territory. This ability of the damselfish and the blenny to take advantage of progressively smaller shelter holes is one way in which coexistence is achieved by different species that utilize the same limited resource, the algae. Perhaps the most pugnacious of the territorial fishes are the so-called "farmer fishes" of the damselfish genera *Stegastes* and *Hemiglyphidodon*. They typically live in colonies among staghorn corals whose dead bases are covered with a mat of filamentous algae. They encourage the growth of the favored filamentous species of algae by "weeding" out the undesirable species - literally snipping and removing them from the territory.

Vision and color are of paramount importance in the social lives of most species of reef fishes. Distinctive color patterns enable each species to recognize its own kind as well as the rank of an individual within a social system. Behaviorally controlled changes in coloration and posturing convey messages among fishes just as facial expressions do among humans. In some species sounds and scents may also play a role in social interactions. Flared operculae and fins are commonly used to convey aggression. Males of many species flash brilliantly intense colors during courtship. At night, most species exhibit a subdued color pattern, often with contrasting blotches or bars that may help them match their background.

Reproduction and Development

Reproduction among fishes is highly varied and often quite complex. The vast majority of fishes lay eggs. The birth of fully developed young is extremely rare among bony fishes and common only among cartilaginous fishes. Eggs of fishes are typically small (about 1 mm in diameter) and generally take about a week to hatch. The eggs hatch into larvae which bear little resemblance to the fishes familiar to most people. Larvae start out as tadpole-like creatures with large eyes, without pigment or scales, and often with an external yolk sack to nourish them until their gut develops. Larvae are adapted to a pelagic life, drifting with the currents and feeding on phytoplankton to progressively larger zooplankton as they grow. Some larvae actively swim, guided by environmental cues that may help them find a suitable settling site. In many species the larvae develop enlarged bony plates or spines that help protect them from predation. In some species larvae settle and transform into juveniles within days of hatching while in others they may go through a prolonged late larval stage that may last up to two months or more. Once they locate a suitable place to settle, larvae become bottom-oriented and rapidly acquire the pigments, scales, and full compliment of fin rays characteristic of juveniles. Juveniles usually resemble adults in form, but in reef species, may often have a color pattern entirely different from that of adults. Growth rate and life span vary among species. Some species grow at a steady rate until they die while others grow more slowly after reaching a certain size. Small species may reach maturity within six months and live to an age of one to two years while large species may take several years to mature and live as long as 80 years or more.

Most species of fishes have the familiar male and female sexes, but only a minority of them go through adult life as monogamous pairs. In fact, the majority of reef fish species so far studied are not only polygamous but undergo sex reversal as a normal part of their sexual development. This is called sequential hermaphroditism. Species in which individuals begin their life as females before changing to males are known as protogynous hermaphrodites whereas those that change from male to female are known as protandrous hermaphrodites. No species exhibit both protogyny and protandry but a few species are simultaneous hermaphrodites, and a very few of these are occasionally self-fertilizing.

Most wrasses and parrotfishes are typical examples of sequential hermaphrodites. In most species individuals begin their adult life as either males or females and each has a similar, relatively dull color pattern. This is known as the primary or initial phase. Primary males are usually incapable of changing sex, but females have the capacity to change sex into brilliantly colored males, known as secondary or terminal phase males. Secondary males are larger than, and dominant over all primary phase individuals. The change of sex is socially controlled - the presence of terminal males inhibits females from changing sex. If the ratio of terminal males to females falls below a certain threshold, the dominant female will change sex. Terminal males generally pair spawn with numerous females of their choice, while primary males often band together and spawn in large groups with the females which on occasion may be "raided" from a courting terminal male. In simpler systems, typified by the anthiases (genus *Pseudanthias*), primary males are absent, and all males are terminal, usually with a distinctive, gaudier coloration. These are known as haremic systems. In most haremic systems there is one male dominant over a group of females, but in some large colonies of Pseudanthias there may be more than one male. If the male is removed, the dominant female changes sex, insuring the constant reproductive capacity of a group of fishes that may spend their entire post-larval lives confined to the safety of a small area of suitable shelter.

In protandrous hermaphrodites such as the anemonefishes, the social hierarchy of the sexes is reversed. In a typical large anemone there is usually a single pair of reproductively active anemone-fishes and often one or more immature individuals. The female is the largest and most dominant. Should she be removed, the male will change sex and the largest of the juveniles will rapidly grow and mature into a male. The presence of the female inhibits the male from changing sex and the presence of the male stunts the growth and development of the juveniles. This is another example of a strategy that insures the reproductive capacity of a small colony of animals confined to a very limited space.

Some species, particularly large roving carnivores, may normally be solitary in their day-to-day lives but migrate to favorite spawning sites at certain times of the year or throughout the year on a lunar rhythm. Some locations, usually current-swept promontories or channel entrances, are the sites of mass spawning aggregations of hundreds or thousands of individuals of some species. Some species may spawn as pairs that break off from the main aggregation while others may spawn en mass.

Most species of reef fishes are pelagic or broadcast spawners, that is they spew their gametes into the water usually at the apex of an ascent well above the bottom. Most species also spawn at a favorable time, usually on an outgoing tide, more often than not near or during dusk. Many species spawn on a lunar rhythm, around full moon, new moon, or both which is when the tidal range is greatest and tide-induced currents the strongest. These strategies increase the chances of the eggs escaping the hungry mouths of the innumerable small diurnal planktivorous fishes and filter feeding invertebrates that populate every reef. The favored sites of migrating spawners may also be near gyres in ocean currents that return the larvae to natal or nearby reefs after they have had two to three weeks to develop and are ready to settle.

There is a rough correlation between adult size and reproductive behavior. Since most fishes have eggs that ripen at a diameter of about a millimeter, large species have a much greater reproductive capacity than smaller ones. A 100 cm grouper may carry a million or more eggs whereas a small goby may only have a few dozen. Since an average of only two progeny per adult pair per generation need to survive to adulthood and spawn to insure the continued survival of the species, the larger species can better afford to spew their gametes into the vastness of the sea than can smaller ones. Many of the smaller species such as the gobies, blennies, and damselfishes therefore spawn in nests that are usually guarded by one or more of the parents. Hatching generally occurs after about a week, usually at night and on an outgoing tide. Cardinalfishes take parental care a step further by brooding the eggs in the mouth of the male until hatching. By providing a measure of protection for their eggs, nesting species greatly reduce egg predation, thereby evening the odds with the more fecund broadcast spawners.

Protective Resemblance and Mimicry

Among the multitude of lifestyles of reef fishes are those that depend on the color of other plants and animals. Protective resemblance and mimicry are ploys utilized by a number of species to capture prey or escape predators. Many species rely on camouflage to blend in with their surroundings. Scorpionfishes and frogfishes have fleshy tassels or warts that resemble fronds of algae and some even have algae growing on them. Many groupers have color patterns that do not resemble any particular background, but when overlain with a series of darker diagonal bands that break up their outline, they become virtually invisible. Some fishes do not match their background at all but closely resemble something else of no interest to a potential predator or prey. The juvenile of the wrasse *Novaculichthys taeniourus* (pl. 93-7) looks like, and swims as if it is a clump of seaweed swaying back and forth in the surge.

Protective resemblance is known as mimicry when an organism resembles another that is protected from predation by virtue of distastefulness, toxicity, or some other characteristic. Mimicry occurs in two basic forms: Batesian mimicry when an otherwise unprotected animal resembles a protected one, and Müllerian mimicry when two or more protected animals closely resemble one another. Among reef fishes Batesian mimicry is the more common of the two. The protected species, or model, generally has a distinctive, often gaudy color pattern (termed aposematic coloration) that potential predators learn to avoid after one or more bad experiences. The similar looking mimic is also avoided.

In Batesian mimicry, the protected species is usually more common than the mimic. This decreases the chances of the mimic encountering an inexperienced predator that may attempt to eat it. A typical example of Batesian mimicry involves the noxious puffer *Canthigaster valentini* (pl. 137-2) and the edible filefish *Paraluteres prionurus* (pl. 135-3). The puffer is distasteful and quite likely toxic; it is a relatively slow swimmer that makes little attempt to hide. The edible filefish not only looks like the puffer, but swims like it as well. In aggressive mimicry, the mimic takes its charade a step further in order to gain an advantage other than protection at the expense of another animal. Aggressive mimicry is perhaps best developed among the sabre-toothed blennies (pl. 114). In a classic example, the cleaner mimic *Aspidontus taeniatus* (pl. 114-2) has evolved a color pattern identical to that of the cleaner wrasse *Labroides dimidiatus* (pl. 104-5). The wrasse makes a living grooming other fishes by removing parasites and pieces of damaged tissue. Large piscivorous fishes will pose with their mouths agape as the cleaner swims inside looking for a meal. The piscivores recognize the cleaner's service and will not attempt to eat it. The blenny uses its disguise to closely approach other fishes expecting to be groomed. But instead of grooming, the blenny darts in to make a meal of a piece of fin or scale! The blenny's disguise is not perfect though; older, more experienced fishes usually learn to distinguish the two and avoid the mimic.

Many juvenile sweetlips, *Plectorhinchus* spp. (pls. 48-49), are possible Müllerian mimics, but it has not yet been demonstrated that they are noxious. They typically have a similar color pattern of highly contrasting light and dark blotches, and swim or hover in the open with distinctive, greatly exaggerated movements of the body and fins. By resembling one another, the effectiveness of their aposematic coloration is reinforced since a predator can learn to avoid them collectively through a bad experience with just one. In Müllerian mimicry each participant therefore acts as both model and mimic.

Symbiosis

The lives of some of the reef's animals are closely associated with, and often dependent upon the life of another species. This is known as symbiosis. There are three basic forms of symbiosis: mutualism when both organisms depend upon each other, commensalism when one organism depends upon the other without harming it, and parasitism when one benefits to the detriment of the other. All three are found among Micronesia's reef fishes

The prawn-associated gobies are a classic example of mutualism (pls. 120-121). The goby lives only in a burrow excavated by a prawn which is blind or nearly so. The prawn spends much of its time maintaining the burrow, and each time it dumps a load of sand out the entrance it is exposed to predation. The goby stands guard at the entrance to the burrow and is quite alert and difficult to approach closely. When at the entrance, the prawn usually maintains contact with the goby by touching it with one of its antennae. If the goby detects danger, it signals the prawn with a flick of its tail before following the prawn into the burrow. The goby also benefits by feeding on small invertebrates exposed by the prawn's digging.

Perhaps the best known example of commensalism is that of the anemonefishes (pl. 75-76). Anemonefishes occur only in the vicinity of certain large sea anemones. The surface of the sea anemones are covered with venomous stinging cells capable of killing most fishes. But the anemonefishes are not stung and utilize the anemone as a predator-free home. The key is a substance acquired from the anemone itself, through a careful process of acclimation, that is present in the anemonefishes mucus. The stinging cells recognize the anemonefish as a part of the anemone and will not sting it. Although anemonefishes have been observed to carry food to their host, the anemone is not dependent upon the anemonefish. Perfectly healthy anemones occur without anemonefish, but the anemonefishes are invariably found with an anemone.

Parasitism on the part of coral reef fishes seems to be limited to the pearlfishes which live within the body cavities of certain invertebrates. The most common species occur within certain sea cucumbers and starfish. While some species occasionally feed on the respiratory tree of their host, others may be harmless.

Reef Fishes as a Resource and Its Conservation

With the advent of cash economies as well as modern diving and fishing equipment, outboard motors, and refrigeration, most coral reefs within range of transportation networks are commercially exploited. A vicious cycle is often set up where the demand for money to pay for consumer goods is satisfied only by selling more fish. As nearby stocks become depleted, the fishermen go further away to get their catch and the depleted area gets larger. It is only a matter of time before the incoming flow of money drops to match whatever sustained level of harvest can be maintained. Many large and vulnerable species are being heavily impacted, particularly by spearfishing with scuba gear or at night. Certain large species such as the giant humphead parrotfish (pl. 105-1) that were once common in many areas and groupers over 25 kg are rarely seen.

Destructive methods of fishing such as the use of explosives or poisons such as chlorine or natural root extracts are widespread in developing countries. These methods are particularly reprehensible because they kill most if not all marine life in the area and may render it unsuitable for normal recolonization. Although these methods are generally illegal, enforcement is difficult and often lax.

Traditional concepts of conservation and ownership are being lost as traditional methods give way to modern ones. Modern methods of management practiced on single- or few-species stocks in temperate regions are impractical on coral reefs where dozens of species are caught by each method, where there is little seasonal variation, and where distinct size classes are absent. Even the most abundant species on coral reefs only comprise a small portion of the harvestable catch. When the cost of learning the population dynamics of an individual species may exceed its annual value, and policymakers and special interest groups demand answers before action, the resource is bound to suffer. Other less species-specific approaches are needed to maximize the sustainable harvest and preserve species for traditional uses. Bag limits, protection for certain vulnerable species, banning the use of scuba diving while spearfishing, limiting the sale of speared fish, and limited entry into a fishery may offer some hope, but the real answer lies in economic diversification and in maximizing the non-consumptive uses of the resource.

The explosive growth of the marine aquarium hobby has been a mixed bag. A well-maintained marine aquarium can have a positive effect by helping those living thousands of miles away develop an appreciation for coral reefs and the environment. In some areas such as Hawaii, where selective collecting techniques are practiced and the resource is well-managed, the resource is able to support a modest number of small businesses with little or no measurable impact on targeted species' populations. However, in other areas such as the Philippines, destructive collecting techniques have decimated virtually all accessible reefs. Unlike many of the larger species exploited for food, most popular aquarium species are small and have a high turnover rate which makes them much less susceptible to overfishing. As long as fish-collecting chemicals are banned or strictly controlled, and catches are monitored, there is little danger of overexploitation. Generally only certain sizes are in demand and only certain habitats are practical for collecting, so most individuals are left to grow and reproduce.

Poor land uses have an adverse impact on coral reefs. Prolonged and continuous infestations of the crown-of-thorns starfish in many areas are most likely the result of increased nutrient flow into reef waters due to erosion caused by construction and modern as well as slash-and-burn agriculture. Sustained widespread destruction of corals has a direct impact on the structure of reef fish communities. Certain herbivorous species such as parrotfishes and surgeonfishes may temporarily benefit from the increased area of dead reef available for algal growth, while others that feed on corals or live within them, particularly many species of butterflyfishes, may disappear. The decrease in the available shelter may limit populations of many species.

For some places, the value of a reef fish resource for non-consumptive activities such as tourism, photography, and education far outweighs its value as a food resource. Scuba diving is one of the world's fastest growing sports. Millions of Americans, Europeans, and Japanese are certified divers. Most of them visit a coral reef at some time in their lives and many return to favorite locations year after year. Partly as a result of lessons learned in the early days of diving, spearfishing has given way to underwater photography and "fish-watching" as the most popular recreational activities of divers. Most divers want to see or photograph large fishes at close range. A place that offers exciting encounters with large tame fish or simply a chance to view a reef in pristine condition is likely to be visited time and time again. A place where large fishes are uncommon or flee at the first sight of a diver is seldom visited twice.

In many parts of the world there are underwater parks where marine life is protected. In the Caribbean and the Maldives, the economic prosperity of entire nations depends on their underwater parks and the tourists they attract.

Underwater parks and marine conservation areas also benefit the fishermen by offering a refuge for heavily exploited species to grow and reproduce so that the species' continued presence outside conservation areas is ensured. The key to the future well-being of many of the worlds coral reef fish resources is clear. The establishment of underwater parks is a necessity if the maximum and well-balanced benefits of food, recreation, education, and economic development of marine resources are to be realized.

Dangerous Marine Fishes

Although some coral reef fishes are potentially harmful, there is rarely any danger to a person that uses common sense and leaves unfamiliar fishes alone. With the possible exception of the tiger shark and bull shark, there are no animals on coral reefs that would consider a human as potential prey. Most bad encounters with marine life are the result of the victim's lack of knowledge of an animal's anatomy, behavior, and defences, and are almost always avoidable. One stands a much greater risk of being killed or maimed on the way to the dive site than as a result of an encounter with a potentially dangerous species of fish. There are three basic types of potentially dangerous fishes: those that bite, those that sting, and those that are poisonous to eat.

Of the potentially dangerous biters, only a few species of sharks get large enough to consider humans as prey. Only one of the world's three most dangerous species of shark, the tiger shark (pl. 3-1), enters diveable coral reef waters. Fortunately, it generally avoids shallow water during the day when most divers are in the water. It is most likely to be encountered in relatively deep water along steep outer reef slopes. The few sightings made in lagoons have usually been in the vicinity of deep channels leading to the seaward reef. Occasionally tiger sharks forage in shallow reef front waters, primarily at night. Even if one does encounter a tiger shark, it more than likely will not attack unless it is stimulated by the presence of speared fish. The best thing to do if one is encountered is to get out of the water. The dreaded great white shark is a cool water species that occurs in the tropics only as a rare wanderer in deeper waters within the thermocline. The world's third most dangerous species of shark, the oceanic whitetip (pl. 2-3) inhabits all offshore tropical waters but very rarely occurs on the edges of deep offshore banks which are generally not visited by divers. Fatal attacks by the bull shark (pl. 140-5) generally occur in murky coastal, estuarine, or even fresh waters.

In the Indo-Pacific, the grey reef shark (pl. 2-2) is the most dangerous species commonly encountered by divers. It is aggressive and territorial and may view man as a competitor. Although it won't hesitate to take a fish off the end of a spear, attacks on people are territorial in nature and are invariably preceded by a distinctive swimming behavior known as threat-posturing. In most popular dive areas, grey reef sharks have become accustomed to divers and generally ignore them. As with most sharks, it is advisable for the diver to be aware of the shark's behavior and to get out of the water if the shark becomes persistently curious. Several other species of reef sharks are potentially dangerous, particularly when stimulated by fish being speared or hooked.

The other "biters" most feared by humans are barracudas and moray eels. Attacks by the great barracuda are invariably the result of mistaken identity or provocation. In murky water, a shiny object such as bracelet may be mistaken for a small fish, resulting in the limb to which it is attached being bitten, or a speared barracuda could attack in self defence. Bites from moray eels are also nearly always the result of some form of provocation or stimuli. Attacks have been attributed to thrusting a hand into a hole occupied by an eel, spearing an eel, and holding speared fish in the hand. Although temperament varies between species and individuals, certain large morays have become popular "pets" among dive tour operators who feed them and pet them.

There are a number of reef fishes that possess venomous spines. The most dangerous of these are the scorpionfishes and rabbitfishes. One species of scorpionfish, the stonefish (pl. 19-8), has caused fatalities among humans.

Most scorpionfishes are extremely well-camouflaged. Several species, including the stonefish are common on shallow reef flats, but they usually station themselves against rocks and are rarely stepped on. Although the dorsal spines of the stonefish are capable of penetrating tennis shoes, sturdy footwear greatly reduces the chances of them penetrating the skin. One group of scorpionfishes, the lionfishes (pl. 20) are quite conspicuous and make little effort to avoid the diver. Rabbitfishes (pls. 129-130) also have highly venomous dorsal and anal spines. Although they have not been implicated in fatalities, the sting of some species is feared as much as that of the stonefish. Surgeonfishes (pls. 124-128) have either a pair of razor-sharp, movable, sheathed spines or two pairs of sharp, fixed bucklers on their sides near the base of the tail. Squirrelfishes (pls. 13-14) have prominent preopercular (cheek) spines. Stingrays have one or more sharp detachable spines on the basal portion of their whiplike tails that are capable of severely wounding a wader who inadvertently steps on one. Although less hazardous than the fishes listed above, most other species of reef fishes have some form of defence in the form of sharp spines, beaks, or teeth, and should be handled cautiously.

A number of reef fishes are poisonous by possessing toxins that make them unpalatable. Toxicity may be due to either substances made by the fish itself, or to substance ingested with other organisms. Puffers (pls. 137-138) and boxfishes (pl. 136) have highly toxic skin or vicera which protects them from predation. The toxin, tetrodotoxin, is among the most powerful poisons known and is responsible for many fatalities throughout the world. Soapfishes and possibly juvenile sweetlips also possess toxic or bitter skin secretions that discourage predation.

Perhaps the most dangerous form of fish poisoning from the standpoint of public health is ciguatera. Ciguatera is a toxin that may be present in a wide variety of fishes, but reaches its highest concentrations in the piscivorous fishes at the top of the food chain. It does not affect the fishes themselves but can cause extreme illness and even death in humans and land animals. Symptoms vary from a tingling of the lips and extremities in the mildest cases to reversal of the sensations of hot and cold, muscular weakness, vomiting, diarrhoea, shortness of breath, and cardiac arrest. There is no known cure, and until very recently, no practical means of detecting the toxin in fishes. Its greatest danger is its unpredictability of occurrence in some of the most valuable food fishes.

The toxin is produced by a small dinoflagellate *Gambierdiscus toxicus* that colonizes the bare surfaces of rock, piers, shipwrecks, or even blades of algae. It is eaten along with filamentous algae by herbivorous fishes which are in turn eaten by predatory fishes. Since the toxin is not metabolized, it accumulates in the flesh and particularly the liver and reproductive organs. Each time a predator eats a smaller fish, it accumulates its victim's lifetime supply of ciguatera. Consequently, the highest concentrations occur in large predatory fishes. The occurrence of ciguatera varies from place to place and through time. In the Indo-Pacific, large red snapper *Lutjanus bohar* (pl. 45-8) and the moray eel, *Gymnothorax javanicus* (pl. 6-1) are the most frequently implicated species and should never be eaten. Large individuals of the larger species of groupers, snappers, emperors, jacks, barracuda, and triggerfishes should be treated with caution. It is wise not to eat any predatory reef fish larger than those that are commonly caught and consumed locally. Fortunately, ciguatera is not present in the offshore pelagic and deep reef food chains that form the basis of the regions largest commercial fisheries.

The System of Classification

In order to efficiently catalogue and understand how the world's millions of varieties of animals relate to one another, scientists classify them in a hierarchical scheme based on kinship, that is, on their common ancestry and evolutionary development. In order to standardize such a scheme, all levels of classification use latinized names. Without such a universal language, any attempt at a conceivable scheme would result in chaos. In order to distinguish between levels of classification, many levels use standardized endings. The names of orders, families, and subfamilies end in "iformes", "idae", and "inae", respectively, as shown in boldface in the example of the emperor angelfish below.

Level of classification	Example	Common name
class	Osteichthyes	Bony fishes
subclass	Actinopterygii	Ray-finned fishes
superorder	Teleostei	"Modern" ray-finned fishes
order	Perciformes	Perch-like fishes
family	Pomacanthidae	Angelfishes
subfamily	Pomacanthiinae	
genus	*Pomacanthus*	genus and species together =
species	*imperator*	Emperor Angelfish

The levels of interest to the non-specialist are the family and species. A family consists of a group of species with a common ancestry. Each species in a family is more closely related to one another than to any other species. The species is a group of "the same kind" of organisms, that is, organisms that are capable of breeding with one another and producing fertile offspring which in turn are capable of producing future generations. The species name always consists of two parts, the genus and the "specific epithet". Both parts are always italicized (or underlined if italic type is not available); the genus is always capitalized, and the specific epithet is never capitalized. The genus name is used for one or more species and denotes a group of very closely related species distinguishable from one another by minor differences in morphology. The specific epithet denotes a single species within a genus; it cannot be used for another member of that genus, but can be used for species in other genera. Together the two parts form a unique name that distinguishes a species from all others. For some species, populations in different geographic regions have become sufficiently isolated from one another to maintain minor differences in coloration or morphology. These are indicated as subspecies by a third part added to the species name which is also latinized and italicized.

Living fishes fall into four major classes: the lampreys (Cephalaspidomorphi), the hagfishes (Pteraspidomorphi), the cartilagenous fishes (Chondrichthyes), and the bony fishes (Osteichthyes). The primitive lampreys and hagfishes, which lack jaws, consist of a few dozen species confined to cold waters. Cartilagenous and bony fishes are well represented in all seas with a few dozen of the former and at least 4,000 of the latter inhabiting coral reefs.

Physiology and Senses

Vision: fishes exhibit a tremendous diversity in eye development. Species active at night (nocturnal) and those that live in deep water (300-1,000 m) tend to have large eyes. Those living at extreme depths (below 2,000 m) or deep within caves where vision is useless have tiny vestigial eyes or none at all. The lens of a fish's eye is spherical and focusing is accomplished by movement of the lens back and forth within the eye. Fishes generally have an extremely wide field of view, but their greatest visual acuity in the forward field where the highest concentration of visual cells is located. Mudskippers have retractable periscope-like eyes on top of the head which give it a 360° field of vision. Shallow water fishes generally have both rods and cones and are thus able to perceive colors. This is particularly true of coral reef species where color plays an important role in species recognition and behavior.

Hearing and vibration: water is 1,000 times as dense as air allowing sound waves to travel five times faster (1,500 m/s) and further. Fishes can detect sound with their inner ears and lateral-line system. The lateral-line is a series of small perforated tubes running just under the skin of the head or midlateral part of the body. Each tube ("neuromast") contains cells("hair cells") which

ANATOMY OF A FISH

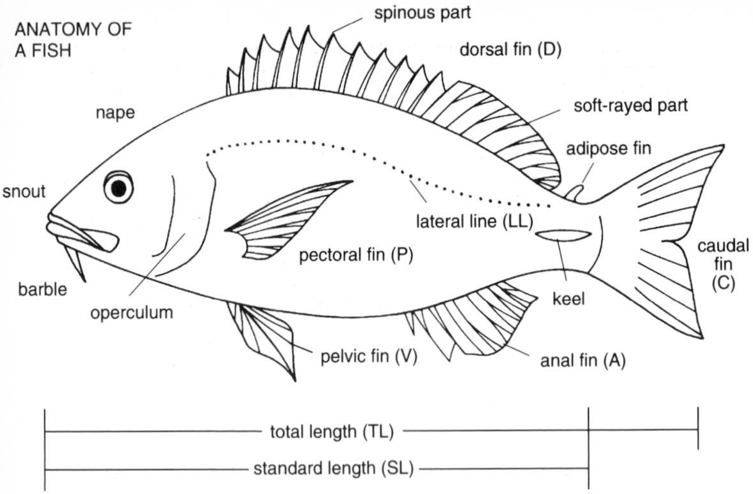
spinous part
dorsal fin (D)
soft-rayed part
nape
adipose fin
snout
lateral line (LL)
pectoral fin (P)
caudal fin (C)
barble
operculum
keel
pelvic fin (V)
anal fin (A)
total length (TL)
standard length (SL)

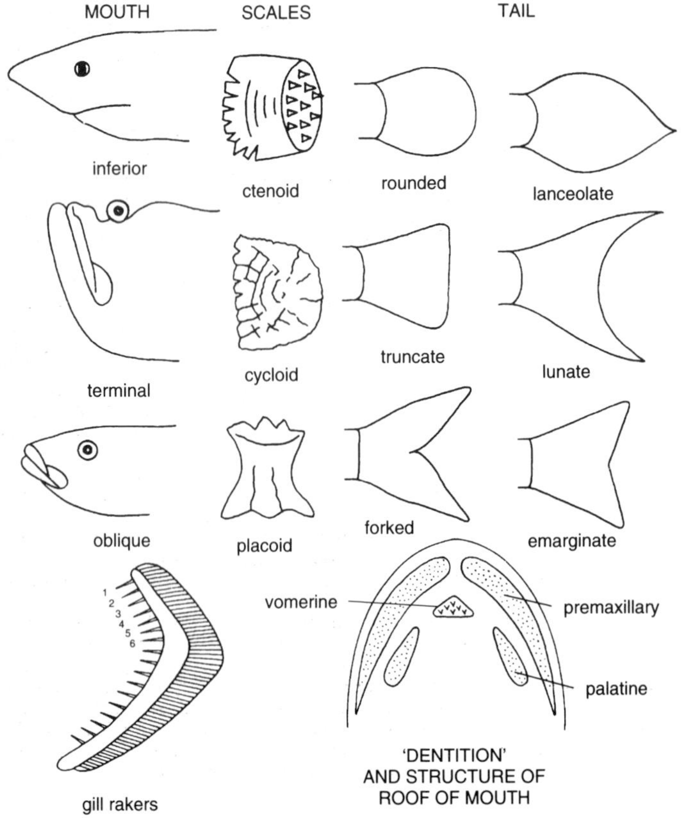
MOUTH
SCALES
TAIL
inferior
ctenoid
rounded
lanceolate
terminal
cycloid
truncate
lunate
oblique
placoid
forked
emarginate
1
2
3
4
5
6
vomerine
premaxillary
palatine
gill rakers
'DENTITION' AND STRUCTURE OF ROOF OF MOUTH

can detect water movement and the motion of nearby animals. The lateral-line is most sensitive to low-frequency near-field sounds. The ears of fishes consist of convoluted fluid-filled organs ("labyrinths") contained in chambers on either side of the skull. They are sensitive to movement and orientation of the fish and to high-frequency far-field sounds. In many fishes, the innermost portion of the ear is connected to the gas bladder which amplifies high-frequency sounds. Many fishes are able to produce a variety of sounds and often utilize the gas bladder for amplification. Recent studies have shown that sound may play an important role in courtship and spawning of many coral reef species.

Smell and taste: the sense of smell is well-developed in most fishes with olfactory organs generally located on the snout. Eels and sharks have a particularly keen sense of smell. Spawning salmon are able to return to their natal streams after years at sea by chemical cues picked up by their nostrils. Taste receptors are located in the mouth as well as on barbels, lips, and even scattered over the body or fins of some fishes. Some fishes (e.g. soapfishes, pls.30, 149; *Pardachirus* soles, pl. 131) are able to secrete bitter or toxic substances from pores in the skin which are extremely effective at deterring predation by other fishes.

Electromagnetic: sharks, rays, and some bony fishes (e.g. Plotosus, pl. 9-1) have electro-receptors sensitive to the minute electrical fields produced by all living things. These organs ("ampullae of Lorenzini"), located in pores in the front of the head enable sharks and rays to locate prey buried in sediment or in open water with no visibility. Migratory fishes are able to detect the magnetic field of the earth as well as magnetic anomalies produced by certain bottom features such as banks or pinnacles. Some fishes (electric rays, pls.3, 141 ; Astroscopus pl. 167-13) have electrical organs capable of producing currents of electricity strong enough to stun prey or deter predators.

Touch and Pain: fishes have a network of free nerve endings in the skin which enable them to register sensations of touch. Barbels and enlarged pectoral or pelvic fin rays are often well-equipped with free nerve endings. While many fishes exhibit behaviors that seem to indicate that they either do not perceive pain or have a high tolerance for it, others, such as the avoidance many adult fish exhibit towards scale-eating blennies indicate that pain may serve a useful function.

Respiration: fishes respire by passing water over the surface of the gills. The feathery red gill filaments consist of numerous convoluted lamellae containing capillaries at the surface where oxygen diffuses into the blood and carbon dioxide diffuses out. Water contains only about 3% of the oxygen contained in an equal volume of air. Fishes can effectively remove about 74% of this from the water. Mudskippers and freshwater eels are able to absorb a considerable portion of their oxygen through the skin. Some fishes adapted to low-oxygen environments have developed the ability to breath air through modifications of the swim bladder.

Swimbladder: most bony fishes have a gas-filled organ known as the swimbladder. Its primary function is to provide buoyancy which enables the fish to remain upright and stay within a given depth range without floating or sinking. The gas bladder of a fish taken rapidly to the surface from deep water will expand to the point where its eyes may bulge and stomach may protrude from the mouth. Sharks have a large oily liver instead of a swimbladder. Many bottom-dwelling fishes lack a swim bladder.

Temperature: nearly all fishes are "cold-blooded", that is they are the same temperature as their surroundings. Most fishes have rather narrow temperature tolerances of only a few degrees Celsius. Many coral reef species can tolerate seasonal temperatures as low as 15°C or as high as 33°C, but are intolerant of rapid changes or prolonged exposure to these extremes. Certain fast-swimming pelagic fishes such as tunas, billfishes, and lamnid sharks (including the great white shark) have high metabolisms and are able to maintain a core body temperature higher than their surroundings.

1 SHARKS

WHALE SHARK (RHINCODONTIDAE): the single species described below.

1 **Whale shark** *Rhincodon typus* (Smith) 12 m
World's largest fish, unconfirmed reports to 18 m; toothless terminal mouth; distinctive pattern of spots and bars on dorsal surface; young probably born fully developed. **Ecology:** feeds on zooplankton, pelagic crustaceans, small fishes and squids seived through a spongy tissue between the gill arches. Pelagic, rarely found near shore in areas of upwelling or convergence. Curious and harmless. **Range:** circumtropical.

ZEBRA SHARK (STEGOSTOMATIDAE): body cylindrical with prominent ridges on sides; tail long without a lower lobe. Young hatch from egg cases at size of 20 to 26 cm. One species.

2 **Zebra shark (juv.); Leopard shark** *Stegastoma fasciatum* (Hermann) 354 cm
Ecology: solitary bottom dweller usually in channels or patches of sand or rubble at depths of 5 to over 30 m. Generally found resting on sand rather than in caves. Forages primarily at night on molluscs and small fishes. Harmless unless molested. **Range:** Red Sea to Samoa, n. to s. Japan, s. to se. Australia.

NURSE SHARKS (GINGLYMOSTOMATIDAE): bottom dwelling sharks lacking a lower tail lobe and with a small mouth bearing multicuspid teeth; young born fully developed.

3 **Nurse shark** *Nebrius ferrugineus* Rüppell 320 cm
Both D fins far back; tail rel. long; barbels long; matures at 250 cm; litters of ⩾4. **Ecology:** lagoon and seaward reefs, 1 to 70 m. On sand where currents flow. Feeds primarily at night on small fishes, crustaceans, cephalopods, or even sea urchins and sea snakes that may be sucked or rooted from shelter. Harmless unless molested. **Range:** Red Sea to Tuamotus, n. to s. Japan, s. to N. Cal.

4 **Short-tail nurse shark** *Ginglymostoma brevicaudatum* Günther 75 cm
Both D fins far back; tail rel. short (<¼TL); barbels short; very small size. **Ecology:** coastal reefs of continental shelf. Diet probably similar to 3. Harmless. **Range:** E Africa; possibly to Seychelles and Mauritius.

WOBBEGONGS (ORECTOLOBIDAE): body flattened with highly variegated pattern and tassels and skin flaps on side of head and around mouth; young born fully developed at 20 to 26 cm. Bottom dwellers with poor eyesight. Generally harmless unless approached too closely.

5 **Tassled wobbegong** *Eucrossorhinus dasypogon* (Bleeker) 366 cm
Sides of head and chin with dermal flaps; large spiracles behind eyes. Ca. 22 cm at birth. **Ecology:** coral reefs, intertidal to ⩾40 m. Solitary, usually in caves by day. Feeds on fishes and crustaceans. **Range:** e. Indonesia, New Guinea and n. Australia to ca. 20° S.

6 **Ornate wobbegong** *Orectolobus ornatus* deVis 288 cm
Orectolobus spp. without chin flaps and with head, P and V fins narrower than 5; similar to *O. japonicus* (s. Jap. to Viet. & Phil.) which has reticulated lines instead of blotches and spots on light areas of back. Ca. 20 cm at birth. **Ecology:** coral and rocky reefs, intertidal to ⩾30 m. Feeds primarily at night on fishes and invertebrates. Solitary or in aggregations. More often in clearer water than 7. **Range:** all Australia except Tasmania; New Guinea and s. Japan.

7 **Spotted wobbegong** *Orectolobus maculatus* Bonnaterre 320 cm
Similar to 6 but with ocellated spots on back and 8-10 dermal flaps forward of eyes; ⩾37 per litter; ♂ mature at 60 cm. **Ecology:** coastal bays and rocky reefs, intertidal to 110 m. Juveniles in estuaries and seagrass beds. Feeds on fishes and invertebrates. Primarily warm-temperate waters. **Range:** all Australia except Tasmania. Possibly Japan and S. China Sea.

BAMBOOSHARKS (HEMISCYLLIDAE): smaller and more elongate than 2-5, nearly cylindrical in cross-section; young hatch from round egg cases. Harmless; used as foodfishes.

8 **Gray bambooshark** *Chiloscyllium griseum* Müller & Henle ⩾ 74 cm
Ecology: common in inshore waters. Probably feeds on invertebrates. **Range:** Arab. G. to PNG, n. to e. China and s. Japan.

9 **Brownbanded bambooshark** *Chiloscyllium punctatum* Müller & Henle 104 cm
Ecology: common in shallow intertidal and inshore waters. Often under coral by day, feeds at night on invertebrates. **Range:** India to ne. Australia, Phil., and s. Japan.

10 **White-spotted bambooshark** *Chiloscyllium plagiosum* (Bennett) 95 cm
Ecology: shallow intertidal and inshore waters, often under coral or in crevices by day. Forages at night on fishes and invertebrates. **Range:** India to w. Indonesia, Phil., and s. Japan.

11 **Epaulette shark** *Hemiscyllium ocellatum* (Bonnaterre) 107 cm
Nostrils smaller and snout shorter and blunter than 8 & 9; shoulder spots distinctive. **Ecology:** inshore waters, intertidal to 10 m. Often under coral by day. Feeds at night on invertebrates. Common on Great Barrier Reef. **Range:** all N. Guinea and Australia n. of 30° S, possibly to Sumatra.

12 See over

1
2 juv
2
3
4
6
5
7
8
9
10
11
12

←12 **Speckled catshark** *Hemiscyllium trispeculare* Richardson 64 cm
Shoulder spots distinctive; snout shorter than other spp. shown. **Ecology:** shallow coral reefs, often under coral by day. Feeds at night on invertebrates. **Range:** Australia n. of 30° S. Possibly also Indonesia.

2 SHARKS

REQUIEM SHARKS (CARCHARHINIDAE): sleek, active swimmers with 1st D fin base located in front of V fins, single cusped teeth in a single functional row in each jaw, and tail with a distinct lower lobe. Young born fully developed. Includes several dangerous species, but most prefer to avoid divers.

1 **Reef blacktip shark** *Carcharhinus melanopterus* (Quoy & Gaimard) 180 cm
Black tips on fins, 1st D fin with white submarginal band; mature at about 110 cm. **Ecology:** reef flats and shallow lagoons and reef margins to 75 m, usually very shallow. Easily frightened, but known to mistakenly bite wader's feet. Feeds on small fishes. **Range:** Red Sea to Hawaiian, Marquesan, and Mangareva Is., n. to s. Japan, s. to N. Cal.

2 **Gray reef shark** *Carcharhinus amblyrhynchos* (Bleeker) 233 cm
Trailing edge of tail dusky, trailing edge of 1st D may be white; matures at 130-140 cm. **Ecology:** lagoon and seaward reefs to a depth of 274 m. Usually encountered along steep outer reef slopes and in channels, particularly common on atolls. Small individuals often in packs. Feeds primarily on fishes, occasionally on crustaceans and cephalopods. Usually curious, but may be aggressive and engage in a threat display before attacking. Among the most likely of sharks to attack divers, but generally gives a single non-fatal bite. **Range:** Red Sea to Hawaiian and Easter Is., s. to L. Howe; primarily at oceanic islands.

3 **Silvertip shark** *Carcharhinus albimarginatus* (Rüppell) 300 cm
White trailing edges of fins distinctive; ♂ matures at 165 cm, ♀ at 170 cm; young of this family born fully developed. **Ecology:** dropoffs and offshore banks at depths of 10 to 400 m, usually below 30 m. Feeds primarily on fishes, including rays and small sharks. May be persistent and potentially dangerous. **Range:** Red Sea to c. America, n. to s. Japan, s. to N. Cal.; primarily at oceanic islands.

4 **Oceanic whitetip shark** *Carcharhinus longimanus* (Poey) 270 cm
Long, rounded fins with white tips distinctive; ♂ mature at <198 cm, ♀ at $\geqslant 180$ cm. **Ecology:** surface layers of open sea over 200-500 m bottom, rare at offshore coral banks. Feeds on pelagic fishes and squids. Aggressive and dangerous. **Range:** all seas warmer than 20°C, rare in waters as cool as 15°C.

5 **Sandbar shark** *Carcharhinus plumbeus* (Nardo) 240 cm
1st D fin tall, snout rounded, and uniform color; matures at 131-144 cm. **Ecology:** intertidal to 280 m. Continental shelf populations migrate to temperate seas in spring. Feeds primarily on small bottomfishes. **Range:** continental shelves of all tropical and temperate seas and Hawaiian Is.

6 **Spinner shark** *Carcharhinus brevipinna* (Müller & Henle) 280 cm
Pointed snout, black tips on both D, P, and A fins and lower tail lobe; C. limbatus similar but has larger D fin and slightly shorter snout; **os** mature at 159 cm, **os** at 170 cm. **Ecology:** coastal-pelagic from shoreline to $\geqslant 75$ m. Feeds on small fishes. **Range:** continental shelves of tropical and warm-temperate Atlantic and Indo-Pacific.

7 **Spot-tail shark** *Carcharhinus sorrah* (Valenciennes) 160 cm
Slightly pointed snout, black tips on 2nd D and P fins and lower tail lobe, narrow black trailing edge on 1st D fin; matures at $\geqslant 106$ cm. **Ecology:** shallow continental shelves, primarily coral reefs to 73 m. Feeds on small fishes and cephalopods. **Range:** Red Sea to e. Australia and Solomon Is.(?), n. to Taiwan.

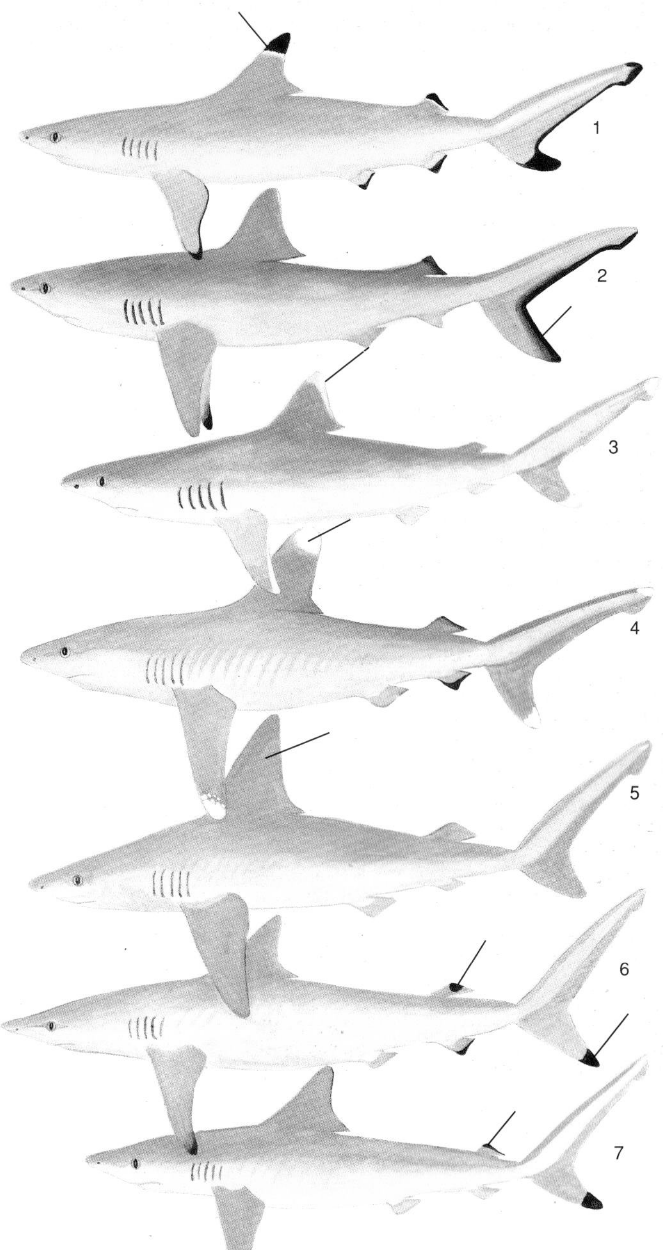
1
2
3
4
5
6
7

3 SHARKS, ELECTRIC RAYS and GUITARFISHES

1 **Tiger shark** *Galeocerdo cuvier* (Peron & Lesueur) ⩾ 550 cm
Head wide, nearly square; dusky bars and wide, serrated teeth distinctive; ♂ mature at 290 cm, ♀ at 340 cm; up to 80 pups per litter. **Ecology:** outer reef slopes and offshore banks, usually remains deep during the day, but may enter shallow water at night to feed. Common seasonally in lagoons of nw. Hawaiian Is. The most dangerous tropical shark, responsible for many fatalities. Feeds on wide range of animals, including porpoises, sea turtles, seabirds, spiny puffers, sharks, and rays. **Range:** all tropical and warm-temperate seas.

2 **Indo-Pacific lemon shark** *Negaprion acutidens* (Rüppell) 310 cm
D fins large, both nearly same size; yellowish hue. **Ecology:** lagoon and seaward reefs, more often turbid lagoons of ⩾30 m. Feeds on bottomfishes and rays. Shy, but easily enraged and potentially dangerous. **Range:** Red Sea to Tuamotus, n. to Marshalls, s. to Queensland.

3 **Reef whitetip shark** *Triaenodon obesus* (Rüppell) 216 cm
White tips on 1st D fin and tail, snout blunt, consipicuous nasal flaps; upper teeth triangular and serrated, lower teeth dagger-like; ♂ mature at 100 cm, ♀ at 125 cm. **Ecology:** inhabits well-developed coral reefs to a depth of 122 m, common on oceanic islands. Often rests on bottom, particularly in channels or caves. Usually docile, but may get aggressive around speared fish. Feeds on fishes, octopuses, and crustaceans. **Range:** Red Sea to Panama, n. to Ryukyus & Bonins, s. to NSW.

HAMMERHEAD SHARKS (SPHYRNIDAE): a laterally expanded blade on either side of head; eyes located at tip of each blade. Young born fully developed. Potentially dangerous.

4 **Scalloped hammerhead shark** *Sphyrna lewini* (Griffith & Smith) 330 cm
Leading edge of head slightly rounded and scalloped, 1st D fin nearly = body depth; ♂ mature at 140 cm, ♀ at 200 cm; up to 30 pups per litter. **Ecology:** adults primarily pelagic, form large shoals in shallow water in Sea of Cortez, but usually remain below thermocline (50-200 m) in Indo-Pacific. Enters shallow turbid inshore backwaters to breed. Young often in schools that forage in protected inshore waters, then migrate to deeper waters to grow. Feeds primarily on fishes, including other sharks and rays, occasionally on cephalopods and crustaceans. Generally non-aggressive. **Range:** circumtropical.

5 **Great hammerhead shark** *Sphyrna mokarran* (Rüppell) 545 cm
Leading edge of head nearly straight, 1st D fin tall, pointed (ca. 1.5 x body depth); matures at 300 cm; up to 38 pups per litter, usually in late spring to summer. **Ecology:** in atoll lagoons and passes in Fr. Polynesia, but rare on most coral reefs. Feeds primarily on fishes, particularly rays, occasionally on cephalopods and crustaceans. Considered dangerous in most areas. **Range:** circumtropical-temperate.

ELECTRIC RAYS (TORPEDINIDAE): rays with 2 large kidney-shaped electric organs on either side of head. Can deliver a dangerous electric shock normally used to stun small fishes on which they feed. Young hatch inside uterus; born fully developed.

6 **Blackspotted electric ray** *Torpedo fuscomaculata* Peters 64 cm
Variable with black spots present or absent. Similar to *T. panthera* (Red Sea). **Ecology:** sandy areas near deep rocky reefs, 25 to 439 m. **Range:** Zanz. to S. Africa (23°E), e. to Seychelles, Mauritius & sw. India.

7 **Marbled electric ray** *Torpedo sinuspersici* Olfers 130 cm
Ecology: common in shallow sandy areas, intertidal to 200 m. **Range:** continental shelves from Red Sea to India, s. to Madagascar and S. Africa.

8 **Numbfish** *Hypnos monopterygium* (Shaw & Nodder) 69 cm
Color variable, from light brown to nearly black. **Ecology:** sandy to muddy bottoms, intertidal to 240 m. **Range:** w., s.& e. Australia n. to s. GBR.

GUITARFISHES (RHINOBATIDAE): elongate rays with pointed depressed heads and sharklike bodies; teeth flattened, pavement-like. Young born fully developed.

9 **White-spotted guitarfish** *Rhynchobatus djiddensis* (Forsskål) 305 cm, 227 kg
♂ mature at 156 cm, ♀ at 177 cm; ca. 55-67 cm at birth. **Ecology:** sandy inshore areas to over 30 m. Feeds on crabs, squids, and small fishes. **Range:** Red Sea to N. Cal., n. to s. Jap., s. to NSW; primarily continental shorelines.

1
2
3
4
5
5
6
7
8
9

4 RAYS

STINGRAYS (DASYATIDAE): body flattened into round or nearly round disc; small mouth with pavement-like teeth; one or more venomous barbs near base of tail. Respire by drawing water through a small hole behind the eye and expelling it through gill slits on underside of disc. Young born fully developed. All species dangerous if stepped on, the larger ones can deliver a fatal sting.

1 **Bluespotted ribbontail ray** *Taeniura lymma* (Forsskål) 243 cm, width 95 cm
Round shape with bright blue spots; A fin in form of long fold on tail. **Ecology:** sandy areas of coral reefs, often in caves or beneath ledges. **Range:** Red Sea to Fiji, n. to s. Jap., s. to GBR & Vanuatu.

2 **Giant reef ray** *Taeniura melanospilos* Bleeker ca. 3 m, width 164 cm
Round shape with dense pattern of black spots; tail somewhat compressed. **Ecology:** sandy areas of coral reefs from shallow flats to 430 m. Feeds on fishes. **Range:** Red Sea to the Galapagos, n. to s. Jap., s. to N. Cal.

3 **Bluespotted stingray** *Dasyatis kuhlii* (Müller & Henle) 80 cm, width 40 cm
Angular shape with less conspicuous blue spots than in 1, black spots may also be present. **Ecology:** sandy areas of coral reefs to a depth of at least 50 m. Feeds on sand-dwelling invertebrates. **Range:** Red Sea to Samoa, n. to s. Jap., s. to N. Cal.

4 **Honeycomb stingray** *Himantura uarnak* (Forsskål) 6 m, width 175 cm; 120 kg
Pattern variable with network of dark spots, ocelli, or blotches; tail extremely long. **Ecology:** mangrove creeks and sandy areas of coral reefs to at least 42 m. **Range:** Red Sea to Fr. Polynesia, n. to Ryukyus, s. to Queensland.

EAGLE RAYS (MYLIOBATIDAE): head protrudes from disc; disc wide and winglike; tail long and slender with one or more venomous barbs at its base in most species; jaws powerful with large platelike crushing teeth in several rows. Young born fully developed.

5 **Flapnose ray** *Rhinoptera javanica* Müller & Henle width: 120 cm; 45 kg.
No markings; head bilobed; barb at base of tail. **Ecology:** above sand and mud bottoms of inshore reefs, sometimes in large aggregations. Feeds on bivalves. **Range:** E. Africa to Indonesia, n. to s. China.

6 **Spotted eagle ray** *Aetobatus narinari* (Euphrasen) width: 229 cm; 227 kg.
White spots become ocelli in some individuals; 2-6 barbs at base of tail. Up to 4 pups per litter born at 17-35 cm. **Ecology:** seagrass flats and sandy areas of coral reefs to 80 m. Usually swims above bottom. Feeds on mollusks and crustaceans. Usually solitary but occasionally in groups. **Range:** circumtropical.

MANTA RAYS (MOBULIDAE): large protruding flaps in front of mouth; disc wide and winglike; small D fin at base of tail; tail spine rudimentary or absent; teeth minute. Mantas feed by flitering plankton from water drawn over filter plates on the inside of gill openings. Young born fully developed. Among the largest of fishes, but harmless.

7 **Manta ray** *Manta birostris* (Donndorff) width: 670 cm; 1,400 kg.
Horn-like flaps in front of mouth; minute teeth in lower jaw only; filter plates on inside of gill openings; species of *Mobula* smaller with smaller head flaps and teeth in both jaws. **Ecology:** swims in mid-water singly or in small groups, most often in or near channels. Harmless, feeds on plankton. **Range:** circumtropical.

8 **Devilray** *Mobula japonica* (Müller & Henle) width: ca. 310 cm
Ca. 9 spp. in genus, 5 in Indo-Pacific. All with smaller head flaps than 7 and teeth in both jaws; some spp. to ca. 310 cm width. This sp. with v. long tail with basal spine; possibly = *M. mobular* (Atlantic & Medit.). **Ecology:** swims in mid-water, primarily pelagic. Harmless, feeds on plankton. **Range:** E. Africa to Calif., n. to s. Japan, s. to N. Z.; W. Africa.

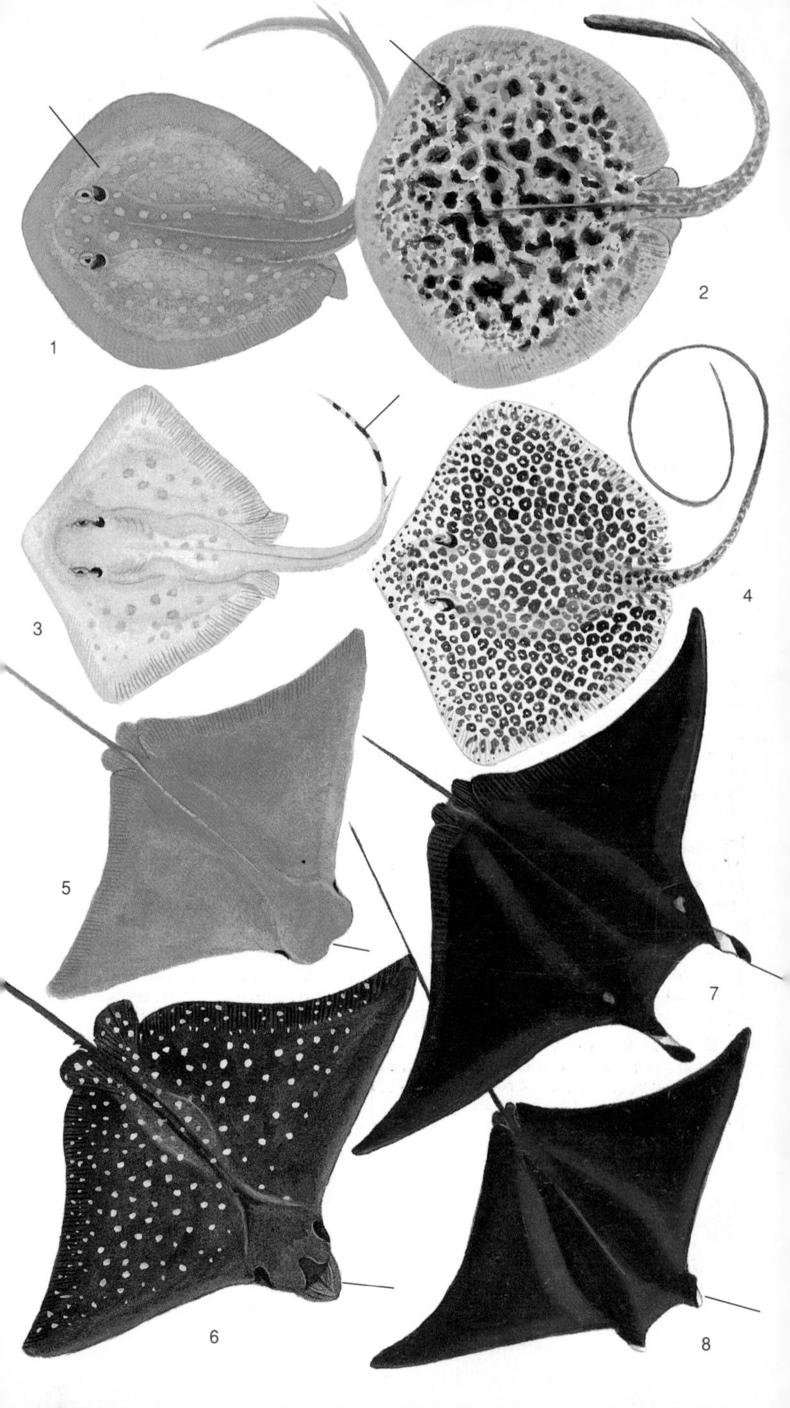
1
2
3
4
5
6
7
8

5 MORAY EELS

MORAY EELS (MURAENIDAE): a diverse group of extremely elongate fishes with large mouths containing numerous teeth, restricted gill openings, and no pectoral or pelvic fins. Most are secretive during the day. Widely used as food, but a few large species may be ciguatoxic. Morays are normally docile, but will bite if provoked. Bites from large morays may require medical attention and result in permanent injury. Generally hardy in captivity.

1 **Snowflake moray** *Echidna nebulosa* (Ahl) 75 cm
Echidna spp. with blunt snouts and short conical teeth, some molar-like and closely packed. **Ecology:** shallow lagoon and seaward reefs, particularly common on intertidal reef flats; feeds primarily on crustaceans. Safely kept with small aquarium fishes. **Range:** Red Sea to Panama, n. to Ryuk. and Hawaiian Is., s. to L. Howe Is.

2 **Barred moray** *Echidna polyzona* (Richardson) 60 cm
Bars become obscure or degenerate to uniform pattern of fine speckles in large individuals. **Ecology:** reef flats and clear shallow lagoon and seaward reefs; feeds primarily on crustaceans during both day and night. **Range:** Red Sea to Marquesas, n. to Ryuk. and Hawaiian Is., s. to GBR and Tuamotus.

3 **Whiteface moray** *Echidna leucotaenia* (Schultz) 75 cm
Ecology: reef flats and outer lagoon and seaward reefs to 24 m; feeds on crustaceans. **Range:** E. Africa to Line and Tuam. Is., n. to Johnston Is.

4 **Bayer's moray** *Enchelycore bayeri* (Schultz) 65 cm
Enchelycore spp. with curved or hooked jaws, numerous long dagger-like teeth, and enlarged nostrils. **Ecology:** lagoon and seaward reefs, 0-20 m. Feeds on fishes. Very secretive. **Range:** Chagos to Line and Society Is., n. to Marianas, s. to GBR.

5 **Dragon moray** *Enchelycore pardalis* (Temminck) 80 cm
Unmistakeable pattern; rear nostrils as long tubes. **Ecology:** coral and rocky reefs, common in warm-temperate s. Japan. Feeds on fishes. **Range:** Reunion to Hawaiian, Line, and Society Is., n. to s. Korea, s. to N. Cal.

6 **Mosaic moray** *Enchelycore ramosus* (Griffin) 150 cm
Ecology: subtropical and warm-temperate coral and rocky reefs. Secretive. **Range:** se. Aust., n. NZ, L. Howe, Norfolk, Kermadec, Rapa, and Easter Is.

7 **White-margined moray** *Enchelycore schismatorhynchus* (Bleeker) 120 cm
Uniformly tan with white margin on fins. **Ecology:** lagoon and seaward reefs. **Range:** Chagos to Marq. and Society Is., n. to Ryukyus.

8 **Viper moray** *Enchelynassa canina* (Quoy & Gaimard) 152 cm
Rear nostrils surrounded by fleshy rim, front nostrils with bilobed fleshy protuberance. **Ecology:** benches, outer reef flats, and shallow reefs exposed to strong surge. Very secretive by day, hunts at night for fishes and octopuses. **Range:** Chagos to Panama, n. to Marcus and Hawaiian, s. to Tonga and Mangareva.

9 **Zebra moray** *Gymnomuraena zebra* (Shaw) 150 cm
Snout blunt, teeth close-set and pebble-like, fins undeveloped, color pattern unique. **Ecology:** seaward reefs from surge zone to at least 39 m. Feeds mainly on xanthid crabs, but will also take other crustaceans, mollusks, or sea urchins. Secretive and quite docile. **Range:** Red Sea to Panama, n. to Ryukyu and Hawaiian, s. to Society Is.

10 **Giant estuarine moray** *Strophidon sathete* (Hamilton) 394 cm
Body extremely elongate; fins low; mouth large. **Ecology:** muddy bottoms of tidal rivers and inner bays, subtidal to 15m. Reported to extend itself vertically from a burrow with its head held horizontally beneath the surface, rising and falling with the tide, giving it the Palauan name of "tide gauge eel". **Range:** Red Sea to Fiji, n. to Ryuk., s. to N. Cal. & s. Qld.

11 **Ribbon Eel** *Rhinomuraena quaesita* Garman 120 cm
Flaps on nostrils, lower chin with barbels; body ribbon-like, fins wide; changes sex from ♂ to ♀; juvs. black, ♂ ($\geqslant$65 cm) blue with yellow fins, and ♀ ($\geqslant$94 cm) yellow. **Ecology:** lagoon and seaward reefs, intertidal to at least 57 m. A secretive dweller of rubble or sand usually seen with only head protruding. Feeds on fishes. Common on Indo-Australian reefs, rare on oceanic islands. A popular aquarium fish but delicate. **Range:** E. Africa to Tuam., n. to s. Japan, s. to N Cal. and Austral Is.

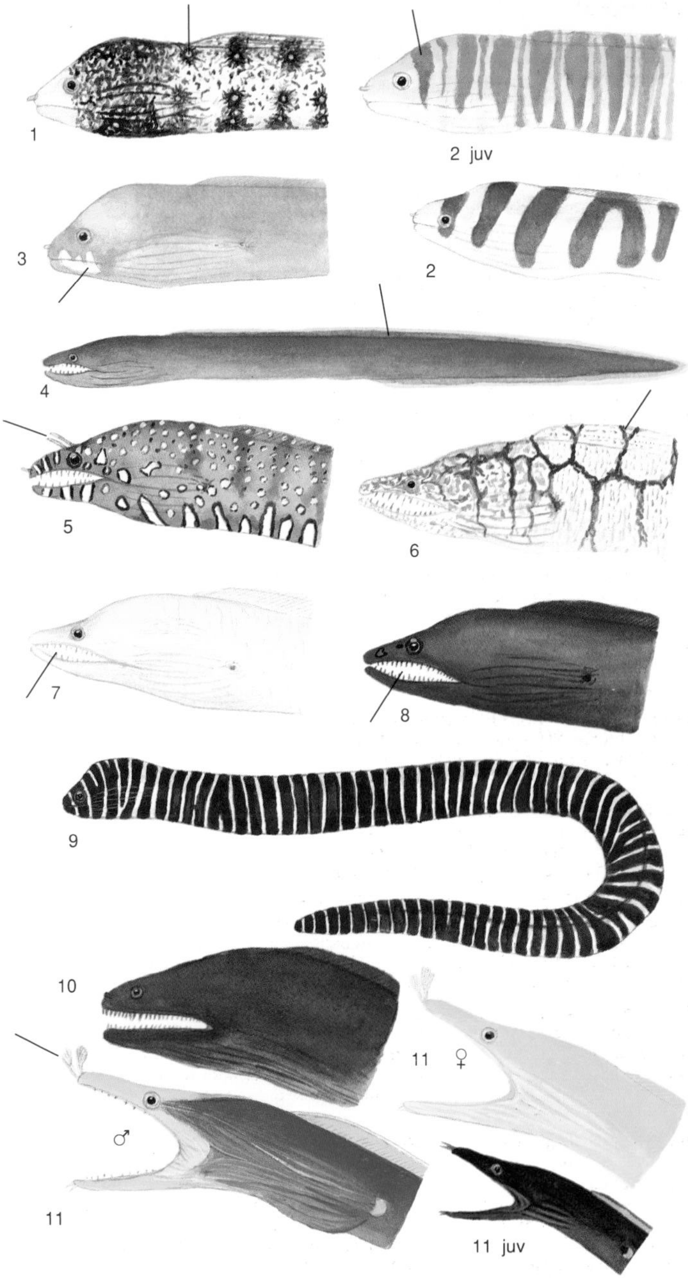
1
2 juv
3
2
4
5
6
7
8
9
10
11 ♀
♂
11
11 juv

6 MORAY EELS

1 **Giant moray** *Gymnothorax javanicus* (Bleeker) 300 cm
Gymnothorax spp. with 1 depressable fang along front midline of upper jaw (which may be lost in old individuals). Juvs. of this sp. uniformly tan to brown with rows of large dark spots on sides; large individuals become quite heavy-set. **Ecology:** shallow lagoon and seaward reefs to ⩾46 m. The most common large moray throughout most of the Indo-Pacific. Feeds primarily on fishes, occasionally on crustaceans. Frequently ciquatoxic. Capable of causing severe injury, but normally docile and tamed by dive guides in certain areas. **Range:** Red Sea to Marq. and Pitcairn Is., n. to Ryuk., s. to N. Cal. and Austral Is.; rare in Hawaiian Is.

2 **Whitemouth moray** *Gymnothorax meleagris* (Shaw & Nodder) 120 cm
Inside of mouth white; rarely spots may be connected to form reticulate pattern. **Ecology:** coral-rich areas of lagoon and seaward reefs from 1 to 36 m. Feeds primarily on fishes, less often on crustaceans. Common in Hawaiian Is., uncommon elsewhere. **Range:** Red Sea to Mangareva and Galapagos; n. to s. Japan and Hawaiian Is., s. to N. Cal.

3 **Salt and pepper moray** *Gymnothorax eurostus* (Abbott) 57 cm
Dark individuals resemble *G. buroensis*, but are covered with numerous yellow specks. **Ecology:** among coral and rubble of seaward reefs. The most common moray in the Hawaiian Islands. Feeds on fishes and crustaceans. **Range:** se. Africa to Isla del Coco (Costa Rica), n. to s. Japan and Hawaiian Is., s. to L. Howe and Easter Is; mainly antitropical.

4 **Yellowmouth moray** *Gymnothorax nudivomer* (Playfair) 180 cm
Inside of mouth yellow, spots on lg. indiv. minute and close-set anteriorly, large and widely-spaced posteriorly; mucus is toxic. **Ecology:** seaward reefs ⩾ 4 m in Red Sea, much deeper (30-165 m) elsewhere. **Range:** Red Sea to Hawaiian and Marq. Is., n. to Ryuk., s. to N Cal.

5 **Yellow-margined moray** *Gymnothorax flavimarginatus* (Rüppell) 123 cm
Differs from 1 by green fringe on fins, orange eyes, and no leopard-like dark blotches. **Ecology:** reef flats and lagoon and seaward reefs to 150 m. Feeds on fishes and crustaceans. Commonest large moray in Hawaiian Is. **Range:** Red Sea to Panama, n. to Ryuk. and Hawaiian Is., s. to N. Cal. and Austral Is.

6 **Undulated moray** *Gymnothorax undulatus* (Lacépède) 150 cm
Ecology: among rocks and rubble of lagoon and seaward reefs to 26 m. Common on reef flats. Primarily nocturnal, feeds on fishes, octopuses, and probably crustaceans. **Range:** Red Sea to Panama, n. to s. Japan and Hawaiian Is., s. to s. GBR and Australs.

7 **Latticetail moray** *Gymnothorax buroensis* (Bleeker) 33 cm
Similar to dark *G. eurostus* but without numerous yellow specks. **Ecology:** shallow lagoon and seaward reefs to at least 24 m, primarily in surge zone. **Range:** E. Africa to Panama, n. to Ryuk. and Hawaiian Is., s. to Tuam.

8 **Barredfin moray** *Gymnothorax zonipectis* (Seale) 47 cm
Facial pattern distinctive, rest of body similar to small *G. undulatus*. **Ecology:** rubble and ledges of seaward reefs to ⩾ 40 m. Usually in caves below 20 m. **Range:** E. Africa to Marq. and Society Is., n. to Phil. & Johnston Is.

9 **Masked moray** *Gymnothorax breedeni* (McCosker & Randall) 75 cm
Black marks behind eye and on corner of mouth distinctive. **Ecology:** clear seaward reefs of oceanic islands from 4 to over 25 m. Aggressive. **Range:** E. Africa, Comore, Seychelles, Maldives, Line, and Marq. Is.

10 **Freckled moray** *Gymnothorax fuscomaculatus* (Schultz) 20 cm
D fin origin close to anus; teeth short and conical, but upper jaw with median row. White spots around posterior nostrils and each pore on sides of jaw. **Ecology:** coral and rubble of seaward reefs to 25 m. Very secretive. **Range:** E. Africa to Tuam., s. to GBR and Fiji.

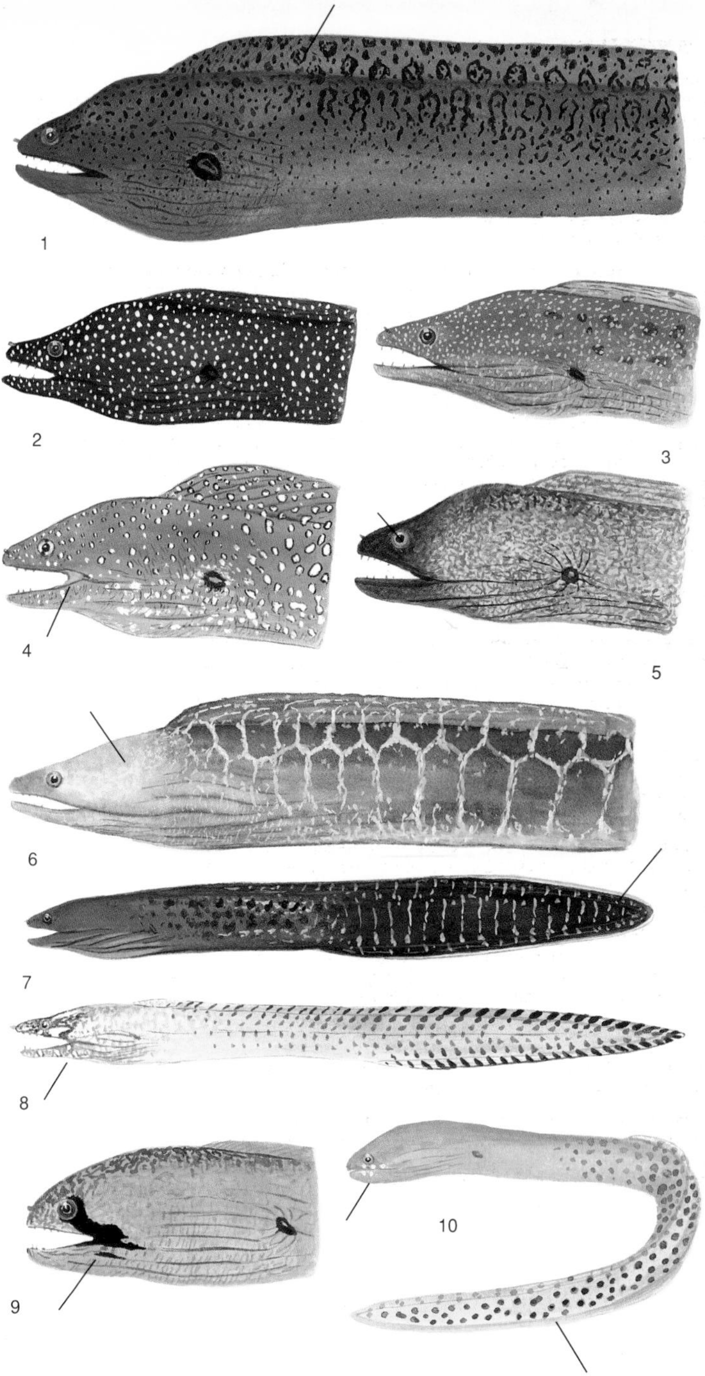
1
2
3
4
5
6
7
8
9
10

7 MORAY EELS

1 **Honeycomb moray** *Gymnothorax favagineus* (Bloch & Schneider) 300 cm
Resembles *G. permistus*, but spots about size of eye and more regular in shape, forming a honeycomb pattern. Large adults may be aggressive. **Ecology:** reef flats and outer reef slopes of continental reefs to over 35 m. **Range:** s. Red Sea & E. Africa to PNG, n. to Oman, s. to s. Mozambique & s. GBR.

2 **Black-blotched moray** *Gymnothorax permistus* (Smith) 66 cm
Smaller and slenderer than *G. favagineus* with relatively larger, irregularly-shaped spots. **Ecology:** rocky reefs of continental coasts, 1 to 12 m. **Range:** Indian Ocean from E. Africa to Sri Lanka.

3 **Blackspotted Moray** *Gymnothorax melanospilus* (Bleeker) 180 cm
Spots widely spaced, becoming curved and clumped into near circles with age. **Ecology:** outer reef slopes of continental reefs; common at Okinawa and se. China. **Range:** Maldives to the s. GBR, n. to s. Japan.

4 **Fimbriated moray** *Gymnothorax fimbriatus* (Bennett) 80 cm
Ecology: reef flats, lagoon and seaward reefs to at least 26 m. Feeds on fishes and crustaceans, probably nocturnal. **Range:** Seychelles & Mauritius to Society Is., n. to Ryuk., s. to ne. Australia.

5 **Yellow-headed moray** *Gymnothorax rueppelliae* (McClelland) 80 cm
Resembles *G. enigmaticus*, but bars on head do not meet on underside and head yellowish. **Ecology:** reef flats and outer lagoon and seaward reefs to at least 30 m. Feeds on fishes and crustaceans, primarily at night. Nervous and aggressive. **Range:** Red Sea to Hawaiian, Marq., and Tuam. Is., n. to Ryuk., s. to GBR.

6 **Dirty yellow moray** *Gymnothorax melatremus* Schultz 18 cm
Teeth short and conical; body dirty yellow with dark area around gill opening. **Ecology:** holes and crevices of seaward reefs to at least 26 m. **Range:** E. Africa to Hawaiian, Marq. and Mangareva Is., s. to Australs.

7 **Tiger moray** *Gymnothorax enigmaticus* (McCosker & Randall) 58 cm
Resembles *G. rueppelliae*, but bars on head complete and head never yellow. **Ecology:** clear intertidal reefs, probably also in other habitats. **Range:** G. Aden to Tuam., n. to Ryuk., s. to Samoa.

8 **Blotchnecked moray** *Gymnothorax margaritophorus* (Bleeker) 70 cm
Ecology: seaward reefs to at least 20 m. Very secretive. **Range:** E. Africa to Line and Society Is., N. to Ryuk. & Johnston Is., s. to s. GBR.

9 **Longsnout moray** *Gymnothorax steindachneri* Jordan & Evermann 65 cm
Ecology: shallow seaward reefs to over 30 m, common in holes or crevices at base of corals or rock. **Range:** Hawaiian Is.

10 **Peppered moray** *Siderea picta* (Ahl) 120 cm
Siderea spp. with blunt snout and stout conical teeth, none molariform or depressible, in 2 rows on vomer. On this species, small juvs. have circles instead of spots; they break up into spots which become proportionately smaller and more numerous with growth. **Ecology:** reef flats and rocky intertidal shorelines. Common on most Pacific reefs. Feeds on small crustaceans and fishes, sometimes leaving the water in pursuit of prey. **Range:** E. Africa, S. Africa to e. Pacific Is., n. to Ryuk. and Hawaiian Is., s. to s. Qld and Mangareva.

11 **Geometric moray** *Siderea grisea* (Lacépède) 65 cm
Ecology: the most common moray in Red Sea where it occurs on seaward reef slopes. **Range:** Red Sea and w. Indian Ocean to S. Africa, e. to Mauritius.

12 **White-eyed moray** *Siderea prosopeion* (Bleeker) 65 cm
Variable, some uniformly darker with white eye; posssibly 3 spp. involved. **Ecology:** a common inhabitant of reef flats on oceanic islands. **Range:** w. Thailand to Tuam., n. to Ryuk., s. to Tonga.

1
2
3
4
5
6
7
8
9
10
11
12

8 MORAY EELS, CONGER EELS and SNAKE EELS

1 **White ribbon eel** *Pseudechidna brummeri* (Bleeker) 103 cm
Body ribbon-like with wide fins but head without ornamentation and color tan to cream. **Ecology:** reef flats and shallow lagoons, usually buried in sand or rubble. **Range:** E. Africa to Cook Is., n. to Yaeyamas, s. to Fiji.

2 **Moon moray** *Uropterygius kamar* McCosker & Randall 37 cm
Uropterygius spp. snakelike with vestigial fins confined to tip of tail and numerous needle-like teeth; ground color of this species mottled to uniformly dark. **Ecology:** coral rubble at depths of 3 to 55 m. **Range:** E. Africa to Pitcairn group, n. to Marshal Is.

3 **Tidepool snake moray** *Uropterygius micropterus* Bleeker 28 cm
Ecology: among rubble of intertidal reef flats. Feeds on small crustaceans and fishes. **Range:** E. Africa to Phoenix and Samoan Is., n. to s. Jap., s. to s. GBR.

4 **Tiger snake moray** *Scuticaria tigrinus* (Lesson) 120 cm
Ecology: lagoon and seaward reefs. Extremely secretive. **Range:** E. Africa to Panama, n. to Phil. and Hawaiian Is., s. to Society Is.

CONGER and GARDEN EELS (CONGRIDAE): round-bodied eels, the conger eels with large P fins and the garden eels with tiny P fins and upturned mouths. Most conger eels occur in deep or temperate waters and are valued as food fishes. Garden eels occur in colonies in sand where they live individually in burrows from which they protrude to feed on plankton.

5 **Moustache conger** *Conger cinereus* Rüppell 130 cm
Dark band over upper lip; broad dark bands on body at night. **Ecology:** reef flats and lagoon and seaward reefs to at least 80 m. Feeds on small fishes and crustaceans, primarily at night. **Range:** Red Sea to Hawaiian, Marq. & Easter Is., n. to s. Japan, s. to L. Howe Is.

6 **Spotted garden eel** *Heteroconger hassi* Klausewitz & Eibl-Eibesfeldt 35 cm
Ecology: in colonies on protected sandy slopes exposed to current, 7 to 45 m. **Range:** Red Sea to Line Is., n. to Ryuk., s. to N. Cal.,Tonga and E. Africa.

7 **Whitespotted garden eel** *Gorgasia maculata* Klause. & Eibl-Eibes. 70 cm
Many similar spp., closest to *G. sillneri* (Red Sea) and *G. hawaiiensis* (Hawaiian Is.). **Ecology:** in colonies on clean sandy slopes exposed to currents. **Range:** Maldives to Sol. Is., n. to Phil.

8 **Splendid garden eel** *Gorgasia preclara* Böhlke & Randall 38 cm
Ecology: in colonies on sand slopes exposed to current, usually below 30 m. **Range:** Maldives, Phil., Ryuk., and Marianas.

SNAKE EELS (OPHICHTHIDAE): a large and diverse group of snakelike eels; most with pointed snouts and downward pointing nostrils. Most species spend their time burried in sand and hunt small fishes and crustaceans by sense of smell. Abundant but seldom noticed.

9 **Banded snake eel** *Myrichthys colubrinus* (Boddaert) 88 cm
Ecology: shallow sand flats. Often confused with the sea snake, *Laticauda colubrina.* **Range:** Red Sea to Society Is., n. to Ryuk., s. to Qld.

10 **Saddled snake eel** *Leiuranus semicinctus* (Lay & Bennett) 66 cm
Ecology: shallow sandy areas. Feeds on small fishes and crustaceans. **Range:** E. Africa to Hawaiian, Marq., and Mangareva Is., n. to s. Japan, s. to NSW.

11 **Dark-shouldered snake eel** *Ophichthus cephalozona* (Bleeker) 100 cm
Ecology: muddy to sandy inshore areas. **Range:** E. Indies to Society Is., n. to Marianas, s. to Qld.

12 **Spotted snake eel** *Myrichthys maculosus* (Cuvier) 100 cm
Spots become proportionately smaller and more numerous with age; several similar spp. **Ecology:** sandy areas, 0 to 262 m. May aggregate in large numbers under a light at night. **Range:** Red Sea to Hawaiian, Marq., and Society Is., n. to s. Japan, s. to L. Howe, Rapa Is.

13 **Crocodile snake eel** *Brachysomophis crocodilinus* (Bennett) 120 cm
Eyes set far forward; median row of large fangs on roof of mouth; tassles on lips. **Ecology:** sandy bottoms from intertidal to over 12 m. Remains buried in sand with only the eyes protruding where it waits to ambush fishes. **Range:** Mauritius to Tahiti; this or similar spp. throughout Indo-Pacific.

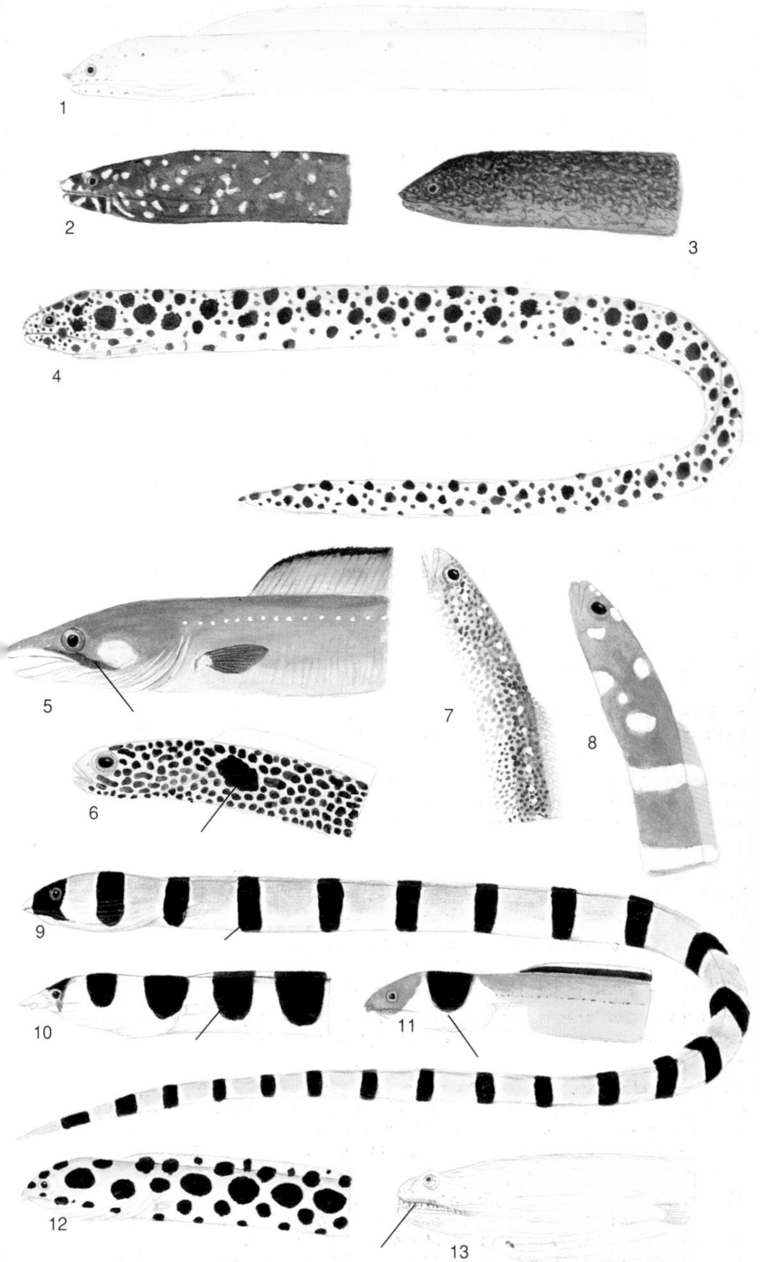
1
2
3
4
5
7
8
6
9
10
11
12
13

9 CATFISHES, PEARLFISHES, CLINGFISHES, LIZARDFISHES and TOADFISHES

EEL CATFISHES (PLOTOSIDAE): elongate fishes with second D and A fins joined at the tail, barbels around the mouth, and venomous spines at front of P fins and first D fin.

1 **Striped catfish** *Plotosus lineatus* (Thunberg) 32 cm
Ecology: coastal reefs, 1 to 35 m. Juveniles in dense ball-shaped schools over reefs and among seagrasses, adults solitary and under ledges by day. **Range:** Red Sea to Samoa., n. to s. Korea, s. to L. Howe Is.

2 **White-lipped catfish** *Paraplotosus albilabrus* (Valenciennes) 134 cm
Other similar spp. in coastal Indo-Australian waters. **Ecology:** coastal reefs, generally among vegetation. **Range:** Malaysia to PNG, n. to Phil., s. to n. Australia.

CUSK EELS (OPHIDIIDAE): elongate tapered fishes with greatly reduced thoracic V fins.

3 **Reef cusk eel** *Brotula multibarbata* Temminck & Schlegel 43 cm
Ecology: lagoon and seaward reefs from 0 to 220 m. Hidden by day, hunts in open by night on small invertebrates and fishes. **Range:** Christmas Is. to Hawaiian and Mangareva Is., n. to s. Japan, s. to L. Howe Is.

PEARLFISHES (CARAPODIDAE): translucent eel-like fishes which lack scales, V fins, and in some spp., P fins. Many species live commensally in the body cavities of invertebrates.

4 **Silver pearlfish** *Encheliophis homei* (Richardson) 14 cm (larvae to 20 cm)
Flesh translucent; *E. mourlani* similar but with numerous melanophores
Ecology: lagoon and seaward reefs, 0 to over 30 m. Inhabits body cavity of large sea cucumbers, entering through anus. Leaves host at night to feed on small fishes and shrimps. **Range:** Red Sea to Hawaiian and Society Is., n. to Ryuk., s. to Queensland.

CLINGFISHES (GOBIESOCIDAE): tiny scaleless fishes with pelvic fins forming a sucking disc.

5 **Urchin clingfish** *Diademichthys lineatus* (Sauvage) 5 cm
This sp. free-swimming, others attach to invertebrate host or to bottom. **Ecology:** associated with long-spined sea urchins or branching corals of sheltered reefs. Feeds on zooplankton and tubed feet of echinoderms. **Range:** Oman to PNG, n. to Ryuk., s. to nw. Australia, GBR, and N. Cal.

6 **Crinoid clingfish** *Discotrema crinophila* Briggs 3 cm
Ground color and intensity of stripes variable according to color of host. **Ecology:** occurs among the arms of crinoids. Reported from depths of 8 to 20 m. **Range:** Christmas Is. to Fiji, n. to Ryuk., s. to GBR.

LIZARDFISHES (SYNODONTIDAE): small cylindrical fishes with spineless fins and large mouth full of slender sharp teeth, even on tongue. Voracious predators of small fishes.

7 **Variegated lizardfish** *Synodus variegatus* Lacépède 20 cm
Color variable, ranging from brown to red; lateral band of blotches often prominent. **Ecology:** hard surfaces of lagoon and seaward reefs from 5 to over 40 m. Often in pairs. **Range:** Red Sea to Hawaiian, Marq., and Ducie Is., n. to Ryuk., s. to L. Howe Is.

8 **Twospot lizardfish** *Synodus binotatus* Schultz 13 cm
Scales large, 3.5 rows above LL (vs. 4.5 in most other spp.). **Ecology:** hard bottoms of seaward reefs from 1 to 30 m. **Range:** G. of Aden to Hawaiian and Mangareva Is., n. to Taiwan, s. to Tonga.

9 **Blackblotch lizardfish** *Synodus jaculum* Waples 14 cm
Distinctive dark blotch at base of tail. **Ecology:** sandy bottoms of sheltered reefs from 2 to 88 m. **Range:** E. Africa to Marq. and Society Is., n. to Izu Is., s. to se. Australia.

10 **Sand lizardfish** *Synodus dermatogenys* Fowler 18 cm
Ecology: sandy bottoms of sheltered and exposed reefs from 1 to over 20 m. Frequently buries in sand leaving only eyes and nostrils exposed. **Range:** Red Sea to Hawaiian, Marq., and Tuam. Is., n. to Ryuk., s. to L. Howe Is.

11 **Indian lizardfish** *Synodus indicus* Day 19 cm
Ecology: soft bottoms, 20 to 100 m. **Range:** Red Sea to Phil. & nw. Australia, s. to S. Africa.

12 **Graceful lizardfish** *Saurida gracilis* Quoy & Gaimard 32 cm
Saurida spp. with rows of small teeth exposed on sides of jaws when mouth is closed. **Ecology:** sand or rubble near rocks or coral. Common on sheltered reefs from 0 to 135 m. **Range:** Red Sea to Hawaiian, Marquesan, and Ducie Is., n. to Ryuk., s. to L. Howe Is.

13 **Orangemouth lizardfish** *Saurida flamma* Waples 29 cm
Ecology: sand or hard bottoms of seaward reefs from 5 to over 12 m. **Range:** Hawaiian Is.

TOADFISHES (BATRACHOIDIDAE): bottom dwellers with large head and mouth, eyes somewhat upturned, and first D fin with III spines. Feed on invertebrates and fishes.

14 **Banded toadfish** *Halophryne diemensis* (Lesueur) 26 cm
Ecology: coastal reefs and among mangroves, sometimes in crevices or caves. **Range:** Burma to PNG, s. to Queensland.

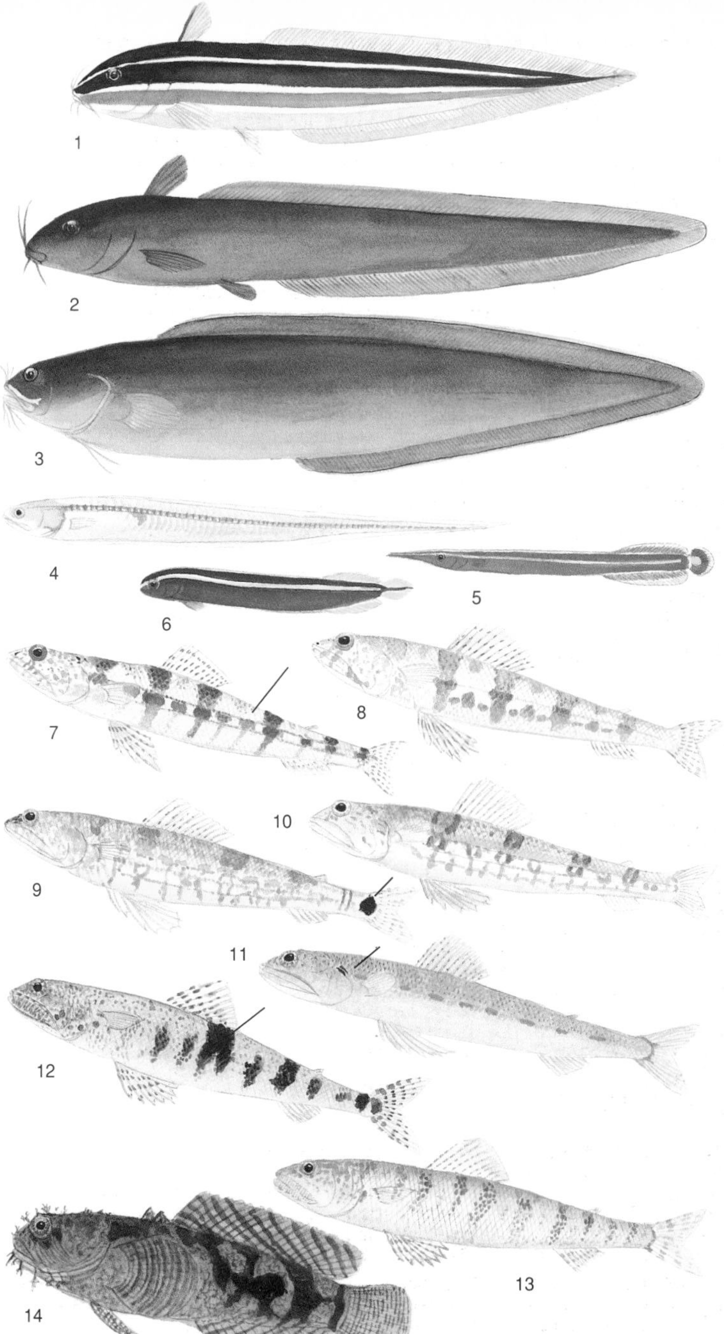
1
2
3
4
5
6
7
8
9
10
11
12
13
14

PRIMITIVE SILVERY FISHES

TARPONS (MEGALOPIDAE): large silvery fishes with ventral P fins, abdominal V fins, forked tail, large mouth with prominent lower jaw, and large scales. Popular sportfishes.

1 **Indo-Pacific Tarpon** *Megalops cyprinoides* (Broussonet) 90 cm
Ecology: inner coastal bays, lower reaches of rivers, and among mangroves in fresh or marine waters. Tolerates oxygen poor water by inhaling air into a lung-like air bladder. **Range:** Red Sea to Society Is., n. to s. Korea, s. to se. Australia; absent from atolls.

BONEFISHES (ALBULIDAE): large silvery fishes with ventral P fins, abdominal V fins, forked tail, and mouth under snout. About 5 very similar species. Highly prized sportfishes.

2 **Indo-Pacific bonefish** *Albula glossodonta* (Forsskål) 90 cm
Ecology: coastal bays and lagoons over sand and mud flats and among mangroves, in fresh to marine waters. Can tolerate oxygen poor water by inhaling air into a lung-like air bladder. Feed on invertebrates by nosing in sediment. Migrates to mass spawn at seaward mouths of channels on lunar cycle. **Range:** Red Sea to Hawaiian & Tuam. Is., n. to s. Japan, s. to L. Howe Is.

MILKFISH (CHANIDAE): large silvery fish with ventral P fins, abdominal V fins, forked tail, small mouth, and small scales. An important se. Asian foodfish raised in ponds from wild-caught fry.

3 **Milkfish** *Chanos chanos* (Forsskål) 180 cm
Ecology: coastal bays and the lower reaches of rivers to outer reef slope in fresh to marine waters. Feeds on benthic algae and invertebrates. Spawns on lunar cycle near surface beyond edge of reef. Fry return to brackish water after 10-14 days. **Range:** Red Sea to Hawaiian, Marq. & Society Is., n. to s. Japan, s. to N. Cal.; w. Atlantic.

HERRINGS, SPRATS, and SARDINES (CLUPEIDAE): small silvery fishes with ventral P fins, abdominal V fins, forked tail, small mouth, and small deciduous scales. Closely related to anchovies (Engraulidae; not included) which have underslung jaw and pre-pelvic scutes and inhabit primarily coastal and brackish waters.

4 **Blue sprat** *Spratelloides delicatulus* (Bennett) 6 cm
Cylindrical body without lateral stripe. **Ecology:** *S. gracilis* similar but with silvery lateral stripe. Relatively clear coastal waters, in large schools. Feeds near surface on plankton. **Range:** Red Sea to Society Is., n. to s. Ryuk., s. to N. Cal.

5 **Gold spot herring** *Herklotsichthys quadrimaculatus* (Rüppell) 15 cm
Ecology: Compressed body, scutes along belly, pair of gold spots on operculum, and lateral blue band. Among mangroves and over silty coastal shallows, in schools. Moves to deeper water at night to feed. **Range:** Red Sea to Samoa, n. to s. Japan, s. to N. Cal.

SILVERSIDES (ATHERINIDAE): small schooling fishes with two D fins, forked tail, small terminal mouth, broad silver lateral band, and no lateral line. Feed on zooplankton. A few species on coral reefs.

6 **Hardyhead silverside** *Atherinomorus lacunosus* (Schneider) 12 cm
2 D fins and silver lateral band. **Ecology:** *Hyperatherina* spp. similar but with narrower bodies. in large schools along sandy shorelines and reef margins in areas of clear water. **Range:** Red Sea to Hawaiian and Samoan Is., n. to s. Japan, s. to N. Cal.

NEEDLEFISHES (BELONIDAE): elongate silvery fishes with greatly elongate jaws full of needle-like teeth, and abdominal V fins. Surface dwelling predators of small fishes. See pl. 143 for the circumtropical species *Platybelone argalus* and *Tylosurus crocodilus*.

7 **Reef needlefish** *Strongylura incisa* (Valenciennes) 100 cm
Base of tail of not flattened, its width depth; body more compressed, jaws longer than 6. **Ecology:** surface waters of lagoon and seaward reefs. **Range:** e. Indian Ocean to Mangareva, n. to Ryukyus, s. to s. GBR.

HALFBEAKS (HEMIRHAMPHIDAE): elongate silvery fishes with small mouth, spikelike lower jaw, and abdominal V fins. Surface dwelling omnivores of algae, zooplankton, and fishes.

8 **Island halfbeak** *Hemiramphus archipelagicus* Collin & Parin 25 cm
Hemirhamphus spp. with scaleless snout; this species lacks markings. **Ecology:** in schools at surface of lagoon and sheltered seaward reefs. **Range:** E. Africa to Samoa, n. to Phil., s. to Tonga.

9 **Spotted halfbeak** *Hemiramphus far* (Forsskål) 40 cm
Ecology: in small groups in coastal waters of high islands and continental shorelines. **Range:** Red Sea to Samoa, n. to Ryuk., s. to N. Cal.

10 **Pacific halfbeak** *Hyporamphus acutus acutus* (Günther) 25 cm
Hyporhamphus spp. with scales on snout; this species with 2 scales between eyes and keel on upper jaw.; similar to *H. gambarur* (Red Sea). **Ecology:** in schools at surface of lagoon and seaward reefs. **Range:** all oceanic Pacific island groups except Hawaii (subsp. *pacificus*).

11 & 12 See over

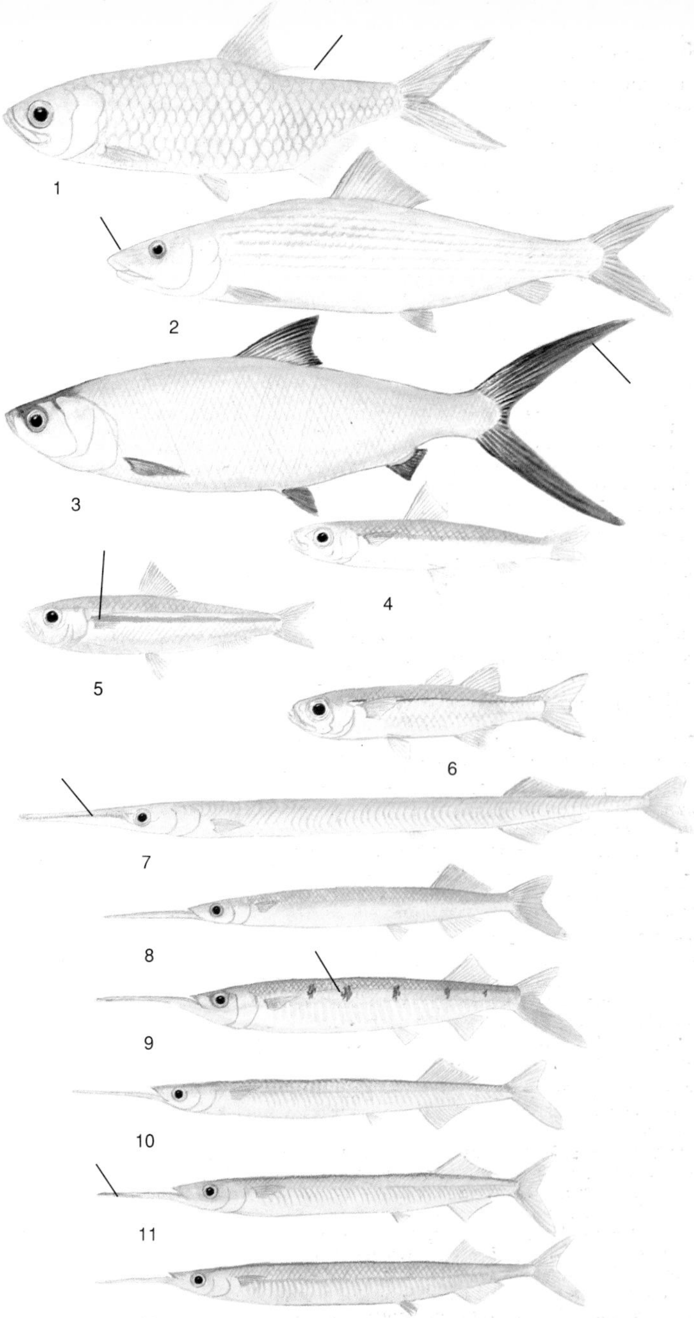
1
2
3
4
5
6
7
8
9
10
11
12

←11 **Insular halfbeak** *Hyporhamphus affinis* (Günther) 26 cm
2 scales on top of head between eyes. **Ecology:** in schools at surface of lagoon and seaward reefs of oceanic islands and atolls. **Range:** E. Africa to Hawaii and Tuam., n. to Ryuk., s. to Austral Is.

←12 **Dussumier's halfbeak** *Hyporhamphus dussumieri* (Valenciennes) 25 cm
Single large scale on top of head between eyes. **Ecology:** in schools at surface of lagoon and seaward reefs. **Range:** E. Africa to Tuam., n. to Ryuk., s. to Australs.

11 FROGFISHES

FROGFISHES (ANTENNARIIDAE): small globular fishes with distensible body, loose prickly skin, limb-like P fins with an elbow-like joint, small round gill openings, very large upward directed mouth, and first D spine highly modified into a moveable fishing rod (illicium) tipped with a lure (esca). The lure is wriggled enticingly above the mouth to attract other fishes that are swallowed whole. Capable of swallowing prey as large as themselves. Extremely well-camouflaged, often adorned with fleshy or filamentous appendages. Gravid females lay thousands of eggs embedded in a large bouyant gelatinous mass.

1 **Giant frogfish** *Antennarius commersonii* (Latreille) 27 cm
Illicium length >2nd D spine; A 8; P 11; color variable: orange, black, brown, yellow or green. **Ecology:** lagoon and seaward reefs to over 30 m. **Range:** Red Sea to C. America, n. to s. Japan and Hawaiian Is., s. to L. Howe and Society Is.

2 **Striped frogfish** *Antennarius striatus* Shaw & Nodder 22 cm
Illicium length ca. = to 2nd D spine; esca has 2-7 (us. 3) worm-like appendages; A 7; ground color highly variable: yellow, orange, green, gray, brown, or black. **Ecology:** rocky and coral reefs, 10 to 219 m, usually below 30 m. **Range:** Red Sea & S. Africa to Hawaiian & Society Is., n. to s. Japan, s. to n. N.Z.; E. Atlantic; replaced by *A. scaber* in W. Atlantic.

3 **Painted frogfish** *Antennarius pictus* (Shaw & Nodder) 16 cm
A 6-7; P us. 10; similar to *A. maculatus*, but body with few if any warts; color variable, often with light-edged spots. **Ecology:** shallow sheltered reefs from as shallow as 0.5 m. **Range:** E. Africa to Hawaiian and Society Is., n. to s. Japan, s. to GBR.

4 **Hispid frogfish** *Antennarius hispidus* (Bloch & Schneider) 18 cm
Illicium length ca. = to 2nd D spine; esca an oval tuft of slender filaments; ground color variable but typically light yellow to brownish orange. **Ecology:** shallow rocky and coral reefs to 90 m. **Range:** S. Africa to Fiji, n. to Taiwan, s. to GBR; absent from oceanic islands.

5 **Freckled frogfish** *Antennarius coccineus* (Lesson) 12 cm
Lacks distinct tail base; otherwise resembles *A. nummifer* but lacks basidorsal spot; A 7. **Ecology:** intertidal as well as lagoon and seaward reefs. **Range:** Red Sea to c. America, n. to Ryuk., s. to L. Howe, Easter, and San Felix Is.

6 **Spotfin frogfish** *Antennarius nummifer* (Cuvier) 10 cm
A 6-7; Illicium length nearly = 2nd D spine; skin with numerous thin tassles; color variable but with dark basidorsal spot. **Ecology:** lagoon and seaward reefs from 0 to 25 m. **Range:** Red Sea to C. America, n. to Ryuk., s. to L. Howe, Easter, and San Felix Is.

7 **Indian frogfish** *Antennarius indicus* Schultz 23 cm
Illicium length ca. = 2nd D spine which is connected by membrane to head; 2-3 dark ocelli on sides; A 8-10; P 12-14, all bifurcate. **Ecology:** coral reefs to at least 25 m, uncommon. **Range:** E. Africa, G. Aden, and Seychelles to se. India and Sri Lanka, n. to G. Oman.

8 **Warty frogfish** *Antennarius maculatus* (Desjardins) 9 cm
A 6-7; illicium length <2nd D spine; skin very warty; color extremely variable, often with large contrasting patches and several round, light-edged spots. **Ecology:** shallow sheltered reefs. **Range:** Mauritius to Solomon Is., n. to Ryuk., s. to GBR.

9 **Bandtail frogfish** *Antennarius dorehensis* Bleeker 5 cm
Illicium length 2nd D spine; color variable: usually ashy grey or light yellow to black. **Ecology:** sandy reef flats. **Range:** Red Sea to C. America, n. to Ryuk., s. to L. Howe, Easter, and San Felix Is.

10 **Bandfin frogfish** *Antennatus tuberosus* (Cuvier) 7 cm
Illicium without esca; A and tail fins with dark margin and broad dark band. **Ecology:** coral reefs, specific ecological data unavailable. **Range:** E. Africa to Hawaiian, Line, and Pitcairn Is., s. to Samoa.

11 **Sargassumfish** *Histrio histrio* (Linnaeus) 14 cm
Covered with leafy and fleshy appendages, resembling floating *Sargassum* seaweed. **Ecology:** surface waters, among floating *Sargassum* seaweed. **Range:** all tropical waters except e. Pacific.

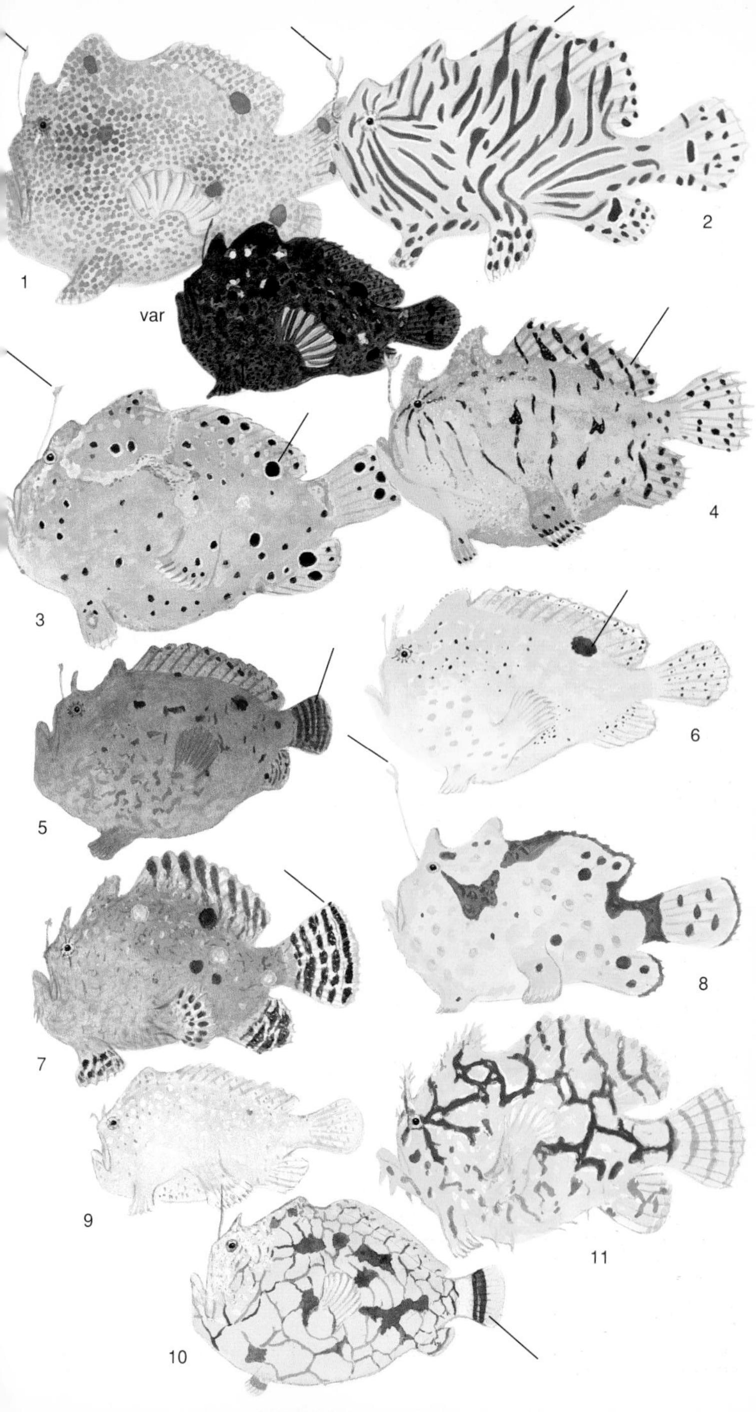
1
2
var
3
4
5
6
7
8
9
10
11

SOLDIERFISHES and SQUIRRELFISHES (HOLOCENTRIDAE): medium-sized fishes with bony heads, stout fin spines, large spiny scales, and large eyes; predominately red in color. Hardy in aquariums. Important subsistence foodfishes in many areas.

Subfamily soldierfishes (Myripristinae): preopercular spine absent, scales large, and snout short and blunt. All species are primarily nocturnal; *Myripristis* spp. swim well above the bottom to feed on large zooplankton at night. By day they hover in groups in or near caves or coral formations.

1 **Bronze soldierfish** *Myripristis adusta* Bleeker 32 cm
The only bronze soldierfish with bronze color and broad black margins on vertical fins. **Ecology:** reef and channel slopes with rich coral growth from 1 to 25 m. Occurs singly or in small groups, sometimes with other species. **Range:** E. Africa to Line & Tuam. Is., n. to Ryuk., s. to N. Cal.

2 **Brick soldierfish** *Myripristis amaena* (Castelnau) 25 cm
Margins of fins uniformly red. **Ecology:** reef flats to 52 m. May aggregate in large numbers in caves by day. **Range:** Phil. & Indonesia to Hawaiian and Ducie Is., n. to Ryuk.

3 **Bigscale soldierfish** *Myripristis berndti* Jordan & Evermann 30 cm
Scales large (LL 28-31), outer portion of spinous D orange; body light red. **Ecology:** subtidal reef flats to 50 m. In loose aggregations in or near shelter by day. **Range:** E. Africa to Line & Tuam. Is., n. to Ryuk., s. to Norfolk Is.

4 **Yellowfin soldierfish** *Myripristis chryseres* Jordan & Evermann 25 cm
Vertical fins mostly to entirely bright yellow. **Ecology:** deep seaward slopes, usually below 30 to 235 m. Rarely as shallow as 12 m. **Range:** E. Africa to Hawaii & Samoa, n. to s. Japan s. to GBR.

5 **Doubletooth soldierfish** *Myripristis hexagona* (Lacépède) 20 cm
2 pairs of tooth patches at tip of lower jaw outside gape; scales large (LL 25-28). **Ecology:** outer reef slopes, in small groups in caves sometimes with other soldierfishes. **Range:** E. Africa to Samoa, n. to Ryuk., s. to GBR.

6 **Pearly soldierfish** *Myripristis kuntee* Cuvier 19 cm (us. ≥15 cm)
Opercular bar prominent and continuous to P axil; pearly sheen; scales small (LL 37-44). **Ecology:** subtidal reef flats to over 30 m. In loose aggregations in or near shelter by day. **Range:** E. Africa to Line & Tuam. Is., n. to s. Japan & Hawaii, s. to L. Howe Is.

7 **Finspot soldierfish** *Myripristis melanosticta* (Forsskål) 30 cm
Light red, but face deep red; scales large (LL 27-29); tips of soft D, A, C fins black. **Ecology:** dead reef areas, 20 to 64 m under coral heads. Uncommon. **Range:** E. Africa to N. Cal., n. to Ryuk., s. to s. GBR.

8 **Red soldierfish** *Myripristis murdjan* (Forsskål) 27 cm
Scales large (LL 27-32); body deep red; outer portion of spinous D red. **Ecology:** subtidal reef flats to 37 m. In loose aggregations in or near shelter by day. **Range:** Red Sea to Samoa, n. to Ryuk., s. to s. GBR.

9 **Scarlet soldierfish** *Myripristis pralinia* Cuvier 20 cm
Similar to *M. kuntee*, but opercular bar reduced to small patch disconnected from P axil. **Ecology:** subtidal reef flats to 40 m. In loose aggregations in or near shelter by day. **Range:** E. Africa to Marq. & Mangareva, n. to Ryuk., s. to N. Cal.

10 **Violet soldierfish** *Myripristis violacea* Bleeker 20 cm
Distinctive violet sheen; tips of soft D, A, C fins orange; opercular bar dark red. **Ecology:** lagoons and seaward slopes, 4 to 25 m, primarily in areas of rich coral growth. **Range:** E. Africa to Tuam., n. to Ryuk., s. to N. Cal. & Austral Is.

11 **White-tipped soldierfish** *Myripristis vittata* Cuvier 20 cm
Lacks dark opercular bar; tips of D spines white. **Ecology:** steep seaward slopes of offshore reefs, usually below 15 to 80 m. In large aggregations in or near caves by day. **Range:** E. Africa to Marq. & Tuam., n. s. Japan, s. to N. Cal.

12 **Pale soldierfish** *Myripristis* sp. 25 cm
Ecology: coral-rich areas, 12 to 30 m. Not rare. **Range:** Thailand to e. Indonesia.

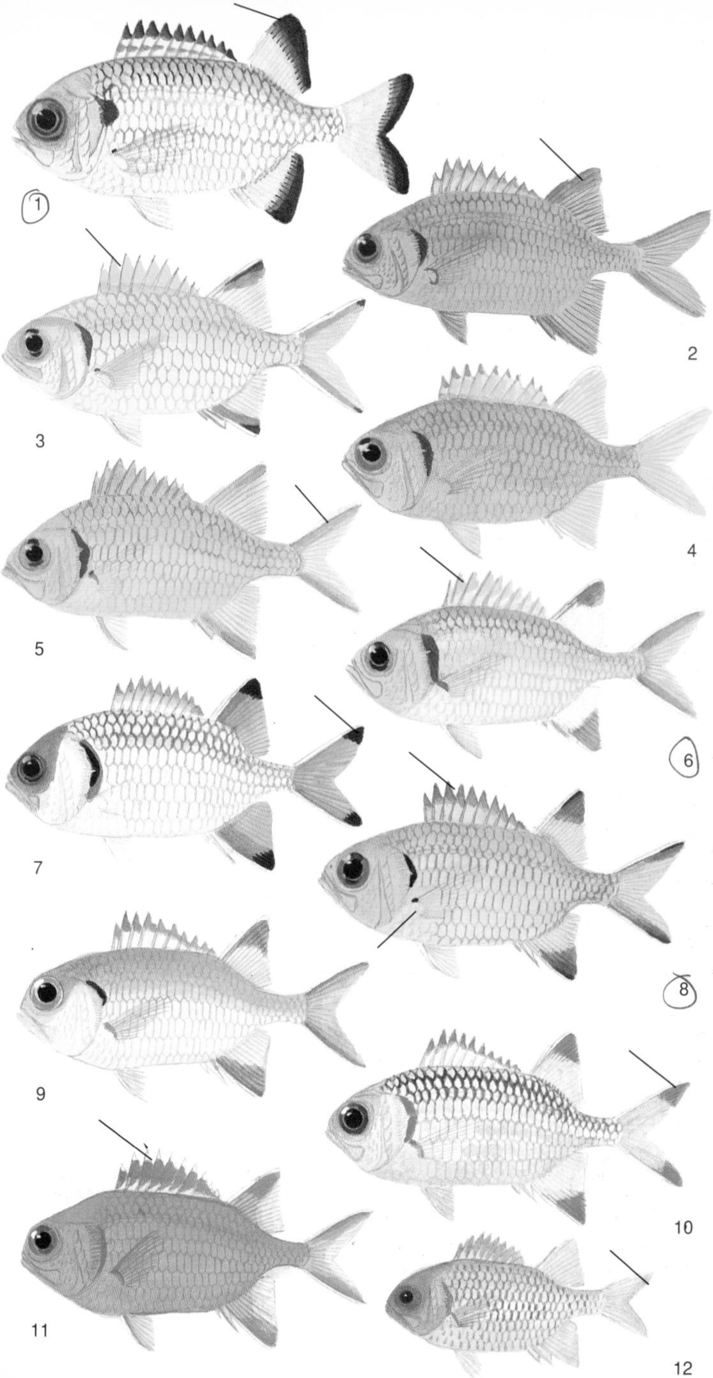
1
2
3
4
5
6
7
8
9
10
11
12

13 SOLDIERFISHES and SQUIRRELFISHES

1 **White-spot soldierfish** *Myripristis woodsi* Schultz 25 cm
Distinctive white spot on upper P axil; scales large (LL30-34). **Ecology:** reef flats and uppermost portions of lagoon and seaward reefs. **Range:** Caroline to Line Is., n. Bonins., s. to Samoa & Tuam. Is.

2 **Yellowtip soldierfish** *Myripristis xanthacrus* Randall & Guezé 20 cm
Tips of soft D, A, C fins yellow; scales large (LL 26-29). **Ecology:** reef flats and slopes with moderate coral growth, 5 to 20 m, usually in caves or under over hangings. **Range:** Middle & s. Red Sea (common) & G. of Aden.

3 **Cardinal soldierfish** *Plectrypops lima* (Valenciennes) 16 cm
Long nearly straight forehead; eyes directed more forward and upward; round tail lobes. **Ecology:** reef flats to 25 m. Deep recesses of reef by day; remains close to the bottom at night to feed on small crustaceans. Uncommon. **Range:** E. Africa to Hawaiian and Easter Is., n. to s. Japan, s. to L. Howe Is.

Squirrelfishes (Subfamily Holocentrinae): preopercle with large spine. All spp. are primarily nocturnal. They roam the reef near the bottom to feed on invertebrates and small fishes at night and hover singly or in groups near or among corals or rocks by day.

4 **Clearfin squirrelfish** *Neoniphon argenteus* (Valenciennes) 22 cm
Similar to *N. sammara*, but D fin clear. **Ecology:** reef flats and sheltered reefs to > 20 m. Among large branching corals often with *N. sammara*,.
Uncommon, primarily from oceanic islands. **Range:** E. Africa to Marq., n. to Ryuk., s. to Samoa & Tuam. Is.

5 **Yellowstriped squirrelfish** *Neoniphon aurolineatus* (Liénard) 25 cm
Yellow stripes; differs from *Sargocentron ensiferum* (S. China Sea to Hawaiian & Pitcairn Is.) which has solid red D fin. Ecology: deep outer reef slopes, 30 to 160 m. **Range:** Comoro Is. to Hawaii, n. to s. Japan., s. to GBR.

6 **Blackfin squirrelfish** *Neoniphon opercularis* (Valenciennes) 35 cm
Spinous D fin black except for tips and along base. **Ecology:** subtidal reef flats and lagoon and seaward reefs to > 20 m. Occurs singly or in small groups in areas of rich coral growth. More wary and secretive than *S. sammara*. **Range:** E. Africa to Tuam., n. to Ryuk., s.to N. Cal.

7 **Bloodspot squirrelfish** *Neoniphon sammara* (Forsskål) 32 cm (us. <26 cm)
Similar to *N. argenteus*, but forward portion of spinous D fin with dark red spot. **Ecology:** reef flats to 46 m. Often among large branching *Acropora* corals. Feeds primarily on crabs. The most common *Neoniphon* in most shallow areas. **Range:** Red Sea to Marq. & Ducie Is., n. to s. Japan & Hawaiian Is., s. to L. Howe Is.

8 **Tailspot squirrelfish** *Sargocentron caudimaculatum* (Rüppell) 25 cm
Rear of body silvery with a white spot on upper tail base. **Ecology:** outer reef slopes and dropoffs in areas of rich coral growth, 6 to >40 m. Abundant in Red Sea and common in w. Indian Ocean and Micronesia. **Range:** Red Sea to Marq. & Tuam. Is., n. to s. Japan, s. to GBR.

9 **Threespot squirrelfish** *Sargocentron cornutum* (Rüppell) 17.3 cm
Large black blotches on bases of soft D, A & tail fins, spinous D dark red with white tips and elongate white spots anteriorly on each membrane; ground color red. **Ecology:** outer reef slopes and dropoffs in areas of rich coral growth, 6 to >40 m. **Range:** Indonesia to Solomon Is, n. to Phil., s. to GBR.

10 **Long-jawed squirrelfish** *Sargocentron spiniferum* (Forsskål) 45 cm
Deep body and v. large opercular spine; the largest squirrelfish. **Ecology:** reef flats and lagoon and seaward reefs to 122 m. Solitary and generaly under ledges by day. Feeds primarily on crabs. Common. **Range:** Red Sea to Hawaiian & Ducie Is., n. to s. Japan, s. to NSW.

11 **Crown squirrelfish** *Sargocentron diadema* (Lacépède) 17 cm
Spinous D fin mostly black or very dark red with white tips and white median band. **Ecology:** subtidal reef flats to >30 m, under ledges or in caves by day. Common. **Range:** Red Sea to Hawaiian, Marq. & Tuam. Is., n. to Ryuk., s. to L. Howe Is.

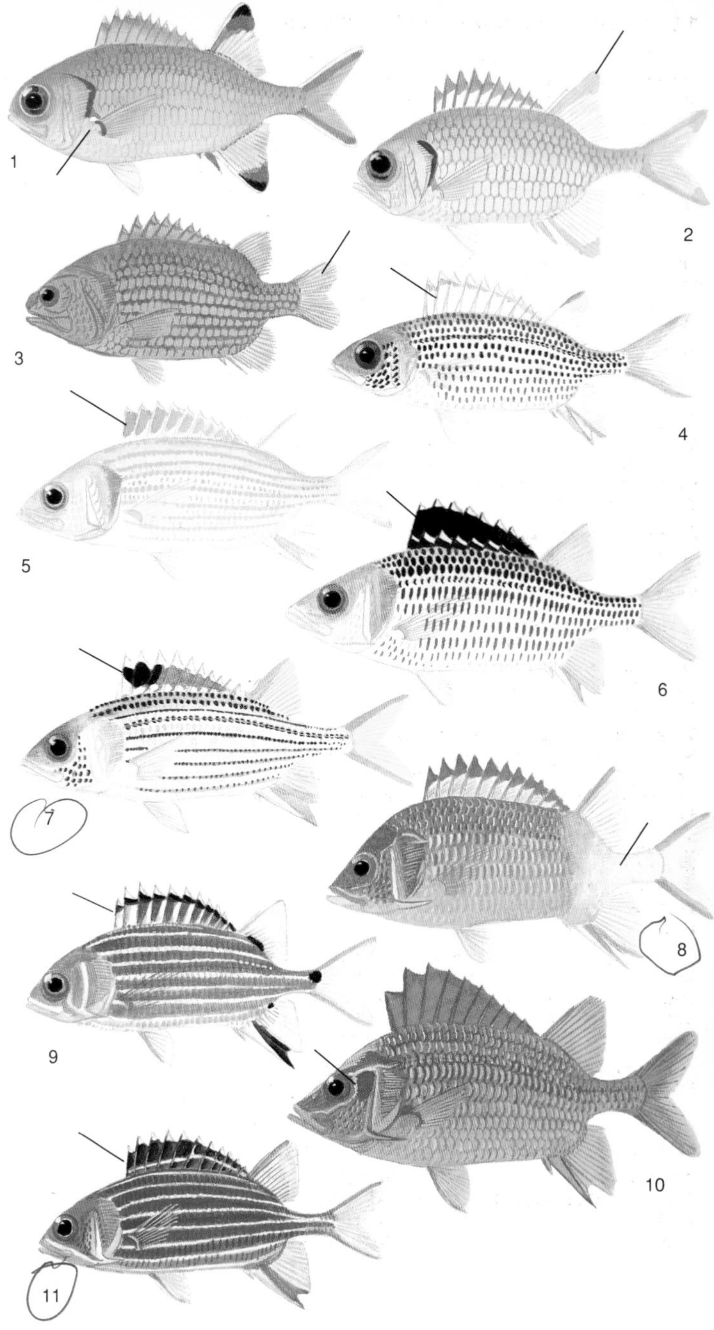
1
2
3
4
5
6
7
8
9
10
11

SQUIRRELFISHES

1 **Samurai squirrelfish** *Sargocentron ittodai* (Jordan & Fowler) 20 cm
Similar to *S. xantherythrum*, but spinous D with narrow white median band and no black spot on inner P axil. Smaller outside Japan ($\geqslant$17 cm). **Ecology:** outer reef slopes, 5-70 m, usually 16 m. Common off s. Japan. **Range:** Red Sea to Marq. Is. & GBR, n. to s. Japan.

2 **Roundfinned squirrelfish** *Sargocentron inaequalis* Randall & Heemstra 10 cm
Soft D, A, and C fins small and round; similar to *S. lepros* from Cocos-Keeling, Christmas Is., Palau and GBR and an undescribed sp. from w. Pacific. **Ecology:** lagoon reefs below 6 m. Uncommon, seen only from poison stations. **Range:** Comoro, Chagos & Seychelles Is.

3 **Blackspot squirrelfish** *Sargocentron melanospilos* (Bleeker) 25 cm
Body with yellowish sheen and large black blotches on bases of soft D, A **and** tail fins; v. similar to *S. marisrubri* from Red Sea. **Ecology:** rocky reefs or areas of rich coral growth, 10 to 22 m. Uncommon. **Range:** S. Africa to Samoa, n. to Ryuk., s. to N. Cal.

4 **Finelined squirrelfish** *Sargocentron microstoma* (Günther) 20 cm
Most of inner spinous D fin clear; outer edge of operculum with orange tinge. **Ecology:** reef flats and lagoon and seaward reefs to 183 m. Common in most areas. **Range:** Chagos & Maldive Is. to Hawaiian, Marq. & Tuam. Is., n. to s. Ryuk., s. to Austral Is.

5 **Dark-striped squirrelfish** *Sargocentron praslin* (Lacépède) 24 cm
Similar to *S. rubrum* and *S. seychellense* but ground color darker and base of D fin clear. **Ecology:** reef flats and shallow protected reefs, often in "dead" reef areas. **Range:** S. Africa to Samoa, n. to s. Japan, s. to GBR.

6 **Speckled squirrelfish** *Sargocentron punctatissimum* (Cuvier) 20 cm
Rear of body pale with a white spot on upper tail base. **Ecology:** exposed rocky shores or reef margin and front, in holes in surge zone. Rare below 30 m, but observed to 183 m. Very secretive during the day. **Range:** Red Sea to Easter Is., n. to s. Japan & Hawaii, s. to GBR & Austral Is.

7 **Redcoat** *Sargocentron rubrum* (Forsskål) 27 cm
Similar to *S. praslin* and *S. seychellense*, but spinous D fin red with clear central band, and white tips. **Ecology:** coastal reefs among rocks or corals, absent from oceanic islands. **Range:** Red Sea to N. Cal., n. to Japan, s. to s. GBR. (absent from w. Indian Ocean Is. where *S. seychellense* is present)

8 **Seychelles squirrelfish** *Sargocentron seychellense* (Smith & Smith) 27 cm
Similar to *S. rubrum*, but ground color not as dark; tips of spinous D fin orange. **Ecology:** coral reefs and rocky shores in shallow, clear areas. Often seen between branched corals. **Range:** Madagascar, Seychelles, Mauritius, Chagos and intervening islands.

9 **Blue-lined squirrelfish** *Sargocentron tiere* (Cuvier) 33 cm
Sides with iridescent blue streaks; light dorsal wedge not always present. **Ecology:** exposed reef margins and outer reef slopes to 183 m. Usually hidden in holes by day. Common at oceanic islands. Feeds primarily on crabs at night. **Range:** Aldabra to Hawaii, Marq. & Ducie Is., n. to s. Japan, s. to Austral Is.

10 **Pink squirrelfish** *Sargocentron tieroides* (Bleeker) 17 cm
Spinous D fin light red, almost clear with deep red submarginal band and white tips. **Ecology:** lagoon and seaward reefs, 15 to 36 m. Uncommon. **Range:** E. Africa to Line & Society Is., n. to Ryuk., s. to GBR.

11 **Violet squirrelfish** *Sargocentron violaceum* (Bleeker) 25 cm
Shape similar to *S. spiniferum*, but body with distinctive violet tinge. **Ecology:** clear outer reef flats and lagoon and seaward reefs in coral-rich areas to 25 m. **Range:** E. Africa to Line and Society Is., n. to Ryuk., s. to GBR.

12 **Hawaiian squirrelfish** *S. xantherythrum* (Jordan & Evermann) 17 cm
Spinous D fin entirely red except for white tips; inner P axil black. **Ecology:** seaward reefs below the surge zone to 100 m, common near caves and ledges. **Range:** Hawaiian Is.

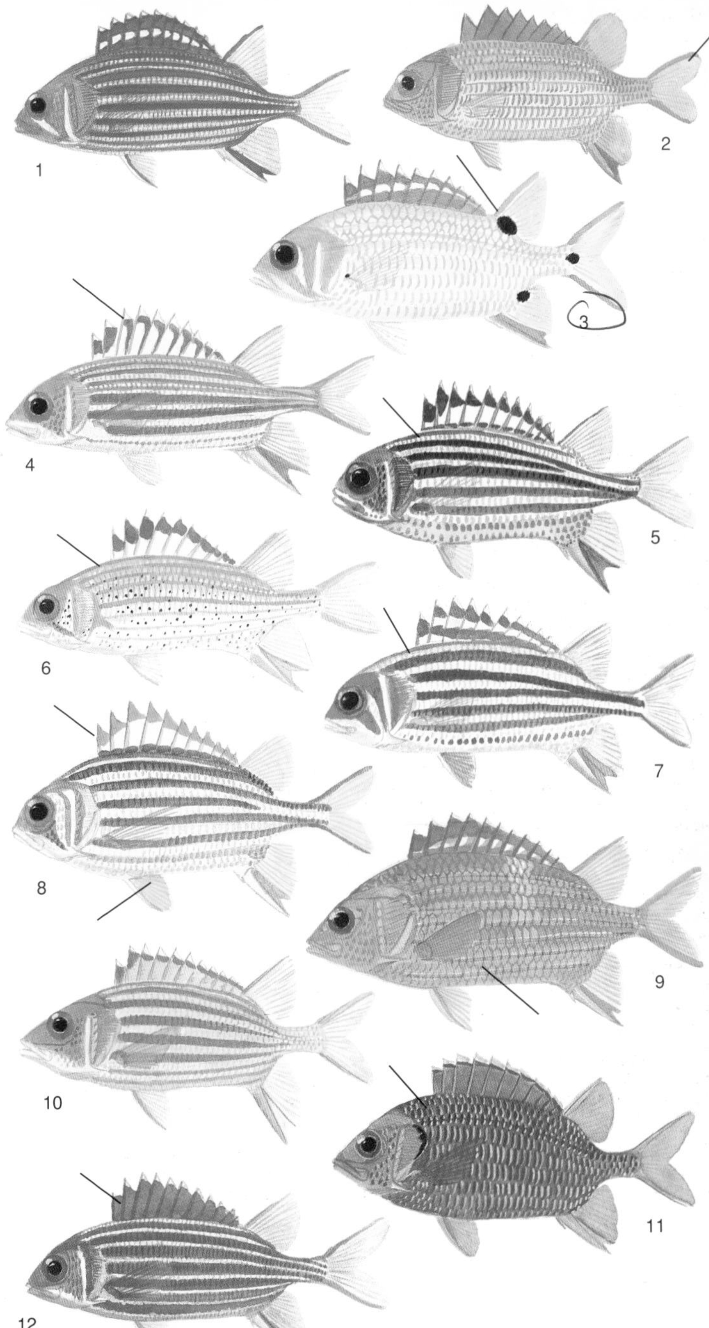
1
2
3
4
5
6
7
8
9
10
11
12

15 FLASHLIGHTFISHES, TRUMPETFISHES and related families

FLASHLIGHTFISHES (ANOMALOPIDAE): small uniformly black fishes with bony heads, small rough scales and a light organ beneath each eye. Symbiotic bacteria produce the light.

1 **Great flashlightfish** *Anomalops katoptron* Bleeker 35 cm
2 D fins and a light organ that operates by rotation. **Ecology:** only a small form under 12 cm seen by divers on moonless nights along steep dropoffs near caves; highly localized. The large form inhabits deep dropoffs at 200-400 m. **Range:** Phil. and Indon. to Tuam., n. to s. Japan, s. to GBR.

2 **Small flashlightfish** *Photoblepharon palpebratus* (Boddaert) 12 cm
1 D fin and flap to operate light organ (which can flash at up to 50 flashes per minute; very similar to *P. steinitzi* (Red Sea and Comoro Is.). **Ecology:** only seen on moonless nights on seaward reefs near or along steep dropoffs with caves. Approaches the surface in some places, but highly localized. **Range:** Phil. to Soc. Is., n. to Marsh. Is., s. to GBR and Rarotonga.

PINECONEFISHES and PINEAPPLEFISHES (MONOCENTRIDAE): small fishes encased in bony armor with 2 D fins, the first consisting of strong spines, a strong locking spine at front of V fins, and a luminescent organ on sides lower jaw. Symbiotic bacteria produce the light.

3 **Pineapplefish** *Cleidopus gloriamaris* (DeVis) 22 cm
Luminous bacteria in light organ on side of lower jaw, hidden when mouth closed. **Ecology:** rocky and occasionally coral reefs, in caves and under ledges, to 100 m. **Range:** e. and w. coasts of Australia; primarily warm-temperate.

4 **Pineconefish** *Monocentris japonicus* (Houttuyn) 17 cm
Luminous bacteria in light organ at corners of mouth. **Ecology:** rocky reefs, in caves and under ledges, 40 to 200 m. Juv. in 10 m. **Range:** Red Sea, s. Africa, s. Japan (common), Mauritius & Sri Lanka.

TRUMPETFISHES (AULOSTOMIDAE): body laterally compressed; distinct tail fin.

5 **Trumpetfish** *Aulostomus chinensis* (Linnaeus) 80 cm
Brown, green, or yellow phases. **Ecology:** among rocks or corals, reef flats to 122 m. A solitary ambusher of small fishes and crustaceans. Often swims behind large herbivorous fishes to sneak up on prey. Mouth opens to diameter of body to suck in prey. **Range:** S. Africa to Panama, n. to s. Japan & Hawaii, s. to L Howe & Easter Is.

CORNETFISHES (FISTULARIIDAE): body wider than deep, oval in x-sect.; tail a long filament.

6 **Cornetfish** *Fistularia commersonii* Rüppell 150 cm
Ecology: hovers above the bottom in wide variety of habitats, reef flats to 128 m. Solitary or in schools, feeds on small fishes and crustaceans. **Range:** Red Sea to Panama, n. to s. Japan & Hawaii, s. to L Howe & Easter Is.

SHRIMPFISHES (CENTRISCIDAE): body thin, with ventral keel; covered with bony plates.

7 **Shrimpfish** *Aeoliscus strigatus* (Günther) 15 cm
Ecology: in small groups near or among long-spined sea urchins, branching corals or other shelter. Swims in vertical head-down position and feed on minute planktonic crustaceans. **Range:** Aldabra & Seychelles to N. Cal., n. to s. Japan, s. to GBR.

8 **Speckled shrimpfish** *Aeoliscus punctulatus* (Bianconi) 15 cm
Ecology: see 7. **Range:** Red Sea & E. Africa.

GHOST PIPEFISHES (SOLENOSTOMIDAE): body thin, covered with bony plates; large pelvic fins, with egg pouch on female. Usually paired and feed on minute invertebrates. 3 species.

9 **Ghost pipefish** *Solenostomus cyanopterus* (Bleeker) 16 cm
C peduncle short; color nearly uniform, usually light green to brown. **Ecology:** among weeds and seagrasses of shallow sheltered waters. Uncommon **Range:** Red Sea to Marianas & Fiji., n. to s. Japan, s. to se. Australia.

10 **Harlequin ghost pipefish** *Solenostomus paradoxus* (Pallas) 12 cm
C peduncle long; body covered with tassles; intricate and variable color pattern. Often swims with head down. **Ecology:** among gorgonians, weeds, or crinoids. Solitary or paired. Uncommon. **Range:** Red Sea to Marshalls & N. Cal., n. to s. Japan, s. to se. Australia.

DRAGONFISHES (PEGASIDAE): flattened body covered with bony plates, proboscis-like snout.

11 **Short dragonfish** *Eurypegasus draconis* (Linnaeus) 7 cm
Ecology: on sheltered sandy bottoms, feeds on minute invertebrates. Often in pairs. **Range:** Red Sea to Marq. & Soc. Is., n. to s. Japan, s. to L. Howe Is.

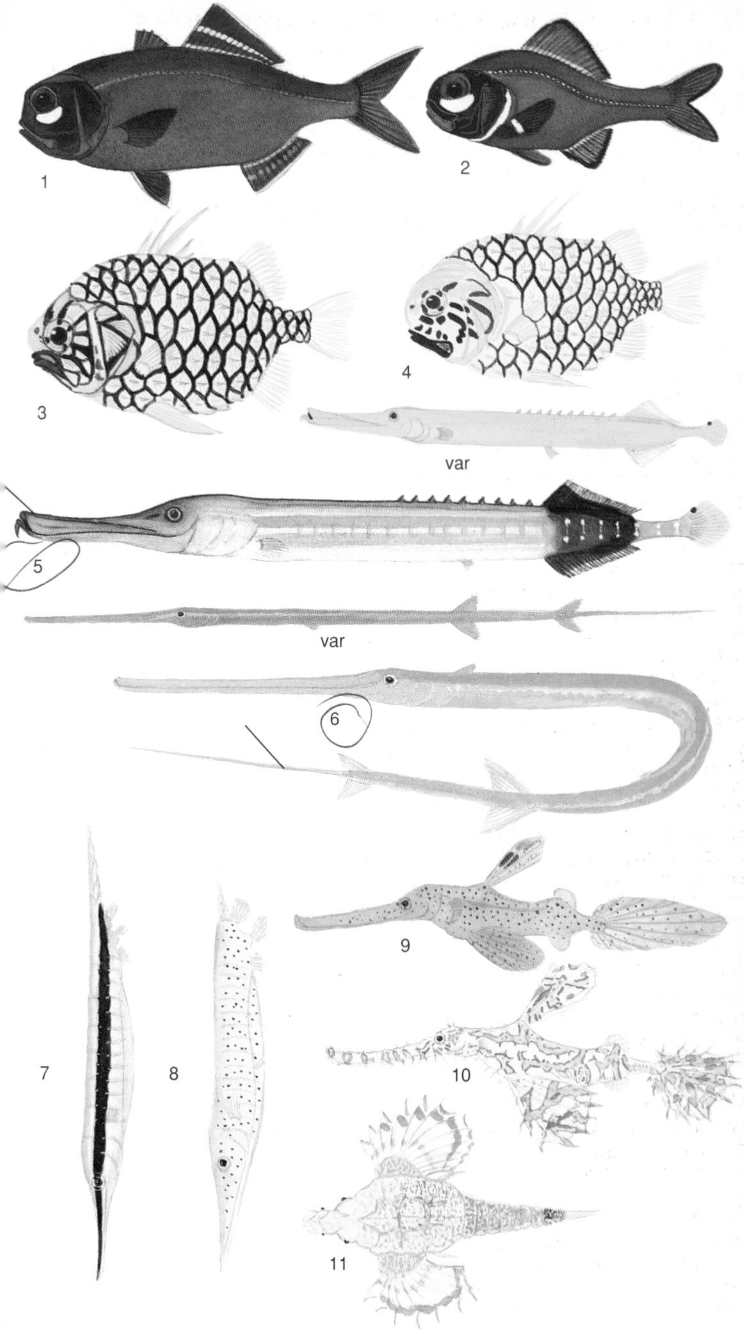
1
2
3
4
var
5
var
6
7
8
9
10
11

16 PIPEFISHES and SEAHORSES

SYNGNATHIDAE (SEAHORSES and PIPEFISHES): small elongate fishes encased in rings of bony plates. Seahorses have an angled head and prehensile tail that lacks a fin. All species feed on minute invertebrates sucked into a tubular snout. Reproduction is highly unusual: the male has a brood pouch in which the eggs are fertilized and incubated after being deposited by the female.

1 **Sculptured pipefish** *Choeroichthys sculptus* (Günther) 8.5 cm
Ecology: intertidal reef flats to about 3 m. **Range:** E. Africa to Line & Gambier Is., n. to s. Japan., s. to GBR & Tonga.

2 **Brown-banded pipefish** *Corythoichthys amplexus* Dawson & Randall 9.5 cm
Ecology: coral reefs. **Range:** E. Africa to Samoa, n. to Ryuk., s. to GBR.

3 **Network pipefish** *Corythoichthys flavofasciatus* (Rüppell) 12 cm
Ecology: subtidal lagoon and seaward reefs to 25 m, on algal-matted rocks and corals. **Range:** Red Sea to Tuam., n. to Ryuk., s. to GBR and Austral Is.

4 **Scribbled pipefish** *Corythoichthys intestinalis* (Ramsay) 16 cm
Ecology: reef flats and shallow sandy lagoons to 20 m, on sand. **Range:** Borneo to Samoa, n. to Phil. and Marianas, s. to GBR and Tonga.

5 **Black-breasted pipefish** *Corythoichthys nigripectus* Herald 11 cm
Ecology: lagoon and seaward reefs, 4 to 28 m. **Range:** Red Sea to Society Is., n. to Marianas.

6 **Guilded pipefish** *Corythoichthys schultzi* Herald 15 cm
Ecology: lagoon and seward reefs to 30 m, among corals or sea fans **Range:** Red Sea to Society Is. and Tonga, n. to Ryuk., s. to GBR.

7 **Ringed pipefish** *Dorhyramphus dactyliophorus* (Bleeker) 18 cm
Ecology: hovers in deep recesses beneath ledges, tidepools to 56 m. **Range:** Red Sea to Austral Is., n. to s. Japan, s. to GBR and N. Cal.

8 **Many-banded pipefish** *Doryramphus multiannulatus* Regan 18 cm
Ecology: hovers in deep recesses beneath ledges or among corals, shallow reefs to 45 m. **Range:** Red Sea to Chagos & Maldive Is., s. to s. Africa.

9 **Bluestripe pipefish** *Doryramphus excisus* Kaup 7 cm
Ecology: subtidal lagoon and seaward reefs to $\geqslant$ 45 m. Hovers in deep recesses beneath ledges. A cleaner that swims with a bobbing motion with tail spread to attract hosts. Picks parasites from other fishes, especially moray eels. **Range:** Red Sea to Mexico, n. to Ruyk. & Hawaiia, s. to GBR & Tuam.

10 **Janss' pipefish** *Doryramphus janssi* (Herald & Randall) 13 cm
Ecology: hovers in deep recesses beneath ledges, tidepools to 35 m. **Range:** G. Thail. to Sol. Is., n. to Phil., s. to GBR.

11 **Ornate pipefish** *Halicampus macrorhynchus* Bamber 16 cm
Numerous leaf-like flaps on upper sides of small indiv. $\geqslant$ 10 cm. **Ecology:** reef flats to 25 m, among seagrasses, coral rubble or algae-covered rocks. **Range:** Red Sea to Sol. Is., n. to Ryuk, s. to GBR.

12 **Double-ended pipefish** *Trachyramphus bicoarctatus* (Bleeker) 39 cm
Ecology: subtidal lagoon and seaward reefs to 42 m, usually among algae or seagrasses. **Range:** Red Sea to N. Cal., n. to s. Japan, s. to GBR.

13 **Gorgonian seahorse** *Hippocampus* sp. 5 cm
Snout very short, head and body with large blunt knobs; mimics a gorgonian. Undescribed. **Ecology:** among the branches of certain gorgonians. **Range:** N. Cal.

14 **Thorny seahorse** *Hippocampus histrix* Kaup 15 cm
Corners of plates with spines; color variable. **Ecology:** shallow sheltered areas among weeds or seagrasses, solitary. **Range:** Red Sea to Hawaiian & Society Is., n. to s. Japan, sw. to PNG.

15 **Spotted seahorse** *Hippocampus kuda* (Bleeker) 30 cm
Corners of plates with small knobs; color variable, with small black dots if light. **Ecology:** coastal reefs and estuaries to 30 m. Occasionally on offshore reefs or pelagic. **Range:** Red Sea to Hawaiian & Society Is., n. to s. Japan, s. to GBR.

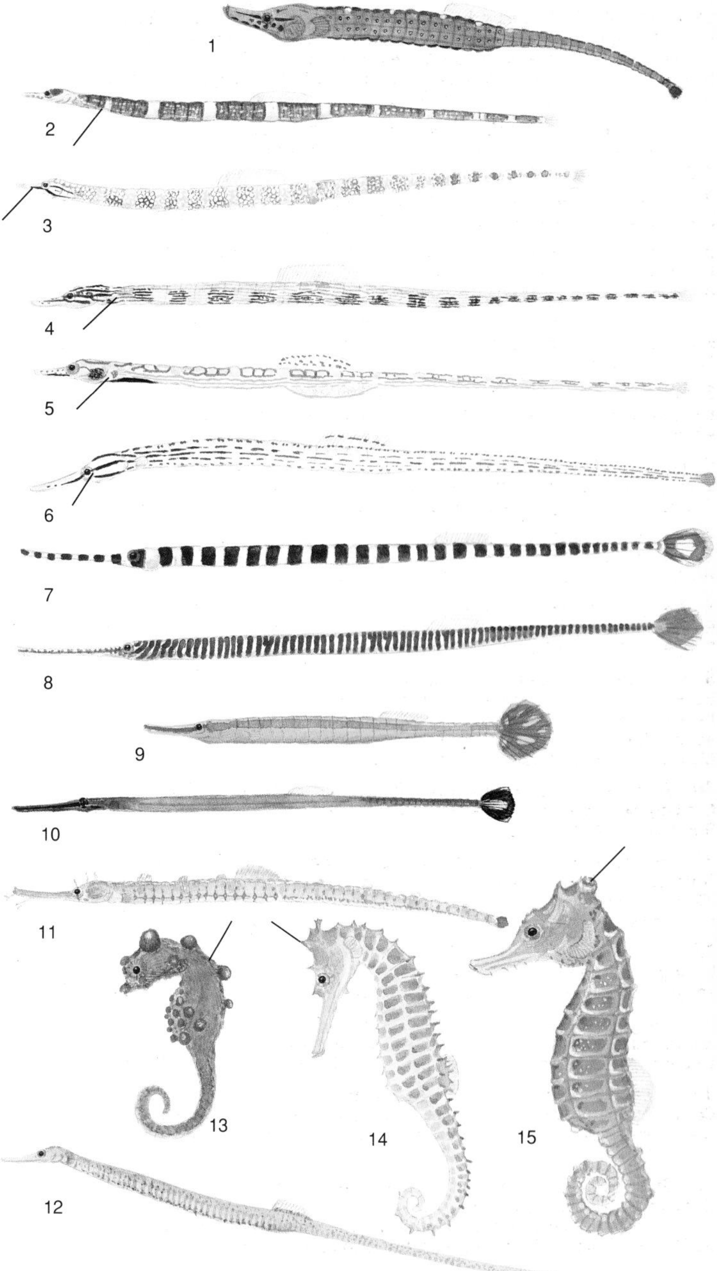
1
2
3
4
5
6
7
8
9
10
11
13
14
15
12

17 FLATHEADS, HELMET GURNARDS, WASPFISHES etc.

FLATHEADS (PLATYCEPHALIDAE): Elongate, depressed fishes with 2 D fins and head with bony ridges and spines. Typically live on sand, often partially burried. Feed mainly on crustaceans and small fishes. Many species in continental seas; identification difficult.

1 **Indian Ocean crocodilefish** *Papilloculiceps longiceps* (Ehrenberg) 70 cm
Resembles *Cymbacephalus* spp.; bony ridge with 1 spine below eye, branched papilla on top of eye; no pit behind eye. **Ecology:** on sand or rubble near coral heads, 1 to 15 m. **Range:** Red Sea to Durban, e. to Seychelles & Madagascar.

2 **Fringlip flathead** *Thysanophrys otaitensis* (Cuvier) 25 cm
Skin flaps on edges of lips; space between eyes ½ to ⅓ eye diameter. **Ecology:** on sand or rubble of lagoon and seaward reefs, 1 to ⩾ 15 m. **Range:** E. Africa to Tuam., n. to Taiwan & Ryuk, s. to GBR.

3 **Broadhead flathead** *Thysanophrys arenicola* Schultz 31 cm
Head and snout broad; space between eyes ½ eye diameter. **Ecology:** on sand or rubble of sheltered or semi-exposed reefs, 1 to ⩾ 15 m. **Range:** E. Africa to Marsh. Is., n. to Taiwan & Ryuk, s. to n. Australia & S. Africa.

4 **Beaufort's crocodilefish** *Cymbacephalus beauforti* (Knapp) 50 cm
Pit behind each eye; head and snout long. **Ecology:** on sand or rubble of sheltered or semi-exposed reefs, 1 to ⩾ 8 m. **Range:** Singapore to N. Cal., n. to Phil.

5 **Longsnout flathead** *Thysanophrys chiltonae* Schultz 23 cm
Space between eyes narrow, eyes nearly touching, spots somewhat large and irregular. **Ecology:** on sand of sheltered or semi-exposed reefs, 1 to 80 m. **Range:** Red Sea to Marq. & Tuam. Is., n. to Taiwan & Ryuk., s. to GBR.

HELMET GURNARDS (DACTYLOPTERIDAE): armored box-like fishes with colorful winglike P fins and rays of V fins free and used to "walk" on bottom.

6 **Common helmet gurnard** *Dactyloptena orientalis* (Cuvier) 38 cm
Ecology: sandy expanses, 1 to 45 m. Solitary, feeds on sand-dwelling inveretebrates. **Range:** Red Sea to Hawaiian, Marq. & Tuam. Is., n. to s. Jap., s. to N. Zeal.

WASPFISHES (TETRAROGIDAE): compressed fishes with venomous D spines. Similar to scorpionfishes, but D fin originates above eyes. Bottom-dwelling predators of crustaceans and fishes.

7 **Redskinfish** *Ablabys binotatus* (Peters) 15 cm
Strongly compressed with sail-like D fin. *Ablabys.* spp. similar to *Tetraroge barbata* (Sumatra to Ryuk. & N. Cal.) which has somewhat deeper body and *Taenianotus triacanthus* (pl. 19-6) with much deeper body. **Ecology:** shallow subtidal areas among weeds. Rocks back and forth. **Range:** E. Africa from Zanzibar to Xora River mouth (S. Africa).

8 **Cockatoo waspfish** *Ablabys taenianotus* (Cuvier) 10 cm
Ecology: shallow subtidal areas with sand rubble and weed. Rocks back and forth. **Range:** Andaman Sea to Fiji, n. to s. Japan; repl. by *A. binotatus* in w. Indian Ocean.

9 **Whiteface waspfish** *Richardsonichthys leucogaster* (Richardson) 10 cm
D fin membranes deeply incised. **Ecology:** silty coastal reefs. **Range:** India to Melanesia, s. to n. Australia.

CORAL CROUCHERS (CARACANTHIDAE): Body covered with tiny tubercles; venomous D spines. Feed on small invertebrates and wedge themselves tightly among coral branches.

10 **Spotted coral croucher** *Caracanthus maculatus* (Gray) 5 cm
Similar to *C. typicus* (Hawaii) and *C. madagascariensis* (w. Indian Oc.), the latter with short lines instead of spots. **Ecology:** among branches of certain *Pocillopora, Stylophora*, and *Acropora* corals. **Range:** Cocos-Keeling Is. & E. Indies to Line Is., n. to s. Jap., s. to Austral Is. & GBR.

11 **Pygmy coral croucher** *Caracanthus unipinna* (Gray) 5 cm
Ecology: among branches of *Stylophora mordax*, and certain *Acropora* corals. **Range:** E. Africa to Tuam., n. to s. Jap., s. to GBR.

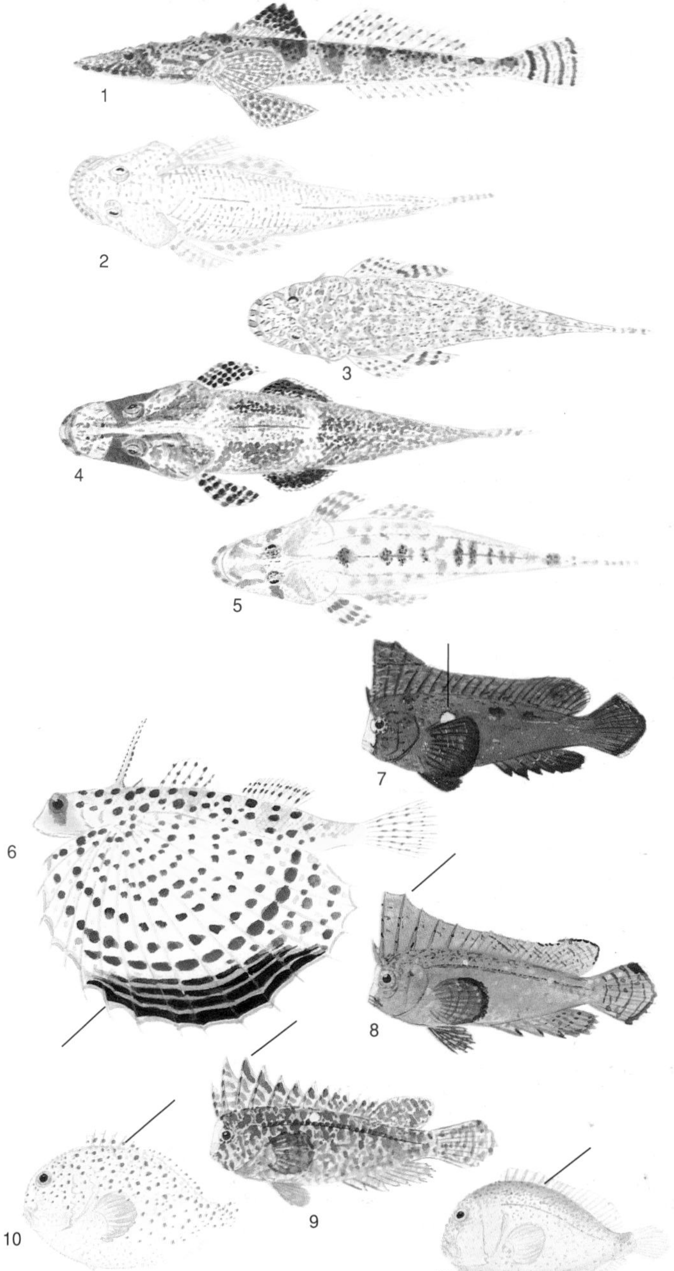
1
2
3
4
5
6
7
8
9
10
11

18 SCORPIONFISHES

SCORPIONFISHES (SCORPAENIDAE): Head large and spiny with bony ridge on cheek; D fin usually notched, fin spines venomous with groove and venom sack. Most spp. live on or near the bottom and feed on crustaceans or fishes. Most are extremely well-camouflaged and remain in or near shelter during the day. Most do well in the aquarium, but some require live foods and others can be trained to take almost anything.

1 **Merlet's scorpionfish** *Rhinopias aphanes* Eschmeyer 24 cm
Body moderately compressed, covered with tassels. **Ecology:** coral slopes, near the bases of coral heads. Possible mimic of crinoids. Rare. **Range:** ne. Australia, PNG, N. Cal., and s. Japan.

2 **Weedy scorpionfish** *Rhinopias frondosa* (Günther) 23 cm
Ecology: seaward reefs, 13 to 90 m. On algal-covered rocks. *R. eschmeyeri* similar but D little incised (Mauritius to Sri Lanka). **Range:** E. Africa to Caroline Is., n. to s. Japan, s. to Mauritius.

3 **Decoy scorpionfish** *Iracundus signifer* Jordan & Evermann 13 cm
4th D spine elongate, anterior part of fin resembles a tiny fish. **Ecology:** seaward reefs, usually below 10 m. On sand and rubble under ledges. D fin mimics a tiny fish and is used as a lure by wiggling the first few spines back and forth. **Range:** Mauritius, Taiwan, Society, Cook, Marq., Tuam., Pitcairn & Hawaiian Is.

4 **Yellowspotted scorpionfish** *Sebastapistes cyanostigma* (Bleeker) 8 cm
Body with numerous small yellow or white specks and scatterd larger yellow patches. **Ecology:** seaward reefs 2 to 20 m, only among branches of robust *Pocillopora* corals. **Range:** Red Sea to Line Is., n. to Ryuk., s. to GBR & Samoa.

5 **Spotfin scorpionfish** *Sebastapistes ballieui* (Sauvage) 11.5 cm
Dark blotch at rear of spinous D fin; no occipital pit. **Ecology:** shallow reefs, common. **Range:** Hawaiian Is.

6 **Mauritius scorpionfish** *Sebastapistes mauritiana* (Cuvier) 7 cm
Dark blotch at rear of spinous D fin; distinct occipital pit. **Ecology:** outer reef flats and shallow lagoon reefs in areas exposed to wave action. **Range:** S. Africa to Marq. & Rapa, n. to Ryuk., s. to GBR & Samoa.

7 **Barchin scorpionfish** *Sebastapistes strongia* (Cuvier) 6 cm
Dark bars on lower jaw; usually a dark spot at front base of spinous D fin; supraorbital tentacles. **Ecology:** reef flats, lagoons, and channels to $\geqslant$ 18 m, areas of sand and rubble. **Range:** Red Sea to Soc. Is., n. to Taiwan, s. to GBR.

8 **Speckled scorpionfish** *Sebastapistes coniorta* Jenkins 10 cm
Ecology: seaward reefs near shore to 24 m, among branches of corals. Feeds mainly on crabs and shrimps. **Range:** Hawaiian Is.

9 **Minor scorpionfish** *Scorpaenodes minor* (Smith) 5 cm
Head and snout elongate; lower P rays elongate & thickened. **Ecology:** reef flats to 18 m, areas of mixed sand and rubble. **Range:** E. Africa to Samoa & Austral Is., n. to Phil., s. to Australia.

10 **Coral scorpionfish** *Scorpaenodes parvipinnis* (Garrett) 14 cm
Usually a large wedge-shaped light area on front half of body and rear of head. **Ecology:** reef flats to 49 m, in areas of rich coral growth. **Range:** Red Sea to Marq., n. to Ryuk. & Hawaiian Is., s. to L. Howe Is.

11 **Guam scorpionfish** *Scorpaenodes guamensis* (Quoy & Gaimard) 14 cm
Conspicuous dark spot on posterior corner of operculum. **Ecology:** reef flats, lagoons, and channels, rocky or rubbly areas. Feeds primarily at night on crustaceans. **Range:** Red Sea to Pitcairn Is., n. to Izu Is., s. to NSW.

12 **Mozambique scorpionfish** *Parascorpaena mossambica* (Peters) 10 cm
Tentacle above eye well-developed; rear spine of preorbital series hooked forward. **Ecology:** reef flats to 18 m, areas of mixed sand and rubble. **Range:** S. Africa to Soc. Is., n. to Izu Is., s. to Australia.

1
2
3
4
5
6
7
8
10a
juv
9
10
11
12

19 SCORPIONFISHES

1 **Devil scorpionfish** *Scorpaenopsis diabolus* (Cuvier) 30 cm
Distinctive humpback; inner P fin bright orange, yellow & black. **Ecology:** reef flats to 70 m, usually on weedy, rubbly bottoms, occasionally on coral. When disturbed, flashes its inner P fins as a warning. Would-be predators learn to associate this with unpalatability after the unpleasant experience of being stung. **Range:** Red Sea to Hawaiian, Marq. & Pitcairn Is., n. to s. Japan, s. to GBR & N. Cal.

2 **Humpback scorpionfish** *Scorpaenopsis gibbosa* Bloch & Schneider 10 cm
Very similar to *S. diabolus*, but inner P fin with complete band of black submarginal spots. **Ecology:** probably like that of *S. diabolus*. **Range:** Red Sea & w. Indian Ocean, s. to s. Africa.

3 **Flasher scorpionfish** *Scorpaenopsis macrochir* Ogilby 13 cm
Larger eye, shorter snout & less humped back than *S. diabolus*; pattern on P fin different. **Ecology:** reef flats and shallow lagoons, on sand and rubble **Range:** Phil. to Marq. & Soc. Is., n. to Ryuk., s. to nw. Aust. & Tonga.

4 **Tassled scorpionfish** *Scorpaenopsis oxycephala* (Bleeker) 36 cm
Juvs. with broad white band on nape and from eye to upper lip; 2nd & 3rd D spines nearly equal in length; 19-20 P rays. Very similar to *S. venosa* (see below), *S. cirrhosa* (Ryuk. to s. Japan), *S. cacopsis* (Hawaii), and other undescribed spp. **Ecology:** seaward reefs and channels, 1 to $\geqslant$ 35 m, on rubble, rock, or coral. **Range:** Red Sea to Mariana Is. & s. GBR, n. to Taiwan.

5 **Raggy scorpionfish** *Scorpaenopsis venosa* (Cuvier) 18 cm
Similar to *S. oxycephalus*, but 1st 3 D spines increase in length evenly; 16-18 P rays, & usually dark blotch on spinous D fin. **Ecology:** coastal reefs, 3 to 25 m. Less common than *S. oxycephala*. **Range:** E. Africa to PNG, n. to Phil,. s. to GBR.

6 **Leaf scorpionfish** *Taenianotus triacanthus* Lacépède 10 cm
Highly compressed; color variable, from white or black to yellow, brown, green, or red. **Ecology:** lagoon and seaward reefs to 134 m. Feeds on small crustaceans and fishes. Rocks from side to side to mimic a piece of debris in a current. May periodically shed the outer layer of skin. **Range:** S. Africa to Galapagos, n. to Ryuk. & Hawaian Is., s. to NSW & Tuam.

7 **Stonefish** *Synanceia verrucosa* Bloch & Schneider 35 cm
Eyes widely separated with deep depression between them; color variable, often mottled with orange. Spines long and stout but normally folded against skin, can penetrate a tennis shoe. World's most venomous fish, has caused human fatalities. Wounds should be treated immediately with hot water or dry heat (cigarette). **Ecology:** reef flats to 20 m, often under rocks and ledges. May bury in sand. Feeds on fishes and crustaceans. Prey are sucked in during a nearly imperceptable split-second movement. **Range:** Red Sea to Mangareva, n. to Ryuk., s. to N. Cal. & Austral Is.

8 **Estuarine stonefish** *Synanceia horrida* (Linnaeus) 30 cm
Bony ridge above and between eyes; prominent raised warts on sides; light to dark brown. As venomous as *S. verrucosa*, stings may be fatal. **Ecology:** coastal reefs, including estuaries. **Range:** India to PNG & ne. Australia, n. to China.

9 **Spiny devilfish** *Inimicus didactylus* (Pallas) 18 cm
Spinous D fin of *Inimicus* spp. deeply incised; inner P fin pale yellow and black. **Ecology:** lagoon and seaward reefs, 5 to 40 m. On sand or silt, sometimes buried to eyes. Ambushes small fishes and crustaceans. **Range:** Thail. to Vanuatu, n. to se. China.

10 **Filament-finned stinger** *Inimicus filamentosus* (Cuvier) 22 cm
Ecology: on sand and rubble of coral reefs to 55 m. **Range:** Red Sea to Maldives, s. to Madag. & Maurit.

11 **Chinese stinger** *Inimicus sinensis* (Valenciennes) 26 cm
I. caledonicus similar but inner P yellow with two dark bands (Andaman Sea to N. Cal.). **Ecology:** on sand near reefs, 5 to 90 m. **Range:** S. India to Phil., n. to Taiwan, s. to nw. Australia.

1
1a
2
3
4
5
6
7
7a
8
9
9a
10
10a
11

1 **Spotfin lionfish** *Pterois antennata* (Bloch) 20 cm
Supraorbital tentacles of *Pterois* and *Dendrochirus* spp. variable, us. longest in juvs., may disappear in large adults; this sp. closest to *P. sphex*, but P membrane always spotted. **Ecology**: reef flats to 50 m, usually under ledges or in holes by day. Feeds primarily on crustaceans. **Range**: E. Africa to Marq. & Mangareva, n. to s. Japan, s. to GBR & Austral Is.

2 **Clearfin lionfish** *Pterois radiata* Cuvier 24 cm
The only lionfish with horiz. white lines on tail base; P fin membranes without markings. **Ecology**: lagoon and seaward reefs, 1 to 15 m, under ledges by day. Feeds primarily on crustaceans. Uncommon in most areas. **Range**: Red Sea to Soc. Is., n. to Ryuk., s. to N. Cal.

3 **Hawaiian turkeyfish** *Pterois sphex* Jordan & Evermann 21 cm
Ecology: lagoon and seaward reefs, 3 to 120 m, usually under ledges by day. Feeds primarily on crustaceans. **Range**: Hawaiian Is.

4 **Lionfish; Turkeyfish** *Pterois volitans* (Linnaeus) 38 cm
Nearly indistinguishable from *P. miles* (Red Sea to Sumatra, n. to Pers. G., s. to S. Africa.); spots on soft vertical fins somewhat larger than on *miles*; soft D rays usually11 and soft A rays usually 7 (vs. 10 and 6 for *miles*). Sting is extremely painful, rarely fatal. **Ecology**: lagoon and seaward reefs, shoreline to 50 m, often under ledges by day. Feeds on fishes and crustaceans, using P fins to "corral" them. Unafraid, often will stand their ground when approached. **Range**: Malaysia & w. Australia to Pitcairn Gp., n. to s. Japan, s. to L. Howe, Kermadec & Austral Is.; replaced by *P. miles* from Red Sea & Indian Ocean to Andaman Sea.

5 **Plaintail, Spotless firefish** *Pterois russelli* Bennett 30 cm
Soft fins & tail without spots, D fin spines not banded; Similar to *P. lunulata* from temperate Japan which has a few spots basally on vert. fins and broad bands on D fin spines. **Ecology**: offshore reefs, usually below 20 m. **Range**: E. Africa to nw. Australia, n. to India.

6 **Deepwater firefish** *Pterois mombasae* (Smith) 16 cm
P fin densely spotted, filamentous tips of rays short; complex pattern on tail base. **Ecology**: deep offshore reefs, usually below 40 m. Rare. **Range**: E. Africa to PNG, n. to Sri Lanka, s. to S. Africa & nw. Australia.

7 **Zebra lionfish** *Dendrochirus zebra* (Cuvier) 18 cm
Dark spot on lower opercle; concentric bands on P fin conspicuous on inner portion. **Ecology**: reef flats to 60 m, on coral, rubble, or rock. **Range**: S. Africa to Samoa, n. to s. Japan, s. to L. Howe Is.

8 **Shortfin lionfish** *Dendrochirus brachypterus* (Cuvier) 17 cm
Cryptic, but concentric bands on P fin conspicuous, esp. on inner portion. **Ecology**: shallow sheltered reefs, often on isolated weed-covered rocks in sandy areas. **Range**: Red Sea to Samoa, n. to s. Japan, s. to L. Howe Is. & Tonga.

9 **Hawaiian lionfish** *Dendrochirus barberi* (Steindachner) 16.5 cm
Cryptic; closest to *D. brachypterus* which is absent from Hawaii. **Ecology**: turbid lagoons to clear seaward reefs, 1 to 45 m, often under ledges. Cryptic. **Range**: Hawaiian Is.

10 **Ocellated lionfish** *Dendrochirus biocellatus* (Fowler) 10 cm
The only lionfish with a pair of ocelli (rarely 3) on soft D fin; inner P membrane conspicuous. **Ecology**: exposed rocky or coral-rich areas, 1 to $\geqslant$ 40 m. Uncommon to rare, generally seen only at night. **Range**: Mauritius to Soc. Is., n. to s. Japan, s. to nw. Australian shelf.

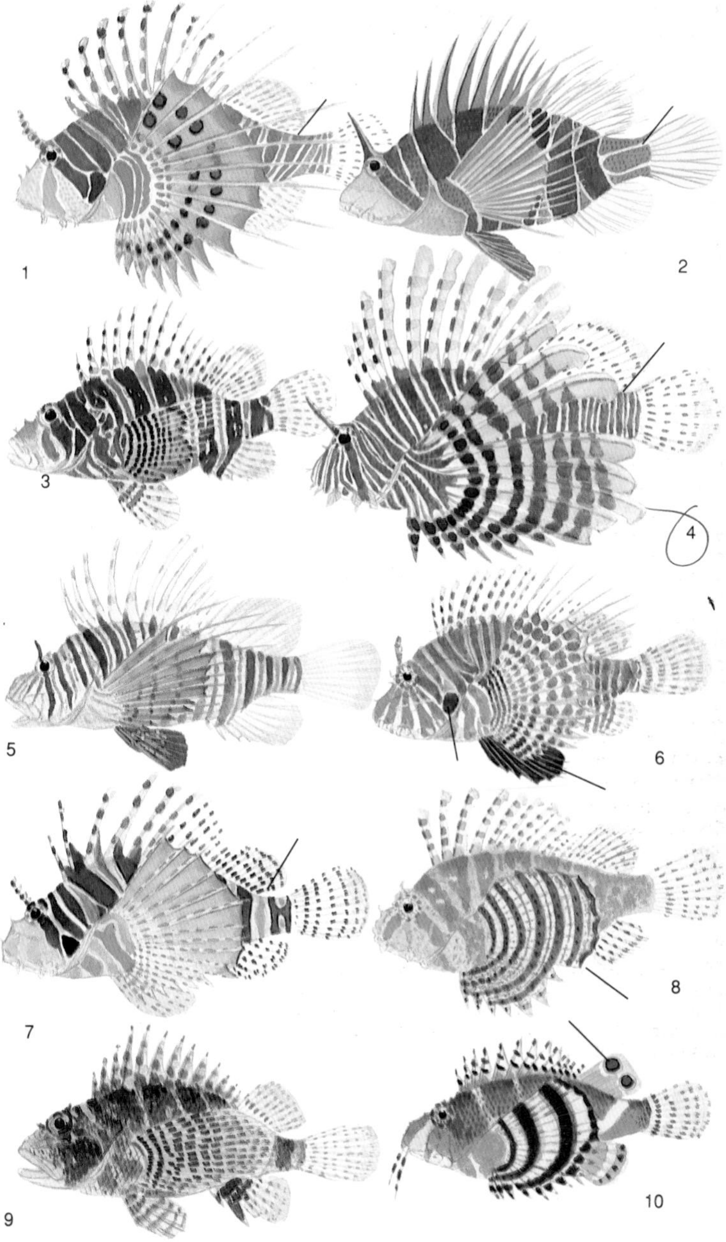
1
2
3
4
5
6
7
8
9
10

21 ANTHIASES

GROUPERS, ANTHIASES, PERCHLETS, BASSLETS, and SOAPFISHES (SERRANIDAE): a large and varied group of fishes typically with a single D fin with well-developed spines, continuous LL, 2-3 small flattened opercular spines, and small ctenoid scales. Hermaphrodites that commence maturity as females then change sex to males later in life.

Anthiases (Subfamily Anthiinae): mostly small colorful planktivores with small mouths and small scales that feed primarily on tiny crustaceans and fish eggs. Typically occur in aggregations of many females with one to a few males. Excluded are *Plectranthias* spp. which are secretive, primarily deep dwelling carnivores with large mouths, larger scales, and thickened lower P rays.

1 **Slender anthias** *Luzonichthys waitei* (Fowler) 7 cm
D fin divided; 5 other spp. in genus, all v. similar, only this one usually with ⩾57 LL scales. Other spp. tend to occur in deeper water. **Ecology:** in aggregations off steep outer reef slopes, 1 to 35 m. **Range:** Aldabra to Loyalty Is., n. to s. Japan.

2 **Threadfin anthias** *Nemanthias carberryi* (Smith) 13 cm
♂ of 2-11 with protruding upper lip and colorful D fin used in courtship. **Ecology:** in aggregations off steep outer reef slopes, 4 to 30 m. **Range:** E. Africa to Maldives.

3 **Purple queen** *Pseudanthias pascalus* (Jordan & Tanaka) 17 cm
♂ with enlarged sail-like red soft D fin; juvs. and ♀ nearly uniformly purple. **Ecology:** in large aggregations around coral outcrops and caves of outer reef slopes, 5 to 60 m. Feeds on planktonic crustaceans and fish eggs. More common at oceanic islands than on continental reefs, sometimes in mixed aggregations with *P. tuka*. **Range:** n. Sulawesi & Taiwan to Fr. Polynesia, n. to s. Japan, s. to GBR & N. Cal.

4 **Yellowstriped anthias** *Pseudanthias tuka* Herre & Montalban 12 cm
♂ similar to 3, but red on D fin confined to a patch and throat yellowish. **Ecology:** in large aggregations on outer reef slopes, 2 to over 30 m. Feeds on planktonic crustaceans and fish eggs. Primarily on continental reefs. **Range:** Indonesia to Sol. Is., n. to s. Japan, s. to n. GBR.

5 **Yellowback anthias** *Pseudanthias evansi* Smith 9.5 cm
Ecology: in large aggregations on outer reef slopes, 4 to 40 m, preferring dropoffs. **Range:** E. Africa to Christmas Is., n. to Andaman Sea, s. to Mauritius.

6 **Flame anthias** *Pseudanthias ignitus* Randall & Lubbock 8 cm
Similar to *P. dispar*, but ♂ with outer lobes of tail broadly red as in rest of upper body. **Ecology:** outer reef slopes, 10 to 30 m. Typically around large coral heads or patch reefs. **Range:** Maldives and Similan Is.

7 **Peach anthias** *Pseudanthias dispar* Herre 9.5 cm
Ecology: upper edges of steep outer reef slopes, 1 to at least 15 m. In large aggregations. **Range:** Christmas Is. to Line Is., n. to Yaeyamas, s. to Loyalty Is.; absent from Marianas and Fr. Polynesia.

8 **Princess anthias** *Pseudanthias smithvanizi* Randall & Lubbock 9.5 cm
Ecology: steep outer reef slopes, 6 to 70 m. In small aggregations close to the reef. **Range:** Cocos-Keeling to s. Marshall Is., n. to Yaeyamas, s. to GBR.

9 **Lori's anthias** *Pseudanthias lori* Randall & Lubbock 12 cm
Ecology: in aggregations near caves or ledges of steep outer reef slopes, 7 to 70 m. **Range:** Phil. and Christmas Is. to Tuam., n. to Yaeyamas, s. to Loyalty Is.

10 **Bartlett's anthias** *Pseudanthias bartlettorum* Randall & Lubbock 9 cm
Ecology: in aggregations off steep outer reef slopes, 4 to 30 m. **Range:** Palau, Caroline, s. Marshall, Nauru, and Line Is.

11 **Sunset anthias** *Pseudanthias parvirostris* Randall & Lubbock 9 cm
Ecology: in aggregations above patch reefs on sand or rubble seaward slopes, 35 to 60 m. **Range:** Maurit., Maldives, Phil., Palau & Sol. Is.

12 **Painted anthias** *Pseudanthias pictilis* (Randall & Allen)15 cm
Pls. 21-12 to 22-11 with upper lip of ♂ normal; ♀ of this sp. without blue body bars. **Ecology:** in aggregations above steep outer reef slopes, 12 to 40 m. **Range:** s. Coral Sea from s. GBR to N. Cal. and L. Howe Is.

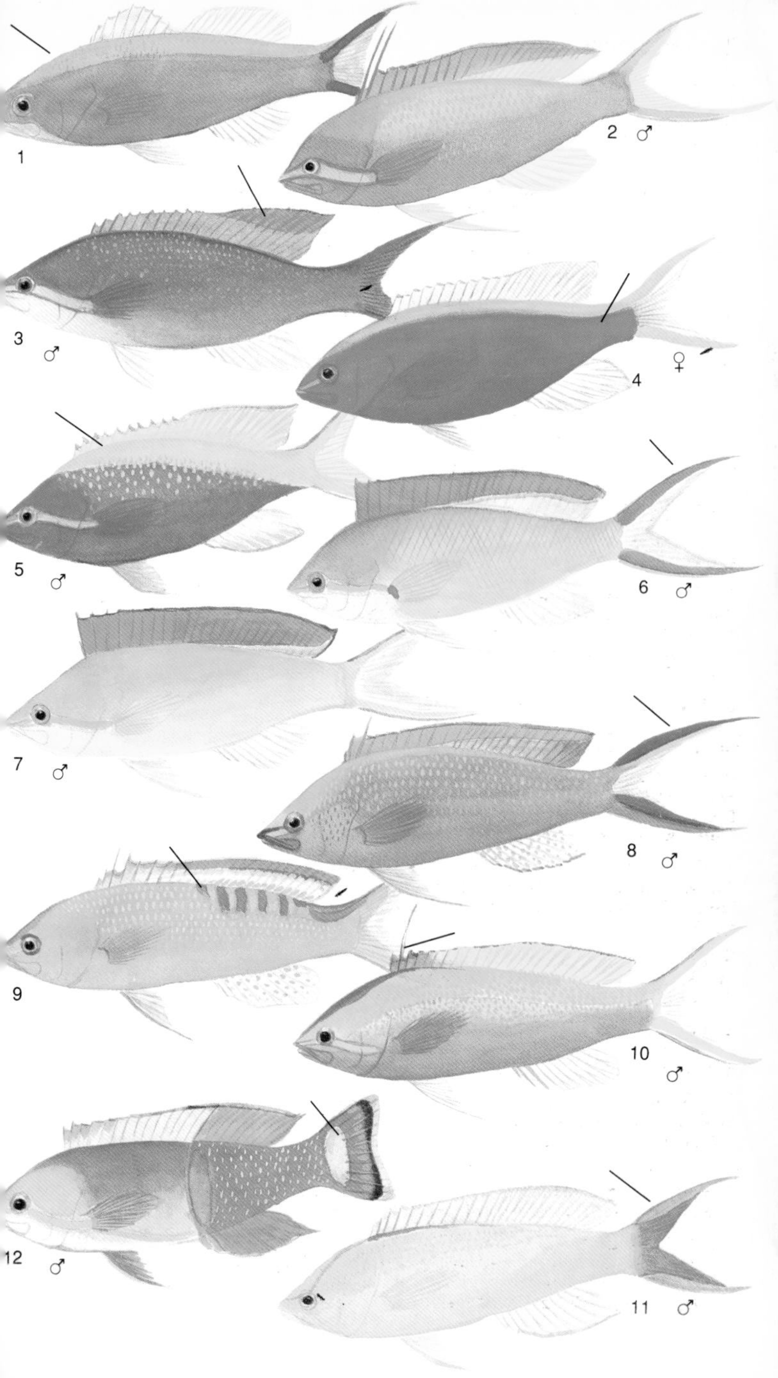
1
2 ♂
3 ♂
4 ♀
5 ♂
6 ♂
7 ♂
8 ♂
9
10 ♂
12 ♂
11 ♂

1 **Goldie; Lyretail anthias** *Pseudanthias squamipinnis* (Peters) 15 cm
Ecology: in large aggregations around coral outcrops of lagoon or outer reef slopes, 2 to 20 m. Males territorial and haremic. *P. lunulatus* similar (Red Sea, Bali & Mauritius) but golden yellow and >50 m. **Range:** Red Sea to Sol. Is., n. to s. Japan, s. to NSW.

2 **Red-cheeked anthias** *Pseudanthias huchti* (Bleeker) 12 cm
♀ with yellow instead of red band on cheek, and yellow P fin. **Ecology:** in large aggregations around coral outcrops of lagoon or outer reef slopes, 0.3 to 20 m. Males territorial and haremic. Abundant on coastal Indonesian and Phil. reefs. **Range:** Indonesia and Phil. to Vanuatu and s. GBR.

3 **Squarespot anthias** *Pseudanthias pleurotaenia* (Bleeker) 20 cm
Similar to *P. sheni* (Rowley Shoals & Scott Reef) with magenta patch extending to tail base. Magenta patch on ♂ seem to glow. Hybridizes with *P. bimaculatus.* **Ecology:** in small aggregations off current-swept dropoffs, 10 to 180 m, usually 25 m. **Range:** Indonesia to Samoa, n. to Ryuk., s. to N. Cal.

4 **Striped anthias** *Pseudanthias taeniatus* (Klunzinger) 13 cm
♀ orange-red dorsally, without stripes. **Ecology:** in aggregations around coral outcrops, 10 to 50 m. Often with *P. squamipinnis.* **Range:** Red Sea.

5 **Luzon anthias** *Pseudanthias luzonensis* (Katayama & Masuda) 14.5 cm
♀ without red patch on D fin and tail, and without dorsal stripes. **Ecology:** in small groups around coral and rubble at base of steep slopes, 10 to 60 m. **Range:** Indonesia and Phil. to PNG, n. to Taiwan, s. to n. GBR.

6 **Red-bar anthias** *Pseudanthias cooperi* (Regan) 14 cm
Ecology: in small groups along current-swept outer reef slopes, 16 to 60 m. **Range:** E. Africa to Line Is., n. to s. Japan, s. to GBR.

7 **Stocky anthias** *Pseudanthias hypselosoma* Bleeker 19 cm
♀ without red D spot of ♂, but often with blue ring around eye. **Ecology:** in aggregations around patch reefs in lagoons or outer reef slopes, 10 to 40 m. **Range:** Maldives to Samoa, n. to Taiwan & Ryuk., s. to GBR and Loyalty Is.

8 **Two-spot anthias** *Pseudanthias bimaculatus* (Smith) 9 cm
♀ pink on lower face and belly becoming orange-red above and yellow-orange postero-dorsally and on D and A fins; Indonesian & Maldives ♂ lack the posteriormost red spot on D fin. Interbreeds with *P. pleurotaenia* at Bali resulting in hybrids. **Ecology:** coastal reefs, including dead reef areas in relatively turbid water, 28 to 54 m, usually below 40 m. **Range:** E. Africa, Maldives & Indonesia (Java & Bali).

9 **Red-belted anthias** *Pseudanthias rubrizonatus* (Randall) 10 cm
♀ lack red band and red patch on A fin of ♂, and have red tips on tail lobes. *P. connelli* (Natal, S. Africa) similar, but with dark red area continuous from mid-body to snout with a light band extending backward from nape. **Ecology:** in aggregations around isolated coral heads and rubble patches, 30 to 133 m, usually below 50 m but as shallow as 20 m in s. Japan and Andaman Sea. **Range:** Andaman Sea to Sol. Is., n. to s. Japan, s. to nw. Australia.

10 **One-stripe anthias** *Pseudanthias fasciatus* (Kamohara) 21 cm
Ecology: in small aggregations in or near caves and ledges of seaward reefs, 30 to 100 m. **Range:** Red Sea, Taiwan, Ryuk., s. Japan, Indonesia & s. GBR.

11 **Orangehead anthias** *Pseudanthias heemstrai* Schumacher, Krupp & Randall 13 cm
♀ yellow dorsally becoming salmon ventrally and without distinctive head color of ♂. **Ecology:** lower forereef slopes, 20 to 67 m. In harems, sometimes with *P. taeniatus.* **Range:** G. Aquaba in Red Sea only.

♀
1
♂
2
♂
3
♂
4
♂
5
♂
6
♂
♀
6
7
♂
8
♂
9
♂
10
11
♂

23 ANTHIASES and BASSLETS

1 **Bicolor anthias** *Pseudanthias bicolor* (Randall & Lubbock) 13 cm
Ecology: in small groups on lagoon patch reefs or outer reef slopes at depths of 5 to 68 m. At Hawaii, around crevices and ledges on barren pavement below 15 m. Uncommon. **Range:** Mauritius to Hawaiian and Line Is., n. to Yaeyamas, s. to Loyalty Is.

2 **Hawaiian anthias** *Pseudanthias thompsoni* (Kamohara) 8 cm
Ecology: in small groups around coral outcrops and escarpments, 14 to 145 m. **Range:** Hawaiian Is.

3 **Long-finned anthias** *Pseudanthias ventralis* (Randall) 7 cm
Ecology: caves or coral rubble along steep slopes at depths of 40 to 120 m. Secretive and rare in less than 60 m, but may be abundant below 90 m. **Range:** (3a) subsp. *ventralis* from Marianas to s. GBR and Pitcairn; (3b) subsp. *hawaiiensis* at Hawaiian and Johnston Is.

4 **Randall's anthias** *Pseudanthias randalli* (Lubbock & Allen) 7 cm
Very close to *P. pulcherrimus* (E. Africa to Maldives & Chagos Is.) & a possible undescribed species (Marianas & Line Is.) but lg. ♂ with distinct magenta and red bands. **Ecology:** in small groups near shelter in caves of dropoffs at depths of 15 to 70 m. **Range:** Phil. and Bali to s. Marshalls, n. to Yaeyamas.

5 **Sailfin anthias** *Rabaulichthys altipinnis* Allen 6 cm
Similar to *Luzonichthys*, but with single D fin which is greatly enlarged in ♂. 2 spp. described; a possible 3rd sp. collected at Condor Reef, Caroline Is. **Ecology:** in small aggregations close to coral rubble on steep outer reef slope, 30 to 40 m. **Range:** New Britain off PNG.

6 **Spotfin anthias** *Rabaulichthys stigmaticus* Randall & Pyle 6 cm
Ecology: current-swept rubble bottoms, 35 to 50 m. **Range:** Mauritius and Maldives.

7 **Hawkfish anthias** *Serranocirrhitus latus* Watanabe 13 cm
One species with single D fin, elongate P fin rays, small mouth and deep body. **Ecology:** in small groups near caves and ledges of dropoffs at depths of 15 to 70 m. **Range:** Indonesia & Taiwan to Fiji, n. to Izu Is., s. to N. Cal.

Basslets, groupers, soapfishes and podges (Subfamily Epinephelinae): bottom dwelling carnivores with large-mouths, robust bodies, and small ctenoid scales. Formerly divided into several families, grouped here as "tribes".

Basslets (Tribe Liopropomini): small elongate forms with a broad head, deeply notched or divided D fin with VIII spines (last one may be scaled over), and continuous LL arched over P region. All species are secretive, many inhabit depths below 60 m.

8 **Flathead perch** *Rainfordia opercularis* McCulloch 15 cm
Ecology: in caves of coral reefs. Secretive. **Range:** n. Australia from Dampier Archip. to Queensland.

9 **Pinstriped basslet** *Liopropoma mitratum* Lubbock & Randall 9 cm
Very similar to *L. pallidum* (Pacific Plate) which has fewer P rays (14 vs 15-16). **Ecology:** caves and crevices, 3 to 46 m, usually below 15 m. **Range:** Red Sea to Tuam., n. to Phil. & Caroline Is., s. to GBR.

10 **Yellowmargin basslet** *Liopropoma aurora* (Jordan & Evermann) 17 cm
Ecology: seaward reefs at depths of 49 to 184 m; rare. **Range:** Hawaiian Is.

11 **Redstriped basslet** *Liopropoma tonstrinum* (Randall & Lubbock) 6.5 cm
Similar to *L. multilineatum* (w. Pacific) which has numerous red pinstripes on its sides. **Ecology:** secretive inhabitant of recesses of caves at depths of 11 to 50 m. **Range:** Christmas Is., Micronesia, Fiji & Samoa.

12 **Meteor basslet** *Liopropoma susumi* (Jordan & Seale) 9 cm
Ecology: in recesses of lagoon and seaward reefs at depths of 2 to 34 m. **Range:** Red Sea to Line Is., n. to Ryuk., s. to N. Cal.

13 **African basslet** *Liopropoma africanum* (Smith) 8 cm
Ecology: in recesses of seaward reefs, 8 to 48 m. **Range:** E. Africa to Chagos & Maldive Is., n. to Djibouti, s. to 15°S.

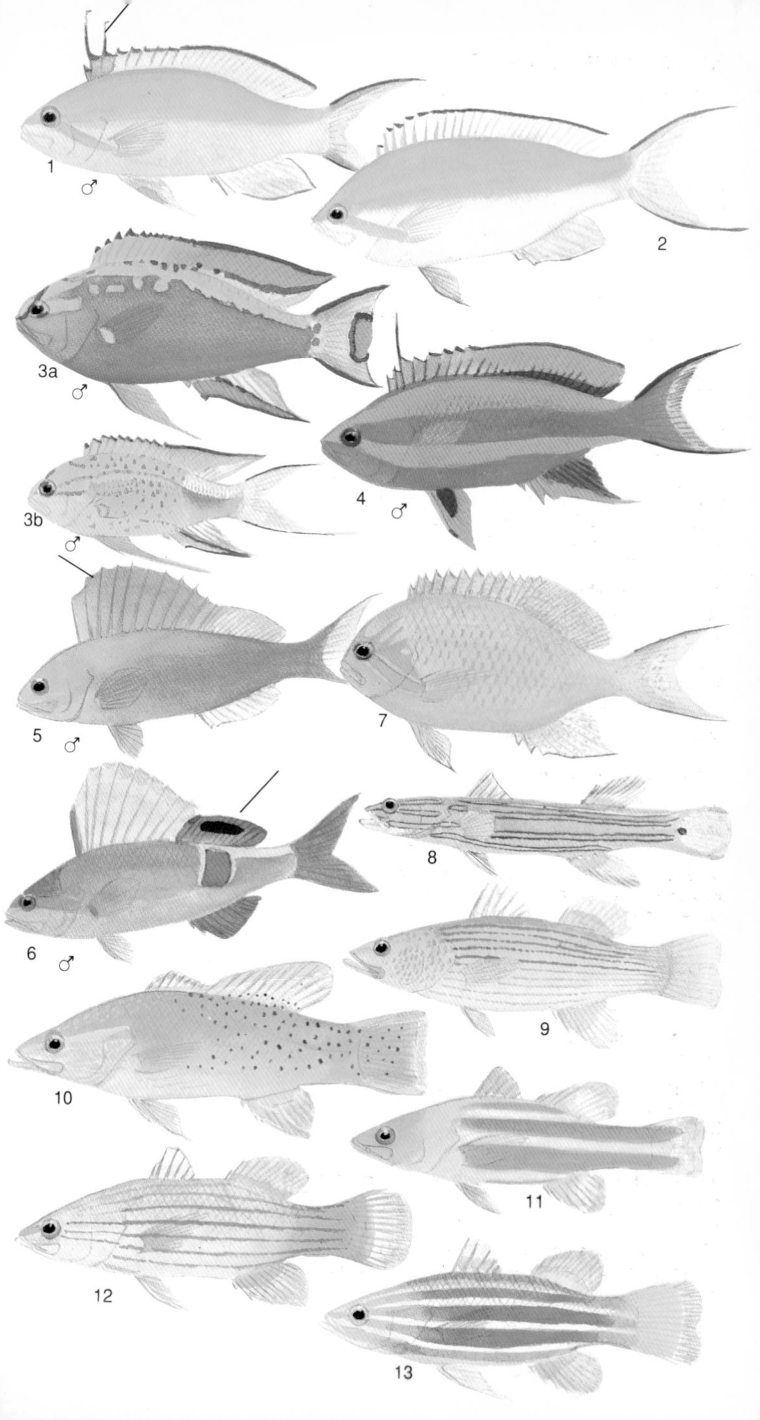

1
♂
2
3a
♂
4
♂
3b
♂
5
♂
7
6
♂
8
9
10
11
12
13

Groupers (Tribe Epinephelini): medium to large robust-bodied forms with large mouths, the jaws typically containing bands of small teeth and canines in front. Typically bottom-dwelling predators of fishes and crustaceans. Important foodfishes, but some species may be ciguatoxic in certain areas. Relatively hardy in aquariums, but grow rapidly.

1 **Redmouth grouper** *Aethaloperca rogaa* (Forsskål) 60 cm
Body deep, inside of mouth red; juvs. with white margin on tail, white bar on side variable. **Ecology:** coral-rich areas of seaward reefs, 1 to 54 m, usually in or near caves, or around coral heads. Feeds primarily on small schooling fishes associated with caves as well as on crustaceans. **Range:** Red Sea to Kiribati & Vanuatu, n. to s. Japan, s. to GBR.

2 **Slender grouper** *Anyperodon leucogrammicus* (Valenciennes) 52 cm
11 D spines; palatine teeth absent; head & body more elongate and compressed than *Epinephelus* spp.; white lines disappear on adults; juvs. mimic i.p. of the wrasses, *Halichoeres purpurascens, H. hoevenii* & *H. vrolikii* (pl. 99). **Ecology:** coral-rich areas of clear lagoon and protected seaward reefs, 1 to 50 m. Feeds primarily on small fishes. Juveniles mimic certain non-piscivorous wrasses in order to get closer to prey. **Range:** Red Sea to Line Is., n. to Ryuk., s. to N. Cal. & Samoa.

3 **Humpback grouper; Pantherfish** *Cromileptes altivelis* (Valenciennes) 70 cm
10 D spines; concave head profile and small head give humpback appearance. **Ecology:** lagoon and seaward reefs, 2 to ⩾ 40 m. More common on dead or silty areas than clear offshore areas. Juveniles popular aquariumfishes. Adults highly valued for food. **Range:** E. Africa to Vanuatu, n. to s. Japan, s. to N. Cal.

4 **Slenderspine grouper** *Gracila albomarginata* (Fowler & Bean) 40 cm
9 D spines, truncate tail. Juvs. purple with broad red stripe on D and A fins and on upper & lower tail lobes and base. **Ecology:** clear outer reef slopes, particularly coral-rich dropoffs, 6 to 120 m, but usually below 15 m. Hovers above the bottom and probably feeds primarily on fishes. **Range:** E. Africa to Marq., n. to Ryuk., s. to N. Cal.

5 **Smooth grouper** *Dermatolepis striolata* (Playfair & Günther) 85 cm
11 D spines; deep bodied; head profile concave with short snout & long nape. **Ecology:** sheltered, turbid coastal rocky or coral reefs. Common at Aldabra. **Range:** s. Red Sea & S. Africa n. to Oman, e. to Seychelles.

6 **Chocolate hind** *Cephalopholis boenak* (Bloch) 26 cm
All *Cephalopholis* have 9 D spines and rounded tails (except truncate in *C. polleni*). **Ecology:** sheltered lagoon reefs, 1 to 20 m, in rocky or coral-rich, often turbid areas. Secretive, feeds primarily on crustaceans. Absent from most oceanic islands. **Range:** E. Africa to Vanuatu, n. to s. Japan, s. to Queensland.

7 **Bluelined hind** *Cephalopholis formosa* (Shaw) 34 cm
Ecology: shallow sheltered coastal reefs, often in dead or silty areas. **Range:** E. Africa & w. India to PNG, n. to s. Japan, s. to GBR.

8 **Harlequin hind** *Cephalopholis polleni* (Bleeker) 35 cm
Ecology: caves and crevices of deep dropoffs, 10 to 120 m, rarely above 25 m. **Range:** Comores to Line Is., n. to Ryuk., s. to Maurit.; absent from Pacific s. of Sol. Is.

9 **Freckled hind** *Cephalopholis microprion* (Bleeker) 23 cm
Ecology: shallow silty reefs. **Range:** Andaman Sea to GBR & N. Cal., n. to Phil.

10 **Starry grouper** *Cephalopholis* sp. ca. 20 cm
Very similar to *C. argus*, but lacks blue spots on portions of tail and soft D & A fins. Often adopts a mottled ground color similar to that of certain *Epinephelus* spp. **Ecology:** patches of coral or porous rock with numerous shelter holes, 3 to at least 20 m. Generally in small groups within the same home patch. **Range:** Andaman Sea from Similan Is. possibly n. Sumatra, w. Indonesia.

11 **Peacock grouper** *Cephalopholis argus* (Schneider) 40 cm
Ecology: lagoon and seaward reefs, 1 to ⩾ 40 m, esp. areas of clear water and rich coral growth. Juvs. usually in shallow protected coral beds. Feeds primarily on fishes. Ciguatoxic in certain areas. Common in most areas except Red Sea. **Range:** Red Sea (uncommon) to Pitcairn Gp., n. to s. Japan, s. to L. Howe Is., introduced to Hawaii.

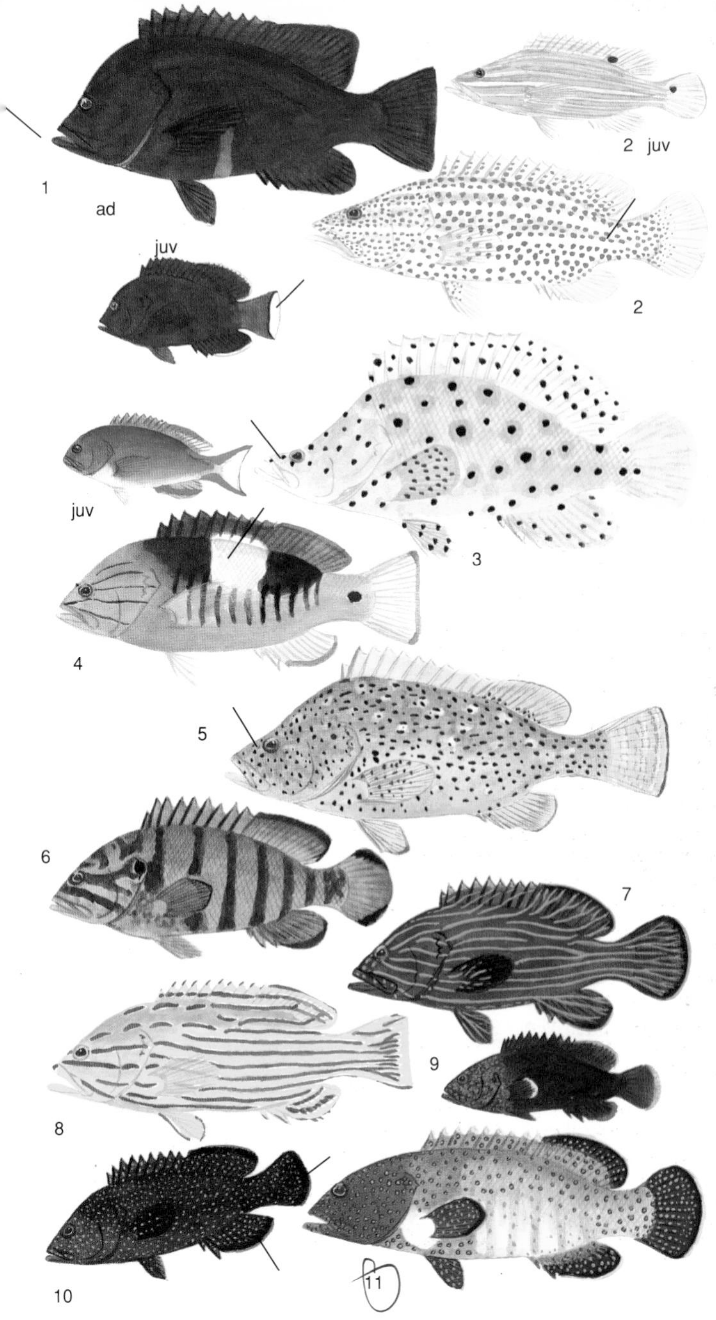
1
ad
juv
2 juv
2
juv
3
4
5
6
7
8
9
10
11

1 **Coral hind** *Cephalopholis miniata* (Forsskål) 41 cm
Juvs. orange with widely scattered blue spots. **Ecology:** channels and seaward reefs in coral-rich areas with clear water, 2 to 150 m. Feeds primarily on fishes, occasionally on crustaceans. Generally common. **Range:** Red Sea to Line Is., n. to s. Japan, s. to L. Howe Is.

2 **Vermilion hind** *Cephalopholis oligosticta* Randall & Ben-Tuvia 30 cm
Similar to *C. miniata*, but blue spots widely scattered. **Ecology:** dead reefs, 15 to 45 m. **Range:** Red Sea.

3 **Sixspot grouper** *Cephalopholis sexmaculata* (Rüppell) 47 cm
Similar to *C. miniata*; but not as red & with blue lines on head & dusky spots or bars dorsally. **Ecology:** caves and crevices of steep outer reef slopes, 6 to 150 m. Occasionally in open water in Red Sea. **Range:** Red Sea to Marq. & Tuam., n. to s. Japan, s. to L. Howe Is.

4 **Halfspotted hind** *Cephalopholis hemistiktos* (Rüppell) 35 cm
Ground color variable, olivaceous in shallow water, becoming red in those from 30 m. **Ecology:** coral reefs, 4 to 55 m. The most common *Cephalopholis* in the Red Sea., primarily in open patchy reefs. Feeds primarily on fishes and crustaceans. **Range:** Red Sea to Pakistan, n. to Arabian Gulf.

5 **Leopard hind** *Cephalopholis leopardus* (Lacépède) 24 cm
May resemble brown indiv. of *C. urodeta*, but that sp. never has saddle at base of tail. **Ecology:** lagoon and seaward reefs in areas of rich coral growth, 1 to 40 m. Secretive. **Range:** E. Africa to Line & Tuam. Is., n. to Yaeyama Is., s. to GBR.

6 **Flagtail grouper; Darkfin hind** *Cephalopholis urodeta* (Forster) 27 cm
Two subsp.: *urodeta* (a) & *nigripinnis* (b) which lacks the white lines on tail. **Ecology:** lagoon and seaward reefs, 1 to 40 m. Common in areas of clear water and rich coral growth, 3 to 15 m. Feeds primarily on fishes, occasionally on crustaceans. **Range:** subsp. *nigripinnis*: E. Africa to Similan & Christmas Is.; subsp. *urodeta*: Christmas Is. to Marq. & Gambier Is., n. to s. Japan, s. to N. Cal. & Rapa.

7 **Strawberry grouper** *Cephalopholis spiloparaea* (Valenciennes) 21 cm
Similar to *C. aurantia*, differing in pattern on tail margin. **Ecology:** seaward reefs, 15 to ⩾ 108 m, common below 30 m. Rare on continental reefs. **Range:** E. Africa to Pitcairn Gp., n. to Ryuk., s. to N. Cal.

8 **Golden hind** *Cephalopholis aurantia* (Valenciennes) 29 cm
Pacific fish (formerly *C. analis*) lack the black submarginal band on tail. **Ecology:** steep seaward reefs, 40 to 250 m, rarely above 100 m. **Range:** E. Africa to Soc. Is., n. to Ryuk., s. to N. Cal.

9 **Tomato grouper** *Cephalopholis sonnerati* (Valenciennes) 57 cm
Deep-bodied, head profile concave; ground color variable from red to brown, juvs. 10 cm dark brown with white tail margin, occas. with white P fin margin & yellow spots on head. During display changes colour rapidly from red, brown to tan. **Ecology:** deep lagoon and seaward reefs, 12 to 150 m. Usually associated with patch reefs on open bottoms below 20 m. Juvs. near sponges or coral heads. **Range:** E. Africa to Samoa., n. to s. Japan, s. to GBR & Tonga.

10 **Bluespotted hind** *Cephalopholis cyanostigma* (Valenciennes) 35 cm
Juvs. with yellow median fins and no blue spots; ground color of adults more tan than *C. argus* and with a different pattern of mottling. **Ecology:** shallow protected coastal reefs, in seagrass beds and coral-rich areas, to 50 m. Feeds on crustaceans and fishes. **Range:** w. Thail. & w. Australia to Sol. Is., n. to Phil., s. to Queensland.

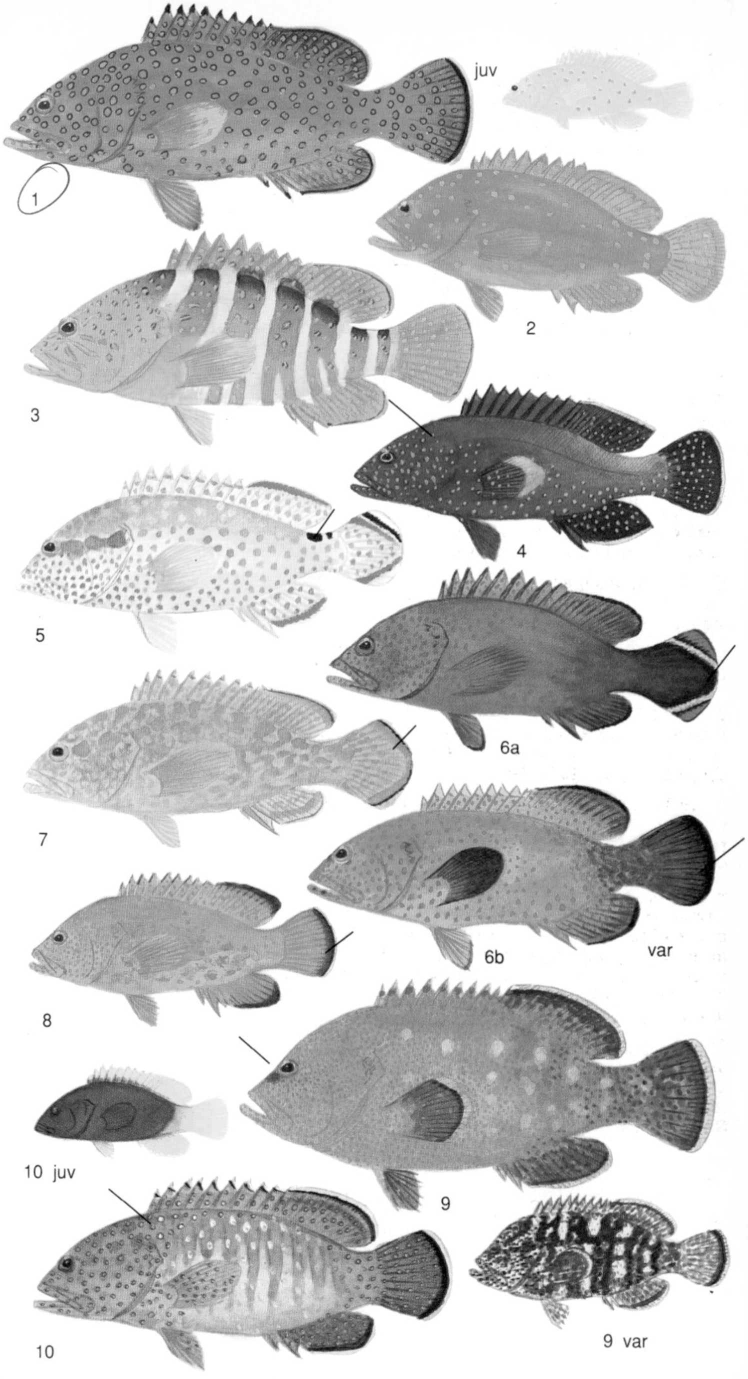
1
juv
2
3
4
5
6a
7
6b
var
8
9
10 juv
10
9 var

1 **Giant grouper** *Epinephelus lanceolatus* (Bloch) ⩾ 270 cm; ca. 300 kg.
All *Epinephelus* with 11 D spines, many v. similar spp. Juvs. of this sp. with black & yellow blotches, becoming mottled brown with age; the only *Epinephelus* with D spines progressively longer from front to back. The largest coral reef dwelling bony fish. **Ecology:** lagoon and seaward reefs, a few to 100 m. Often occurs in a home cave or wreck. Juveniles may occur in brackish water, adults in deep estuaries. Feeds on fishes, larger crustaceans such as spiny lobsters, and even small sharks and sea turtles. Large ones often ciguatoxic. Unconfirmed reports of fatal attacks on humans. Rare. Nearly wiped out in areas - heavily spear fished. **Range:** Red Sea to Hawaiian, Line & Pitcairn. Is., n. to s. Japan, s. to NSW & N. Cal.

2 **Potato grouper** *Epinephelus tukula* Morgans 200 cm; 110 kg
Ecology: clear, coral-rich areas from shallow water to 150 m. Feeds primarily on fishes, occasionally on crustaceans and cephalopods. Uncommon and localized, but bold and easily approached. Hand fed by divers in certain areas, but potentially dangerous to the inexperienced. A diver has drowned after being knocked in the chest by a large individual. **Range:** Red Sea to GBR, n. to s. Japan; absent from many intervening areas.

3 **Speckled grouper** *Epinephelus cyanopodus* (Richardson) 100 cm
Juvs. light gray with yellow fins, becoming speckled & losing yellow with age; similar to *E. flavocaeruleus* which is not speckled. **Ecology:** lagoon and seaward reefs, 2 to 150 m. Generally around isolated coral heads. **Range:** S. China Sea to Kiribati, n. to Ryuk. & Bonin Is., s. to L. Howe Is.

4 **Blue-and-yellow grouper** *Epinephelus flavocaeruleus* (Lacépède) 90 cm
Ecology: rocky or coral reefs, 10 to 150 m. Juveniles shallow, adults generally deeper. Feeds primarily on fishes, occasionally on crustaceans and cephalopods. **Range:** E. Africa to w. Thail. & Sumatra, incl. w. Ind. Oc. islands, n. to Pers. G., s. to Maurit.

5 **White-blotched grouper** *Epinephelus multinotatus* (Peters) 100 cm
Deep body, truncate tail; juvs. yellow posteriorly. **Ecology:** coastal to deep offshore reefs. May mimic the damselfish *Neopomacentrus sindensis* (pl. 84-8; Persian G. to Pakistan), enabling it to closely approach prey. **Range:** E. Africa to w. Australia incl. Ind. Oc. islands, n. to Arab. G.

6 **Specklefin grouper** *Epinephelus ongus* (Bloch) 35 cm
Juvs. black with white spots, these merging to form squiggly longit. bands in adults. P 15-17 (us 17) similar to *E. caeruleopunctatus* (P 18) & *E. summana* (Red Sea only). **Ecology:** shallow coastal and inner lagoon reefs, 5 to 25 m. Enters brackish water. **Range:** E. Africa to Marsh. Is., n. to Ryuk., s. to GBR & N. Cal.

7 **Whitespotted grouper** *Epinephelus caeruleopunctatus* (Bloch) 76 cm
Similar to *E. ongus* and *E. summana*. P fin us. 18., unspotted except basally on adults. **Ecology:** coral-rich areas of lagoon and seaward reefs, 4 to 65 m. Juveniles occasionally in tidepools. Stays close to shelter. **Range:** E. Africa to Kiribati, n. to Pers. G. & s. Japan, s. to GBR & N. Cal.

8 **Summana grouper** *Epinephelus summana* (Forsskål) 52 cm
Ecology: lagoon and protected reefs, 1 to 20 m. Common on rocky reefs (Yemen). Enters brackish water. **Range:** Red Sea & G. Aden.

9 **Saddled grouper** *Epinephelus daemelii* (Günther) 200 cm
Similar to *E. brunneus* (S. China to s. Japan) which lacks dark saddle on tail base. **Ecology:** rocky reefs, around caves. Large ones aggressive and often attracted to divers. **Range:** NSW, n. N. Zeal. & L. Howe, Norfolk & Kermadec Is., Elizabeth & Middleton Rfs.

10 **Halfmoon grouper** *Epinephelus rivulatus* (Valenciennes) 39 cm
Ecology: rocky or weedy areas and coral reefs, 1 to 150 m. **Range:** S. Africa to Bonin & Sol. Is., n. to s. Japan, s. to se. Aust. & n. N. Zeal.

11 **Blacktip grouper** *Epinephelus fasciatus* (Forsskål) 40 cm
May be uniformly light with upper head & nape abruptly dark (b). Similar to the deepwater (us. 80 m, to 40 at Maurit.) *E. retouti* which has more angular truncate tail, & straight head profile. **Ecology:** primarily seaward reefs, 1 to 160 m. Common. Feeds on fishes and crustaceans. **Range:** Red Sea to Marq. & Pitcairn gp., n. to s. Japan, s. to L. Howe Is.

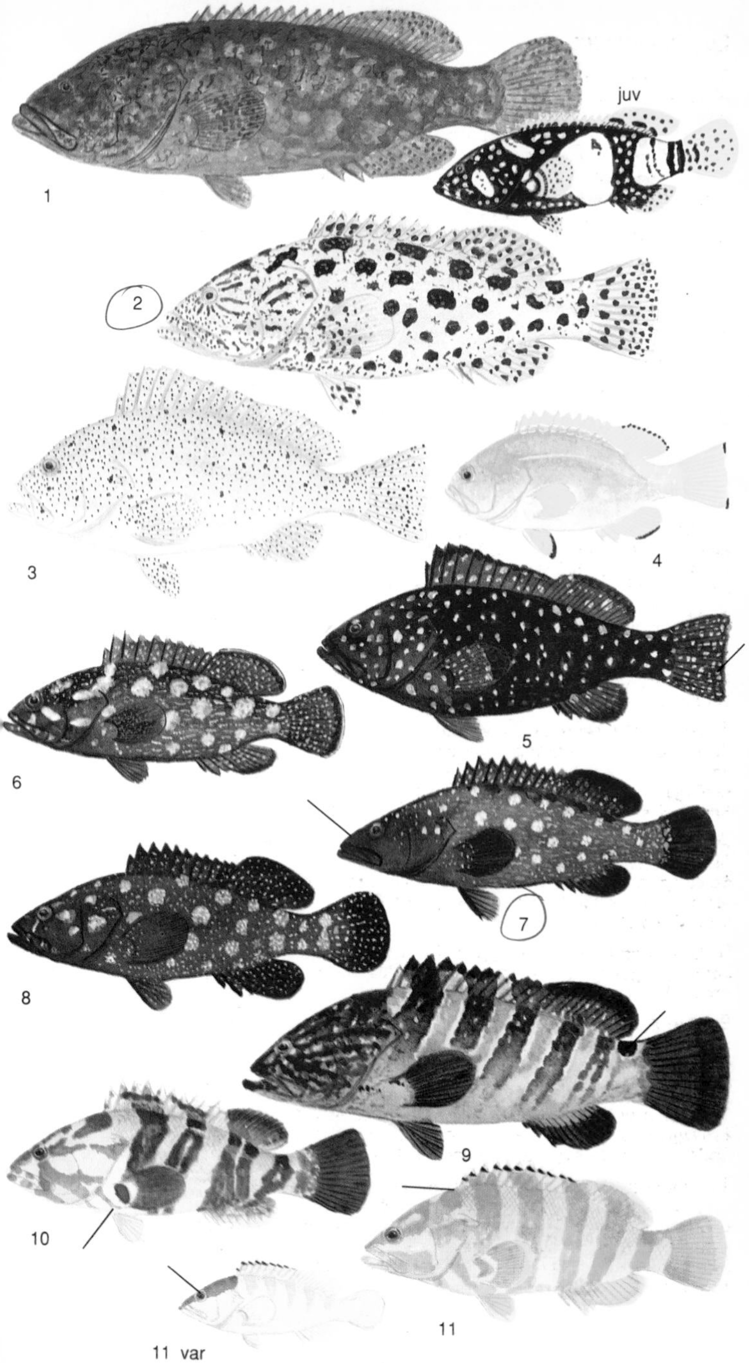

juv
1
2
3
4
5
6
7
8
9
10
11
11 var

27 GROUPERS

1 **Malabar grouper** *Epinephelus malabaricus* (Bloch & Schneider) >120 cm; 150 kg
Diag. dark bands bifurcate ventrally; black spots increase in no. with age. Similar to *E. coioides*, which has larger orange spots and lacks whitish spots. **Ecology:** primarily coastal reefs, occasionally estuaries or clear offshore reefs to 60 m. Feeds primaily on fishes and crustaceans, occasionally on cephalopods. **Range:** Red Sea to PNG, n. to Pers. G. & Ryuk., s. to N. Cal.

2 **Brown-marbled grouper** *Epinephelus fuscoguttatus* (Forsskål) ⩾ 90 cm
Similar to *E. polyphekadion*, but head profile indented at eye & color more yellowish-tan. **Ecology:** lagoon and seaward reefs, in areas of rich coral growth and clear water, 1 to 60 m. Uncommon and wary. Feeds on fishes, crustaceans, and cephalopods. May be ciguatoxic. **Range:** Red Sea to Phoenix & Samoan Is., n. to Ryuk., s. to GBR.

3 **Marbled grouper** *Epinephelus polyphekadion* (Bleeker) 75 cm
Ecology: clear lagoon and seaward reefs, in areas of rich coral growth, 1 to 46 m. Feeds primarily on crustaceans, occasionally on fishes. Common. **Range:** Red Sea to Line & Gambier Is., n. to s. Japan, s. to L. Howe & Rapa.

4 **Greasy grouper** *Epinephelus tauvina* (Forsskål) 75 cm
Fins similar to *E. hexagonatus* & *E. spilotoceps*, but spots on body not close-set hexagons; large ones resemble *E. malabaricus* and *E. coioides*. **Ecology:** coral-rich areas of clear lagoon and seaward reefs, 1 to 46 m. Feeds primarily on fishes, occasionally on crustaceans. May be ciguatoxic. **Range:** Red Sea to Marq. & Ducie Is., n. to s. Japan, s. to N. Cal. & Rapa.

5 **Blacksaddle grouper** *Epinephelus howlandi* (Günther) 44 cm
Snout short; similar to *E. corallicola*, but spots much larger at equiv. size; juvs. with large white patches, resembling juv. *E. maculatus*. **Ecology:** lagoon and seaward reefs, 3 to 30 m. More common than *E. corallicola*. **Range:** Andaman Sea to Marsh. Is. & Samoa, n. to Ryuk., s. to N. Cal.

6 **Highfin grouper** *Epinephelus maculatus* (Bloch) 50 cm
D fin higher than other hexagon-spotted groupers. Juvs. with large white patches. **Ecology:** lagoon and seaward reefs, 2 to 80 m. Usually around isolated coral heads. Juveniles in shallow lagoon rubble. **Range:** Cocos-Keeling to Samoa, n. to s. Japan, s. to L. Howe Is.

7 **Snubnose grouper** *Epinephelus macrospilos* (Bleeker) 51 cm
Projecting lower jaw; no lg. dark spot on back; W. Ind. Oc. subsp. (*E. m. cylindricus*) more closely resembles *E. quoyanus*, but with even larger, more closely-set hexagonal spots. **Ecology:** lagoon and seaward reefs, 5 to 25 m. Feeds primarily on crustaceans. **Range:** S. Africa to Marquesas, n. to Ryuk., s. to GBR.

8 **Coral grouper** *Epinephelus corallicola* (Valenciennes) 49 cm
Snout short; similar to *E. howlandi*, but spots much smaller at equiv. size. **Ecology:** typically in shallow silty coastal reefs, occasionally clear coral slopes to 23 m. **Range:** G. Thail. to Sol. Is., n. to Taiwan, s. to nw. Aust. & NSW.

9 **Orange-spotted grouper** *Epinephelus coioides* (Hamilton) ⩾ 100 cm
Most similar to *E. malabaricus* which has smaller orange dots as well as whitish spots. **Ecology:** turbid coastal reefs to 100 m, even in brackish water. Common in Arabian Gulf. **Range:** Arab. Gulf to GBR, s. to NSW.

10 **Epaulet grouper** *Epinephelus stoliczkae* (Day) 38 cm
Ecology: shallow sandy areas, around small rocks or coral heads. **Range:** Red Sea to G. Oman & Pakistan.

11 **Longspined grouper** *Epinephelus longispinis* (Kner) 55 cm
D spines long; widely scattered small black spots, those on rear 3rd as diag. streaks. **Ecology:** coral or rocky reefs, 1 to 70 m. Occasionally trawled from open bottom. **Range:** E. Africa to Indonesia (Aru Is.), n. to Laccadive & Andaman Is.

12 **Cloudy grouper** *Epinephelus erythrurus* (Valenciennes) 43 cm
Ecology: coral or rocky reefs on muddy bottoms, 10 to 18 m. **Range:** Pakistan & Laccadives to Sulawesi, s. to Sumatra.

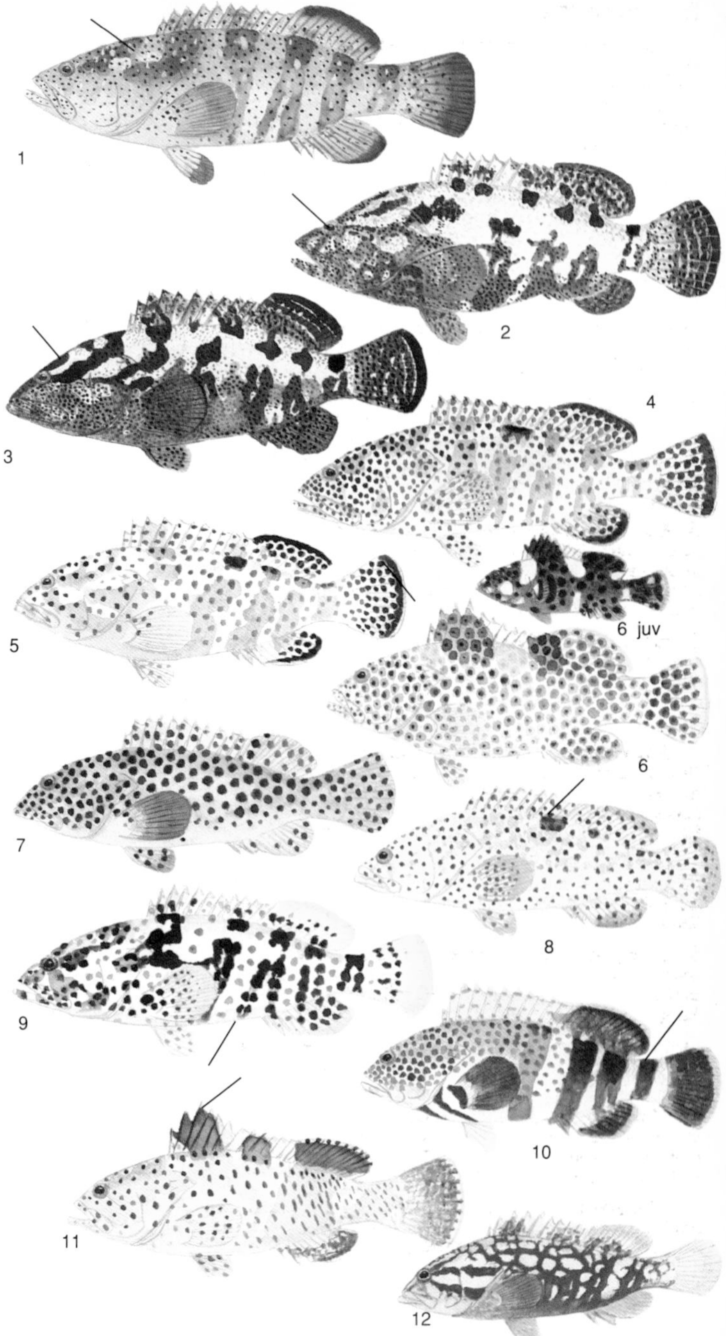
1
2
3
4
5
6 juv
6
7
8
9
10
11
12

1 **Honeycomb grouper** *Epinephelus merra* (Bloch) 31 cm
No white spots at corners of hexagons; hexagons on sides may coalesce into short rows. **Ecology:** shallow lagoon and semi-protected seaward reefs, intertidal to 50 m. Common. Feeds primarily on crustaceans and fishes. **Range:** S. Africa to Line & Gambier Is., n. to s. Japan, s.. to L. Howe & Rapa Is.

2 **Hexagon grouper** *Epinephelus hexagonatus* (Bloch & Schneider) 26 cm
Similar to *E. melanostigma* & *E. spilotoceps* but corners of hexagons with white dots and large tan blotch behind eye. **Ecology:** outer reef flats and clear lagoon and seaward reefs, usually less than 6 m. **Range:** S. Africa to Marq. & Pitcairn gp. n. to Ryuk. & Izu Is., s. to N. Cal. & Rapa.

3 **Longfin grouper** *Epinephelus quoyanus* (Valenciennes) 39 cm
Polygonal spots v. lg.; white margin on tail v. thin, absent on P fin. *E. faveatus* (s. India & Cocos-Keeling to Lombok) similar but lacks dark margins on P & soft A fins & has more spots on snout. **Ecology:** primarily coastal reefs, often in very shallow or intertidal water. **Range:** Andaman Is. to PNG, n. to s. Korea & s. Japan, s. to nw. Aust. & NSW; absent from oceanic is.

4 **Blackspot grouper** *Epinephelus melanostigma* Schultz 33 cm
Similar to *E. hexagonatus* & *E. spilotoceps*, but a single dark blotch at spinous D fin base. **Ecology:** reef flats and shallow lagoon and seaward reefs, 0.3 to 7 m. Uncommon. **Range:** S. Africa to Line & Tokelau Is., n. to s. Japan, s. to L. Howe Is.

5 **Foursaddle grouper** *Epinephelus spilotoceps* Schultz 31 cm
Similar to *E. hexagonatus* but lacks large brown blotch behind eye & has darker spots on snout. **Ecology:** outer reef flats and shallow lagoon and seaward reefs to 30 m. **Range:** S. Africa to Line Is., n. to Laccadive & Marsh. Is., s. to Cook Is.; primarily oceanic; not yet known from mainland of Asia or Australia.

6 **Netfin grouper** *Epinephelus miliaris* (Valenciennes) 53 cm
Hexagonal spots small & close-set on body & spinous D fin, but large on other fins. **Ecology:** seagrass beds and mangrove swamps to deep coastal reefs, 1 to 200 m. Uncommon to rare. **Range:** E. Africa to Gilbert & Samoa Is., n. to Ryuk.; unknown from mainland of Asia or Australia.

7 **Areolate grouper** *Epinephelus areolatus* (Forsskål) 40 cm
Large light yellowish spots, slightly emarginate tail. **Ecology:** seagrass beds and small coral heads on silty sand, 6 to 200 m. **Range:** Red Sea to Fiji, n. to s. Japan, s. to N. Cal.

8 **Brownspotted grouper** *Epinephelus chlorostigma* (Valenciennes) 75 cm
Dark close-set hexagonal spots very small; tail slightly emarginate. Similar to *E. polylepis* (Pers. G. & Oman to w. India) but has fewer LL scales (48-53 vs. 65-72) and to *E. gabriellae* (Somalia & Oman) which has a more emarginate tail & fewer D soft rays (14-15 vs. 16-18). **Ecology:** seagrass beds to seaward reefs, 4 to 280 m. Generally uncommon, but abundant in certain areas such as coral rubble habitats in the Seychelles. **Range:** S. Africa to Samoa, n. to s. Japan, s. to N. Cal.

9 **Surge grouper** *Epinephelus socialis* (Günther) 52 cm
Ecology: reef flats and surge pools to 3 m. More common on atolls than on high islands. **Range:** Oceanic Islands from Bonin & Mariana Is. to Line Is. & Pitcairn gp.

10 **Maori grouper** *Epinephelus undulatostriatus* (Peters) 61 cm
Ecology: rocky reefs and outer reef slopes, 5 to 73 m. **Range:** s GBR & NSW only; primarily warm-temperate.

11 **Palemargin grouper** *Epinephelus bontoides* (Bleeker) 30 cm
Often dark with a blotched pattern. **Ecology:** coastal reefs, 0.3 to 30 m, particularly on shallow cobble bottoms. **Range:** Indonesia & Phil. to Sol. Is., n. to Taiwan.

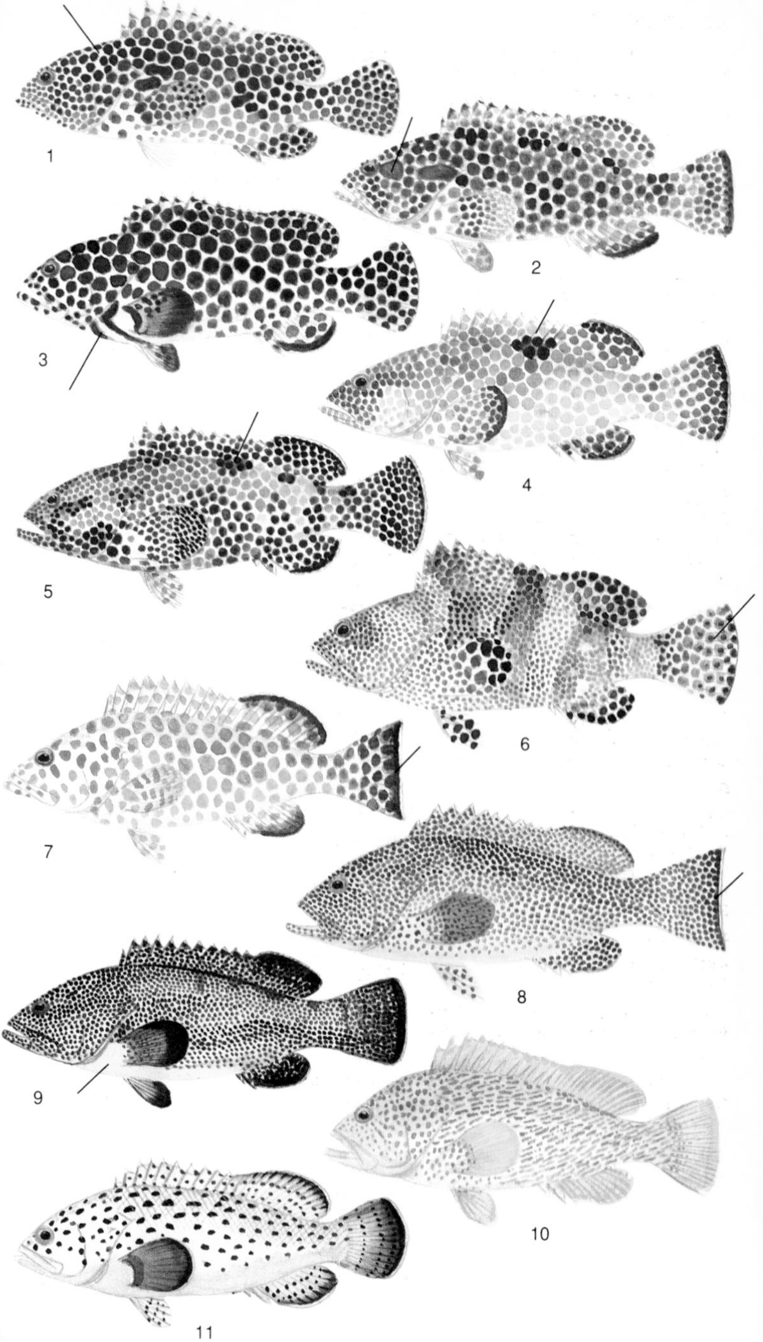
1
2
3
4
5
6
7
8
9
10
11

29 GROUPERS

1 **Lyretail grouper** *Variola louti* (Forsskål) 80 cm
Variola spp. with 9 D spines & lunate tails; posterior margins of all fins broadly yellow; ground color variable, lavender to red; blue dots may coalesce into short squiggly lines; juvs. abruptly white ventrally with narrow white mid-dorsal line from mouth to D fin and nearly clear fins. **Ecology:** coral-rich areas of lagoon and seaward reefs, 1 to ⩾ 150 m. Feeds primarily on fishes, occasionally on crustaceans. Common in many areas. May be ciguatoxic in certain areas. **Range:** Red Sea to Marq. & Pitcairn group., n. to s. Japan, s. to L. Howe & Rapa Is.

2 **Whitemargin lyretail grouper** *Variola albimarginata* Baissac 60 cm
Tail dusky submarginally with narrow white margin; P fin yellow becoming red basally; ground color variable as in *V. louti*; juvs. white ventrally. **Ecology:** seaward reefs, 2 to 100 m, rarely above 20 m. Uncommon. **Range:** E. Africa to Samoa, n. to s. Japan, s. to GBR.

3 **Saddleback coralgrouper** *Plectropomus laevis* (Lacépède) 110 cm
All *Plectropomus* with 8 D spines, prominent canines on sides of lower jaw & angular head. They feed almost exclusively on fishes and typically hover above the bottom. This sp. with saddleback ph. (a) to ca. 60 cm, but spotted ph. (b) may be as small as 13 cm.; ground color of spotted ph. variable, with dark saddles or mottled brown to bright red. **Ecology:** coral-rich areas of lagoon and seaward reefs, 4 to ⩾ 90 m. Encountered most frequently in channels. Can eat surprisingly large fishes. Large ones often ciguatoxic in many areas. Usually wary. **Range:** S. Africa to Mangareva, n. to Ryuk., s. to N. Cal. & Rapa.

4 **Squaretail coralgrouper** *Plectropomus areolatus* (Rüppell) 100 cm
Large dark-edged spots; truncate tail usually with narrow white margin. **Ecology:** lagoon and seaward reefs in areas of rich coral growth, 1 to 20 m. Most frequently encountered in channels and along the reef front. Aggregates to spawn. **Range:** Red Sea to Phoenix Is. & Samoa, n. to Ryuk. & Marsh. Is., s. to GBR.

5 **Leopard coralgrouper** *Plectropomus leopardus* (Lacépède) 70 cm
Blue dots smaller and more numerous than in other *Plectropomus*; usually a blue ring around eye. Ground color variable & generally uniform during day, from pale to dark brown or red. **Ecology:** coral-rich areas of lagoon reefs, 3 to 100 m. Inactive at night, hiding under ledges. The most common *Plectropomus* on mid reefs of the GBR and in the Coral Sea. **Range:** Indochina & Bali to Fiji, n. to s. Japan, s. to w. Aust., s. GBR & N. Cal.

6 **Roving coralgrouper** *Plectropomus pessuliferus* (Fowler) 90 cm
Subsp. *marisrubri* (a) with blue dots on head numerous, may radiate from snout as short lines; ground color with light blotches and bars. Subsp. *pessuliferus* (b) with blue dots on head widely spaced; ground color variable, brown to red. **Ecology:** shallow lagoon and seaward reefs to 147 m. Common in Red Sea, uncommon to rare elsewhere. **Range:** subsp. *marisrubri*: Red Sea; subsp. *pessuliferus*: E. Africa, St. Brandon's Shoals, Maldives, Sri Lanka, Similan Is., Sumatra & Fiji.

7 **Blue-lined coralgrouper** *Plectropomus oligacanthus* (Bleeker) 61 cm
Blue lines on head and vertical lines on sides; ground color brown to bright red; fins elevated. **Ecology:** dropoffs and steep channel slopes, 5 to 35 m. Rare in most areas. **Range:** e. Java to Sol. Is., n. to Phil., Carol. & s. Marsh. Is., s. to nw. Aust. shelf & n. GBR.

8 **Spotted coralgrouper** *Plectropomus maculatus* (Bloch) 70 cm
Blue spots relatively large and horizontally elongate, esp. on head; tail margin white. **Ecology:** coastal reefs. Absent from clear offshore reefs. **Range:** w. Thail. to Sol. Is., n. to Phil., s. to Cocos-Keeling, w. Aust. & GBR.

9 **Marbled coralgrouper** *Plectropomus punctatus* (Quoy & Gaimard) 96 cm
Blue margins on fins distinctively blue. **Ecology:** shallow coral or rocky reefs, particularly patch reefs, 3 to 62 m. Solitary or in small groups. Often drifts well above bottom. **Range:** E. Africa & w. Indian Ocean e. to Seychelles & Maurit.

1
2
juv
3
4
5 var
5
6a
6b
7
8
9

30 SOAPFISHES and PRETTYFINS

Soapfishes (Tribe Diploprionini, Grammistini and Pseudogrammatini): Small grouper-like fishes that produce a skin toxin, grammistin. This bitter toxin protects them from predators and can kill other fishes in a confined space. Solitary predators of crustaceans and fishes. Species of *Grammistops*, *Aporops*, and *Pseudogramma* are always hidden deep in the reef and never seen by divers.

1 **Sixstripe soapfish** *Grammistes sexlineatus* (Thunberg) 30 cm
White stripes break up into series of short dashes in lg. indiv. **Ecology:** reef flats and lagoon and seaward reefs to 20 m. In holes and crevices. **Range:** Red Sea to Marq. & Gambier Is., n. to s, Japan, s. to N. Cal.

2 **Golden-ribbon soapfish** *Aulacocephalus temmincki* (Bleeker) 40 cm
Ecology: rocky reefs, 20 to 120 m. In caves and crevices. **Range:** Primarily subtropical: Red Sea, S. Africa, Mascarenes, se. Asia, N.Z. & Rapa.

3 **Two-banded soapfish** *Diploprion bifasciatum* (Cuvier) 25 cm
Occas. entirely black or black with yellow soft-rayed portions of fins. **Ecology:** rocky and coral reefs, 1 to 18 m. Near caves and crevices. **Range:** India to PNG, n. to s, Japan, s. to Maldives & L. Howe Is.

4 **Yellowface soapfish** *Diploprion drachi* (Estève) 14 cm
Ecology: rocky and coral reefs. Swims behind large non-predatory fishes to ambush prey. Solitary or in pairs, leaving caves at sunset. **Range:** Red Sea & G. of Aden.

5 **Arrowhead soapfish** *Belonoperca chabanaudi* (Fowler & Bean) 15 cm
Ecology: coral-rich areas of steep slopes, 4 to 50 m. Hovers in mid water in caves. Often comes out at sunset. **Range:** E. Africa to Samoa, n. to Ryuk., s. to N. Cal.

6 **Spotted soapfish** *Pogonoperca punctata* (Valenciennes) 35 cm
Ecology: clear seaward reefs, 25 to 120 m. Rare in Oceania. **Range:** Comores to Marq. & Soc. Is., n. to s, Japan, s. to N. Cal.

PRETTYFINS (PLESIOPIDAE): elongate fishes with large mouth, large eyes, elongate pelvic fin, and disjunct LL. Most tropical species are small and secretive; a few warm-temperate Australian species are large and spectacular. Feed on small crustaceans and fishes.

7 **Comet** *Calloplesiops altivelis* (Steindachner) 20 cm
Sometimes with a white spot on tail, described as *C argus*. **Ecology:** seaward reefs, 3 to 45 m. Under ledges and in holes by day. Comes out at night. When alarmed, will poke its head into a hole and expose its tail end which mimics the head of the moray eel, *Gymnothorax meleagris* (pl. 6-2). **Range:** Red Sea to Line Is., n. to s. Japan, s. to GBR & Tonga.

8 **Bluegill longfin** *Plesiops corallicola* Bleeker 16 cm
Ecology: exposed areas of outer reef flats and seaward reefs to 23 m. Common, but hidden in holes by day. Ventures out to feed on small invertebrates and fishes at night. **Range:** Madagascar to Line Is., n. to s. Japan, s. to GBR & Tonga.

9 **Whitespotted longfin** *Plesiops nigricans* (Rüppell) 14 cm
Ecology: coral reefs, 5 to 30 m. Hidden in holes by day. **Range:** Red Sea.

10 **Red-tipped longfin** *Plesiops caeruleolineatus* Rüppell 8 cm
Ecology: exposed areas of outer reef flats and seaward reefs to 23 m. Common, but hidden in holes by day. Ventures out to feed on small invertebrates and fishes at night. **Range:** Red Sea to Samoa, n. to s. Japan, s. to the sGBR.

11 **Yellow devilfish** *Assessor flavissimus* Allen & Kuiter 5.5 cm
Ecology: lagoon and seaward reefs, 5 to 20 m. In aggregations in caves, often upside down. Males incubate the egg mass in their mouth. **Range:** n. GBR.

12 **Blue devilfish** *Assessor macneilli* Whitley 6 cm
Ecology: same as for *A. flavissimus*. **Range:** GBR and N. Cal.; a similar sp., *A. randalli* from the Ryuk. Phil.

1
2
3
var
4
5
7
8
9
10
11
12

31 DOTTYBACKS

DOTTYBACKS and EEL BLENNIES (PSEUDOCHROMIDAE): small often brilliantly colored elongate fishes with a single D fin. *Congrogadus* and *Haliophis* spp. are greatly elongate eel-like forms. Most species remain near crevices or among coral or rubble. They feed on small invertebrates and fishes. The male guards a ball off eggs deposited by the female.

1 **Orchid dottyback** *Pseudochromis fridmani* Klausewitz 6 cm
Similar: *Chrlidichthys johnvoelcheri* (Pemba s. to Natal), without eye-stripe. **Ecology:** vertical rock faces or beneath overhangs, or near holes, 1 to 60 m. Common. **Range:** Red Sea.

2 **Magenta dottyback** *Pseudochromis porphyreus* Lubbock & Goldman 6 cm
Ecology: steep outer reef slopes and channel walls, 6 to 65 m. Hovers close to coral or rubble. Common in Belau, uncommon in e. Caroline Is. **Range:** e. Phil., Moluccas & n. PNG to Samoa, n. to Ryuk. & Caroline Is.

3 **Royal dottyback** *Pseudochromis paccagnellae* Axelrod 7 cm
Ecology: steep outer reef slopes, 5 to 40 m. Hovers close to coral or rubble. **Range:** Indonesia to PNG & Sol. Is., n. to n. Sulawesi, s. to n. Australia & Vanuatu.

4 **Diadem dottyback** *Pseudochromis diadema* Lubbock 6 cm
Ecology: reef slope and base, in small groups among corals or rocks, 10 to 30 m. **Range:** e. Malay Penin. & w. Phil.

5 **Sunrise dottyback** *Pseudochromis flavivertex* Rüppell 7 cm
♀ resembles yellow ph. of *P. fuscus*, a species that does not occur west of India. **Ecology:** around bases of small rocks or corals on sand, 2 to 30 m. **Range:** Red Sea & G. Aden.

6 **Surge dottyback** *Pseudochromis cyanotaenia* Bleeker 6 cm
♀ brown with reddish tail often with yellowish margins. **Ecology:** exposed outer reef flats and reef fronts to 10 m. Common, but secretive, usually in pairs. Feeds on small crustaceans. **Range:** Indonesia to Fiji, n. to Ryuk., s. to GBR.

7 **Blackmargin dottyback** *Pseudochromis tapienosoma* Bleeker 6 cm
♀ without black band on D and tail fins. **Ecology:** intertidal and lagoon reefs, among corals, 2 to 60 m. Common in the Ryukyus. **Range:** Timor & Moluccas to e. Carol. Is., n. to Ryuk.

8 **Dutoiti** *Pseudochromis dutoiti* Smith 9 cm
Ecology: common among shoreline rocks and corals. Guards eggs laid in empty shells. **Range:** E. Africa, s. to S. Africa.

9 **Yellowspeckled dottyback** *Pseudochromis marshallensis* Schultz 8 cm
Ecology: lagoon and seaward reefs to $\geqslant$ 10 m. **Range:** Phil. to Marsh. Is. & Vanuatu, n. to Taiwan, s. to N. Cal.

10 **Dusky dottyback** *Pseudochromis fuscus* Müller & Troschel 9 cm
Colour variable: dark brown to dusky yellow with longitudinal rows of small blue spots. **Ecology:** among corals of subtidal lagoon and seaward reefs to 30 m. **Range:** India to the Solomons, n. to Taiwan, s. to GBR.

11 **Olive dottyback** *Pseudochromis olivaceus* Rüppell 9 cm
V. similar to *P. linda* which occurs in Arab. G. & coasts of Oman & Somalia. **Ecology:** shallow coral-rich areas to 20 m, among branches of corals. Timid. **Range:** Red Sea.

12 **Dark dottyback** *Pseudochromis melas* Lubbock 9 cm
Dark blue opercular spot shared with several spp., but this sp. much darker than the others. **Ecology:** only 3 specimens known, collected between 15 and 20 m. **Range:** E. Africa from Kenya to S. Africa.

13 **Midnight dottyback** *Pseudochromis paranox* Lubbock & Goldman 7 cm
Similar to *P. melas* which is all black except for a blue ocellus on upper edge of operculum. **Ecology:** in or near holes or among corals to $\geqslant$ 20 m. Mimics the angelfish *Centropyge nox* (pl. 69-2). **Range:** sw. Pacific; Sol. Is. & GBR.

14 **Yellowfin dottyback** *Pseudochromis wilsoni* (Whitley) 8 cm
Ecology: among rubble and in crevices of coastal reefs. **Range:** n. Australia, sw. to Shark Bay.

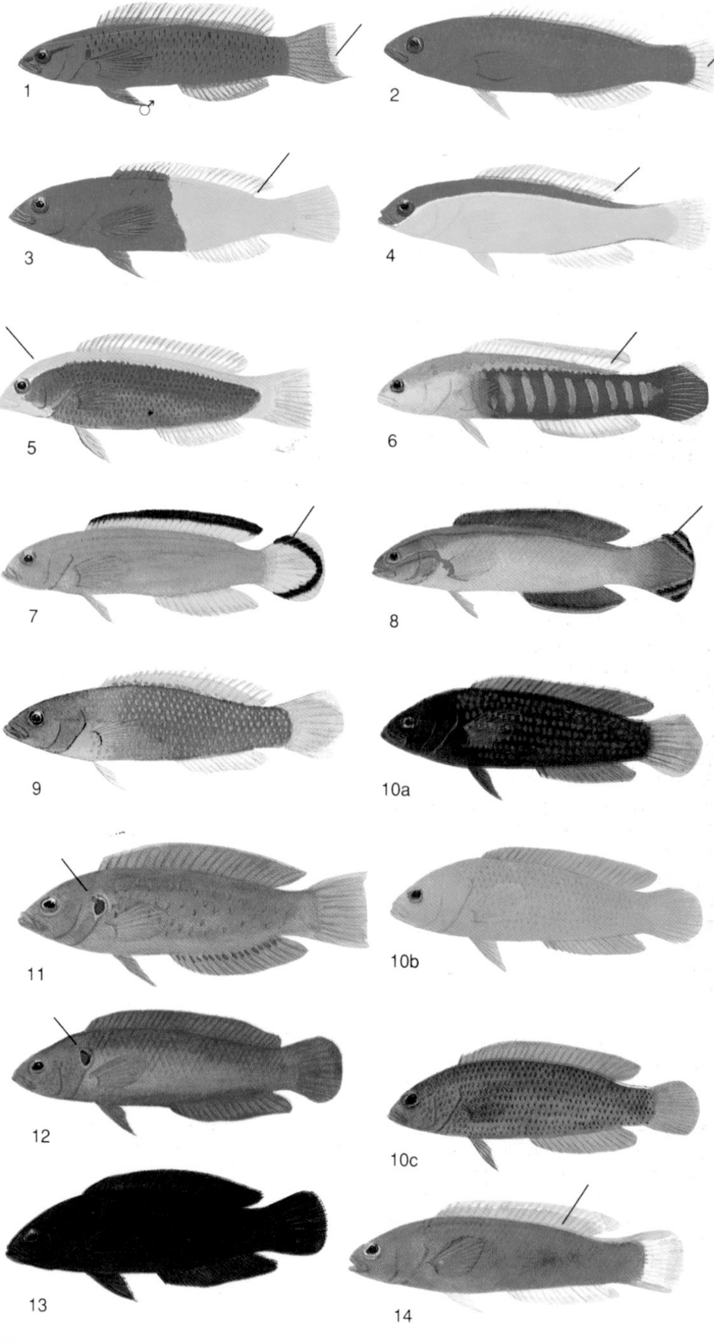
1
2
3
4
5
6
7
8
9
10a
11
10b
12
10c
13
14

32 DOTTYBACKS

1 **Blue-striped dottyback** *Pseudochromis springeri* (Lubbock) 5.5 cm
Ecology: among corals of lagoon and seaward reefs, 2 to 60 m. Solitary around coral heads. Common. **Range:** Red Sea & Gulf of Aden.

2 **Pale dottyback** *Pseudochromis pesi* Lubbock 10 cm
Ecology: around small isolated rocks or corals on sand, 10 to 45 m. Singly or in pairs. **Range:** G. Aqaba, s. Africa, Eritrea & Yemen.

3 **Forktail dottyback** *Pseudochromis dixurus* Lubbock 9 cm
Ecology: in caves or around silt-covered rocks, 5 to 60 m. **Range:** Red Sea.

4 **Striped dottyback** *Pseudochromis sankeyi* Lubbock 7 cm
Ecology: rock and coralline ledges and caves, 2 to 20 m. Often in colonies, up to 25 per sq. m, prefers limestone rocks. **Range:** s. Red Sea & G. Aden (very common in Yemen).

5 **Double-striped dottyback** *Pseudochromis bitaeniatus* (Fowler) 7 cm
Ecology: coral-rich coastal reefs, 1 to 20 m. A possible mimic of *Pholidichthys leucotaenia*. (118-8). Common at Flores. **Range:** Indonesia to Queensland, n. to Phil.

6 **Blackstripe dottyback** *Pseudochromis perspicillatus* Günther 12 cm
Ecology: coral and rocky patches on sand, rubble, or silt bottoms, 3 to 18 m, often around small coral heads. **Range:** Indonesia & Phil.

7 **Lighthead dottyback** *Pseudochromis tauberae* Lubbock 6 cm
Ecology: inside shallow fringing reefs to 6 m where *P. natalensis* is absent. **Range:** E. Africa & Madagascar, s. to S. Africa.

8 **Firetail dottyback** *Pseudochromis flammicauda* Lubbock & Goldman 5.5 cm
Ecology: in or near holes of coral or rock, 3 to 10 m. **Range:** GBR.

9 **Spotted dottyback** *Pseudochromis quinquedentatus* McCulloch 9.5 cm
Ecology: coastal reefs, around outcrops on sand or rubble. **Range:** n. Australia.

10 **Pyle's dottyback** *Pseudochromis pylei* Randall & McCosker 8 cm
Ecology: steep dropoffs and reef base, coral rock and sand, 40 to 55 m. **Range:** Indonesia, in Banda & Flores Seas.

11 **Lyretail dottyback** *Pseudochromis steenei* Gill & Randall 12 cm
Large canine teeth in jaws; sexually dimorphic as shown. Similar to *P. moorei* (Phil.) and *P. quinquedentatus* (n. Australia). **Ecology:** coastal reefs, on patch reefs on soft bottom slopes, 15 to 100 m. Highly territorial and aggressive. This and related species have been known to bite camera housings of divers and kill aquarium tankmates. **Range:** Indonesia, from Bali to Flores.

12 **Bluespotted dottyback** *Pseudochromis persicus* Murray 10 cm
Ecology: coastal reefs, 1 to 25 m. **Range:** Arab. G. to Pakistan.

13 **Spot-tailed dottyback** *Pseudochromis jamesi* Schultz 5.5 cm
♀ light purplish brown with a dark area beneath the white C ped. spot. **Ecology:** reef flats and lagoon reefs. **Range:** Great Barrier Reef to Samoa.

14 **Longfin dottyback** *Pseudochromis polynemus* Fowler 12 cm
Ecology: among dense coral growths of steep outer reef slopes to ⩾ 15 m. Uncommon. **Range:** Moluccas, Phil. & Belau.

15 **Splendid dottyback** *Pseudochromis splendens* Fowler 13 cm
Ecology: lagoon and seaward reefs, reef flats to ⩾ 40 m. Prefers dropoffs, usually close to corals and sponges. Usually solitary, occasionally in pairs. Wary. **Range:** Flores, Moluccas, Irian-Jaya s. to nw. Australia.

1

2

3

4

5

6

7

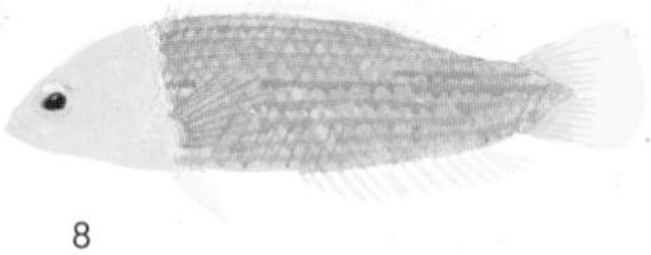

8

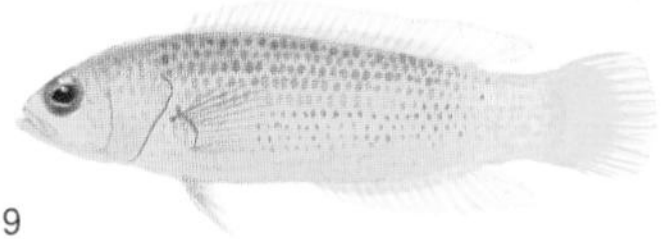

9

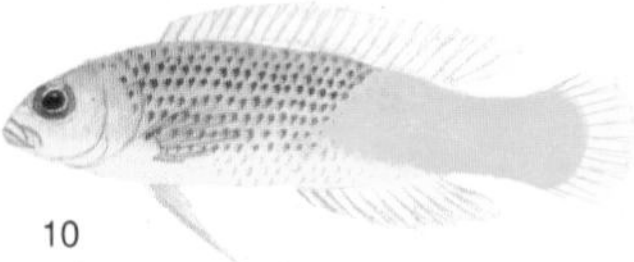

10

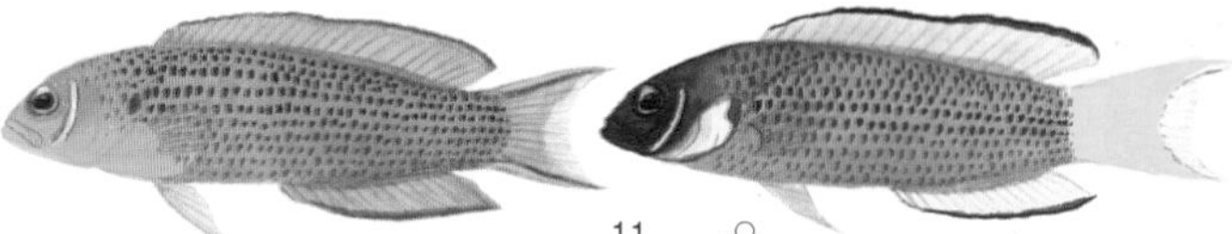

♂ 11 ♀

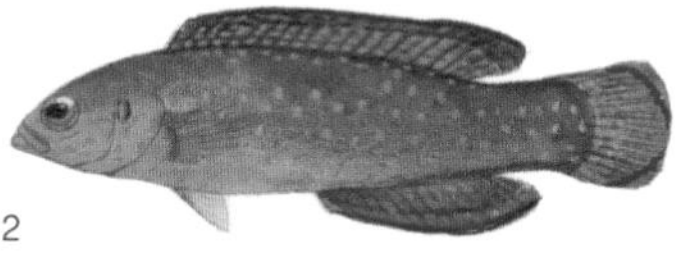

12

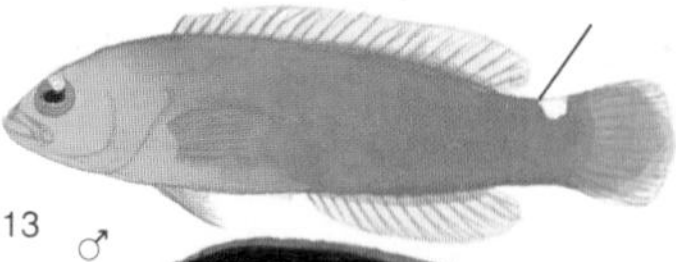

13 ♂

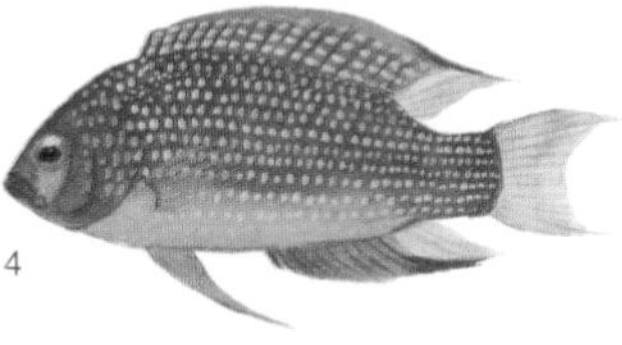

14

15

33 DOTTYBACKS and MORWONGS

1 **Oblique-lined dottyback** *Cypho purpurascens* (DeVis) 7.5 cm
Ecology: in or near holes of coral reefs, 5 to 35 m. **Range:** Admiralty Is., PNG, GBR & Vanuatu.

2 **Giant dottyback** *Labracinus cyclophthalmus* (Müller & Troschel) 20 cm
Ecology: near shelter of coral or rock of shallow reefs, 2 to 20 m. Feeds on small fishes. **Range:** Indonesia, Phil. & PNG, n. to s. Japan.

3 **Lined dottyback** *Labracinus lineatus* (Castelnau) 25 cm
Ecology: in or near crevices of coral or rock of shallow reefs. **Range:** nw. Australia.

4 **Darkstriped dottyback** *Labracinus melanotaenia* (Bleeker) 20 cm
Ecology: in or near crevices of coral or rock of shallow reefs, 1 to 15 m. **Range:** Phil., Borneo, Sulawesi & Moluccas.

5 **Nosey dottyback** *Chlidichthys bibulus* (Smith) 6 cm
Ecology: among corals and seagrasses. **Range:** E. Africa, 3 to 22°S; probably further s & n.

6 **Multicolored dottyback** *Ogilbyina novaehollandiae* (Steindachner) 10 cm
Lg. ♀ may be dark grey to black with red belly. **Ecology:** in or near holes. **Range:** sw. Pacific incl. GBR.

7 **Queensland dottyback** *Ogilbyina queenslandiae* (Saville-Kent) 15 cm
Ecology: in or near holes of coral reefs, 10 to 20 m. **Range:** GBR.

8 **Sailfin dottyback** *Ogilbyina velifera* (Lubbock) 12 cm
Ecology: around formations of rock and coral on sand, 12 to 35 m. **Range:** GBR.

9 **African eel blenny** *Haliophis guttatus* (Forsskål) 14 cm
Ecology: among rocks and rubble of shallow reefs. **Range:** Red Sea, e. Africa & Madagascar.

10 **Carpet eel blenny** *Congrogadus subducens* Richardson 45 cm
Ecology: lives in caves or crevices. **Range:** Nicobar Is. to PNG, s. to nw. Australia & s. GBR, n. to Ryuk.

MORWONGS (CHEILODACTYLIDAE): moderately elongate and compressed fishes with small mouths, thick lips, thickened elongate lower P rays, long continuous D fins and forked tails. Feed on small benthic invertebrates. Hide in holes at night. Most species inhabit subtropical and temperate seas.

11 **Crested morwong** *Cheilodactylus vestitus* (Castelnau) 30 cm
Ecology: rocky and coral reefs, 5 to 30 m. **Range:** se. Australia, s. GBR to L. Howe & Norfolk Is. & N. Cal.

12 **Hawaiian morwong** *Cheilodactylus vittatus* Garrett 41 cm
Ecology: seaward reefs, usually below 18 m. Uncommon. **Range:** N. Cal., L. Howe, Kermadec & Hawaiian Is.

13 **Plessis' morwong** *Cheilodactylus plessisi* Randall 43 cm
Ecology: rocky bottoms and adjacent sandy areas, 0.5 to 22 m. **Range:** Ilots de Bass, Rapa & Easter Is.

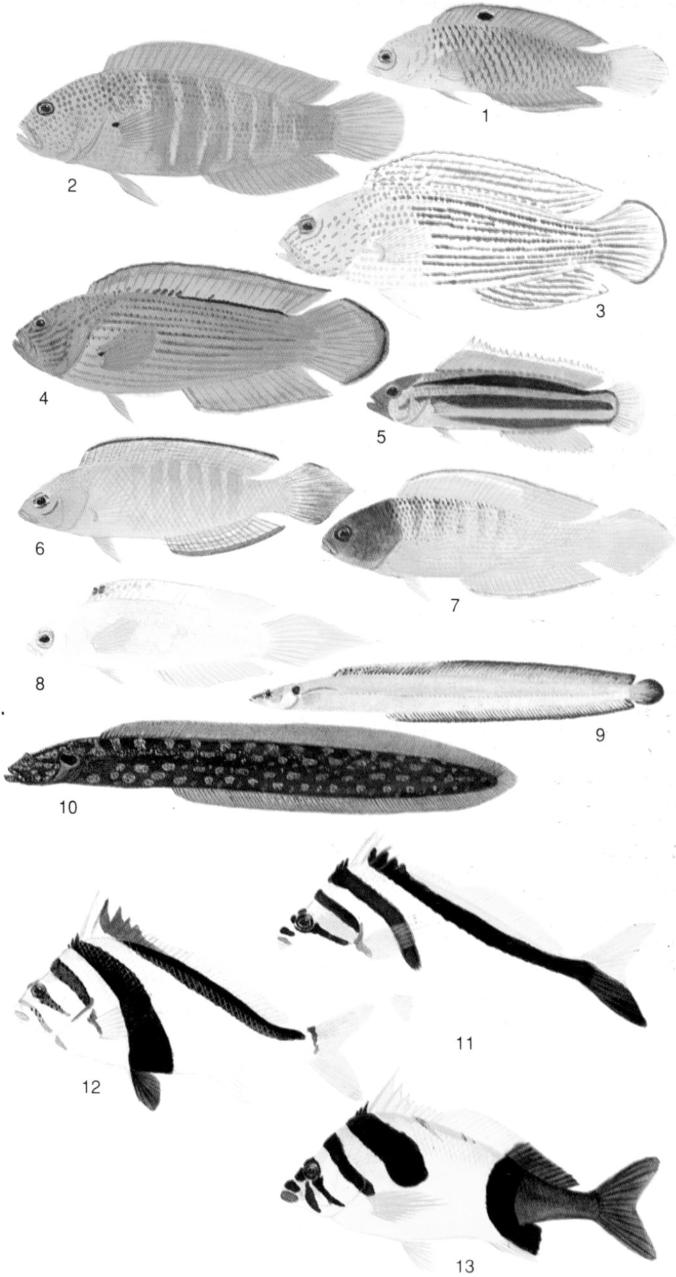
1
2
3
4
5
6
7
8
9
10
11
12
13

HAWKFISHES (CIRRHITIDAE): small grouper-like fishes with tuft of cirri at tip of D fin spines, thickened elongate lower P fin rays, continuous LL and single D fin. Typically perch on the edges of coral heads or other prominences and feed on benthic crustaceans and fishes during the day. Sequential hermaphrodites, the terminal phase is male and is territorial and maintains a harem of females. Spawning and courtship occur at dusk or shortly thereafter. Adapt well to the aquarium but need well-oxygenated high-quality water.

1 **Arc-eye hawkfish** *Paracirrhites arcatus* (Cuvier) 14 cm
Variable: olive to reddish-brown with or without white stripe posteriorly. Other spp. with arc-eye pattern are *P. bicolor* (Caroline atoll) which is dark anteriorly, light posteriorly, *P. nisus* (Tuam.) which has a dark-bordered light longit. band posteriorly & *P. xanthus* (Phoenix, Soc., Tuam. & Gambier Is.) which is yellow. **Ecology:** clear lagoon and seaward reefs, 1 to ⩾ 33 m. Typically perches on small heads of *Stylophora, Pocillopora*, and *Acropora* corals. Feeds primarily on crustaceans. **Range:** E. Africa to Hawaiian & Gambier Is., n. to s. Japan, s. to Norfolk & Rapa Is.

2 **Freckled hawkfish** *Paracirrhites forsteri* (Schneider) 22.5 cm
Variable: *typee* ph. (b) dark brown with red spots anteriorly becoming yellow posteriorly. Indo-Aust. juvs. brownish-red dorsally; Pacific juvs. brown to green dorsally. **Ecology:** clear lagoon and seaward reefs, 1 to ⩾ 33 m. Typically perches on small heads of *Stylophora, Pocillopora*, and *Acropora* corals. Feeds primarily on small fishes and occasionally on shrimps. Common in most areas. **Range:** Red Sea to Hawaiian, Marq. & Ducie Is., n. to s. Japan, s. to L. Howe & Austral Is.

3 **Flame hawkfish** *Neocirrihites armatus* Castlenau 9 cm
Ecology: inhabits heads of *Stylophora* and *Pocillopora* corals on exposed seaward reefs, 1 to 10 m. Retreats deep into the corals when approached. **Range:** Phil., Sunda Is. & GBR to Samoa, n. to Ryuk. & Bonin Is., s. to N. Cal.

4 **Longnose hawkfish** *Oxycirrhites typus* Bleeker 13 cm
Ecology: dropoffs, 12 to 100 m, usually below 30 m. Inhabits gorgonians and black corals and feeds on small benthic or planktonic crustaceans. Uncommon to rare. **Range:** Red Sea to Panama, n. to s. Japan & Hawaiian Is., s. to N. Cal.

5 **Stocky hawkfish** *Cirrhitus pinnulatus* (Bloch & Schneider) 28 cm
Small dark spots more red in Hawaiian popul. **Ecology:** rocky shorelines and reef fronts exposed to surge, 0.3 to 3 m. Feeds primarily on crabs but also takes small fishes, shrimps, sea urchins, and brittle stars. **Range:** Red Sea to Hawaiian, Marq. & Gambier Is., n. to s. Japan, s. to Kermadec & Rapa Is.

6 **Whitespot, halfspotted hawkfish** *Paracirrhites hemistictus* (Günther) 29 cm
Two morphs: light (a. *hemistictus* ph.) or dark (b. *polystictus* ph.)
Ecology: exposed seaward reefs, 1 to 18 m. On corals or rock. Uncommon. **Range:** Cocos-Keeling & Christmas Is. to Marq. & Ducie Is., n. to Bonins, s. to N. Cal. & Austral Is. Absent from most large continental islands.

7 **Yellow hawkfish** *Cirrhitichthys aureus* Temminck & Schlegel 14 cm
Ecology: rocky cliffs in deep water. Common off s. Japan. **Range:** s. China & s. Japan, s. Korea, Java.

8 **Redbar hawkfish** *Cirrhitops fasciatus* Bennett 11 cm
C. hubbardi (Bonin, Phoenix & Tuam. Is.) similar but more brown than red. **Ecology:** seaward reefs, in areas of moderate to rich coral growth to ⩾ 30 m. Typically at the bases of coral heads on hard bottom. Feeds primarily on fishes and crustaceans. Common in Hawaiian Is. **Range:** Madagascar, Maurit., Réunion, s. Japan & Hawaiian Is.

9 **Two-spotted hawkfish** *Amblycirrhitus bimacula* (Jenkins) 8.5 cm
Ecology: clear exposed seaward reefs, 2 to 20 m. Secretive, hidden in or near holes. **Range:** E. Africa to Hawaiian & Gambier Is., n. to Ryukyun, s. to GBR.

10 **Threadfin hawkfish** *Cirrhitichthys aprinus* (Cuvier) 12.5 cm
Ecology: subtidal coastal reefs, in rocky or coralline areas to 40 m. Common. **Range:** E. Indies, n. to s. Japan, s. to Cocos-Keeling, nw Aust. & GBR.

11 **Pixy hawkfish** *Cirrhitichthys oxycephalus* (Bleeker) 9.5 cm
Variable: spots dark or light-centered. Similar to *C. guichenoti* (Maurit. & Réunion) with longer snout & *C. bleekeri* (India & Sri Lanka) with lighter, poorly defined brown blotches. **Ecology:** lagoon and seaward reefs, in areas of moderate to rich coral growth, 1 to 40 m. Typically at the bases of coral heads on hard bottoms. **Range:** Red Sea & S. Africa to Panama, n. to s. Japan, s. to N. Cal.

12 & 13 See over

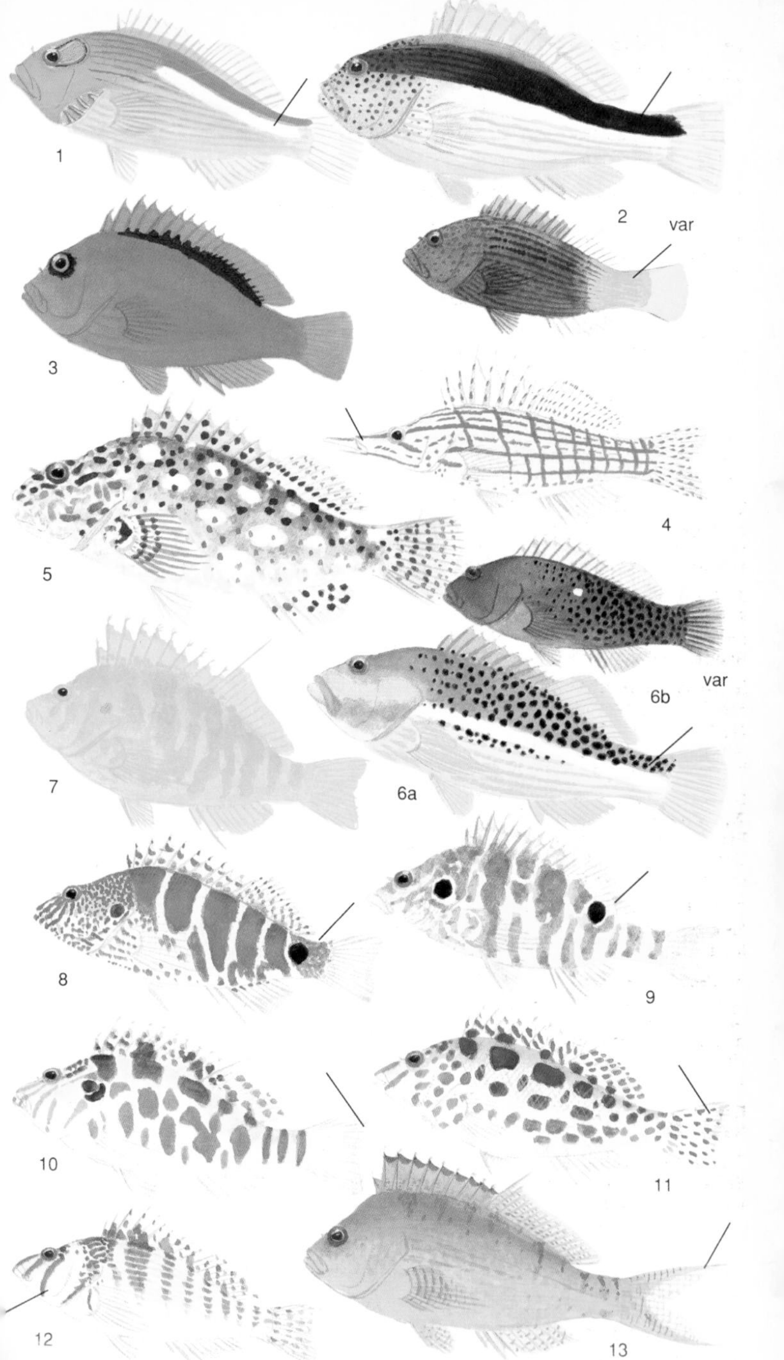
1
2
var
3
4
5
6b
var
7
6a
8
9
10
11
12
13

←12 **Falco or dwarf hawkfish** *Cirrhitichthys falco* Randall 7 cm
Ecology: seaward reefs, in areas of moderate to rich coral growth, 4 to 46 m. Typically at the bases of coral heads on hard bottom. **Range:** Maldives to Caroline Is. & Samoa, n. to Ryuk. & Bonin Is., s. to N. Cal.

←13 **Swallowtail hawkfish** *Cyprinocirrhites polyactis* (Bleeker) 15 cm
Ecology: steep slopes and around small coral heads exposed to currents, 10 to 132 m. The only hawkfish that hovers in water column to feed on planktonic crustaceans and larvae. **Range:** E. Africa to Austalia, n. to s. Japan, s. to nw. Aust. shelf & GBR.

35 CARDINALFISHES

CARDINALFISHES (APOGONIDAE): small moderately elongate fishes with 2 D fins, a single LL, large mouth, and large eyes. Most species remain hidden during the day and venture out to feed on zooplankton or small benthic invertebrates at night. Some species form dense aggregations above and among branching corals. Males incubate the eggs in the mouth until hatching. They generally do well in the aquarium.

1 **Broad-striped cardinalfish** *Apogon angustatus* (Smith & Radcliffe) 10 cm
Numerous v. similar spp. differing in details of striping. **Ecology:** clear seaward reefs, reef flat to 65 m. Feeds on benthic invertebrates. **Range:** Red Sea to Line & Gambier Is., n. to Taiwan, s. to N. Cal.

2 **Seven-striped cardinalfish** *Apogon novemfasciatus* Cuvier 9 cm
Ecology: reef flats and shallow lagoons to 4 m. Common in sandy, rubbly areas. In groups under ledges or in holes by day. Feeds on small fishes and crustaceans by night. **Range:** Cocos-Keeling Is. to Line Is., n. to Izu Is., s. to GBR & Samoa.

3 **Blackbanded cardinalfish** *Apogon cookii* Macleay 10 cm
Ecology: coastal and lagoon reefs, 1 to 8 m. Common in w. Indian Ocean. **Range:** E. Africa to GBR, n. to Arabian G. & Ryuk.

4 **Reef-flat cardinalfish** *Apogon taeniophorus* Regan 11 cm
Ecology: exposed seaward reefs, in holes and under ledges. **Range:** Red Sea to Line & Pitcairn Is., n. to s. Japan, s. to NSW & Rapa.

5 **Blackstripe cardinalfish** *Apogon nigrofasciatus* Lachner 10 cm
Indiv. from Pacific oceanic islands with white stripes (see plate). **Ecology:** shallow sheltered reefs, solitary or in pairs. **Range:** Red Sea to Tuam., n. to s. Japan, s. to N. Cal. & Rapa.

6 **Doederlein's cardinalfish** *Apogon doederleini* Jordan & Snyder 14 cm
Ecology: rocky inshore areas, around ledges. Common, solitary or paired. **Range:** Taiwan to s. Japan and GBR & NSW to N. Cal, s. to Kermadec Is.

7 **Yellow-striped cardinalfish** *Apogon cyanosoma* Bleeker 8 cm
Micronesian form solid yellow. Similar to *A. nitidus* which has stripe through tail. **Ecology:** sheltered clear lagoon and seaward reefs, 1 to 49 m. In small aggregations under ledges, in holes, or among sea urchin spines by day. **Range:** Red Sea to Marsh. Is., n. to s. Japan, s. to GBR.

8 **Bluespot cardinalfish** *Apogon nitidus* (Smith) 8 cm
Ecology: among corals. Only 3 specimens known, taken from about 15 m. **Range:** E. Africa to Seychelles.

9 **Ochre-striped cardinalfish** *Apogon compressus* (McCulloch) 12 cm
Ecology: shallow sheltered reefs, in small groups among branching corals, 0.3 to 7 m. **Range:** Malaysia to Sol. Is., n. to Ryuk., s. to GBR.

10 **Candystripe cardinalfish** *Apogon endekataenia* Bleeker 13 cm
Ecology: coral reef crevices. **Range:** E. Indies, n. to s. Japan, s. to nw. Aust.

11 **Hartzfeld's cardinalfish** *Apogon hartzfeldii* Bleeker 10 cm
Ecology: sheltered reef flats and shallow lagoons, in small groups among debris or corals. **Range:** Phil. to w. NG, s. to nw. Aust.

12 **Many-lined cardinalfish** *Apogon chrysotaenia* Bleeker 10 cm
Ecology: crevices of reef flats and coral slopes. **Range:** Indonesia s. to nw. Aust & Philipp..

13. **Semi-lined cardinalfish** *Apogon semilineatus* Temminck & Schlegel 12 cm
Ecology: rocky areas, 3 to 100 m, in schools. Common in s. Japan. **Range:** Phil. n. to s. Japan.

14 **Broad-banded cardinalfish** *Apogon fasciatus* (Shaw) 10 cm
Ecology: coastal reefs, in sandy or weedy areas. **Range:** Red Sea to Line & Tuam. Is., n. to Ryuk., s. to NSW.

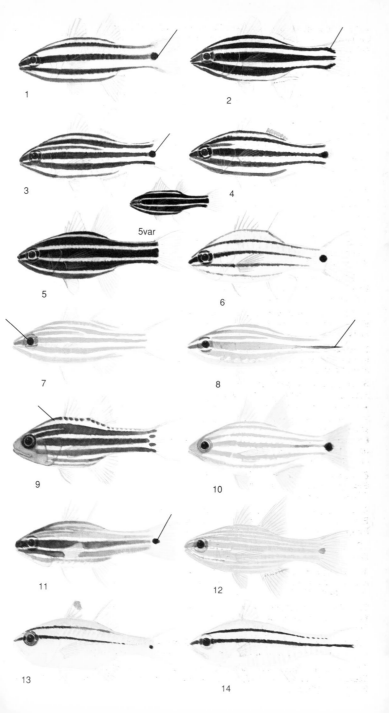

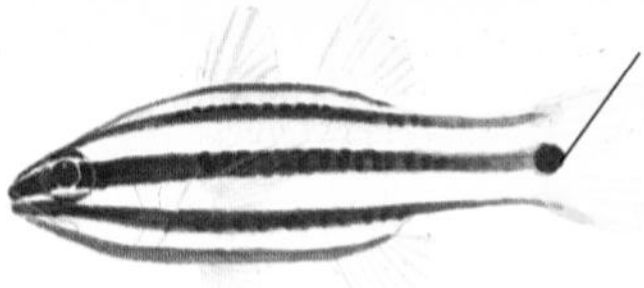

1

2

3

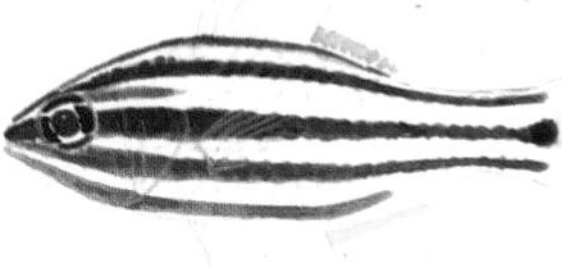

4

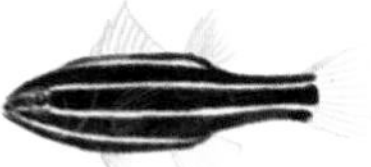

5var

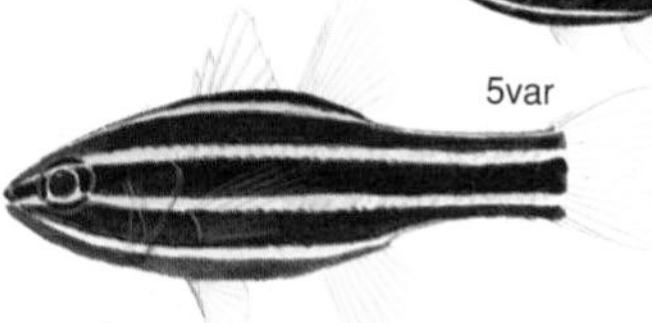

5

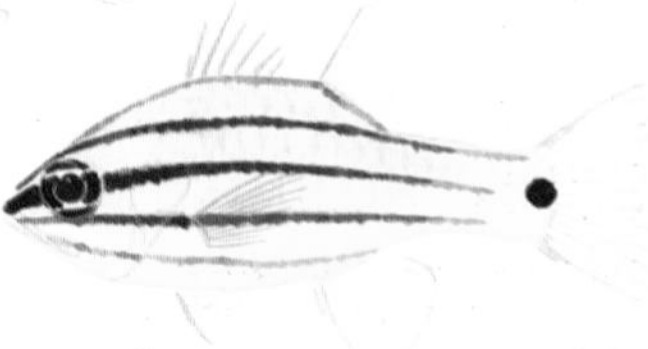

6

7

8

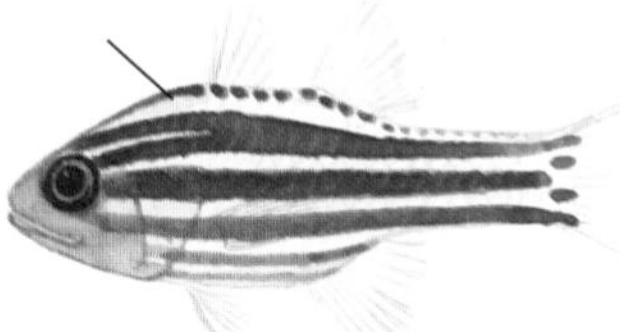

9

10

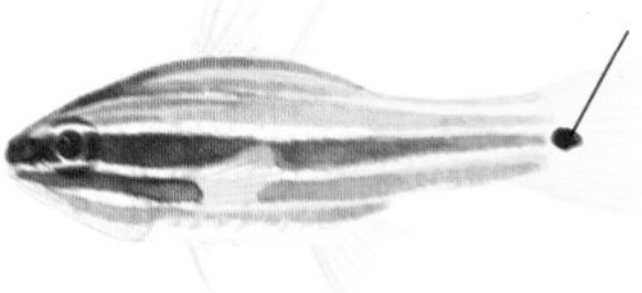

11

12

13

14

CARDINALFISHES

1 **Ring-tailed cardinalfish** *Apogon aureus* (Lacépède) 12 cm
V. similar to *A. fleurieu* (Red Sea to Moluccas), which has a slightly hourglass-shaped black bar at the tail base. **Ecology:** sheltered reefs near caves or crevices, 1 to 40 m. Feeds on zooplankton. **Range:** E. Africa to Tonga, n. to s. Japan, s. to NSW & N. Cal.

2 **Goldbelly cardinalfish** *Apogon apogonides* (Bleeker) 10 cm
Ecology: coastal reefs, 3 to 30 m. In aggregations among branching corals and soft corals. **Range:** E. Africa to e. Indonesia, n. to Izu Is., s. to GBR.

3 **Spotnape cardinalfish** *Apogon notatus* (Houttuyn) 10 cm
Ecology: among corals. **Range:** S. Japan to Coral Sea.

4 **White-saddled cardinalfish** *Apogon ventrifasciatus* Allen & Randall 10 cm
Ecology: shallow coral reefs in silty water, 2 to 10 m. **Range:** E. Africa to PNG, s. to n. Australia.

5 **Iridescent cardinalfish** *Apogon kallopterus* Bleeker 15 cm
Ecology: lagoon and seaward reefs below surge zone to 45 m. Solitary, near holes by day. **Range:** Red Sea to Hawaiian, Marq. & Pitcairn Is., n. to s. Japan, s. to L. Howe & Rapa Is.

6 **Bridled cardinalfish** *Apogon fraenatus* Valenciennes 10 cm
Ground color pinkish; spot on tail base centered at level of lateral stripe. **Ecology:** reef flats and lagoon and seaward reefs to 25 m. Common in clear water areas of mixed sand, rubble, and coral. Under ledges by day, solitary or in small groups. **Range:** Red Sea & Arabian G. to Line & Tuam. Is., n. to Ryuk., s. to NSW.

7 **Eyeshadow cardinalfish** *Apogon exostigma* (Jordan & Starks) 11 cm
Spot on tail base centered above level of lateral stripe, body color with pinkish cast. **Ecology:** under ledges or among isolated coral heads in shallow inner reef areas. **Range:** Red Sea to Line & Gambier Is., n. to Ryuk., s. to S. GBR & Austral Is.

8 **Three-saddle cardinalfish** *Apogon bandanenis* Bleeker 10 cm
Similar to *A. annularis* (Red Sea) and 10. **Ecology:** shallow sheltered reefs, among branching corals. Solitary. **Range:** E. Indies to Samoa, n. to Ryuk., s. to GBR.

9 **Gray cardinalfish** *Apogon fuscus* (Quoy & Gaimard) 10 cm
Eyebar wide, light bars on sides, dark saddle on tail base. Often id. as *A. savayensis.* **Ecology:** outer reef slopes, hidden in crevices or among corals by day. Feeds above the bottom on free-swimming invertebrates by night. **Range:** Red Sea to Line & Tuam. Is., n. to Ryuk., s. to GBR & Rapa.

10 **Guam cardinalfish** *Apogon guamensis* Valenciennes 10 cm
Ecology: reef flats and shallow lagoons, among corals or in holes during the day. **Range:** Red Sea to Samoa, n. to Ryuk., s. to s. GBR.

11 **Bandfin cardinalfish** *Apogon taeniopterus* Bennett 18 cm
Ecology: rocky and coralline areas of seaward reefs, 1 to 35 m, in or near shelter by day. Common in Hawaiian Is., uncommon elsewhere. **Range:** Maurit. to Haw., Marq. & Pit. Is., s. to N. Cal.

12 **Threespot cardinalfish** *Apogon trimaculatus* (Cuvier) 16 cm
Ecology: clear lagoon and seaward reefs, in coral-rich areas. Hidden by day. Uncommon. **Range:** Malaysia to Samoa, n. to Ryuk., s. to nw. Aust. shelf & GBR.

13 **Twobelt cardinalfish** *Apogon taeniatus* Ehrenberg 12.5 cm
Ecology: coastal reefs, in shallow silty areas and among mangroves. **Range:** Red Sea & E. Africa to Comores & Madag., s. to S. Africa.

14 **Inshore cardinalfish** *Apogon lateralis* Valenciennes 11 cm
Ecology: in aggregations among algae and rubble in shallow sheltered lagoons. **Range:** E. Africa to Samoa, n. to Taiwan s. to L. Howe.

15 **Bluestreak, threadfin cardinalfish** *Apogon leptacanthus* Bleeker 6 cm
Ecology: in large aggregations among branching corals in sheltered lagoons and bays. **Range:** Red Sea to Samoa, n. to Ryuk, s. to N. Cal. & Tonga.

16 **Fragile cardinalfish** *Apogon fragilis* Smith 5.5 cm
Ecology: in large aggregations among branching corals in sheltered lagoons and bays. **Range:** E. Africa to Marsh. Is. & Samoa, n. to Ryuk., s. to GBR.

17 **Frostfin cardinalfish** *Apogon hoevenii* (Bleeker) 5 cm
Ecology: in aggregations near crinoids, sea urchins, or sponges sheltered weedy areas. **Range:** Indonesia and Phil. to the n. GBR, n. to s. Japan.

1
2
3
4
5
6
7
8
9
10
11
12
13
14
15
16
17

37 CARDINALFISHES

1 **Seale's cardinalfish** *Apogon sealei* Fowler 8 cm
A. chrysopomus similar (Bali to Philippines), but lateral stripes broader. **Ecology:** shallow sheltered reefs, in small groups among branching corals. Uncommon. **Range:** Malaysia to Sol. Is., n. to Ryuk., s. to GBR.

2 **Rifle cardinalfish** *Apogon kiensis* Jordan & Snyder 8 cm
Similar to *A. quadrifasciatus* from deep sheltered areas (⩾ 50 m). **Ecology:** rocky and coral reefs. **Range:** Red Sea to Phil., n. to s. Japan.

3 **Gobbleguts** *Apogon rueppelli* Günther 12 cm
Ecology: estuaries and inshore reefs, in aggregations in weedy areas. **Range:** PNG, s. to sw. Australia.

4 **Spotted cardinalfish** *Apogon maculiferus* Garrett 14 cm
Ecology: under ledges or in caves by day, 1 to 29 m. **Range:** Hawaiian Is.

5 **Sangi cardinalfish** *Apogon sangiensis* Bleeker 9 cm
Ecology: in groups among rocks or corals of reef flats and shallow sheltered lagoons. **Range:** E. Africa to Vanuatu, n. to Ryuk., s. to GBR.

6 **Bullseye cardinalfish** *Apogon nigripinnis* Cuvier 8 cm
Ecology: inshore to deep offshore reefs. **Range:** Red Sea to nw. Aust.

7 **Multistriped cardinalfish** *Apogon multitaeniatus* (Cuvier & Valenciennes) 18 cm
Ecology: remains hidden by day. **Range:** Red Sea & w. Indian Ocean.

8 **Cryptic cardinalfish** *Apogon coccineus* Rüppell 6 cm
Body transparent red; numerous similar spp. including *A. doryssa* (w-c. Pacific), *A. crassiceps* (Hawaiian Is.) & *A. caudicinctus* (w. Ind. Oc. to Pitcairn Gp.). **Ecology:** lagoon and seaward reefs to 17 m. Always hidden by day, stays near bottom to feed on smalll benthic crustaceans at night. **Range:** Red Sea to Marq. & Easter Is., n. to Ryuk, s. to L. Howe Is.

9 **Ocellated cardinalfish** *Apogonichthys ocellatus* (Weber) 4 cm
Ecology: shallow sheltered reefs among rocks, rubble or weed, primarily in "dead" areas. **Range:** E. Africa to Marq., n. to s. Japan, s. to GBR & Rapa.

10 **Bay cardinalfish** *Foa brachygramma* (Jenkins) 8 cm
Ecology: common in shallow inshore dead silty or weedy reefs, but known to 90 m. **Range:** E. Africa to Hawaiian Is., n. to s. Japan.

11 **Variegated cardinalfish** *Fowleria variegata* (Valenciennes) 8 cm
5-6 other spp. in genus, all very similar and rather cryptic. **Ecology:** reef flats, bays, and shallow lagoons, among rubble, corals or seagrasses. **Range:** Red Sea to Samoa, n. to Ryuk., s. to GBR.

12 **Sea urchin cardinalfish** *Siphamia versicolor* (Smith & Radcliffe) 7 cm
Siphamia spp. with elongate luminous organ on ea. side of belly. Many ssp. in E. Indies. Similar to *S. mossambica* (E. Africa), which also occurs among sea urchins, *S. majimai* (Indo-Aust.) & *S. fuscolineata* (w. Pacific), the latter two found among the spines of the crown of thorns starfish, *Acanthaster planci*. **Ecology:** shallow sheltered reefs, in groups exclusively among the spines of the sea urchin *Diadema setosum*. **Range:** Red Sea, Maldives, Phil., Marianas & Ryuk.

13 **Luminous cardinalfish** *Rhabdamia gracilis* (Bleeker) 6 cm
2 to 3 spp. in genus, all transparent with a luminous organ beneath the end of ea. operculum. **Ecology:** among rocks or corals of lagoon and coastal reefs, in dense aggregations. **Range:** E. Africa to Marsh. Is., n. to Ryuk., s. to Indonesia & PNG.

14 **Paddlefin cardinalfish** *Pseudamia zonata* Randall, Lachner & Fraser 14 cm
This sp. in subfamily Pseudaminae which includes numerous delicate elongate forms, some lacking LL or scales, many transparent. Most of these spp. seldom venture out in the open. **Ecology:** deep in caves, 10 to 31 m. **Range:** Phil. & Palau to Sol. Is., n. to Ryuk., s. to Vanuatu.

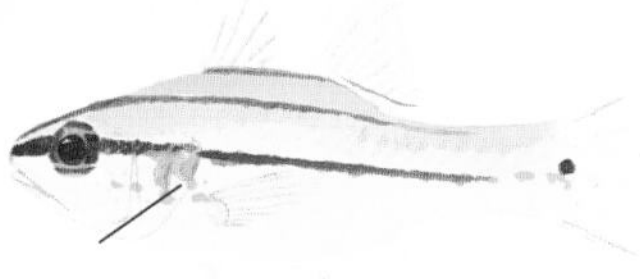

1

2

3

4

5

6

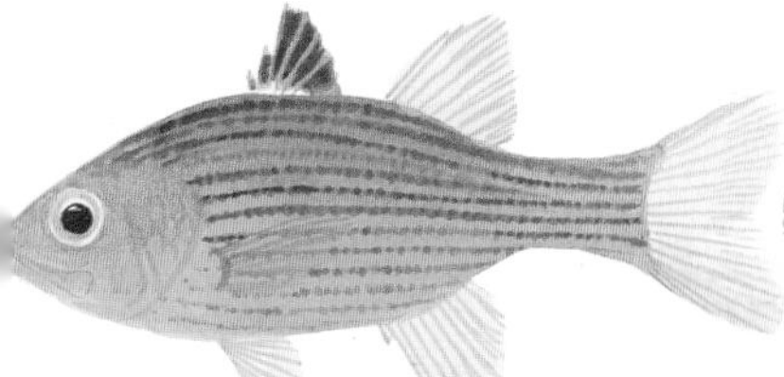

7

8

9

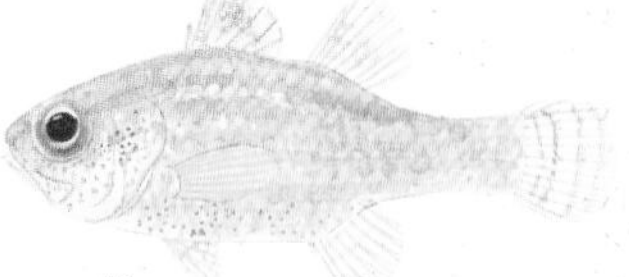

10

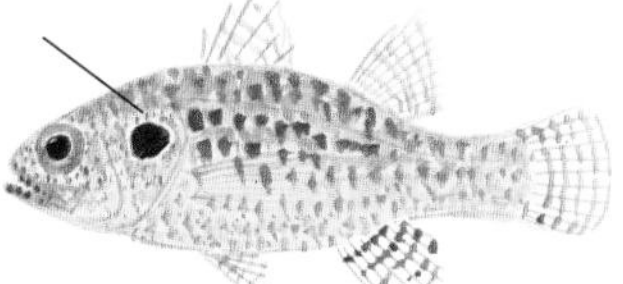

11

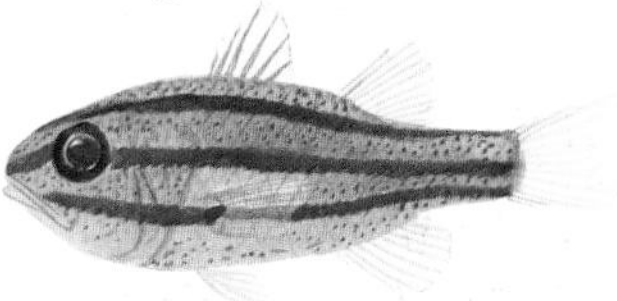

12

13

14

38 CARDINALFISHES

1 **Lea's cardinalfish** *Archamia leai* Waite 9 cm
Ecology: shallow coastal and lagoon reefs to 15 m. In groups among corals. **Range:** s. GBR & Coral Sea to N. Cal.

2 **Blackbelted cardinalfish** *Archamia zosterophora* (Bleeker) 8 cm
Ecology: in large aggregations among branching corals in sheltered lagoons and bays. **Range:** Phil. & Moluccas to Sol. Is., n. to Ryuk., s. to N. Cal.

3 **Orange-lined cardinalfish** *Archamia fucata* (Cantor) 8 cm
Ca. 23 orange bars; similar to *A. lineolata* (Red Sea to Samoa) which has ca.13 bars. **Ecology:** sheltered coastal and lagoon reefs, 2 to 60 m. In dense aggregations at entrances of caves and among branching corals. **Range:** Red Sea to Samoa, n. to Ryuk., s. to n. Cal.

4 **Twinspot cardinalfish** *Archamia biguttata* Lachner 11 cm
Similar to *A. dispilus* (Indo-Aust.) which lacks the dark bar below eye
Ecology: shallow coastal and lagoon reefs to 18 m. In small groups in recesses of caves. **Range:** Sumatra to Samoa, n. to Ryuk. & Marianas.

5 **Mozambique cardinalfish** *Archamia mozambiquensis* Smith 8 cm
Ecology: in loose aggregations between branching corals or coralline rocks, 1 to 20 m. Common. **Range:** E. Africa s. to Sodwana Bay.

6 **Blackspot cardinalfish** *Archamia melasma* Lachner & Taylor 9 cm
Ecology: inshore rocky areas and among branching corals. **Range:** PNG & n. Australia s. to Dampier Archip. & GBR.

7 **Pajama cardinalfish** *Sphaeramia nematoptera* (Bleeker) 8 cm
Ecology: sheltered coastal and lagoon reefs, 1 to 6 m, in groups among branching corals by day. Disperses at night to feed close to the bottom. **Range:** Java and Cocos-Keeling to PNG, n. to Ryuk., s. to GBR.

8 **Orbiculate cardinalfish** *Sphaeramia orbicularis* (Cuvier) 10 cm
Ecology: sheltered coastal waters, 0 to 5 m. In groups among mangroves, rocks, piers, or debris. **Range:** E. Africa to Kiribati, n. to Ryuk., s. to N. Cal.

9 **Large-toothed cardinalfish** *Cheilodipterus macrodon* (Lacépède) 24 cm
Cheilodipterus spp. with large canine teeth. Several similar spp., many difficult to identify. This sp. with dark squiggly lines wider than interspaces & more brown than copper. **Ecology:** clear subtidal lagoon and seaward reefs to ⩾ 40 m, in caves and under ledges. Species of *Cheilodipterus* feed primarily on small fishes **Range:** Red Sea to Marsh. Is., n. to s. Japan, s. to GBR.

10 **Eight-lined cardinalfish** *Cheilodipterus* sp. 22 cm
Lg. well defined dark area on 1st D fin; leading edge of 2nd D fin & outer tail lobes dark. **Ecology:** coastal reefs with dropoffs, to 15 m. **Range:** Flores, Indonesia; probably more widespread in Indo-Aust. region.

11 **Five-lined cardinalfish** *Cheilodipterus quinquelineatus* (Cuvier) 12 cm
Lacks canines at tip of lower jaw; *C. isostigma* similar but has canines at tip of lower jaw. **Ecology:** reef flats and lagoon and seaward reefs to ⩾ 40 m. In aggregations among rocks, corals, or spines of sea urchins. Feeds on small invertebrates as well as fishes. Common. **Range:** Red Sea to Ducie Is., n. to s. Japan, s. to L. Howe & Rapa Is.

12 **Lined cardinalfish** *Cheilodipterus artus* Smith 12 cm
Dark copper lines narrower than interspaces. Similar spp. incl. *C. lachneri* & *C. subulatus*, each with more numerous dark lines. **Ecology:** sheltered bays and lagoon reefs, 5 to 20 m. In caves or among corals. **Range:** Red Sea to Tuam., n. to Ryuk., s. to GBR.

13 **Dogtooth cardinalfish** *Cheilodipterus caninus* Smith 18 cm
13-15 dark stripes of variable width. Juv. with yellow spot on peduncle. **Ecology:** in small groups among corals, 3 to 18 m. Common. **Range:** Red Sea to s. Mozambique.

14 **Mimic cardinalfish** *Cheilodipterus zonatus* Smith & Radcliffe 8 cm
Ecology: among corals of coastal reefs below 5 m. Mimics the venomous blenny, *Meiacanthus vittatus* (pl. 114-16). **Range:** Indonesia to PNG, n. to Phil., s. to GBR.

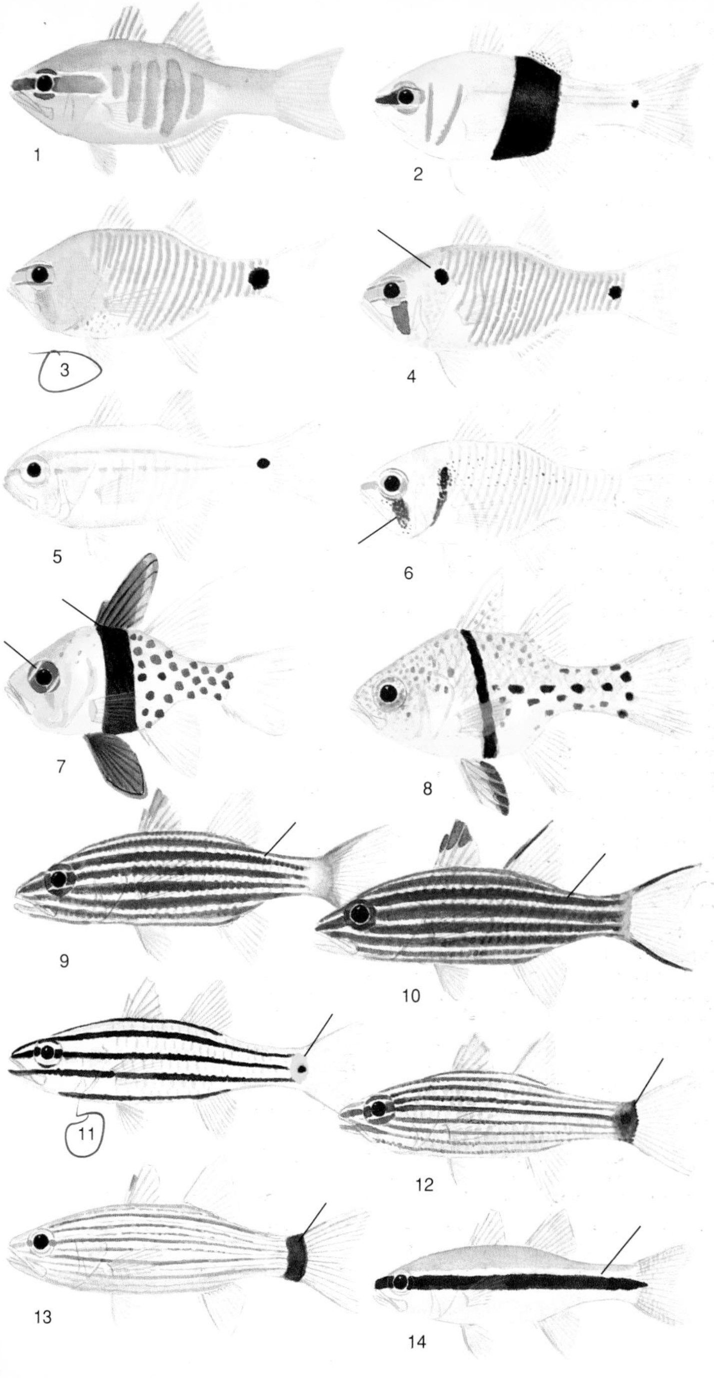
1
2
3
4
5
6
7
8
9
10
11
12
13
14

39 BARRAMUNDI, GRUNTERS, FLAGTAILS, BIGEYES, and MOJARRAS

BARRAMUNDI (CENTROPOMIDAE): perchlike fishes with concave snout profile, separate D fins, and complete LL. Primarily estuarine. Important foodfishes.

1 **Sand bass; Glasseye perch** *Psammoperca waigiensis* (Cuvier) 47 cm
Barramundi (*Lates calcarifer*; n. Indian Oc. to w. Pacific) similar, but has larger eyes, smaller scales, gets much larger (150 cm), is primarily in estuarine & freshwater. **Ecology:** rocky inshore areas and coastal reefs, often in weedy areas. In crevices or holes by day, forages on fishes and crustaceans at night. **Range:** Sri Lanka to PNG, n. to Ryuk., s. to GBR.

TIGER PERCHES; GRUNTERS (THERAPONIDAE): perchlike fishes with two opercular spines, a notched D fin. Most marine species silvery with black stripes. Many freshwater species.

2 **Crescent-banded grunter** *Terapon jarbua* (Forsskål) 36 cm
Ecology: shallow sandy areas near river mouths, in schools. Juveniles common in sandy intertidal areas. Feeds on fishes, insects, algae, and sand-dwelling invertebrates. **Range:** Red Sea to Samoa, n. to s. Japan, s. to L. Howe Is.

FLAGTAILS (KUHLIIDAE): small compressed silvery fishes with a deeply notched D fin, scaly sheath on D and A fins, and forked tail. In schools in surgy areas by day, dispersed to feed on free-swimming crustaceans at night. Juveniles are often in tidepools. Some species enter fresh water.

3 **Dark-margined flagtail** *Kuhlia marginata* (Cuvier) 24 cm
Similar to *K. sandvicensis* (Hawaiian Is.). **Ecology:** exposed rocky shorelines and reef margins, schools in caves and surge channels. **Range:** Sri Lanka to Line & Ducie Is., n. to s. Japan, s. to Rapa.

4 **Barred flagtail** *Kuhlia mugil* (Schneider) 27 cm
Ecology: exposed rocky shorelines and reef margins, schools in caves and surge channels. **Range:** Red Sea to Panama, n. to s. Japan, s. to L. Howe & Rapa Is.

BIGEYES (PRIACANTHIDAE): bigeyes have compressed bodies, large mouths, large eyes, a continuous D fin, and small scales. They remain near shelter by day and migrate away from the reef to feed on large zooplankton at night. Usually red by day, blotched or silvery at night. Foodfishes.

5 **Glasseye** *Heteropriacanthus cruentatus* (Lacépède) 32 cm
Ecology: lagoon and seaward reefs, subtidal to 20 m. Under or near ledges by day. **Range:** Circumtropical; n. to Ryuk. & Bonin Is., s. to L. Howe & Easter Is.

6 **Bloch's bigeye** *Priacanthus blochii* Bleeker 35 cm
Similar to *P. nazca* (Easter Is.). Sev. other spp. in genus, many in deep water. **Ecology:** lagoon and seaward reefs, 15 to 30 m. Under ledges or in caves by day. **Range:** Red Sea to Samoa; n. to Phil., s. to nw. Aust. & GBR.

7 **Goggle-eye** *Priacanthus hamrur* (Forsskål) 40 cm
Similar to *P. meeki* (Hawaiian Is.) and *P. zaizerae* (n. Phil. to Ryuk. & Izu Is.). **Ecology:** lagoon and seaward reefs, 15 to 250 m. Often with broad silvery bars. **Range:** Red Sea to Marq. & Gambier Is.; n. to s. Japan, s. to L. Howe & Easter Is.

8 **Hawaiian bigeye** *Priacanthus meeki* Jenkins 33 cm
Ecology: clear lagoon and seaward reefs, 3 to $\geqslant$ 50 m. Under ledges by day. **Range:** Hawaiian Is.; strays to Johnston Atoll.

MOJARRAS (GERREIDAE): small silvery fishes with highly protrusible mouth, single D fin, and deeply forked tail. They feed by sorting benthic invertebrates from sand. Foodfishes.

9 **Slenderspine mojarra** *Gerres acinaces* Bleeker 35 cm
Ecology: shallow, sheltered sandy areas, singly or in groups. **Range:** Red Sea to Samoa, n. to s. Japan, s. to GBR.

10 **Blacktip mojarra** *Gerres oyena* (Forsskål) 23 cm
Ecology: shallow, sheltered sandy areas, singly or in groups. **Range:** Red Sea to Marsh. & Gilbert Is., s. to GBR.

SLIPMOUTHS (LEIOGNATHIDAE): similar to mojarras but with luminescent organs on the throat. They feed on benthic invertebrates. Foodfishes.

11 **Common slipmouth** *Leiognathus equulus* (Forsskål) 28 cm
Ecology: in groups on shallow, sheltered silty bottoms. **Range:** Red Sea to Samoa, s. to GBR & N. Cal.

1
2
3
4
5
6
7
var
8
9
10
11

SAND TILEFISHES (MALACANTHIDAE): elongate fishes with long continuous D & A fins. *Hoplolatilus* spp. feed on zooplankton, *Malacanthus* spp. feed on invertebrates. All species live in a burrow, some in a large rubble mound of their own construction, in pairs or colonies. Most aquarium specimens are collected with poisons and soon die.

1 **Striped blanquillo** *Malacanthus latovittatus* (Lacépède) 45 cm
Juvs. resemble juvs. of the wrasse *Hologymnosus annulatus* (pl. 100-3). **Ecology:** seaward reefs, on sand and rubble patches below 5 m. Hovers above bottom. Solitary or in pairs. Adults wary, juveniles more approachable. **Range:** Red Sea to Line Is.; n. to s. Japan, s. to N. Cal. & Cook Is.

2 **Quakerfish** *Malacanthus brevirostris* (Guichenot) 30 cm
Ecology: seaward reefs, in barren open areas, 14 to 45 m. In pairs, usually remains close to the bottom, retreating in a hole or under a rock when threatened. **Range:** Red Sea to Panama; n. to s. Japan & Hawaiian Is., s. to L. Howe Is.

3 **Chameleon sand tilefish**. *Hoplolatilus chlupatyi* Klausewitz *et al.* 13 cm
Can instantly change colors ranging from salmon to orange, green, blue or violet. Us. pale ventrally. **Ecology:** probably sandy, silty or rubbly areas at bases of reefs near 30 m. **Range:** Phil.

4 **Pale sand tilefish** *Hoplolatilus cuniculus* Randall & Dooley 15 cm
Color variable, may be pale olive to brown or yellow, or a combination. **Ecology:** outer reef slopes, in muddy or rubbly areas, 25 to 115 m. **Range:** S. Africa & Maurit. to Soc. Is.; n. to Ryuk. & Marsh. Is.

5 **Yellow-blotched sand tilefish** *Hoplolatilus fourmanoiri* Smith 14 cm
Similar to *H. luteus* (Flores, Indon.) which is mostly yellow, with white blotches ventrally. **Ecology:** silty sand bottoms with coral rocks, 5 to 55 m. **Range:** s. Vietnam, Phil, Flores & Sol. Is.

6 **Stocky sand tilefish** *Hoplolatilus fronticinctus* Günther 20 cm
Ecology: sandy areas at bases of reefs, to 60 m. Builds a mound of rubble 1 m high. **Range:** Maurit to Sol. Is.; n. to Phil & Palau. & Marsh. Is.

7 **Yellow sand tilefish** *Hoplolatilus luteus* Allen & Kuiter 11 cm
Ecology: hovers above burrow in flat soft silty bottom, 30 to 35 m. **Range:** Flores, Indonesia.

8 **Redback sand tilefish** *Hoplolatilus marcosi* Burgess 12 cm
Ecology: sandy and rubble areas, 18 to 80 m. **Range:** Phil., Sulawesi, Sol. Is & Palau.

9 **Purple sand tilefish** *Hoplolatilus purpureus* Burgess 13 cm
Ecology: outer reef slopes, in muddy or rubbly areas, 18 to 80 m. **Range:** Phil. & Sol. Is.

10 **Purple-headed sand tilefish** *Hoplolatilus starcki* Randall & Dooley 15 cm
Juvs. entirely blue, resemble *Pseudanthias pascalus* (pl. 21-3) and school with them. **Ecology:** sand and rubble patches of steep seaward slopes, 21 to 105 m. Usually in pairs. **Range:** Celebes & Phil. to Pitcairn Gp.; n. to Mariana Is., s. to N. Cal.

REMORAS (ECHENEIDAE): elongate fishes with a laminated sucking disc on top of the head which is used to attach themselves to the surfaces of larger fishes, turtles or mammals.

11 **Sharksucker** *Echeneis naucrates* Linnaeus 110 cm
Ecology: occasionally free-swimming over coral reefs. Usually associated with sharks, rays, other large fishes, or sea turtles. May follow divers. **Range:** Circumglobal.

12 **Remora** *Remora remora* Linnaeus 50 cm
Ecology: usually associated with sharks. **Range:** Circumglobal.

1
1 juv
2
3
4
5
6
7
8
9
10
11
12

41 JACKS and TREVALLYS

JACKS and TREVALLYS (CARANGIDAE): medium to large compressed silvery fishes with 2 D fins (the 1st fitting into a groove), a narrow caudal peduncle usually reinforced by a series of bony scutes, and a forked tail. Fast-swimming predators of the waters above the reef and in open sea; a few root in sand. Only juveniles of a few species suitable for aquariums. Important foodfishes. The following circumtropical species are featured in the W. Atlantic section: *Alectis ciliaris* (pl. 154-4), *Caranx lugubris* (pl. 155-1), *Decapterus macarellus* (pl. 154-9), *Elagatis bipinnulatus* (pl. 155-9), *Naucrates ductor* (pl. 154-3), *Selar crumenophthalmus* (pl. 154-8), *Seriola dumerili* (pl. 155-7), and *Seriola rivoliana* (pl. 155-8).

1 **Yellow-dotted trevally** *Carangoides fulvoguttatus* (Forsskål) 100 cm
Carangoides spp. with teeth in broad villiform bands in both jaws and no canines. This sp. yellowish spots in 4 vertical bands on sides, lg. adults with 3 black mid-lateral blotches. **Ecology**: schools along outer reef slopes, rocky coasts, and offshore banks to 100 m. **Range:** Red Sea to N. Cal., n. to Ryuk.

2 **Bludger trevally** *Carangoides gymnostethus* (Cuvier) 90 cm
Ecology: deeper offshore reefs. Juveniles in small schools, adults usually solitary. **Range:** E. Africa to PNG, s. to GBR.

3 **Club-nosed trevally** *Carangoides chrysophrys* (Cuvier) 60 cm
Ecology: open waters of coastal reefs. **Range:** E. Africa to PNG, n. to s. Japan, s. to GBR.

4 **Bar jack** *Carangoides ferdau* (Forsskål) 70 cm
Usually lacks yellow spots as shown here. **Ecology**: in schools in open waters of lagoons and outer reef slopes. **Range:** Red Sea to Hawaiian & Tuam. Is., n. to s. Japan, s. to N. Cal.

5 **Yellow-spotted trevally** *Carangoides orthogrammus* Jordan & Gilbert 71 cm
Lg. adults with prominent upper jaw, and blueish soft D and A fins with elongate points. **Ecology:** generally in small groups that frequent sandy channels of lagoon and seaward reefs, 3 to 168 m. Large adults usually deep. Roots in sand for invertebrates and fishes. **Range:** w. Indian Ocean to Mexico, n. to s. Japan & Hawaii, s. to L. Howe & Austral Is.

6 **Barcheek trevally** *Carangoides plagiotaenia* (Bleeker) ⩾ 40 cm
Ecology: generally along the edges of lagoon and seaward reef slopes, singly or in groups. **Range:** Red Sea to Samoa, n. to Ryuk., s. to N. Cal.

7 **Shadow trevally** *Carangoides dinema* Bleeker 60 cm
Similar to *C. humerosus* which replaces this sp. in n. Aust.to s. PNG. This sp. with series of black rectangles along soft D fin base, A fin and sometimes lower P fin dark. **Ecology:** solitary or in schools along steep dropoffs. **Range:** E. Africa to Samoa, n. to s. Japan, s. to Tonga.

8 **Orangespotted trevally** *Carangoides bajad* (Forsskål) 53 cm
Round orange spots on sides, not in rows; ground color usually silvery, but occasionally almost entirely orange-yellow. **Ecology:** in groups along reef slopes, 2 to 50 m. Occasionally with yellow goatfishes. **Range:** Red Sea to PNG, n. to Phil.

9 **Golden trevally** *Gnathanodon speciosus* (Forsskål) 110 cm
Juvs. yellow with black bars; adults lack teeth, yellowish silver, lg. ones loose dark bars. **Ecology:** tiny juveniles live among the tentacles of jellyfish. Those over 5 cm accompany large groupers or sharks; they are probably too small and maneuverable to be eaten by their hosts and gain protection from likely predators. Adults inhabit deep lagoon and seaward reefs where they feed by rooting in the sand for invertebrates. **Range:** Red Sea to Panama, n. to Ryuk. & Hawaiian Is., s. to N. Cal. & Austral Is.

10 **Indian threadfin** *Alectis indicus* (Rüppell) 165 cm
Alectis spp. with small lateral keels on C ped. & extremely compressed. Similar to *A. ciliaris* (circumtropical; pl. 154-4) which has a less angular head profile. Subadults of *Carangoides hedlandensis* (E. Africa to Samoa) also with streamers on D & A fins, but with scutes on C ped. **Ecology:** juveniles inhabit surface waters and may mimic a jellyfish. Adults move to bottom waters below 60 m. **Range:** Red Sea to PNG, n. to s. Japan, s. to GBR.

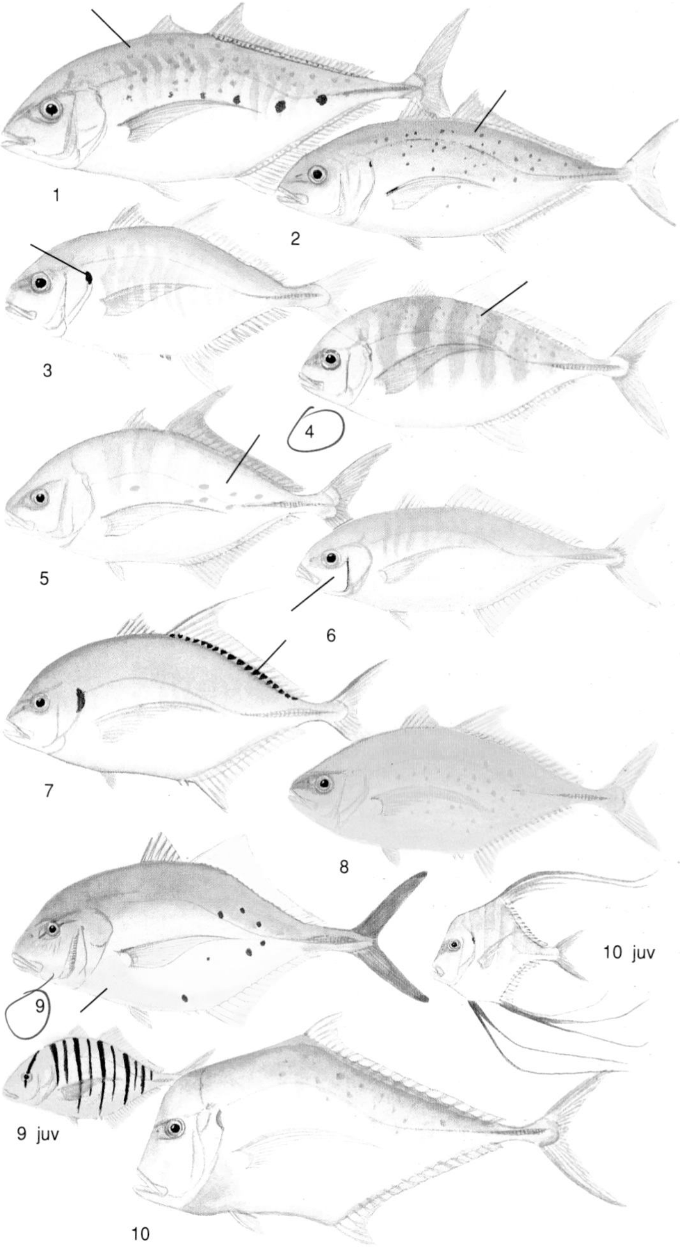
1
2
3
4
5
6
7
8
9
10 juv
9 juv
10

42 JACKS and TREVALLYS

1 **Giant trevally** *Caranx ignobilis* (Forsskål) 170 cm; 68 kg
Caranx spp. with single row of canines in both jaws & several inner bands of villiform teeth in jupper jaw. This spp. with mostly naked breast & steep head profile. Similar *C. lugubris* (see pl.155-1) **Ecology:** juveniles in small schools over sandy inshore or estuarine areas; adults solitary in clear lagoon and seaward reef waters to 80 m. Feeds primarily on fishes and crustaceans. Large ones may be ciguatoxic. Uncommon in heavily fished areas. **Range:** Red Sea to Hawaiian, Marq. & Pitcairn Is., n. to s. Japan, s. to N. Cal.

2 **Bluefin trevally** *Caranx melampygus* (Cuvier) 100 cm
Resembles *C. papuensis* but fins usually blue, blue speckles on sides & breast fully scaled. **Ecology:** lagoon and seaward reefs, shoreline to 190 m. Solitary or in small groups, common throughout most of its range. Feeds on fishes and crustaceans. Large adults may be ciguatoxic. Juveniles seasonal in shallow sandy inshore waters. **Range:** Red Sea to Panama, n. to Izu Is., s. to N. Cal. & Ducie Is.

3 **Brassy trevally** *Caranx papuensis* Alleyne & MacLeay 88 cm
Resembles *C. melampygus*, but breast mostly naked, spots & fins not blue & distal margin of A and tail fins white. **Ecology:** shallow lagoon and seaward reefs. Less common than bluefin trevally. **Range:** Red Sea, E. Africa to Marq., n. to Ryuk., s. to N. Cal. & Samoa.

4 **Bigeye trevally** *Caranx sexfasciatus* Quoy & Gaimard 94 cm
Eye relatively large; dark spot on upper edge of opercle; 2nd D fin often with white tip. **Ecology:** adults generally in schools by day along lagoon, channel, or seaward reef dropoffs, 1 to 90 m. Feeds primarily at night on fishes and crustaceans. Juveniles in shallow inshore areas, even entering freshwater as well as offshore around floating objects. **Range:** Red Sea to c. America, n. to s. Japan & Hawaiian Is., s. to N. Cal.

5 **Tille trevally** *Caranx tille* Cuvier 80 cm
Head steep, body more elongate than other *Caranx* spp. **Ecology:** inshore coastal waters of continental coasts. **Range:** E. Africa to Fiji, n. to Ryuk., s. to GBR.

6 **Silver pompano** *Trachinotus blochii* (Lacépède) 110 cm
Trachinotus spp. lack scutes, have distinctive ovoid bodies. Adults of *T. blochii* have yellowish fins. **Ecology:** juveniles in sandy inshore and estuarine areas. Large adults in schools off seaward reefs. Feeds primarily on sand on mollusks and other hard-shelled invertebrates. **Range:** E. Africa to Marsh. Is. & Samoa, n. to s. Japan, s. to Norfolk Is.

7 **Small-spotted pompano** *Trachinotus bailloni* (Lacépède) 54 cm
Ecology: surge zone along sandy beaches and near surface waters of clear lagoon and seaward reefs. Feeds on small fishes. **Range:** Red Sea to Line & Gambier Is., n. to s. Japan, s. to L. Howe & Rapa Is.

8 **Leatherback** *Scomberoides lysan* (Forsskål) 77 cm
Scomberoides spp. lack scutes; D and A fin spines venomous. **Ecology:** juveniles in shallow inshore and brackish waters where they feed on scales torn from schooling fishes. Adults in clear lagoon and seaward reef waters, usually near surface, but to 100 m. They feed on small fishes and crustaceans. **Range:** Red Sea to Hawaiian, Marq. & Tuam. Is., n. to Japan, s. to NSW.

9 **Talang queenfish** *Scomberoides commersonianus* Lacépède 120 cm
Several similar spp. including *S. tol* (Indian Ocean to Fiji) with one row of dark spots on side. **Ecology:** waters above reefs and offshore islands, usually in small groups. **Range:** E. Africa to PNG, n. to Taiwan, s. to GBR.

10 **Smooth-tailed trevally** *Selaroides leptolepis* (Cuvier) 20 cm
Resembles *Selar crumenophthalmus* (pl. 154-8) but eye smaller and prominent yellow stripe along back. **Ecology:** in large mid-water schools in coastal waters, 1 to 25 m. **Range:** Arab. G. to n. Australia and s. Japan.
See also pl. 154-5.

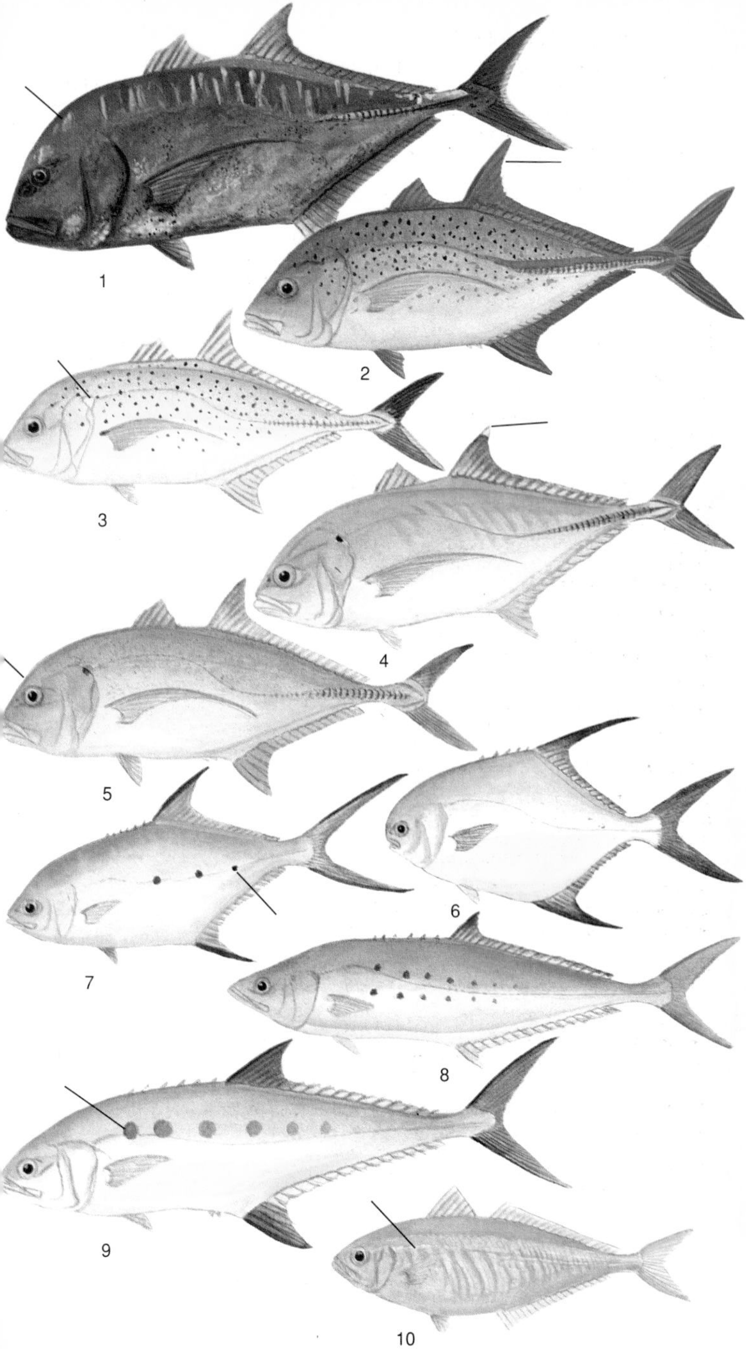
1
2
3
4
5
6
7
8
9
10

43 SNAPPERS

SNAPPERS (LUTJANIDAE): medium to large perchlike fishes with a continuous D fin, large coarse scales, large canine teeth, a maxillary mostly covered by the cheek, and an emarginate to forked tail. Most species are predators of crustaceans and fishes, several are planktivores. Most inhabit inshore and reef waters, but many occur at depths of 90 to 360 m. Among the most important of commercial bottomfishes. Most do well in aquaria, but grow too fast.

1 **Smalltooth jobfish** *Aphareus furca* (Lacépède) 40 cm
Small ones occasionally with bright yellow patches on snout or head. **Ecology:** mid-waters of clear lagoon and seaward reefs, 1 to ⩾ 122 m. Solitary or in groups, feeds on small fishes and crustaceans. Often curiuos and approachable. **Range:** E. Africa to Panama, n. to Ryuk., s. to L. Howe & Austral Is.

2 **Green jobfish; Uku** *Aprion virescens* Valenciennes 100 cm
Ecology: open waters of deep lagoons, channels, or seaward reefs, 3 to 180 m. Predators of fishes that also take crustaceans and cephalopods. Large ones may be ciguatoxic. **Range:** Red Sea to Hawaiian, Marq. & Tuam. Is., n. to Ryuk., s. to L. Howe Is.

3 **Chinamanfish** *Symphorus nematophorus* (Bleeker) 80 cm
Ecology: coastal reefs. Frequently ciguatoxic in certain areas. Its sale is banned in Australia. **Range:** Malaysia to PNG, n. to Ryuk., s. to GBR.

4 **Blue-lined sea bream** *Symphorichthys spilurus* Günther 60 cm
Juvs. tan with black mid-lateral stripe and filament. D & A fin rays shorten with age. **Ecology:** sand and rubble areas of coastal, lagoon, and channel reefs. Aggregates to spawn along seaward reefs. **Range:** n. Sumatra & Phil. to N. Cal., n. to Ryuk, s. to n. Australia.

5 **Black snapper** *Macolor niger* (Forsskål) 66 cm
Juvs. 10 cm with black P fins & shorter fins than *M. macularis*; subadults with 4-5 white blotches dorsally; adults with darker background. Juvs. may be mimics of *P. picus* (pl. 49-10). **Ecology:** adults in large aggregations along steep outer lagoon, channel and seaward slopes, 3 to 90 m. Juveniles solitary. Feeds primarily on large zooplankton at night. **Range:** Red Sea to Samoa, n. to Ryuk., s. to N. Cal.

6 **Black-and-white-snapper** *Macolor macularis* Fowler 55 cm
Juvs. 10 cm with elongate fins, deeply notched D fin & clear P fins; subadults with 6 white blotches dorsally; adults with blue squiggly lines on yellow background. V. similar to *M. niger*, juvs. may be mimics of v. similar juv. *P. picus* (pl. 49-10) which might be toxic. **Ecology:** along steep slopes of lagoon, channel, or seaward reefs, 3 to 50 m. Juveniles solitary, adults may be in small groups. Feeds primarily on large zooplankton at night. **Range:** Maldives to Sol. Is., n. to Ryuk., s. to N. Cal.

7 **Checkered snapper** *Lutjanus decussatus* (Cuvier) 30 cm
Ecology: inshore and offshore reefs, 2 to 30 m. Solitary or in schools. **Range:** se. India & Sri Lanka to w. NG, n. to Ryuk., s. to GBR.

8 **Emperor snapper** *Lutjanus sebae* (Cuvier) 80 cm; 27 kg
Lg. adults become uniformly red. **Ecology:** lagoon sand flats near coral reefs, 10 to 100 m. Juveniles on shallow reefs and in mangroves, those 5 cm often among the spines of sea urchins. **Range:** Red Sea to PNG, n. to s. Japan, s. to NSW; absent from oceanic is.

9 **Timor snapper** *Lutjanus timorensis* (Quoy & Gaimard) 35 cm
Similar to *L. malabaricus* (Arab. G to Fiji) which lacks the black P fin axil & white blotch on upper tail base. **Ecology:** coral and rubble bottoms, 30 to 130 m. Uncommon. **Range:** Andaman Sea to Samoa, n. to Phil.

10 **Humphead or blood snapper** *Lutjanus sanguineus* (Cuvier) 100 cm; 23 kg
Gibbous forehead of adults distinctive. Several similar spp., mostly in deep water. **Ecology:** coral banks, often in turbid areas, 9 to 100 m. Active at night when it feeds over sandy or rubbly bottoms. **Range:** Red Sea to w. India, n. to Arab. G., s. to S. Africa.

1
2
3
4
5 juv
5
6 juv
6
7
8
9 juv
10
9

1 **Bluelined snapper** *Lutjanus kasmira* (Forsskål) 35 cm
4 blue stripes, lower belly often white with dusky narrow lines. Numerous similar spp. **Ecology:** shallow sheltered reefs to exposed seaward reefs below surge zone to 265 m. Often in large aggregations around prominent coral formations by day. Disperses at night to feed on benthic crustaceans and fishes. Juveniles in seagrasse beds or around patch reefs. **Range:** Red Sea to Marq. & Tuam. Is., n. to s. Japan, s. to L. Howe Is; introduced to Hawaiian Is.

2 **Bengal snapper** *Lutjanus bengalensis* (Bloch) 21 cm
4 blue lines, belly entirely white below lowest line; *L. kasmira* has yellow band below lowest blue line and several narrow dusky stripes on belly. **Ecology:** coral and rocky reefs, 10 to 30 m. Solitary or in small groups. **Range:** Red Sea to Moluccas, n. to G. of Oman, s. to Maurit. Absent from atolls.

3 **Five-lined snapper** *Lutjanus quinquelineatus* (Bloch) 38 cm
5 blue lines, belly pale yellow; most similar to *L. notatus* with 6 lines. **Ecology:** sheltered lagoons and exposed seaward reefs, 2 to 40 m. In aggregations. Common on the GBR. **Range:** Arab. G. to Fiji, n. to s. Japan, s. to NSW. Absent from oceanic Is.

4 **Bluestriped snapper** *Lutjanus notatus* (Cuvier) 22 cm
6 blue lines, belly pale yellow. Most similar to *L. quinquelineatus* with 5 blue lines. **Ecology:** coral reefs, 10 to 40 m. Solitary or in small groups. **Range:** E. Africa to 30°S, Madagascar, Réunion & Maurit.

5 **Blueline snapper** *Lutjanus coeruleolineatus* (Rüppell) 35 cm
7-8 blue lines, belly white. All other similar spp. with ⩾ 6 blue lines. **Ecology:** clear coastal reefs, 10 to 20 m. Solitary or in small groups. **Range:** Red Sea & G. Aden n. to G. of Oman.

6 **Spanish flag; Stripey** *Lutjanus carponotatus* (Richardson) 40 cm
Ecology: sheltered lagoon and seaward reefs, 2 to 80 m. Usually in aggregations. **Range:** se. India to PNG, n. to s. China, s. to nw. Aust. & GBR.

7 **Blackspot snapper** *Lutjanus ehrenbergi* (Peters) 31 cm
Similar to *L. fulviflamma*, but scale rows above LL aligned horizontally. **Ecology:** coastal, lagoon, and seaward reefs of high islands, 5 to ⩾ 20 m. Juveniles in inshore silty or rubbly areas, and occasionally in estuarine or mangrove areas. **Range:** Red Sea to PNG & e. Caroline Is., n. to Ryuk., s. to GBR.

8 **Black-spot snapper** *Lutjanus fulviflamma* (Forsskål) 35 cm
Scale rows above LL aligned diagonally. **Ecology:** coral reefs, 3 to 35 m. Often in large aggregations with *L. kasmira* and *L. lutjanus*. Juveniles enter brackish water streams. Abundant in E. Africa and Australia. **Range:** Red Sea to Samoa & Tonga, n. to Taiwan, s. to Perth NSW & L. Howe Is.

9 **Golden-lined snapper** *Lutjanus rufolineatus* (Valenciennes) 24 cm
Ecology: coastal reefs, 15 to 50 m. Usually in aggregations near outcrops or dropoffs, often with other species. **Range:** Sumatra to Samoa, n. to s. Japan, s. to nw. Aust. & Tonga.

10 **Onespot snapper** *Lutjanus monostigma* (Cuvier) 53 cm
Ecology: outer lagoon and seaward reefs, 1 to 60 m. Enters reef flats at night to feed primarily on fishes. Common along reef margins with deep cuts and holes. May be ciguatoxic. **Range:** Red Sea to Marq. & Tuam. Is., n. to Ryuk., s. to N. Cal.

11 **Russell's snapper** *Lutjanus russelli* (Bleeker) 50 cm
Ecology: inshore rocky and coral reefs to 80 m. Juveniles in coastal shallows and estuarine or brackish areas. Common on GBR. **Range:** Red Sea to Fiji, n. to s. Japan, s. to S. Africa & NSW.

12 **John's snapper** *Lutjanus johnii* (Bloch) 63 cm
Ecology: adults on coral reefs, juveniles enter brackish streams. **Range:** G. Aden & n. S. Africa to Fiji, n. to s. China & Taiwan, s. to n. GBR.

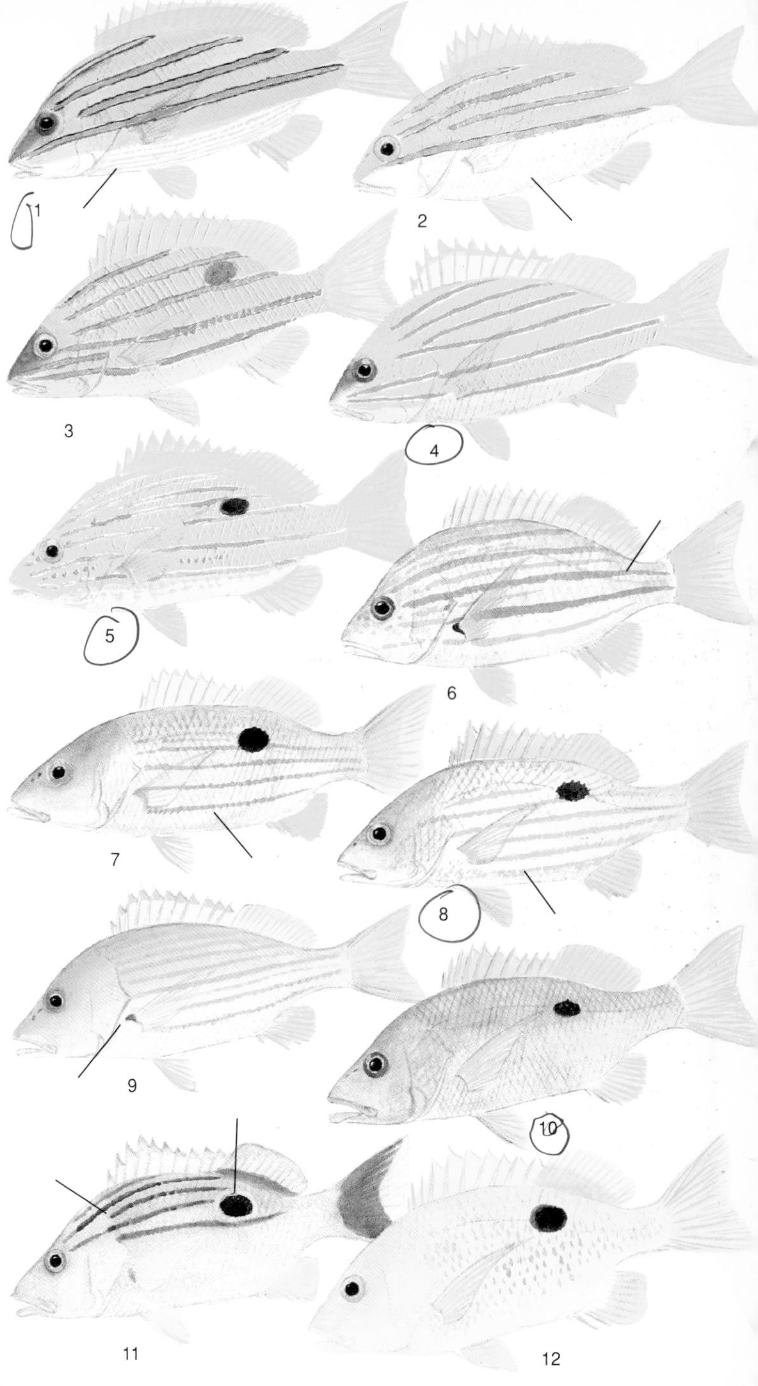
1
2
3
4
5
6
7
8
9
10
11
12

45 SNAPPERS

1 **Two-spot snapper** *Lutjanus biguttatus* (Valenciennes) 20 cm
Ecology: seaward reef slopes, 3 to 36 m. In small to large groups. Uncommon. **Range:** Maldives to Sol. Is., n. to Phil. & Palau, s. to n. GBR.

2 **Humpback or Paddletail snapper** *Lutjanus gibbus* (Forsskål) 50 cm
Juvs. grey with oblique dark pinstrips and black behind line from soft D fin to lower tail base. **Ecology:** juveniles in seagrass beds and sand and coral areas of shallow sheltered reefs. Adults often in large aggregations along steep lagoon, channel and seaward reef slopes, 1 to 150 m. Large ones may be ciguatoxic. Feeds on benthic invertebrates and fishes. **Range:** Red Sea to Line & Tuam. Is., n. to Ryuk., s. to N. Cal.

3 **Lunulate snapper** *Lutjanus lunulatus* (Park) 30 cm
Ecology: coral reefs, 10 to 30 m. Solitary or in small groups. **Range:** Pakistan to Vanuatu, n. to Phil.; continental Islands & coasts only.

4 **Flametail snapper** *Lutjanus fulvus* (Schneider) 40 cm
Similar to *L. lemniscatus* (India to GBR) which gets larger and is silvery grey instead of yellowish pink. **Ecology:** lagoon and semi-protected seaward reefs, 1 to 75 m. Enters estuarine areas. Fees on benthic invertebrates and fishes. **Range:** Red Sea to Marq. & Tuam. Is., n. to s. Japan, s. to NSW; introd. to Hawaii.

5 **Hussar** *Lutjanus adetii* (Castelnau) 50 cm
Ecology: shallow coastal rocky reefs and lagoon and seaward reefs, to 20 m. In large aggregations around coral or rock outcrops by day. Disperses to feed at night. **Range:** e. Aust. (ca. 10 to 36°S), L. Howe Is. & Coral Sea to N. Cal.

6 **Bigeye snapper** *Lutjanus lutjanus* Bloch 30 cm
Similar to the deeper-bodied *L. adetii*, & *L. madras* & *L. vitta* which have smaller eyes. **Ecology:** exposed reefs of continental shelves to 90 m. Often in aggregations with other *Lutjanus* spp. **Range:** Red Sea to Sol. Is., n. to Ryuk., s. to nw. Aust. & GBR. Not at atolls.

7 **One-lined or brownstripe snapper** *Lutjanus vitta* (Quoy & Gaimard) 40 cm
Similar to *L. lutjanus* which has larger eye much closer to mouth. **Ecology:** rubble slopes or flat areas with coral outcrops, 10 to 72 m. Often in groups. **Range:** Seychelles (?), w. India to Vanuatu, n. to s. Japan, s. to N. Cal.

8 **Twinspot snapper; Red snapper** *Lutjanus bohar* (Forsskål) 90 cm
Has 2 light spots dorsally when below 20 cm; juvs. mimic *Chromis ternatensis* (pl. 78-12). **Ecology:** outer lagoon, channel and seaward reefs, 1 to 180 m. Singly or in roving groups. A voracious predator of fishes that also takes crustaceans and cephalopods. Among the most frequently ciguatoxic fishes in many areas. Common at atolls. **Range:** Red Sea to Marq. & Tuam. Is., n. to Ryuk., s. to L. Howe Is.

9 **River snapper; Mangrove jack** *Lutjanus argentimaculatus* (Forsskål) 120 cm
Juvs. with blue streaks on face. **Ecology:** juveniles in estuaries or rivers. Adults along coastal and lagoon reefs and channels to 120 m, often in groups at the base of reefs by day. **Range:** Red Sea to Samoa & Line Is., n. to Ryuk., s. to NSW.

10 **Scribbled snapper** *Lutjanus rivulatus* (Cuvier) 76 cm; 11 kg
Similar to *L. stellatus* (s. China to s. Jap.) which lacks the squiggly blue lines on head & small white dots in center of scales. **Ecology:** seaward reefs to ⩾ 100 m. Occasionally on shallow inshore flats. Solitary or in small groups. Matures at ca. 45 cm. Uncommon. **Range:** Red Sea to Soc. Is., n. to Ryuk., s. to GBR.

11 **Half-barred snapper** *Lutjanus semicinctus* Quoy & Gaimard 35 cm
Ecology: shallow lagoon and seaward reefs to 36 m. Uncommon except in e. Caroline Is. **Range:** Phil. & Moluccas to Gilbert Is. & Fiji, n. to Caroline Is., s. to N. Cal.

2 juv
2
1
4
3
6
5
7
8 juv
8
9
10
11

1 False fusilier snapper *Paracaesio sordidus* Abe & Shinohara 48 cm
Paracaesio spp. resemble *Caesio* spp., members of a different family. **Ecology:** a schooling midwater planktivore of deep current-swept reefs and dropoffs. Observed in as little as 5 m, but usually in less than 100 m. **Range:** Red Sea to Samoa, n. to Ryuk.

2 Yellowtail false fusilier *Paracaesio xanthura* (Bleeker) 48 cm
Ecology: a schooling midwater planktivore, below 100 m in tropics, but to 10 m in se. Australia. **Range:** E. Africa to Samoa, n. to s. Japan, s. to NSW, L. Howe & Kermadec Is.

FUSILIERS (CAESIONIDAE): elongate fusiform fishes with small protrusible mouths, small scales, continuous D fins, and forked tails. Fast-swimming mid-water planktivores that occur in vast, often mixed-species schools during the day. They shelter on the reef at night and assume a red ground color. Require unrestricted space, hence unsuitable for home aquaria. Important foodfishes in some areas.

3 Deep-bodied fusilier *Caesio cuning* (Bloch) 28 cm
Head profile steep, body deeper than *C teres*; blue marks on head darker than background. **Ecology:** in schools in mid-water in deep lagoons and along seaward reefs. **Range:** Sri Lanka to Vanuatu, n. to Ryuk. s. to GBR, E. Africa, Arab. Gulf.

4 Lunar fusilier *Caesio lunaris* Cuvier 30 cm
Tail lobes with black tips, some indiv. with yellow tail and base. **Ecology:** more common along steep seaward reefs than in lagoons. In large schools. **Range:** Red Sea, Arabian G. to Sol. Is., n. to Ryuk., s. to GBR.

5 Suez fusilier *Caesio suevica* Klunzinger 25 cm
Yellow stripe on back extends on to tail lobes which have white-edged black tips. **Ecology:** in schools in mid-water along reef slopes, 2 to 25 m. **Range:** Red Sea (common).

6 Yellowtop fusilier *Caesio xanthonota* Bleeker 30 cm
Tail and top of head and back yellow at all sizes. **Ecology:** in schools in mid-water in deep lagoons and along seaward reefs. **Range:** s. Red Sea & E. Africa to Moluccas, n. to Maldives & Andaman Sea.

7 Yellowback fusilier *Caesio teres* Seale 31 cm
Yellow area extends to nape only in juvs., retreating to tail and its base with growth. **Ecology:** in schools in mid-water in deep lagoons and along seaward reefs. Spawns *en masse* near the surface in the entrances of deep channels during outgoing tides on a lunar cycle. **Range:** E. Africa to Line Is., n. to s. Japan, s. to N. Cal.

8 Scissor-tailed fusilier *Caesio caerulaurea* Lacépède 28 cm
Blue-edged yellow stripe dorsally; ea. tail lobe with longit. black streak. **Ecology:** in schools in mid-water in deep lagoons and along seaward reefs. **Range:** E. Africa to Samoa, n. to s. Japan, s. to N. Cal.

9 Yellow lined fusilier *Caesio varilineata* Carpenter 25 cm
Ca. 6 yellow stripes on back & upper sides; tips of tail black. **Ecology:** in schools in mid-water in deep lagoons and along seaward reefs (1 to 25 m). **Range:** Red Sea to Sumatra, n. to Arab. G., s. to Seychelles & E. Africa.

10 Striated fusilier *Caesio striata* Rüppell 18 cm
4 dark stripes on back; ea. tail lobe with longit. black streak. Juv. with distinctive yellow spot on upper C peduncle. **Ecology:** in schools in mid-water along reef slopes, 2 to 30 m. Common on half-protected coral and rocky reefs. Juvs. in large schools. **Range:** Red Sea (common in s. Red Sea).

1
2
3
4
5
6
7
8
9
10

47 FUSILIERS

1 **Bluestreak fusilier** *Pterocaesio tile* (Cuvier) 25 cm
Broad iridescent blue band on middle of sides; belly pearly white to red; the only *Pterocaesio* without dark tips on tail lobes, but longit. dark stripes instead. **Ecology:** in schools in mid-water in deep lagoons and along seaward reefs. Juveniles occasionally appear in large numbers on shallow lagoons and reef flats. **Range:** E. Africa to Marq. & Gambier Is., n. to s. Japan, s. to N. Cal. & Rapa.

2 **Goldband fusilier** *Pterocaesio chrysozona* (Cuvier) 18 cm
Broad yellow stripe below LL except posteriorly; closely resembles *P. lativittata*. **Ecology:** in schools in mid-water in lagoons and along seaward reefs. **Range:** Red Sea to PNG, n. to e. China, s. to nw. Aust. & s. GBR.

3 **Two-lined fusilier** *Pterocaesio digramma* (Bleeker) 24 cm
Lower yellow stripe below LL for most of its length; closely resembles *P. marri*. **Ecology:** in schools in mid-water in lagoons and along seaward reefs. **Range:** Phil. & nw. Aust. to Sol. Is., n. to Taiwan & Bonin Is., se. to N. Cal. & Norfolk Is.

4 **Tessellated fusilier** *Pterocaesio tessellata* Carpenter 21 cm
A single narrow yellow stripe over LL; resembles *P. capricornis* (w. Indian Ocean). **Ecology:** in schools in mid-water in deep lagoons and along seaward reefs. **Range:** Sri Lanka to Vanuatu, n. to Phil., s. to Indonesia & PNG.

5 **Twinstripe fusilier** *Pterocaesio marri* Schultz 32 cm
Lower yellow stripe over LL for most of its length; closely resembles *P. digramma*. **Ecology:** in schools in mid-water in clear lagoons and along seaward reefs. **Range:** E. Africa to Marq., n. to s. Japan, s. to Samoa.

6 **Widestripe fusilier** *Pterocaesio lativittata* Carpenter 13 cm
Broad yellow stripe extends above LL; closely resembles *P. chrysozona*. **Ecology:** in schools along steep outer reef slopes to at least 40 m. **Range:** Chagos Is. to PNG, n. to Palau.

7 **Yellowpatch fusilier** *Pterocaesio randalli* Carpenter 23 cm
Broad oblong yellow patch from top of eye to middle of side. **Ecology:** in schools in mid-water in deep lagoons and along seaward reefs, 5 to 30 m. **Range:** Andaman Sea to Phil. & Moluccas, s. to Flores.

8 **Ruddy fusilier** *Pterocaesio pisang* (Bleeker) 17 cm
LL conspicuous, inner P fin axil and tips of tail black to dark red, otherwise uniformly red to blueish grey. **Ecology:** in schools in mid-water in deep lagoons and along seaward reefs. **Range:** E. Africa to Gilbert Is. & Fiji, n. to Ryuk., s. to N. Cal.

9 **Three-striped fusilier** *Pterocaesio trilineata* Carpenter 15 cm
3 alternating dark and light stripes dorsally. **Ecology:** in schools in mid-water in clear lagoons and along seaward reefs. **Range:** Phil. & Indonesia to Gilbert Is. & Fiji, n. to Caroline Is., s. to N. Cal. & Norfolk Is.

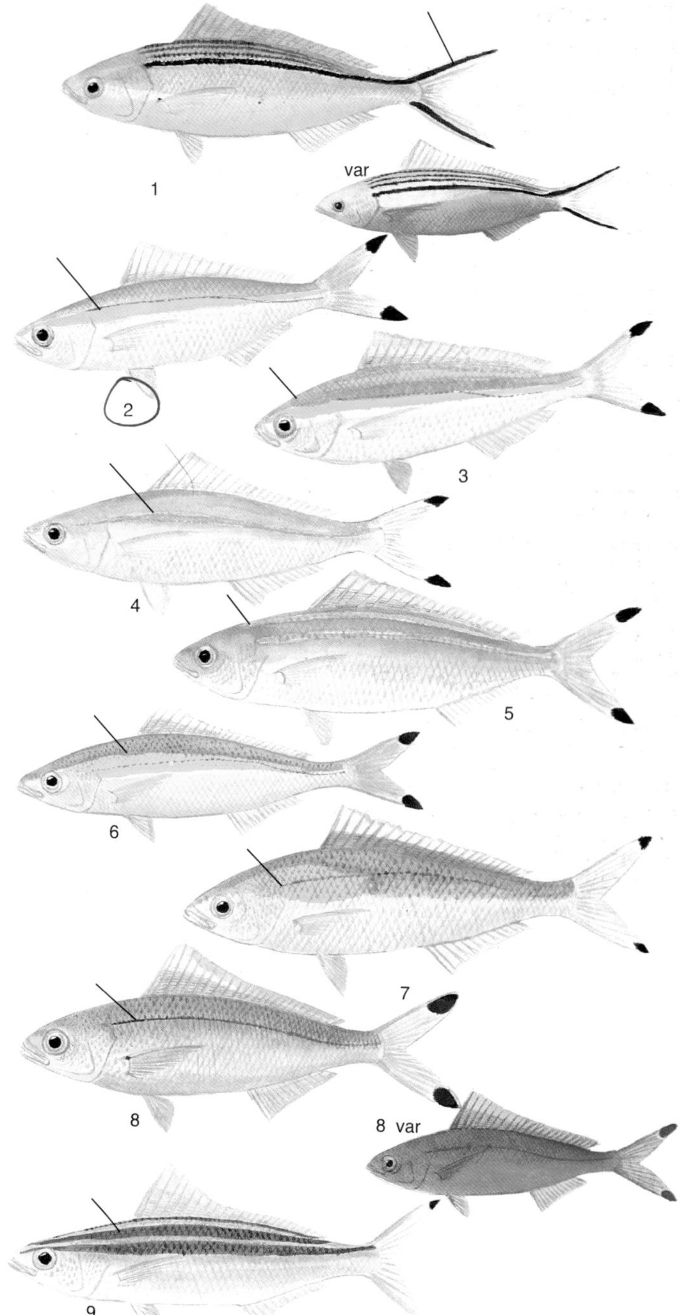
1
var
2
3
4
5
6
7
8
8 var
9

SWEETLIPS and GRUNTS (HAEMULIDAE): Medium to large fishes with thickened lips, small conical jaw teeth, pharyngeal teeth (in throat), small to medium scales, continuous D fins, and usually truncate to rounded tails. Juveniles of *Diagramma* and *Plectorhinchus* spp. undergo dramatic changes in color with growth. They typically swim with a conspicuous undulating motion and might be distastful to predators. Adults are typically inactive by day when they shelter near or under ledges, and disperse to feed on benthic invertebrates at night. Juveniles are popular in home aquaria and reasonably easy to maintain, but adults require a large tank. Important foodfishes.

1 **Paintes or Slatey sweetlips** *Diagramma pictum* (Thunberg) 94 cm
Juvs. 10 cm similar to juv. *P. albovittatus*; subadults silvery-grey with orange-yellow spots, lg. adults uniformly silvery-grey. Similar to *D. punctatum* which retains spots. **Ecology**: sandy to silty bottoms near coastal and lagoon reefs to 40 m. In aggregations around patch reefs or coral slopes by day. Juveniles in weedy areas. **Range**: Red Sea to N. Cal., n. to s. Japan, s. to L. Howe Is. & NSW.

2 **Harlequin sweetlips** *Plectorhinchus chaetodonoides* (Lacépède) 72 cm; 7 kg
Ecology: adults in coral-rich areas of clear lagoon and seaward reefs, 1 to 30 m. Solitary, near under ledges or caves by day. Juveniles among corals of sheltered coastal and inner lagoon reefs. Small ones may mimic a toxic flatworm. Forages at night on sand-dwelling invertebrates. **Range**: Maldives to Fiji, n. to Ryuk., s. to GBR & N. Cal.

3 **Crescent sweetlips** *Plectorhinchus cinctus* (Temminck & Schlegel) 60 cm
Ecology: coastal reefs, near rocky and coral areas. Common in s. Japan. **Range**: Arab. Sea to Taiwan & s. Japan, s. to Sri Lanka; continental areas only.

4 **Giant sweetlips** *Plectorhinchus albovittatus* (Bleeker) 100 cm; 15 kg
Juvs. (see pl. 49-5) dk grey to brown with 2 thin white lines on back, the lowermost from above eye to upper tail base, the uppermost just below D fin; tip of soft D, A & tail fins black. **Ecology**: clear lagoon and seaward reefs, 2 to 50 m. Adults usually solitary, occasionally in pairs. Juveniles in shallow turbid coastal areas. **Range**: Red Sea to s. Marsh. Is. & Fiji, n. to s. Japan, s. to NSW & N. Cal.

5 **Whitebarred sweetlips** *Plectorhinchus playfairi* (Pellegrin) 90 cm
Ecology: coral reefs, tidepools to 80 m. Solitary. **Range**: G. Aden s. to ca. 32°S, e. to Seychelles & Maurit.

6 **Somber sweetlips** *Plectorhinchus schotaf* (Forsskål) 40 cm, rare 80 cm
Head of juv. scarlet; ad. with hind edge of operculum & inside of mouth red; head profile well-rounded, body deepest behind tip of P fin; longest D spine depth of tail base. **Ecology**: rocky and coral reefs, surf zone to 80 m. Juveniles in tide pools. **Range**: Red Sea to GBR, n. to Ryuk, s. to L. Howe Is.

7 **Red-lined sweetlips** *Plectorhinchus plagiodesmus* (Fowler) ⩾ 90 cm
Juvs. of this sp. black with reddish lips; adults with orange spongelike lips; orange bars dissappear at 40 cm. **Ecology**: coastal, generally turbid reefs. Singly or in pairs, adults under ledges by day. **Range**: Somalia s. to ca. 30°S, e. to Aldabra & Madagascar.

8 **Gibbus sweetlips** *Plectorhinchus gibbosus* (Lacépède) 75 cm
Sev. similar spp., but lips thicker, head profile straighter, and body deepest at P fin origin. **Ecology**: shallow coastal reefs, 3 to 25 m. Solitary or in small groups. **Range**: Red Sea to Samoa, n. to Ryuk., s. to GBR & Norfolk Is.

9 **Dusky sweetlips** *Plectorhinchus chubbi* (Regan) 75 cm; 5 kg
Head profile rounded; most similar to *P. sordidus*, but normally D XI. **Ecology**: juveniles in shallow weedy areas. Adults on coastal reefs. Rare. **Range**: E. Africa s. to 32°S, n. to India, e. to se. Indonesia.

10 **Black sweetlips** *Plectorhinchus sordidus* (Klunzinger) 60 cm
Juvs. with incomplete white circles on body and large white blotches on D and A fins, white tail; adults with orange opercular margin & lips; head profile well-rounded; longest D spines depth of tail base. **Ecology**: shallow weedy areas and coral and rocky reefs, 2 to 25 m. Solitary or in small groups close to shelter. **Range**: Red Sea to 32°S, e. to Seychelles (common) & Maurit.

juv
1
1
2
juv
2
3
4
5
6
7
8
9
10

49 SWEETLIPS

1 **Oriental sweetlips** *Plectorhinchus vittatus* (Bloch) 86 cm
Juvs. <13 cm dark brown with cream blotches; adult with stripes extending to belly. **Ecology:** adults on clear outer lagoon and seaward reefs, 2 to 25 m. Juveniles in clear sheltered areas. Usually solitary, but occasionally occur in large groups. **Range:** E. Africa to Samoa, n. to Ryuk., s. to Maurit. & N. Cal.

2 **Lesson's sweetlips** *Plectorhinchus lessonii* (Cuvier) 48 cm
Juvs. similar to juv. *P. albovittata* and *P. lineatus*, but with 3 to 4 thick black stripes; belly of adults unstriped. **Ecology:** adults under coral ledges of shallow clear lagoon and seaward reefs, 1 to 35 m. Solitary. Forages on benthic invertebrates in open sand flats and seagrass beds at night. **Range:** Malaysia to N. Cal., n. to Ryuk., s. to GBR.

3 **Lined sweetlips** *Plectorhinchus lineatus* (Linnaeus) 72 cm
Juvs. similar to juv. *P. albovittata* & *P. lessonii* but with 5 horizon. black stripes on sides; belly becoming white & unstriped at ca. 10 cm; stripes break up & become diagonal at ⩾ ca. 22 cm. **Ecology:** singly or in aggregations along coral slopes of clear lagoon and seaward reefs, 2 to ⩾ 30 m. Forages at night over reef flats and sand patches primarily for crustaceans. **Range:** Moluccas & Phil. to N. Cal., n. to Ryuk.

4 **Blackspotted sweetlips** *Plectorhinchus gaterinus* (Forsskål) 45 cm
Juvs. 12 cm with 3 pairs of black stripes on head and body which become spots with age. **Ecology:** often in large groups under ledges or along coral slopes by day. **Range:** Red Sea to Comores, Mad., & Maurit, n. to G. Oman, s. to 30°S; absent from Seychelles.

5 **Giant sweetlips** *Plectorhinchus albovittatus* (Rüppell) 30 cm
Juvs. similar to juv. *P. lineatus* & *P. lessonii* with 4 thick horizon. black stripes on sides; belly becoming white & unstriped at ca. 12 cm. See pl. 48-4 for lge adult. **Ecology:** clear lagoon and seaward reefs, 2 to 50 m. Adults usually solitary, occasionally in pairs. Juveniles in shallow turbid coastal areas. **Range:** Red Sea to s. Marsh. Is. & Fiji, n. to s. Japan, s. to NSW & N. Cal.

6 **Ribbon sweetlips** *Plectorhinchus polytaenia* (Bleeker) 48 cm
Juvs. similar to adults, but with fewer stripes. **Ecology:** coastal and seaward reefs, 5 to 20 m. Solitary or in small groups, usually under ledges by day. **Range:** Phil. & Bali to PNG, s. to nw. Australia.

7 **Celebes sweetlips** *Plectorhinchus celebicus* (Bleeker) 49 cm
Ecology: sheltered reefs, 8 to 80 m. Solitary or in aggregations. **Range:** Moluccas to N. Cal., n. to Ryuk., s. to GBR.

8 **Gold-spotted sweetlips** *Plectorhinchus flavomaculatus* (Ehrenberg) 60 cm
Juvs. striped; gold spots of adults extend to D fin and tail, fused as oblique stripes on head. **Ecology:** juveniles in weedy areas, adults on sheltered coastal reefs below 4 m. **Range:** Red Sea to PNG, s. to S. Africa (32°S), w. Aust.& NSW, n. to s. Japan.

9 **Many-lined sweetlips** *Plectorhinchus multivittatum* (Macleay) 50 cm
Juvs., subadults striped; adults resembles *P. flavomaculatus* but fins yellow & spots yellow rather than orange. **Ecology:** coastal reefs. **Range:** nw. Australia.

10 **Spotted sweetlips** *Plectorhinchus picus* (Cuvier) 84 cm
Juvs. <25 cm black with large rounded white blotches; spots of adults smaller than those on *P. chaetodonoides*. **Ecology:** adults on clear lagoon and seaward reefs, 3 to 50 m. Juveniles in shallow lagoons. Adults usually under coral heads or in caves. Solitary. Rare or absent from most of the western Indian Ocean, but common in the Seychelles. **Range:** Seychelles to Soc. Is., n. to s. Japan, s. to L. Howe & Rapa Is.

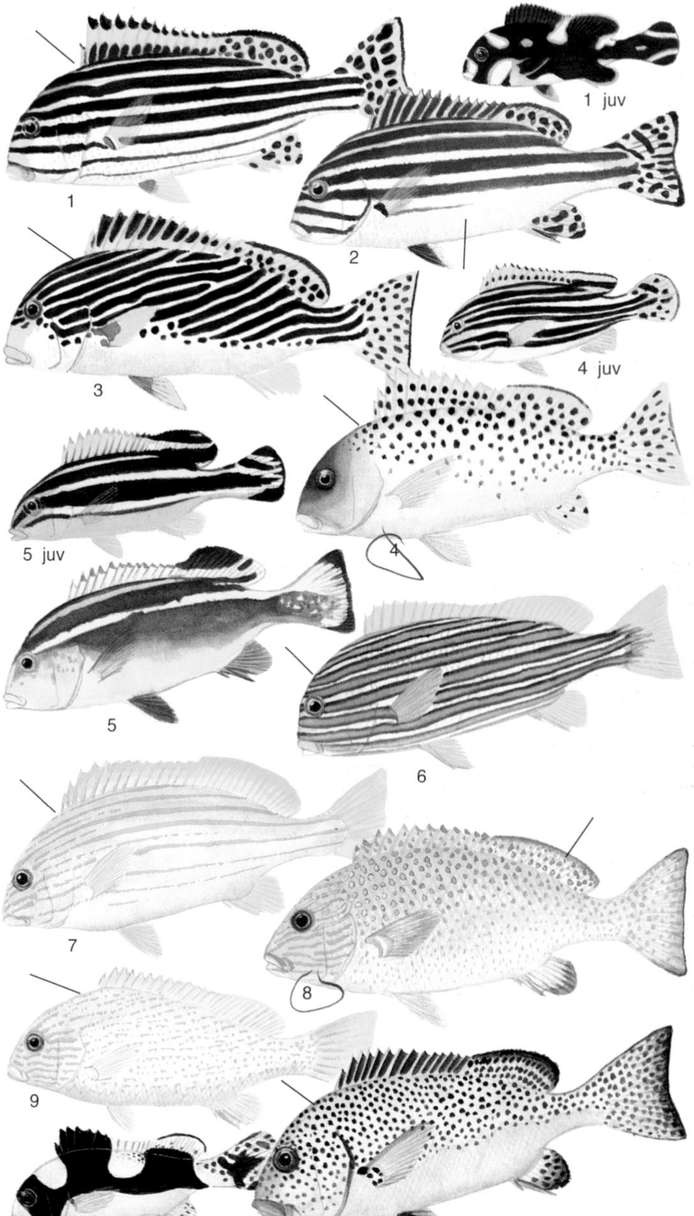
1 juv
1
2
3
4 juv
4
5 juv
5
6
7
8
9
10 juv
10

MONOCLE BREAMS and SPINECHEEKS

MONOCLE BREAMS and SPINECHEECKS (NEMIPTERIDAE): small to medium moderately elongate fishes with small mouths, large scales, continuous D fins with X spines and 11 rays, and emarginate to forked tails. Carnivores of benthic invertebrates or planktivores. Not generally kept in aquaria, but potentially hardy. Important foodfishes in some areas.

1 **Twoline spinecheek** *Scolopsis bilineatus* (Bloch) 23 cm
Scolopsis spp. with spine below eye. Juvs. of this sp. similar to juv. *S. lineatus*. Juvs. mimic poison-fang blennies, Fiji pop. yellow (*Meiacanthus* spp.; pl. 114). Adults variable in shade, may be almost entirely pale except for single dark stripe dorsally above eye. **Ecology:** *Scolopsis* species feed on benthic invertebrates and small fishes. Juveniles of this species near corals on sheltered reefs. Adults near sand patches of lagoon and sheltered seaward reefs, 1 to 25 m. Solitary. **Range:** Laccadive & Maldive Is. to Fiji, n. to Ryuk., s. to L. Howe Is.

2 **Threelined spinecheek** *Scolopsis trilineatus* Kner 20 cm
Ecology: protected reef flats and lagoons, on shallow sandy bottoms with scattered corals. Solitary or in small groups. **Range:** Bali & Borneo to Samoa, n. to Phil., s. to nw. Austral., N. Cal. & Tonga.

3 **Black-and-white spinecheek** *Scolopsis lineatus* Quoy & Gaimard 23 cm
Juvs. similar to juv. *S. bilineatus*. **Ecology:** juveniles solitary near shelter of corals on clear shallow lagoon reefs. Adults on outer lagoon, reef flat, and seaward reefs to 20 m, often in groups. **Range:** Andaman & Cocos-Keeling Is. to Gilbert Is. & Tuvalu, n. to Ryuk. & Mariana Is., s. to GBR & Vanuatu.

4 **Arabian spinecheek** *Scolopsis ghanam* (Forsskål) 18 cm
Ecology: shallow sandy inshore areas near coral reefs, 1 to 20 m. Abundant in Arabian Gulf. **Range:** Red Sea to Pakistan, n. to Arab. G, s to 27°S; Andaman Is.

5 **Bridled spinecheek** *Scolopsis frenatus* (Cuvier) 26 cm
Juvs. bright blue with 2 yellow stripes dorsally, fading with growth. **Ecology:** coral or rocky reefs, 5 to ⩾20 m. Adults in large groups, juveniles and suabadults solitary over sand and coral rubble. Common at the Seychelles. **Range:** E. Africa to Seychelles & Chagos Is., s. to Madag. & Maurit.

6 **Pearl-streaked spinecheek** *Scolopsis xenochrous* Günther 21 cm
Ecology: sand or rubble areas near coral reefs, 5 to 50 m, usually below 15 m. Feeds primarily on benthic crustaceans. **Range:** Maldives & Sri Lanka to Sol. Is., n. to Taiwan, s. to nw Australia & GBR.

7 **Saw-jawed spinecheek** *Scolopsis ciliatus* (Lacépède) 19 cm
Ecology: sandy areas of shallow sheltered reefs near corals. Solitary or in small groups. **Range:** Andaman Sea to Sol. Is., n. to Ryuk., s. to Vanuatu.

8 **Pearly spinecheek** *Scolopsis margaritifer* (Cuvier) 28 cm
Juvs. mimic poison-fang blennies (*Meiacanthus* spp.; pl. 114). **Ecology:** lagoon reefs, solitary near shelter of corals near sand. **Range:** Sumatra & G. Thail. to Vanuatu, n. to Taiwan, s. to nw. Aust. atolls & GBR.

9 **Thumbprint spinecheek** *Scolopsis bimaculatus* Rüppell 31 cm
S. taeniatus (Red Sea & Arab. G. to Pakistan) similar but with dark dorsal blotch extended to above P axil & a blue line from eye to corner of mouth. **Ecology:** shallow sand or mud bottoms of coastal reefs to 60 m. Feeds on benthic Invertebrates. Spawns during spring and fall. **Range:** Red Sea to s. India & Sri Lanka, n. to Arab. G., s. to 27°S & Madag.

10 **Whitecheek monocle bream** *Scolopsis vosmeri* (Bloch) 20 cm
Ecology: sand or mud bottoms of coastal rocky or coral reefs, 2 to 25 m. Absent from mid-oceanic islands. **Range:** Red Sea to PNG, n. to Arab. G. & Ryuk., s. to nw. Austral.

11 **Pale spinecheek** *Scolopsis affinis* Peters 24 cm
S. auratus (Maldives to s. Indon.) similar but with golden-yellow midlateral stripe. **Ecology:** sheltered lagoon and seaward reefs, in sandy areas with scattered corals from shoreline to 60 m. Solitary or in small groups. **Range:** Andaman Sea to Sol. Is., n. to Ryuk., s. to n. Australia & GBR.

12 **Monogrammed monocle bream** *Scolopsis monogramma* (Cuvier) 31 cm
S. temporalis (Sulawesi to Sol. Is. & Fiji) similar but with naked area extend. behind eye. **Ecology:** shallow sandy areas near coastal reefs to 50 m. **Range:** Andaman Sea to PNG, n. to Ryuk., s. to nw. Austral., N. Cal.

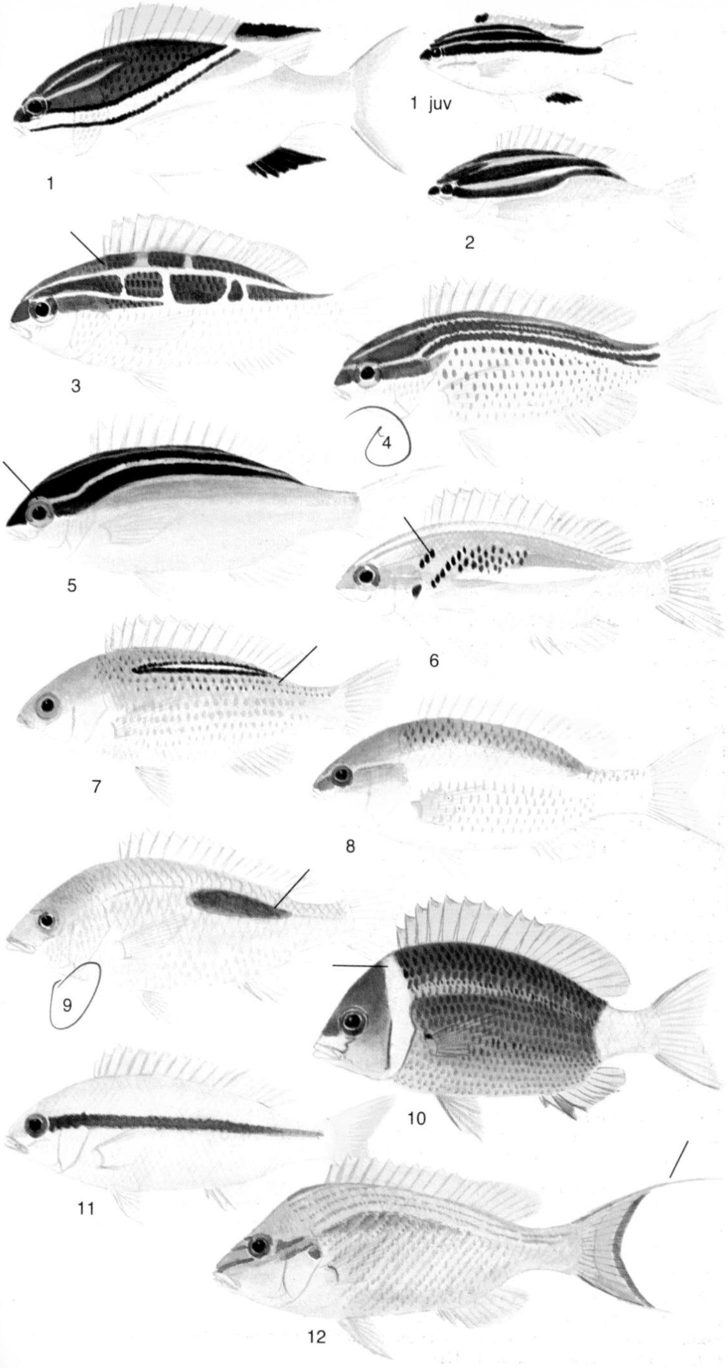
1
1 juv
2
3
4
5
6
7
8
9
10
11
12

51 WHIPTAILS

1 **White-shoulder whiptail** *Pentapodus bifasciatus* (Bleeker) 18 cm
Ecology: shallow coastal reefs. Feeds on small fishes and benthic invertebrates including crustaceans and polychaetes. **Range:** Singapore to Bali & Sulawesi, n. throughout Phil.

2 **Northwest Australian whiptail** *Pentapodus porosus* (Valenciennes) 27 cm
Ecology: over sand and rubble bottoms near coastal and offshore reefs. **Range:** nw. Australia to Aru Is.

3 **Paradise whiptail** *Pentapodus paradiseus* (Günther) 30 cm
Similar to *P. setosus* (G. Thail. to Moluccas, n. to Phil., s. to Timor.) but has 3 instead of 2 blue bands across snout. **Ecology:** mid-water near coastal reefs. Juveniles in rubble areas. **Range:** Arufura Sea to ne. Australia, n. to PNG & Sol. Is.

4 **Blue whiptail** *Pentapodus* sp. 20 cm
Juvs. similar to juv. *P. emeryii*; adult also similar but without filamentous tail lobes. **Ecology:** mid-waters over sand bottoms near reefs. **Range:** ne. Australia to Fiji & Samoa.

5 **Double whiptail** *Pentapodus emeryii* (Richardson) 30 cm
Juvs. similar to juv. *Pentapodus* sp.; ad. also similar but with filamentous tail lobes. **Ecology:** coastal reefs. Solitary. Feeds on small fishes and benthic invertebrates. **Range:** Java & Borneo to Timor, n. to Phil., PNG & n. Australia.

6 **Japanese whiptail** *Pentapodus nagasakiensis* (Tanaka) 20 cm
Ecology: in aggregations in mid-water above rocky and coral reefs, below 15 to 100 m. **Range:** s. Japan, s. to nw Aust., GBR & Coral Sea.

7 **Three-striped whiptail** *Pentapodus trivittatus* Bloch 25 cm
P. bifasciatus (Sing. to Bali & Phil.) similar but with white bar on upper margin of opercle. **Ecology:** mid-waters above lagoon and sheltered bay reefs. Feeds on zooplankton by day and shelter in the reef at night. **Range:** s. S. China Sea to Sol. Is., n. to Phil. & Palau, s. to Timor & PNG.

8 **Small-toothed whiptail** *Pentapodus caninus* (Cuvier) 35 cm
Ecology: in loose aggregations high above lagoon and sheltered bay patch reefs, 3 to 30 m. Feeds on small fishes, larger zooplankton, and benthic invertebrates. **Range:** s. S. China Sea to Marsh. Is. & Vanuatu, n. to Ryuk., s. to Timor & N. Cal.

9 **Striped whiptail** *Pentapodus vitta* Quoy & Gaimard 26 cm
Ecology: sandy weedy areas or rocky bottoms near shore in coastal bays. **Range:** W. Australia, ca. 20 to 34°S.

PORGIES and SEA BREAMS (SPARIDAE): stocky snapper-like fishes with conical to incisiform teeth, some with molars, medium to large scales, continuous D fins, and emarginate to forked tails. Carnivores of hard-shelled benthic invertebrates. Most species from temperate waters. Important foodfishes.

10 **Arabian pinfish** *Diplodus noct* (Cuvier & Valenciennes) 25 cm
Ecology: shallow waters of exposed rocky or dead coral shores, 1 to 8 m. **Range:** Red Sea, e Med.

11 **Doublebar bream** *Acanthopagrus bifasciatus* (Forsskål) 50 cm
Ecology: sand and rubble areas near reefs, 2 to 20 m. Solitary or in small groups. Often several meters from reef slopes. **Range:** Red Sea, n. to Arab. G., s. to 30°S.

12 **Yellowfin bream** *Rhabdosargus sarba* (Forsskål) 40 cm; 12 kg
Ecology: Sand and rubble areas near reefs, enters brackish water. Often in schools **Range:** Red Sea & E. Africa to 34°S.

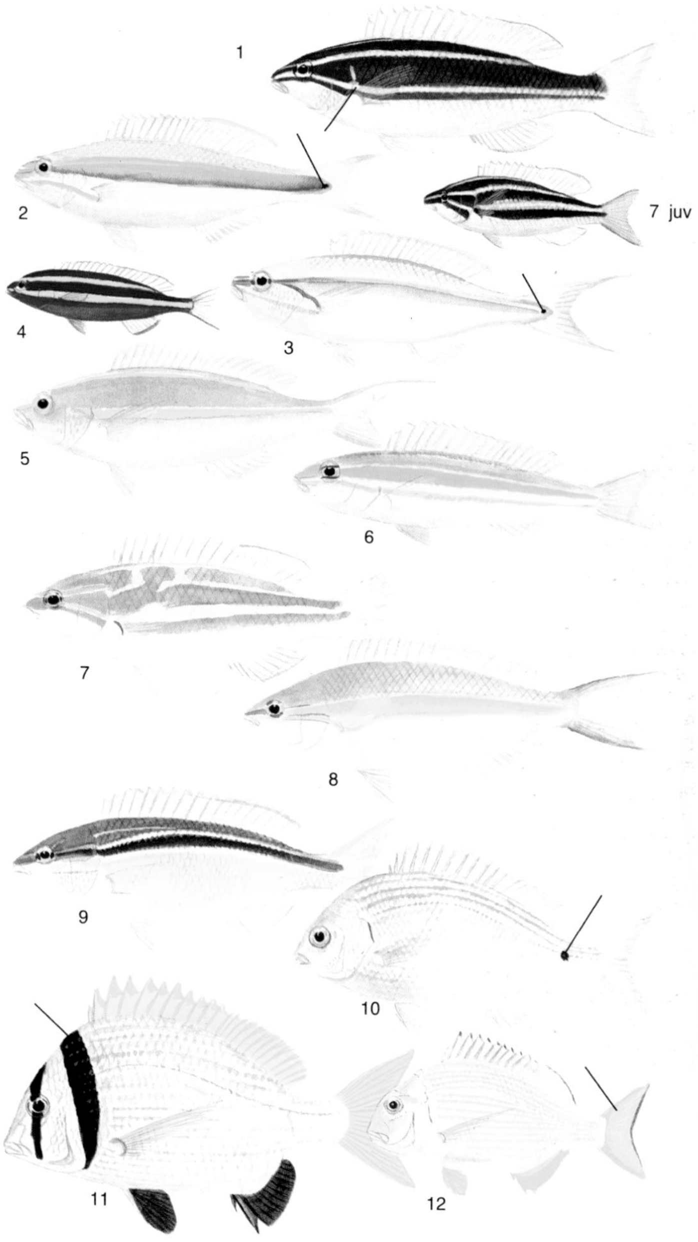

1
2
7 juv
4
3
5
6
7
8
9
10
11
12

EMPERORS (LETHRINIDAE): Medium to large snapper-like fishes with the maxillary completely hidden by a naked or near naked preopercle, thickened lips, canine teeth in the front of the jaws and conical to molariform teeth on the sides, large scales, a continuous D fin (always X, 9-10), and emarginate to forked tails. They typically feed primarily at night on benthic invertebrates or fishes, those with molariform teeth primarily on hard-shelled invertebrates. Many spp. of *Gymnocranius* and *Lethrinus* are difficult to distinguish and able to change color instantly. At least 39 spp., many are important foodfishes.

1 **Bigeye emperor** *Monotaxis grandoculis* (Forsskål) 60 cm
Juvs. distinctively barred; adults silvery, with wide dusky saddles or uniformly pale. **Ecology:** lagoon and seaward reefs near sand patches, 1 to 100 m. Juveniles solitary, adults solitary or in aggregations on reef slopes near sand by day. They disperse over sand at night to feed on hard-shelled invertebrates. **Range:** Red Sea to Hawaiian, Marq. & Pitcairn Is., n. to Ryuk., s. to N. Cal.

2 **Yellowspot emperor** *Gnathodentex aurolineatus* (Lacépède) 24 cm
Ecology: subtidal reef flats, lagoons, and seaward reefs to 30 m. Hovers in aggregations near coral heads by day. Disperses at night to feed on benthic invertebrates. Common. **Range:** E. Africa to Marq. & Gambier Is., n. to s. Japan, s. to NSW & Norfolk & Rapa Is.

3 **Collared large-eye bream** *Gymnocranius audleyi* Ogilby 40 cm
Ecology: areas of sand and rubble near coastal to offshore reefs, 8 to 40 m. **Range:** Bali to coastal Queensland & GBR.

4 **Japanese large-eye bream** *Gymnocranius euanus* Günther 45 cm
Subad. occas. with faint blue band across front of snout; scattered dark scales; tail lobes rounded; the only *Gymnocranius* with 41/2 scale rows above LL (all other with 51/2). **Ecology:** sand or rubble bottoms near coral or rocky reefs, 15 to 50 m. **Range:** G. Thail. to Samoa, n. to s. Japan, s. to N. Cal. & Tonga; unknown from Indonesia.

5 **Blacknape large-eye bream** *Gymnocranius* sp. 45 cm
Nape dusky; fins & tail reddish; tail lobes blunt. **Ecology:** sand and rubble near reefs, 15 to 40 m. Feeds primarily on gastropods. **Range:** s. Japan, Marianas, PNG, GBR, N. Cal.

6 **Blue-lined large-eye bream** *G. grandoculis* (Valenciennes) 80 cm
Blue squiggly lines on snout; tail lobes pointed. **Ecology:** offshore reefs and rocky bottoms, 50 to 100 m. Feeds on invertebrates and fishes. **Range:** Red Sea to Fr. Polynesia, n. to s. Japan, s. to N. Cal.

7 **Pacific yellowtail emperor** *Lethrinus atkinsoni* Seale 45 cm
Ad. us. with dark head; often yellow on sides not apparent; similar to *L. crocineus*. **Ecology:** seagrasss beds and sandy areas of lagoon and seaward reefs to 30 m. **Range:** Sumatra and Cocos-Keeling to Tuam., n. to Ryuk., s. to nw. Aust. & L. Howe Is.

8 **Snubnose emperor** *Lethrinus borbonicus* Valenciennes 40 cm
Ecology: sandy areas near reefs to 40 m. Solitary or in small groups. Enters reef flats to feed on hard-shelled invertebrates at night. **Range:** Red Sea & Arab. G. s. to Maurit., e. to Seychelles.

9 **Orange-fin emperor** *Lethrinus erythracanthus* Valenciennes 70 cm
Ecology: deep lagoon and seaward reefs, 18 to 120 m. Solitary in or near ledges or caves by day. Feeds on shelled or armored benthic invertebrates, probably mostly at night. **Range:** E. Africa to Tuam., n. to Ryuk., s. to GBR.

10 **Longspine emperor** *Lethrinus genivittatus* Valenciennes 25 cm
The only *Lethrinus* with an elongate 2nd D spine. **Ecology:** seagrass beds, mangroves, and shallow sandy areas of coastal reefs to 25 m. **Range:** Sumatra to e. Caroline Is., n. to s. Japan, s. to nw. Aust. & N. Cal.

11 **Longfin emperor** *Lethrinus erythropterus* Valenciennes 50 cm
Ecology: coral reefs and nearby sandy areas, 2 to 25 m. Solitary or in groups. Feeds on benthic invertebrates and fishes. **Range:** E. Africa to Sol. Is., n. to Phil. & Caroline Is, s. to Indonesia.

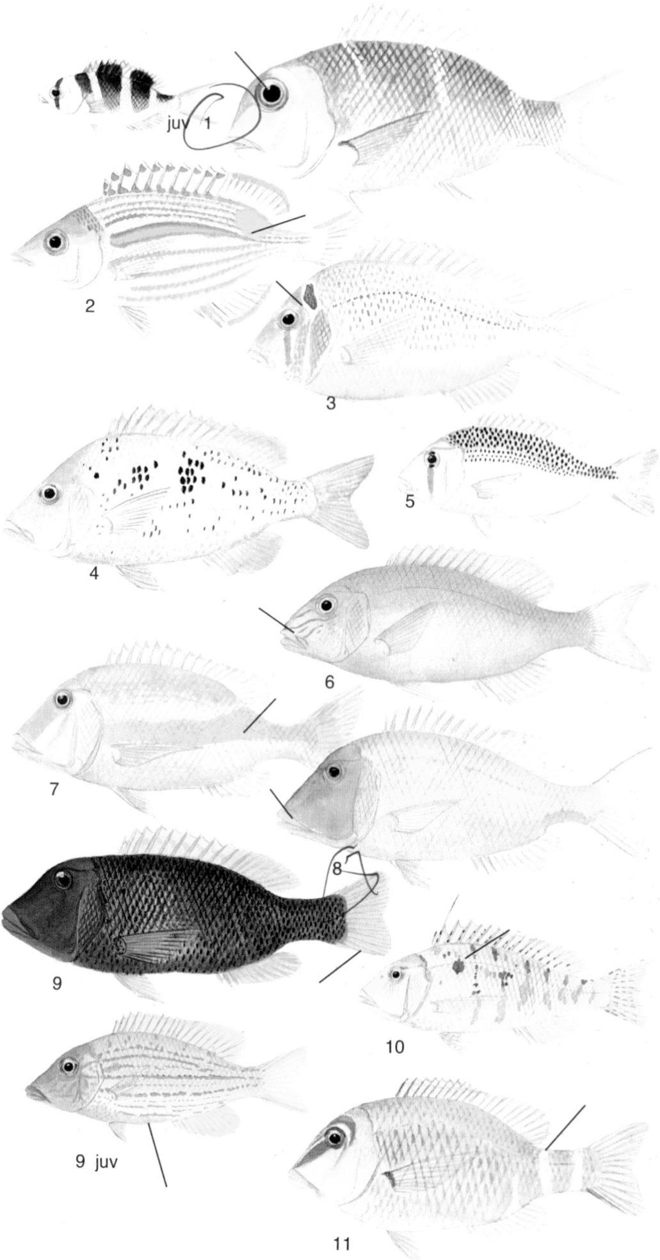
juv 1
2
3
4
5
6
7
8
9
10
9 juv
11

53 EMPERORS

1 **Blackspot emperor** *Lethrinus harak* (Forsskål) 50 cm
Lg. spot on sides variable, may be pale and indistinct. **Ecology:** seagrass beds and shallow sandy or rubbly areas of reef flats and shallow lagoons and channels to 20 m. Solitary or in small groups. Feeds on benthic invertebrates. **Range:** Red Sea to Samoa, n. to s. Japan, s. to Maurit. & N. Cal.

2 **Pink-ear emperor** *Lethrinus lentjan* (Lacépède) 50 cm
Ecology: sandy areas of shallow coastal and lagoon reefs to 50 m. Juveniles and subadults in loose aggregations in mangroves and seagrases, adults solitary in deeper water. Feeds primarily on crustaceans and mollusks. **Range:** Red Sea to Tonga, n. to Ryuk., s. to N. Cal.

3 **Sky emperor** *Lethrinus mahsena* (Forsskål) 65 cm
Dusky bars on upper sides, otherwise may resemble *L. crocineus*, or *L. borbonius*. **Ecology:** coral reefs and nearby seagrass beds and sand areas, 2 to 100 m. Feeds on echinoderms, crustaceans and fishes. Wary. **Range:** Red Sea & Arab. G. to Sri Lanka, s. to Maurit. & Chagos. Is.

4 **Smalltooth emperor** *Lethrinus microdon* Valenciennes 70 cm
Resembles *L. olivaceus*, but has shorter snout with straight head profile. **Ecology:** sandy areas near reefs to 80 m. Occasionally in groups with *L. olivaceus*. **Range:** Red Sea & Arab. G. to PNG, n. to s. Japan, s. to Maurit. & nw. Aust.

5 **Trumpet emperor** *Lethrinus miniatus* (Schneider) 90 cm
Ecology: in aggregations around coral heads and reefs by day, 5 to 30 m. Disperses over sand and rubble at night and occasionally by day to feed on crabs, sea urchins, and fishes. **Range:** Ryuk.; w. Aust. n. of 32°S to GBR & N. Cal.

6 **Orange-stripe emperor** *Lethrinus obsoletus* (Forsskål) 30 cm
May have 2-3 additional faint yellow stripes; can make all stripes dissappear at will. **Ecology:** seagrass beds and sand or rubble areas of shallow lagoon and seaward reefs to 30 m. Feeds mainly on hard-shelled benthic invertebrates. Solitary or in groups. Common. **Range:** Red Sea to Samoa, n. to Ryuk., s. to N. Cal. & Tonga.

7 **Spangled emperor** *Lethrinus nebulosus* (Forsskål) 86 cm
Ecology: mangroves, seagrass beds, weedy reef flats, and lagoon and seaward reefs to 75 m. Feeds primarily on echinoderms, crustaceans, and mollusks. Often in groups. **Range:** Red Sea & Arab. G. to Samoa, n. to s. Japan, s. to NSW (36°S) & N. Cal.

8 **Ornate emperor** *Lethrinus ornatus* Valenciennes 40 cm
Ecology: seagrass beds and sandy or silty bottoms near reefs in coastal bays and shallow lagoons. Feeds on benthic invertebrates and fishes. **Range:** Sri Lanka to N. Brit., n. to Ryuk., s. to n. GBR.

9 **Grass emperor** *Lethrinus laticaudis* Alleyne & Macleay 56 cm
Resembles *L. nebulosus*, but body deeper & snout shorter. **Ecology:** juveniles in mangroves and seagrasses, adults on reefs. Feeds primarily on crustaceans and fishes. **Range:** Andaman Sea to PNG & Sol. Is., s. to nw. Aust. & N. Cal.

10 **Longface emperor** *Lethrinus olivaceus* Valenciennes 100 cm; 14 kg
Longest snout in genus; snout profile concave; body may be mottled (also see *L. microdon*). **Ecology:** lagoon and seaward reefs, 1 to 185 m. Juveniles in shallow sandy areas, often in schools. Feeds primarily on fishes, less on crustaceans and cephalopods. **Range:** Red Sea to Samoa, n. to s. Japan, s. to N. Cal.

11 **Redgill emperor** *Lethrinus rubrioperculatus* Sato 50 cm
Body may be mottled; occas. with dark head; red opercular spot always present. **Ecology:** sand and rubble areas of seaward reefs, 12 to 160 m. Common in Micronesia. **Range:** E. Africa to Marq., n. to s. Japan, s. to N. Cal.

12 **Red-axil emperor** *Lethrinus conchyliatus* Smith 76 cm
Ecology: coral reefs to 220 m. Feeds on fishes and crustaceans. **Range:** E. Africa to Maldives, s. to Madag.; Andaman Is. to Timor.

13 **Yellowlip emperor** *Lethrinus xanthochilus* Klunzinger 60 cm
P axil orange; lips yellow-orange; body with scattered dark scales; may be mottled. Similar to *L. amboinensis* which lacks the orange P axil. **Ecology:** shallow lagoon and seaward reefs, in seagrass beds and sand, rubble or coral areas. Often in small groups. Feeds primarily on hard-shelled invertebrates and fishes. **Range:** Red Sea to Marq., n. to Ryuk., s. to N. Cal.

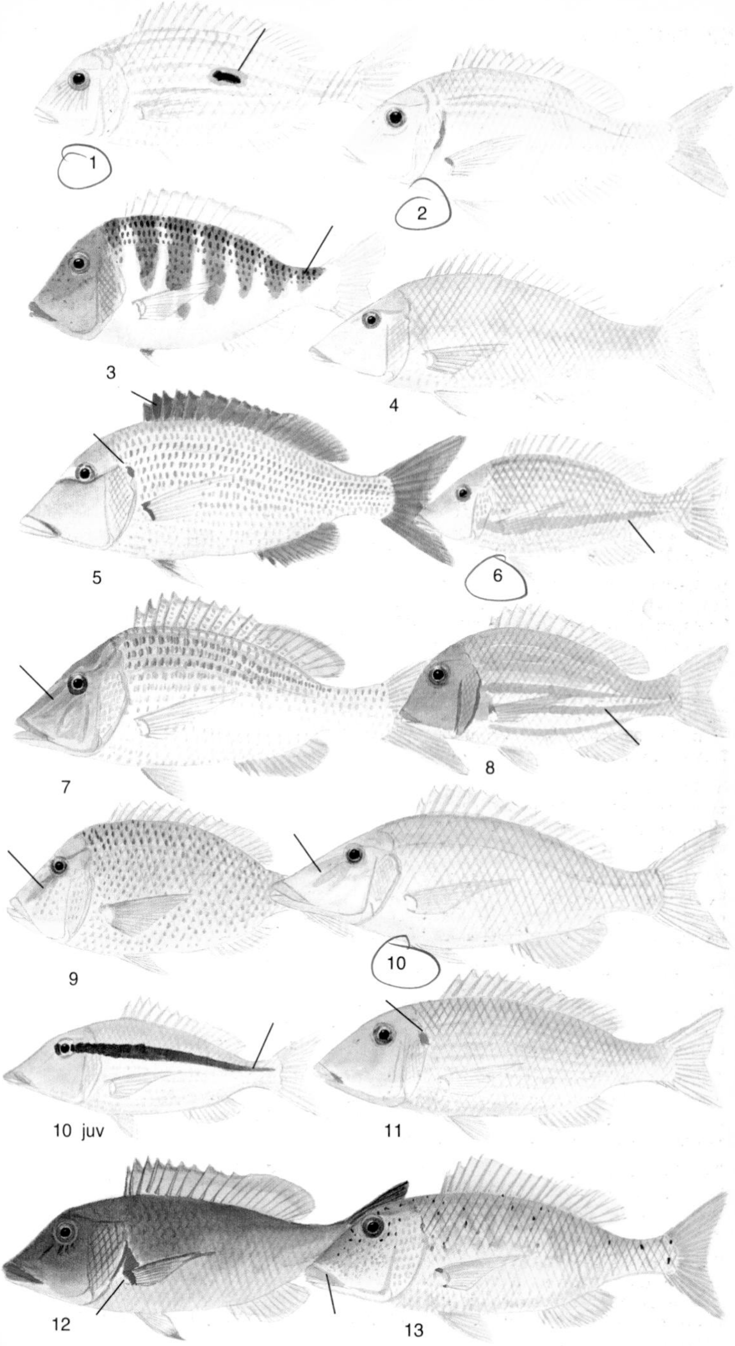
1
2
3
4
5
6
7
8
9
10
10 juv
11
12
13

GOATFISHES (MULLIDAE): medium elongate fishes with pair of barbels on chin; 2 D fins, large scales, and forked tails. The chemosensory barbels are thrust in sand or holes to detect prey. Important food fishes. Not popular for aquariums, but do well in right setting.

1 **Yellowstripe goatfish** *Mulloidichthys flavolineatus* (Lacépède) 43 cm
Closely resembles *M. vanicolensis* when black blotch is "turned off", but snout is longer. **Ecology:** shallow sandy areas of lagoon and seaward reefs to 35 m. Often in large inactive aggregations by day. Feeds singly or in small groups on benthic invertebrates by day or night. When feeding, the yellow stripe is replaced by an oblong midlateral black blotch. Common throughout most of its range. **Range:** Red Sea to Hawaiian, Marq. & Pitcairn Is., n. to Ryuk., s. to L. Howe & Rapa Is.

2 **Yellowfin goatfish** *Mulloidichthys vanicolensis* (Valenciennes) 38 cm
Fins yellow; body pale to orange-pink; may resemble *M. vanicolensis* but snout is shorter. **Ecology:** reef flats and lagoon and seaward reefs to 113 m. In large inactive aggregations by day, dispersing to sand flats to feed on benthic invertebrates by night. Common. **Range:** Red Sea to Hawaiian, Marq. & Tuam. Is., n. to s. Japan, s. to L. Howe & Kerm. Is.

3 **Mimic goatfish** *Mulloidichthys mimicus* (Randall & Gueze) 30 cm
Ecology: rocky and coral reefs, 12 to 15 m. Mimics *Lutjanus kasmira* (pl. 44-1), which is less desirable to some predators, and aggregates with it by day. Probably disperses at night to feed. **Range:** Line & Marq. Is. only.

4 **Half-and-half goatfish** *Parupeneus barberinoides* (Bleeker) 30 cm
Ecology: shallow sand and rubble areas of lagoon and coastal reefs. **Range:** Phil. & e. Indonesia to Samoa, n. to s. Japan, s. to N. Cal. & Tonga.

5 **Dash-and-dot goatfish** *Parupeneus barberinus* (Lacépède) 60 cm
Yellow area above black bar variable; bar and dot occasionally dark red; *P. forskalli* (Red Sea) similar but spot at tail base higher and more forward. **Ecology:** sandy areas of reef flats and lagoon and seaward reefs to 100 m. Forages in small groups by day. Common. **Range:** E. Africa to Marq. & Tuam. Is., n. to s. Japan, s. to L. Howe Is.

6 **Longbarbel goatfish** *Parupeneus macronema* (Lacépède) 30 cm
Ecology: lagoon and seaward reefs to over 25 m. On sand or rubble. **Range:** Red Sea & Arab. G. to Phil. & PNG.

7 **Indian goatfish** *Parupeneus indicus* (Shaw) 35 cm
Ecology: shallow sandy or silty areas of coastal and inner lagoon reefs to 20 m. **Range:** E. Africa to Samoa, n. to Phil. & Caroline Is., s. to N. Cal. & Tonga.

8 **Sidespot goatfish** *Parupeneus pleurostigma* (Bennett) 33 cm
Ecology: shallow sandy or rubbly areas of lagoon and seaward reefs to ⩾ 46 m. Feeds on wide variety of benthic invertebrates and fishes. **Range:** E. Africa to Hawaiian, Marq. & Tuam. Is., n. to Ryuk., s. to L. Howe & Rapa Is.

9 **Two-barred goatfish** *Parupeneus bifasciatus* (Lacépède) 35 cm
Pacific plate popul. less distinctly barred (b); odd indiv. may be redddish-brown to black on anterior 2/3; deepwater indiv. may be nearly uniformly red. **Ecology:** lagoon and seaward reefs, 1 to 80 m. Often resting on corals or rocks by day. Feeds on crustaceans by day and fishes and crab larvae by night. **Range:** E. Africa to Hawaiian, Marq. & Ducie Is., n. to s. Japan, s. to N. Cal.

10 **Multibarred goatfish** *Parupeneus multifasciatus* (Quoy & Gaimard) 30 cm
Contrast of pattern and color extr. variable, ranging from grey to, red, purple, or brown. **Ecology:** reef flats and shallow lagoon and seaward reefs to 140 m. On sand patches, rubble, rock, or coral bottoms. Feeds mainly during the day on small crustaceans. Common. **Range:** Cocos-Keeling to Hawaiian, Marq. & Tuam. Is., n. to s. Japan, s. to L. Howe & Rapa Is.

11 **Whitesaddle goatfish** *Parupeneus porphyreus* (Jenkins) 45 cm
Closely resembles *P. ciliatus* (pl. 55-1), *P. spilurus* (w. Pacific) which has well-defined white stripes on head & distinct black saddle behind white spot on tail base, *P. ischyurus* (s. Japan), and *P. rubescens*. **Ecology:** lagoon and seaward reefs, 1 to 140 m. In small groups under ledges or among corals by day, dispersing at night to feed among rocks and corals on benthic crustaceans. **Range:** Hawaiian Is. only.

12 **Rosy goatfish** *Parupeneus rubescens* (Lacépède) 43 cm
Ecology: sandy areas. Solitary or in aggregations, sometimes with other goatfishes. Common in S. Africa. **Range:** Red Sea & Indian Ocean, sw. to 34°S, e. to e. Indonesia.

13 **Redspot goatfish** *Parupeneus heptacanthus* (Lacépède) 28 cm
Ecology: sandy or silty bottoms of lagoon and seaward reefs, below 20 to 350 m. **Range:** Red Sea to Samoa, n. to s. Japan, s. to L. Howe Is.

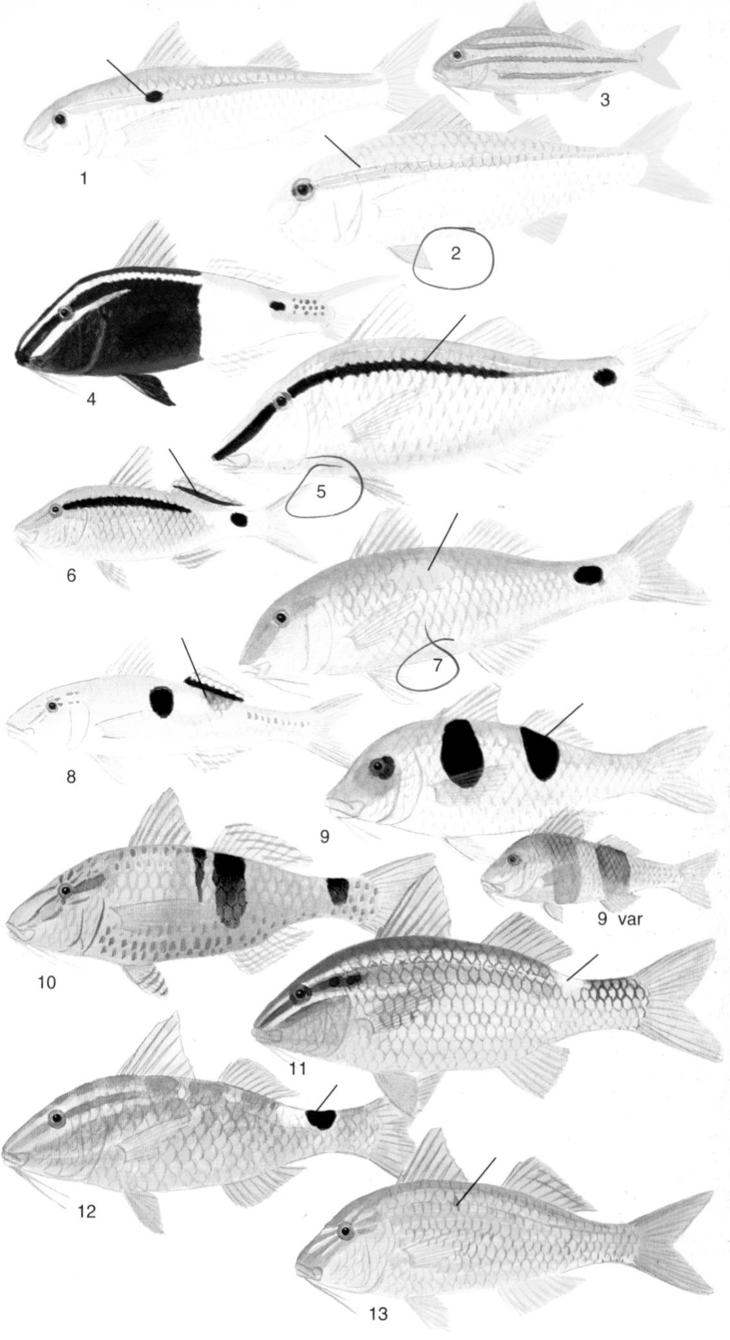
1
3
2
4
5
6
7
8
9
10
9 var
11
12
13

55 GOATFISHES, SWEETLIPS and RUDDERFISHES

1 **White-lined goatfish** *Parupeneus ciliatus* (Lacépède) 38 cm
Ecology: seagrass beds and sandy, rubbly, or coralline areas of lagoon and seaward reefs to 40 m. Rests on corals by day. **Range:** e. Indian Ocean to Marq. & Tuam. Is., n. to s. Japan, s. to L. Howe. & Rapa Is.

2 **Yellowsaddle goatfish** *Parupeneus cyclostomus* (Lacépède) 50 cm
Deepwater indiv. may be primarily pink; yellow ph. absent from Hawaii. **Ecology:** clear reef flats and lagoon and seaward reefs to 92 m. On coral, rock, or rubble bottoms. Feeds primarily by day on small fishes driven from holes by the thrusting barbels. **Range:** Red Sea to Hawaiian, Marq. & Tuam. Is., n. to Ryuk., s. to N. Cal. & Rapa.

3 **Goldband goatfish** *Upeneus moluccensis* (Bleeker) 20 cm
Ecology: shallow sandy or weedy areas of coastal reefs. **Range:** Red Sea to PNG, n. to s. Japan, s. to nw. Aust.

4 **Blackstriped goatfish** *Upeneus tragula* Richardson 30 cm
Ecology: shallow sandy or silty areas of lagoon and sheltered coastal reefs. Enters rivers. **Range:** Red Sea to Vanuatu & N. Cal., n. to s. Japan, s. to NSW & Norfolk Is.

5 **Yellowbanded goatfish** *Upeneus vittatus* (Forsskål) 28 cm
U. taeniopterus (E. Africa to Hawaii & Tuam.) similar but with more dark bars on tail. **Ecology:** shallow sandy areas of lagoon and coastal reefs to 100 m. Often in groups. Feeds primarily on small crustaceans. **Range:** Red Sea to Hawaiian, Marq. & Soc. Is., n. to s. Japan, s. to N. Cal.

SWEEPERS (PEMPHERIDAE): small compressed ovoid fishes with large eyes, small oblique mouth, single D fin, and slightly forked tail. Aggregate in caves by day and disperse to feed on zooplankton at night. Many s. Australian species. Not popular for aquariums.

6 **Pygmy sweeper** *Parapriacanthus ransonneti* (Steindachner) 10 cm
Similar to *P. guentheri* (Red Sea to Maldives). **Ecology:** coastal and lagoon reefs, in dense aggregations under ledges and in caves by day. **Range:** Seychelles to Marsh. Is. & N. Cal., n. to s. Japan, s. to w. Aust. & L. Howe Is.

7 **Copper sweeper** *Pempheris oualensis* Cuvier 20 cm
P base dark; scales above LL 6-9, LP 60-68. **Ecology:** lagoon and seaward reefs, 1 to 36 m. Common along seaward reef margin. **Range:** Red Sea to Marq. & Ducie Is., n. to Ryuk., s. to L. Howe & Rapa Is.

8 **Vanikoro sweeper** *Pempheris vanicolensis* Cuvier 20 cm
D fin tip and outer A fin dark; LP 55-60. **Ecology:** shallow rocky and coral reefs. **Range:** Red Sea to Samoa, n. to Phil.

9 **Schwenk's sweeper** *Pempheris schwenkii* Bleeker 15 cm
A fin base dark, tail yellowish, P base unmarked; scales large, LL 44-50 (vs. $\geq$ 53). **Ecology:** rocky and coral reefs, 5 to 40 m. **Range:** E. Africa to Fiji, n. to Indonesia, s. to GBR.

RUDDERFISHES (KYPHOSIDAE): moderately large fishes with small heads, small terminal mouth with incisiform teeth, single D fin, small scales, and slightly forked tail. Omnivores characteristic of exposed seaward reefs. Foodfishes in some areas, trash fishes in others.

10 **Lowfin rudderfish** *Kyphosus vaigiensis* (Quoy & Gaimard) 61 cm
Us. D14, A13, LP 56-58; resembles *K. bigibbus*(us. D12, A11; widespread Indo-Pac.), *K. lembus* (LP 50-55; s. Japan-PNG), *K. cornelii* (dark tail lobes; w. Aust.) & *K. sydneyanus* (dark fins; s. Aust.). **Ecology:** coastal and lagoon reefs, in dense aggregations under ledges and in caves by day. **Range:** Red Sea to Hawaiian & Tuam. Is., n. to Marianas, s. to Norfolk & Rapa Is.

11 **Highfin rudderfish** *Kyphosus cinerascens* (Forsskål) 45 cm
Soft D & A fins taller than in other spp. **Ecology:** outer lagoon and exposed seaward reefs and rocky shores, in aggregations in surgy areas to 24 m. Often high in water. Solitary at night. **Range:** Red Sea to Hawaiian & Tuam. Is., n. to s. Japan, s. to L. Howe Is.

1
2 var
2
3
4
5
6
7
8
9
10
11

56 SPADEFISHES, MONOS, STRIPEYS, and ARCHERFISHES

SPADEFISHES (EPHIPPIDAE): highly compressed deep-bodied fishes with a small terminal mouth with small brushlike teeth and small scales. Omnivores of algae and small invertebrates. Juveniles of *Platax* species popular and easily kept in aquaria.

1 **Longfin spadefish** *Platax teira* (Forsskål) 60 cm
Ad. resembles *P. orbicularis*, but with vertical black blotch in front of A fin; Recently distinguished from v. similar *P. boersi* (LP44-52 vs. 56-66; Red Sea to PNG). **Ecology:** juveniles in shallow protected areas. adults on lagoon and seaward reefs to 20 m. Solitary or in groups. **Range:** Red Sea to PNG, n. to Ryuk., s. to GBR & Norfolk Is.

2 **Circular spadefish; Batfish** *Platax orbicularis* (Forsskål) 57 cm
Ad. resembles *P. teira*, but without a vertical black blotch in front of A fin. **Ecology:** juveniles among mangroves and in inner sheltered lagoons. They closely resemble a floating leaf in appearance and behavior. Subadults move out to deeper lagoons and channels. Large adults solitary or in groups in open water over sandy areas of deep lagoon and seaward reefs to 30 m. Feeds on algae, invertebrates and small fishes. **Range:** Red Sea to Tuam., n. to s. Japan, s. to N. Cal.

3 **Pinnate spadefish** *Platax pinnatus* (Linnaeus) 45 cm
Ad. snout profile concave before eyes, ground color more silvery than brown. **Ecology:** juveniles among mangroves and on inner sheltered reefs. They resemble a toxic flatworm. Adults solitary near caves or ledges of seaward reef slopes to 20 m. **Range:** W. Pac. to Sol. Is., n. to Ryuk., s. to GBR; doubtfully in w. Indian Ocean.

4 **Hump-headed spadefish** *Platax batavianus* Cuvier 50 cm
Juvs. with vertical white lines in areas between bars; ad. elongate with hump on head. **Ecology:** juveniles in inshore waters; adults to deeper water. Strictly continetal reefs. **Range:** Malay Penin. to PNG, s. to GBR.

5 **Orbiculate spadefish** *Ephippus orbis* (Bloch) 25 cm
Ecology: shallow inshore areas over silty bottoms near reefs, 10 to 30 m. **Range:** Arab. G & E. Africa to Indonesia, n. to s. Japan, s. to n. Australia.

SICKLEFISHES (DREPANIDAE): similar to Ephippidae, but mouth protrudes downward.

6 **Sicklefish** *Drepane punctata* Linnaeus 50 cm
Similar to *D. longimanus* (E. Af.-PNG) which lacks spots, having vertical bars dorsally. **Ecology:** shallow inshore waters over silty bottoms near reefs. Eats small invertebrates. **Range:** Red Sea to PNG (Samoa?), n. to Ryuk., s. to nw. Aust.

MONOS (MONODACTYLIDAE): highly compressed silvery diamond-shaped fishes with a small terminal mouth and small scales. Commonly kept in freshwater aquaria.

7 **Mono** *Monodactylus argenteus* (Linnaeus) 22 cm
Ecology: primarily in brackish estuaries, occasionally in groups on silty coastal reefs. **Range:** Red Sea to Samoa, n. to Ryuk., s. to N. Cal.

SCATS (SCATOPHAGIDAE): highly compressed deep-bodied fishes with a small terminal mouth and small scales. Feed on algae and faeces. Commonly kept in freshwater aquaria.

8 **Scat** *Scatophagus argus* (Linnaeus) 22 cm
Ecology: primarily in brackish estuaries, occasionally in groups on silty coastal reefs. **Range:** Red Sea to Samoa, n. to Ryuk., s. to N. Cal.

STRIPEYS (SCORPIDIDAE): related to kyphosids but differ by possessing brushlike teeth.

9 **Stripey** *Microcanthus strigatus* (Cuvier) 16 cm
Ecology: coastal and lagoon reefs, in dense aggregations under ledges and in caves by day. **Range:** Antiequatorial: s. China to s. Japan, Hawaii, w. & e. Aust., s GBR to N. Cal.

ARCHERFISHES (TOXOTIDAE): small oblong fishes with elongate pointed mouths and single D fin set far back. Renowned for their ability to dislodge insects from overhanging vegetation with a jet of water squirted from the mouth. Popular in aquariums; best in brackish water.

10 **Banded archerfish** *Toxotes jaculator* Pallas 20 cm
Similar to *T. chatareus* (India to PNG) but us. with black blotches dorsally instead of bars. **Ecology:** surface waters of mangrove estuaries, and lower reaches of streams. On reefs only near overhanging vegetation. **Range:** India to Vanuatu, n. to Phil. & s. Ryuk., s. to n. Aust.; Palau.

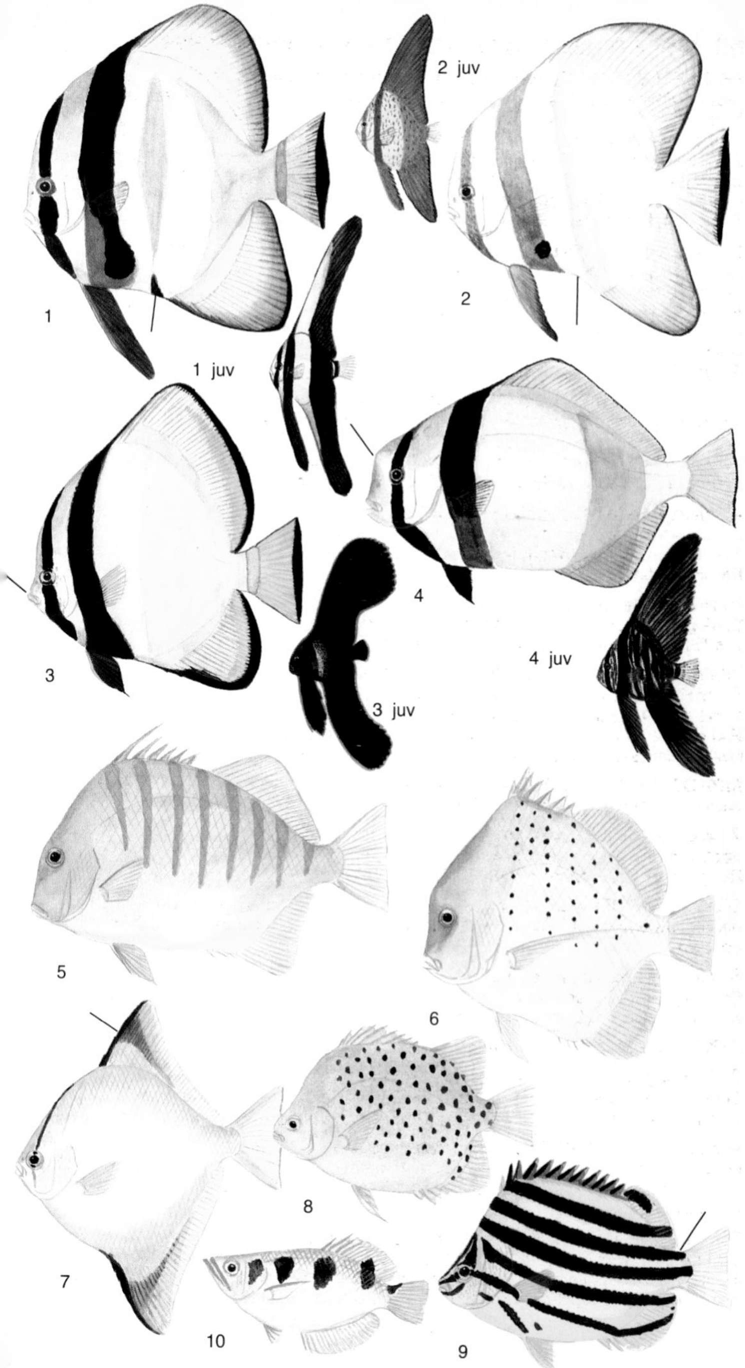
2 juv
1
2
1 juv
4
4 juv
3
3 juv
5
6
7
8
10
9

BUTTERFLYFISHES (CHAETODONTIDAE): small, colorfull, disclike fishes with small protractile mouths with small brush-like teeth, continuous D fins, body and head covered with small scales extending onto the median fins, and rounded to emarginate tails. Most species are diurnal and rest among corals or rocks during the night. Diet differs greatly among the species. Many feed on a variety of coelenterate polyps or tentacles, small invertebrates, fish eggs, and filamentous algae. Others are specialists with some feeding exclusively on coral polyps. Coral polyp feeders tend to be highly territorial around the areas of their food source. Most species patrol a home range. Some species are planktivores that aggregate in large schools high in the water and may range into deep water. Many species occur as heterosexual pairs that may remain together for years, if not life. Larval stage lengthy, from a few weeks to perhaps 2 months, and with distinctive late tholichthys stage in which head and front of body are covered in bony plates. Some of the planktivores and generalists do well in the aquarium, but most species are difficult to maintain, and obligate corallivores nearly impossible.

1 **Lined butterflyfish** *Chaetodon lineolatus* Cuvier 30 cm
Ecology: lagoon and seaward reefs, 2 to 171 m. Usually in pairs in areas of rich coral growth. Feeds primarily on coral polyps and small anemones, but also eats other invertebrates and algae. The largest species in genus. **Range:** R. Sea to Hawaiian, Marq. & Ducie Is., n. to s. Japan, s. to L. Howe Is.

2 **Spot-nape butterflyfish** *Chaetodon oxycephalus* Bleeker 25 cm
Similar to *C. lineolatus*, but bar through eye separate from bar on nape. **Ecology:** areas of rich coral growth of lagoon and seaward reefs, 10 to 40 m. Feeds primarily on corals and usually paired. **Range:** Maldives & Sri Lanka to PNG, n. to Phil. & Palau, s. to GBR.

3 **Saddleback butterflyfish** *Chaetodon falcula* Bloch 20 cm
Ecology: coral-rich areas of lagoon and seaward reefs, 1 to 15 m. Paired or in groups. **Range:** E. Africa s. to 27°S, e. to Nicobar & Andaman Is., n. to India, se. to Maurit.

4 **Pacific double-saddle butterflyfish** *Chaetodon ulietensis* Cuvier 15 cm
Ecology: coral-rich areas of lagoon and seaward reefs, 2 to 30 m. Common on lagoon reefs. Solitary, paired, or in groups. Feeds on wide variety of invertebrates and algae. **Range:** Cocos-Keeling Is.; Indonesia & Phil. to Tuam., n. to s. Japan, s. to L. Howe Is.

5 **Black-backed butterflyfish** *Chaetodon melannotus* Bloch 15 cm
Ecology: reef flats and lagoon and seaward reefs in areas of rich coral growth to 20 m. Solitary or paired, feeds primarily on soft and hard coral polyps. **Range:** R. Sea to Samoa, n. to s. Japan, s. to L. Howe Is.

6 **Spot-tail butterflyfish** *Chaetodon ocellicaudus* Cuvier 14 cm
Similar to *C. melannotus*, but with black spot on center of ea. side of tail base. **Ecology:** lagoon and seaward reefs in areas of rich coral growth, 3 to 15 m. Solitary or paired, feeds primarily on soft and hard coral polyps. **Range:** Malaysia to PNG, n. to Phil. & Palau; questionably reported from Zanzibar.

7 **Vagabond butterflyfish** *Chaetodon vagabundus* Linnaeus 23 cm
Ecology: reef flats and lagoon and seaward reefs to 30 m. Sometimes in turbid "dead" areas, but not common anywhere. Often paired and feeds primarily on anemones, coral polyps, polychaetes and algae. **Range:** s. R. Sea to Line & Tuam. Is., n. to s. Japan, s. to L. Howe & Austral Is.

8 **Threadfin butterflyfish** *Chaetodon auriga* Forsskål 23 cm
R. Sea popul. (8b) lacks an ocellus on soft D fin. **Ecology:** reef flats and lagoon and seaward reefs to 30 m in areas of mixed sand coral and rubble. Feeds by tearing pieces from polychaetes, anemones, coral polyps, and algae. Common throughout most of range. **Range:** R. Sea to Hawaiian, Marq. & Ducie Is., n. to s. Japan, s. to L. Howe & Rapa Is. Galapagos (rare).

9 **Indian vagabond butterflyfish** *Chaetodon decussatus* Cuvier 20 cm
Ecology: rubble and rocky to coral-rich areas, 1 to 30 m. More common in turbid areas. Often paired. **Range:** Sri Lanka to Bali, n. to Andaman Sea, s. to Maldives.

10 ·**Yellow-dotted butterflyfish** *Chaetodon selene* Bleeker 16 cm
Ecology: coastal reefs, 8 to 50 m. Primarily on rubble slopes below 20 m. Rare. **Range:** Indonesia to w. NG, n. to s. Japan.

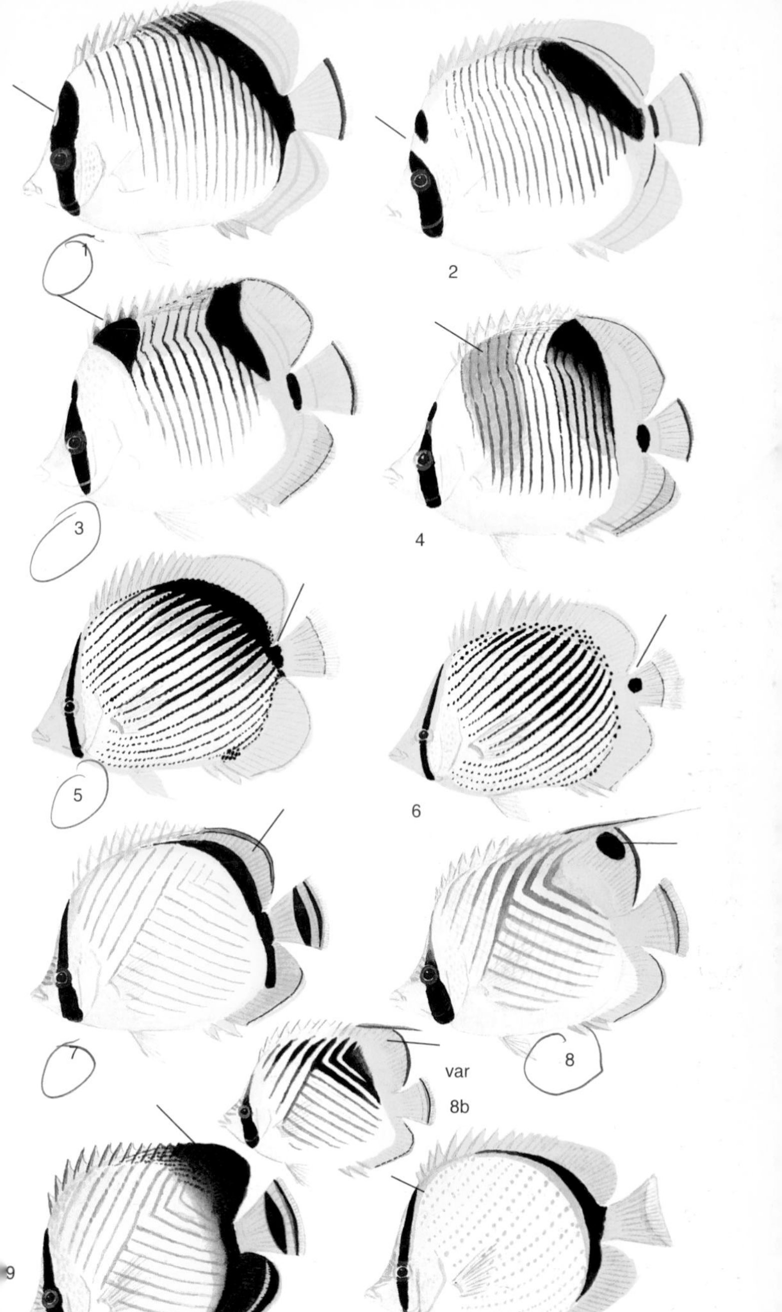
1
2
3
4
5
6
7
8
var
8b
9
10

1 **Teardrop butterflyfish** *Chaetodon unimaculatus* Bloch 20 cm
Ind. Oc. form is a deeper yellow than the Pacific form & lacks white around the dark spot. Large adults have deformed snout. **Ecology:** reef flats and lagoon and seaward reefs to 60 m. Feeds primarily on hard and soft corals as well as other invertebrates and algae. Common where ther are abundant soft leather corals (*Sarcophyton* and *Sinularia* spp.). **Range:** E. Africa to Hawaiian, Marq. & Ducie Is., n. to s. Japan, s. to L. Howe & Rapa Is.

2 **Bennett's butterflyfish** *Chaetodon bennetti* Cuvier 18 cm
Ecology: lagoon and seaward reefs in areas of rich coral growth, 5 to 30 m. Solitary or paired. Juveniles occasionally among shallow staghorn corals. Feeds primarily on coral polyps. **Range:** E. Africa to Pitcairn gp., n. to s. Japan, s. to L. Howe & Rapa Is.

3 **Zanzibar butterflyfish** *Chaetodon zanzibariensis* Playfair 12 cm
Ecology: coral-rich areas of lagoon and seaward reefs, particularly among staghorn *Acropora* thickets, 3 to 40 m. Usually solitary, occasionally in pairs or small groups. Feeds primarily on coral polyps. **Range:** E. Africa s. to 30°S, e. to Maurit. & Chagos Is.

4 **Ovalspot butterflyfish** *Chaetodon speculum* Cuvier 18 cm
Ecology: clearwater coral-rich areas of outer lagoon and seaward reefs, 3 to 30 m. Generally solitary and uncommon. Feeds on coral polyps and small invertebrates. **Range:** Christmas Is. to Tonga, n. to s. Japan, s. to L. Howe Is.

5 **Bluespot butterflyfish** *Chaetodon plebeius* Cuvier 15 cm
Juvs. & Indian Ocean popul. lacks the blue spot. **Ecology:** shallow coastal and lagoon and seaward reefs to 10 m. Will clean parasites from other fishes. Feeds primarily on coral polyps. Often paired. Common. **Range:** Maldives to Fiji, n. to s. Japan, s. to nw. Aust., GBR, L. Howe Is & N. Cal.

6 **Merten's butterflyfish** *Chaetodon mertensii* Cuvier 12.5 cm
Ecology: lagoon and seaward reefs, 10 to 120 m. Solitary or paired. Feeds on small benthic invertebrates and algae. Common. **Range:** Phil. to Tuam., n. to Ryuk., s. to L. Howe & Rapa Is.

7 **Yellowtail butterflyfish** *Chaetodon xanthurus* Bleeker 14 cm
Ecology: coral reefs below 15 m. Around staghorn corals in Ryukyus. **Range:** Indonesia & Phil. to Ryuk., juvs. to s. Japan.

8 **Crown butterflyfish** *Chaetodon paucifasciatus* Ahl 14 cm
Similar to *C. madagascariensis* (E. Africa to Cocos-Keeling & Christmas Is.) which replaces it in the Indian Ocean outside the R. Sea & G. Aden. **Ecology:** areas of coral and rubble, 4 to 30 m. In pairs or groups. Feeds on hard and soft coral polyps, algae, polychaetes, and crustaceans. **Range:** R. Sea & G. Aden.

9 **Klein's butterflyfish** *Chaetodon kleinii* Bloch 14 cm
Ecology: lagoon and seaward reefs, 4 to 61 m, usually below 10 m. Feeds primarily on soft corals, algae and zooplankton. Solitary, paired, or often in groups. **Range:** E. Africa to Hawaii & Samoa, n. to s. Japan, s. to L. Howe Is. Galapagos (rare).

10 **Yellowhead butterflyfish** *Chaetodon xanthocephalus* Bennett 20 cm
Ecology: algae-covered rocky and coral-rich areas, 1 to 25 m. Usually solitary, occasionally paired. Hybrids of this species and *C. ephippium* (pl. 63-1) have been found in the Similan Islands and Sri Lanka where the latter has not yet been reported. **Range:** E. Africa, Somalia to 30°S, e. to Maldives & Sri Lanka, se. to Maurit.

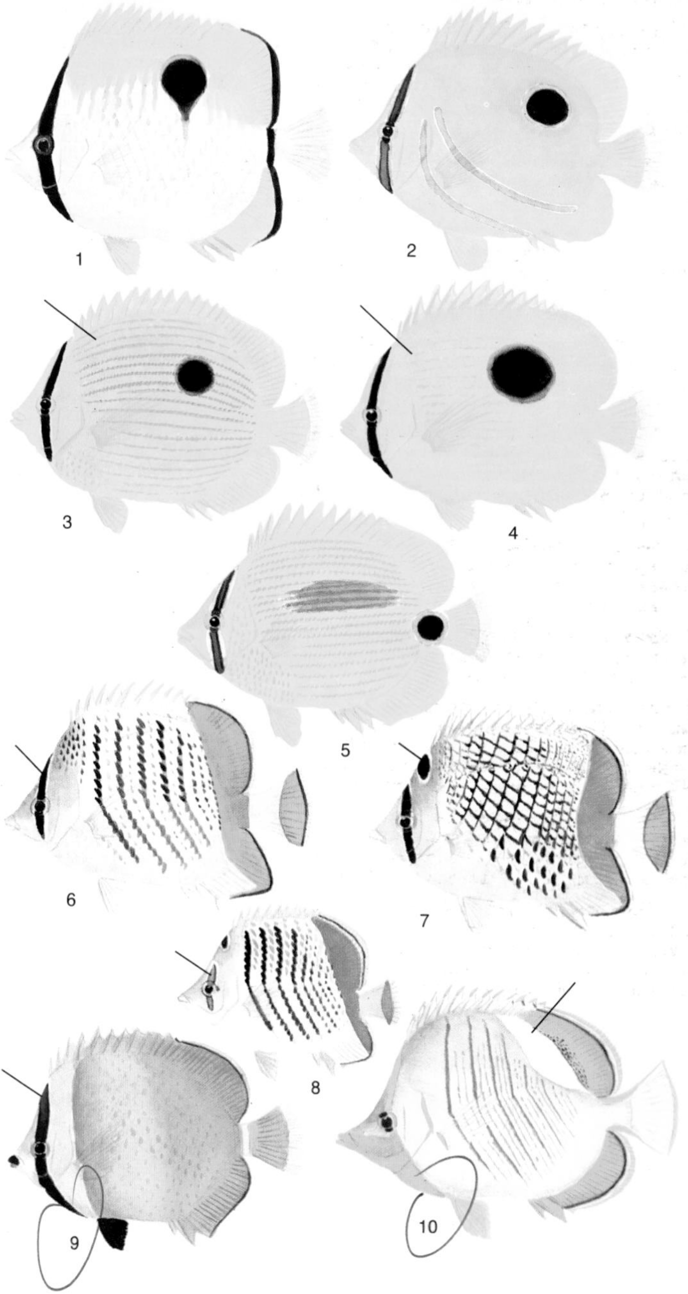
1
2
3
4
5
6
7
8
9
10

59 BUTTERFLYFISHES

1 **Racoon butterflyfish** *Chaetodon lunula* (Lacépède) 20 cm
Black spot on caudal peduncle. Juvs. with an ocellus on the soft D fin. **Ecology:** lagoon and seaward reefs, 0 to 30 m, primarily on exposed rocky slopes. Juveniles often among intertidal rocks. Often in inactive aggregations by day. Feeds at night as well as day on nudibranchs, worm tentacles, coral polyps and algae. **Range:** E. Africa to Hawaiian, Marq. & Ducie Is., n. to s. Japan, s. to L. Howe & Rapa Is. Galapagos (rare).

2 **Red Sea racoon butterflyfish** *Chaetodon fasciatus* Forsskål 22 cm
Short white band above eye. **Ecology:** coral-rich areas, 2 to >25 m. Solitary or paired. Feeds on coral polyps, algae, and small invertebrates. Common on reef flats. **Range:** R. Sea & G. Aden.

3 **Weibel's butterflyfish** *Chaetodon weibeli* Kaup 18 cm
Distinctive black band on caudal fin. **Ecology:** shallow rocky and coral reefs, 4 to 25 m. Solitary, paired or in groups. Feeds at least partially on algae. Rare in Ryukyus and s. Japan. **Range:** G. Thail. & S. China Sea to Ryuk. & s. Japan.

4 **Oriental butterflyfish** *Chaetodon auripes* Jordan & Snyder 20 cm
Juv. with ocellus on soft D fin. **Ecology:** rocky reefs with algae and corals. Solitary or in groups. Feeds on benthic invertebrates. Juveniles among shallow sheltered rocks. Can survive temp. as low as 10°C. **Range:** s. China Sea, s. China & Taiwan ne. to Tokyo & Izu Is., s. Japan.

5 **Fourspot butterflyfish** *Chaetodon quadrimaculatus* Gray 16 cm
During the night the two white spots disappear. **Ecology:** exposed seaward reefs, often in moderately surgy areas, 2 to 15 m. Solitary or paired. Feeds primarily on polyps of *Pocillopora* corals. **Range:** Taiwan to Hawaiian, Marq., & Pitcairn Is., n. to Ryuk. & Bonin Is., s. to Samoa & Austral Is.

6 **Latticed butterflyfish** *Chaetodon rafflesi* Bennett 15 cm
Juv. similar to adult. **Ecology:** areas of rich coral growth of reef flats, and lagoon and seaward reefs to 15 m. Feeds on sea anemones, polychaetes and polyps of soft and hard corals. Uncommon, but often in pairs. **Range:** Sri Lanka to Tuam., n. to s. Japan, s. to GBR.

7 **Dotted butterflyfish** *Chaetodon semeion* Bleeker 26 cm
Blue nape is distinctive. **Ecology:** areas of clear water and rich coral growth of lagoon and semi-protected seaward reefs, 2 to 25 m. Usually in pairs or small groups. Uncommon. Wary. **Range:** Maldives to Tuam., n. to Ryuk., s. to GBR.

8 **Golden butterflyfish** *Chaetodon semilarvatus* Cuvier 23 cm
Orange bars may be irregular. **Ecology:** coral-rich areas, 3 to 20 m. In pairs or aggregations. Often inactive under tabular *Acropora* corals. Common and approachable. **Range:** R. Sea & G. Aden.

9 **Panda butterflyfish** *Chaetodon adiergastos* Seale 16 cm
Juvs. show an ocellus in dorsal fin. **Ecology:** coral reefs, 3 to 25 m. In pairs or groups, usually near soft corals. **Range:** Indonesia, n. toTaiwan & Ryuk., s. to nw. Aust.

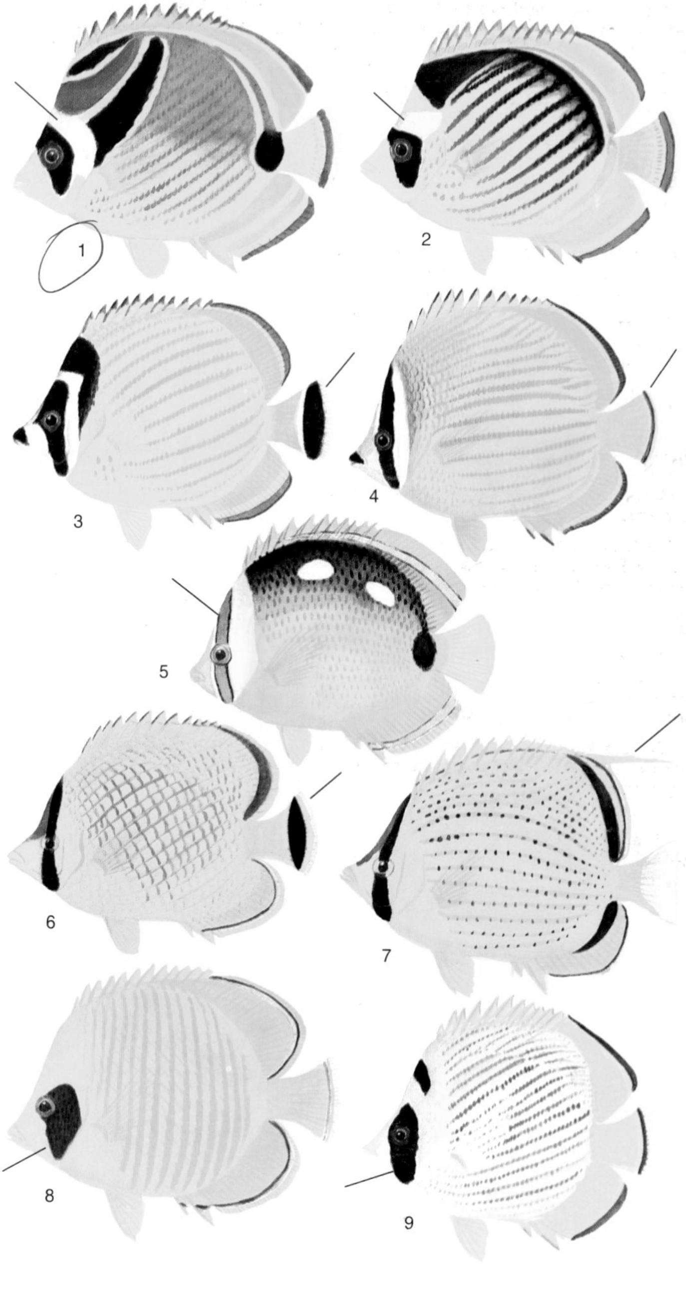
1
2
3
4
5
6
7
8
9

1 **Spot-banded butterflyfish** *Chaetodon punctatofasciatus* Cuvier 12 cm
Ecology: areas of clear water and rich coral growth of lagoon and seaward reefs, 1 to 45 m. Usually paired, feeds on benthic invertebrates, coral polyps, and algae. Occasionally hybridizes with *C. pelewensis* in the southern parts of its range. **Range:** Christmas Is. to Line Is., n. to Ryuk., s. to n. GBR.

2 **Dot-and-dash butterflyfish** *Chaetodon pelewensis* Kner 12.5 cm
Ecology: seaward reefs, 1 to 30 m. Usually paired. Feeds on coral polyps and benthic invertebrates. Abundant on Great Barrier Reef. **Range:** GBR to Tuam., n. to PNG, s. to L. Howe Is. & n. NSW.

3 **Spotted butterflyfish** *Chaetodon guttatissimus* Bennett 12 cm
Ecology: lagoon and seaward reefs, to 25 m. In pairs or small groups. Feeds on polychaetes, coral polyps, and algae. **Range:** E. Africa to 30°S, e. to Christmas Is., n. to Sri Lanka & w. Thail.

4 **Speckled butterflyfish** *Chaetodon citrinellus* Cuvier 13 cm
Ecology: moderately exposed areas of shallow reef flats and lagoon and seaward reefs to 36 m. Prefers open areas with scattered corals. Usually paired. Feeds on coral polyps, benthic invertebrates, and algae. **Range:** E. Africa to Hawaiian, Marq., & Tuam. Is., n. to s. Japan, s. to L. Howe Is.

5 **Lemon butterflyfish** *Chaetodon miliaris* Quoy & Gaimard 13 cm
May lose yellow colour in captivity. **Ecology:** reef flats and lagoon and seaward reefs to 250 m. Singly, in pairs or aggregations of up to several hundred. Feeds on the bottom on small invertebrates and fish eggs as well as high in the water on zooplankton. Among the most abundant of Hawaiian fishes, often swarming around divers. Juveniles appear from April to June. Rare at Johnston Atoll. **Range:** Hawaiian Is. and Johnston Atoll.

6 **Multiband butterflyfish** *Chaetodon multicinctus* Garrett 12 cm
Ecology: coral-rich areas of lagoon and seaward reefs, 5 to 30 m. In pairs or small groups. Feeds on coral polyps, polychaetes, small shrimps, and algae. Juveniles present from April to Sept. Very common. **Range:** Hawaiian & Johnston Is.

7 **African butterflyfish** *Chaetodon dolosus* Ahl 14 cm
Ecology: deep offshore reefs, 40 to 200. Over rocks and coral rubble. Usually paired, occasionally with *C. mitratus*. Common at Mauritius, otherwise uncommon to rare. **Range:** E. Africa from Somalia to Natal & Mauritius.

8 **Günther's butterflyfish** *Chaetodon guentheri* Ahl 18 cm
Ecology: seaward reefs in areas of rich coral growth, 40 m off GBR. Rare in tropics, more common at L. Howe Is. and NSW, from 5 to 40 m. **Range:** Antiequatorial: Taiwan & Ryuk. to s. Japan; PNG & GBR to L. Howe Is. & NSW.

9 **Gardiner's butterflyfish** *Chaetodon gardineri* Norman 17 cm
Ecology: deep reefs, below 25 m, rarely as shallow as 15 m. Paired or in groups. **Range:** G. Aden to G. Oman, e. to Sri Lanka.

10 **Somali butterflyfish** *Chaetodon leucopleura* Playfair 18 cm
Ecology: deep coral-rich reefs, often near base of slopes over coral rubble. 7 to 75 m. Usually solitary or in pairs over open bottoms. Often at the base of coral-rich slopes. Uncommon. **Range:** s. R. Sea (uncommon), Oman & E. Africa (common) s. to Zanzibar; Aldabra & Seychelles.

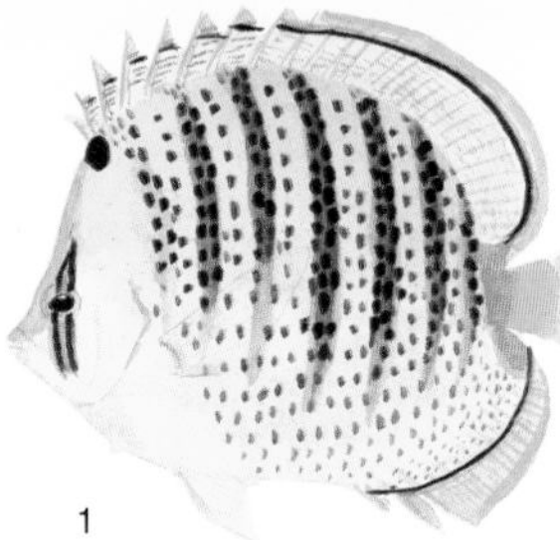
1

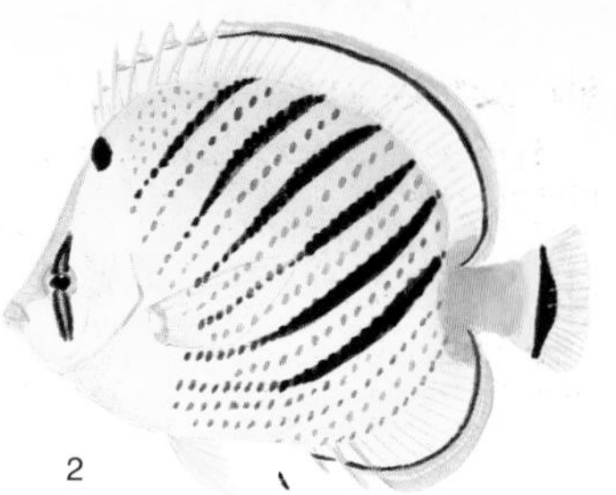
2

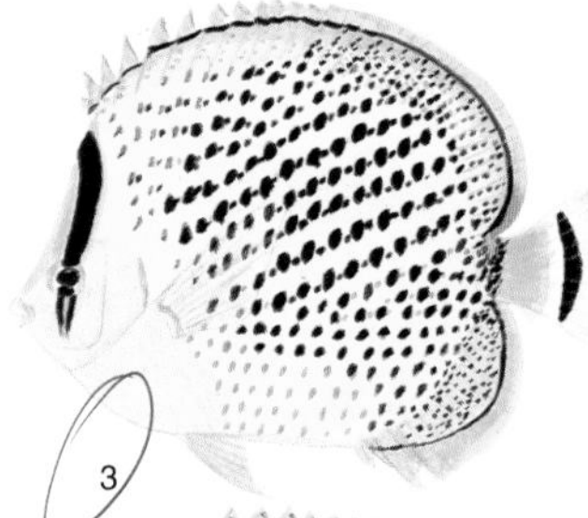
3

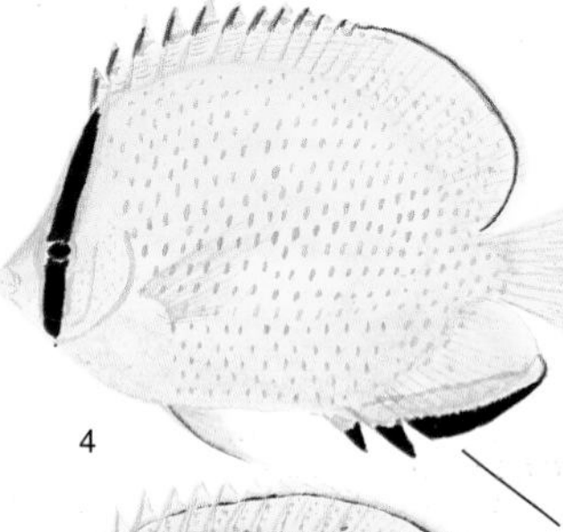
4

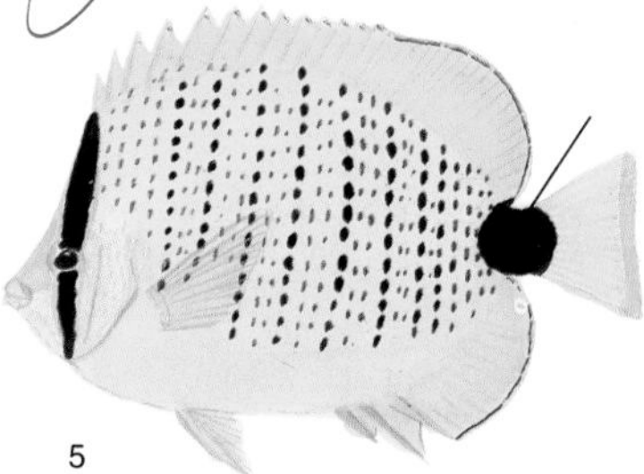
5

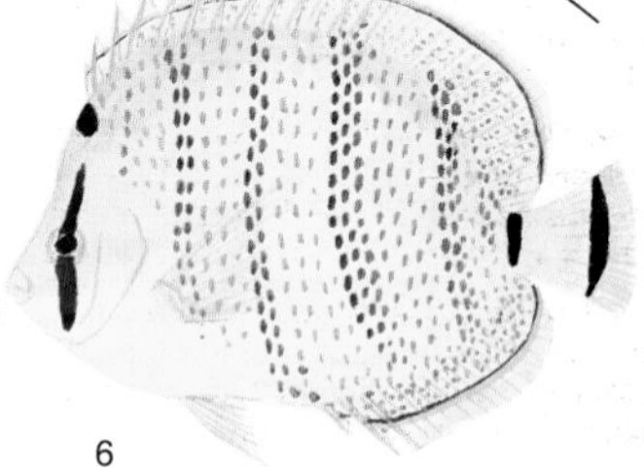
6

7

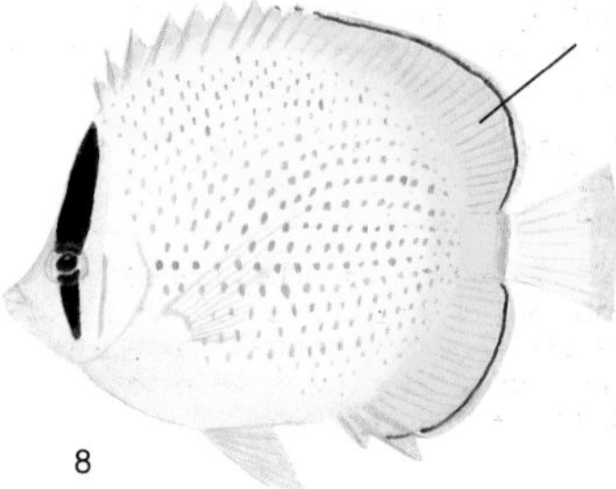
8

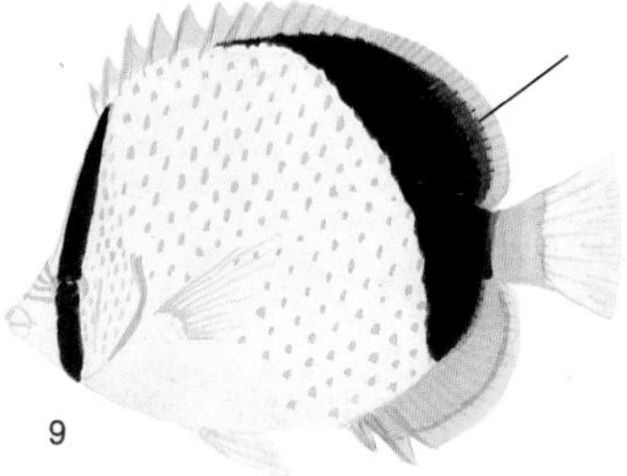
9

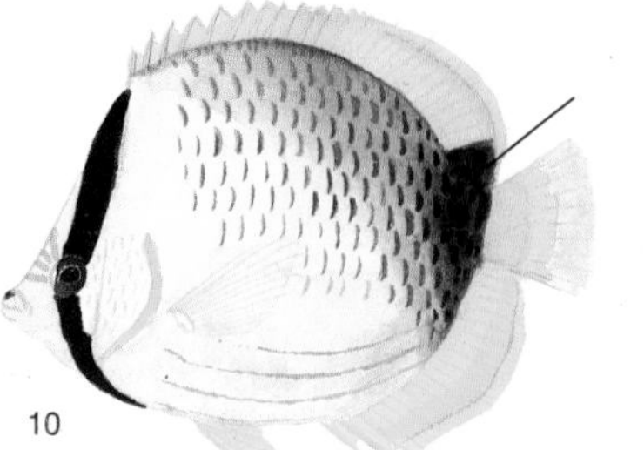
10

61 BUTTERFLYFISHES

1 **Collared butterflyfish** *Chaetodon collare* Bloch 16 cm
Ecology: rocky as well as coral-rich areas, 3 to 15 m. Often in pairs, sometimes in large aggregations. Feeds primarily on coral polyps. **Range:** se. Arab. Penin. & G. Oman, n. to Pakistan, e. to Bali, s. to Maldives & Christmas Is.

2 **Reticulated butterflyfish** *Chaetodon reticulatus* Cuvier 16 cm
Ecology: areas of clear water and rich coral growth of exposed lagoon and seaward reefs, 1 to >30 m. Feeds primarily on coral polyps. Usually paired. Easily approached. **Range:** Phil. & Taiwan to Hawaiian, Marq. & Ducie Is., n. to Ryuk. & Bonin Is., s. to N. Cal. & Austral Is.

3 **Eastern triangle butterflyfish** *Chaetodon baronessa* Cuvier 15 cm
Ecology: lagoon and seaward reefs only where there are tabular *Acropora* corals. In pairs and territorial. Feeds exclusively on the polyps of these corals. **Range:** Cocos-Keeling Is. & Indonesia to Fiji, n. to s. Japan, s. to N. Cal.

4 **Triangular butterflyfish** *Chaetodon triangulum* Cuvier 15 cm
Possibly a subspecies of *C. baronessa.* **Ecology:** lagoon and seaward reefs only where there are tabular *Acropora* corals. In pairs and territorial. Feeds exclusively on the polyps of these corals. **Range:** Madagascar to Java, n. to Andaman Sea.

5 **Black butterflyfish** *Chaetodon flavirostris* Günther 20 cm
Ecology: coral-rich to algae-covered rocky areas of lagoon and seaward reefs including lower estuarine areas, 2 to 20 m. Usually paired, but in groups at Lord Howe Island. Omnivorous. Feeds on algae, coral polyps, and small benthic invertebrates. **Range:** GBR to NSW, L. Howe Is.to N. Cal., Fiji, Samoa, Rapa & Pitcairn Is.

6 **Oman butterflyfish** *Chaetodon dialeucos* Salm & Mee 15 cm
Ecology: coral and rocky reefs, 1 to 10 m. Solitary, paired or in small aggregations. **Range:** Arabian Sea coast of Oman.

7 **Orange-face butterflyfish** *Chaetodon larvatus* Cuvier 12 cm
Ecology: coral reefs, 4 to 12 m only where there are tabular *Acropora* corals. In pairs and territorial. Seem to occupy a home-range. Feeds exclusively on the polyps of these corals. Common in central R. Sea and Yemen/Erithrea. **Range:** R. Sea, from Hurghada south & G. Aden.

8 **Wrought-iron butterflyfish** *Chaetodon daedalma* Jordan & Fowler 15 cm
Ecology: clear outer rocky reefs, 7 m. Adults in wide-ranging aggregations. Common only in the Bonin (Ogasawara) Is., rare elsewhere. **Range:** s. Japan, Ryuk., Izu & Bonin Is.

9 **White-face butterflyfish** *Chaetodon mesoleucos* Forsskål 13 cm
Ecology: coral-rich fringing reefs. Uncommon on algae-covered, rocky reefs. 1 to 20 m. Usually paired. Home-ranging. **Range:** R. Sea (common in Yemen and Erithrea) & G. Aden.

10 **Black-spotted butterflyfish** *Chaetodon nigropunctatus* Sauvage 13 cm
Ecology: coral reefs, 3 to 15 m. Solitary or paired. Home-ranging. Feeds at least partially on coral polyps. **Range:** Arab. G., G. Oman & se. Arab. Pen. s. to E. Africa.

11 **Tahiti butterflyfish** *Chaetodon trichrous* Günther 12 cm
Ecology: lagoon reefs, usually solitary or paired. Uncommon. **Range:** Society Is.

12 **Japanese butterflyfish** *Chaetodon nippon* Steindachner & Döderlein 15 cm
Ecology: shallow rocky reefs. Moderately common in Izu Is. Spawning occurs in groups at sunset when water temp. 23°C. **Range:** n. Phil. to s. Korea, s. Japan & Izu Is.

1
2
3
4
5
6
7
8
9
10
11
12

1 **Redfin butterflyfish** *Chaetodon trifasciatus* Park 15 cm
Longitudinal fins may be purplish. **Ecology:** coral-rich areas of shallow lagoon and semi-protected seaward reefs to 20 m. Feeds exclusively on coral polyps. Usually paired and home-ranging. **Range:** E. Africa to Hawaiian & Tuam. Is., n. to s. Japan, s. to L. Howe & Rapa Is.

2 **Exquisite butterflyfish** *Chaetodon austriacus* Rüppell 13 cm
Ecology: coral-rich areas, 1 to 15 m. Juveniles confined to single coral heads, adults home-ranging. Feeds exclusively on coral polyps. Common. **Range:** R. Sea.

3 **Arabian butterflyfish** *Chaetodon melapterus* Guichenot 12 cm
Ecology: coral-rich areas of shallow coastal reefs, 2 to 20 m. Occasionally in aggregations. Common in s. Arab. G., Oman & Yemen. Feeds exclusively on coral polyps. **Range:** s. R. Sea, Arab. G., G. Oman & w. Ind. Oc. to Seychelles & Réunion.

4 **Meyer's butterflyfish** *Chaetodon meyeri* Schneider 18 cm
Ecology: coral-rich areas of clear lagoon and seaward reefs, 2 to 25 m. Juveniles usually among branching corals, adults usually paired and home-ranging. Feeds exclusively on coral polyps. **Range:** E. Africa to Line Is., n. to Ryuk. & Marsh. Is., s. to GBR. Galapagos (rare).

5 **Ornate butterflyfish** *Chaetodon ornatissimus* Solander 20 cm
Ecology: areas of clear water and rich coral growth of lagoon and seaward reefs, 1 to 36 m. Juveniles solitary among branching corals, adults paired and home-ranging. Feeds exclusively on coral tissue. **Range:** Maldives to Hawaiian, Marq. & Ducie Is., n. to s. Japan, s. to L. Howe & Rapa Is.

6 **Indian butterflyfish** *Chaetodon mitratus* Günther 14 cm
Ground color of Mauritius popul. more yellowish than in other areas. **Ecology:** steep dropoffs with black coral or gorgonian growth, 30 to 68 m, rarely above 50 m. Often in pairs, occasionally in small groups. Feeds on a wide variety of benthic and planktonic invertebrates. **Range:** Amirante, Cosmoledo, Maurit., Chagos, Maldives, Cocos-Keeling & Christmas Is.

7 **Burgess' butterflyfish** *Chaetodon burgessi* Allen & Stark 14 cm
Ecology: precipitous dropoffs characterized by abundant gorgonian and black coral growth, 20 to 80 m. Sometimes in big caves. Apparent hybrids between this species and *C. flavocoronatus* and *C. tinkeri* have been recently found at Tarawa in the Gilbert Islands where the parent species remain unknown. **Range:** Indonesia (Sipadau, Flores, Sulawesi, Mollucas), Phil., Palau & Pohnpei.

8 **Tinker's butterflyfish** *Chaetodon tinkeri* Schultz 15 cm
Marshall Is. popul. with more extensive submarginal yellow area on D fin. **Ecology:** steep dropoffs with black coral or gorgonian growth, 27 to 135 m, rarely 40 m. Often in pairs. Feeds on a wide variety of benthic and planktonic invertebrates. **Range:** Marshall, Johnston & Hawaiian Is.

9 **Yellow-crowned butterflyfish** *Chaetodon flavocoronatus* Myers 12 cm
Ecology: precipitous dropoffs where there is an abundance of gorgonian and black coral growth below 36 m to 75 m. Solitary or paired. **Range:** Marianas.

10 **Marquesan butterflyfish** *Chaetodon declivis* Randall 12 cm
Two subspp.: *declivis* (Marq.) and *wilderi* (Line Is.), the latter with a more yellow eyeband and with more black pigment above the diagonal demarcation. **Ecology:** reported from 23 m over rock and sand bottom at base of vertical rock wall. **Range:** Marquesas & Line Is.

1
2
3
4
5
6
7
8
9
10

63 BUTTERFLYFISHES

1 **Saddled butterflyfish** *Chaetodon ephippium* Cuvier 23 cm
Ecology: lagoon and seaward reefs to 30 m, in areas of rich coral growth and clear water. Solitary, paired, or in small groups. Feeds on coral polyps, sponges, invertebrates, fish eggs, and algae. Hybrids of this species and *C. xanthocephalus* (pl. 58-10) have been found in the Similan Islands and Sri Lanka where this species has not yet been reported. **Range:** Thailand, Cocos-Keeling to Hawaiian, Marq. & Tuam. Is., n. to s. Japan, s. to NSW & Rapa Is.

2 **Bluestriped butterflyfish** *Chaetodon fremblii* Bennett 13 cm
Ecology: areas of rock or coral, 4 to 65 m. Juveniles on reef flats from April to Sept. Feeds on benthic invertebrates, coral polyps, and fish eggs. Solitary or in small groups. Common. **Range:** Hawaiian Is.

3 **Chevroned butterflyfish** *Chaetodon trifascialis* (Quoy & Gaimard) 18 cm
At night it displays two white lateral spots on a dark background. **Ecology:** shallow lagoon and semi-protected seaward reefs to 30 m. Closely associated with tabular and branching *Acropora* corals and feeds exclusively on their polyps and mucus. Solitary or paired and highly territorial. Common, but in Hawaii found only on the few central archipelago atolls where *Acropora* occurs. **Range:** R. Sea to Hawaiian & Society Is., n. to s. Japan, s. to L. Howe & Rapa Is.

4 **Blackburn's butterflyfish** *Chaetodon blackburni* Desjardins 13 cm
Ecology: outer reef slope with moderate coral growth, below 10 to 30 m. **Range:** E. Africa, Kenya to 33°S, Madagascar & Maurit.

5 **Asian butterflyfish** *Chaetodon argentatus* Smith & Radcliffe 20 cm
Ecology: rocky and coral reefs, 5 to 20 m. Often in pairs or groups. Rare in Philippines. **Range:** Phil. to s. China, Taiwan, Ryuk., s. Japan & Izu Is.

6 **West Australian butterflyfish** *Chaetodon assarius* Waite 13 cm
Ecology: seaward reefs, 1 to 40 m. In aggregations. Feeds on algae and zooplankton. Recently discovered in deep water in cold upwelling areas of Bali. **Range:** w. Australia: Shark Bay s. to Perth; strays to s. Indonesia.

7 **Rainford's butterflyfish** *Chaetodon rainfordi* McCulloch 15 cm
Ecology: coastal and offshore reefs, 1 to 15 m, frequently in areas of sparse coral growth. Usually paired. Feeds on algae and small benthic invertebrates. **Range:** GBR, PNG & L. Howe Is.

8 **Golden-striped butterflyfish** *Chaetodon aureofasciatus* Macleay 12.5 cm
Ecology: coastal and inner reefs, 5 to 15 m. Juveniles among branching corals. Solitary or paired. Feeds on coral polyps. **Range:** nw. Aust. to GBR, n. NSW & PNG.

9 **Eight-banded butterflyfish** *Chaetodon octofasciatus* Bloch 12 cm
Ground color variable: cream to yellow. **Ecology:** coral-rich areas of sheltered lagoon and inshore reefs, 3 to 20 m. Juveniles in groups among branching *Acropora* corals, adults paired. Feeds exclusively on coral polyps. **Range:** Maldives to PNG & Sol. Is., n. to s. China & Ryuk.

10 **Three-striped butterflyfish** *Chaetodon tricinctus* Waite 15 cm
Ecology: coral-rich areas of lagoon and seaward refs, 3 to 15 m. In pairs or aggregations. Abundant at Lord Howe Island. **Range:** L. Howe & Norfolk Is.

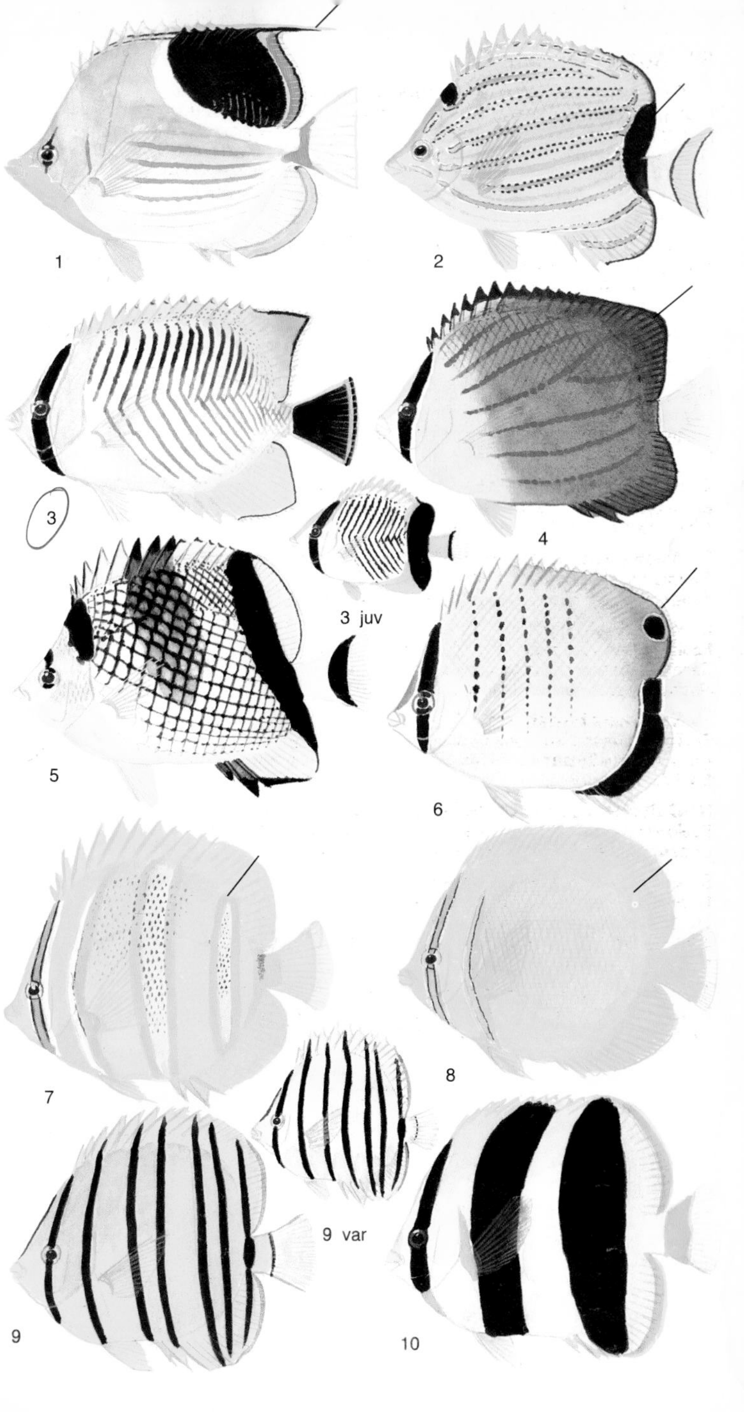
1
2
3
4
3 juv
5
6
7
8
9 var
9
10

1 **Doubledash butterflyfish** *Chaetodon marleyi* Regan 20 cm
Ecology: subtropical rocky and coral reefs to 120 m and disappears among weeds in estuaries. Probably just a subspecies of *C. hoefleri* from the e. Atlantic from Angola to Mauritania. **Range:** S. Africa, 27°S to Atlantic side of Cape of Good Hope.

2 **Brown-banded butterflyfish** *Chaetodon modestus* Temmink & Schlegel 17 cm
Ecology: deep rocky reefs, 120 to 190 m in tropics, but to 40 m in temperate Japan. Often in aggregations. **Range:** s. Arab. Pen. & India (as *C. jayakari*), Phil., s. Jap. to w. Aust. (as *C. modestus*) & Mariana & Hawaiian Is. (as *C. excelsa*).

3 **Smith's butterflyfish** *Chaetodon smithi* Randall 17 cm
Ecology: algal-covered rocky and coral reefs, 10 to 30 m. In large aggregations, common. **Range:** Rapa, Ilots de Bass & Pitcairn Is.

4 **Easter Island butterflyfish** *Chaetodon litus* Randall & Caldwell 15 cm
Ecology: algal covered rocky reefs, 1 to 25 m. Juveniles in tide pools, observed to pick bodies of other fishes for parasites. **Range:** Easter Is.

5 **Gueze's butterflyfish** *Chaetodon guezei* Maugé & Bauchot 11 cm
A closely related sp., *C. guyotensis*, occurs at a depth of ca. 320 m on the Palau -Kyushu Ridge (ca. 27°N). **Ecology:** deep reefs, below 80 m. Observations from a submersible indicates that it is common below 100 m in the Comores. **Range:** Comores, Réunion & Maurit.

6 **Ocellate coralfish** *Parachaetodon ocellatus* (Cuvier) 18 cm
Ecology: coastal and inner reefs on flat silty bottoms. Usually in pairs **Range:** India & Sri Lanka to Fiji, n. to Ryuk. & Bonin Is., s. to n. GBR, NSW.

7 **Lord Howe butterflyfish** *Amphichaetodon howensis* (Waite) 18 cm
Ecology: rocky reefs,usually with corals, 10 to 50 m. Feeds on small invertebrates. **Range:** s. Queensland to NSW, L. Howe, Norfolk & Kermadec Is., n. NZ.

8 **Black pyramid butterflyfish** *Hemitaurichthys zoster* (Bennett) 16 cm
Ecology: steep seaward and channel reef slopes, 1 to >35 m. In large aggregations above the upper edges of slopes or coral patches on sand. Feeds on zooplankton. **Range:** E. Africa to Andaman Sea, n. to India, s. to Maurit. & 28°S.

9 **Pyramid butterflyfish** *Hemitaurichthys polylepis* (Bleeker) 18 cm
Head occasionally yellow. **Ecology:** seaward reef slopes, usually along the upper edges of dropoffs, 3 to 40 m. In large aggregations high in water. Feeds on zooplankton. Common. **Range:** Cocos-Keeling to Hawaiian & Pitcairn Is., n. to s. Japan, s. to N. Cal.

10 **Thompson's butterflyfish** *Hemitaurichthys thompsoni* Fowler 18 cm
Ecology: steep outer reef slopes, 10 to 300 m, rarely in clear lagoons as shallow as 4 m (Johnston Is.). In aggregations in mid-water. Feeds on zooplankton. Uncommon and highly localised. **Range:** Mariana, Samoan, Johnston, Hawaiian, Line & Tuam. Is.

11 **Many-spined butterflyfish** *Hemitaurichthys multispinosus* Randall 20 cm
D 15-16 spines. Long body resembles a surgeonfish underwater. **Ecology:** seaward reefs to 45 m. **Range:** Pitcairn Is.

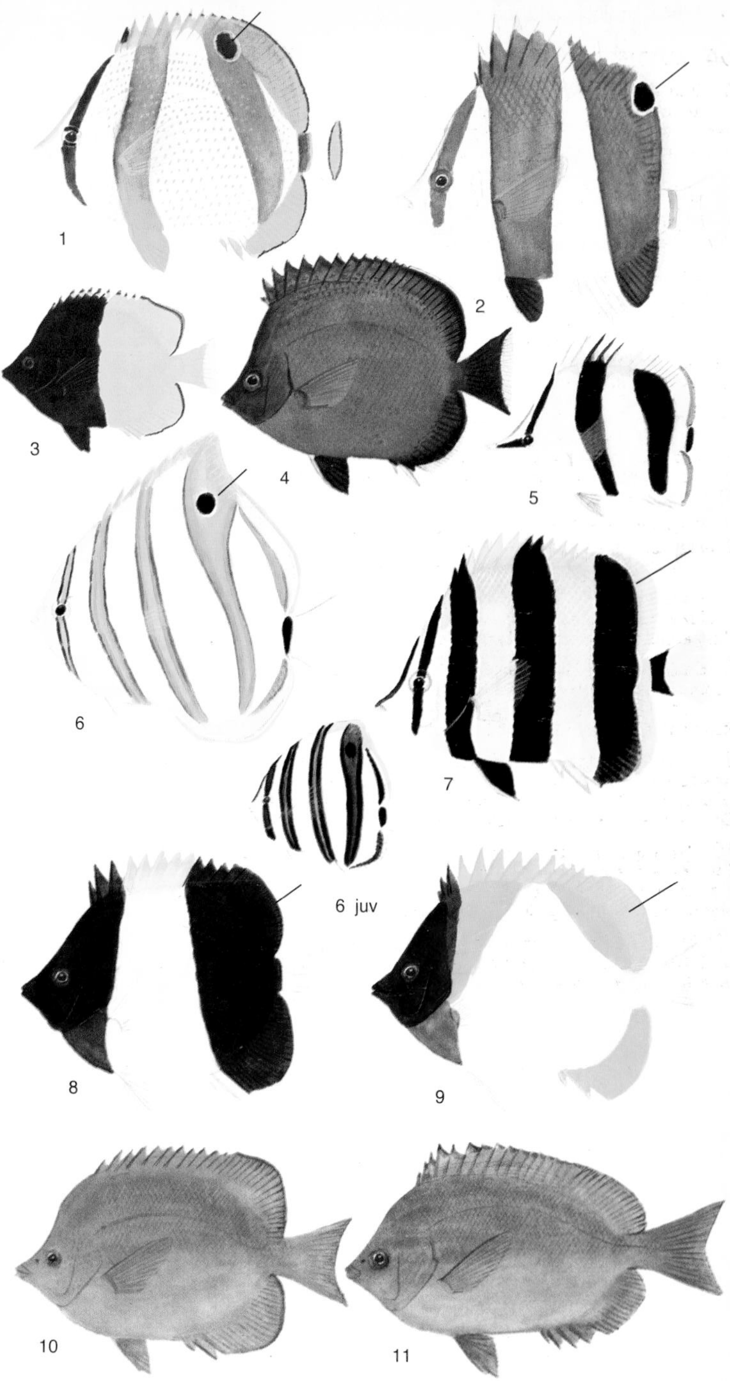
1
2
3
4
5
6
7
6 juv
8
9
10
11

1 **Long-nosed butterflyfish** *Forcipiger flavissimus* Jordan & McGregor 22 cm
Snout shorter, but gape of mouth larger than in *F. longirostris*; no dark phase. **Ecology:** exposed seawrd reefs, 2 to 114 m. Occasionally on lagoon reefs. Solitary or in small groups near ledges and caves. Feeds on benthic invertebrates, particularly pieces of soft parts snipped from sedentary forms. **Range:** R. Sea to c. America, n. to s. Japan & Hawaii, s. to L. Howe, Kermadec & Easter Is.

2 **Big long-nosed butterflyfish** *Forcipiger longirostris* (Broussonet) 22 cm
Snout longer, gape smaller than in *F. flavissimus*; has a rare reversible dark phase (b). **Ecology:** seaward reefs, 5 to >60 m, more often on deep dropoffs. Generally uncommon. Feeds on small invertebrates, taking whole organisms. **Range:** E. Africa to Hawaiian, Marq. & Pitcairn Is., n. to Bonin Is., s. to N. Cal. & Austral Is.

3 **Beaked or Copper-banded butterflyfish** *Chelmon rostratus* (Linnaeus) 20 cm
Ecology: estuaries, coastal reefs, and silty inner reefs, 1 to 25 m. Common. Solitary or in pairs. **Range:** Andaman Sea to PNG., n. to Ryuk., s. nw. Aust. & GBR.

4 **Margined coralfish** *Chelmon marginalis* Richardson 18 cm
Ecology: coastal reefs, 1 to 30 m. Solitary or paired. **Range:** s. to nw. Aust. (20°S) & GBR.

5 **Müller's coralfish** *Chelmon mülleri* (Klunzinger) 18 cm
Ecology: algal-covered and mud-bottomed areas of estuaries and coastal reefs. Feeds on small benthic invertebrates. **Range:** nw. Aust. n. of 14°S to Queensland only.

6 **Highfin coralfish** *Coradion altivelis* McCulloch 15 cm
Third bar of equal size. This genus with D and A fins somewhat elevated; this sp. lacks an ocellus on soft D fin, but subadult and juv. show an ocellus. **Ecology:** coastal reefs, often in silty water, 3 to 15 m. **Range:** Andaman Sea & Sumatra to PNG, n. to s. Japan, s. to nw. Aust. & GBR.

7 **Orange-banded coralfish** *Coradion chrysozonus* (Cuvier) 15 cm
Third bar wider and mostly orange-yellow rather than brown. **Ecology:** coastal reefs, in rocky or rubbly areas with poor to good coral growth, 3 to 60 m. Feeds on sponges. **Range:** Thail. & Malaysia to Sol. Is., n. to Ryuk. & Bonin Is., s. to nw. Aust. & GBR.

8 **Two-eyed coralfish** *Coradion melanopus* (Cuvier) 15 cm
Ocellus at A fin base; center rear double orange bar may be light or dusky. **Ecology:** coastal lagoon and seaward reefs, 12 to >30 m. More common along dropoffs in the vicinity of sponges on which they feed. Usually in pairs. **Range:** Bali to PNG, n. to Phil.

9 **Western talma** *Chelmonops curiosus* Kuiter 26 cm
Similar to *C. truncatus*, but bands dk. brown, not black; juvs. lose ocellus at ca. 7.5 cm. **Ecology:** vertical rock faces. Feeds on small worms and crustaceans. Common. **Range:** s. & w. Aust. from Adelaide to 26°S.

10 **Eastern talma** *Chelmonops truncatus* (Kner) 22 cm
Bands and centers of scales black and gray, resp.; juvs. retain ocellus to near adult size. *C. curiosus* similar but bands dark brown, not black & juvs. louse ocellus at ca. 7.5 cm. **Ecology:** vertical rock faces. Feeds on small worms and crustaceans. **Range:** NSW, Australia from 26° to 35°S.

1
2
2 var
3
4
5
6
7
8
9
10

1 **Longfin bannerfish** *Heniochus acuminatus* (Linnaeus) 25 cm
2nd black band ends behind tip of A fin; us. 11 D spines, rarely 12 as in *H. diphreutes.* Snout longer than H. diphreutes. **Ecology:** deep lagoon and seaward reefs, 2 to 75 m, usually below 15 m. Adults solitary or paired, rarely in large groups. Juveniles sometimes pick parasites from the bodies of other fishes, adults feed primarily on zooplankton, occasionally on benthic invertebrates. **Range:** s. Red Sea to Soc. Is., n. to Arab. G. & s. Japan, s. to L. Howe Is.

2 **Schooling bannerfish** *Heniochus diphreutes* (Jordan) 18 cm
2nd black band ends at tip of A fin; us. 12 D spines. Snout broader, breast more rounded. **Ecology:** seaward reefs, 5 to 210 m, usually below 15 m. Generally shallow only in cool upwelling areas in tropics. Juveniles in aggregations around isolated patch reefs, adults in large schools well above the bottom. Feeds primarily on zooplankton. Juveniles may act as cleaners. **Range:** R. Sea & S. Africa, to s. Japan, NSW & Kermadec Is.; Hawaiian Is.

3 **Red Sea bannerfish** *Heniochus intermedius* (Steindachner) 18 cm
1st black band reaches eye; interspaces diffused with yellow. **Ecology:** coral slopes, 3 to 50 m. Juveniles in large groups at base of reef, sometimes with *H. diphreutes.* Adults usually solitary or paired, occasionally in groups. Feeds on zooplankton and benthic invertebrates. **Range:** R. Sea.

4 **Pennant bannerfish** *Heniochus chrysostomus* (Cuvier) 18 cm
1st balck band reaches eye, 2nd begins in front of D fin pennant; soft D fin base black. **Ecology:** coral-rich areas of shallow lagoon and seaward reefs, reef flats to 40 m. Usually solitary, occasionally in small groups. Feeds on coral polyps. **Range:** w. India to Pitcairn gp., n. to s. Japan, s. to N. Cal.

5 **Masked bannerfish** *Heniochus monoceros* (Cuvier) 23 cm
Juvs. similar to juvs. of *H. singularis,* but middle black band behind D fin pennant. **Ecology:** coral-rich areas of lagoon and seaward reefs, 2 to 25 m, occasionally in areas of dead coral with plenty of holes. Feeds on benthic invertebrates, especially polychaetes. **Range:** E. Africa to Tuam., n. to s. Japan, s. to NSW, Norfolk Is. & Tonga.

6 **Singular bannerfish** *Heniochus singularis* (Smith & Radcliffe) 25 cm
Juvs. similar to juvs. of *H. monoceros,* but middle black band in front of D fin pennant; posterior light interspace with dark-centered scales. **Ecology:** lagoon and seaward reefs, 2 to 40 m, usually below 15 m. Solitary or paired. Feeds on coral polyps. Uncommon. **Range:** Maldives to Samoa, n. to s. Japan, s. to N. Cal.

7 **Phantom bannerfish** *Heniochus pleurotaenia* (Ahl) 17 cm
Incomplete white band between V and A fins.; adult with horn and knob on forehead. **Ecology:** coral-rich areas of lagoon and seaward reef, 1 to 25 m. In pairs or aggregations. **Range:** Maldives & Sri Lanka to Java, n. to Andaman Sea.

8 **Humphead bannerfish** *Heniochus varius* (Cuvier) 19 cm
No white band between V and A fins; adults with horn & knob on forehead. **Ecology:** coral-rich areas of deep lagoon and seaward reefs, 2 to 20 m. Solitary or in small groups. Feeds on corals and other invertebrates. **Range:** Indonesia & Phil. to Soc. Is., n. to s. Japan, s. to N. Cal.

1

2

3

4

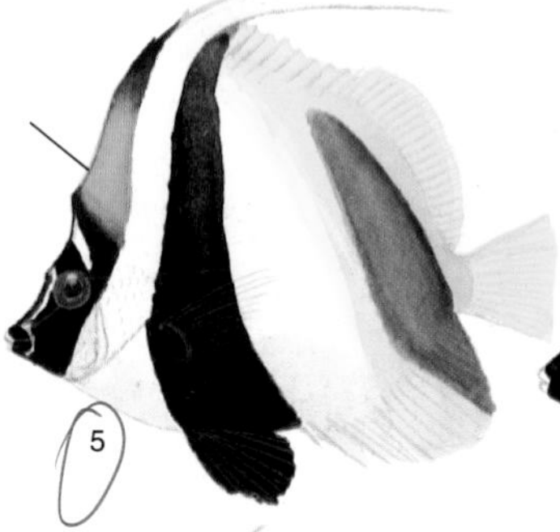

5

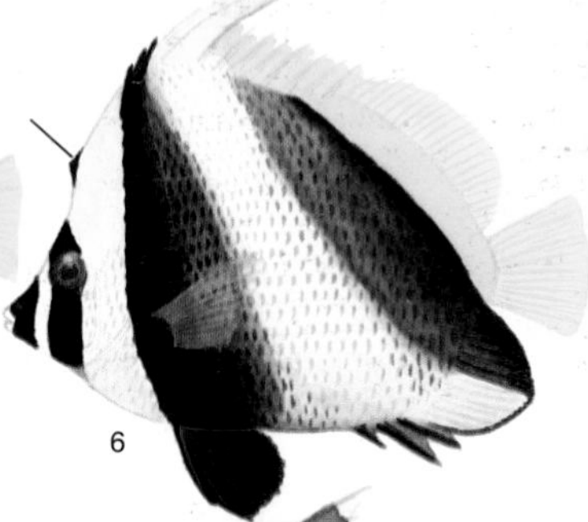

6

7

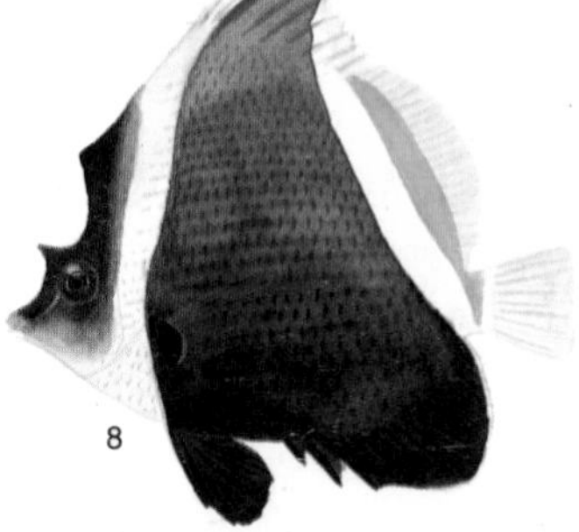

8

ANGELFISHES (POMACANTHIDAE): small to medium fishes with deep compressed bodies, small mouths with brush-like teeth, continuous D fins, small coarsely ctenoid scales extending onto the median fins, and a prominent spine at corner of preopercle as well as smaller spines on adjacent regions of the head. The head spines, more coarsely ctenoid scales and absense of a *tholichthys* larval stage set them apart from the superficially similar butterflyfishes. All species studied to date are protogynous hermaphrodites with haremic social systems. Males typically defend a territory containing 2 to 5 females. Territory size ranges from a few square meters (*Centropyge*) to over 1,000 square meters (large *Pomacanthus*). Spawn in pairs, usually at sunset. Eggs are pelagic and larval stage lasts 3 to 4 weeks. Species of *Centropyge* feed on filamentous algae, species of *Genicanthus* feed primarily on zooplankton supplemented by small benthic invertebrates and algae, and most other species feed primarily on sponges supplemented by soft-bodied invertebrates, fish eggs, and algae. Most *Centropyge, Genicanthus*, and a few species of *Pomacanthus* do well in aquariums, but others are difficult to maintain.

1 **Three-spot angelfish** *Apolemichthys trimaculatus* (Lacépède) 25 cm
Similar to *A. armitagei* (pl. 139-3) which has a black D fin. **Ecology:** clear lagoon and seaward reefs, 3 to 40 m. Prefers areas of high vertical relief and feeds primarily on sponges and tunicates. **Range:** E. Africa s. to 28°S, e. to Samoa, n. to s. Japan, s. to N. Cal.

2 **Bandit angelfish** *Holacanthus arcuatus* (Gray) 18 cm
Questionably placed in this genus; probably more closely related to *Apolemichthys*. **Ecology:** seaward reefs, 12 to 50 m. Sometimes among corals, but usually around ledges and caves below 25 m. Feeds primarily on sponges. **Range:** Hawaiian & Johnston Is.

3 **Indian yellowtail angelfish** *Apolemichthys xanthurus* (Bennett) 15 cm
Ecology: coral-rich areas, 5 to 20 m. Solitary or paired. **Range:** Mauritius, India, Maldives & Sri Lanka.

4 **Red Sea angelfish** *Apolemichthys xanthotis* (Fraser-Brunner) 15 cm
Ecology: semi-protected coral or rubble slopes with whip corals. Common offshore Is. of Yemen. Occasionally in loose colonies, 5 to 30 m. Often in pairs or small groups. Probably feeds on algae, sponges, and benthic invertebrates. **Range:** R. Sea; G. Aden & Oman.

5 **Griffis angelfish** *Apolemichthys griffisi* (Carlson & Taylor) 25 cm
Ecology: steep seaward reef slopes, 10 to 60 m, usually below 40 m. Solitary. Uncommon to rare. **Range:** e. Caroline, Gilbert, Nauru & Line Is.; ne. Indonesia & PNG.

6 **Tiger angelfish** *Apolemichthys kingi* Heemstra 20 cm
Ecology: seaward reefs at about 23 to 30 m. Uncommon. **Range:** S. Africa, on reefs near Durban.

7 **Golden spotted angelfish** *Apolemichthys xanthopunctatus* Burgess 25 cm
Ecology: lagoon and seaward slopes below 3 m. Solitary or in small groups. **Range:** Kapingamarangi (e. Caroline Is.), Nauru, Tarawa (Gilbert Is.) & Line Is.

8 **Réunion angelfish** *Apolemichthys guezei* (Randall & Maugé) 15 cm
Ecology: deep seaward reefs, 60 to 80 m. **Range:** Réunion, but probably also at nearby islands.

9 **Purple-mask angelfish** *Centropyge venustus* Yasuda & Tominaga 11 cm
Hybridizes with *C. multifasciatus*. **Ecology:** steep outer reef slopes, 15 to 35 m. Secretive, usually solitary. Common at Kerama Island in the Ryukyus. **Range:** n. Luzon to Taiwan, Ryuk. & Izu Is.

10 **Peppermint angelfish** *Centropyge boylei* Pyle & Randall 7 cm
Ecology: among rubble of steep seaward reefs, 56 to 120 m. **Range:** Rarotonga, Cook Is.

11 **Multibarred angelfish** *Centropyge multifasciatus* (Smith & Radcliffe) 11 cm
Hybridizes with *C. venustus*. **Ecology:** common in caves and crevices of steep seaward reefs, 7 to 70 m, usually below 20 m. Occasionally on clear lagoon reefs. Secretive, always near escape hole. **Range:** Cocos-Keeling Is. to Soc. Is., n. to Ryuk., s. to GBR.

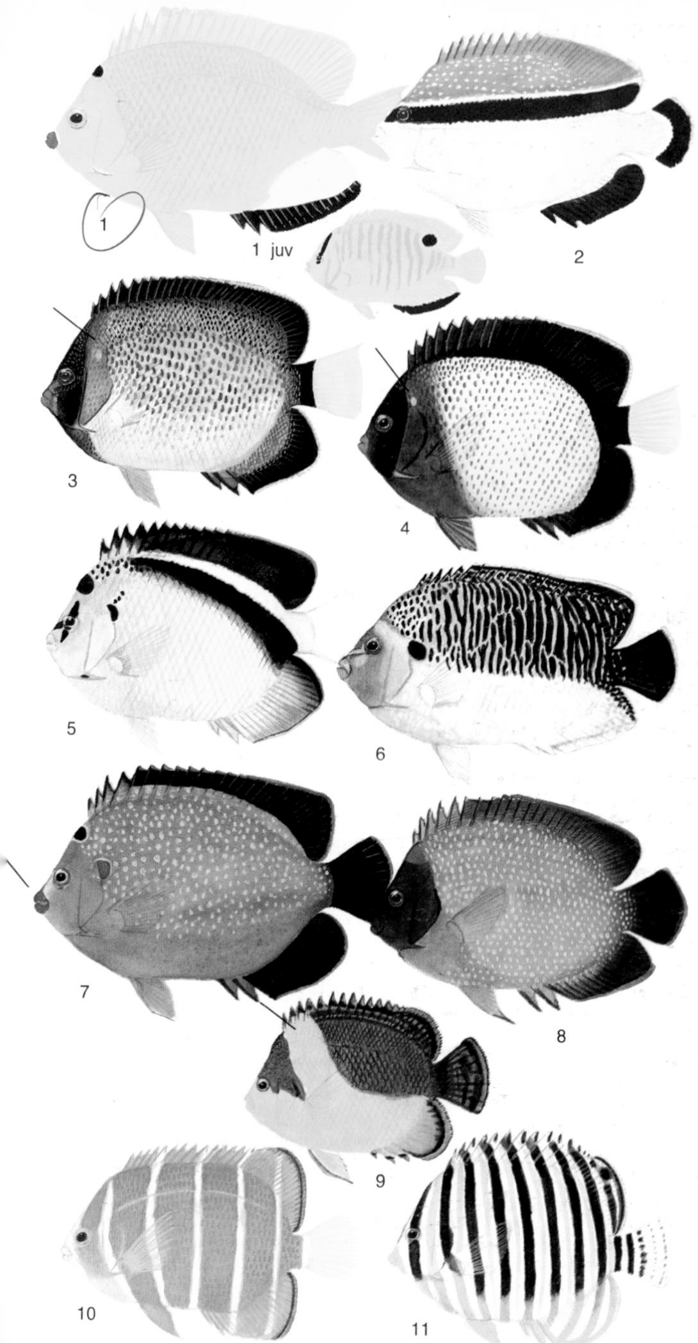
1
1 juv
2
3
4
5
6
7
8
9
10
11

1 **Lemonpeel angelfish** *Centropyge flavissimus* (Cuvier) 14 cm
Species of *Centropyge* typically occur in harems of 1 ♂ and several ♀. They feed primarily on filamentous algae. Juvs. of this sp. with blue-edged black ocellus in center of ea. side. Cocos-Keeling & Christmas Is. popul. lacks blue ring around eye, but has blue iris and black mark behind operculum. The ground colour is orange. Closely related to & hybridizes with *C. vroliki* (pl. 70-1) and *C. eibli* (pl. 70-2). These 3 spp. mimicked by juvs. of sympatric popul. of *Acanthurus pyroferus* (pl. 126-1) or *A. tristis* (pl. 126-2). **Ecology:** coral-rich areas of shallow lagoon and exposed seaward reefs from lower surge zone to 30 m. Common at most oceanic islands except the Carolines. Juveniles secretive. **Range:** Cocos-Keeling & Christmas Is., Ryuk. & Marianas to Marq. & Ducie Is., straying to Easter Is., s. to N. Cal. & Rapa; absent from most of Indo-Australian region.

2 **Herald's angelfish** *Centropyge heraldi* Woods & Schultz 10 cm
Lacks blue trim of *C. flavissimus*; ♂ with angular D & A fins and dusky patch behind eye. **Ecology:** moderately common on steep seaward slopes, 15 to 40 m. Occasionally on clear lagoon reefs as shallow as 5 m. **Range:** Taiwan to Tuam., n. to s. Japan, s. to GBR.

3 **Bicolor angelfish** *Centropyge bicolor* (Bloch) 15 cm
Ecology: lagoon and semi-protected seaward slopes, 3 to 25 m. Among small patches of rubble or rocks with holes. Never far from shelter. Common in many areas. **Range:** Malaysia to Phoenix Is. and Samoa, n. to s. Japan, s. to nw. Aust. & N. Cal.

4 **Cocos pymy angelfish** *Centropyge joculator* Smith-Vaniz & Randall 9 cm
Ecology: coral and rubble areas of steep outer reef slopes, 15 to 70 m. Occasionally above slope in 8 m. Solitary or in small groups. Abundant at Christmas Is. **Range:** Cocos-Keeling & Christmas Is. only.

5 **Hotumatua's angelfish** *Centropyge hotumatua* Randall & Caldwell 8 cm
Ecology: coral rock with numerous crevices, 14 to 45 m. Moderately common. **Range:** Rapa, Austral, Pitcairn & Easter Is.

6 **African pygmy angelfish** *Centropyge acanthops* (Norman) 7 cm
Closely related to *C. flavicauda* (pl. 69-5) & *C. fisheri* (pl. 69-7). **Ecology:** areas of coral or rubble, 6 to 40 m. Often in small groups, sometimes among the branches of corals. Common off E. Africa. **Range:** E. Africa, Somalia to 34°S, e. to Maurit., Seychelles & Chagos Is.

7 **Colin's angelfish** *Centropyge colini* Smith-Vaniz & Randall 9 cm
Ecology: steep outer reef slopes, 24 to 75 m. In or near crevices in large caves. Secretive. **Range:** Cocos-Keeling Is., Palau, Guam, Marshalls & Fiji.

8 **Blue Mauritius angelfish** *Centropyge debelius* Pyle 9 cm
Ecology: steep rocky outer reef slopes, 46 to 90 m. Uncommon. **Range:** Mauritius & Réunion.

9 **Multicolor angelfish** *Centropyge multicolor* Randall & Wass 6 cm
Ecology: steep outer reef slopes, 20 to 90 m. Secretive, typically among rubble. **Range:** Palau, e. Caroline, Marshall, Gilbert, Fiji, Cook & Society Is.; strays to Hawaii.

10 **Nahacky's angelfish** *Centropyge nahackyi* Kosaki 9 cm
Ecology: seaward slopes, 25 to 75 m. In groups on barren bottom with rubble. **Range:** Johnston Atoll; strays to Hawaiian Is.

11 **Flame angelfish** *Centropyge loriculus* (Günther) 10 cm
Ecology: coral-rich areas of clear lagoon and seaward reefs from lower surge zone to 57 m. Somewhat secretive, stays close to shelter. Common from Palau to e. Carolines and s. Marshalls, and at Johnston Island. Rare in Marianas and Hawaii. **Range:** Palau to Hawaiian, Marq. & Ducie Is., sw. to GBR & Samoa.

12 **Golden angelfish** *Centropyge aurantius* Randall & Wass 10 cm
Ecology: among coral and sponges, 3 to 15 m. Extremely secretive. **Range:** e. Indonesia, PNG, GBR & Samoa.

1
juv
2
3
4
5
6
7
8
9
10
11
12

1 **Keyhole angelfish** *Centropyge tibicen* (Cuvier) 19 cm
Ecology: areas of mixed coral and rubble of lagoon and seaward reefs, 4 to 30 m. Uncommon at oceanic Islands. **Range:** Christmas Is. to Vanuatu & N. Cal., n. to s. Japan, s. to L. Howe Is.

2 **Midnight angelfish** *Centropyge nox* (Bleeker) 9 cm
Ecology: among rubble in coral-rich areas of clear lagoon & shelteR. Seaward reefs, 5 to 70 m. Common in some areas, but not often noticed. **Range:** Indonesia to N. Cal., n. to Ryuk., Palau & Kapingamarangi.

3 **Many-spined angelfish** *Centropyge multispinis* (Playfair) 9 cm
Ecology: coral-rich and rubbly areas of lagoon and seaward reefs, 1 to 30 m. Common in the Maldive and Chagos Islands. More approachable than most species in the genus. **Range:** Red Sea & E. Africa s. to 27.5°S, n. to Sri Lanka, e. to w. Thail.

4 **Yellowfin angelfish** *Centropyge flavipectoralis* Randall & Klausewitz 10 cm
Very similar to *C. multispinis* which has dusky P. fins. **Ecology:** rubbly areas, 3 to 12 m. **Range:** Sri Lanka & Maldives.

5 **White-tail angelfish** *Centropyge flavicauda* Fraser-Brunner 8 cm
Ground color variable, greenish to blueish brown; ♂ with blue trim on fins. Closley related to *C. acanthops* (pl. 68-6) and *C. fisheri*. **Ecology:** rubble bottoms of channel or seaward reef slopes, 10 to 60 m. Sometimes in small groups and close to the bottom. Secretive. Superficially resembles a damselfish. **Range:** E. Africa to Tuam., n. to s. Japan, s. to GBR.

6 **Black-spot angelfish** *Centropyge nigriocellus* Woods & Schultz 6 cm
Ecology: coral rubble of clear lagoon and exposed seaward reefs, 4 to 15 m. Quite secretive, never seen alive without the use of chemicals to flush it from hiding. **Range:** Mariana, Admiralty, Samoan, Society, Line & Johnston Is.

7 **Two-spined or dusky angelfish** *Centropyge bispinosus* (Günther) 10 cm
Ground color variable, with blue covering most of sides to just the edges; dark lines occas. reduced to a small patch above P fin base, or broken into spots. **Ecology:** coral-rich areas of lagoon and seaward reefs, 5 to 45 m. Common in Seychelles, Indonesia, Philippines and Marshall Islands. At Guam where this species is rare it has been known to spawn with the common *C. shepardi*. **Range:** E. Africa to Tuam., n. to Izu Is., s. to L. Howe Is.

8 **Fisher's angelfish** *Centropyge fisheri* (Snyder) 6 cm
Ecology: among rubble of seaward reefs below 10 m. Common in below 30 m. **Range:** Hawaiian Is.; rarely at Johnston Atoll.

9 **Rusty angelfish** *Centropyge ferrugatus* Randall & Burgess 10 cm
Resembles *C. shepardi*, but dark markings on sides consistently broken into spots. ♂ with blue trim. **Ecology:** seaward reefs, 10 to 30 m. **Range:** Taiwan, Ryuk. & Bonin Is. to s. Japan; strays to Izu Is.

10 **Shepard's angelfish** *Centropyge shepardi* Randall & Yasuda 9 cm
Ground color variable, reddish-orange to light orange; extent of dark markings ranging from a few behind P fin to entire upper 2/3rds of sides. ♂ with blue trim on fins. **Ecology:** exposed seaward reefs, 18 to 56 m. Prefers areas of mixed dead and living coral with numerous holes for shelter. Common. Rarely in coral-rich areas of lagoon reefs in as little as 1 m. **Range:** Mariana & Bonin Is., straying to Izu Is.

11 **Potter's angelfish** *Centropyge potteri* Jordan & Metz 10 cm
Ecology: rock, coral, or rubble areas of seaward reefs below 10 m. Juveniles occasionally in 5 m. Abundant. **Range:** Hawaiian Is.; rarely at Johnston Atoll.

12 **Japanese pygmy angelfish** *Centropyge interruptus* (Tanaka) 15 cm
♂ with heavy blue lines on opercular region; black bars on rear blue margins of D & A fins. **Ecology:** rocky and coral reefs, 12 to 60 m. **Range:** Izu Penin. s. to Izu & Bonin Is.; far nw. Hawaiian Is. (Midway & Kure).

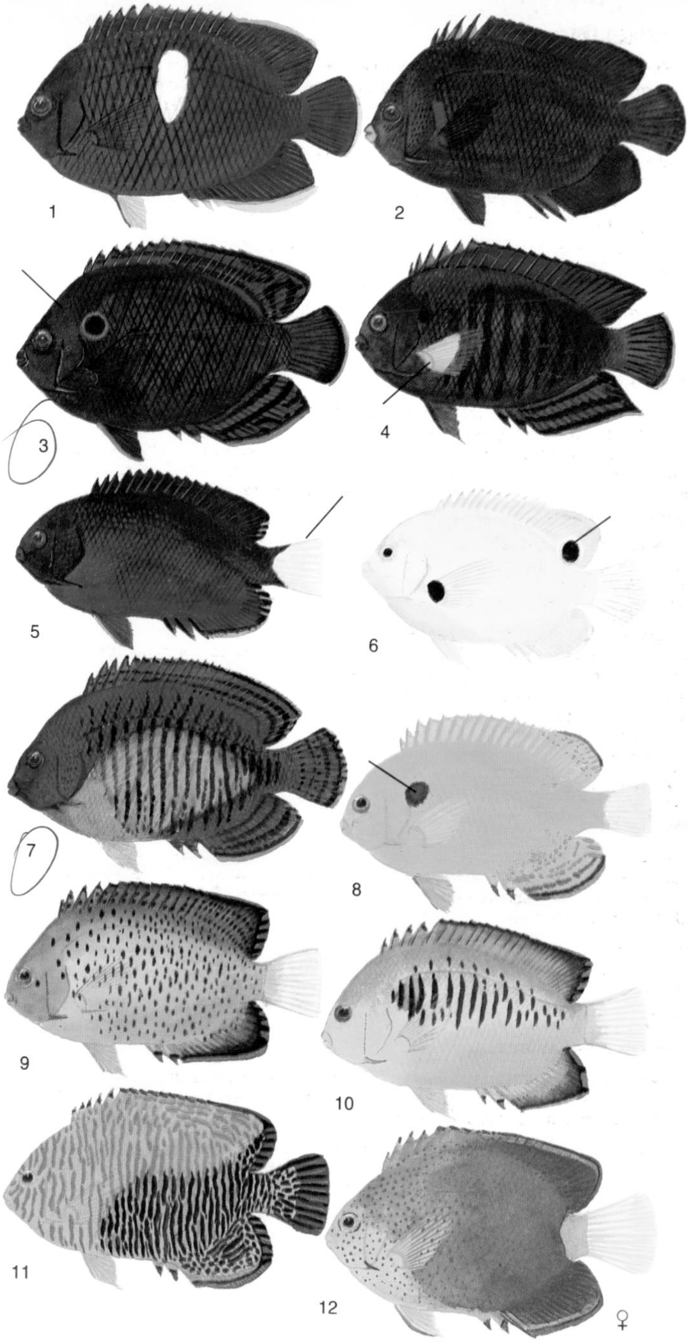
1
2
3
4
5
6
7
8
9
10
11
12
♀

1 **Pearlscale angelfish** *Centropyge vrolikii* (Bleeker) 9 cm
Ecology: coral-rich areas of lagoon and seaward reefs, 3 to 25 m. Common from Palau to e. Carolines. Hybridizes with *C. flavissimus* (pl. 68-1) and *C. eibli.* Mimicked by juvenile *Acanthurus pyroferus* (pl. 126-1). **Range:** Sumatra, Christmas Is., Marsh. Is. & Vanuatu, n. to s. Japan, s. to L. Howe Is.

2 **Eibl's angelfish** *Centropyge eibli* Klausewitz 15 cm
Ecology: coral-rich and rocky areas of seaward reefs, 1 to 30 m. Mimicked by juvenile *Acanthurus tristis* (pl. 126-2). *Hybridizes* with *C. flavissimus* (pl. 68-1) at Christmas and Cocos-Keeling Islands. **Range:** Sri Lanka to e. Indonesia (Flores), n. to Andaman Sea, s. to nw. Australia.

3 **Vermiculated angelfish** *Chaetodontoplus mesoleucus* (Bloch) 18 cm
Spp. of *Chaetodontoplus* have an incomplete lateral line and small scales (LL >85). They inhabit continental shelf reefs and are generally absent from oceanic islands. Individuals in parts of Indonesia have a white tail. **Ecology:** coral-rich areas of protected reefs, 1 to 20 m. Feeds on sponges, tunicates, and filamentous algae. Difficult to approach. **Range:** Malaysia to Sol. Is., n. to Ryuk., s. to Indonesia & PNG.

4 **Black velvet angelfish** *Chaetodontoplus melanosoma* (Bleeker) 20 cm
Specimens from s. Japan with yellow tail. **Ecology:** coastal reefs and dropoffs over coral rubble. Uncommon and solitary. **Range:** Sumatra to PNG, n. to s. Japan.

5 **Scribbled angelfish** *Chaetodontoplus duboulayi* (Günther) 28 cm
Ecology: shallow coastal and continental shelf reefs, on open flat bottoms with rock, coral, sponge, or seawhip outcrops to 20 m. May be found in small groups. **Range:** n. Australia to Aru Is. (Indonesia) & s. PNG.

6 **Blue-spotted angelfish** *Chaetodontoplus caeruleopunctatus* Yasuda & Tominaga 14 cm
Ecology: unknown, probably coastal reefs. **Range:** Cebu, probably throughout the central Phil.

7 **Blue-striped angelfish** *Chaetodontoplus septentrionalis* (Schlegel) 22 cm
Similar to *C. chrysocephalus* which may be the male of this sp. Juv. similar to *C. melanosoma* but without dark band in caudal fin. **Ecology:** coastal rocky and coral reefs, 5 to 15 m. **Range:** s. China, Taiwan, Ryuk. & s. Japan.

8 **Queensland yellowtail angelfish** *Chaetodontoplus meredithi* Kuiter 25 cm
Juv. 12 cm identical to juv. of *C. personifer*; adults similar but with entirely yellow tail. **Ecology:** coastal reefs and open bottoms with rock, coral, sponge or seawhip outcrops to >35 m. Juveniles in shallow coastal and inner reef areas, often among sponges under jetties. Adults often in pairs, generally in deeper water. **Range:** Queensland s. to NSW (Sydney) & L. Howe Is.

9 **Yellowtail angelfish** *Chaetodontoplus personifer* (McCulloch) 35 cm
Juv. 12 cm identical to juv. of *C. meredithi*; adults similar but with middle or front 2/3 of tail black. **Ecology:** coastal reefs and adjacent open bottoms with rock, coral, sponge or seawhip outcrops. Large adults, probably males, become slightly elongate. **Range:** nw. Australia.

10 **Orange-faced angelfish** *Chaetodontoplus chrysocephalus* Bleeker 22 cm
May possibly be the male of *C. septentrionalis.* **Ecology:** deep rocky reefs. Rare. **Range:** Indonesia (Java) to s. Japan.

11 **Conspicuous angelfish** *Chaetodontoplus conspicillatus* (Waite) 10 cm
Ecology: seaward reefs, 20 to 40 m. Juveniles as shallow as 1 m on lagoon reefs. **Range:** s. GBR, N. Cal., Norfolk & L. Howe Is.

1
2
3
4
4 juv
5
6
7
8
9
10
11

71 ANGELFISHES

1 **Black-spot angelfish** *Genicanthus melanospilos* (Bleeker) 18 cm
Species of *Genicanthus* feed primarily on zooplankton supplemented by small benthic invertebrates and algae. **Ecology:** steep seaward slopes in coral-rich or rubble areas interspersed with sand, 20 to 45 m. Often in pairs or small groups 1 to 2 m above the bottom at the base of dropoffs. **Range:** Malaysia to Fiji, n. to Ryuk., s. to Rowley Sh. & N. Cal.

2 **Zebra angelfish** *Genicanthus caudovittatus* (Günther) 20 cm
Ecology: coral-rich areas of seaward reef slopes, 15 to 70 m. Usually in small aggregations of one male and several females that swim a few m above the bottom. Feeds on zooplankton. Common in R. Sea. **Range:** R. Sea, E. Africa, Mauritius, s. to Mozambique.

3 **Lamarck's angelfish** *Genicanthus lamarcki* (Lacépède) 23 cm
♀ with white pelvic fins. **Ecology:** steep seaward reef slopes, 2 to 40 m, but below 10m in most areas. In aggregations that swim well above the bottom. Feeds on zooplankton. **Range:** Indonesia to Vanuatu, n. to s. Japan, s. to n. GBR.

4 **Watanabe's angelfish** *Genicanthus watanabei* (Yasuda & Tominaga) 15 cm
Ecology: current-swept seaward reef slopes, 12 to 81 m. In small to large aggregations that swim high above the bottom. Common outside the main passes of New Caledonia, but rare in less than 25 m in the Micronesia. **Range:** Taiwan to Tuam., n. to Ryuk., s. to N. Cal. & Austral Is.

5 **Ornate angelfish** *Genicanthus bellus* Randall 17 cm
Ecology: steep seaward reef dropoffs, 24 to 97 m. Rare in less than 50 m. Solitary or in aggregations a few m out from the slope. Feeds on zooplankton. ♀ more common than ♀. **Range:** Cocos-Keeling, Mariana, and Society Is.

6 **Japanese swallow** *Genicanthus semifasciatus* (Kamohara) 21 cm
Ecology: seaward rocky and coral reefs, 15 to 100 m. **Range:** n. Phil., Taiwan, Ryuk., s. Japan & Izu Is.

7 **Spotted angelfish** *Genicanthus* n. sp. <25 cm
Ecology: coral-rich areas of seaward reefs below 36 m. In groups of one male and several females. In the Bonin Islands, found only at Chichi-Jima, in a current-swept channel between two islands characterized by cool (20°C) upwelling water. **Range:** Bonin & Marcus Is. only

8 **Half-banded angelfish** *Genicanthus semicinctus* (Waite) 20 cm
Approximately 10 dark bars. Fins and belly yellowish. **Ecology:** seaward reefs, 10 to 100 m, usually below 35 m. **Range:** L. Howe & Kermadec Is. only.

9 **Pitcairn angelfish** *Genicanthus spinus* Randall 35 cm
Belly whitish, fins show little yellow. **Ecology:** rocky and coral reefs, 30 to >60 m. In aggregations high above the bottom. **Range:** Austral Is. & Pitcairn Group. to Ducie.

10 **Masked angelfish** *Genicanthus personatus* Randall 21 cm
The ♀ may lose their dark head pattern. **Ecology:** seaward reefs, 23 to 84 m. Common in northwest Hawaiian Is., but rare to the south. **Range:** Hawaiian Is.

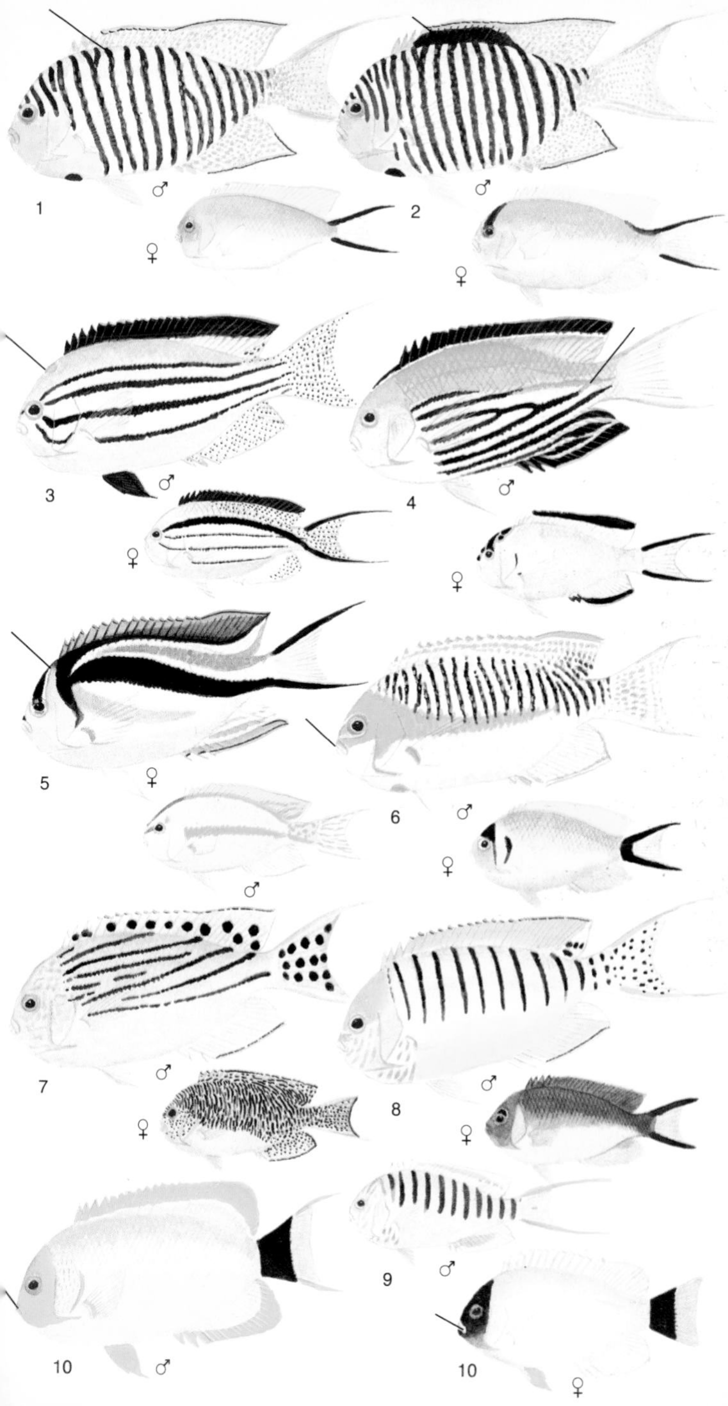
1
♂
♀
2
♂
♀
3
♂
♀
4
♂
♀
5
♀
♂
6
♂
♀
7
♂
♀
8
♂
♀
9
♂
10
♂
10
♀

1 **Regal angelfish** *Pygoplites diacanthus* (Boddaert) 25 cm
Juvs. resemble adults but have a large ocellus and less blue on soft D fin. **Ecology:** coral-rich areas of clear lagoon and seaward reefs, 1 to 48 m. Often near caves and crevices. Solitary or in pairs. Feeds on sponges and tunicates. Juveniles secretive, usually in caves along dropoffs. **Range:** R. Sea to Tuam., n. to Ryuk., s. to N. Cal.

2 **Emperor angelfish** *Pomacanthus imperator* (Bloch) 40 cm
The only juv. *Pomacanthus* with concentric white rings on sides; transformation occurs at 8-12 cm. Soft D fin of adults of Indian Ocean popul. remains rounded. Makes knocking sounds when disturbed. **Ecology:** juveniles solitary and under ledges or in holes of shallow reef flats and lagoon and channel reefs. Adults generally in coral-rich areas of deep lagoon and seaward reefs, 3 to 70 m, usually near caves or ledges or large boulders. Haremic, but usually seen singly or in pairs. Not uncommon. **Range:** R. Sea to Hawaiian (2 cases), Line & Tuam. Is., n. to s. Japan, s. to N. Cal. & Austral Is.

3 **Blue-face angelfish** *Pomacanthus xanthometopon* (Bleeker) 38 cm
Juv. resembles juv. *P. sexstriatus*, but soft D & A fins not as elevated posteriorly; transformation at 7-12 cm. **Ecology:** coral-rich areas of lagoon and seaward reefs, 5 to 25 m. Often near caves, generally solitary. Hybridizes with *P. navarchus.* **Range:** Maldives to Vanuatu, n. to Ryuk. & Caroline Is., s. to GBR.

4 **Blue-girdled angelfish** *Pomacanthus navarchus* (Cuvier) 28 cm
Juv. with clear tail, all bars blue; transformation at 3-8 cm. **Ecology:** coral-rich areas of lagoon, channel, and steep seaward reefs, 3 to 40 m. Juveniles in shallow protected areas. Usually solitary and relatively shy. Feeds on sponges and tunicates. Uncommon except in Indonesia. Hybridizes with *P. xanthometopon.* **Range:** Indonesia to PNG, n. to Phil., Palau & Yap, s. to Rowley Sh. & GBR.

5 **Bluering angelfish** *Pomacanthus annularis* (Bloch) 45 cm
Juv. resembles juv. *P. rhomboides* (pl. 73-3), but the two spp. occur together only in E. Africa. **Ecology:** coastal reefs to >30 m. Adults often in pairs in caves or wrecks. **Range:** E. Africa s. to Natal, e. to Sol. Is., n. to Ryuk., s. to PNG.

6 **Semicircle angelfish** *Pomacanthus semicirculatus* (Cuvier) 38 cm
Curvature of white lines of juvs. intermediate between juvs. of *P. imperator* and other spp.; transformation at 8-16 cm. **Ecology:** juveniles among rocks or coral of shallow sandy protected reefs to 30 m, secretive when very small. Adults in coral-rich areas of coastal reefs, often in caves or wrecks. Solitary. Common in the Seychelles, s. Japan to GBR. **Range:** E. Africa to Fiji, n. to s. Japan, s. to w. Aust., NSW & L. Howe Is.

7 **Ear-spot angelfish** *Pomacanthus chrysurus* (Cuvier) 33 cm
Juvs. with yellow tail bisected by white stripe; white lines relatively widely spaced. **Ecology:** coral-rich reefs, 1 to 25 m. Hybridizes with *P. maculosus* (pl. 73-1). Uncommon. **Range:** E. Africa from G. Aden to Natal, e. to Seychelles.

8 **Six-banded angelfish** *Pomacanthus sexstriatus* (Cuvier) 46 cm
Juv. resembles juv. *P. xanthometopon*, but soft D and A fins more elevated posteriorly; transformation at 8-15 cm. **Ecology:** lagoon and seaward reefs, 3 to 50 m, in coral-rich areas of high vertical relief, in silty as well as clear areas. Juveniles in shallow inner reefs and secretive. Adults usually paired and wide-ranging. Hybridizes with *P. xanthometopon.* **Range:** Malaysia to Sol. Is., n. to Ryuk., Palau & Yap, s. to Rowley Shoals & N. Cal.

1
juv
2
juv
juv
3
juv
4
5
6
juv
7
8 juv
8

73 ANGELFISHES, BOARFISHES, and KNIFEJAWS

1 **Yellowbar angelfish** *Pomacanthus maculosus* (Forsskål) 50 cm
Resembles *P. asfer* but tail of juvs. clear & adults lack iridescent blue scales; yellow bar appears at ca. 6 cm. **Ecology:** in the R. Sea, an uncommon inhabitant of shallow coastal reefs and wrecks in silty bays. In Oman, common in coral-rich areas, 4 to >20m. Solitary. **Range:** R. Sea & E. Africa, n. to Arab. G.& G. Oman, s. to 13°S.

2 **Arabian angelfish** *Pomacanthus asfur* (Forsskål) 40 cm
Resembles *P. maculosus*; juv. stage unknown; adult with iridescent blue scales on forward part of body, color complete at 5cm. **Ecology:** turbid inshore reefs with little coral growth, 3 to 25m. Often in pairs. Occasionally in areas of rich soft and hard coral growth. **Range:** c. & s. Red Sea & G. Aden, s. to Zanzibar.

3 **Old woman angelfish** *P. rhomboides* (Gilchrist & Thompson) 46 cm
Body depth & soft D and A fins more elevated than most similar spp.; juv. nearly identical to juv. *P. annularis* (pl. 72-5), the two spp. occur together only in E. Africa s. to 27°S. **Ecology:** coastal reefs, adults to >12m. Feeds in midwater on plankton. Common in n. S. Africa. **Range:** s. R. Sea & E. Africa, s. to 34°S (Knysna).

BOARFISHES (PENTACEROTIDAE): compressed fishes with bony heads and protrusible mouths. Primarily deep slopes, seamounts, and pelagic. Shallow primarily in temperate areas. Foodfishes.

4 **Striped boarfish** *Evistius acutirostris* (Temminck & Schlegel) 60 cm
Ecology: deep rocky dropoffs, 40 m in Hawaii. In pairs or small groups. **Range:** s. Japan & Bonin Is.; Hawaii; Aust. to Kermadec Is. & n. NZ.

5 **Sailfin boarfish** *Histiopterus typus* Temminck & Schlegel 42 cm
Juv. with large brown spots and long fins. **Ecology:** deep rocky reefs, 40 to 400 m, 100 m only in temperate areas. **Range:** R. Sea to Phil. & nw. Aust., n. to s. Japan, s. to Capetown, S. Africa.

KNIFEJAWS (OPLEGNATHIDAE): large fishes with teeth fused into a strong beak and small scales. Feed on barnacles and mollusks. Foodfishes. Usually not kept in aquaria. Juveniles brightly colored. Primarily warm-temperate.

6 **Spotted knifejaw** *Oplegnathus punctatus* (Temminck & Schlegel) 86 cm
Ecology: rocky and coral reefs. Common at s. Japan and Midway, but extremely rare in the s. Hawaiian and s. Mariana Is. **Range:** S. China Sea to s. Japan e. to Hawaii & Johnston Atoll, s. to n. Phil. & Marianas.

7 **Cape knifejaw** *Oplegnathus conwayi* Richardson 90 cm
2 other African spp: *O. peaolopesi* (n. of 27°S) & *O. robinsoni* (deep-bodied; ad. n. of 31°S) both with more angular soft D & A fins and tail lobes. Both are found on rocky reefs. **Ecology:** rocky and coral reefs. **Range:** se. Africa s. of 28°S.

1 juv
1
2
2 juv
3
4
5
juv
6
juv
7
juv

DAMSELFISHES (POMACENTRIDAE): small often colorful fishes with moderately deep, compressed bodies, small terminal mouths with conical or incisiform teeth, moderately large scales, continuous D fins, and an interupted LL. Conspicuous and numerous on all rocky or coral reefs. Includes herbivores (some *Abudefduf*; all *Plectroglyphidodon* and *Stegastes*) that are typically highly territorial and often pugnacious, omnivores (many *Chrysiptera* and *Pomacentrus*) that occur in small groups near shelter, and planktivores (*Acanthochromis, Chromis, Dascyllus, Lepidozygus, Neopomacentrus* and *Pomachromis*) that aggregate high in the water. The anemonefishes (subfamily Amphiprioninae, *Amphiprion* and *Premnas*; see also pl. 75) live in close association with one or more species of sea anemones. Damselfishes lay demersal eggs that are guarded by the male. They are among the hardiest of aquarium fishes, but some species are extremely aggressive.

1 **Indo-Pacific sergeant** *Abudefduf vaigiensis* (Quoy & Gaimard) 20 cm
Ecology: rocky lagoon shorelines and lagoon and seaward reefs to 12 m. Feeds on zooplankton, benthic algae, and small invertebrates, often in aggregations high in the water. **Range:** R. Sea to Marq. & Tuam., n. to s. Japan, s. to L. Howe Is.

2 **Scissor-tail sergeant** *Abudefduf sexfasciatus* (Lacépède) 17 cm
Ecology: coral-rich areas of upper lagoon and seaward slopes to 15 m. Feeds on zooplankton and benthic algae, often aggregating high in water. **Range:** R. Sea to Tuam., n. to s. Japan, s.to L. Howe & Rapa Is.

3 **Natal sergeant** *Abudefduf natalensis* Hensley & Randall 17 cm
Ecology: rocky inshore and offshore reefs, 1 to 25 m. **Range:** Se. Africa n. of 31.5°S, e. to s. Madag.

4 **Yellow-tail sergeant** *Abudefduf notatus* (Day) 17 cm
Ecology: rocky inshore reefs with moderate wave action, 1 to 12 m. In roving aggregations and somewhat difficult to approach. **Range:** E. Africa to N. Britain, n. to G. Aden & s. Japan, s. to Indonesia & Natal.

5 **Pearly sergeant** *Abudefduf margariteus* (Cuvier) 19 cm
Ecology: coastal coral reefs with moderate wave action, 2 to 8 m. In loose aggregations. **Range:** Mauritius & Réunion.

6 **Maomao** *Abudefduf abdominalis* (Quoy & Gaimard) 30 cm
Ecology: rocky bottoms of inshore and offshore reefs, shoreline to 50 m. Juveniles in surge pools. Often in aggregations. **Range:** Hawaiian Is.

7 **Whitley's sergeant** *Abudefduf whitleyi* Allen 17 cm
Ecology: seaward reef margins and surge channels, 1 to 5 m. Often in aggregations. **Range:** GBR, Coral Sea & N. Cal.

8 **Bengal sergeant** *Abudefduf bengalensis* (Bloch) 17 cm
Ecology: inshore and lagoon reefs, 1 to 6 m. Highly territorial. **Range:** Pakistan to PNG, n. to s. Japan, s. to nw. and ne. Australia.

9 **Blacktail sergeant** *Abudefduf lorenzi* Hensley & Allen 18 cm
Ecology: sheltered rocky shorelines, often around piers and breakwaters, intertidal to 6 m. Highly territorial. **Range:** Phil. & Moluccas to Sol. Is.

10 **Black-spot sergeant** *Abudefduf sordidus* Forsskål 20 cm
Ecology: shallow rocky lagoon and reef flat shorelines exposed to mild surge, intertidal to 3 m. Feeds on benthic algae and associated small invertebrates. Highly territorial. **Range:** R. Sea to Hawaiian, Marq. & Tuam. Is., n. to s. Japan, s. to L. Howe & Rapa Is.

11 **Banded sergeant** *Abudefduf septemfasciatus* (Cuvier) 19 cm
Ecology: shallow rocky lagoon and reef flat shorelines exposed to mild surge, intertidal to 3 m. Feeds on benthic algae and associated small invertebrates. Highly territorial. **Range:** E. Africa to Line & Tuam. Is., n. to s. Japan, s. to the GBR.

12 **False-eye sergeant** *Abudefduf sparoides* (Quoy & Gaimard) 15 cm
Ecology: coral and rocky reefs with moderate wave action, 1 to 12 m. Juveniles in shallow lagoons among soft corals, 0.3 to 2 m. Solitary or in loose aggregations. **Range:** E. Africa from Kenya to Natal, e. to Aldabra, Maurit. & Réunion.

1
2
3
4
5
6
7
8
9
10
11
12

75 DAMSELFISHES

Anemonefishes (subfamily Amphiprioninae: *Amphiprion*, pl. 75-76, and *Premnas*, pl. 89) live in close association with one or more of 10 host species of sea anemones. They are protected from the anemone's stinging cells by their mucus which carries the anemones' chemical signature. This inhibits the stinging cells from firing and is acquired by the larvae during settlement at the anemones base. Anemonefishes are protandrous hermaphrodites, that is all mature as males, then may reverse sex later. The female is the largest most dominant fish of each colony, and her presence inhibits the sex reversal of the males. Anemonefishes feed primarily on zooplankton and filamentous algae and are among the hardiest and most popular of aquarium fishes.

1 **False clown anemonefish** *Amphiprion ocellaris* Cuvier 11 cm
Melanistic popul. in vicinity of Darwin, n. Australia. **Ecology:** lagoon and seaward reefs, including turbid coastal areas, 1 to 15 m. Occurs with the anemones *Heteractis magnifica, Stichodactyla gigantea,* and *S. mertensii.* **Range:** Andaman & Nicobar Is. to Moluccas, n. to Ryuk., s. to nw. Australia.

2 **Clown anemonefish** *Amphiprion percula* (Lacépède) 11 cm
Ecology: lagoon and seaward reefs, 1 to 15 m. Occurs with the anemones *Heteractis magnifica, H. crispa,* and *Stichodactyla gigantea.* **Range:** n. PNG, Sol. Is., Vanuatu & GBR.

3 **Tomato anemonefish** *Amphiprion frenatus* Brevoort 14 cm
Ecology: 1 to 2 m. Exclusively with *Entacmaea quadricolor.* **Range:** se. Thailand to Indonesia & Phil., n. to s. Japan.

4 **Red saddleback anemonefish** *Amphiprion ephippium* (Bloch) 14 cm
Small juvs. with 1-3 white bands, the first the last to dissappear with growth. **Ecology:** protected reefs, 2 to 15 m. With *Entacmaea quadricolor* and *Heteractis crispa.* **Range:** Andaman & Nicobar Is. to w. Malaysia & Java.

5 **Dusky anemonefish** *Amphiprion melanopus* Bleeker 12 cm
Sm. juvs. red with 2-3 white bars; lg. ad. dull reddish-brown; Coral Sea popul. orange with lg. brown blotch posteriorly & occas. lack white bar; s. Oceania popul. orange-red. **Ecology:** reef flats and lagoon reefs to 18 m. Typically in large colonies among clusters of *Entacmaea quadricolor;* occasionally with *Heteractis crispa* and *H. magnifica.* **Range:** Sulawesi & Moluccas to Society Is., n. to Marianas, s. to GBR, N. Cal. & Tonga.

6 **Australian anemonefish** *Amphiprion rubrocinctus* Richardson 12 cm
Ecology: 1 to 8 m. With *Entacmaea quadricolor* and *Stichodactyla gigantea.* **Range:** nw. Australia.

7 **Skunk anemonefish** *Amphiprion akallopisos* Bleeker 11 cm
Ecology: 3 to 25 m. Occas. with *A. allardi* and with *Heteractis magnifica* and *Stichodactyla mertensii.* **Range:** E. Africa s. to 30°S, e. to Bali, n. to India & w. Thailand.

8 **Orange anemonefish** *Amphiprion sandaracinos* Allen 14 cm
Ecology: lagoon and seaward reefs, 3 to 20 m, often on reef crests. With *Heteractis crispa* and *Stichodactyla mertensii.* **Range:** Sumatra to Sol. Is., n. to Ryuk., s. to nw. Australia.

9 **Pink anemonefish** *Amphiprion perideraion* Bleeker 10 cm
Ecology: lagoon and seaward reefs, 3 to 30 m, below the influence of surge. Typically with *Heteractis magnifica,* but rarely with *Heteractis crispa, Macrodactyla doreensis,* and *Stichodactyla gigantuea.* **Range:** se. Thailand and Cocos-Keeling to Samoa, n. to Ryuk., Marianas & Marshalls, s. to GBR & N. Cal.

10 **Maldives anemonefish** *Amphiprion nigripes* Regan 11 cm
Ecology: lagoon and seaward reefs, 2 to 25 m. Exclusively with *Heteractis magnifica.* **Range:** Maldives, Laccadives & Sri Lanka.

11 **Thielle's anemonefish** *Amphiprion thiellei* Burgess 9 cm
Ecology: described from aquarium specimens; no ecological information available. **Range:** Philippines.

12 **White-bonnett anemonefish** *Amphiprion leucokranos* Allen 9 cm
Ecology: lagoon and seaward reefs, 2 to 12 m. With *Heteractis crispa, H. magnifica,* and *Stichodactyla mertensii.* **Range:** ne. PNG, N. Britain & Sol. Is.

13 **Saddleback anemonefish** *Amphiprion polymnus* (Linnaeus) 13 cm
Bali popul. black with yellow P fins, orange face, and broad white bar instead of saddle. **Ecology:** lagoon and coastal reefs, often in silty areas, 2 to 30 m. With *Heteractis crispa* and *Stichodactyla haddoni.* **Range:** se. Thailand to Sol. Is., n. to Taiwan & Ryuk., s. to Indonesia, PNG, n. Australia. 14 See over

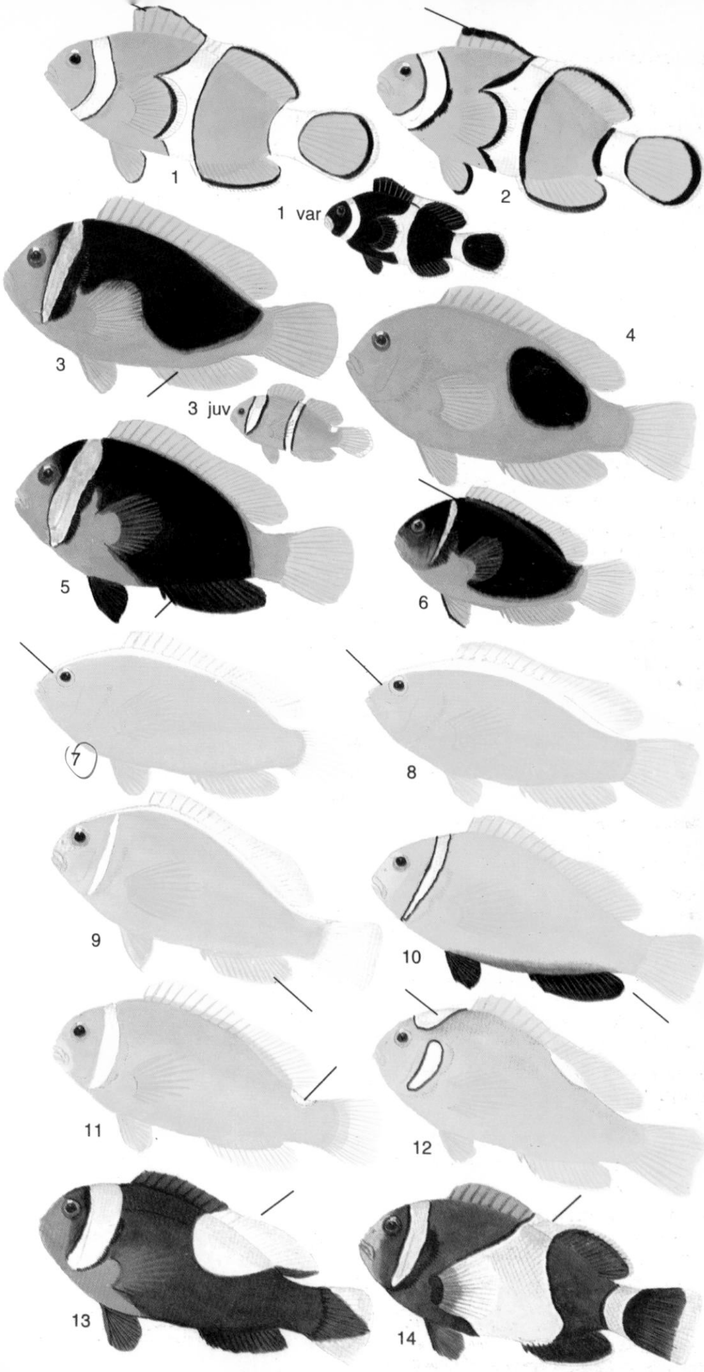
1
2
1 var
3
4
3 juv
5
6
7
8
9
10
11
12
13
14

←14 **Wideband anemonefish** *Amphiprion latezonatus* Waite 14 cm
Ecology: rocky and coral reefs, 10 to 45 m. With *Heteractis crispa*. **Range:** L. Howe Is. & s. Queensland to n. NSW.

76 DAMSELFISHES

1 **Two-banded anemonefish** *Amphiprion bicinctus* Rüppell 14 cm
In Yemen with a forked tail and orange-brown ground color. **Ecology:** protected fringing reefs, 1 to 30 m. With *Entacmaea quadricolor, Heteractis aurora, H. crispa, H. magnifica,* and *Stichodactyla gigantea*. **Range:** R. Sea, G. Aden & Chagos Is.

2 **Oman anemonefish** *Amphiprion omanensis* Allen 14 cm
Us. a white spot on upper C peduncle; tail forked. **Ecology:** coastal reefs, 2 to 10 m. With *Entacmeaea quadricolor* and *Heteractis crispa*. **Range:** Oman coast of Arabian Sea.

3 **Allard's anemonefish** *Amphiprion allardi* Klausewitz 15 cm
Ecology: protected reefs, 1 to 30 m. With *Entacmaea quadricolor, Heteractis aurora,* and *Stichodactyla mertensii*. Common in Kenya. **Range:** E. Africa s. to 30°S.

4 **Chagos anemonefish** *Amphiprion chagosensis* Allen 11 cm
Ecology: primarily seaward reef slopes, 10 to 25 m, but occasionally on lagoon reefs and reef tops. Host anemone species unknown. **Range:** Chagos Is.

5 **Seychelles anemonefish** *Amphiprion fuscocaudatus* Allen 14 cm
Ecology: lagoon and seaward reefs, particularly patch reefs, 5 to 30 m. Exclusively with *Stichdactyla mertensii*, occasionally with *A. akallopisos*. **Range:** Seychelles & Aldabra.

6 **Mauritian anemonefish** *Amphiprion chrysogaster* Cuvier 15 cm
Ecology: lagoon and seaward reefs, 2 to 40 m, usually 10 m. With *Heteractis aurora, H. magnifica, Macrodactyla doreensis, Stichodactyla haddoni,* and *S. mertensii*. **Range:** Mauritius & probably Réunion.

7 **Clark's anemonefish** *Amphiprion clarkii* (Bennett) 13 cm
Highly variable, ground color dusky orange to black with or without orange-yellow fringe; tail orange, white, or black. **Ecology:** seaward and clear lagoon reefs, 1 to 55 m. Occurs with all 10 host anemone species: *Cryptodendrum adhaesivum, Entacmaea quadricolor, Heteractis aurora, H. crispa, H. magnifica, H. malu, Macrodactyla doreensis, Stichodactyla gigantea, S. haddoni,* and *S. mertensii*. Common from E. Indies to s. Japan. **Range:** Arab. G. to Fiji, n. to s. Japan, s. to Maldives, w. Australia, GBR & N. Cal.

8 **Sebae anemonefish** *Amphiprion sebae* Bleeker 16 cm
Ecology: 2 to 25 m. With *Stichodactyla haddoni*. **Range:** s. Arab. Peninsula to Java, n. to Pakistan, India & Andaman Is, s. to Maldives.

9 **Madagascar anemonefish** *Amphiprion latifasciatus* Allen 13 cm
Ecology: coral-rich protected areas, 1 to 8 m. Occasionally on silty reef flats. Exclusively with *Stichdactyla mertensii*. **Range:** Madagascar & Comoro Is.

10 **Orange-fin anemonefish** *Amphiprion chrysopterus* Cuvier 17 cm
Juvs. dull orange, adults brown with bright orange fins; bars white to blue. **Ecology:** seaward reefs, from lower surge zone to >30 m. Most often with *Heteractis crispa*, but also with *Entacmaea quadricolor, H. aurora, H. magnifica, Stichodactyla haddoni,* and *S. mertensii*. Common in the insular Pacific, rare in the Coral Sea. **Range:** Palau to Tuam., n. to Marianas, s. to GBR.

11 **Three-band anemonefish** *A. tricinctus* Schultz & Welander 12 cm
Two color phases: orange or black. **Ecology:** lagoon and seaward reefs, 3 to 38 m. The black phase with *Stichodactyla mertensii*, the orange phase with *Heteractis aurora, H. crispa* and *Entacmaea quadricolor*. **Range:** Marshall Is.

12 **Barrier Reef anemonefish** *Amphiprion akindynos* Allen 12 cm
Ecology: lagoon and seaward reefs, 1 to 25 m. Occurs in *Entacmaea quadricolor, Heteractis aurora, H. crispa, H. magnifica, Stichodactyla haddoni,* and *S. mertensii*. **Range:** GBR to N. Cal. & Loyalty Is., s. to n. NSW.

13 **McCulloch's anemonefish** *Amphiprion mccullochi* Whitley 12 cm
Ecology: lagoon and outer rocky reefs, 2 to 45 m. With *Entacmaea quadricolor* only. **Range:** L. Howe & Norfolk Is.

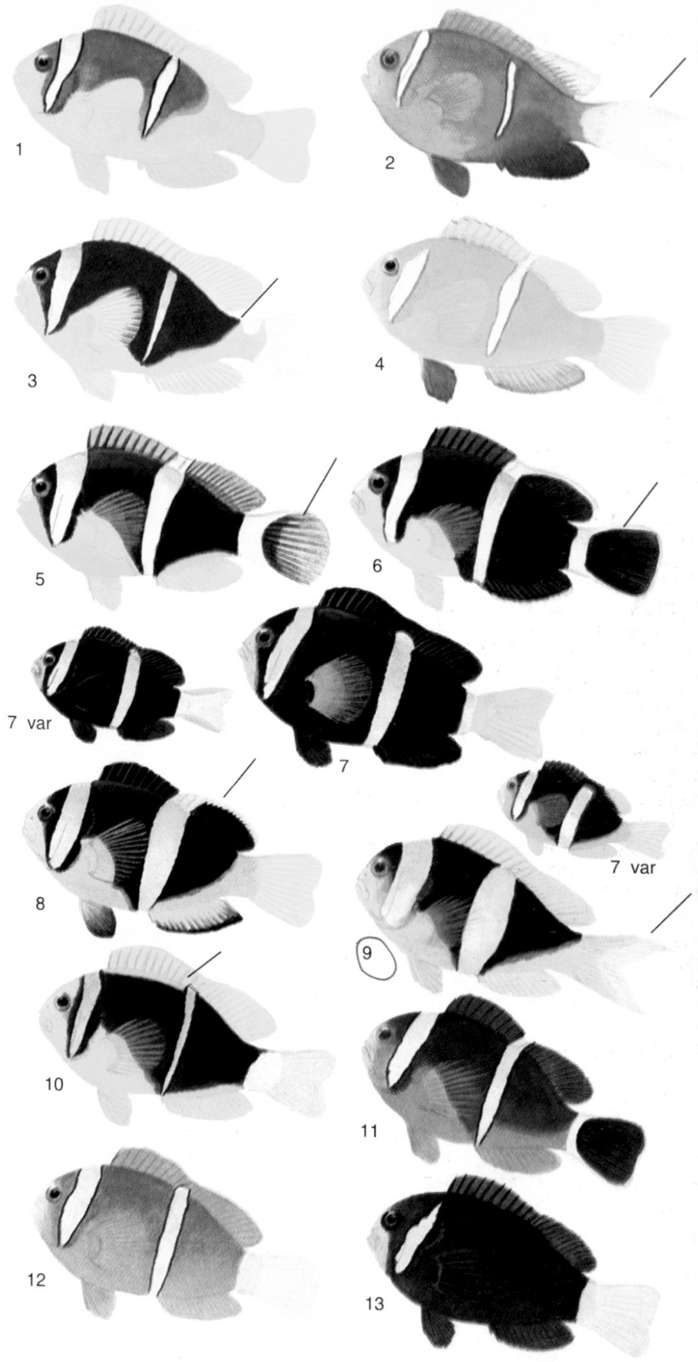
1
2
3
4
5
6
7 var
7
8
7 var
9
10
11
12
13

77 DAMSELFISHES

1 **Golden damsel** *Amblyglyphidodon aureus* (Cuvier) 14 cm
Color on Cocos-Keeling darker. **Ecology:** steep outer reef slopes, 3 to at least 45 m, usually below 12 m. Juveniles often near gorgonians. Occasionally in deep lagoon and channel slopes. Feeds on zoo plankton. **Range:** Cocos-Keeling, Similan Is. to Fiji, n. to Ryuk., s. to N. Cal.

2 **Staghorn damsel** *Amblyglyphidodon curacao* (Bloch) 12 cm
Ecology: coral-rich areas of lagoons and sheltered bays to 40 m. Feeds primarily on zooplankton, often in large aggregations. **Range:** Malaysia to Samoa, n. to Ryuk., s. to Rowley Shoals & s. GBR.

3 **White-belly damsel** *Amblyglyphidodon leucogaster* (Bleeker) 13 cm
Indian Ocean form uniformly greenish, possibly a distinct sp.; both forms at Similan Is. **Ecology:** singly or in small groups in coral-rich areas of deep clear lagoons and seaward reefs, 2 to 34 m. **Range:** R. Sea to Samoa, n. to Ryuk., s. to GBR.

4 **Ternate damsel** *Amblyglyphidodon ternatensis* (Bleeker) 13 cm
Ecology: coral-rich areas of shallow sheltered coastal reefs, in small groups. **Range:** Indonesia to Sol. Is., n. to Ryuk.

5 **Yellowfin damsel** *Amblyglyphidodon flavilatus* Allen & Randall 10 cm
Ecology: inshore coral reefs and steep outer reef slopes, 12 to 20 m. **Range:** R. Sea & G. Aden.

6 **Brighteye damsel** *Plectroglyphidodon imparipennis* (Vaillant & Sauvage) 6 cm
Marq. pop. with 2-3 pale bars on sides & dark saddle on tail base. **Ecology:** surge zone of seaward reefs, 0 to 6 m, near small holes and sea urchin furrows. **Range:** E. Africa to Hawaiian, Marq., & Pitcairn Is., n. to Ryuk. & Bonin Is., s. to N. Cal. & Rapa Is.

7 **Dick's damsel** *Plectroglyphidodon dickii* (Liénard) 11 cm
Ecology: coral-rich areas of seaward reefs, 1 to 12 m. Among robustly branching *Pocillopora* and *Acropora* corals, often in surgy areas. Species of *Plectroglyphidodon* are territorial omnivores that feed primarily on filamentous algae and small benthic invertebrates. **Range:** E. Africa to Line, Marq. & Tuam. Is., n. to s. Japan, s. to L. Howe Is.

8 **Johnston damsel** *Plectroglyphidodon johnstonianus* Fowler & Ball 9 cm
Some indiv. in w. Pacific and in E. Africa lack the dark posterior band. **Ecology:** shallow exposed seaward reefs to 18 m, often among closely spaced *Pocillopora, Acropora,* or *Stylophora* corals. **Range:** E. Africa to Hawaiian, Marq. & Pitcairn Is., n. to Ryuk. & Bonin Is., s. to L. Howe & Rapa Is.

9 **Jewel damsel** *Plectroglyphidodon lacrymatus* (Quoy & Gaimard) 10 cm
Ecology: clear lagoon and seaward reefs, 1 to 40 m in areas of mixed coral and rubble or dead coral rock. Occupies algae-covered substrates between coral heads. **Range:** R. Sea to Marq., Society & Austral Is., n. to Ryuk., s. to L. Howe Is.

10 **Whiteband damsel** *Plectroglyphidodon leucozonus* (Bleeker) 11 cm
Juvs. with conspicuous dorsal ocellus; white band disappears in large indiv.; tail & posterior D & A fins yellow in R. Sea subsp.(*P. l. cingulum*). A similar surge zone sp., *P. Randall i* (Maurit.) has more subdued colors. **Ecology:** surgy shorelines and reef margins to 3 m. Juveniles in intertidal pockets, adults in ridges between surge channels. **Range:** R. Sea to Marq. & Pitcairn Is., n. to s. Japan, s. to L. Howe & Rapa Is.

11 **Hawaiian rock damsel** *P. sindonis* (Jordan & Evermann) 12 cm
Ecology: rocky inshore reefs exposed to surge, 0 to 3 m. **Range:** Hawaiian Is.

12 **Phoenix damsel** *Plectroglyphidodon phoenixensis* (Schultz) 9 cm
Ecology: exclusively in surge zone of seaward reef margins to 3 m, always near corals or algae-rich rocks. **Range:** E. Africa to Line, Marq. & Tuam. Is., n. to Ryuk., strays to Johnston & Hawaiian Is.

13 **Mauritian damsel** *Plectroglyphidodon Randall i* Allen 9 cm
Ecology: rocky inshore reefs exposed to wave action, 1 to 4 m. **Range:** Mauritius & probably Réunion.

1
2
3
4
5
6
7
8
9
10
11
12
13

1 **Black-axil chromis** *Chromis atripectoralis* Welander & Schultz 11 cm
Dorsal fin darkens in courting males. **Ecology:** clear lagoon and protected seaward reefs, 1 to 29 m. In aggregations above staghorn *Acropora* corals. Common. **Range:** E. Africa, Seychelles to Line & Tuam. Is., n. to Ryuk., s. to L. Howe & Rapa Is.

2 **Blue-green chromis** *Chromis viridis* (Cuvier) 9 cm
Ecology: reef flats and shallow lagoon and shelteR. Seaward reefs to 12 m. In large aggregations near branching corals, often well above the bottom. Juveniles closely tied to individual coral heads. Abundant. **Range:** R. Sea to Marq. & Soc. Is., n. to Ryuk., s. to N. Cal.

3 **White-tail chromis** *Chromis leucura* Gilbert 7 cm
Ecology: outer reef slopes, 20 to 119 m. In aggregations near ledges and deep patch reefs. **Range:** Madag., Maurit., Réun., Ryuk., Hawaiian & Marq. Is.

4 **Green chromis** *Chromis cinerascens* (Cuvier) 13 cm
Ecology: coastal reefs, 3 to 15 m. **Range:** Sri Lanka, Thail. & Indonesia, n. to Phil., s. to nw. Australia.

5 **Blacktail chromis** *Chromis nigrura* Smith 6 cm
C. lineata (Indon., Melan & n. Aust.) similar but without dusky upper and lower C peduncle. **Ecology:** seaward reefs, particularly coral-rich outer reef crests, 1 to 30 m. In small or large aggregations close to corals. **Range:** E. Africa s. to 32°S, e. to Christmas Is.

6 **Vanderbilt's chromis** *Chromis vanderbilti* (Fowler) 6 cm
Ecology: exposed seaward reefs, 2 to 20 m. In aggregations above prominent coral heads. **Range:** Taiwan to Hawaiian & Pitcairn Is., n. to Izu Is., s. to L. Howe & Rapa Is.

7 **Midget chromis** *Chromis acares* Randall & Swerdloff 5.5 cm
Ecology: exposed seaward reefs, 2 to 37 m. In aggregations close to corals. Uncommon. **Range:** Marianas to Hawaiian & Society Is., s. to Vanuatu & Austral Is.

8 **Doublebar chromis** *Chromis opercularis* (Günther) 16 cm
Yellow blotch on C ped. variable, absent in many areas. V. similar to Marianas *C. xanthura*. **Ecology:** seaward reefs and deep lagoons, 4 to 40 m. **Range:** E. Africa s. to 28°S, e. to Christmas Is. & Bali, n. to India & Andaman Sea.

9 **Weber's chromis** *Chromis weberi* Fowler & Bean 12 cm
Ecology: channels and seaward reef slopes, 3 to 25 m. Singly or in small groups. **Range:** R. Sea to Line & Pitcairn Is., n. to s. Japan, s. to N. Cal.

10 **Yellow-axil chromis** *Chromis xanthochira* (Bleeker) 13 cm
Ecology: steep outer reef slopes, 10 to 48 m. Singly or in small groups. **Range:** Indonesia to Sol. Is., n. to Phil.

11 **Scaly chromis** *Chromis lepidolepis* Bleeker 8 cm
Ecology: coral-rich areas of lagoon and seaward reefs, 2 to 43 m. Aggregates close to shelter. **Range:** R. Sea to Line Is., n. to Izu Is., s. to N. Cal.

12 **Ternate chromis** *Chromis ternatensis* (Bleeker) 10 cm
Ecology: upper margins of clear lagoon and seaward reefs, 2 to 36 m. In aggregations above branching corals. **Range:** E. Africa to Samoa, n. to Ryuk., s. to N. Cal.

13 **Dark-fin chromis** *Chromis atripes* Fowler & Bean 7 cm
Similar to *C. xutha* (E. Africa to Maldives; pl.80-8). **Ecology:** coral-rich areas of seaward reefs and channels, 2 to 40 m. Solitary near bottom. **Range:** Thail., w. Indonesia & Cocos-Keeling Is. to Gilbert Is., n. to Izu Is., s. to N. Cal.

14 **Ambon chromis** *Chromis amboinensis* (Bleeker) 8 cm
Ecology: coral-rich areas of clear lagoon and seaward reefs, 5 to 70 m. Abundant on steep outer reef slopes below 24 m, uncommon in lagoons. In aggregations. **Range:** Cocos-Keeling Is. to Samoa, n. to Marianas, s. to N. Cal.

15 **Philippines chromis** *Chromis scotochiloptera* Fowler 16 cm
Ecology: seaward reef slopes, 2 to 20 m. In aggregations. **Range:** Indonesia & Phil.

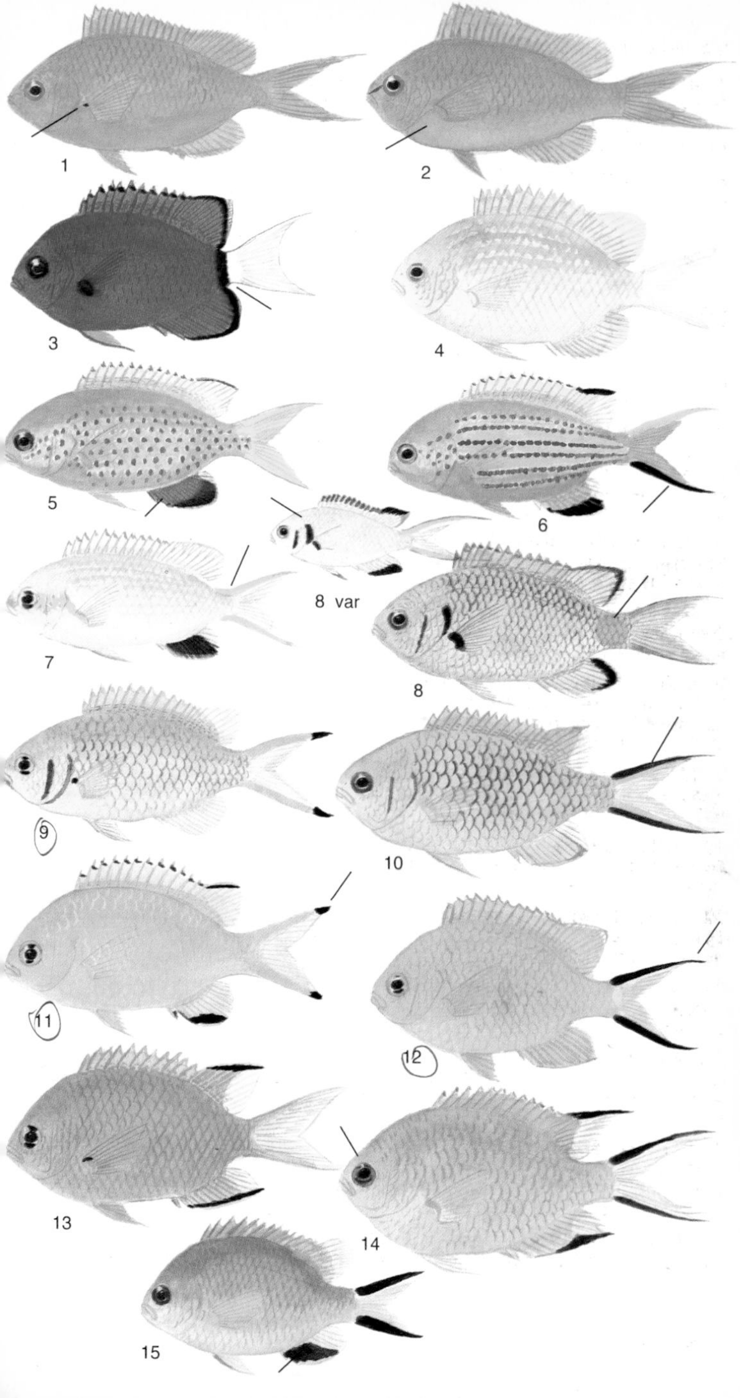
1
2
3
4
5
6
8 var
7
8
9
10
11
12
13
14
15

79 DAMSELFISHES

1 **Yellow-edge chromis** *Chromis pembae* Smith 13 cm
Ecology: steep outer reef slopes, 12 to 50 m. In small loose groups near shelter. Often above reef pinnacles. Uncommon. **Range:** R. Sea & E. Africa to Chagos Is.

2 **Yellow chromis** *Chromis analis* (Cuvier) 15 cm
Uniformly yellow to brown with yellow median fins and eyes. **Ecology:** steep outer reef slopes, 10 to 144 m. In small aggregations. Uncommon. **Range:** Seychelles to Fiji, n. to s. Japan, s. to N. Cal.

3 **Black-bar chromis** *Chromis retrofasciata* Weber 5 cm
Ecology: coral-rich areas of clear lagoon and seaward reefs, 3 to 65 m. Singly or in small groups, always close to thickly branching coral shelter. **Range:** Indonesia to Fiji, n. to Ryuk., s. to N. Cal.

4 **Barrier Reef chromis** *Chromis nitida* (Whitley) 8 cm
Ecology: coral-rich areas of lagoon and seaward reefs, 5 to 25 m. In aggregations above branching corals. Abundant on seaward reef slopes of s. GBR, occasionally in lagoons. **Range:** GBR, n. NSW & L. Howe Is.

5 **Twotone chromis** *Chromis dimidiata* (Klunzinger) 9 cm
Ecology: lagoon and seaward reefs, 1 to 36 m. Abundant, in large aggregations over reef tops and upper edges of slopes. **Range:** R. Sea & E. Africa s. to Durban, e. to Thail.

6 **Half and half chromis** *Chromis iomelas* Jordan & Seale 7 cm
Ecology: seaward reefs and channels, 3 to 35 m. Singly or in small groups. **Range:** GBR to Society Is., n. to n. PNG & Vanuatu.

7 **Bicolor chromis** *Chromis margaritifer* Fowler 9 cm
Ecology: lagoon and seaward reefs, 2 to 20 m. Common on exposed seaward reefs, uncommon in lagoons. Solitary or in large aggregations. **Range:** Cocos-Keeling Is. to Line & Tuam. Is., n. to Izu Is., s. to L. Howe Is.

8 **Black chromis** *Chromis xanthura* (Bleeker) 15 cm
Juvs. slate gray to brilliant metallic blue (Marianas) with orange-yellow tail; white tail of ad. absent in some areas (Marianas). V. similar to *C. opercularis* (pl. 78-8). **Ecology:** steep outer reef slopes, 3 to 40 m. Adults typically in loose aggregations well above bottom, juveniles close to shelter. Nests in small patches of loose sand under ledges or at base of slopes. **Range:** Cocos-Keeling Is. & s. Indonesia to Marq. & Pitcairn Is., n. to Izu Is., s. to N. Cal.

9 **Stout-body chromis** *Chromis chrysura* (Bliss) 13 cm
Ecology: seaward reefs and channels, 6 to 45 m. In large aggregations above bottom, usually below 15 m in tropics. Common in shallow subtropical waters. **Range:** Maurit. & Réunion; Taiwan to Izu Is.; GBR & NSW to Fiji.

10 **Deep-reef chromis** *Chromis delta* Randall 7 cm
Ecology: steep outer reef slopes, 10 to 80 m, usually below 25 m. **Range:** Cocos-Keeling to Fiji, n. to Taiwan, s. to Vanuatu.

11 **Malayan chromis** *Chromis flavipectoralis* Randall 7 cm
Similar to *C. amboinensis* (pl. 78-14), but A fin, posterior D fin & tail white. **Ecology:** seaward reef slopes, 2 to 15 m. **Range:** Maldives, Thail., w. Indonesia & Malaysia.

12 **Hawaiian chromis** *Chromis hanui* Randall & Swerdloff 8 cm
Ecology: seaward reefs, 6 to 50 m. In aggregations above corals. Abundant. **Range:** Hawaiian Is.

13 **Ovate chromis** *Chromis ovatiformis* (Fowler) 10 cm
Ecology: seaward rocky or coral reefs, 10 to 40 m. **Range:** Taiwan, Ryuk. & Izu Is.

14 **Blue-axil chromis** *Chromis caudalis* Randall 10 cm
The only chromis with a blue inner P axil. **Ecology:** steep outer reef slopes, 10 to 55 m. In small groups near ledges and small caves. Locally common. **Range:** Indonesia to Sol. Is., n. to Phil., s. to Christmas Is.

1
2
3
4
5
6
7
8
9
10
11
12
13
14

1 **Twin-spot chromis** *Chromis elerae* Fowler & Bean 7 cm
Ecology: in small aggregations at the entrances to caves and crevices of steep outer reef slopes, 12 to 70 m. Uncommon. **Range:** Maldives to Marshall Is. & Fiji, n. to Taiwan.

2 **Trispot chromis** *Chromis trialpha* Allen & Randall 6 cm
Ecology: seaward reefs, 3 to 50 m. **Range:** R. Sea.

3 **Pearl-spot chromis** *Chromis notata* Temminck & Schlegel 17 cm
Similar to *C. hypsilepis* (se. Aust., L. Howe & Norf. Is., n. N. Z.)
Ecology: inshore and offshore rocky and coral reefs, 2 to 15 m. **Range:** se. China & Taiwan to Ryuk. & s. half of Japan.

4 **Smokey chromis** *Chromis fumea* Tanaka 13 cm
Ecology: lagoon and seaward coral and rocky reefs, 3 to 25 m. **Range:** Malaysia, Indonesia, Taiwan & Ryuk. n. to s. Japan; w. & s. Aust.

5 **Three-spot chromis** *Chromis verator* Jordan & Metz 20 cm
Ecology: rocky areas, near caves, ledges and outcrops, 6 to 160 m. In large aggregations well above the bottom. Abundant below 18 m, uncommon shallower. **Range:** Hawaiian & Johnston Is.

6 **Duskytail chromis** *Chromis pelloura* Randall & Allen 14 cm
Similar to *C. axillaris* (Ind. Oc. & N. Cal.) which has a larger eye. **Ecology:** seaward reef slopes, 30 to 50 m. Known only from the Gulf of Aqaba, R. Sea. **Range:** G. of Aqaba (R. Sea) only.

7 **Yellow-spotted chromis** *Chromis flavomaculata* Kamohara 16 cm
Ecology: seaward rocky and coral reefs, 6 to 40 m. In large aggregations well above bottom. Abundant. **Range:** Antitropical: Ryuk. & Bonin Is. to s Japan; GBR & NSW to L. Howe Is., N. Cal.

8 **Buff chromis** *Chromis xutha* Randall 7 cm
Ecology: offshore coral reefs with rich growth, always close to the bottom, 2 to 20 m. Always close to corals. Solitary or in small groups. **Range:** Tanzania, Kenya, Seychelles & Maldives.

9 **Bronze reef chromis** *Chromis agilis* Smith 10 cm
Ecology: clear lagoon and seaward reefs, 3 to 65 m. In loose aggregations near caves or ledges. Common. In Hawaiian Is. abundant over branching corals of leeward coasts. **Range:** E. Africa to Hawaiian & Pitcairn Is., n. to Marianas, s. to N. Cal. & Rapa.

10 **Arabian chromis** *Chromis xanthopterygia* Randall & McCarthy 11 cm
Ecology: inshore rocky and coral reefs, 5 to 20 m. Abundant. **Range:** Arab. G. & G. Oman.

11 **Hawaiian chromis** *Chromis ovalis* (Steindachner) 18 cm
Ecology: rocky areas, 7 to 45 m. In aggregations. Common. Nests from Feb. to May. **Range:** Hawaiian Is.

12 **Yellow-speckled chromis** *Chromis alpha* Randall 12 cm
Similar to *C. nigroanalis* which has mostly black A fin. **Ecology:** in aggregations a few meters above steep outer reef slopes, 12 to 95 m. Nests on small patches of loose sand. Common. **Range:** Cocos-Keeling to Society Is., n. to Marianas, s. to n. Cal.

13 **Kenyan chromis** *Chromis nigroanalis* Randall 12 cm
V. similar to *C. alpha*, but with anterior 2/3 of A fin black. **Ecology:** outer reef slopes, 20 to 40 m. **Range:** E. Africa, Maldives & Java Sea.

1
2
3
4
5
6
7
8
9
10
11
11 juv
12
13

81 DAMSELFISHES

1 **Blue devil** *Chrysiptera cyanea* (Quoy & Gaimard) 8 cm
Ecology: rubble and coral of clear sheltered lagoons and reef flats to 10 m. In groups. **Range**: Indonesia to Sol. Is., n. to Ryuk. & w. Caroline Is., s. to nw. Aust. shelf & GBR.

2 **Goldtail demoiselle** *Chrysiptera parasema* (Fowler) 7 cm
Ecology: coral-rich areas of sheltered lagoon and inshore reefs, 1 to 16 m. **Range**: Phil. & Sulawesi to n. New Guinea & Sol Is., n. to Ryuk.

3 **Springer's demoiselle** *Chrysiptera springeri* (Allen) 5.5 cm
Ecology: sheltered lagoon and inshore reefs, 4 to 30 m. Among finely branching corals. **Range**: Phil., Moluccas & Flores.

4 **Starck's demoiselle** *Chrysiptera starcki* (Allen) 10 cm
Ecology: rocky outcrops & crevices in sand channels of outer reef slopes, 20 to 60 m. **Range**: Taiwan to Ryuk. & s. Japan; Coral Sea, N. Cal., Loyalty Is. & Fiji.

5 **South Seas devil** *Chrysiptera taupou* (Jordan & Seale) 8 cm
Spinous D fin yellow in mature ♀, blue in ♂. **Ecology:** lagoon and offshore reefs, 1 to 10 m. **Range:** n. GBR to Samoa, s. to N. Cal.

6 **Yellowfin damsel** *Chrysiptera flavipinnis* (Allen & Robertson) 8 cm
Ecology: rubble and dead coral outcrops, often in sandy areas, 3 to 38 m. **Range**: se. PNG to GBR, Coral Sea & se. Australia (Sydney).

7 **Azure demoiselle** *Chrysiptera hemicyanea* (Weber) 7 cm
Ecology: sheltered coral reefs, 1 to 15 m. **Range**: Indonesia & nw. Austalian shelf reefs.

8 **Blueline demoiselle** *Chrysiptera caeruleolineata* (Allen) 6 cm
Rowley Shoals popul. dark blue over anterior 2/3 of body. **Ecology**: rubble and rocky outcrops in sand channels of steep outer reef slopes, 24 to 65 m. **Range**: Rowley Shoals to N. Guinea, Sol. Is. & Samoa, n. to Ryuk., Mariana & Marshall Is.

9 **Surge demoiselle** *Chrysiptera leucopoma* (Lesson) 8 cm
Color pattern variable, two major phases; some indiv. black except for orange operc. bar. **Ecology**: exposed reef flats and seaward reef margins and slopes to 12 m, abundant in surgy areas. Feeds primarily on benthic algae and small crustaceans. **Range**: E. Africa to Marq., Soc. & Austral Is., n. to s. Japan, s. to N. Cal.

10 **Bluespot demoiselle** *Chrysiptera oxycephala* (Bleeker) 9 cm
Ecology: sheltered inshore reefs, 1 to 16 m, near corals. Feeds primarily on zooplankton. **Range**: Indonesia to PNG, n. to Phil. & Palau.

11 **King demoiselle** *Chrysiptera rex* (Snyder) 7 cm
Ecology: reef margins and upper seaward slopes subject to mild surge, 1 to 6 m. **Range**: Indonesia to Vanuatu, n. to Ryuk., s. to nw. Australia & N. Cal.

12 **Talbot's demoiselle** *Chrysiptera talboti* (Allen) 6 cm
Ecology: coral-rich areas of seaward reef slopes and deep lagoons, 3 to 35 m. Feeds on zooplankton. **Range**: Andaman Sea to Fiji, n. to Palau & N. Britain, s. to Timor Sea & GBR.

13 **Tracey's demoiselle** *Chrysiptera traceyi* (Woods & Schultz) 6 cm
Ecology: coral, rock, or rubble habitats of lagoon and seaward reefs, below surge zone to 40 m. Usually in small groups close to bottom. Abundant in Mariana and Marshall Islands. **Range**: Caroline, Mariana & Marshall Is.

14 **Rolland's demoiselle** *Chrysiptera rollandi* (Whitley) 6 cm
Loyalty Is. & N. Cal. popul. with yellow forehead & nape. **Ecology**: among corals and coral rubble of inshore and outer reefs, 2 to 35 m. **Range**: Andaman Sea to Society Is., n. to Phil., s. to GBR & N. Cal.

15 **Onespot demoiselle** *Chrysiptera unimaculata* (Cuvier) 8 cm
Ecology: rubble and rocky areas of shallow inner reefs exposed to mild surge. **Range**: R. Sea to Fiji, n. to Ryuk., s. to GBR.

16 **Twospot demoiselle** *Chrysiptera biocellata* (Quoy & Gaimard) 11 cm
Ecology: rubbly areas of lagoon and inner reef flats to 5 m. Feeds on filamentous algae. **Range**: E. Africa to Samoa, n. to Ryuk., s. to Rowley Shoals & N. Cal.

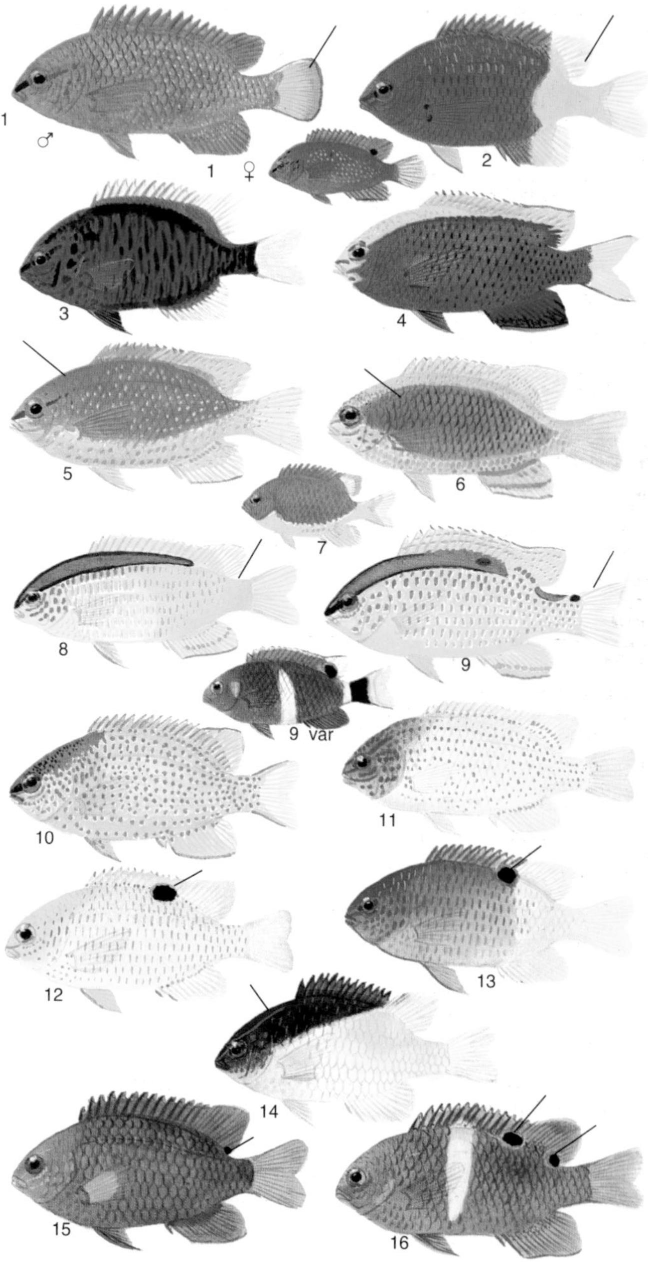
1
♂
1 ♀
2
3
4
5
6
7
8
9
9 var
10
11
12
13
14
15
16

1 **Threeband demoiselle** *Chrysiptera tricincta* (Allen & Robertson) 6 cm **Ecology:** coral or rock outcrops on sand of lagoon and inshore reefs, 10 to 38 m. **Range:** Indonesia to Samoa, n. to s. Japan, s. to se. Australia & N. Cal.

2 **Footballer demoiselle** *Chrysiptera annulata* (Peters) 8 cm **Ecology:** inshore and lagoon flats, in weedy and sandy areas, to 2 m. Common. **Range:** R. Sea & E. Africa s. to Durban, e. to Aldabra, Maurit. & Réunion.

3 **Grey demoiselle** *Chrysiptera glauca* (Cuvier) 11 cm **Ecology:** rubble and rocky areas of inner intertidal reef flats subject to mild surge. **Range:** E. Africa to Line Is., n. to s. Japan, s. to se. Australia & Pitcairn Is.

4 **Southern demoiselle** *Chrysiptera notialis* Allen 9 cm **Ecology:** outer rocky reefs, to 45 m. **Range:** L. Howe & Norfolk Is., to N. Cal.

Bleekers demoiselle *Chrysiptera bleekeri* (Fowler & Bean) 8 cm Similar to *C. flavipinnis*, but blue with a yellow back. **Ecology:** protected inner reef, 3-35 m. **Range:** Bali to Timor, Phillipines.

Black demoiselle *Chrysiptera niger* (Allen) 7 cm Blackish grey with a black spot at base of P fin. **Ecology:** shallow coastal reefs, 0-2 m. **Range:** se. New Guinea.

5 **Humbug dascyllus** *Dascyllus aruanus* (Linnaeus) 8 cm All species in genus feed on zooplankton, benthic inverts. and algae. **Ecology:** sheltered waters, 0.5 to 20 m. Among branching corals, primarily on subtidal reef flats. **Range:** R. Sea to Line, Marq. & Tuam. Is., n. to Ryuk., s. to L. Howe & Rapa Is.

6 **Black-tail dascyllus** *Dascyllus melanurus* Bleeker 8 cm **Ecology:** shallow sheltered waters to 10 m., among branching corals. Often with *D. aruanus*, but less common. **Range:** Sumatra to Vanuatu & e. Caroline Is., n. to Ryuk., s. to N. Cal.

7 **Three-spot dascyllus** *Dascyllus trimaculatus* (Rüppell) 14 cm *D. strasburgi* (Marq.) similar but lighter. **Ecology:** lagoon and seaward reefs, 1 to 55. Juveniles associated with large anemones which they share with species of *Amphiprion*. Adults in small groups around prominent coral mounds or rocks. **Range:** R. Sea to Line & Pitcairn Is., n. to s. Japan, s. to L. Howe Is.

8 **Yellow-tailed dascyllus** *Dascyllus flavicaudus* Randall & Allen 12 cm **Ecology:** coral and rocky reefs, 3 to 40 m. **Range:** se. Oceania: Soc., Tuam., Pitcairn & Rapa Is.

9 **Hawaiian dascyllus** *Dascyllus albisella* Gill 13 cm **Ecology:** coral and rocky areas below surge zone, 1 to 45 m. Juveniles associated with *Pocillopora* coral heads, or occasionally with the sand dwelling anemone *Heteractis malu*. **Range:** Hawaiian & Johnston Is.

10 **Red Sea dascyllus** *Dascyllus marginatus* (Rüppell) 6 cm **Ecology:** coral reefs, 1 to 15 m, usually associated with branching corals of the genera *Stylophora*, *Acropora*, and *Porites*. **Range:** R. Sea & G. of Oman.

11 **Indian dascyllus** *Dascyllus carneus* Fischer 6 cm **Ecology:** lagoon and seaward reefs, associated with branching corals, 5 to 35 m. **Range:** E. Africa s. to Durban, e. to Maldives, Andaman Sea & Java.

12 **Reticulated dascyllus** *Dascyllus reticulatus* (Richardson) 8 cm **Ecology:** outer lagoon and seaward reefs, 1 to 50 m. In colonies associated with heads of branching corals, particularly *Pocillopora eydouxi*. Abundant on exposed reefs. **Range:** Cocos-Keeling Is. to Samoa and Line Is., n. to s. Jap., s. to L. Howe Is.

1
2
3
4
5
6
7
7 juv
8
9
10
11
12

83 DAMSELFISHES

1 **White-spot damsel** *Dischistodus chrysopoecilus* (Schlegel & Müller) 15 cm
Ecology: coral outcrops and seagrass beds of silty lagoon and coastal reefs, 1 to 5 m. **Range:** Indonesia to Sol. Is., n. to Phil., s. to Ashmore Reef.

2 **Monarch damsel** *D. pseudochrysopoecilus* (Allen & Robertson) 17 cm
Ecology: among scattered live corals on sand or dead coral of reef flats and lagoon and inshore reefs, 1 to 5 m. **Range:** Phil., N. Guinea, Sol. Is. & GBR.

3 **Black-vent damsel** *Dischistodus melanotus* (Bleeker) 16 cm
Ecology: lagoon reefs, 1 to 10 m, usually around small patch reefs on sand or rubble. Feeds on benthic algae which it aggressively guards against other herbivores. **Range:** Indonesia to Sol. Is., n. to Yaeyama Is., s. to s. GBR.

4 **Honey-head damsel** *Dischistodus prosopotaenia* (Bleeker) 19 cm
Ecology: silty or sandy bottoms of lagoon and inshore reefs, 1 to 12 m. **Range:** Nicobar Is. to Vanuatu, n. to Ryuk., s. to nw. Australian shelf reefs & GBR.

5 **White damsel** *Dischistodus perspicillatus* (Cuvier) 20 cm
Ecology: small patch reefs of shallow sandy lagoons and seagrass beds to 10 m. **Range:** Andaman Is. to Sol. Is. & Vanuatu, n. to s. China, s. to Rowley Shoals & GBR.

6 **Banded damsel** *Dischistodus fasciatus* (Cuvier) 14 cm
Ecology: coral outcrops and seagrass beds of silty lagoon and coastal reefs, 1 to 5 m. **Range:** Indonesia, Phil. & nw. Australia.

7 **Lagoon damsel** *Hemiglyphidodon plagiometopon* (Bleeker) 20 cm
Juveniles orange-yellow posteroventrally with numerous blue lines and spots on face. **Ecology:** protected lagoon and coastal reefs, among branching corals with dead algae-covered bases, 1 to 20 m. Actively tends its algal garden by weeding out undesirable species and aggressively guarding against other herbivores. Also known as giant farmer fish. **Range:** Andaman Sea to Sol. Is., n. to s. China & Phil., s. to nw. Austalia & GBR.

8 **Black damsel** *Neoglyphidodon melas* (Cuvier) 16 cm
Ecology: lagoon and seaward reefs near soft corals, 1 to 12 m. Juveniles among staghorn *Acropora* corals. Feeds on soft corals. Adults often near *Tridacna* clams and may feed on their faeces. **Range:** R. Sea to Sol. Is. & Vanuatu, n. to Ryuk, s. to n. Australia.

9 **Behn's damsel** *Neoglyphidodon nigroris* (Cuvier) 13 cm
Ecology:coral-rich areas of lagoon and seaward reefs, 2 to 23 m. Usually solitary. Feeds on algae, plankton, and small crustaceans. **Range:** Andaman Sea to Sol. Is., n. to Ryuk., s. to N. Australia & Vanuatu.

10 **Ocellated damsel** *Neoglyphidodon bonang* (Bleeker) 14 cm
Ecology: coral reefs, 1 to 20 m. Uncommon. **Range:** Sri Lanka to Indonesia & Sol. Is.

11 **Cross' damsel** *Neoglyphidodon crossi* Allen 13 cm
Ecology: in shallow gutters of rocky areas or coral reefs in protected bays and lagoons, 1 to 5 m. Solitary and shy. **Range:** Bali, Sulawesi & Molucca Is.

12 **Carlson's damsel** *Neoglyphidodon carlsoni* (Allen) 13 cm
Ecology: fringing reefs on leeward sides of islands, generally around caves, 0.5 to 5 m. **Range:** Fiji.

1
2
3
4
5
6
7 juv
7
9 juv
8
juv
8
9
10
11
11 juv
12 juv
12

1 **Javanese damsel** *Neoglyphidodon oxyodon* (Bleeker) 15 cm
Ecology: protected reef flats of lagoon and inshore reefs to 4 m. **Range:** Indonesia, Phil. & Ashmore Reef.

2 **Barhead damsel** *Neoglyphidodon thoracotaeniatus* (Fowler & Bean) 12 cm
Ecology: coral-rich areas of seaward reef slopes, 15 to 45 m. **Range:** Indonesia, Phil, N. Guinea & Sol. Is.

3 **Multispine damsel** *Neoglyphidodon polyacanthus* (Ogilby) 15 cm
Ecology: coral and rocky reefs, 2 to 30 m. **Range:** s. GBR, L. Howe & Norfolk Is. & N. Cal.

4 **Yellowtail demoiselle** *Neopomacentrus azysron* (Bleeker) 8 cm
Resembles *N. bankieri* & *N. xanthurus* which lack the prominent dark opercular spot. **Ecology:** coastal reefs, often in surge channels and near ledges, 1 to 12 m. Species of *Neopomacentrus* occur in aggregations and feed on zooplankton. **Range:** E. Africa to Vanuatu, n. to Taiwan, s. to nw. Australia & GBR.

5 **Silver demoiselle** *Neopomacentrus anabatoides* (Bleeker) 10.5 cm
Resembles *N. filamentosus* & *N. metallicus* (Fiji & Samoa) which lack the dark operc. spot. **Ecology:** coral or rock outcrops on soft bottoms, 2 to 15 m. **Range:** Andaman Sea to Malaysia & c. Indonesia, n. to Phil.

6 **Chinese demoiselle** *Neopomacentrus bankieri* (Richardson) 8 cm
Queensland-PNG popul. us. with small dark spot in front of LL orig. **Ecology:** coastal reefs around coral or rock outcrops on soft bottoms, 3 to 12 m. **Range:** S. China & Java Seas; se. PNG to Queensland.

7 **Regal demoiselle** *Neopomacentrus cyanomos* (Bleeker) 10 cm
Ecology: inshore and outer coral reefs, 5 to 18 m. **Range:** R. Sea to Sol. Is., n. to s. Japan, s. to n. Australia.

8 **Red Sea Demoiselle** *Neopomacentrus xanthurus* Allen & Randall 6 cm
Similar to *N. azysron* and *N. sindensis* (Arab.G.), but lacks dark patch at top of operculum. **Ecology:** coral reefs, 1 to 15 m. In groups under overhangs. **Range:** s. R. Sea to G. Aden.

9 **Miry's demoiselle** *Neopomacentrus miryae* Dor & Allen 10.5 cm
Resembles *N. nemurus* which has dark opercular spot & lacks white spot behind D base. **Ecology:** inshore coral reefs, 2 to 25 m. In groups close to bottom. **Range:** n. & c. R. Sea.

10 **African demoiselle** *Neopomacentrus fuliginosus* (Smith) 10 cm
Resembles *N. sindensis* (Arab. G. & Arab. Sea). **Ecology:** near rock outcrops and weed beds of shallow sheltered coastal reefs, 1 to 10 m. **Range:** E. Africa, Kenya to Mozambique.

11 **Coral demoiselle** *Neopomacentrus nemurus* (Bleeker) 8 cm
Resembles *N. miryae* which has white spot behind D base & lacks dark opercular spot. **Ecology:** over coral outcrops of silty sheltered lagoon and coastal reefs, 1 to 10 m. **Range:** Indonesia to Sol. Is., n. to Phil., s. to n. Australia & N. Cal.

12 **Violet demoiselle** *Neopomacentrus violascens* (Bleeker) 7 cm
Ecology: protected coastal bays, lagoons, and harbors, 1 to 30 m. **Range:** Indonesia to Sol. Is., n. to s. China, s. to n. Australia & Vanuatu.

13 **Brown demoiselle** *Neopomacentrus filamentosus* (Macleay) 8 cm
Resembles *N. metallicus* (Fiji & Samoa) which has a dark outer P axil. **Ecology:** coral and rock outcrops on soft bottoms of coastal reefs, 5 to 12 m. **Range:** Andaman Sea to Sol. Is., n. to Phil., s. to N. Cal.

14 **Banded scalyfin** *Parma polylepis* Günther 21 cm
Ecology: rocky and coral reefs, 1 to 40 m. Several other species in temperate waters. **Range:** s. GBR to NSW, e. to L. Howe & Norfolk Is., N. Cal. & n. NZ.

15 **Bigscaled scalyfin** *Parma oligolepis* Whitley 21 cm
P. alboscapularis similar (L. Howe to NZ), but with white spot on opercle. **Ecology:** rocky and occasionally coral reefs, 2 to 20 m. **Range:** e. Australia from s. Queensland to Sydney.

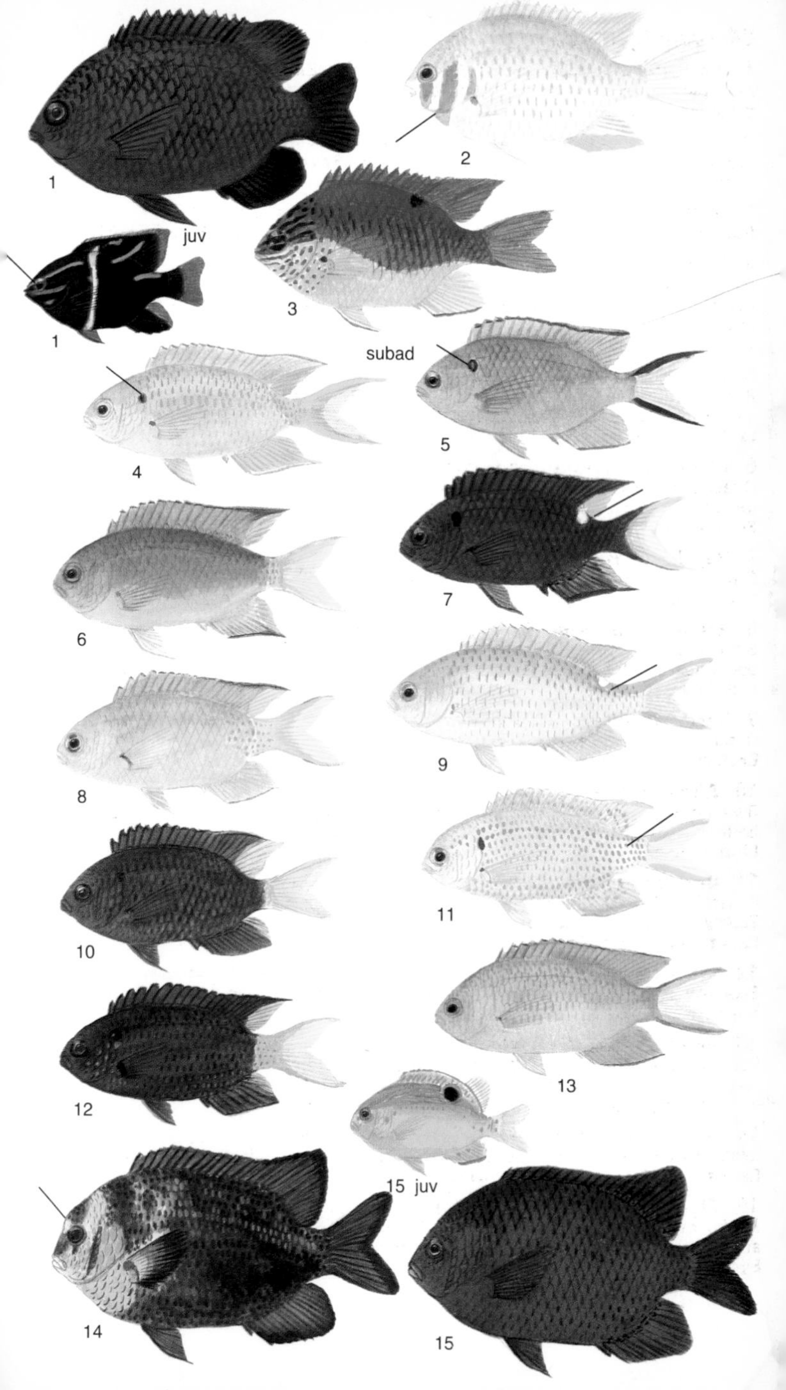
1
2
juv
1
3
subad
4
5
7
6
9
8
11
10
13
12
15 juv
14
15

1 **Caerulean damsel** *Pomacentrus caeruleus* Quoy & Gaimard 8 cm
Ecology: lagoon and outer reef slopes, usually over rubble near base of reefs, 1 to 20 m. In loose aggregations. **Range:** G. Aden & E. Africa s. to Durban, e. to Maldives.

2 **Neon damsel** *Pomacentrus coelestis* Jordan & Starks 9 cm
Ecology: rubbly areas of clear reefs exposed to mild surge or currents, 1 to 20 m. In aggregations near the bottom. **Range:** Sri Lanka to Line & Tuam Is., n. to s. Japan, s. to n. Australia

3 **Goldbelly damsel** *Pomacentrus auriventris* Allen 7 cm
Ecology: rubble slopes, 1 to 15 m. In aggregations, often with *P. coelestis* (Seychelles & n. Austr). Common. **Range:** Christmas Is. & Bali to Flores & Moluccas, n. to Palau.

4 **Andaman damsel** *Pomacentrus alleni* Burgess 6 cm
Similar to *P. coelestis* but with black lower lobe of tail. **Ecology:** rubble and dead reef areas of inshore and outer reef slopes, 3 to 15 m. **Range:** Similan Is.

5 **Similar damsel** *Pomacentrus similis* Allen 7 cm
Resembles *P. coelestis* but has dark D & A fins & dusky tail margin. **Ecology:** coral reefs, 2 to 10 m. In small groups. **Range:** Sri Lanka & Andaman Sea.

6 **Australian damsel** *Pomacentrus australis* Allen & Robertson 8 cm
Ecology: coral or rock outcrops in sandy areas, 5 to 35 m. **Range:** e. Australia from GBR s. to Sydney.

7 **Philippine damsel** *Pomacentrus philippinus* Evermann & Seale 10 cm
Maldives fish black with yellow tail; GBR fish nearly black, lacking yellow entirely **Ecology:** lagoon, channel, and seaward reef slopes, 1 to 12 m. In groups near overhangs. **Range:** Maldives to Fiji, n. to Ryuk., s. to nw. Aust. shelf reefs & N. Cal.

8 **Blue damsel** *Pomacentrus pavo* (Bloch) 11 cm
Lg. ♂ may have bright yellow P fins; yellow on tail variable, occas. absent; ground color variable, pale green (Andaman Sea) to deep blue. **Ecology:** shallow lagoon reefs, 1 to 16 m. In groups among coral outcrops and patch reefs surrounded by sand. Feeds on zooplankton and filamentous algae. **Range:** E. Africa to Tuam., n. to Mariana & Marshal Is., s. to L. Howe Is.

9 **Creole damsel** *Pomacentrus agassizi* Bliss 11 cm
Ecology: inshore and lagoon reefs, 1 to 4 m. Usually among staghorn *Acropora* corals. **Range:** Madag., Maurit. & Réunion.

10 **Indonesian damsel** *Pomacentrus melanochir* Bleeker 7 cm
Ecology: inshore coral reefs subject to strong currents, 1 to 8 m. **Range:** Bali & Sulawesi to Moluccas & Timor.

11 **Brackish damsel** *Pomacentrus taeniometopon* Bleeker 12 cm
♂ occasionally with a yellow tail. Juvs. with turquoise stripes on nape. **Ecology:** mangrove creeks, brackish lagoons and reefs exposed to runoff, 0 to 5 m. **Range:** Indochina to Indonesia (Sulawesi), n. to Taiwan & Ryuk.

12 **Blue-spotted damsel** *Pomacentrus azuremaculatus* Allen 10 cm
Ecology: offshore coral reefs, 5 to 30 m. **Range:** Andaman Sea (Similan Is.; Phuket) to Java Sea (Seribu Is.).

13 **Reid's damsel** *Pomacentrus reidi* Fowler & Bean 11 cm
Ecology: steep lagoon and outer reef slopes, 3 to 70 m. Solitary or in small loose groups. **Range:** Indonesia to Vanuatu, n. to Phil. & Palau, s. to n. GBR.

14 **Baensch's damsel** *Pomacentrus baenschi* Allen 10 cm
Ecology: coastal and offshore coral-rich reefs, 1 to 20 m. Solitary and close to substrate. Uncommon. **Range:** E. Africa (Kenya to Mozambique), Comore & adjacent Is.

15 **Princess damsel** *Pomacentrus vaiuli* Jordan & Seale 9 cm
Variable in intensity of blue and tan, may be dark or light; juvs. similar to *P. bankanensis*. **Ecology:** lagoon and seaward reefs, 1 to 40 m. Solitary but common in areas of mixed coral and rubble. Feeds on filamentous algae and small invertebrates. **Range:** Moluccas to Samoa, n. to Izu Is., s. to nw. Aust. shelf reefs, N. Cal. & GBR.

1
2
3
4
5
6
7
8
8 var
9
10
11
12
13
14
15

1 **Sulphur damsel** *Pomacentrus sulfureus* Klunzinger 11 cm
Ecology: inshore coral reefs in areas of rich coral growth, 0.5 to 15 m. **Range**: R. Sea & E. Africa s. to 21°S, e. to Seychelles & Maurit.

2 **Lemon damsel** *Pomacentrus moluccensis* Bleeker 7 cm
Some indiv. (Fiji & Tonga) mostly purplish brown with yellow tail. Resembles *P. pikei.* **Ecology**: clear lagoon and seaward reefs, 1 to 14 m. In small groups among branching corals. Feeds on algae and planktonic crustaceans. **Range**: Andaman Sea to Fiji, n. to Ryuk. & Carol. Is., s. to N. Cal.

3 **Blacklip damsel** *Pomacentrus pikei* Bliss 11 cm
Ecology: inshore coral and rocky reefs, 1 to 6 m. Rare. **Range**: Mauritius & Réunion.

4 **Ambon damsel** *Pomacentrus amboinensis* Bleeker 10 cm
Highly variable in color, ranging from yellow to light blue or dark brown, often yellowish ventrally; juvs. with blue ocellus on soft D which is retained in adults from Andaman Sea. **Ecology**: sheltered reefs, 3 to 40 m. In groups around coral outcrops bordering sand. **Range**: Andaman Sea to Vanuatu, n. to Ryuk., s. to nw. Aust. shelf, GBR & N. Cal.

5 **Scaly damsel** *Pomacentrus lepidogenys* Fowler & Bean 9 cm
Ecology: lagoon, coastal, and seaward reefs, 1 to 12 m, near branching corals. **Range**: Andaman Sea to Fiji & Tonga, n. to Phil. & Palau (rare), s. to GBR & N. Cal.

6 **Blackmargined damsel** *Pomacentrus nigromarginatus* Allen 8 cm
Fish outside Indonesia are primarily gray with little or no yellow posteriorly. **Ecology**: outer reef slopes around coral and rock outcrops, 10 to 50 m. **Range**: Indonesia to Sol. Is., n. to Ryuk., s. to nw. Australian shelf reefs & n. GBR.

7 **Black-axil damsel** *Pomacentrus nigromanus* Weber 9 cm
Ecology: lagoon and seaward reef slopes, 6 to 60 m. In groups. Feeds on plankton, algae, and small invertebrates. **Range**: Indonesia to Sol. Is., n. to Phil. & Palau, s. to nw. Australia & Vanuatu.

8 **Bluespot damsel** *Pomacentrus grammorhynchus* Fowler 11 cm
Light blue spot on upper C peduncle present at all sizes; juvs. similar to *P. simsiang;* adults from Seribu Is. dark with orange tail. **Ecology**: lagoon and inshore reefs, 2 to 12 m, often among branching corals. **Range**: Indonesia to Sol. Is., n. to Taiwan, s. to n. GBR.

9 **Speckled damsel** *Pomacentrus bankanensis* Bleeker 9 cm
Juv. similar to *P. vaiuli* but with blue stripe on midline of snout & forehead. **Ecology**: clear lagoon and semi-protected seaward reefs, 1 to 12 m. In small groups among patches of rubble or sand with scattered corals. Feeds primarily on benthic algae. **Range**: Christmas Is. to Fiji, n. to s. Japan, s. to nw. Aust. shelf reefs & N. Cal.

10 **Colombo damsel** *Pomacentrus proteus* Allen 10 cm
Similar to *P. milleri* (n. & w. Aust.) which has a smaller D ocellus in ad. **Ecology**: silty coastal reefs among coral or rubble, 2 to 10 m. **Range**: Sri Lanka.

11 **Whitefin damsel** *Pomacentrus albicaudatus* Baschieri-Salvadori 6 cm
Ecology: inshore and offshore reefs, 1 to 12 m. **Range**: R. Sea.

12 **Whitetail damsel** *Pomacentrus chrysurus* Cuvier 9 cm
Ecology: reef flats and shallow lagoon and coastal reefs to 3 m. In small groups in sandy areas near corals. Feeds primarily on benthic algae. **Range**: Sri Lanka & Maldives to Sol. Is., n. to Ryuk., s. to N. Cal.

13 **Molucca damsel** *Pomacentrus simsiang* Bleeker 9 cm
Resembles *P. grammorhynchus* but lacks blue spot on C peduncle. **Ecology**: silty lagoon and inshore reefs, 1 to 10 m. Feeds primarily on benthic algae. **Range**: Indonesia & Phil. to Sol. Is., n. to Ryuk., s. to Vanuatu.

14 **Pailtail damsel** *Pomacentrus trichrous* Günther 11 cm
Tail ranges from white to yellow; resembles *P. albicaudatus* and *P. leptus*. **Ecology**: inshore and offshore coral reefs, 1 to 43 m. **Range**: R. Sea & w. Indian Ocean s. to Natal.

15 **Slender damsel** *Pomacentrus leptus* Allen & Randall 7 cm
Ecology: primarily inshore reefs, 1 to 10 m. In large aggregations close to substrate. Sometimes solitary. **Range**: s. R. Sea (common) to G. Aden & G. Oman, s. to E. Africa.

1
2
3
4
5
6
7
8 juv
8
9
10
11
12
12 juv
13
14
15

87 DAMSELFISHES

1 **Obscure damsel** *Pomacentrus adelus* Allen 8 cm
Juv. with blue streaks on head and blue speckles on body. **Ecology:** lagoon, coastal, and seaward reefs, 0 to 8 m. **Range:** w. Thail. to Vanuatu, n. to Phil. & Palau, s. to nw. Aust. shelf reefs, GBR & N. Cal.

2 **Threespot damsel** *Pomacentrus tripunctatus* Cuvier 10 cm
Black blotch on upper C ped. distinct; juvs. with blue ocellus. Many similar non-descript grey to black spp. that lack C ped. spot incl. *P. aquilus* (G. Oman), *P. arabicus* (R. Sea to Mad.), *P. colini* (s. PNG), *P. cuneatus* (Ambon) & *P. javanicus* (Seribu Is.). **Ecology:** shallow inshore reefs, in "dead" areas, 0 to 3 m. **Range:** Sri Lanka to Vanuatu, n. to Andaman Sea & Phil., s. to GBR.

3 **Whitespot damsel** *Pomacentrus albimaculus* Allen 10 cm
Ecology: inshore areas, among rocky outcrops and debris on sand, 10 to 20 m. **Range:** n. PNG & possibly Taiwan.

4 **Dark damsel** *Pomacentrus aquilus* Allen & Randall 11 cm
Closely resembles *P. arabicus* (G. Oman). **Ecology:** inshore coral reefs, 0 to 15 m. **Range:** R. Sea & E. Africa, e. to Madag., n. to Arab. G.

5 **Indian damsel** *Pomacentrus indicus* Allen 11 cm
Juvs. with orange on head & back, this area shrinking with age. **Ecology:** lagoon and seaward reefs, 1 to 15 m, solitary or in small groups. **Range:** Sri Lanka & Seychelles, Chagos & Maldive Is.

6 **Charcoal damsel** *Pomacentrus brachialis* Cuvier 10 cm
Ecology: channel and seaward reef slopes, 6 to 40 m. Feeds on zooplankton and algae. **Range:** Indonesia to Fiji, n. to Ryuk. & Marshall Is, s. to N. Cal.

7 **Nagasaki damsel** *Pomacentrus nagasakiensis* Tanaka 11 cm
Ecology: sandy areas near reefs, 3 to 35 m. Feeds primarily on zooplankton. **Range:** Sri Lanka to Vanuatu, n. to s. Japan, s. to nw. Aust. & N. Cal.

8 **Imitator damsel** *Pomacentrus imitator* (Whitley) 11 cm
Similar to *P. philippinus* but never with bright yellow on D, A & tail fins. **Ecology:** outer reef slopes, 2 to 15 m. **Range:** GBR, Coral Sea, N. Cal., Rotuma, Fiji & Tonga.

9 **Alexander's damsel** *Pomacentrus alexanderae* Evermann & Seale 9 cm
Ecology: lagoon, inshore, and offshore reefs, 5 to 30 m. **Range:** Indonesia n. to Taiwan & Ryuk.

10 **Smith's damsel** *Pomacentrus smithi* Fowler & Bean 7 cm
Ecology: lagoon and inshore reefs, 2 to 14 m. In live coral patches in silty areas. **Range:** Indonesia to Sol. Is., n. to Phil., s. to Vanuatu.

11 **Outer-reef damsel** *Pomacentrus emarginatus* Cuvier 10 cm
Ecology: outer reef slopes, 4 to 12 m. Singly or in groups. Feeds on zooplankton and algae. **Range:** Palau & N. Guinea.

12 **Threeline damsel** *Pomacentrus trilineatus* Cuvier 10 cm
Ad. variable, yellowish to brown or blue-grey. **Ecology:** rocky inshore areas and coral reefs, 0 to 4 m. **Range:** R. Sea s. to Mozambique and Madag.

13 **Blackspot damsel** *Pomacentrus stigma* Fowler & Bean 13 cm
Ecology: coastal reefs, 2 to 10 m. in small groups around coral outcrops. **Range:** Phil.

14 **Burrough's damsel** *Pomacentrus burroughi* Fowler 8 cm
P. colini (New Guinea) and *P. wardi* (GBR to Sydney) similar, but both are brown. **Ecology:** lagoon and coastal reefs, 2 to 16 m. Feeds primarily on benthic algae. **Range:** Phil., New Guinea, Sol. Is. & Palau.

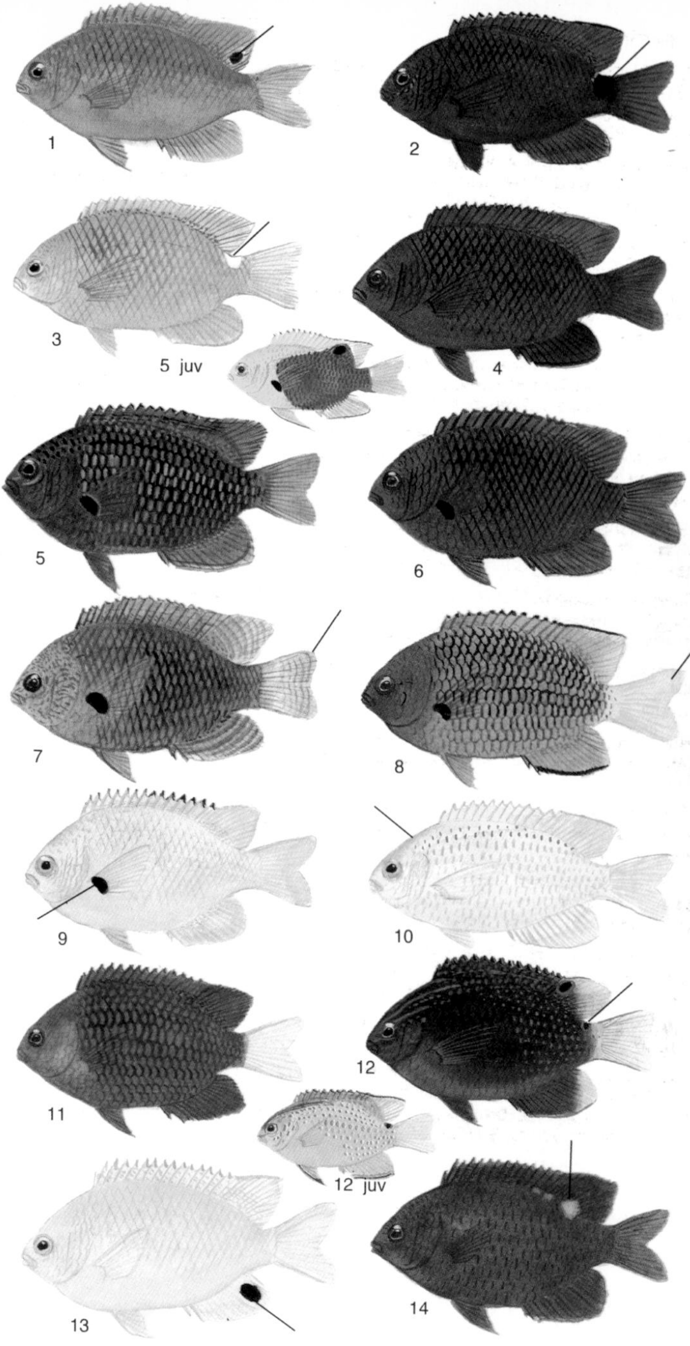
1
2
3
4
5 juv
5
6
7
8
9
10
11
12
12 juv
13
14

1 **Whitebar gregory** *Stegastes albifasciatus* (Schlegel & Müller) 13 cm
Ecology: reef flats, lagoons and semi-shelteR. Seaward reefs to 4 m. Common around rock or rubble surrounded by coral and exposed to mild surge. **Range:** Seychelles & Réunion to Line & Tuam. Is., n. to Ryuk., s. to N. Cal.

2 **Pacific gregory** *Stegastes fasciolatus* (Ogilby) 15 cm
W.-c. Indian Ocean popul. with rear of D, A & tail fins variably yellow. **Ecology:** rocky and coral reefs exposed to moderate surge, 1 to 30 m, but usually under 5 m. Territorial around a filamentous algae-covered patch of rock or dead coral. **Range:** E. Africa to Hawaiian & Easter Is., n. to Ryuk., s. to L. Howe & Kermadec Is.

3 **Bluntsnout gregory** *Stegastes lividus* (Bloch & Schneider) 13 cm
Ecology: shallow reef flats and lagoon reefs to 5 m, usually in colonies among partially dead staghorn corals. Extremely aggressive and pugnacious, will attempt to chase all intruders, even a diver. Also known as the "farmer fish" because of its habit of "weeding" an algal garden growing on dead coral branches by removing undesirable species in order to promote the growth of preferred species. Makes loud staccato sounds. Common. **Range:** R. Sea to Line & Society Is., n. to Ryuk. & Bonin Is., s. to N. Cal. & Tonga.

4 **Dusky gregory** *Stegastes nigricans* (Lacépède) 13 cm
Snout shorter than *S. lividus*; breeding males develop a broad light band on middle of sides and light streak from mouth to top of P axil. **Ecology:** reef flats and lagoon reefs to 10 m. Pugnacious and territorial, maintains and "weeds" a patch of filamentous algae growing on dead coral. **Range:** R. Sea to Line, Marq. & Tuam. Is., n. to Ryuk. & Bonin Is., s. to N. Cal. & Tonga.

5 **Golden gregory** *Stegastes aureus* (Fowler) 11 cm
Ecology: inshore and offshore reefs, 1 to 5 m. **Range:** N. Cal. & Gilbert, Phoenix, Samoan, Line, Marq. & Tuam. Is.

6 **Coral Sea gregory** *Stegastes gascoynei* (Whitley) 15 cm
Ecology: coral and rocky reefs, 2 to 30 m. **Range:** e. Australia from s. GBR to Sydney, e. to N. Cal., s. to n. N. Zeal

7 **Island gregory** *Stegastes insularis* Allen & Emery 11 cm
Ecology: seaward reefs, 1 to 10 m, usually in less than 3 m. **Range:** Christmas & Marcus Is. only.

8 **Emery's gregory** *Stegastes emeryi* (Allen & Randall) 10 cm
Ecology: outer rocky and coral reefs, 1 to 18 m. **Range:** Tuam., Pitcairn Is., Oeno & Ducie Atolls.

9 **Australian gregory** *Stegastes apicalis* (DeVis) 15 cm
Juv. with ocellus on front of D fin and lack yellow on posterior D fin and tail margins. Similar to *S. altus* which lacks the bright yellow margins on D fin & tail. **Ecology:** inshore and coastal reefs, 1 to 5 m on inner portions of GBR. **Range:** E. Australia from Cape York to Sydney.

10 **Mauritian gregory** *Stegastes pelicieri* Allen & Emery 14 cm
Juv. resembles *Plectroglyphidodon lacrymatus* but distal margins of A fin & tail yellow. **Ecology:** rocky reefs with little coral cover, 2 to 20 m. Close to crevices and holes. **Range:** Maurit.

11 **Western gregory** *Stegastes obreptus* (Whitley) 15 cm
Snout shorter than *S. lividus*; breeding males develop a broad light band on middle of sides and light streak from mouth to top of P axil. **Ecology:** reef flats and lagoon reefs to 10 m. Pugnacious and territorial, maintains and "weeds" a patch of filamentous algae growing on dead coral. **Range:** India to Moluccas., n. to Ryuk., s. to w. Austr.

12 **Ebony gregory** *Stegastes limbatus* (Cuvier) 13 cm
Ecology: surge zone of inshore boulder areas, 1 to 2 m. Pugnacious. Common. **Range:** Madagascar, Mauritius & Réunion.

13 **Japanese gregory** *Stegastes altus* (Okada & Ikeda) 15 cm
Similar to juv. *S. apicalis*. **Ecology:** rocky reefs, 5 to 20 m. **Range:** Ryuk. & Izu Is. to s. Japan.

1
2
2a
3
4
4 var
5
6
7
8
9
10
11
12
13

89 DAMSELFISHES

1 **Spiny chromis** *Acanthochromis polyacanthus* (Bleeker) 15 cm
Color highly variable, depending on geog. locality. May be entirely black or greenish. Juv. with yellow stripes. **Ecology:** inshore and offshore coral reefs, 1 to 65 m. Lacks a larval stage, the only coral reef fish in which the fry are guarded by the parents. **Range:** Indonesia & Phil. to Sol. Is. & Vanuatu, s. to GBR.

2 **Black banded demoiselle** *Amblypomacentrus breviceps* (Schlegel & al.) 7 cm
Chrysiptera rapanui similar (Kermadec, Easter Is.), but on rocky and coral reefs. **Ecology:** lagoon and coastal areas, 2 to 35 m. Usually in small groups around rock or sponge outcrops on silty bottoms. **Range:** w. Indonesia to Sol. Is., n. to Phil., s. to Queensland.

3 **Big-lip damsel** *Cheiloprion labiatus* (Day) 11 cm
Lips enlarged and curled, may be lighter than rest of body. **Ecology:** shallow lagoon reefs to 3 m, among branching corals. Feeds on coral polyps. **Range:** Sri Lanka to Solomon Is., n. to Phil. & Palau, s. to n. Australia & Vanuatu.

4 **Fusilier damsel** *Lepidozygus tapeinosoma* (Bleeker) 10 cm
Ecology: clear lagoon and seaward reefs along upper slopes in areas exposed to currents, 1 to 25 m. In aggregations that feed on zooplankton. **Range:** E. Africa to Line, Marq. & Tuam. Is., n. to Ryuk., s. to N. Cal.

5 **Slender reef-damsel** *Pomachromis exilis* (Allen & Emery) 7 cm
Ecology: lagoon and seaward reefs, 8 to 12 m. An aggregating planktivore. **Range:** Marshall and Caroline Is.

6 **Tahiti damsel** *Pomachromis fuscidorsalis* (Allen & Randall) 8 cm
Ecology: seaward and outer channel reefs, 1 to 18 m. In surgy and current-swept areas. **Range:** Society, Tuam. & Pitcairn Is.

7 **Guam damsel** *Pomachromis guamensis* (Allen & Larson) 8 cm
Ecology: exposed seaward reefs, 3 to 33 m. Abundant on barren terraces swept by surge or currents. In large groups, feeds on zooplankton. **Range:** Marianas.

8 **Richardson's damsel** *Pomachromis richardsoni* (Snyder) 8 cm
Ecology: coral and rocky reefs exposed to surge, 5 to 25 m. In small loose groups close to the bottom. Common. **Range:** Maurit., Ryuk. & Taiwan, GBR, Loyalty Is., Fiji & Samoa.

9 **Bluedotted damsel** *Pristotis cyanostigma* Rüppell 11 cm
Ecology: inshore and offshore coral reefs, 5 to 10 m. **Range:** R. Sea & G. Aden.

10 **Gulf damsel** *Pristotis jobtusirostris* (Günther) 14 cm
Ecology: lagoon and coastal bottoms, around patch reefs on flat sand or rubble bottoms, 2 to 80 m. **Range:** R. Sea to N. Cal., n. to Arab. G. & Ryuk.; primarily continental margins.

11 **Jordan's damsel** *Teixeirichthys jordani* (Rutter) 14 cm
Ecology: seagrass beds and sandy bottoms, 10 to 20 m. Primarily continental coasts. **Range:** R. Sea to s. Japan, s. to E. Africa.

12 **Spinecheek anemonefish** *Premnas biaculeatus* (Bloch) 17 cm
♂ smaller and bright red with brilliant white bars; large ♀ become dark, almost black with subdued bars, sometimes barely visible; Sumatra popul. with yellow bars (var.). **Ecology:** lagoon and seaward reefs, 1 to 16 m. Exclusively with *Entacmaea quadricolor.* **Range:** w. Indonesia to Vanuatu, n. to Taiwan, s. to n. GBR.

1
2
3
3 juv
4
5
6
7
8
9
10
11
12
♀
12

WRASSES (LABRIDAE): a large and diverse group in both size and form. Typically with terminal mouth, somewhat thickened lips, one or more pairs of protruding canine teeth, nodular pharyngeal teeth, elongate body, continuous or interupted LL and single unnotched D fin. Most species change color with growth and sex. Typically a drab initial phase (IP) of both males and females, the latter able to change sex into a brilliant terminal male phase (TP). All species inactive at night, the smaller ones often sleep beneath the sand. Includes carnivores, planktivores, and cleaners. Most species do well in aquariums. Medium to large species important foodfishes in many areas.
Tribe Hypseginyini: characterized by rather large mouths with one or more pairs of canines in front of jaws, continuous LL, and relatively large scales (24-57). Carnivores of benthic invertebrates. Some species change color with growth but sexes generally similar.

1 **Lyretail hogfish** *Bodianus anthioides* (Bennett) 21 cm
Color pattern does not change much with growth. **Ecology:** seaward reefs, usually around dropoffs, 6 to 60 m. Species of *Bodianus* are generally solitary and feed primarily on benthic invertebrates that are crushed with their pharyngeal teeth. **Range:** R. Sea to Line and Tuamotu Is., n. to s. Japan, s. to N. Cal.

2 **Diana's hogfish** *Bodianus diana* (Lacépède) 25 cm
B. prognathodes (Line Is.) has an identical color pattern, but with a much longer snout. **Ecology:** coral-rich areas of seaward reefs, 6 to 25 m. Juveniles often near black corals or gorgonians. **Range:** R. Sea to Samoa, n. to s. Japan, s. to N. Cal. and Tonga.

3 **Mesothorax hogfish** *Bodianus mesothorax* (Schneider) 19 cm
Ecology: steep outer reef slopes, 5 to over 20 m. **Range:** Christmas Is. to PNG, n. to s. Japan, s. to s. GBR.

4 **Axilspot hogfish** *Bodianus axillaris* (Bennett) 20 cm
Ecology: clear lagoon and seaward reefs, 2 to 40 m. Juveniles usually in caves or under ledges and sometimes serve as cleaners. **Range:** R. Sea to Marq. and Pitcairn Is., n. to s. Japan, s. to L. Howe Is.

5 **Goldspot pigfish** *Bodianus perditio* (Quoy & Gaimard) 80 cm
Ecology: seaward reefs, often near patches of sand and rubble below 10 m. **Range:** disjunct, fringes of tropics and warm-temperate seas: n. Mozambique to s. Africa, e. to Maurit.; s. Japan to Taiwan; w. and e. Australia to N. Cal. and L. Howe Is; Tuamotus and Rapa to Pitcairn gp.

6 **Saddleback hogfish** *Bodianus bilunulatus* (Lacépède) 55 cm
Large ♂ become mostly dark reddish brown; similar to *B. macrourus* (Mauritius). **Ecology:** clear lagoon and seaward reefs, 8 to at least 108 m. Common on coral-rich slopes or over rubble and sand. **Range:** subsp. *bilunulatus*: E. Africa to Marq. & Pitcairn gp., n. to s. Japan, s. to Natal, w. Aust. and N. Cal.; subsp. *albotaeniatus*: Hawaiian Is.

7 **Blackfin hogfish** *Bodianus loxozonus* (Snyder) 47 cm
Large ♂ become mostly dark reddish brown, retaining the black areas of fins. **Ecology:** clear lagoon and seaward reefs, 3 to over 40 m. **Range:** subsp. *loxozonus* from Viet. to Marshall Is. & Tonga., n. to Ryuk. & Bonin Is., subsp. *trotteri* from Line Is., Cook Is., and Fr. Polynesia.

8 **Blackspot pigfish** *Bodianus vulpinus* (Richardson) 60 cm
B. leucostictus (sw. Indian Oc.; s. Jap.), *B. frenchii* (s. Aust.), and 1-2 undescribed deep water spp. (Aust., N. Z., s. Jap., Hawaii) are similar but lack the dark blotch on D fin **Ecology:** deeper reefs with high vertical relief, generally below 30 m. **Range:** warm-temperate seas, s. China to s. Jap., Hawaiian Is. (us. >100 m), sw. and se. Aust. to n. NZ, Rapa, and Easter Is.

9 **Mauritius hogfish** *Bodianus macrourus* (Lacépède) 32 cm
Large ♂ become mostly dark reddish brown, retaining the black areas of fins **Ecology:** exposed seaward reefs with sand patches, 10 to 40 m, generally below 15 m. **Range:** Maurit., Réunion & St. Brandon's Shoals.

10 **Red-striped hogfish** *Bodianus opercularis* (Guichenot) 18 cm
Several similar elongate spp. occur below 100 m in tropical and warm-temperate reefs. **Ecology:** rubble bottoms of steep outer reef slopes, 35 to 70 m. **Range:** R. Sea to Christmas Is., s. to Maurit.

11 **Two-spot slender hogfish** *Bodianus bimaculatus* Allen 10 cm
Closely related to *B. opercularis* and other small elongate mostly deep-water species. **Ecology:** steep outer reef slopes, 30 to 60 m. Typically around rubble and sand. **Range:** Maurit. & Maldives to PNG, n. to s. Japan.

1
2 juv
2
3
juv
juv 4
juv 5
6
6 juv
7
8
9
10
11

1 **Harlequin tuskfish** *Choerodon fasciatus* (Günther) 25 cm
Ecology: seaward reefs, 1 to 15 m. Common in s. GBR but rare elsewhere. Species of *Choerodon* have large protruding canines used for moving rubble to expose invertebrate prey and prying mollusks from the bottom. Hard-shelled prey is crushed by pharyngeal teeth. They are generally solitary and territorial, but range over a large area of reef. **Range:** Taiwan, Ryuk., Vanuatu, GBR, N. Cal. & L. Howe Is.

2 **Yellow-cheek tuskfish** *Choerodon anchorago* (Bloch) 38 cm
Ecology: reef flats and lagoon reefs to 25 m, in areas of seagrasses or mixed sand, rubble, and coral. Occasionally in small groups. **Range:** India to PNG, n. to Ryuk., s. to to N. Cal.

3 **Azure tuskfish** *Choerodon azurio* (Jordan & Snyder) 40 cm
Ecology: coastal reefs, on patches of sand and rubble. **Range:** s. China, Taiwan to s. Korea & s. Japan.

4 **Jordan's tuskfish** *Choerodon jordani* (Snyder) 17 cm
Similar to *C. zosterophorus* (Phil. to PNG) which has a black patch restricted to the rear upper body. **Ecology:** small coral heads and rubble bottoms of outer reef slopes, 15 to 30 m, usually below 20 m. Common in s. GBR. **Range:** Phil. to Samoa, n. to s. Japan, s. to N. Cal.

5 **Graphic tuskfish** *Choerodon graphicus* (DeVis) 46 cm
Ecology: lagoon and seaward reefs, on patches of sand and rubble. Relatively common and easily approached. **Range:** s. GBR & N. Cal. only.

6 **Purple tuskfish** *Choerodon cephalotes* (Castelnau) 38 cm
Ecology: coastal reefs and shallow flat bottoms in areas of seagrasses or sand and rubble. Rare on the GBR. **Range:** Indonesia & n. Australia s. to s. Queensland.

7 **Blackspot tuskfish** *Choerodon schoenleinii* (Valenciennes) 90 cm
Ecology: flat sandy or weedy areas near lagoon and seaward reefs, 10 to 60 m. Will overturn large rocks in search of food. Also known to rest on the bottom during the day. Uncommon in the s. GBR. **Range:** Indonesia to PNG, n. to Ryuk., s. to w. Aust. & s. GBR.

8 **Venus tuskfish** *Choerodon venustus* (DeVis) 65 cm
Ecology: common on outer reef slopes, in areas of sand and rubble. **Range:** Australia from GBR to n. NSW only.

9 **Baldchin groper** *Choerodon rubescens* (Günther) 90 cm
Ecology: coral reefs and weedy rocky reefs. **Range:** w. Aust. only.

10 **Blue tuskfish** *Choerodon cyanodus* (Richardson) 71 cm
Ecology: reef flats and flat shelf bottoms of outer reef slopes in areas of sand and rubble. Feeds on mollusks. Common. **Range:** Sri Lanka to PNG, n. to Ryuk., s. to N. Cal.

11 **Zamboanga tuskfish** *Choerodon zamboangae* (Seale & Bean) 25 cm
May be the male of *C. robusta* (Persian Gulf to Ryuk.). **Ecology:** flat sandy or weedy areas. **Range:** Phil. to nw. Aust. shelf.

Tribe Cheilinini: characterized by an interupted LL with posterior section along axis of tail-base. Species range in size from 5 to 229 cm. Most are carnivores of benthic invertebrates, but *Cirrhilabrus* and *Paracheilinus* (pls. 94-95) are planktivores. Species of *Cheilinus* and *Oxycheilinus* have relatively large scales, large canines in the front of their jaws, and do not change greatly in color with growth or sex. Species of *Epibulus* and *Wetmorella* have large scales and undergo major changes in color with growth or sex.

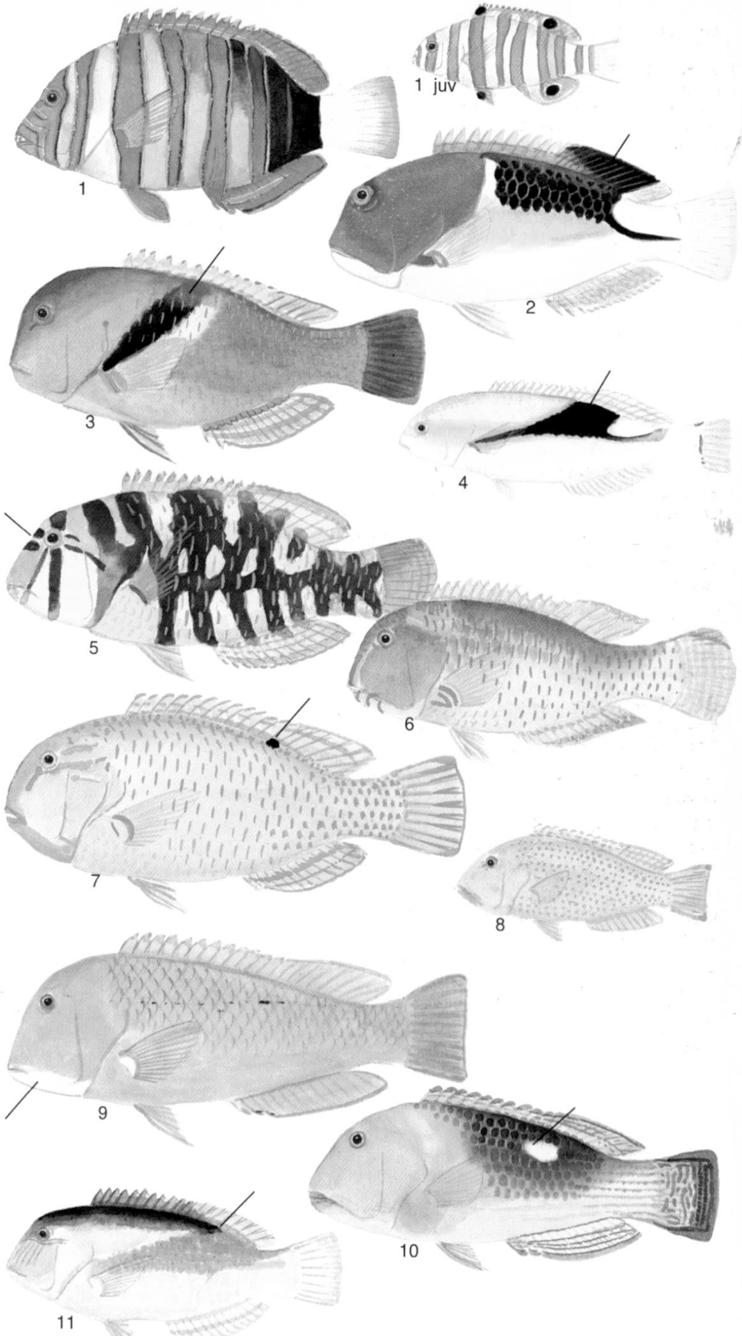
1 juv
1
2
3
4
5
6
7
8
9
10
11

See previous page for introduction to the Tribe Cheilinini

1 **Humphead wrasse; Napoleonfish** *Cheilinus undulatus* Rüppell 229 cm
Among the largest of reef fishes, weighing up to 191 kg. Adults with prominent hump on forehead. Juvs. distinguished from other spp. by two black lines extending behind eye. **Ecology:** lagoon and seaward reefs from 1 to at least 60 m. Juveniles occur among branching corals in shallow lagoons, adults prefer upper margins of clear lagoon pinnacles and steep coral slopes and usually have a home cave in which they sleep. Usually solitary. Feeds primarily on mollusks and a wide variety of well-armored invertebrates; even will take toxic prey such as crown-of-thorns starfish, boxfishes, or sea hares. Extremely wary except where protected and fed by divers. May be ciguatoxic in certain areas. **Range:** R. Sea to Tuamotus, n. to Ryuk., s. to N. Cal.

2 **Red-banded wrasse** *Cheilinus fasciatus* (Bloch) 38 cm
Ecology: lagoon and seaward reefs, 4 to at least 40 m. Common in areas of mixed coral, sand, and rubble. Often follows divers to prey on invertebrates exposed by divers fins. **Range:** R. Sea to Samoa, n. to Ryuk., s. to N. Cal.

3 **Tripletail wrasse** *Cheilinus trilobatus* Lacépède 45 cm
Very similar to *C. abudjubbe* (R. Sea). **Ecology:** lagoon and seaward reefs, 1 to over 30 m. Prefers shallow clear reef margins with good coral covers. Quite wary and difficult to approach. **Range:** E. Africa to Tuamotus, n. to Ryuk., s. to N. Cal. & Austral Is.

4 **Broomtail wrasse** *Cheilinus lunulatus* (Forsskål) 50 cm
Ecology: seaward reefs, 2 to 30 m. Typically along the edges of coral-rich fringing reef slopes. **Range:** R. Sea to G. of Oman.

5 **Floral wrasse** *Cheilinus chlorourus* (Bloch) 45 cm
The only *Cheilinus* with X D spines (all others with IX). Juvs. resemble juv. *C. trilobatus.* **Ecology:** lagoon and coastal reefs in areas of mixed sand, rubble, and coral, 2 to 30 m. **Range:** E. Africa to Marq. & Tuam., n. to Ryuk., s. to N. Cal. & Rapa.

6 **Bandcheek wrasse** *Oxycheilinus digrammus* (Lacépède) 30 cm
Species of *Oxycheilinus* more elongate than *Cheilinus.* This sp. similar to some phases of *O. unifasciatus*, but without area free of red lines behind eye. **Ecology:** coral-rich areas of lagoon and shelteR. Seaward reefs, 3 to possibly 120 m. **Range:** R. Sea to Samoa, n. to Ryuk., s. to N. Cal.

7 **Ringtail wrasse** *Oxycheilinus unifasciatus* (Streets) 46 cm
Light bar usually present on base of tail; elongate area behind eye clear of red markings. Similar to *O. digrammus.* **Ecology:** clear lagoon and seaward reefs, 1 to 160 m in coral-rich as well as rubbly areas. Often hovers well above bottom and feeds primarily on fishes. **Range:** Cocos-Keeling to Hawaiian, Marq. & Tuamotu Is., n. to Ryuk., s. to N. Cal. & Rapa.

8 **Celebes wrasse** *Oxycheilinus celebicus* (Bleeker) 24 cm
Concave head profile with red lines radiating from eye. **Ecology:** coral-rich areas of protected reefs, 3 to 30 m. **Range:** Borneo & Moluccas to Solomons, n. to s. Japan, s. to Rowley Shoals.

9 **Twospot wrasse** *Oxycheilinus bimaculatus* (Valenciennes) 15 cm
Ecology: clear lagoon and seaward reefs, 2 to 110 m, usually in weedy rubbly areas. **Range:** E. Africa to Hawaiian & Marq. Is., n. to s. Japan, s. to Vanuatu.

10 **Arenatus wrasse** *Oxycheilinus arenatus* (Valenciennes) 19 cm
Ecology: steep outer reef dropoffs, 25 to over 46 m, usually in caves. **Range:** R. Sea to Samoa, n. to Phil.

11 **Mental wrasse** *Oxycheilinus mentalis* (Rüppell) 20 cm
Similar to *O. orientalis* (W. Pacific). Red lines radiating from eye. **Ecology:** fringing reefs near coral heads, 1 to 20 m. Solitary. Common in R. Sea. **Range:** R. Sea & w. Indian Ocean.

12 **Snooty wrasse** *Cheilinus oxycephalus* Bleeker 17 cm
Concave head profile, but with deeper body than *O. celebecus*; no red lines radiating from eye and generally with a deeper red hue. **Ecology:** coral-rich areas of lagoon and seaward reefs, 1 to over 40 m. Quite secretive. **Range:** E. Africa to Marq. and Society Is., n. to Taiwan, s. to s. GBR.

juv 1
2
3
4
5
6
7
8
9
♂
10
11
12

1 **Slingjaw wrasse** *Epibulus insidiator* (Pallas) 35 cm
Has a unique protractible jaw that forms a tube half the length of the body. Small juvs. similar to *Wetmorella* spp.; ♀ yellow to brown; large ♂ with white head. A possible 2nd sp. occurs along coral-rich lagoon slopes at Palau. **Ecology:** lagoon and seaward reefs in coral-rich areas from 1 to 42 m. Uses tubular mouth to feed on small coral-dwelling crustaceans and fishes. **Range:** R. Sea to nw. Hawaiian & Tuamotu Is., n. to s. Japan, s. to N. Cal.

2 **Whitebarred pigmy wrasse** *Wetmorella albofasciata* Schultz & Marshall 6 cm
Similar to juv. *Epibulus* and juv. *W. nigropinnata*, the latter with 4 vertical stripes. **Ecology:** lagoon and seaward reefs, 8 to 42 m. Very secretive, in caves and crevices. **Range:** E. Africa to Hawaiian & Society Is., s. to GBR.

3 **Blackspot pigmy wrasse** *Wetmorella nigropinnata* (Seale) 8 cm
Ecology: lagoon and seaward reefs, 1 to 30 m. Very secretive, in caves and crevices. **Range:** R. Sea to Marq. Pitcairn Is., n. to Ryuk., s. to s. GBR, N. Cal.

Tribe Cheilinini: continued on Pl. 94

Tribe Novaculini: characterized by highly compressed bodies with steep, keeled foreheads that facilitate rapid burrowing beneath the sand and large protruding canines at tip of jaws.

4 **Finescale razorfish** *Cymolutes torquatus* (Valenciennes) 12 cm
Ecology: sandy areas of reef flats and shallow lagoons to at least 6 m. Most species of razorfishes do well in aquariums with a loose sand bottom and docile tankmates. They will learn to take food from owner's hand, but remain extremely nervous. **Range:** E. Africa to N. Brit. (& Marq?), n. to s. Japan, s. to L. Howe Is.

5 **Knife razorfish** *Cymolutes praetextatus* (Quoy & Gaimard) 20 cm
Similar to *C. leclusei* (Hawaiian Is.). **Ecology:** reef flats and shallow lagoons to 6 m, in sandy, current-swept areas with rubble and weed. **Range:** E. Africa to Society Is., s. to Rowley Shoals.

6 **Seagrass wrasse** *Novaculichthys macrolepidotus* (Bloch) 15 cm
Ecology: shallow lagoons and channels, on sandy flats with seagrass and algae to 4 m. **Range:** R. Sea to PNG, n. to the Ryuk., s. to L. Howe Is.

7 **Dragon or rockmover wrasse** *Novaculichthys taeniourus* (Lacépède) 27 cm
Hawaiian juvs. usually green; w. Pac. juvs. usually brown. **Ecology:** semi-exposed reef flats, and lagoon and seaward reefs to over 14 m, in areas of mixed sand and rubble. Feeds on a wide variety of benthic invertebrates, often moving rocks to expose them. Juveniles mimic a clump of detached drifting algae. **Range:** R. Sea to Panama, n. to Ryuk. & Hawaiian Is., s. to L. Howe & Tuamotu Is.

8 **Yellowblotch razorfish** *Xyrichtys aneitensis* (Günther) 24 cm
Ecology: lagoon and seaward slopes, on expanses of fine sand, 12 to 92 m. Uncommon. **Range:** Chagos to Hawaiian Is., n. to Ryuk.

9 **Indianfish (juv.); Blue razorfish (adult)** *Xyrichtys pavo* Valenciennes 41 cm
Ecology: clear lagoon and seaward reefs, on large expanses of coarse sand. Juv. in as little as 2 m, adults rare in less than 20 m, common deeper to at least 100 m. Juv. mimic a waterlogged leaf by swimming with a swaying motion, head-down or on their sides **Range:** R. Sea to Mexico, n. to s. Japan and Hawaiian Is., s. to L. Howe and Society Is.

10 **Fivefinger razorfish** *Xyrichtys pentadactylus* (Linnaeus) 25 cm
Ecology: sandy slopes of mainly continental coastlines, 2 to over 18 m. **Range:** R. Sea to PNG, n. to Bonin Is., s. to Natal.

11 **Black-barred razorfish** *Xyrichtys tetrazona* (Bleeker) 15 cm
Juvs. bright yellow, green or white with distinct ocelli; large ♂ without black bars and with black spot above mid LL. **Ecology:** coastal sand slopes to over 15 m. Rare. **Range:** Bali & Phil.(?).

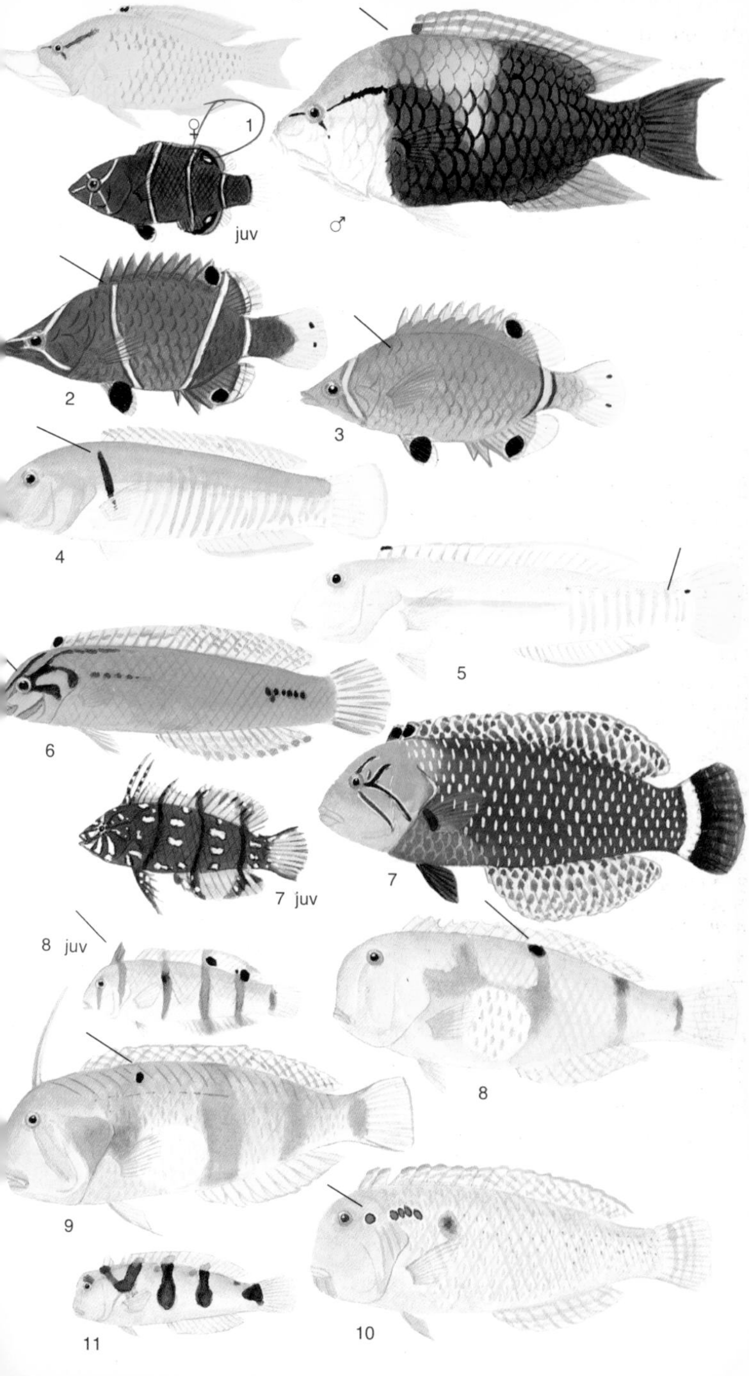

1
♀
juv
♂
2
3
4
5
6
7 juv
7
8 juv
8
9
10
11

Tribe Cheilinini, genera *Cirrhilabrus Coniella, Paracheilinus, Pseudocheilinus* (continued from pl. 93): six genera with a distinct "double cornea" of the eye which may serve as a close-up lens to facilitate in feeding on minute animals. Species of *Cirrhilabrus* and *Paracheilinus* typically aggregate 1 to 2 m above the bottom to feed on zooplankton. Males territorial and haremic and larger, more colorful and often quite differently colored than females. Females of many species nearly indistinguishable. Several species of *Cirrhilabrus* are undescribed. Species of *Pseudocheilinus* remain close to the bottom always near shelter. They are generally solitary and feed on small benthic invertebrates.

1 **Purple-boned wrasse** *Cirrhilabrus blatteus* Springer & Randall 16 cm
Ecology: rock and coral bottoms, 40 to 50 m. **Range:** R. Sea only.

2 **Girdled wrasse** *Cirrhilabrus balteatus* Randall 10 cm
Ecology: lagoon and seaward reefs, 7 to 22 m. Above coral, rubble or algae. **Range:** Marshall Is.

3 **Blueside wrasse** *Cirrhilabrus cyanopleura* (Bleeker) 15 cm
Ecology: in aggregations along the edges of clear lagoon and seaward reefs, 2 to 20 m **Range:** Andaman Sea to PNG, n. to Izus, s. to Rowley Shoals.

4 **Exquisite wrasse** *Cirrhilabrus exquisitus* Smith 12 cm
Ecology: seaward reefs, 6 to 32 m. Often in large aggregations over rubble. **Range:** E. Africa to Tuam., n. to Izus, s. to GBR.

5 **Johnson's wrasse** *Cirrhilabrus johnsoni* Randall 6 cm
Only 1 other sp. with lunate tail, *C. lunatus* (Ryuk. & Bonin Is.) in which ♂ are orange yellow dorsally to end of D fin base & dusky to black below & on tail. **Ecology:** among dense algal beds of deep lagoons, 18 to 28 m. **Range:** Marshall Is.

6 **Flame wrasse** *Cirrhilabrus jordani* Snyder 10 cm
Ecology: seaward reefs below 18 m, in aggregations above rubble at base of dropoffs. **Range:** Hawaiian Is.; strays to Johnston Atoll.

7 **Yellowband wrasse** *Cirrhilabrus luteovittatus* Randall 12 cm
Ecology: in aggregations above lagoon patch reefs on rubble, 7 to 30 m. **Range:** e. Caroline & Marshall Is.; strays to Johnston Atoll.

8 **Rhomboid wrasse** *Cirrhilabrus rhomboidalis* Randall 8.5 cm
Ecology: steep outer reef slopes, near sand and rubble at about 38 to 40 m. Near bottom. **Range:** Kwajalein Atoll (Marshall Is.).

9 **Social wrasse** *Cirrhilabrus rubriventralis* Springer & Randall 7.5 cm
Ecology: over coral or rubble of fringing reefs, 3 to 43 m. **Range:** n. R. Sea.

10 **Redfin wrasse** *Cirrhilabrus rubripinnis* Randall & Carpenter 8 cm
Ecology: rubble and coral slopes at base of reef, ca. 30 m. **Range:** Phil.

11 **Peacock wrasse** *Cirrhilabrus temminckii* Bleeker 10 cm
Similar to *C. katherinae* (Mariana, Ruyuk. & Izu Is.) which has shorter V fin in ♂, a dark P axil & is more solidly red above an abruptly pale ventral 1/3 of body. **Ecology:** seaward reefs, in aggregations over loose rubble. **Range:** Indonesia to PNG, n. to s. Japan, s. to nw. Australia.

12 **Laboute's wrasse** *Cirrhilabrus laboutei* Randall & Lubbock 11 cm
Ecology: over rubble patches of seaward and back reef slopes, 7 to 55 m. **Range:** GBR, Coral Sea, N. Cal. & Loyalty Is.

13 **Scott's wrasse** *Cirrhilabrus scottorum* Randall & Pyle 12 cm
Similar to *C. melanomarginatus* (Taiwan, s. China Sea & Phil.) which lacks the yellow on the head & has a red tail. **Ecology:** outer reef slopes, 3 to 40 m, in small aggregations over coral or rubble. **Range:** Coral Sea, Fiji, Samoa, Society & Tuamotu Is. & Pitcairn group.

14 **Lubbock's wrasse** *Cirrhilabrus lubbocki* Randall & Carpenter 8 cm
♂ from Celebes bright yellow on top of head & back with yellow D & A fins. **Ecology:** seaward reefs, 4 to 45 m. In groups close above rubble or finely branched coral. **Range:** Phil. & Celebes.

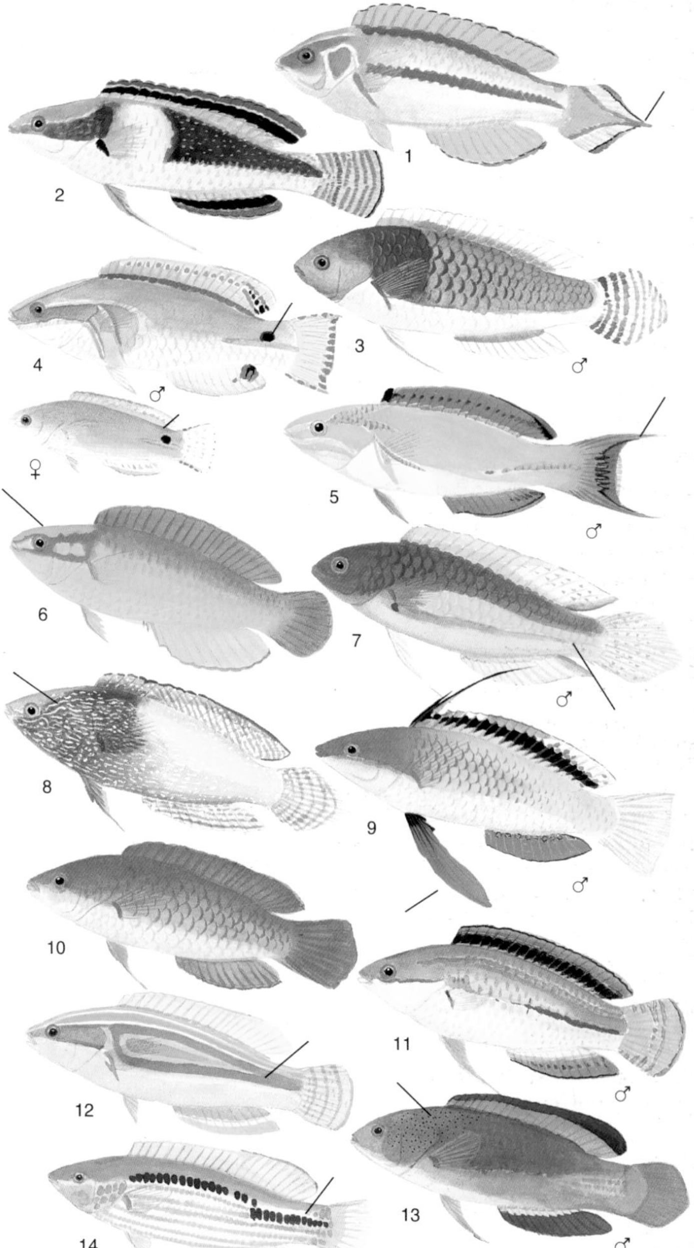
1
2
3
♂
4
♂
♀
5
♂
6
7
♂
8
9
♂
10
11
♂
12
13
♂
14
♀

95 WRASSES

1 **Mutant wrasse** *Coniella apterygia* Allen 8 cm
A "mutant" species that lacks pelvic fins, otherwise identical to the genus *Cirrhilabrus*. **Ecology**: steep outer reef slopes over rubble with patches of live coral, 30 to 40 m. **Range:** Rowley Shoals off nw. Australia only.

2 **Bell's flasher** *Paracheilinus bellae* Randall 6.5 cm
Ecology: among dense algal beds of deep lagoons, 18 to 31 m. **Range:** Kwajalein Atoll (Marsh. Is.).

3 **Filamented flasher** *Paracheilinus filamentosus* Allen 8 cm
Ecology: seaward and outer channel reef slopes, 5 to 35 m. **Range:** Phil., Bali, Moluccas, PNG & Solomon Is.

4 **Pink flasher** *Paracheilinus carpenteri* Randall & Lubbock 8 cm
Ecology: bases of steep outer reef slopes, close above rubble or coral, 27 to 40 m. **Range:** Phil.

5 **Spot-lined flasher** *Paracheilinus lineopunctatus* Randall & Lubbock 6.5 cm
Ecology: base of steep outer reef slopes, close above rubble or coral, 12 to 40 m. **Range:** Phil.

6 **Red Sea eightline flasher** *Paracheilinus octotaenia* Fourmanoir 9 cm
Often shows orange spots instead of lines. **Ecology:** coral-rich areas of seaward reefs, 8 to over 25 m. Common. **Range:** n. R. Sea.

7 **McCosker's flasher** *P. mccoskeri* Randall & Harmelin-Vivien 7 cm
Ecology: outer reef slopes, 12 to 35 m, close above rubble, algae, or coral. **Range:** Arab. G., Comores, Seychelles, Maldives, Similan Is., Bali to Flores & Fiji.

8 **Angular flasher** *Paracheilinus angulatus* Randall & Lubbock 7 cm
Similar to *P. hemitaeniatus* (Madagascar, 42 to 45 m) which has rounded soft D & A fins and a lunate tail with filamentous upper-and lowermost rays. **Ecology:** unknown, presumably similar to others in genus. **Range:** Phil.

9 **Striated wrasse** *Pseudocheilinus evanidus* Jordan & Evermann 8 cm
Ecology: species of *Pseudocheilinus* remain close to the bottom always near shelter. They are generally solitary and feed on small benthic invertebrates. This species occurs in patches of rubble or among branching corals of seaward slopes from 6 to over 40 m. **Range:** R. Sea to Hawaiian & Tuam. Is., n. to Izu Is.

10 **Sixline wrasse** *Pseudocheilinus hexataenia* (Bleeker) 7 cm
Ecology: seaward reefs, 2 to 35 m, among branches of live corals. Secretive. **Range:** R. Sea to Tuam., n. to Ryuk., s. to L. Howe & Austral Is.

11 **Eightline wrasse** *Pseudocheilinus octotaenia* Jenkins 12 cm
Indian Ocean populations often with orange spots. **Ecology:** seaward reefs, among coral or rubble, 2 to 50 m. **Range:** E. Africa to Hawaiian & Ducie Is., n. to Ryuk.

12 **Fourline wrasse** *Pseudocheilinus tetrataenia* Schultz 7.5 cm
Ecology: seaward reefs, among coral or rubble, 6 to 44 m. Very secretive. **Range:** Palau to the Hawaiian & Tuamotu Is., s. to Austral Is.

13 **Whitebarred wrasse** *Pseudocheilinus* sp. 5 cm
Ecology: seaward reefs among coral or rubble, below 25 m. Secretive. **Range:** Guam, GBR & other w. Pacific localities.

14 **Flagfin wrasse** *Pteragogus flagellifera* (Valenciennes) 20 cm
♀ relatively drab & cryptic brown to red. **Ecology:** among patches of algae on coral or rocky reefs. Males are territorial, and may range over a very large area of reef containing up to 30 females. **Range:** E. Africa to PNG, n. to s. Japan, s. to nw. Aust. & s. GBR.

15 **Cryptic wrasse** *Pteragogus cryptus* Randall 9.5 cm
Similar spp. incl. *P. guttatus* (Indo-Aust.) which has concave head profile, *P. pelycus* (R. Sea to Maurit.), *P. enneacanthus* (w. Pac.) & *P. taeniops* (w. Indian Ocean). **Ecology:** rubbly areas with algae, soft corals or branching corals, 2 to 67 m. Secretive. **Range:** R. Sea; Indonesia to Samoa, n. to Phil. & Marianas, s. to GBR.

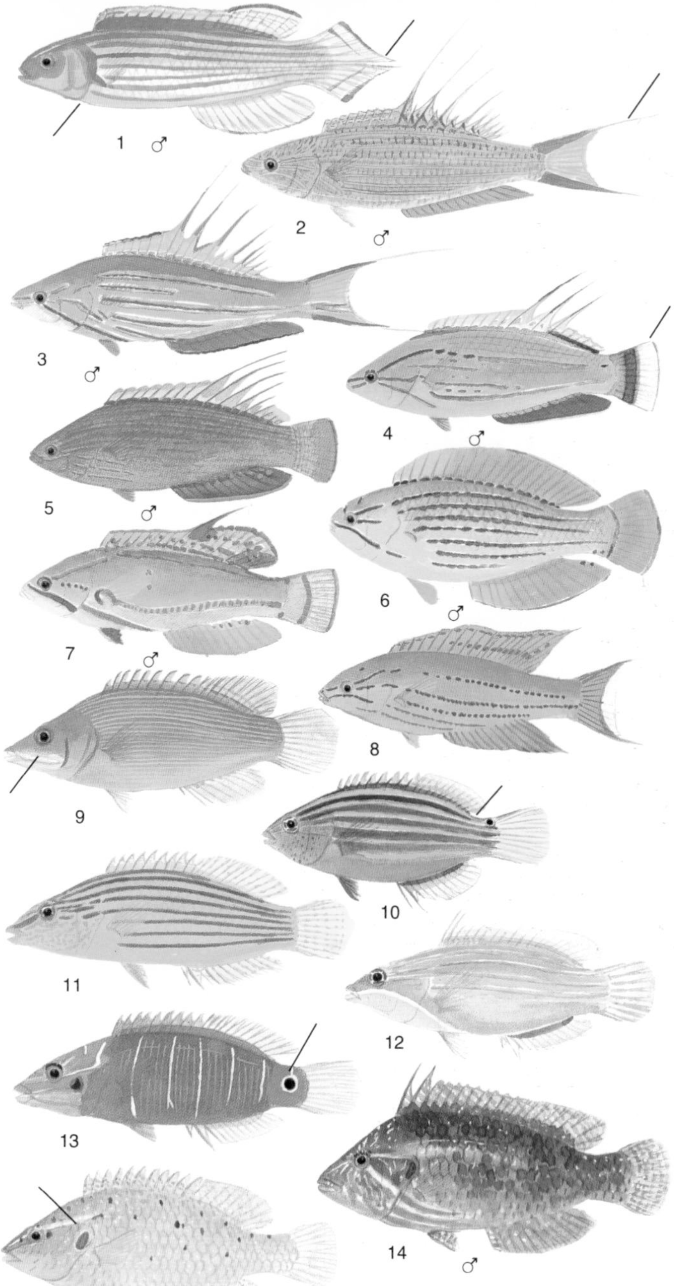
1 ♂
2 ♂
3 ♂
4 ♂
5 ♂
6 ♂
7 ♂
8
9
10
11
12
13
14 ♂
15

Tribe Julidini: characterized by a continuous LL with most species having one or more pairs of prominent canines in front of jaws and well-developed pharyngeal teeth. Most species feed on benthic invertebrates or fishes.

1 **Yellowtail wrasse** *Anampses meleagrides* Valenciennes 22 cm
This genus with a single pair of flattened teeth projecting from front each jaw; scaleless head; most spp. sexually dichromatic. ♂ of this sp. similar to ♂ *A. geographicus*. **Ecology:** seaward reefs in areas of mixed coral, rubble, rock or sand, from 4 to 60 m. **Range:** R. Sea to Tuamotus., n. to s. Japan, s. to NW Australia & L. Howe Is.

2 **White-spotted wrasse** *Anampses melanurus* Bleeker 12 cm
Ecology: solitary or in pairs in surge zone, rarely to 30 m. Feeds on small crustaceans, mollusks, and polychaetes. Bury in sand at night. **Range:** R. Sea to Easter Is., n. to Ryukyus, s. to L. Howe Is.

3 **Lined wrasse** *Anampses lineatus* Randall 12 cm
Ecology: lagoon and seaward reefs, usually deeper than 20 m to at least 42 m, over coral and rubble areas. **Range:** R. Sea & Indian Ocean s. to Natal and e. to Bali.

4 **Psychedelic wrasse** *Anampses chrysocephalus* Randall 17 cm
Ecology: seaward reefs, usually below 15 m. Females in small groups usually accompanied by a single male. Very important in Hawaiian aquarium fish trade. **Range:** Hawaiian Is.

5 **New Guinea wrasse** *Anampses neoguinaicus* Bleeker 15 cm
♂ similar to ♀ but with electric blue lines on head and no ocelli on soft D & A fins. **Ecology:** deep coral-rich slopes. Solitary. Generally uncommon except in Fiji where it is moderately common. **Range:** Taiwan to Fiji, n. to Izu Is., s. to GBR & N. Cal.

6 **Yellowbreasted wrasse** *Anampses twistii* Bleeker 18 cm
♂ not as radically different from ♀ as with other species in genus. **Ecology:** clear lagoon and seaward reefs in areas of mixed coral, rubble, or rock and sand from below surge zone to 30 m. **Range:** R. Sea to Tuamotus., n. to Ryukyus, s. to Maurit. & Rapa.

7 **Geographic wrasse** *Anampses geographicus* Valenciennes 31 cm
Ecology: coastal reefs, often in weedy areas. **Range:** Mauritius to Fiji, n. to Ryukyus, s. to sw. Aust. & L. Howe Is.

8 **Blue-spotted wrasse** *Anampses caeruleopunctatus* Rüppell 42 cm
Ecology: surge zone of coral reefs or rocky coasts, rarely to 30 m. Solitary or in pairs, feeds on small crustaceans, mollusks, and polychaetes. All species so far studied bury in sand at night. **Range:** R. Sea to Easter Is., n. to s. Japan, s. to L. Howe Is.

9 **Feminine wrasse** *Anampses femininus* Randall 24 cm
♀ more brilliantly colored than ♂. **Ecology:** rocky and coral reefs, 10 to 30 m. Usually in small groups. Uncommon at GBR. **Range:** s. GBR, L. Howe, N. Cal., Rapa, Pitcairn & Easter Is.

10 **Blue-and-yellow wrasse** *Anampses lennardi* Scott 28 cm
♂ blue without yellow stripes, but with diffuse yellowish area above P fin. **Ecology:** solitary or in pairs from surge zone to at least 24 m. Feeds on wide variety of small invertebrates, especially crustaceans. **Range:** nw. Australia.

11 **Elegant wrasse** *Anampses elegans* Ogilby 29 cm
Ecology: 2 to 35 m, primarily in lagoons. Females in groups of up to 80 or more, males territorial. Second most abundant wrasse at L. Howe Is. **Range:** GBR, N. Cal, L. Howe Is., Norfolk Is., n. NZ, Rapa, Mangareva, Pitcairn & Easter Is.

12 **Pearl wrasse** *Anampses Cuvier* Quoy & Gaimard 31 cm
Similar to *A. caeruleopunctatus*, esp. ♂. **Ecology:** solitary or in pairs in surge zone of rocky areas to at least 24 m. Feeds on wide variety of very small invertebrates, especially crustaceans. **Range:** Hawaiian Is., where *A. caeruleopunctatus* is absent.

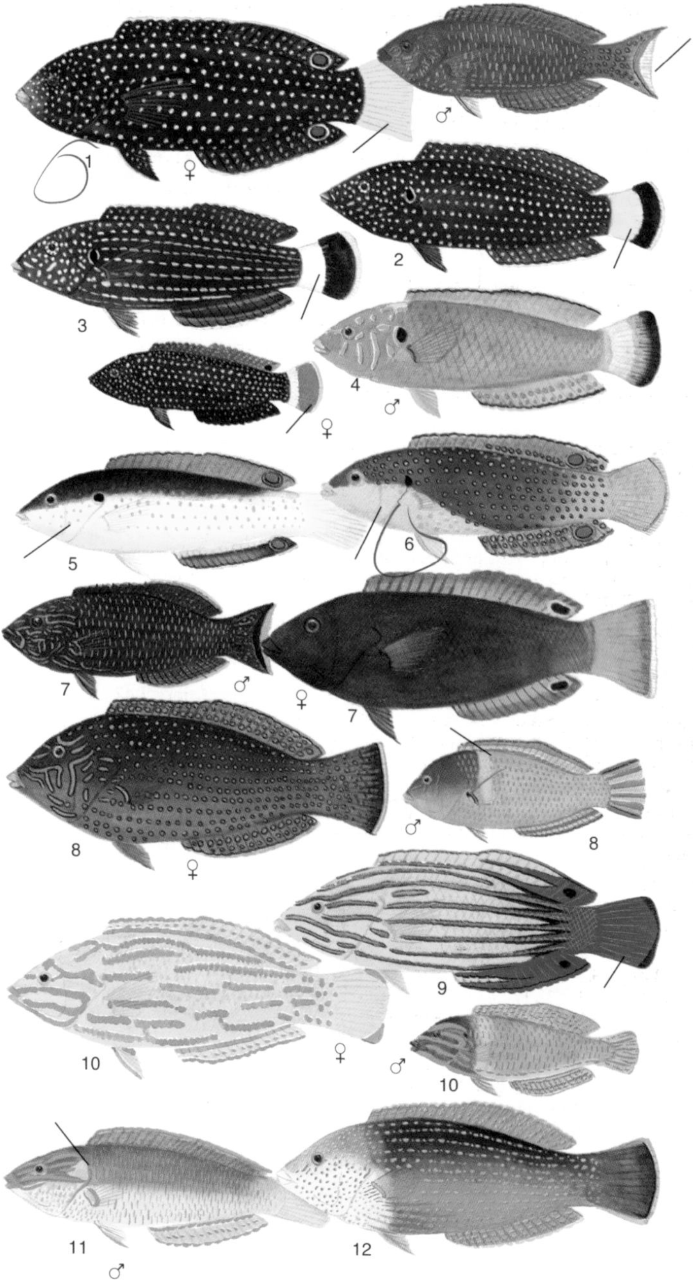

1
♀
♂
2
3
4
♂
♀
5
6
7
♂
♀
7
8
♂
8
♀
9
10
♀
♂
10
11
♂
12

97 WRASSES

1 **Clown coris** *Coris aygula* Lacépède 120 cm
Coris spp. with single pair of canines projecting from front each jaw; head scaleless below eye; scales small (~50 in LL); most spp. sexually dichromatic; all spp. sleep beneath sand. **Ecology:** exposed outer reef flats and lagoon and seaward reefs to at least 30 m, usually near patches of sand and rubble. Feeds on hard-shelled invertebrates such as mollusks, crustaceans, and sea urchins. **Range:** Cocos-Keeling, R. Sea to Line & Ducie Is., n. to s. Japan, s. to L. Howe & Rapa Is.

2 **Yellowtail coris** *Coris gaimard* (Quoy & Gaimard) 38 cm
Similar to *Coris africana* but juvs. with less black & ad. with yellow tail. **Ecology:** areas of mixed coral, sand, and rubble of exposed outer reef flats and lagoon and seaward reefs to 50 m. Feeds on hard-shelled invertebrates such as mollusks, crustaceans, and sea urchins. **Range:** Christmas Is. & Indonesia to Hawaiian, Marq. & Tuamotu Is., n. to s. Japan, s. to N. Cal. & Austral Is.

3 **African coris** *Coris africana* Smith 38 cm
Similar to *Coris gaimard* but juvs. with more black & ad. without yellow tail. **Ecology:** areas of mixed coral, sand, and rubble of exposed outer reef flats and lagoon and seaward reefs, 5 to 50 m. Feeds on hard-shelled invertebrates such as mollusks, crustaceans, and sea urchins. **Range:** R. Sea to Andaman Sea, s. to S. Africa.

4 **Queen coris** *Coris frerei* Günther 60 cm
Juvs. similar to juv. *C. gaimard*, but with larger areas of black. **Ecology:** shallow, exposed outer reefs with areas of sand and rubble. Common in E. Africa and Seychelles. **Range:** s. R. Sea to Maldives & Sri Lanka, s. to S. Africa.

5 **Elegant coris** *Coris venusta* Vaillant & Sauvage 19 cm
Ecology: common in shallow areas of sand and rubble. Feeds on sand dwelling invertebrates, primarily on mollusks, crustaceans, and urchins. **Range:** Hawaiian Is.

6 **Batu coris** *Coris batuensis* Günther 17 cm
Similar to *C. variegata* (R. Sea) which is paler with widely scattered dark speckles on sides and ca. 6 faint light bars along upper back. **Ecology:** clear lagoon and seaward reefs to over 15 m. **Range:** E. Africa to Marshall Is., n. to s. Japan, s. to s. GBR & Tonga.

7 **Spottail coris** *Coris caudimacula* (Quoy & Gaimard) 20 cm
Similar to *C. dorsomacula* & *C. venusta*, but without dark spot at rear of D fin. **Ecology:** areas of rubble, sand, and seaweed, 2 to 25 m. Usually close to bottom. **Range:** R. Sea to Indonesia and nw. Australia, s. to S. Africa.

8 **Spotfin coris** *Coris dorsomacula* (Fowler) 20 cm
Ecology: areas of rubble, weed, and sand of rocky and coral reefs, 2 to 32 m. **Range:** s. Japan, s. to Indonesia.

9 **Lined coris** *Coris ballieui* Vaillant & Sauvage 33 cm
TP primarily blue with slightly elongate first 2 D spines. **Ecology:** areas of sand and rubble, rare in depths of less than 20 m, to at least 81 m. **Range:** Hawaiian Is.

10 **Blackstripe coris** *Coris pictoides* Randall & Kuiter 10.5 cm
IP of *C. picta* (Taiwan-s. Japan & se Aust.-n. N.Z.) closely resembles this sp. **Ecology:** around small coral heads in sandy to rubbly areas, 9 to 33 m. In groups. **Range:** Malaysia & Indonesia to nw. & se. Australia, n. to Phil.

11 **Yellowstripe coris** *Coris flavovittata* Bennett 51 cm
Similar to juv. *C. bulbifrons* (pl. 139-6; s. Coral Sea). **Ecology:** reefs with areas of sand and rubble. Feeds primarily on sea urchins, heart urchins, as well as mollusks, brittle stars, and hermit crabs. **Range:** Hawaiian Is.

12 **Western king wrasse** *Coris auricularis* (Valenciennes) 40 cm
Ecology: shallow rocky and coral reefs with sand patches. Juveniles and females set up cleaning stations and remove surface parasites from other fishes. **Range:** W. Australia (Coral Bay s. to Recherche Arch.).

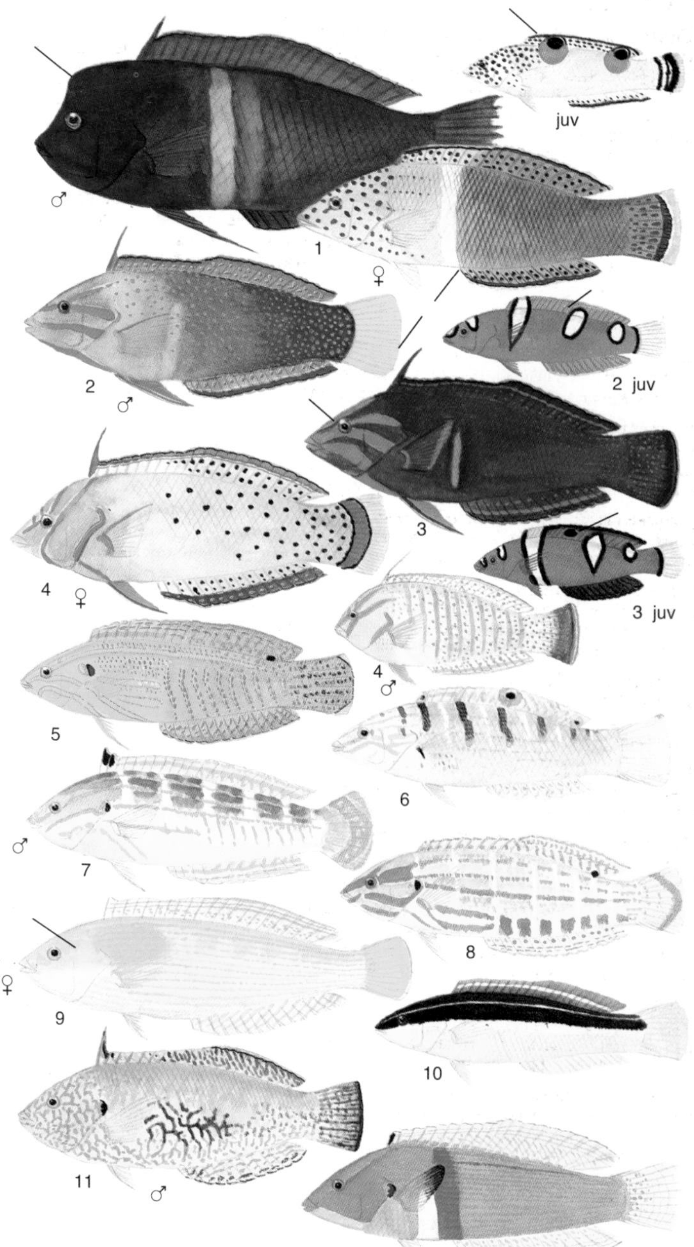
juv
♂
1
♀
2
♂
2 juv
3
4
♀
3 juv
4
♂
5
6
♂
7
8
♀
9
10
11
♂
12
♂

1 **Checkerboard wrasse** *Halichoeres hortulanus* (Lacépède) 27 cm
Canines of *Halichoeres* spp. not as well developed as in *Anampses* and *Coris*. They feed on small invertebrates and sleep buried beneath the sand. Ad. of Indian Oc. form (*centriquadrus*; R. Sea to Bali) lacks the 2nd yellow spot beneath mid D fin of Pacific form. **Ecology:** sand patches of clear lagoon and seaward reefs, 1 to over 30 m. Juveniles often at bottom of surge channels. Common. **Range:** R. Sea to Marquesa and Tuamotu Is., n. to s. Japan, s. to s. GBR.

2 **Three-spot wrasse** *Halichoeres trimaculatus* (Quoy & Gaimard) 27 cm
Ecology: sandy areas of reef flats, lagoons, and protected seaward reefs to 18 m. Often accompany goatfishes in order to capture prey exposed by their excavating activities. **Range:** Cocos-Keeling to Line & Ducie Is., n. to s. Japan, s. to L. Howe Is.

3 **Dusky wrasse** *Halichoeres marginatus* Rüppell 17 cm
TP usually with yellow bar on P fin (missing in Micron. popul.); Marianas TP with red blotch behind P fin; Palau TP with dark-edged white spot behind tip of P fin. **Ecology:** lagoon and seaward reefs to 30 m, particularly along upper edge of reef in coral-rich areas. **Range:** R. Sea to Line & Tuamotu Is., n. to s. Japan, s. to s. GBR and Austral Is.

4 **Zigzag wrasse** *Halichoeres scapularis* (Bennett) 20 cm
Ecology: reef flats and shallow lagoon reefs in areas of mixed sand, rubble or coral. **Range:** R. Sea to PNG, n. to s. Japan, s. to GBR.

5 **Pastel-green wrasse** *Halichoeres chloropterus* (Bloch) 19 cm
Dark blotch on sides of ad. variable, often absent. ♂ lack the black dots of ♀. **Ecology:** lagoon reefs, 0.5 to 10 m, in areas of mixed sand, rubble, algae, and coral. **Range:** Sumatra to Solomon Is., n. to Phil., s. to GBR.

6 **Canarytop wrasse** *Halichoeres leucoxanthus* Randall & Smith 11 cm
Very similar to *H. chrysus* which is uniformly yellow on sides & belly. **Ecology:** areas of sand and rubble at edge of reefs, 7 to 60 m. **Range:** Maldives & Andaman Sea to Java.

7 **Canary wrasse** *Halichoeres chrysus* Randall 12 cm
Very similar to *H. leucoxanthus* which is white ventrally. IP with 1 to 2 black ocelli on soft D fin & black dot on upper C ped. **Ecology:** areas of sand and rubble at edge of reefs, 2 to 60 m. Usually deeper than 20 m. **Range:** Christmas Is. to Marshall Is., n. to s. Japan, s. to se Aust.

8 **Twotone wrasse** *Halichoeres prosopeion* (Bleeker) 13 cm
Juvs. with 4 broad black longitudinal stripes; both sexes similar. **Ecology:** coral-rich areas of lagoon and seaward reefs, 2 to 40 m. **Range:** Indonesia to Samoa, n. to Ryuk., s. to s. GBR.

9 **Rainbow wrasse** *Halichoeres iridis* Randall & Smith 11.5 cm
Ecology: steep seaward reefs, 6 to 43 m. Usually in sand and rubble areas below 20 m, close to bottom. **Range:** s. Red Sea to s. Africa, e. to Chagos & Maurit.

10 **Black wrasse** *Halichoeres melanochir* Fowler & Bean 10 cm
Ecology: edges of sand patches on coral reefs of outer reef slopes. **Range:** Phil. n. to Taiwan & s. Japan, s. to nw. Australia.

11 **Axil spot wrasse** *Halichoeres podostigma* (Bleeker) 18.5 cm
Juvs. reddish-tan with 5 to 9 white stripes on front half, becoming pale green posteriorly; dark spot on P axil and V fins distinctive & present at all sizes. **Ecology:** outer reef flats and upper slopes of coastal reefs, 2 to over 25 m. Common. **Range:** Philippines & Indonesia.

12 **Black-ear wrasse** *Halichoeres melasmapomus* Randall 24 cm
Juvs. with 3 ocelli on D fin, otherwise similar at all sizes. **Ecology:** sand and rubble patches of steep outer reef slopes, 10 to 55 m. Usually below 33 m at the base of steep slopes. **Range:** Cocos-Keeling to Marq. & Tuam. Is., n. to Phil. & Micronesia.

13 **Threespot wrasse** *Halichoeres trispilus* Randall & Smith 9 cm
Male with a yellow band in tail. **Ecology:** sandy or rubble areas, with little coral growth, of deep lagooon and seaward reefs, 24 to 56 m. **Range:**E. Africa to Java, s. to Maurit. & Cocos-Keeling.

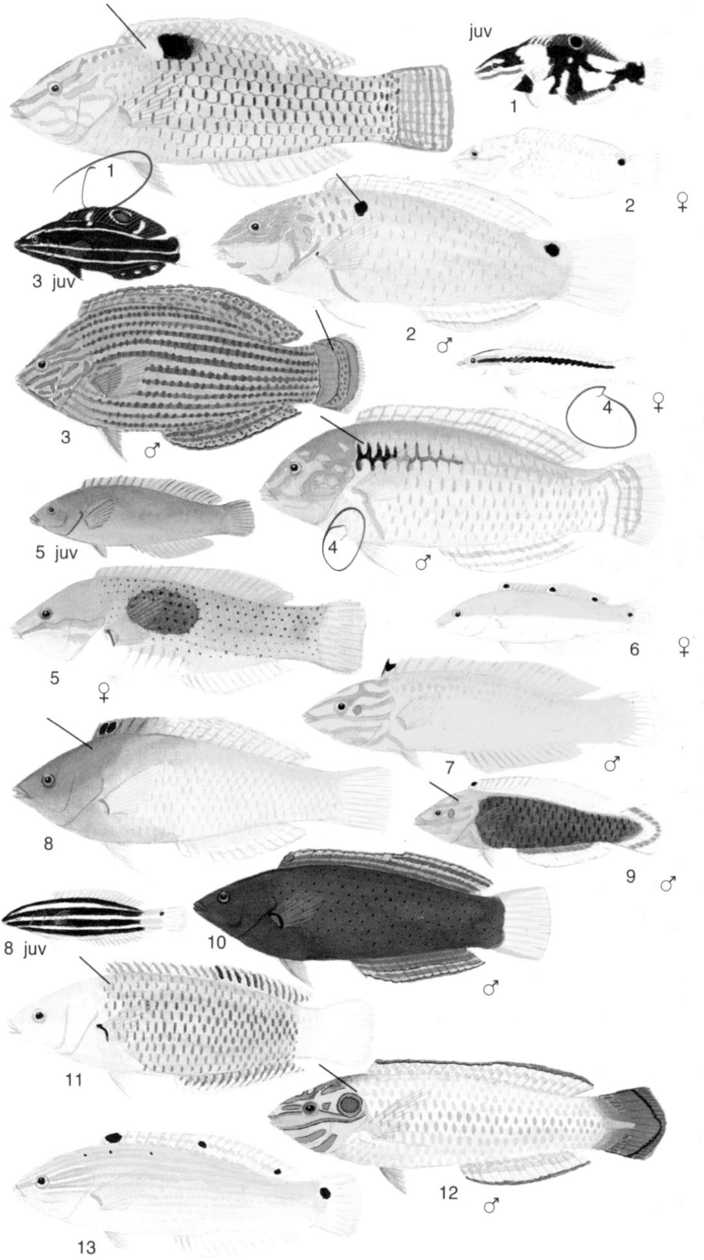
juv
1
1
2 ♀
3 juv
2 ♂
4 ♀
3 ♂
4
♂
5 juv
6 ♀
5 ♀
7 ♂
8
9 ♂
8 juv
10 ♂
11
12 ♂
13

99 WRASSES

1 **Nebulous wrasse** *Halichoeres nebulosus* (Valenciennes) 12 cm
Very similar to *H. margaritaceus* but with boomerang-shaped salmon pink mark on cheek below eye; ♂ also similar to ♂ *H. miniatus* (Ryukyus to coastal ne. Aust.). **Ecology:** reef flats, reef margins, and rocky shores, primarily in inshore weedy areas, but occasionally as deep as 40 m. **Range:** R. Sea to PNG, n. to s. Japan, s. to GBR.

2 **Weedy surge wrasse** *Halichoeres margaritaceus* (Valenciennes) 13 cm
Very similar to *H. nebulosus*; ♂ similar to ♂ *H. miniatus* (Ryukyus to coastal ne. Aust). **Ecology:** reef flats, reef margins, and rocky shores, in weedy areas exposed to surge. **Range:** Cocos-Keeling Is. to Line & Tuamotu Is., n. to s. Japan, s. to se. Aust.

3 **Two-spotted wrasse** *Halichoeres biocellatus* Schultz 12 cm
Similar to *H. ornatissimus*, but green streaks on head less iridescent & color generally darker; ocelli on D fin disappear in ad. & broad dusky bars appear on rear half of body. **Ecology:** seaward reefs, 7 to over 35 m, usually in areas of mixed coral and reef rock with sand patches. **Range:** Phil. to Fiji, n. to s. Japan, s. to the s. GBR.

4 **Argus wrasse** *Halichoeres argus* (Bloch & Schneider) 11 cm
Ecology: shallow coastal reefs and seagrass flats of continental plate shorelines. **Range:** Sri Lanka to Fiji, n. to Taiwan, s. to n Aust.

5 **Ornate wrasse** *Halichoeres ornatissimus* (Garrett) 17 cm
Similar to *H. biocellatus*; series of iridescent green spots along back; juvs. with more green than adults and with prominent dark spot on mid D fin; color pattern changes slowly with growth, sexes similar. Hawaiian form with darker green and red. **Ecology:** lagoon and seaward reefs, in areas of rich coral with sand patches. **Range:** Ryuk, s. Japan, Cocos-Keeling, Mariana, Marq., Society, Tuamotu & Hawaiian Is.

6 **Adorned wrasse** *Halichoeres cosmetus* Randall & Smith 13 cm
♂ similar to ♂ of *H. vrolikii*. **Ecology:** common on shallow coral and rocky reefs, 2 to 31 m. **Range:** E. Africa to Chagos and Maldives, s. to Mauritius and s. Africa.

7 **Pinstriped wrasse** *Halichoeres melanurus* (Bleeker) 12 cm
IP of this and *H. richmondi, H. purpurascens* and *H. vrolikii* nearly indistinguishable. IP of all 4 spp. mimicked by juvs. of the grouper *Anyperodon leucogrammicus* (pl. 24-2). **Ecology:** lagoon patch reefs and areas of coral near sand, 1 to over 15 m. **Range:** Indonesia to Samoa, n. to Ryuk., s. to nw Aust. and s. GBR.

8 **Indian Ocean pinstriped wrasse** *Halichoeres vrolikii* (Bleeker) 13 cm
Closest to *H. melanurus*, but TP without dark spot on tail margin. **Ecology:** shallow lagoon and channel reefs in areas of mixed coral and sand. **Range:** Maldives to Moluccas, n. to Andaman Sea.

9 **Diamond wrasse** *Halichoeres dussumieri* (Valenciennes) 13 cm
Ecology: shallow weedy areas of rocky shorelines, not around rich coral growth. **Range:** se. India to Phil., n. to Hong Kong, s. to nw. Aust.

10 **Timor wrasse** *Halichoeres timorensis* (Bleeker) 14 cm
Ecology: shallow coastal reefs to at least 7 m. **Range:** Sri Lanka, Thail., Malaysia, Indonesia & PNG.

11 **Goldstripe wrasse** *Halichoeres zeylonicus* (Bennett) 20 cm
Juvs. white with broad yellow longitudinal stripe; Pacific (*hartzfeldii*) & Indian Oc. forms slightly different, possibly distinct spp.; similar to *H. pelicieri* (Mauritius) in which TP has dark D fin and looses the yellow lateral stripe. **Ecology:** open sandy and rubbly areas of seaward reefs, 11 to over 34 m. **Range:** R. Sea to Samoa, n. to Arab. G. & s. Japan, s. to GBR.

12 **Red-head wrasse** *Halichoeres rubricephalus* Kuiter & Randall10 cm
Ecology: areas of rich coral growth on detached coastal reefs to at least 35 m. **Range:** known only from ne. Flores, Indonesia.

13 **Purple striped wrasse** *Halichoeres purpurascens* (Schneider) 13 cm
Head of TP not concave, pattern on tail distinctive. **Ecology:** shallow lagoon and channel reefs in areas of rich coral growth with sand patches, to at least 15 m **Range:** Indonesia, Phil. & Palau.

14 **Chain-lined wrasse** *Halichoeres leucurus* (Walbaum) 19 cm
Head of TP concave; this sp. reaches a larger size than the other 3 spp. in complex. **Ecology:** shallow lagoon and channel reefs to at least 12 m. **Range:** Java & Phil. to s. Marshall Is., n. to Ryuk.

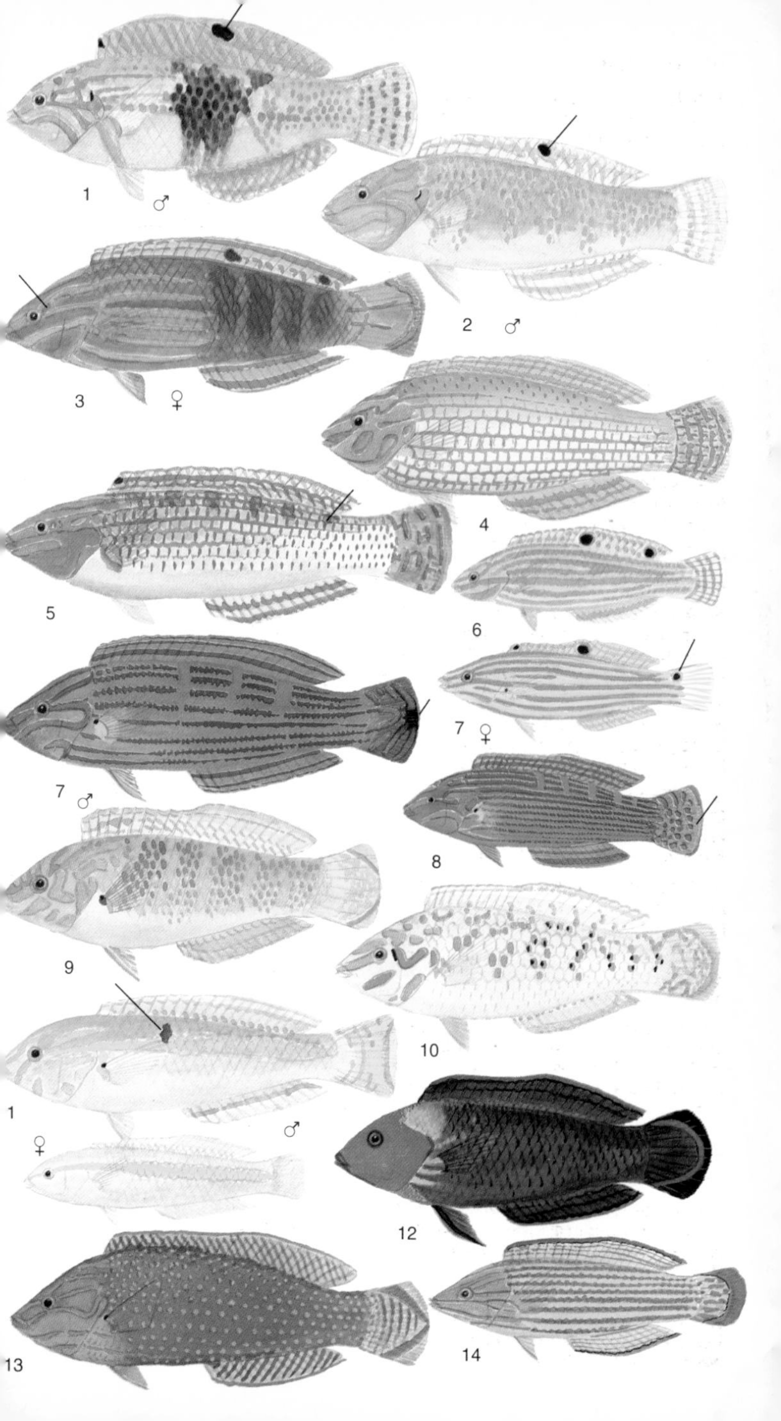
1 ♂
2 ♂
3 ♀
4
5
6
7 ♀
7 ♂
8
9
10
1
♂
♀
12
13
14

1 **Barred thicklip wrasse** *Hemigymnus fasciatus* (Bloch) 50 cm
Nuptial ♂ striking with dark and light areas on sides reversed as in a photo negative. **Ecology:** lagoon and seaward reefs, 1 to over 18 m. Juveniles usually among branching corals and feed on demersal planktonic crustaceans. Adults in areas of mixed sand, rubble, and coral and feed on benthic invertebrates. **Range:** R. Sea to Line & Ducie Is., n. to s. Japan, s. to L. Howe Is.

2 **Blackedge thicklip wrasse** *Hemigymnus melapterus* (Bloch) 50 cm
Ecology: lagoon and seaward reefs, 1 to 30 m. Juveniles usually among branching corals and feed on demersal planktonic crustaceans. Adults in areas of mixed sand, rubble, and coral. Feed on benthic invertebrates, especially hard-shelled forms. **Range:** R. Sea to Society Is., n. to Ryuk, s. to L. Howe Is.

3 **Ring wrasse** *Hologymnosus annulatus* (Lacépède) 40 cm
Juvs. mimic juv. *Malacanthus latovittatus* (pl. 40-2). **Ecology:** seaward reefs in areas of mixed sand, rubble, and coral. Feeds mainly on fishes and occasionally on small crustaceans. Juveniles generally solitary. **Range:** R. Sea to Pitcairn Is., n. to s. Japan, s. to se Australia.

4 **Candycane (juv.), Longface wrasse** *Hologymnosus doliatus* (Lacépède) 38 cm
M. similar to m. *H. annulatus* but with light band midway between P base and A origin. **Ecology:** seaward reefs in areas of mixed sand, rubble, and coral. Feeds mainly on fishes and occasionally on small crustaceans. Juveniles in groups close to bottom, adults often high in water. **Range:** s. Red Sea & E. Africa to Samoa & Line Is., n. to s. Japan, s. to se. Australia.

5 **Redback longface wrasse** *Hologymnosus rhodonotus* Randall 32 cm
H. longipes similar, but with red on back broken by numerous light bars & ocellate spot above end of P fin on TP. **Ecology:** seaward reefs in areas of mixed sand, rubble, and coral. **Range:** Indonesia (Bali & Lombok), Phil. & Ryuk..

6 **Sidespot longface wrasse** *Hologymnosus longipes* (Günther) 32 cm
IP variable, very pale in shallow water over light sand, but pale blue-purple with orange stripes & bright yellow tail when over dark bottoms or in deeper water. *H. rhodonotus* similar, but more uniformly red on back & no spot above P fin on TP. **Ecology:** lagoon and seaward reefs, 5 to 30 m. Over sand and rubble near coral outcrops. **Range:** s. GBR, Coral Sea, N. Cal., Loyalty Is. & Vanuatu.

7 **Shoulderspot wrasse** *Leptojulis cyanopleura* Bleeker 11 cm
Similar spp. include *C. chrysotaenia* (Sri-Lanka to Andaman Sea) which has a broader more golden lateral stripe, *L. lamdastigma* (Phil.) & an undescribed sp. (Indonesia) which have distinctive dark marks on the nape & behind P fin. **Ecology:** turbid coastal reefs, 6 to 45 m. Aggregates above reefs to feed on zooplankton. **Range:** Oman to Solomon Is., n. to Phil., s. to NSW.

8 **Rainbow slender wrasse** *Suezichthys arquatus* Russell 13.5 cm
Similar to *S. russelli* (n. R. Sea) and *S. cyanolaemus* (nw. Aust.). **Ecology:** sand patches of shallow reefs to 100 m. **Range:** NSW, L. Howe & Norfolk Is. to N. Cal. & n. N. Z.

9 **Slender wrasse** *Suezichthys gracilis* (Steindachner & Döderlein) 10 cm
Similar to *S. devisi* (s. GBR & NSW to N. Cal.) & *S. soelae* (nw. Aust. shelf); at least 5 other spp. are primarily warm-temperate or deep-dwelling. **Ecology:** around coral and rock patches in shallow protected sandy areas. **Range:** s. Red Sea & Arab. G. to s. Japan & s. Korea.

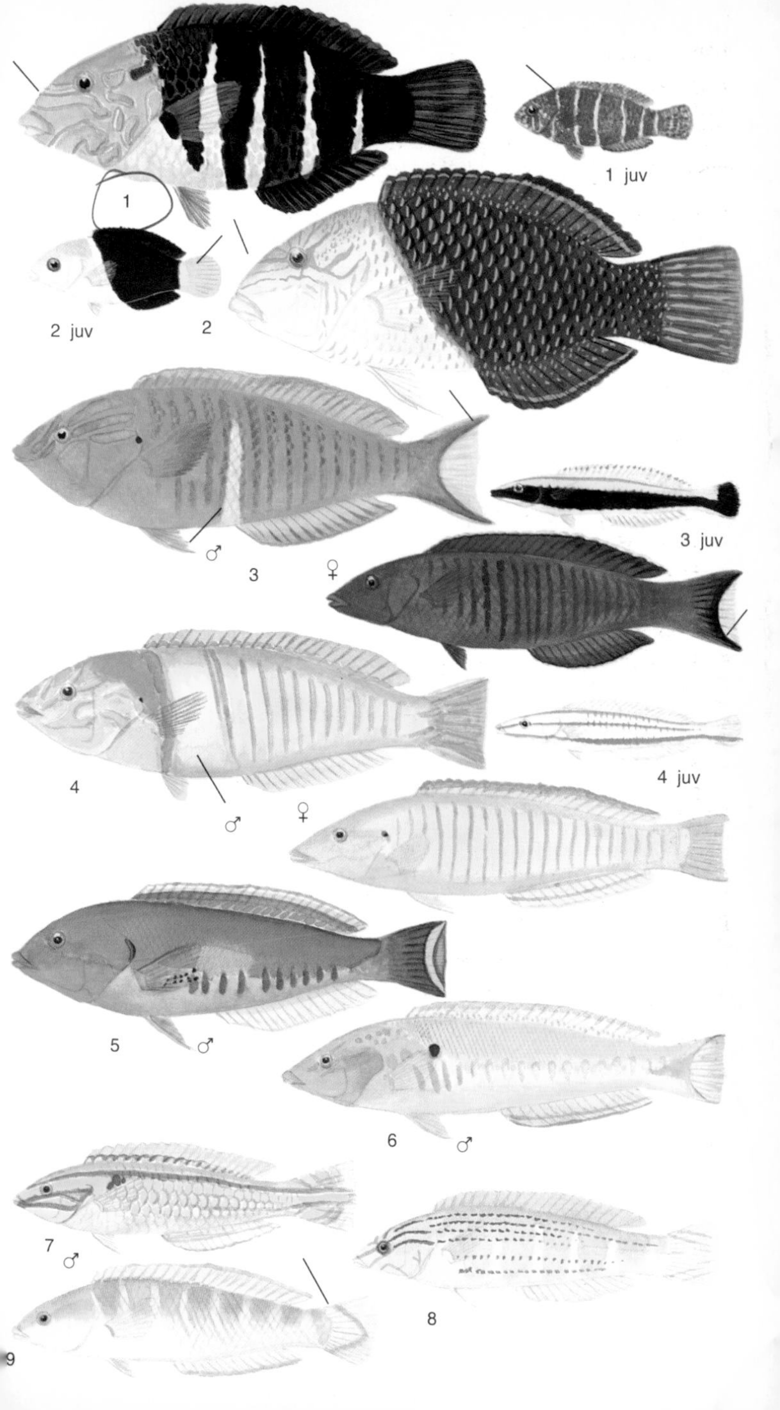
1
1 juv
2 juv
2
♂
3
♀
3 juv
4
♂
♀
4 juv
5
♂
6
♂
7
♂
8
9

101 WRASSES

1 **Cigar wrasse** *Cheilio inermis* (Forsskål) 50 cm
♂ may be tan to gray with orange, white, and black patch on sides; also a yellow phase. **Ecology:** weedy and grassy areas of lagoon and seaward reefs, intertidal to over 30 m. **Range:** R. Sea to Hawaiian & Easter Is., n. to s. Japan, s. to L. Howe Is.

2 **Indian Ocean Bird wrasse** *Gomphosus caeruleus* Lacépède 28 cm
Similar to *G. varius*, but IP is tan postero-ventrally & TP is more blue than green. **Ecology:** coral-rich areas of lagoon and seaward reefs to at least 30 m. **Range:** R. Sea (subsp. *keunzingeri*); E. Africa to Andaman Sea.

3 **Bird wrasse** *Gomphosus varius* Lacépède 28 cm
G. caeruleus similar, but IP is dark postero-ventrally & TP is more blue than green. **Ecology:** coral-rich areas of lagoon and seaward reefs to at least 30 m. **Range:** Indonesia & Cocos-Keeling to Hawaiian, Marq., and Tuamotu Is., n. to s. Japan, s. to L. Howe and Rapa Is.

4 **Vermiculate wrasse** *Macropharyngodon bipartitus* Smith 13 cm
Ecology: lagoon and shelteR. Seaward reefs. ♀ often in small groups. **Range:** R. Sea & w. Indian Ocean, e. to Maldives, s. to Mauritius.

5 **Choat's wrasse** *Macropharyngodon choati* 10 cm
Ecology: channels and seaward reefs, 6 to 28 m. **Range:** GBR s. to n. NSW only.

6 **Shortnose wrasse** *Macropharyngodon geoffroyi* (Quoy & Gaimard) 16 cm
♂ similar to ♂ *M. cyanoguttatus* from Mauritius. **Ecology:** seaward reefs, 6 to 30 m in areas of mixed sand, rubble, and coral. Feeds mainly on mollusks and foraminifera. **Range:** Hawaiian Is.

7 **Leopard wrasse** *Macropharyngodon meleagris* (Valenciennes) 14 cm
Ecology: lagoon and seaward reefs, subtidal to 30 m in areas of mixed sand, rubble, and coral. Feeds mainly on hard-bodied invertebrates and foraminifera. **Range:** Cocos-Keeling Is. to Marq. & Pitcairn Is., n. to s. Japan, s. to se. Australia.

8 **Ornate wrasse** *Macropharyngodon ornatus* Randall 12 cm
Similar to *M. cyanoguttatus* (E. Africa to Maurit.). **Ecology:** lagoon and shelteR. Seaward reefs in areas of mixed sand, rubble, and coral, 3 to at least 30 m. Solitary or in small groups. **Range:** Sri Lanka to PNG, s. to nw. Aust., n. to Andaman Sea.

9 **Black leopard wrasse** *Macropharyngodon negrosensis* Herre 12 cm
Ecology: lagoon and shelteR. Seaward reefs, 8 to 32 m in areas of mixed sand and coral. **Range:** Andaman Sea to Samoa., n. to Ryuk, s. to s. GBR.

10 **Ear-spot leopard wrasse** *Macropharyngodon kuiteri* Randall 10 cm
Similar to *M. moyeri* (Izu Is. & possibly Ryuk.) in which opercular spot is not an ocellus. **Ecology:** areas of mixed sand, rubble, and algae, 5 to 55 m. **Range:** s. GBR to NSW & N. Cal.

Subfamily Pseudodacinae: a single species characterized by teeth fused into chisel-like incisors in front of jaws and into a bony ridge on sides of jaws.

11 **Chiseltooth wrasse** *Pseudodax moluccanus* Valenciennes 25 cm
Ecology: clear channels and seaward reefs, 3 to 40 m. Juveniles usually along dropoffs below 18 m. Probably feeds on hard-shelled benthic invertebrates. **Range:** R. Sea to Marq. & Tuamotus., n. to s. Japan.

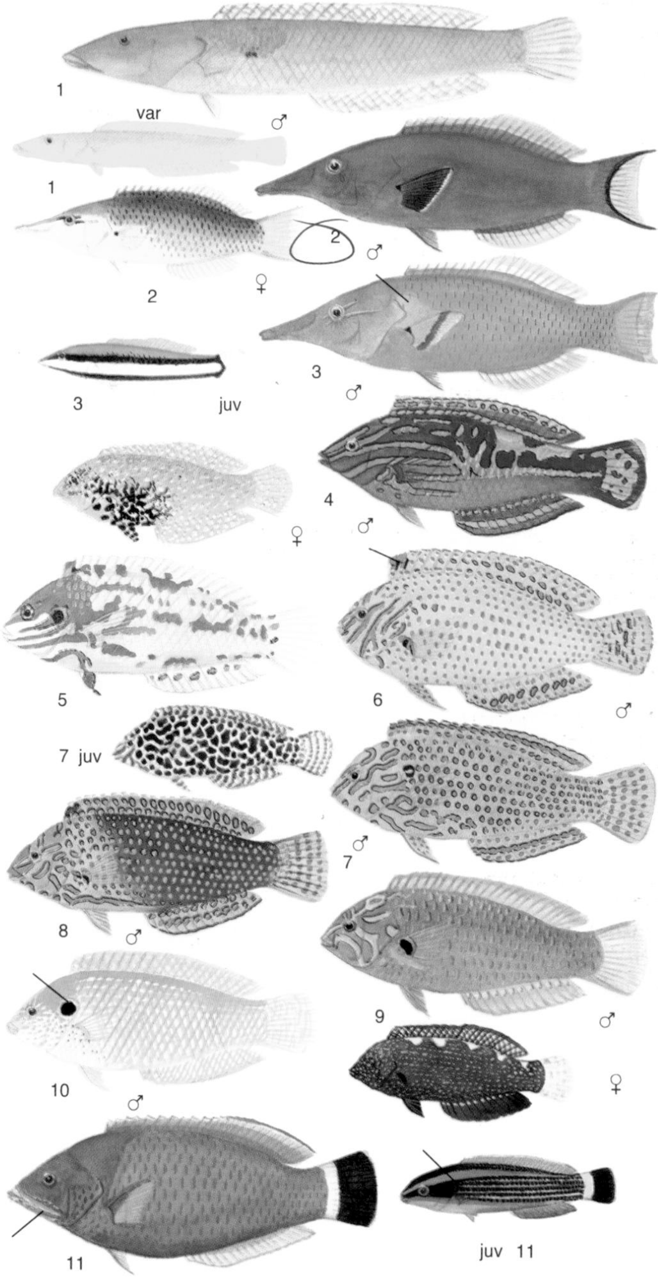
1
var
♂
1
2
♂
♀
2
3
juv
3
♂
4
♂
♀
5
6
♂
7 juv
7
♂
8
♂
9
♂
10
♀
♂
11
juv 11

1 **Minute wrasse** *Minilabrus striatus* Randall & Dor 6 cm
Ecology: in aggregations above upper reef slopes to 12 m. Feeds on zooplankton. **Range:** c. and s. R. Sea only.

2 **Philippine wrasse** *Pseudocoris philippina* Fowler & Bean 15 cm
IP light brown, pale below and with brown band from snout tip to eye and black blotch on end of operculum and upper base of tail. **Ecology:** coral reefs, little specific information available. Apparently rare. **Range:** Phil. & Ryuk.

3 **Rust-banded wrasse** *Pseudocoris aurantiofasciata* Fourmanoir 23 cm
IP brown with yellowish fins. Juv. white with 3 brown lateral stripes. **Ecology:** in small aggregations along deep outer reef dropoffs to >35 m. **Range:** Indonesia to Tuam., Cocos-Keeling, n. to s. Japan.

4 **Yamashiro's wrasse** *Pseudocoris yamashiroi* (Schmidt) 15 cm
Ecology: outer lagoon, channel and seaward reefs to at least 25 m. Aggregates along upper edge of coral slopes to feed on zooplankton. **Range:** E. Africa, Maurit. to Samoa, n. to s. Japan, s. to Kermadec & NSW.

5 **Polynesian wrasse** *Pseudojuloides atavai* Randall & Randall 13 cm
TP orange-yellow with purplish to red squiggly lines and bars on head and body, becoming abruptly bluish-black further back; IP may mimic IP of *T. amblycephalum*. **Ecology:** exposed seaward reefs and clear lagoons, 12 to 31 m. Often swims well above the bottom. **Range:** Marianas & Wake Is. to Society, Tuamotu, Austral, Rapa & Ducie Is.

6 **Smalltail wrasse** *Pseudojuloides cerasinus* (Snyder) 12 cm
IP similar to IP of *P. pyrius* (Marq.), *P. mesostigma* (Phil.), and *P. erythrops* (Maurit.), but TP of all 3 distinctive & all 3 known from few specimens in relatively deep water. **Ecology:** clear lagoon and seaward reefs, 2 to 61 m. Usually over rubble with clumps of weed and scattered corals. **Range:** E. Africa to c. America, n. to the Izu and Hawaiian Is., s. to L. Howe & the Austr. Is.

7 **Redeye wrasse** *Pseudojuloides erythrops* Randall & Randall 10 cm
IP similar to IP of *P. pyrius* (Marq.), *P. mesostigma* (Phil.), and *P. cerasinus*. **Ecology:** seaward reefs, over rubble with some rock and coral, 52 to 57 m. **Range:** Maurit.

8 **Bluelined wrasse** *Stethojulis albovittata* (Bonnaterre) 12 cm
Ecology: reef flats and clear lagoon and seaward reefs to 10 m. This and other species of *Stethojulis* occur in small groups of a male and a few females and are constantly on the move. At night they retire beneath the sand to sleep. **Range:** R. Sea to Maldives & Chagos Is., s. to Natal.

9 **Belted wrasse** *Stethojulis balteata* (Quoy & Gaimard) 15 cm
Ecology: reef flats and clear lagoon and seaward reefs to 15 m. Feeds on small hard-shelled benthic invertebrates and foraminifera. **Range:** Hawaiian & Johnston Is.

10 **Red-shoulder wrasse** *Stethojulis bandanensis* (Bleeker) 16 cm
Ecology: reef flats and lagoon and seaward reefs to 30 m, generally in shallow clear water areas of mixed sand, rubble, and coral. Feeds primarily on demersal planktonic crustaceans and small benthic invertebrates. **Range:** Cocos-Keeling to the Galapagos and Cocos Is., n. to s. Japan, s. to L. Howe & Ducie Is.

11 **Three-ribbon wrasse** *Stethojulis strigiventer* (Bennett) 14 cm
Ecology: inner reef flats and shallow lagoons to 6 m, usually in weedy areas of mixed sand and rubble or seagrass beds. **Range:** E. Africa to Samoa, n. to s. Japan, s. to the s. GBR.

12 **Three-blueline wrasse** *Stethojulis trilineata* (Bloch & Schneider) 14 cm
Ecology: shallow clear-water reefs. Apparently rare in most of its range, only common in the Adaman Sea. **Range:** Maldives to Samoa, n. to s. Japan, s. to GBR.

13 **Cutribbon wrasse** *Stethojulis interrupta* (Bleeker) 13 cm
Ecology: in s. Japan, common in areas of mixed sand, rock and coral, 2-20m. **Range:** R. Sea to PNG, s. to s. Africa, n. to s. Japan (ssp. *terina*).

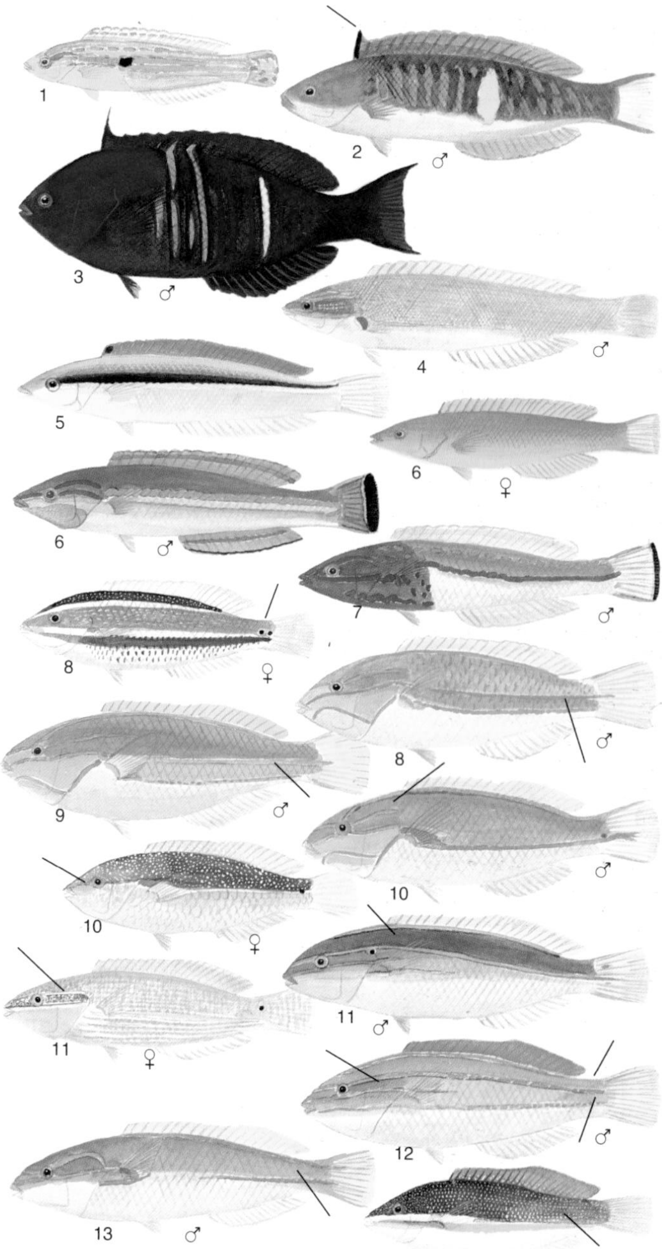
1
2 ♂
3 ♂
4 ♂
5
6 ♀
6 ♂
7 ♂
8 ♀
8 ♂
9 ♂
10 ♂
10 ♀
11 ♂
11 ♀
12 ♂
13 ♂
12 ♀

1 **Twotone wrasse** *Thalassoma amblycephalum* (Bleeker) 14 cm
Ecology: species of *Thalassoma* are active and rapid swimmers. Terminal males spawn individually with females in their harem, primary males group-spawn. This species inhabits shallow lagoon and seaward reefs to 15 m, typically near the tops of isolated coral pinnacles and upper edge of steep slopes. Feeds primarily on crustacean zooplankton. **Range:** E. Africa, Seychelles to Marq. & Tuamotu Is., n. to s. Japan, s. to n. N. Zeal.

2 **Red-cheek wrasse** *Thalassoma genivittatum* (Valenciennes) 20 cm
♂ overall greenish. **Ecology:** rocky reefs with sparse coral cover, 4 to 30 m. Usually in small groups. **Range:** Seychelles, Mauritius & Natal (S. Africa).

3 **Saddle wrasse** *Thalassoma duperrey* (Quoy & Gaimard) 25 cm
Ecology: clear lagoon and seaward reefs from surge zone to 21 m. Feeds on wide variety of benthic invertebrates and small fishes. Juveniles as well as adults occasionally clean other fishes. One of the most abundant Hawaiian inshore reef fishes. **Range:** Hawaiian & Johnston Is.

4 **Goldbar wrasse** *Thalassoma hebraicum* (Lacépède) 23 cm
Ecology: lagoon and seaward reefs, 1 to 30 m. Usually on patch reefs or rocks. **Range:** E. Africa to Maldives & Chagos Is., s. to Algoa Bay (S. Africa).

5 **Sunset wrasse** *Thalassoma lutescens* (Lay & Bennett) 30 cm
Ecology: clear outer lagoon and seaward reefs to 30 m, over open sand and rubble as well as coral. Most common in shallow exposed areas. Feeds on small benthic invertebrates. **Range:** E. Africa (rare), Sri Lanka to Hawaiian Is., n. to s. Japan, s.to sw. Aust., L. Howe, Kermadec & Rapa Is.

6 **Crescent wrasse** *Thalassoma lunare* (Linnaeus) 25 cm
Ecology: lagoon and coastal reefs to 20 m, usually on upper portions of ledges and coral heads. Feeds primarily on small benthic invertebrates. **Range:** R. Sea to Line Is., n. to s. Japan, s.to sw. Aust. & n. NZ.

7 **Jansen's wrasse** *Thalassoma jansenii* (Bleeker) 20 cm
Basic color pattern changes little with growth and sex. **Ecology:** exposed crests of shallow lagoon and seaward reefs to 15 m. **Range:** Maldives to Fiji, n. to s. Japan, s.to L.Howe Is.

8 **Sixbar wrasse** *Thalassoma hardwicke* (Bennett) 20 cm
Basic color pattern changes little with growth and sex, territorial males more colorful. **Ecology:** shallow lagoon and seaward reefs to 15 m in areas of clear water. Feeds on benthic and planktonic crustaceans, small fishes, and foraminifera. **Range:** E. Africa to Tuamotu Is., n. to s. Japan, s. to L. Howe Is.

9 **Surge wrasse** *Thalassoma purpureum* (Forsskål) 43 cm
IP of this sp. and *trilobatum* nearly identical, differing in details of head markings. **Ecology:** surge zone of outer reef flats, reef margins, and clear rocky coastlines. Feeds on wide variety of benthic invertebrates and small fishes. **Range:** R. Sea to Hawaiian, Marq. & Easter Is., n. to s. Japan, s. to L. Howe & Kermadec Is. Galapagos (rare).

10 **Christmas wrasse** *Thalassoma trilobatum* (Lacépède) 29 cm
Ecology: surge zone of outer reef flats, reef margins, and clear rocky coastlines. Feeds on wide variety of benthic invertebrates and small fishes. **Range:** E. Africa to Picairn group, n. to Ryuk., s. to Rapa Is.

11 **Fivestripe wrasse** *Thalassoma quinquevittatum* (Lay & Bennett) 16 cm
Similar to *T. cupido* (s. Japan to Taiwan), *T. heiseri* (Pitcairn group) & *T. klunzingeri*. **Ecology:** clear outer lagoon and seaward reefs to 40 m. Most abundant in shallow exposed areas with surge channels. Feeds on small benthic invertebrates and fishes. **Range:** E. Africa to Hawaiian Is. (rare), n. to Ryuk., s. to L. Howe Is.

12 **Blacktail wrasse** *Thalassoma ballieui* (Vaillant & Sauvage) 39 cm
Juvs. yellowish-green, IP with lighter head and tail than TP. **Ecology:** clear lagoon and seaward reefs. Feeds on wide variety of benthic invertebrates and small fishes. **Range:** Hawaiian & Johnston Is.

13 **Klunzinger's wrasse** *Thalassoma klunzingeri* (Fowler & Steinitz) 20 cm
Similar to *T. quinquevittatum*. **Ecology:** abundant on reef margins and seaward slopes. 0.5 to 20 m. Easy to approach. **Range:** R. Sea.

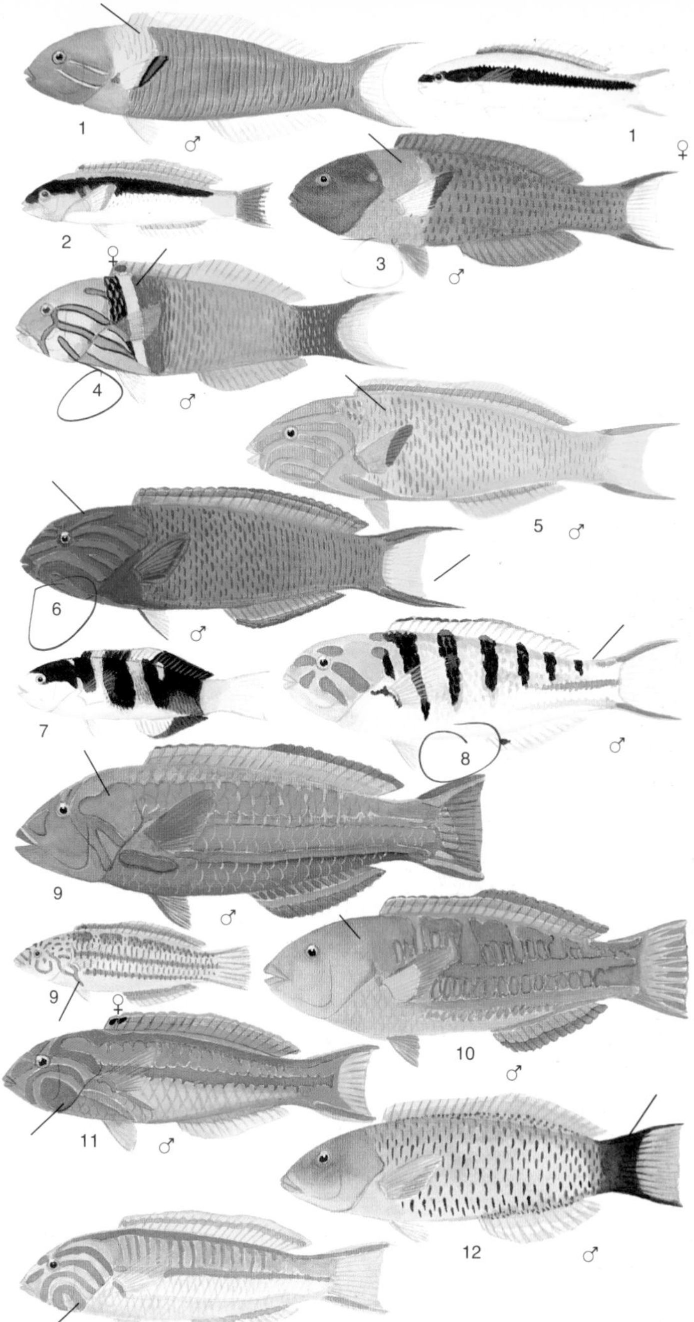
1 ♂
1 ♀
2 ♀
3 ♂
4 ♂
5 ♂
6 ♂
7
8 ♂
9 ♂
9 ♀
10 ♂
11 ♂
12 ♂
13 ♂

Tribe Labrichthyini (remaining genera): small species with a distinctive bilobed lower lip or pursed fleshy lips that form a short tube when the mouth is closed.

1 **Tubelip wrasse** *Labrichthys unilineatus* (Guichenot) 16 cm
Ecology: coral-rich areas of lagoon and semi-protected seaward reefs, 0.5 to 20 m. Usually in the vicinity of branching corals and feeds on coral polyps. **Range:** E. Africa to Samoa, n. to Ryuk., s. to L. Howe Is.

2 **Wandering cleaner wrasse** *Diproctacanthus xanthurus* (Bleeker) 8 cm
Ecology: shallow lagoons and sheltered reefs. Seaward reefs in areas of rich coral growth. Feeds on coral polyps and ectoparasites picked from the bodies of other fishes (see *Labroides* spp.). Has a large home range and services primarily small territorial fishes. **Range:** Phil., Indonesia, N. Guinea & Palau, s. to n. GBR.

3 **Fourline wrasse** *Larabicus quadrilineatus* (Rüppell) 11.5 cm
♂ dark blueish. **Ecology:** coral heads and coral-rich areas of fringing reefs, 0.5 to 22 m. Juveniles are cleaners and usually found in small groups; adults feed on coral polyps. **Range:** R. Sea & G. of Aden.

4 **Bicolor cleaner wrasse** *Labroides bicolor* Fowler & Bean 12 cm
Ecology: species of *Labroides* are known as "cleaner wrasses" because they feed on external parasites or diseased or damaged tissue of other fishes. They are typically territorial around a prominent coral formation termed "cleaning stations" and advertise their trade by swimming with a distinctive up-and-down motion. This attracts fishes of all sizes that may solicit the cleaner's services by posing in unusual positions. Cleaners safely enter the mouths of large predators that value their services enough to resist the temptation to eat them. Juvenile cleaners are generally solitary and somewhat secretive. Adults of this species may wander over a large area of reef in pursuit of customers. **Range:** E. Africa to Marq. & Society Is., n. to s. Japan, s. to L. Howe Is.

5 **Bluestreak cleaner wrasse** *Labroides dimidiatus* (Valenciennes) 11 cm
Ecology: nearly all coral reef habitats from inner lagoons and reef flats to seaward reefs as deep as 40 m. The most common cleaner wrasse on most reefs. Mimicked by the fin-nipping blenny *Aspidontus taeniatus* (pl. 114-2). **Range:** R. Sea to Marq. & Ducie Is., n. to s. Japan, s. to L. Howe Is.

6 **Blackspot cleaner wrasse** *Labroides pectoralis* Randall & Springer 8 cm
Ecology: coral-rich areas of seaward and clear lagoon reefs, 2 to 28 m. Usually in pairs. **Range:** Cocos-Keeling to Line & Pitcairn Is., n. to Bonins, s. to GBR.

7 **Hawaiian cleaner wrasse** *Labroides phthirophagus* Randall 10 cm
Ecology: most coral reef habitats except surge zone, 0.5 to 90 m. An obligate cleaner. **Range:** Hawaiian Is. only.

8 **Redlip cleaner wrasse** *Labroides rubrolabiatus* Randall 9 cm
Ecology: lagoon and seawar reefs, 1 to at least 32 m. **Range:** disjunct: Marcus Is.; Fiji e. to Marq. & Ducie Is., n. to Line Is.

9 **Allen's wrasse** *Labropsis alleni* Randall 10 cm
Ecology: coral-rich areas of steep lagoon and seaward reefs, 4 to 52 m. **Range:** Phil. & Indonesia to Solomon & Marshall Is.

10 **Micronesian wrasse** *Labropsis micronesica* Randall 12 cm
Very similar to *L. manabei* (pl. 139-9) and *L. australis* (sw. Pacific). **Ecology:** clear lagoon and seaward reefs, 7 to over 33 m. A cleaner of small fishes. **Range:** Palau, Caroline, Mariana & Marshall Is.

11 **Wedge-tailed wrasse** *Labropsis xanthonota* Randall 12 cm
Ecology: coral-rich areas of lagoon and seaward reefs, 7 to 55 m. Juveniles are cleaners, adults feed on coral polyps. Males generally solitary. **Range:** E. Africa to Solomon & Marshall Is., n. to Andaman Sea & Phil., s. to GBR, Mauritius.

1
1 juv
2
3
♀
4 juv
4
5
5 juv
6
7
8
9
10
10 juv
11
♂
11 juv

105 PARROTFISHES (widespread species)

PARROTFISHES (SCARIDAE): medium to large wrasse-like fishes differing by having teeth fused into a beaklike plates with a median suture and unique pavement-like pharyngeal teeth. All species have large cycloid scales, a continuous D fin, single LL, and are herbivores. Most species graze on the algal film growing on coral rock, a few eat leafy algae or living coral. Bits of rock eaten with the algae are crushed into sand and ground with the algae to aid in digestion, making parrotfishes among the most important producers of sand on coral reefs. Many species occur in large mixed species schools, often with surgeonfishes. At night they sleep wedged into holes or crevices. Many species secrete a mucus cocoon around themselves which may inhibit the sense of smell of predators. Like the wrasses, most parrotfishes change color with growth and sex. Typically a drab grey, brown, or reddish initial phase (IP) consisting of both females and males, the latter able to change sex into a brilliant blue to green terminal male phase (TP). Juveniles and IP of many species very similar and often very difficult to identify, TP generally more distinctive. Important foodfishes. Difficult to maintain in aquariums as the fused teeth need to constantly graze dead coral rock in order to keep from growing to long.

1 **Bumphead parrotfish** *Bolbometopon muricatum* (Valenciennes) 130 cm, 46 kg
Juvs. brown with two rows of whitish spots on upper half of body, and steep head profile. Differs from other "humpheaded" spp. by having raised bumps on outer surface of beak. **Ecology:** juvs. in lagoons, adults on clear lagoon and seaward reefs, 1 to over 30 m. Typically in schools. Feeds on live corals as well as encrusting algae. May ram its head into corals to break them to facilitate feeding. Quite wary and vulnerable to overfishing. **Range:** R. Sea to Line & Tuam. Is., n. to Taiwan & s. Ryuk., s. to N. Cal.

2 **Bicolor parrotfish** *Cetoscarus bicolor* (Rüppell) 80 cm
Ecology: clear lagoon and seaward reefs, 1 to 30 m. Juvs. usually solitary, adults in harems, usually along upper reaches of coral slopes. **Range:** R. Sea to Tuam., n. to Izus, s. to s. GBR.

3 **Indian Ocean steephead parrotfish** *Chlorurus strongylocephalus* Bleeker 70 cm
Similar to *C.gibbus* (R. Sea) & *C. microrhinos* (w.-c. Pacific; pl. 109-1). **Ecology:** lagoon and seaward reefs, 2 to 35 m. Juveniles usually solitary, adults may occur in schools. Common. **Range:** E. Africa to sw. Indonesia, n. to Andaman Sea, and s. to Cocos-Keeling

4 **Redlip parrotfish** *Scarus rubroviolaceus* Bleeker 70 cm
Snout profile of adults angular with angle closer to mouth than to eye; both sexes often bicolored with the forward half abruptly dark. **Ecology:** seaward reefs, 1 to 30 m. Solitary or in large schools. **Range:** s. Red Sea & E. Africa to Panama, n. to Ryuk. & Hawaiian Is., s. to s. GBR & Tuam.

5 **Bluebarred parrotfish** *Scarus ghobban* Forsskål 75 cm
Ecology: shallow lagoon and seaward reefs to 30 m. Often near sandy areas in silty environments. Usually solitary, but juveniles in groups. **Range:** R. Sea to Panama, n. to s. Japan, s. to sw. & se. Aust., L. Howe & Rapa Is.

6 **Bullethead parrotfish** *Scarus sordidus* Forsskål 40 cm
IP highly variable, may lack the small white dots on sides or light C peduncle, or both; TP also quite variable, cheek and sides often more uniformly green than as shown. **Ecology:** reef flats and lagoon and seaward reefs to over 25 m. In coral-rich as well as open pavement areas. Juveniles among coral rubble of reef flats and lagoons. Juveniles and initial phase fishes often in large groups which may migrate over great distances between feeding and sleeping grounds. One of the most common parrotfishes throughout its range. **Range:** R. Sea to Hawaiian, Line & Ducie Is., n. to Ryuk., s. to sw. & se. Aust., L. Howe & Rapa Is.

7 **Bridled parrotfish** *Scarus frenatus* Lacépède 47 cm
Juvs. light blue posteriorly. **Ecology:** seaward reefs and reef crests. Juveniles among coral and coral rubble of clear lagoon reefs. Usually solitary. **Range:** R. Sea to Line & Ducie Is., n. to s. Japan, s. to nw. Aust, L. Howe & Rapa Is.

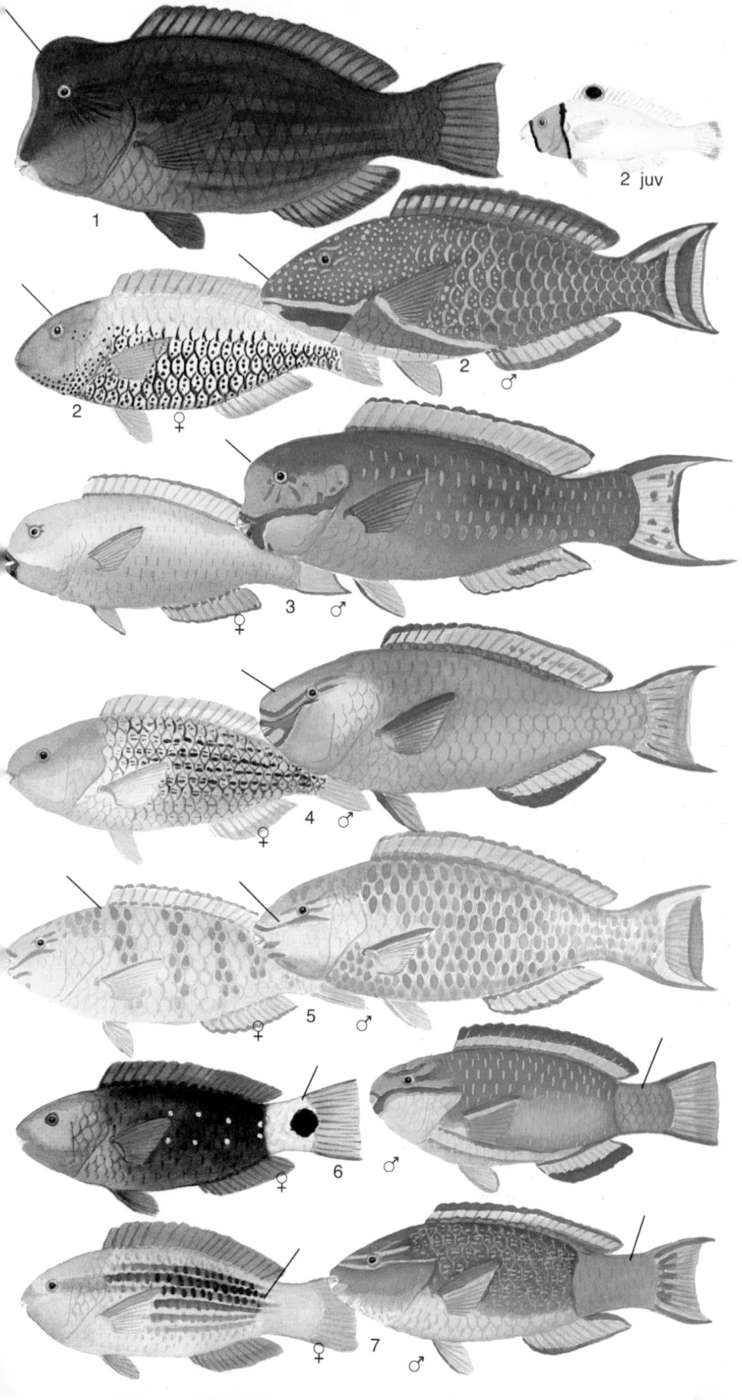
1
2 juv
2
♂
2
♀
3
♂
♀
4
♂
♀
5
♂
♀
6
♀
♂
7
♀
♂

1 **Greenthroat parrotfish** *Scarus prasiognathus* Valenciennes 70 cm
Juv. & IP closely resemble juv. & IP of *S. altipinnis* (pl. 108-2) & *S. falcipinnis* (pl. 107-2). **Ecology:** upper edges of steep outer reef dropoffs and adjacent sandy flats to at least 20 m. Often in large schools. **Range:** Seychelles to N. Ireland, n. to Ryuk., s. to Cocos-Keeling Is.

2 **Festive parrotfish** *Scarus festivus* Valenciennes 43 cm
Brown coloration only in indiv. with distinctive lump on forehead. **Ecology:** clear lagoon and seaward reefs, 3 to 30 m. Uncommon. **Range:** E. Africa to Tuam., n. to Ryuk.

3 **Swarthy parrotfish** *Scarus niger* Forsskål 35 cm
IP of Pacific popul. more closely resembles the TP than IP in the R. Sea & Indian Ocean. **Ecology:** coral-rich areas of clear lagoons, channels, and outer reef slopes, 0.5 to 15 m. Usually solitary except during courtship. **Range:** R. Sea to Society Is., n. to Ryuk., s. to nw. Aust & s. GBR.

4 **Tricolor parrotfish** *Scarus tricolor* Bleeker 55 cm
TP similar to TP of *S. forsteni* (pl. 109-6). **Ecology:** coral-rich areas of lagoon and seaward reefs. Usually solitary, occasionally in groups. **Range:** E. Africa to Indonesia & Belau, Nauru & Line Is. in Pacific.

5 **Palenose parrotfish** *Scarus psittacus* Forsskål 30 cm
Ecology: reef flats and lagoon and seaward reefs toat least 25 m. Often in large mixed-species schools over open hard bottoms near coral heads. Secretes a mucus cocoon at night. **Range:** R. Sea to Hawaiian, Marq. & Tuam. Is., n. to s. Japan, s. to nw. Aust. & L. Howe Is.

6 **Violet-lined parrotfish** *Scarus globiceps* Valenciennes 27 cm
IP similar to IP of *S. psittacus* and *S. rivulatus*. **Ecology:** clear outer reef flats and lagoon and seaward reefs to 12 m. **Range:** E. Africa to Line & Society Is., n. to Ryuk. s. to nw. Aust., s. GBR & Rapa.

7 **Pale bullethead parrotfish** *Chlorurus japanensis* Bleeker 31 cm
Most similar to *C. atrilunula* (pl. 107-4) but front of snout of IP solid brownish red & TP without black crescent on tail & without blue-green line extending from corner of mouth to near P base. Also similar to *C. genazonatus* (pl. 110-4), *C. pyrrhurus* (pl. 109-8) & *C. sordidus* (pl. 105-6). The invalid name *C. capistratoides* is often mistakenly applied to this species. **Ecology:** seaward coral and rocky reefs, 2 to 20 m. **Range:** E. Africa to Bali, s. to Maurit., n. to Andaman Sea; absent from Japan & Pacific.

8 **Stareye parrotfish** *Calotomus carolinus* (Valenciennes) 50 cm
C. viridescens (pl. 110-2) is similar, but TP with small red dots on body and fins and reaches only 27 cm; *C. spinidens* also similar but much smaller (~19 cm) and drably colored. **Ecology:** lagoon and seaward reefs on coral and rubble as well as seagrass and weedy areas to at least 27 m. Solitary or in small groups. Feeds on algae and seagrasses. **Range:** E. Africa to Mexico, n. to s. Japan, s. to S. Africa & Pitcairn Is.

9 **Spinytooth parrotfish** *Calotomus spinidens* (Quoy & Gaimard) 19 cm
Ecology: shallow seagrass and seaweed beds. **Range:** E. Africa to Marshall Is., Fiji & Tonga, n. to Ryuk., s. to GBR.

10 **Seagrass parrotfish** *Leptoscarus vaigiensis* (Quoy & Gaimard) 35 cm
The only parrotfish sp. known not to change sex. **Ecology:** shallow seagrass and seaweed beds. **Range:** R. Sea to Easter Is., n. to Ryuk., s. to L. Howe Is. & n. NZ.

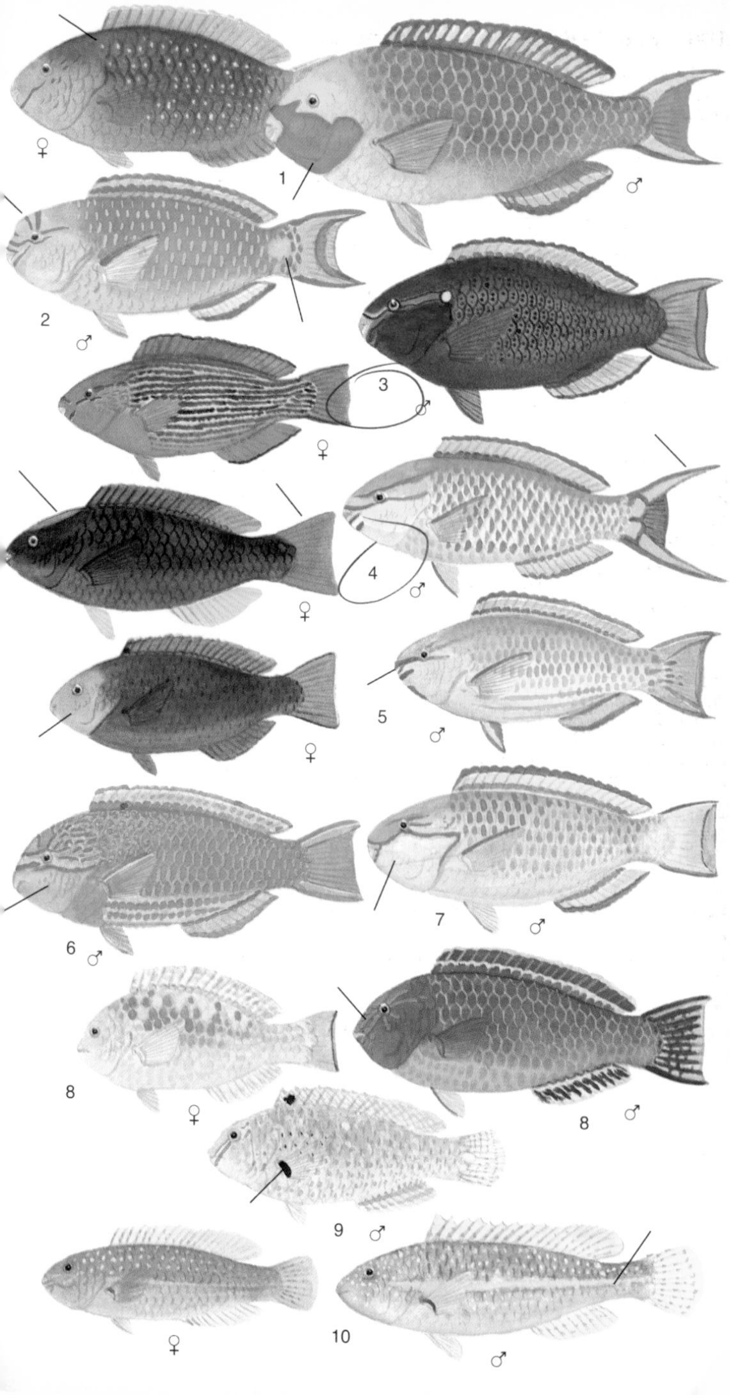

♀
1
♂
2
♂
3
♂
♀
♀
4
♂
♀
5
♂
6
♂
7
♂
8
♀
8
♂
9
♂
♀
10
♂

107 PARROTFISHES (Indian Ocean species)

1 **Indian Ocean Longnose parrotfish** *Hipposcarus harid* (Forsskål) 75 cm
Similar to *H. longiceps* (Pacific; pl. 108-1), but tail of TP emarginate with very long lobes. Indian Ocean TP has horizontal orange band across cheek and operculum. **Ecology:** protected waters, often over sand near reefs, 1 to 25 m. Usually in mobile groups of 1 TP and numerous IP fish. **Range:** R. Sea to Java, s. to Maldives & Mozambique, Cocos-Keeling.

2 **Greenbelly parrotfish** *Scarus falcipinnis* (Playfair) 60 cm
Closely related to *S. prasiognathos* (pl. 106-1) & *S. altipinnis* (pl. 108-2), all with very similar juvs. & IPs. **Ecology:** steep seaward reef slopes, 6 to over 20 m. **Range:** E. Africa to Chagos Is., s. to Mozambique & Maurit.

3 **Saddled parrotfish** *Chlorurus cyanascens* Bleeker 34 cm
Similar to *C. oedema* (pl. 110-9) and *C. ovifrons* (pl. 110-10). **Ecology:** deep rocky reefs, 5 to over 30 m. Solitary or in small groups. **Range:** E. Africa to Madag. & Maurit., s. to Natal.

4 **Black crescent parrotfish** *Chlorurus atrilunula* Randall & Bruce 30 cm
Black crescent shape on tail of TP distinctive. Otherwise very similar to *S. japanensis.* Both closely related to *S. sordidus, S. genazonatus, S. pyrrhurus* & *S. bowersi.* **Ecology:** silty protected reefs, 1 to 15 m. Usually over sand and rubble. Wary. **Range:** E. Africa to Seychelles & Maldives, s. to Chagos, Madagascar.

5 **Dusky-capped parrotfish** *Scarus scaber* Valenciennes 37 cm
Closely related to *S. oviceps* and *S. dimidiatus* with IPs very similar. **Ecology:** reef flats and shallow lagoon reefs with rich coral growth, 1 to 20 m. Initial phase usually in groups. **Range:** G. Aden & E. Africa to Maldives, s. to Natal & Mauritius.

6 **Greenlip parrotfish** *Scarus viridifucatus* Smith 32 cm
Similar to *S. spinus* (w. Pacific), possibly subspecies of it, but both spp. occur at Bali. **Ecology:** shallow reefs, on flats and reef fronts or rocky shores of high Islands. **Range:** s. Red Sea, E. Africa to Bali.

7 **Tail-barred parrotfish** *Scarus caudofasciatus* (Günther) 70 cm
Ecology: steep outer reef slopes, 8 to 40 m. Solitary and wary. **Range:** E. Africa to Maldives, s. to Mozambique.

8 **Green parrotfish** *Chloruruss enneacanthus* Lacépède 50 cm
Similar to *S. frontalis* with little or no change in color between IP and TP. **Ecology:** clear seaward reefs, particularly over areas of dead coral and rubble of reef fronts, reef flats and reef tops to at least 7 m. Uncommon. **Range:** E. Africa to Chagos & Maldives, s. to Maurit & s. to Cocos-Keeling.

9 **Russell's parrotfish** *Scarus russelli* Valenciennes 51 cm
TP often bicolored with front portion darker. **Ecology:** shallow coastal reefs. Grazes on algae on sand or coral rubble. Wary. Usually solitary. Moderately common. **Range:** E. Africa to Similan Is. (Andaman Sea), n. to India.

10 **Arabian parrotfish** *Scarus arabicus* (Steindachner) 40 cm
Ecology: coastal coral-rich reefs. Poorly known. **Range:** G. Aden to Oman.

11 **Troschel's parrotfish** *Scarus troschelii* Bleeker 35 cm
IP like *S. bleekeri*; TP also similar but without distinctive light patch on cheek. **Ecology:** coral-rich areas of clear shallow seaward reefs, 5 to 25 m. Solitary. **Range:** Similan Is. to Java.

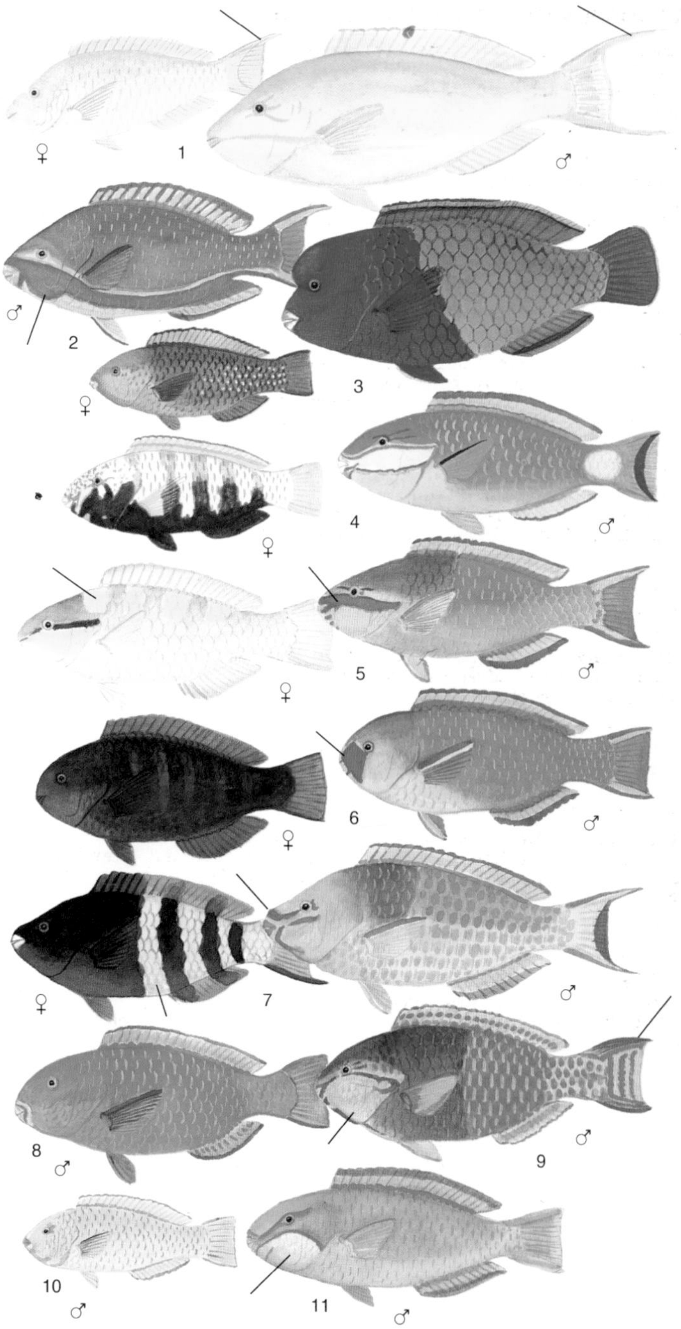

♀
1
♂
♂
2
♀
3
♀
4
♂
♀
5
♂
♀
6
♂
♀
7
♂
♂
8
♂
9
10
♂
11
♂

1 **Pacific longnose parrotfish** *Hippopscarus longiceps* (Valenciennes) 60 cm
Similar to *H. harid* (R. Sea to Java; pl. 107-1), but tail of TP double emarginate with short lobes. **Ecology:** lagoon and seaward reefs to over 40 m. Typically in groups in relatively turbid lagoons over sandy areas near reefs. Juveniles among coral rubble of lagoon patch reefs. **Range:** Indonesia & Cocos-Keeling to Line & Tuam. Is., n. to Ryuk., s. to Rowley Shoals & N. Cal.

2 **Filament-fin parrotfish** *Scarus altipinnis* (Steindachner) 60 cm
The only sp. in family in which a mid-dorsal ray of lg. adults is produced into a filament. Otherwise similar to *S. ferrugineus* (pl. 110-1), *S. persicus* & *S. prasiognathos* (pl. 106-1). **Ecology:** juveniles and subadults occur on shallow protected reefs, adults common on seaward reefs, particularly the reef margin. Juveniles solitary, subadults and adults often in large groups. **Range:** Ryuk. to Line & Ducie Is., n. to s. Japan, s. to L. Howe & Rapa Is.

3 **Red (IP) or Bluechin (TP) parrotfish** *Scarus atropectoralis* Schultz 52 cm
Similar to *S. caudofasciatus* (Indian Oc.; pl. 107-7), but IP more red, often bright red, & without distinct bands posteriorly. **Ecology:** clear lagoon and seaward reefs, usually along dropoffs. Solitary and rare. **Range:** Taiwan to Marshall Is., n. to Ryuk., s. to Indonesia & Cocos-Keeling.

4 **Bleeker's parrotfish** *Chlorurus bleekeri* (deBeaufort) 49 cm
Most similar to *C. troschelii*, but TP with distinctive light patch on cheek. Belly of TP may become purplish during courtship. **Ecology:** lagoon and channel reefs. Common from Palau to e. Caroline Is. **Range:** Borneo to Fiji, n. to Marshalls, s. to GBR & Vanuatu.

5 **Surf parrotfish** *Scarus rivulatus* Valenciennes 40 cm
IP similar to IPs of *S. globiceps* & *S. psittacus*; courting IP with dark hood, the male IP with a darker horizontal stripe through eye; courting TP abruptly dark green on forward part of body. **Ecology:** lagoon and seaward reefs, usually in schools on reef flats and upper reef slopes. More common on coastal reefs than offshore reefs. **Range:** Andaman Sea to N. Cal., n. to Ryuk., s. to sw. & se. Aust. & L. Howe Is.

6 **Pygmy parrotfish** *Scarus spinus* Kner 30 cm
Similar to *S. viridifucatus* which may possibly be a subspecies of this. **Ecology:** coral-rich areas of outer lagoon and seaward reefs, 2 to 25 m. Usually solitary. **Range:** Phil. to Samoa, n. to Ryuk., s. to sGBR.

7 **Quoy's parrotfish** *Scarus quoyi* Valenciennes 21 cm
Ecology: coral-rich areas of outer channels and seaward reefs, 2 to 18 m. Solitary or in small groups. **Range:** India to Vanuatu, n. to Ryuk., s. to N. Cal.

8 **Tan-faced-parrotfish** *Chlorurus frontalis* Valenciennes 50 cm
Color changes little with growth; IP predominately green like TP; lg. TP develop a vertical head profile & elongate tail filaments silmilar to lg. *C. microrhinos*. (pl. 109-1). **Ecology:** exposed reef flats and seaward reefs to 40 m. Often in small groups. **Range:** Ryuk. to Line & Ducie Is., s. to s. GBR.

9 **Highfin parrotfish** *Scarus longipinnis* Randall & Choat 40 cm
Ecology: seaward reefs below 10 m to at leat 55 m. The most abundant parrotfish on Coral Sea Atolls. **Range:** GBR, L. Howe Is., N. Cal., Rapa & Pitcairn Is.

10 **Bower's parrotfish** *Chlorurus bowersi* (Snyder) 31 cm
One of the *Scarus sordidus* complex, but color pattern of TP more similar to *S. hypselopterus*. **Ecology:** channel and lagoon reef slopes, usually in coral-rich areas. Solitary. **Range:** Phil., Java, Ryuk. & Palau.

11 **East-Indies parrotfish** *Scarus hypselopterus* Bleeker 31 cm
Ecology: coral-rich areas of coastal reefs and outer reef slopes to 30 m. Rare. **Range:** Borneo & Phil. to Moluccas, n. to Ryuk. & Pelau.

12 **Stripedbelly parrotfish** *Scarus* sp. ca. 32 cm
Ecology: steep seaward reefs and offshore banks, 18 to over 40 m. **Range:** Phil., Ryuk., PNG & Guam.

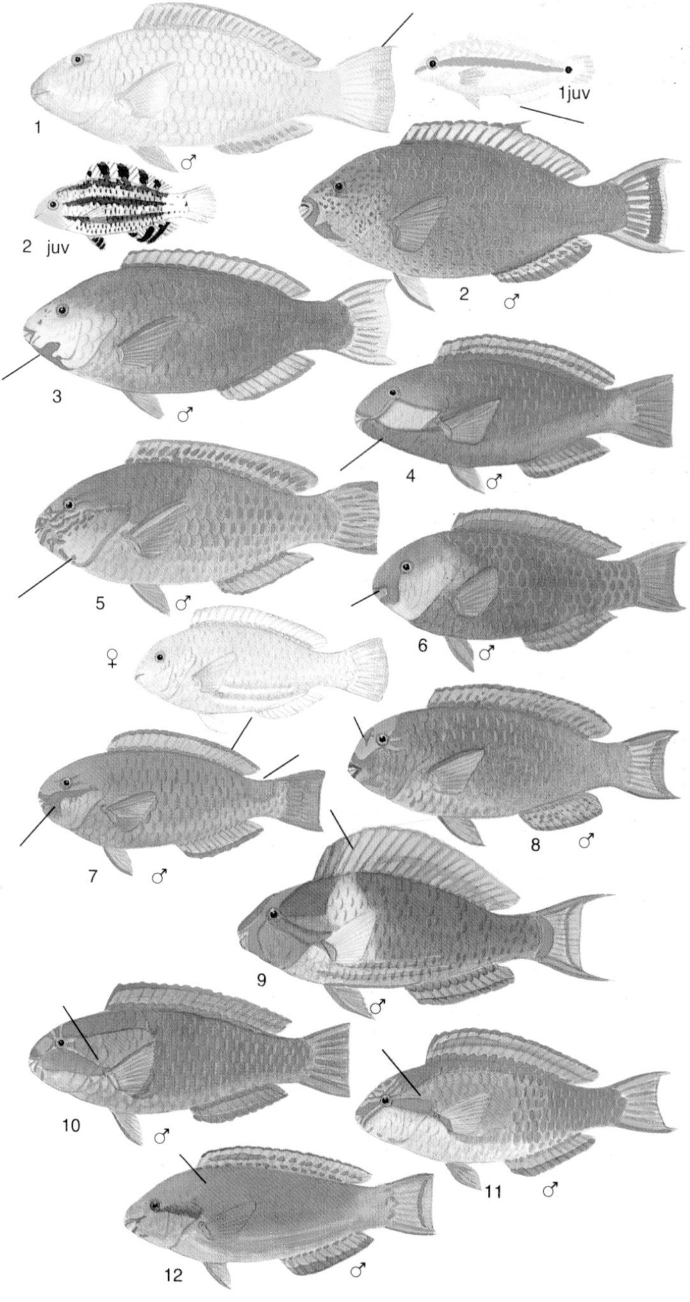
1
♂
1juv
2 juv
2
♂
3
♂
4
♂
5
♂
6
♂
♀
7
♂
8
♂
9
♂
10
♂
11
♂
12
♂

109 PARROTFISHES (Pacific species)

1 **Pacific Steephead parrotfish** *Chlorurus microrhinos* Bleeker 70 cm
Similar to *C. strongylocephalus* (Indian Oc.; pl. 105-3), but IP usually blue-green (rarely a tan phase), and TP with horiz. blue line extending from corner of mouth to edge of operc.; D and A fins of TP may be tan or blue. **Ecology:** lagoon and seaward reefs, 2 to 35 m. Juveniles usually solitary, adults may occur in schools. **Range:** e. Indonesia to Line & Pitcairn Is., n. to Ryuk., s. to L. Howe & Rapa Is.

2 **Schlegel's parrotfish** *Scarus schlegeli* (Bleeker) 38 cm
Closely related to *S. fuscopurpureus* & *S. russelli,* both with similar IP. IP also similar to IPs of *S. globiceps* and *S. spinus*, but usually more distinctly barred. 2nd yellow bar of TP absent in S. Pacific popul. (s. of ca. 15°S). **Ecology:** lagoon and seaward reefs, 1 to over 50 m. Adults common in areas of rich coral growth and high vertical relief. Often feed on rubble bottoms. **Range:** Bali, Cocos-Keeling & Flores to Tuam. & Austral Is., n. to Ryuk., s. to s. GBR & Rapa.

3 **Dark-capped parrotfish** *Scarus oviceps* Valenciennes 30 cm
IP very similar to IPs of *S. dimidiatus* and *S. scaber*. **Ecology:** clear reef flats and outer lagoon and seaward reefs to at least 10 m. **Range:** Phil. and Cocos-Keeling to Line & Society Is., n. to Ryuk., s. to nw. Aust & GBR.

4 **Turquois-capped parrotfish** *Scarus dimidiatus* Bleeker 30 cm
Closely related to *S. scaber* and *S. oviceps*. **Ecology:** coral-rich areas of clear, protected reefs to over 12 m. **Range:** Indonesia to Samoa, n. to Ryuk., s. to nw. Australia & GBR.

5 **Yellowfin parrotfish** *Scarus flavipectoralis* Schultz 30 cm
Ecology: lagoon and channel reefs, usually below 20 m. Generally solitary. **Range:** Andaman Sea to Solomon Is., n. to Marshalls, s. to Scott Reef & GBR.

6 **Rainbow parrotfish** *Scarus forsteni* (Bleeker) 55 cm
TP similar to TP of *S. tricolor* (pl. 106-5); head of TP deep violet during courtship. **Ecology:** clear outer lagoon and seaward reefs, 3 to 30 m. Usually solitary. **Range:** Phil. and Cocos-Keeling & Borneo to Ducie Is., n. to Ryuk. & Marcus Is., s. to s. GBR.

7 **Chameleon parrotfish** *Scarus chameleon* Choat & Randall 31 cm
Ecology: outer reef flats and exposed lagoon and seaward reef slopes to at least 30 m. **Range:** Phil. to Fiji, n. to Ryuk., s. to w. Aust., NSW (juvs.) & L. Howe Is.

8 **Redtail parrotfish** *Chlorurus pyrrhurus* (Jordan & Seale) 30 cm
IP has orange-red tail; often misnamed *S. japanensis* (pl. 106-7). **Ecology:** upper reef slopes; common in Samoa, but rare elsewhere. **Range:** Phil. & Sulawesi to Samoa, n. to Ryuk. & Palau, s. to GBR.

9 **Marquesan parrotfish** *Scarus koputea* Randall & Choat 31 cm
IP very similar to IP of *S. rubroviolaceus*. **Ecology:** inner bays and outer reef slopes, 0-18 m. **Range:** Marq. only.

10 **Black-tail parrotfish** *Scarus sp.* 25 cm
Tail of IP dark with broad green central margin; tail of juv. distinctly black. Andaman Sea pop. without yellow patch on side. **Ecology:** deep coastal reef slopes to 35 m. **Range:** Andaman Sea & Indonesia, n. to Ryuk.

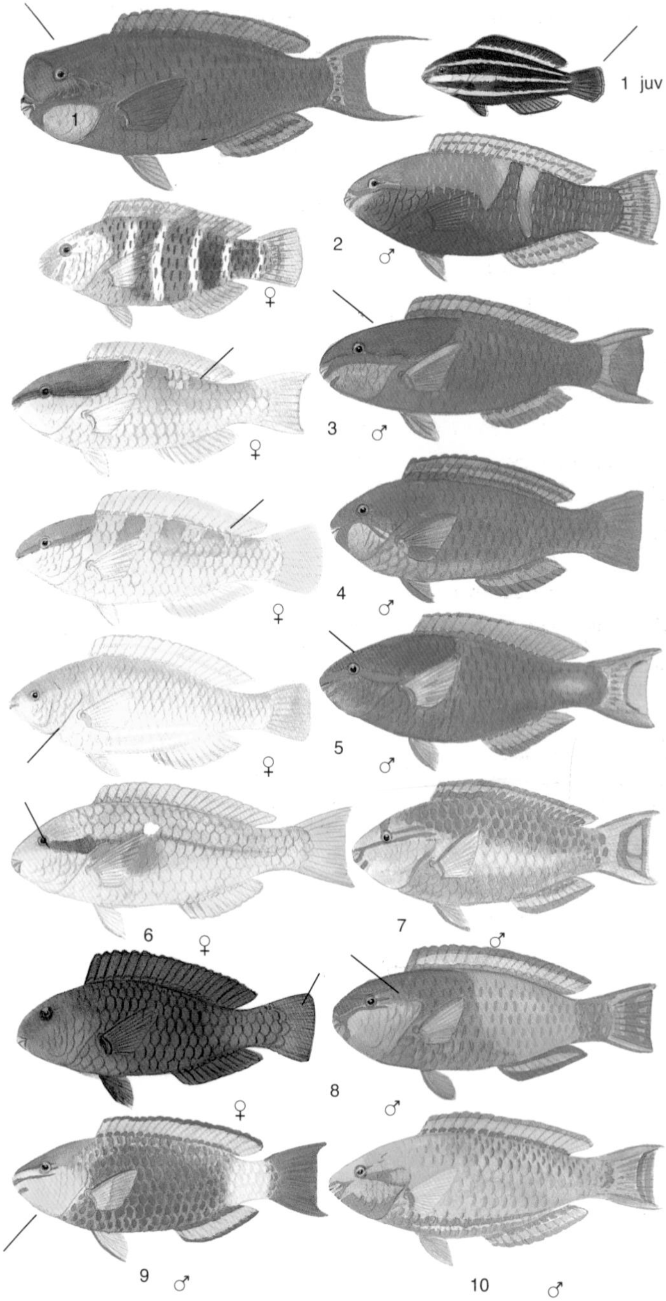
1
1 juv
2 ♂
♀
3 ♂
♀
4 ♂
♀
5 ♂
♀
6 ♀
7 ♂
8 ♂
♀
9 ♂
10 ♂

1 **Rusty parrotfish** *Scarus ferrugineus* Forsskål 41 cm
Similar to *S. persicus* of Persian Gulf and *S. zufar* of Oman. **Ecology:** protected coral slopes, 1 to 60 m. IP in harems. Quite common. **Range:** R. Sea, G. of Aden to Arab. G..

2 **Dotted parrotfish** *Calotomus viridescens* (Rüppell) 27 cm
Similar to *C. carolinus* (pl. 106-8) which lacks black and red spots on the body as well as the black dot on front of D fin; IP can change color instantly. **Ecology:** shallow seagrass beds as well as rocky and coral reefs to ~ 30 m. Feeds on seagrasses and epiphytic algae. Solitary or in small groups. **Range:** R. Sea.

3 **Purple-brown parrotfish** *Scarus fuscopurpureus* (Klunzinger) 38 cm
Closely related to *S. russelli* (pl. 107-9.). Can rapidly change color. **Ecology:** usually over open sand and weedy bottoms with coral heads, 2 to 20 m. In pairs or small groups. Common but wary. **Range:** R. Sea to Arab. G.

4 **Purplestreak parrotfish** *Chlorurus genazonatus* Randall & Bruce 31 cm
Most similar to *C. sordidus*, differing in details of color. **Ecology:** deeper reef slopes, usually below 20 m, occasionally as shallow as 6 m - uncommon. Very shy. **Range:** R. Sea & G. of Aden.

5 **Greenband parrotfish** *Scarus collana* Rüppell 33 cm
Ecology: typically near small coral heads or dead coral rock on silty sand of inshore reefs, 1 to 15 m. Solitary and fast-swimming. **Range:** R. Sea.

6 **Spectacled parrotfish** *Chlorurus perspicillatus* Steindachner 54 cm; 7 kg
Blue bar on snout of TP distinctive; IP with broad light band on base of tail. **Ecology:** clear lagoon and seaward reefs, intertidal to at least 45 m. **Range:** Hawaiian Is.

7 **Yellowbar parrotfish** *Calotomus zonarchus* (Jenkins) 33 cm
See also *C. carolinus* (pl. 106-8) & *C. japonicus*. **Ecology:** areas of coral rock with coral or rubble, lower surge zone to at least 10 m. Uncommon. **Range:** Hawaiian Is.

8 **Regal parrotfish** *Scarus dubius* Bennett 36 cm
Ecology: seaward reefs. Uncommon. **Range:** Hawaiian Is.

9 **Knobsnout parrotfish** *Scarus ovifrons* (Temmink & Schlegel) 78 cm
Juvs. with 2-3 rows of white spots posteriorly; IP orange with blue trim; TP with distinct knob on snout rather than forehead as in *Chlorurus. cyanescens* & *C. oedema*. **Ecology:** in small groups around rocky areas. **Range:** Ryuk. n. to s. Japan (Tokyo area).

10 **Knothead parrotfish** *Chlorurus oedema* (Snyder) 42 cm
Very similar to *C. cyanascens* (pl. 107-3). **Ecology:** coastal rocky and coral reefs. In Sri Lanka on deep rocky reefs, 20-35m. Feeds solitary on algae from hard substratum. Shy. **Range:** Sri Lanka to Phil., n. to Ryuk.

11 **Japanese parrotfish** *Calotomus japonicus* (Valenciennes) 39 cm
Ecology: rocky areas with seaweeds. **Range:** s. Japan & s. Korea only.

1
♀
♂
2
♂
3
♂
4
♂
5
♂
♀
6
♂
7
♂
8
♂
9
10
11
♂

BARRACUDAS and MULLETS

BARRACUDAS (SPHYRAENIDAE): elongate silvery fishes with two widely spaced D fins, small scales, and pointed head with large mouth and long knife-like teeth. Voracious predators of other fishes. Most species in schools by day. Juveniles often in estuaries. Food and gamefishes, but large *S. barracuda* may be ciguatoxic.

1 **Great barracuda** *Sphyraena barracuda* (Walbaum) 190 cm; 40 kg
Ecology: wide range of habitats from turbid inshore waters to open sea. Juveniles in sheltered inner reef and estuarine waters. Solitary and diurnally active. Curious, but not dangerous in clear water unless provoked. Capable of inflicting severe wounds. **Range:** Entire tropical Indo-Pacific & Atlantic; absent from E. Pacific.

2 **Blackfin barracuda** *Sphyraena qenie* Klunzinger 170 cm
Similar to *S. putnamiae* but first rays of 2nd D & A fin the longest & tail dark. **Ecology:** in large schools by day near prominent current-swept lagoon or seaward reefs. **Range:** R. Sea to Panama, n. to Micronesia, s. to GBR, N. Cal. & Tuam. Is.

3 **Pickhandle barracuda** *Sphyraena jello* Cuvier 150 cm
Tail yellowish. **Ecology:** in large schools by day near prominent current-swept lagoon or seaward reefs. **Range:** R. Sea to w. Pacific, n. to Ryukyus, s. to GBR.

4 **Sawtooth barracuda** *Sphyraena putnamiae* Jordan & Seale 87 cm
Similar to *S. qenie* but last rays of 2nd D & A fin the longest. **Ecology:** in large schools by day near prominent current-swept lagoon or seaward reefs. **Range:** R. Sea to w. Pacific, n. to Phil., s. to GBR. Exact dist. uncertain.

5 **Blackspot barracuda** *Sphyraena forsteri* Cuvier 75 cm
Ecology: in schools by day near lagoon pinnacles and seaward reef slopes. Feeds at night. **Range:** E. Africa to Marq. & Society Is., n. to Ryuk., s. to GBR & N. Cal.

6 **Sharpfin barracuda** *Sphyraena acutipinnis* Day 75 cm
Ecology: in schools over lagoon and seaward reefs by day, disperses to feed at night. **Range:** E. Africa to Hawaiian, Marq. & Tuam. Is., n. to s. Japan, s. to GBR.

7 **Yellowtail barracuda** *Sphyraena flavicauda* Rüppell 37 cm
Tail yellowish, side with 2 brown stripes; many similar spp. (*S. obtusata, S. chrysotenia*). **Ecology:** in schools above lagoon and shelteR. Seaward reefs. **Range:** R. Sea to Samoa, n. to Ryuk., s. to N. Cal.

MULLETS (MUGILIDAE): silvery somewhat cylindrical fishes with a short snout, small mouth with or without minute teeth, two widely spaced D fins, large scales, and no LL. Travel in schools and feed on fine algae, diatoms, and detritus of bottom sediments. Many species are estuarine or freshwater. Important food fishes.

8 **Fringelip mullet** *Crenimugil crenilabis* (Forsskål) 60 cm
Upper lip wide with prominent papillae; A fin base 11 in SL (vs. 8 in SL for remaining spp.); dark spot on upper P base. **Ecology:** sandy areas of lagoons and reef flats, usually in small schools. **Range:** R. Sea to Line & Tuam. Is., n. to s. Japan, s. to L. Howe Is.

9 **Squaretail mullet** *Liza vaigiensis* (Quoy & Gaimard) 63 cm
P fin dark; tail truncate (vs. forked in most other spp.) **Ecology:** sandy shorelines and bottoms of lagoons and reef flats, in small schools. **Range:** E. Africa to Tuam., n. to s. Japan, s. to s. GBR & N. Cal.

10 **Foldlip mullet** *Oedalechilus labiosus* (Valenciennes) 25 cm
Lips with folds and lobes; dark spot on upper base; tail slightly forked. **Ecology:** reef flats and lagoons, usually at the surface in small schools. **Range:** R. Sea to Marshall Is., n. to s. Japan, s. to s. GBR.

11 **Bluespot mullet** *Valamugil seheli* (Forsskål) 60 cm
Dark blueish spot on upper P base; tail prominently forked; upper lip without papillae. **Ecology:** shallow sandy lagoons. **Range:** R. Sea to Samoa, n. to s. Japan, s. to N. Cal.

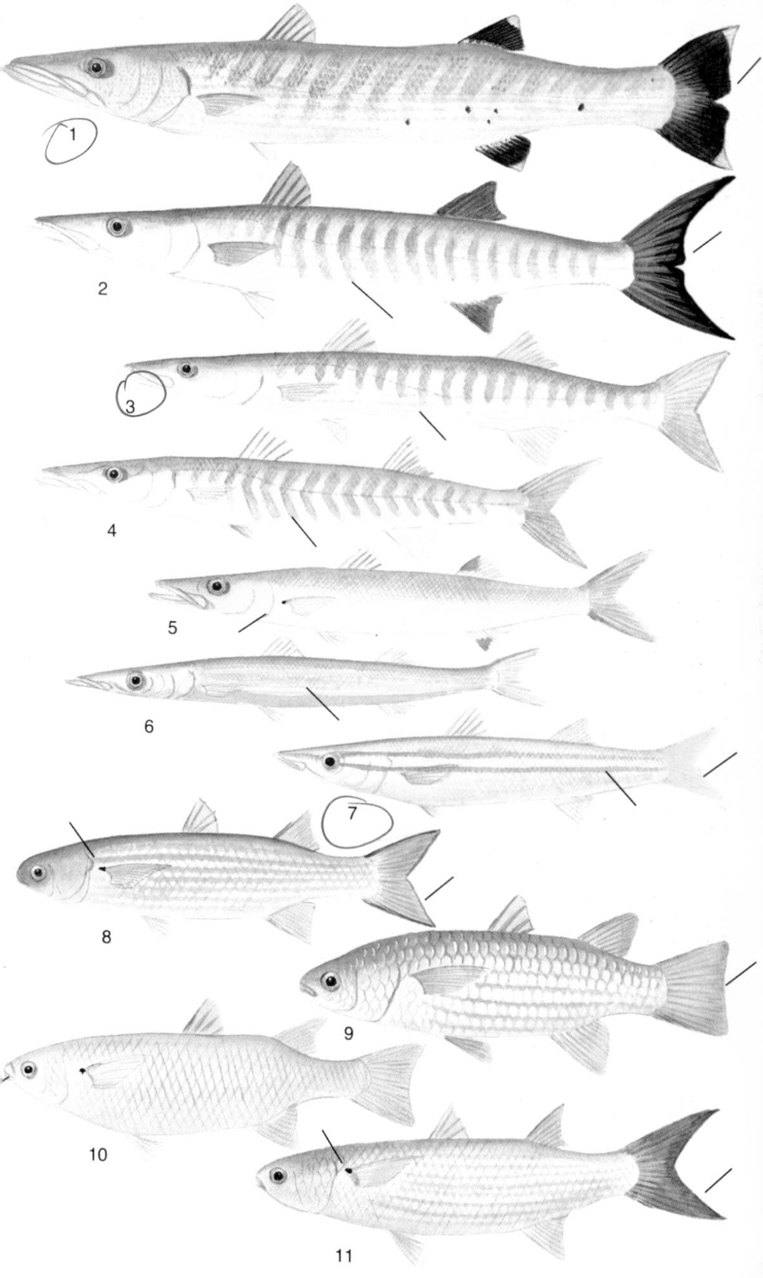
1
2
3
4
5
6
7
8
9
10
11

SANDPERCHES (PINGUIPEDIDAE): elongate cylindrical fishes with long continuous D fin, long A fin, large mouths with thick lips, small scales, complete LL, and truncate to emarginate tail. Benthic carnivores of small invertebrates and fishes. Territorial and haremic.

1 **Blackflag sandperch** *Parapercis signata* Randall 13 cm
Ecology: rubble bottoms near reefs, common below 30 to 50 m, occasionally to 12 m. **Range:** Maldives.

2 **Latticed sandperch** *Parapercis clathrata* Ogilby 17.5 cm
Ecology: clear lagoon and seaward reefs, 3 to 50 m. On sand, rubble, or bare rock. **Range:** Arab. G. to Phoenix & Samoa Is., n. to Ryuk., s. to GBR.

3 **Multispotted sandperch** *Parapercis multiplicata* Randall 12 cm
Ecology: rubble bottoms in clear water, 4 to 30 m, usually below 27 m. **Range:** Bali & nw. Australia to Marianas & N. Cal., n. to Ryuk.

4 **Speckled sandperch** *Parapercis hexophthalma* Cuvier 26 cm
Ecology: shallow lagoon and protected seaward reefs, on sand and rubble, 2 to 22 m. **Range:** R. Sea to Fiji, n. to Ryuk., s. to L. Howe Is.

5 **Black-dotted sandperch** *Parapercis millepunctata* (Günther) 18 cm
Ecology: seaward reefs, 3 to 50 m. Usually on rubble or hard bottoms between corals. **Range:** Maldives to Society Is., n. to Ryuk., s. to GBR.

6 **Cylindrical sandperch** *Parapercis cylindrica* (Bloch) 15 cm
Ecology: sand and rubble areas of lagoons and bays, 1 to 20 m, common in seagrass beds. **Range:** Maldives to Fiji, n. to Ryuk., s. to L. Howe Is.

7 **Redspotted sandperch** *Parapercis schauinslandi* (Steindachner) 14 cm
Ecology: open sand and rubble bottoms, usually below 16 m. Often hovers above bottom. **Range:** se. Africa (Durban) to Hawaiian, Marq. & Society Is., n. to s. Japan, s. to GBR.

8 **Spotted sandperch** *Parapercis punctulata* (Cuvier) 13 cm
Ecology: common on rubble bottoms of coral reefs. **Range:** E. Africa s. to Natal, e. to Seychelles, Amirantes & Maurit.

9 **Blackbarred sandperch** *Parapercis tetracantha* (Lacépède) 25 cm
Ecology: clear shallow lagoon and shelter. Seaward reefs to 20 m. On sand and rubble. **Range:** India to Fiji, n. to s. Japan.

10 **Nebulous sandperch** *Parapercis nebulosa* (Quoy & Gaimard) 27.5 cm
Ecology: silty sand and rubble bottoms, 15 to 60 m. **Range:** Arab. Gulf & E. Africa to e. Australia, s. to Durban, nw. Australia & NSW.

11 **U-mark sandperch** *Parapercis snyderi* Jordan & Starks 10 cm
Japan popul. with more red ground color. **Ecology:** silty sand and rubble areas near reefs, shallow coastal reefs to at least 25 m. **Range:** Andaman Sea & Indonesia, n. to s. Japan, s. to GBR.

12 **Yellowbar sandperch** *Parapercis xanthozona* Bleeker 23 cm
Midlateral whitish stripe from lower part of eye to tip of tail. **Ecology:** shallow protected sandy areas near reefs of lagoons and bays to at least 28 m. **Range:** E. Africa to Fiji, n. to s. Japan, s. to NSW.

JAWFISHES (OPISTOGNATHIDAE): mostly small fishes with enlarged head and mouth and narrow tapering body, and long continuous D fin. Live in burrows in sand which they enter tail-first. Feed on benthic and planktonic invertebrates and incubate their eggs orally. Over 70 species, most of them undescribed, but few species known from any given area.

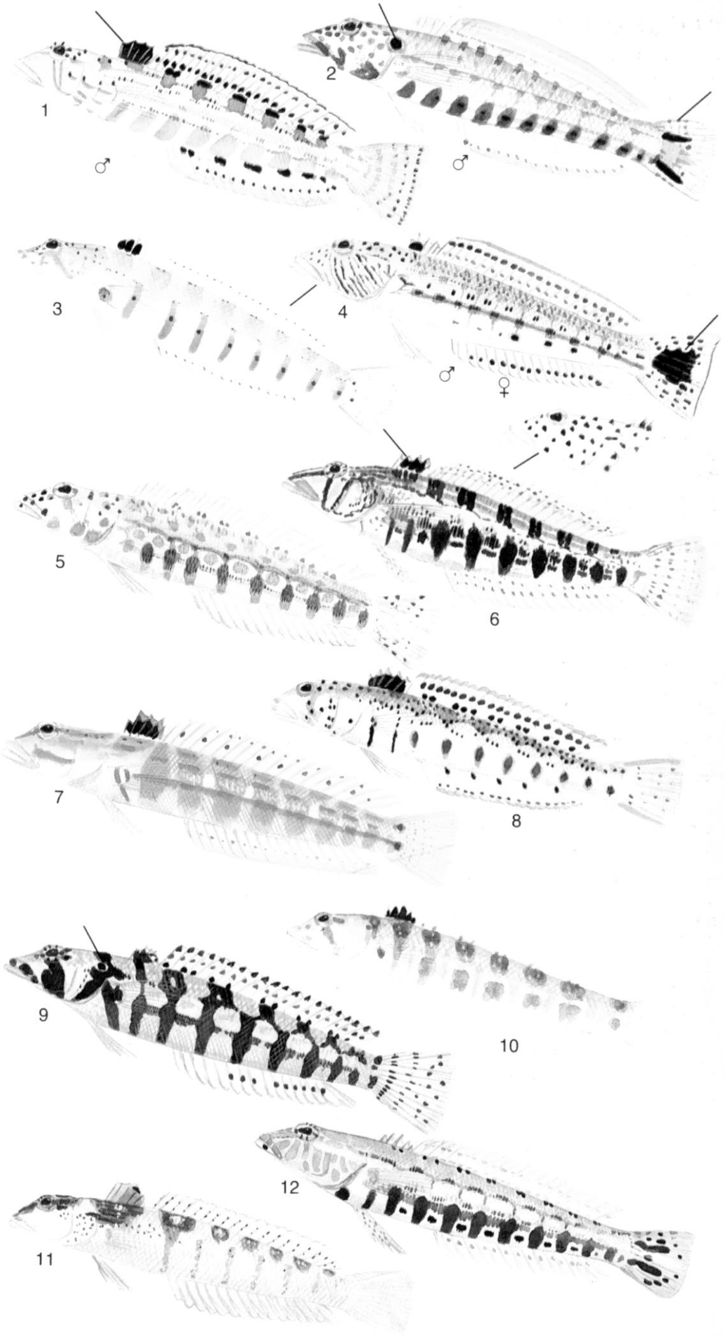
1
♂
2
♂
3
4
♂
♀
5
6
7
8
9
10
11
12

113 JAWFISHES, STARGAZERS, SAND-DIVERS, and TRIPLEFINS

1 **Papuan jawfish** *Opistognathus papuensis* (Bleeker) 40 cm
Ecology: sand patches of coastal reefs. **Range:** s. PNG & ne. Queensland.
2 **Robust jawfish** *Opistognathus muscatensis* Boulenger 45 cm
Ecology: sand patches in weedy areas of coastal reefs, 15 to 50 m. **Range:** R. Sea & Arab. G. e. to Seychelles, s. to Durban (30°S).
3 **Gold-specs jawfish** *Opistognathus* sp. <10 cm
Ecology: patches sand with small pieces of rubble, 6 to over 25 m. **Range:** Bali to Flores; n. to Similian Is., Philipp.

STARGAZERS (URANOSCOPIDAE): thick bodied with massive armored head, large vertically oriented mouth with fringed lips and small teeth, a large venomous spine on shoulder girdle, 2 D fins and no LL. Some with wormlike tentacle on lower jaw. Feed on fishes and invertebrates. Few species near reefs.
4 **Whitemargin stargazer** *Uranoscopus sulphureus* Valenciennes 35 cm
Ecology: reef flats and coastal bottoms. Lies buried in sand, wriggles lure to entice prey. **Range:** R. Sea to Samoa, s. to GBR & Tonga.

SAND-DIVERS (TRICHONOTIDAE): extremely elongate slightly compressed with projecting lower jaw, long continuous D fin with first few spines elongate and filamentous, large fanlike pelvic fins, continuous LL. Hover in groups 1 to 3 m. Dive into sand when alarmed.
5 **Spotted sand-diver** *Trichonotus setiger* (Bloch & Schneider) 15 cm
Similar to *T. arabica* (Arab. G.) which lacks filamentous D spines. **Ecology:** over open sand. **Range:** Arab. G. to Melanesia, s. to GBR.
6 **Threadfin sand-diver** *Trichonotus* sp. 18 cm
Similar to *T. elegans* (Ryuk.). **Ecology:** clear lagoon and seaward reefs, over open sand, 5 to 20 m. **Range:** Mariana and Marshall Is. to Coral Sea.

TRIPLEFINS (TRIPTERYGIIDAE): tiny moderately elongate fishes with 3 D fins and divided or continuous LL. Cryptic bottomdwellers that feed on small inveretebrates. Perhaps 150 species in temperate and tropical seas, many coral reef species poorly known.
7 **Striped triplefin** *Helcogramma striata* Hansen 4 cm
Ecology: on corals, sponges, and other hard surfaces of coral reefs. **Range:** Indonesia to Line Is., n. to Izu Is., s. to GBR; a similar sp. at Maldives & Sri Lanka.
8 **Bigmouth triplefin** Unnamed genus & sp. Holleman (in press) 5 cm
Ecology: clear lagoon and seaward reefs to 18 m, on surface of live corals. **Range:** St. Brandon Shoals to Samoa, n. to Phil. & Marianas, s. to N. Cal, GBR & Tonga.

BLENNIES (BLENNIIDAE): small elongate scaleless fishes with a long continuous D fin. Territorial bottom dwellers. Two subfamilies: the sabretoothed blennies (Blenniinae) which are mostly small-mouthed large-fanged carnivores, and the combtooth blennies (Salariinae) which are wide-mouthed blunt-headed herbivores. Well over 100 species on Indo-Pacific coral reefs, but only a few of the more conspicuous ones are included here. Identification of many species difficult. Subfamily Blenniinae possess large fangs in lower jaw.
9 **Variable fangblenny** *Petroscirtes variabilis* Cantor 15 cm
Ecology: seagrass beds of shallow lagoons. Feeds on small crustaceans but will also nip scales from fishes. **Range:** Sri Lanka to Fiji, n. to Ryuk., s. to s. GBR.
10 **Floral fangblenny** *Petroscirtes mitratus* Rüppell 7 cm
Ecology: sandy areas of reef flats and shallow lagoons. Lives among clumps of algae and nests in empty mollusk shells. **Range:** R. Sea to Phoenix Is. & Samoa, n. to Ryuk., s. to Perth, s. GBR & N. Cal.
11 **Xestus sabretooth blenny** *Petroscirtes xestus* Jordan & Seale 7 cm
Ecology: sandy areas of reef flats and shallow lagoons. Nests in empty mollusk shells. **Range:** E. Africa to Line & Society Is., n. to Marianas, s. to nw. Aust. shelf & s. GBR.
12 **Elongate oyster blenny** *Omobranchus elongatus* (Peters) 5.5 cm
Ecology: shallow coastal areas among rocks or oysters to 4 m. Enters brackish waters. **Range:** E. Africa to Moluccas, n. to Ryuk.
13 **Spotted oyster blenny** *Omobranchus punctatus* (Valenciennes) 9 cm
Ecology: coastal and brackish waters among rocks or mangroves. **Range:** R. Sea to Sol. Is., n. to s. Japan & s. Korea, s. to nw. Australia & s. Queensland.
14 **Hepburn's blenny** *Parenchelyurus hepburni* (Snyder) 4.5 cm
Ecology: beneath rocks of intertidal zone. **Range:** Madag. & Maurit. to Marshall Is. & Samoa, n. to s. Japan, s. to GBR.
15 **Snakeblenny** *Xiphasia setifer* Swainson 53 cm
Similar to *X. matsubarai* (R. Sea to Samoa) which has fewer D spines (11 vs. 13-14). **Ecology:** in tube-like burrows in sand or mud as shallow as 2 m. Free swimming at night. **Range:** R. Sea to Vanuatu & N. Cal., n. to s. Japan, s. to GBR.

1
2
3
4
5
6
♂
6
♀
7
8
9
10
11
12
13
14
15

1 **Lance blenny** *Aspidontus dussumieri* (Valenciennes) 12 cm
Ecology: feeds on algae and detritus. **Range:** R. Sea to Tuam., n. to s. Japan, s. to NSW.
2 **Cleaner mimic** *Aspidontus taeniatus* Quoy & Gaimard 11.5 cm
Resembles *Labroides dimidiatus* (pl. 104-5), but mouth inferior with lg. canines in lower jaw. **Ecology**: lagoon and seaward reefs, 1 to over 20 m. A remarkable mimic of the cleaner wrasse, *Labroides dimidiatus*. This charade enables it to approach naive fishes in order to nip of pieces of fin, skin, or scales as well as gain protection from predation. Also feeds on tubeworms and demersal fish eggs. Lives in pairs in empty worm tubes. **Range:** R. Sea to Marq. & Tuam. Is., n. to s. Japan, s. to NSW.
3 **Scale-eating fangblenny** *Plagiotremus tapeinosoma* (Bleeker) 14 cm
P. goslinei (Hawaiian Is.) nearly identical. **Ecology:** all species in the genus use their lower jaw fangs to feed by tearing pieces of fins, skin, and scales from other fishes. This species inhabits clear shallow lagoon and seaward reefs to 20 m. Swims with a wriggling motion a few meters above the bottom. Attacks divers as well as fishes. Shelters in a worm tube. **Range:** R. Sea to Marq., & Tuam. Is., n. to s. Japan, s. to n. NZ & Rapa.
4 **Bluestriped fangblenny** *Plagiotremus rhinorhynchus* (Bleeker) 12 cm
2 color ph.: ground color black or orange; nearly identical to *P. ewaensis* (Hawaiian Is.). **Ecology**: clear, coral-rich areas of lagoon and seaward reefs, 1 to 40 m. Juveniles are aggressive mimics of the cleaner wrasse, *Labroides dimidiatus*. **Range**: R. Sea to Marq. & Society Is., n. to s. Japan, s. to L. Howe Is.
5 **Poison-fang blenny mimic** *Plagiotremus laudandus* (Whitley) 8 cm
Resembles *Meiacanthus atrodorsalis*, but more elongate. Unif. yellow subsp. *flavus* in Fiji. **Ecology**: mimics the innoffensive poison-fang blenny, *Meiacanthus atrodorsalis* in order to approach its victims. Lagoon and seaward reefs below surge zone to 30 m. Uncommon. **Range**: Phil. & Ryuk. to Gilbert Is. & Samoa, n. to Izu Is., s. to L. Howe Is.
6 **Imposter fangblenny** *Plagiotremus phenax* (Smith-Vaniz) 5 cm
Ecology: an aggressive mimic of the poison-fang blenny *Meiacanthus smithi*. **Range**: Maldives, Sri Lanka & Similan Is.
7 **Townsend's fangblenny** *Plagiotremus townsendi* (Regan) 5 cm
Ecology: an aggressive mimic of *Meiacanthus nigrolineatus*. Coral reefs with poor coral growth, close to bottom, 5 to 55 m. **Range**: R. Sea & G. Oman.
8 **Yellowtail poison-fang blenny** *Meiacanthus atrodorsalis* (Günther) 11 cm
All spp. in genus with pair of large venomous grooved fangs in lower jaw used for defense. This sp. has several geog. variants. Close to the uniformly yellow *M. ovalauensis* (Fiji) & the yellow-green with black D fin base *M. tongaensis* (Tonga). **Ecology**: lagoon and seaward reefs, 1 to 30 m. Feeds on zooplankton. Innoffensive, but immune from predation. Mimicked by the sabre-toothed blenny *Plagiotremus laudandus*. **Range**: Phil. & Bali to Samoa, n. to Ryuk., s. to GBR & N. Cal.
9 **Bundoon blenny** *Meiacanthus bundoon* Smith-Vaniz 8 cm
Ecology: swims above bottom and feeds on zooplankton. **Range:** Fiji.
10 **Blackline fangblenny** *Meiacanthus nigrolineatus* Smith-Vaniz 9.5 cm
Ecology: swims above bottom and feeds on zooplankton. Mimiced by *Ecsenius gravieri* and *Plagiotremus townsendi*. Remains close to shelter. **Range**: R. Sea & G. Aden.
11 **Striped poison-fang blenny** *Meiacanthus grammistes* (Valenciennes) 11 cm
Several similar spp., some undescribed; mimiced by *Petroscirtes breviceps* (pl. 113-10). **Ecology**: sheltered lagoon and seaward reefs. Solitary. **Range**: Indochina to PNG, n. to Ryuk., s. to nw. Aust. & GBR.
12 **Mozambique fangblenny** *Meiacanthus mossambicus* Smith 10 cm
Ecology: coral reefs with poor to moderate growth, often over coral rubble. 1 to 25 m. **Range**: E. Africa, Comore Is. & Madagascar.
13 **Two-striped poison-fang blenny** *Meiacanthus ditrema* Smith-Vaniz 5 cm
Ecology: shallow protected reefs to 15 m. Hovers in groups above bottom. **Range**: Phil. & Moluccas to Samoa, n. to Ryuk., s. to nw. Aust. shelf reefs, GBR & Tonga.
14 **Lined fangblenny** *Meiacanthus lineatus* (Devis) 9.5 cm
Many similar spp. in w. Pacific, some undescribed. **Ecology**: mimiced by *Petroscirtes fallax* & juv. *Scolopsis bilineatus* (pl. 50-1). **Range**: GBR.
15 **Smith's fangblenny** *Meiacanthus smithi* Klausewitz 8 cm
Ecology: coral Reefs. **Range**: Maldives, se. India & w. Indonesia.
16 **One-striped fangblenny** *Meiacanthus vittatus* Smith-Vaniz 6 cm
Ecology: mimiced by juveniles of *Cheilodipterus zonatus* (pl. 38-13) & *Scolopsis margaritifer* (pl. 50-8). **Range**: ne. PNG & Bismark Archip.

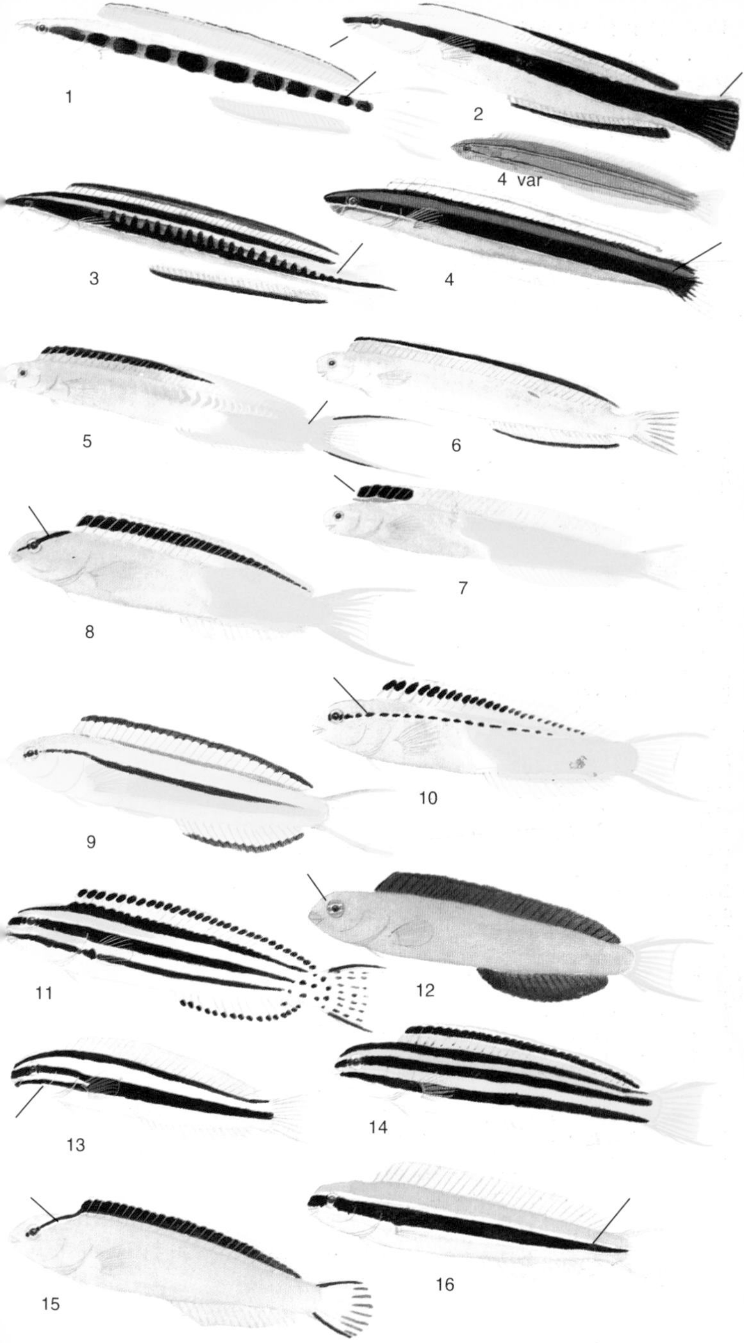
1
2
4 var
3
4
5
6
7
8
9
10
11
12
13
14
15
16

115 COMBTOOTH BLENNIES

Combtooth blennies (Subfamily Salariinae): blunt heads and wide mouths with comb-like teeth. Many similar species, the positive identification of some requires a specimen in hand.

1 **Eared blenny** *Cirripectes auritus* Carlson 9 cm
Ecology: shallow seaward reefs to 20 m but usually 10 m. **Range**: E. Africa, w. Thail., Phil. & Line Is.

2 **Filamentous blenny** *Cirripectes filamentosus* (Alleyne & Macleay) 9 cm
Ecology: shallow coral or rocky reefs to 20 m. **Range**: s. R. Sea & Arab. G. to GBR.

3 **Chestnut blenny** *Cirripectes castaneus* (Valenciennes) 12.5 cm
Ad. ♀ nearly identical to ♀ *C. imitator* & some ♀ *C. stigmaticus*; ad. ♂ highly variable, often with lighter interspaces between reddish bars on front half of body. **Ecology**: surge-swept algal ridge of outer reef flats. Darts into holes when alarmed. **Range**: R. Sea to Caroline Is. & Tonga, n. to s. Japan, s. to L. Howe Is.

4 **Imitator blenny** *Cirripectes imitator* Williams 12 cm
♀ indistinguishable from ♀ of *C. castaneus* & some *C. polyzona* & *C. stigmaticus* by color alone. **Ecology**: shallow coral and rocky reefs. **Range**: n. Phil., s. Japan & Bonin Is.

5 **Dusky spotted blenny** *Cirripectes fuscoguttatus* Strasburg & Schultz 15 cm
Ecology: surge zone of seaward reefs to 8 m. **Range**: s. Taiwan to Tuam., s. to Tonga.

6 **Flaming blenny** *Cirripectes perustus* Smith 12 cm
Ecology: shallow seaward reefs, intertidal to 24 m. **Range**: E. Africa to Gilbert Is., n. to Taiwan.

7 **Gargantuan blenny** *Cirripectes obscurus* (Borodin) 17 cm
Similar to *C. alboapicalis* (GBR to Easter Is.) & *C. viriosus* (Phil.). **Ecology**: surge zone of rocky and coral reefs to 6 m. **Range**: Hawaiian Is.

8 **Barred blenny** *Cirripectes polyzona* (Bleeker) 13 cm
Ecology: algal ridge and crests between surge channels of seaward reef margin to 3 m. **Range**: G. Aden & E. Africa to Line Is. & Samoa, n. to s. Japan, s. to GBR.

9 **Zebra blenny** *Cirripectes quagga* Fowler & Ball 10 cm
Highly variable, either spotted or with narrow squiggly bars. **Ecology**: algal ridge and crests between surge channels of seaward reef margin to 19 m. **Range**: E. Africa to Hawaiian, Marq. & Pitcairn Is., n. to Taiwan & Marcus Is.

10 **Redstreaked blenny** *Cirripectes stigmaticus* Strasburg & Schultz 13 cm
Ecology: among corals of algal ridges between surge channels. **Range**: E. Africa to Samoa, n. to Micronesia, s. to GBR & N. Cal.

11 **Red-speckled blenny** *Cirripectes variolosus* (Valenciennes) 10 cm
Similar to *C. vanderbilti* (Hawaiian & Johnston Is.). **Ecology**: exposed seaward reefs, 0.5 to 5 m, near bases of *Pocillopora* corals. **Range**: Palau to Johnston Is., Marq. & Pitcairn Is., n. to Bonin Is., s. to Rapa.

12 **Lady Musgrave blenny** *Cirripectes chelomatus* Williams & Maugé 12 cm
Similar to *C. springeri* (Phil. & Moluccas to PNG & N. Britain). **Ecology**: shallow rocky and coral reefs, 0 to 16 m, usually 7 m. **Range**: GBR & e. PNG to Fiji & Tonga, s. to L. Howe Is.

1
2
♂
3
4
5
7
6
8
var
8
9
10
11
12

1 **Red Sea mimic blenny** *Ecsenius gravieri* (Pellegrin) 8 cm
Ecology: mimics *Meiacanthus nigrolineatus* in swimming behavior and color pattern. **Range:** R. Sea & G. Aden.

2 **Aron's blenny** *Ecsenius aroni* Springer 5.5 cm
Ecology: coral reefs to 35 m. Relatively secretive. **Range:** R. Sea.

3 **Midas blenny** *Ecsenius midas* Stark 13 cm
Highly variable, some individuals brownish or dark slate-blue anteriorly or entirely. **Ecology:** coral reefs, 2 to 30 m. Orange-yellow individuals often schools with *Pseudanthias squamipinnis*. Feeds on zooplankton. **Range:** R. Sea to Fr. Polynesia, s. to Natal, Mauritius.

4 **Smoothfin blenny** *Ecsenius frontalis* (Ehrenberg) 8 cm
3 color ph.: may be dark brown with white tail (*albicaudatus* form), brown with pale-edged black stripe (*nigrovittatus* form), or yellow (resembles juv. *Atrosalarias fuscus*). **Ecology:** among corals, 3 to 27 m. Close to bottom of mixed corals and rubble. Very common in Yemen. **Range:** R. Sea and G. Aden (only *nigrovittatus* form in s. R. Sea & G. Aden).

5 **Namiye's blenny** *Ecsenius namiyei* (Jordan & Evermann) 10 cm
Ecology: coral reefs, 1 to 30 m. **Range:** Phil. & Moluccas to Sol. Is., n. to Izu Is.

6 **Bicolor blenny** *Ecsenius bicolor* (Day) 10 cm
3 color phases as shown or uniformly dark brown. **Ecology:** clear lagoon and seward reefs, 1 to 25 m, on mixed coral and rock bottoms. **Range:** Maldives to Phoenix Is., n. to Ryuk., s. to GBR.

7 **Linear blenny** *Ecsenius lineatus* Klausewitz 8 cm
Dark lateral stripe may be continuous or interrupted posteriorly. **Ecology:** coral reefs. **Range:** Maurit. & Maldives to nw. Aust., Phil. & Izu & Bonin Is.

8 **Ocular blenny** *Ecsenius oculus* Springer 6 cm
Similar to *monoculus* (Viet., Phil. & Moluccas), *oculatus* (Christmas Is. & w. Aust.), *pardus* (Fiji), *paroculus* (Malaysia & w. Indonesia), *portenoyi* (Rotuma & Samoa), *sellifer* (Palau, PNG & Sol. Is) & *tessera* (N. Cal. & Loyalty Is.)
Ecology: coral Reefs. **Range:** Ryuk., s. Taiwan & Batan Is. (Phil. Strait).

9 **Nalolo blenny** *Ecsenius nalolo* Smith 6.5 cm
Similar to *stictus* (GBR), *dentex* (n. R. Sea), *minutus* (Maldives). **Ecology:** coral reefs. **Range:** R. Sea & w. Indian Ocean, s. to S. Africa, e. to Maldives.

10 **Comical blenny** *Ecsenius opsifrontalis* Chapman & Schultz 5 cm
Many similar spp.: *alleni* (nw. Aust. shelf), *australianus* (n. GBR), *axelrodi* (Sol. Is.), *bathi* (Bali to Moluccas), *dilemma* (Phil.), *fijiensis* (Fiji), *fourmaniori* (N. Cal., s. Fiji & Tonga) & *tigris* (n. Coral Sea). **Ecology:** coral-rich areas of lagoon and seaward reefs below surge zone to ~30 m. **Range:** Micronesia to Rotuma & Samoa.

11 **Pictus blenny** *Ecsenius pictus* McKinney & Springer 5 cm
Ecology: among corals, 11 to 40 m. **Range:** Phil., Moluccas & Sol. Is.

12 **Yaeyama blenny** *Ecsenius yaeyamaensis* (Aoyagi) 6 cm
Similar to *E. stictus* (GBR). **Ecology:** shallow coastal reefs, 0 to 15 m. Sits on rocks and living corals. **Range:** Sri Lanka to Vanuatu,n. to Taiwan & Yaeyama Is., s. to Shark Bay.

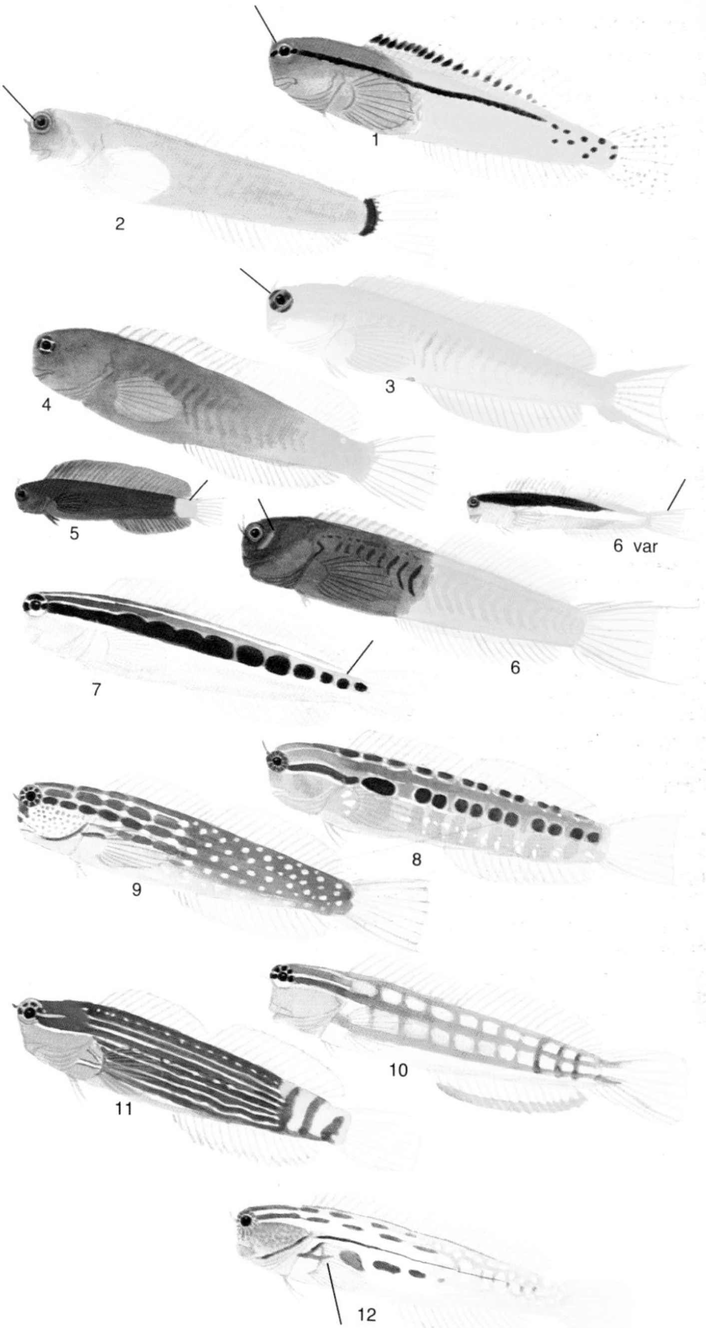
1
2
3
4
5
6 var
6
7
8
9
10
11
12

117 COMBTOOTH BLENNIES

1 **Leopard blenny** *Exallias brevis* (Kner) 14.5 cm
♀ less colorful than ♂; spots of Hawaiian ♂ bright red except on head. **Ecology:** seaward reefs from lower surge zone to 20 m. Lives on corals of the genera *Acropora, Pocillopora, Seriatopora, Porites,* and *Millepora* and feeds on coral polyps. Males are territorial and prepare a nest site by killing a patch of coral by overgrazing. Several females may lay eggs in the same nest which are guarded by the male. **Range:** R. Sea to Hawaiian, Marq. & Society Is., n. to Ryuk. & Bonin Is., s. to N. Cal. & Rapa.

2 **Highfin blenny** *Atrosalarias fuscus* (Rüppell) 14.5 cm
Juvs. yellow, ad. dark brown, GBR popul. with yellow tail persisting in ad. **Ecology:** among branching corals of shallow lagoon and protected seaward reefs. **Range:** R. Sea to Pakistan (subsp. *fuscus*); Sumatra to Society Is., n. to Ryuk., s. to N. Cal. & Tonga (subsp. *holomelas*).

3 **Wavyline rockskipper** *Entomacrodus decussatus* (Bleeker) 19 cm
Many other spp. in genus, primarily in exposed rocky intertidal zone and reef margin. **Ecology:** intertidal zone of rocky shores, benches, and wave-swept seaward reefs. **Range:** G. Thail. to Society Is., n. to Ryuk., s. to N. Cal. & Tonga.

4 **Blackspotted rockskipper** *Entomacrodus striatus* (Quoy & Gaimard) 11 cm
Ecology: intertidal zone of lagoons and wave-swept seaward reefs. **Range:** E. Africa to Line & Ducie Is., n. to Ryuk. & Bonin Is., s. to L. Howe & Rapa Is.

5 **Tattoo-chin rockskipper** *Entomacrodus niuafooensis* (Fowler) 12 cm
Ecology: intertidal zone of rocky shores, benches, and wave-swept seaward reefs. **Range:** Comoro Is. to Easter Is., n. to Ryuk. & Bonin Is., s. to Kermadec & Rapa Is.

6 **Reef margin blenny** *Entomacrodus thalassinus* (Jordan & Seale) 5 cm
Ecology: wave-swept seaward reef margins. **Range:** Seychelles to Line & Tuam., n. to s. Japan, s. to s. GBR.

7 **Seale's rockskipper** *Entomacrodus sealei* Bryan & Herre 8 cm
Ecology: intertidal zone of rocky shores, benches, and wave-swept seaward reefs. **Range:** Caroline & Mariana Is. to Line & Pitcairn Is., s. to Rapa Is.

8 **Delicate blenny** *Glyptoparus delicatulus* Smith 5 cm
Ecology: clear outer lagoon reefs in areas of mixed coral and sand. **Range:** E. Africa to Rotuma, n. to Ryuk., s. to Rowley Shoals.

9 **Tripplespot blenny** *Crossosalarias macrospilus* Smith-Vaniz & Springer 10 cm
Ecology: seaward reefs, 1 to 25 m, usually in less than 10 m. **Range:** S. China Sea (Pratas Reef) to Tonga, n. to Ryuk., s. to GBR.

10 **Red-spotted blenny** *Istiblennius chrysospilos* (Bleeker) 13 cm
Many other spp. in genus, primarily in exposed rocky intertidal zone and reef margin. This sp. most similar to *S. insulinus* (w. Indian Ocean). **Ecology:** outer intertidal reef flats and surge-swept seaward reefs to 6 m. **Range:** Cocos-Kelling & Indonesia to Samoa, n. to Ryuk., s. to nw. Aust. shelf reefs & s. GBR.

11 **Rippled rockskipper** *Istiblennius edentulus* (Bloch & Schneider) 17 cm
Ecology: rocky intertidal areas, 0 to 5 m, but rarely deeper than 1 m. **Range:** R. Sea to Marq. & Tuam. Is., n. to s. Japan, s. to L. Howe & Rapa Is.

12 **Lined rockskipper** *Istiblennius lineatus* (Valenciennes) 14 cm
Ecology: intertidal zone of rocky shores, and rocky areas of reef flats. **Range:** E. Africa to Line & Society Is., n. to s. Japan, s. to GBR.

13 **Blue-dashed rockskipper** *Istiblennius periophthalmus* (Valenciennes) 15 cm
Similar to *I. paulus* (Micronesia & GBR to Marq. & Tuam. Is.) which lacks red and black dots. **Ecology:** reef flats, on rock and rubble. Feeds on filamentous algae and minute benthic invertebrates. Darts into a hole when alarmed. **Range:** R. Sea to Indonesia, n. to Ryuk.

14 **Picture rockskipper** *Istiblennius gibbifrons* Schultz & Chapman 12 cm
Ecology: rocky intertidal areas. **Range:** E. Africa to Hawaiian, Line & Ducie Is., n. to Marcus Is.

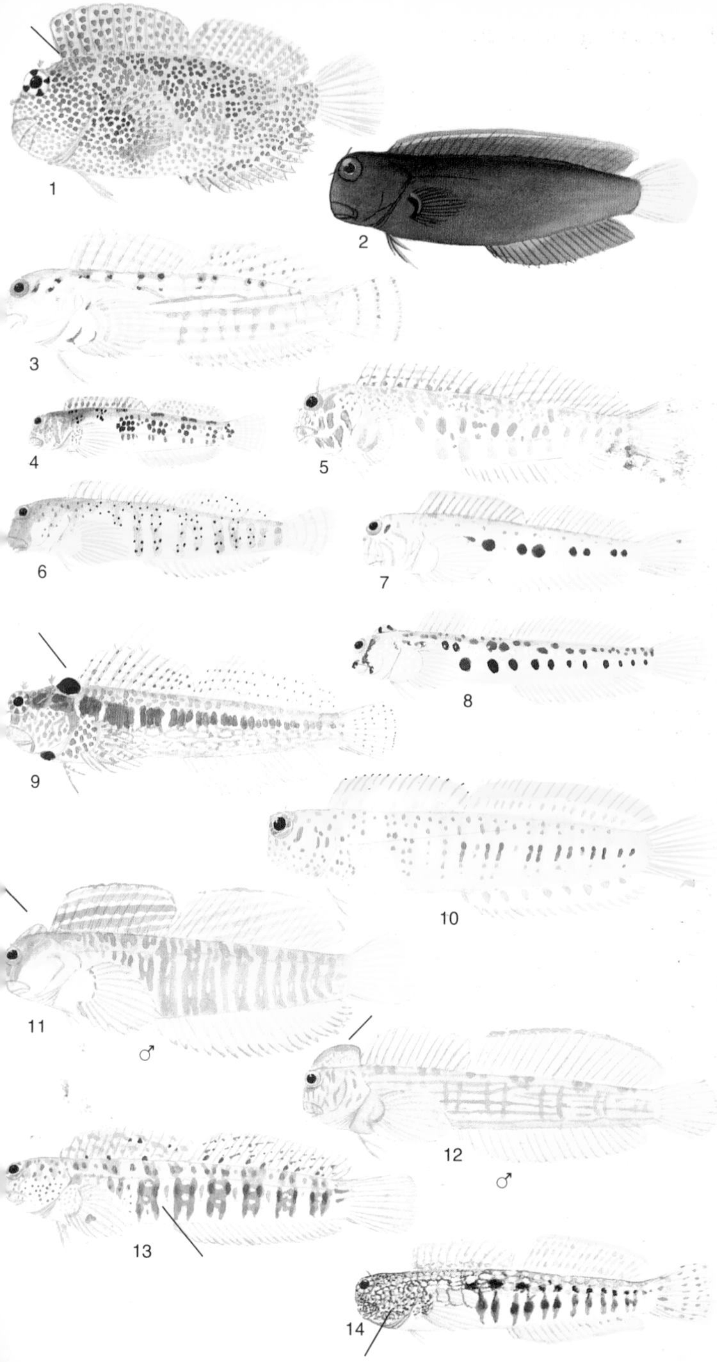
1
2
3
4
5
6
7
8
9
10
11
♂
12
♂
13
14

1 **Throatspot blenny** *Nannosalarias nativittatus* (Regan) 5 cm
Ecology: shallow reefs exposed to surge. **Range:** Christmas Is. to Tonga, n. to, s. to GBR.

2 **Jeweled blenny** *Salarias fasciatus* (Bloch) 13 cm
Ecology: areas of mixed coral, sand, and rubble of reef flats and shallow lagoon and seaward reefs to 8 m. Feeds on filamentous algae. **Range:** R. Sea to Samoa, n. to Ryuk., s. to GBR & N. Cal.

3 **Segmented blenny** *Salarias segmentatus* Bath & Randall 6 cm
Ecology: shallow lagoon reefs, 0 to 12 m. On algal-covered rocks and rubble. **Range:** ne. Borneo, Sulawesi, Aru Is., New Guinea, Sol. Is. & Palau.

4 **Fringelip blenny** *Salarias sinuosus* Snyder 6 cm
Ecology: shallow protected reefs, 0.3 to 5 m. Typically in intertidal areas. **Range:** w. Pacific n. to Ryuk., s. to GBR.

5 **White-spotted blenny** *Salarias alboguttatus* Kner 9 cm
Ecology: shallow lagoon reefs, on algal covered rocks and rubble. **Range:** Sri Lanka to Samoa, n. to s. Japan.

6 **Talbot's blenny** *Stanulus talboti* Springer 5 cm
Ecology: surge channels of exposed seaward reefs, 3 to 15 m. **Range:** Ryuk. & Bonin Is., s. GBR, L. Howe Is. & Marq. Is.

7 **Seychelles blenny** *Stanulus seychellensis* Smith 4 cm
Ecology: exposed outer reef flats and surge zone of shallow seaward reefs. **Range:** Seychelles to Tuam., n. to s. Taiwan, s. to s. GBR.

CONVICT BLENNY (PHOLIDICHTHYIDAE): a single eel-like species with confluent D & A fins.

8 **Convict blenny** *Pholidichthys leucotaenia* (Bleeker) 34 cm
Juvs. resemble *Plotosus lineatus* (pl. 9-1) but lack venomous spines & barbels. **Ecology:** shallow lagoon and coastal reefs. Juv. in schools near bottom, often under ledges or around coral head. **Range:** Phil. & e. Borneo to PNG & Sol Is., s. to Flores.

DRAGONETS (CALLIONYMIDAE): small depressed broad-headed scaleless fishes with two D fins, a large serrated spine on preopercle, and gill openings restricted to a small hole. The first D fin of males is usually enlarged with a colorful and intricate pattern. Dragonets typically live on sandy bottoms and feed on small benthic invertebrates. Most species are intricately but cryptically colored, but a few are spectacular.

9 **Picturesque dragonet** *Synchiropus picturatus* (Peters) 6 cm
Ecology: shallow sheltered reefs. **Range:** Phil., e. Indonesia & nw. Australia.

10 **Mandarinfish** *Synchiropus splendidus* (Herre) 6 cm
Ecology: shallow sheltered reefs to 18 m. On silty bottoms with coral and rubble. **Range:** Phil. & Java to e. Caroline Is. & N. Cal. (& Tonga?), n. to Ryuk., s. to s. GBR.

11 **Starry dragonet** *Synchiropus stellatus* Smith 6 cm
Ecology: algal-covered rock between coral heads. **Range:** E. Africa to w. Pac., s. to GBR; Pac. popul. possibly a distinct undescribed species.

12 **Ocellated dragonet** *Synchiropus ocellatus* (Pallas) 8 cm
Ecology: sandy areas of lagoon and seaward reefs, 1 to 30 m. **Range:** Vietnam to Marq. & Pitcairn Is., n. to Izu Is., s. to s. GBR & Tonga.

13 **Morrison's dragonet** *Synchiropus morrisoni* Schultz 7 cm
Ecology: algal covered rocks of seaward reefs, 12 to 33 m. **Range:** nw. Australia & Ryuk. to Marsh. Is., Fiji & Samoa, n. to Izu Is.

14 **Japanese dragonet** *Synchiropus ijimai* Jordan & Thompson 10 cm
Ecology: algal covered rocks and boulders, 10 to 20 m. **Range:** s. Japan.

15 **Delicate dragonet** *Callionymus delicatulus* Smith 6 cm
Ecology: sandy areas near reefs, 1 to 20 m. **Range:** R. Sea to Palau & Sol. Is.

16 **Simple-spined dragonet** *Callionymus simplicicornis* Valenciennes 5 cm
Ecology: on sand of subtidal reef flats to 40 m. Common in shallow protected areas. **Range:** Phil. to Marq. & Tuam. Is., n. to Marianas.

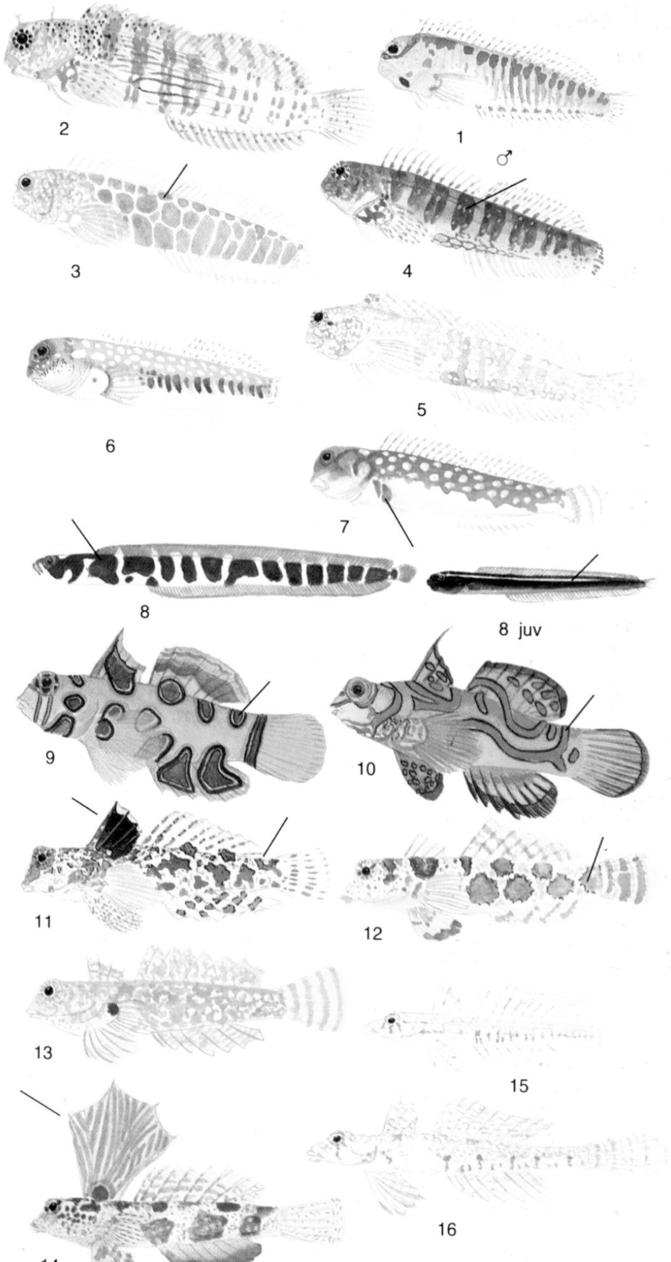
2
1
♂
3
4
5
6
7
8
8 juv
9
10
11
12
13
15
14
♂
16

DARTFISHES and WORMFISHES (MICRODESMIDAE): small elongate fishes with oblique mouths, one or two D fins, and tiny partly embedded scales. Live in holes or burrows and hover in the water to feed on zooplankton. Dartfishes are hardy in the aquarium.

Subfamily Ptereleotrinae: two D fins; moderately elongate, depth 1/10 length to tail base.

1 **Decorated dartfish** *Nemateleotris decora* Randall & Allen 9 cm
Ecology: hovers near hole over patches of sand, rubble, or hard open bottom at the bases of reefs, 28 to 70 m. **Range:** Maurit. & Maldives to Samoa, n. to Ryuk., s. to N. Cal.

2 **Helfrich's dartfish** *Nemateleotris helfrichi* Randall & Allen 6 cm
Ecology: hovers near hole over patches of sand, rubble, or hard open bottom of steep seaward reefs, 25 to 69 m, but rare in less than 40 m. Often in pairs. **Range:** Palau to Tuam., n. to Ryuk., sw. to Samoa & Austral Is.

3 **Fire dartfish** *Nemateleotris magnifica* Fowler 7 cm
Ecology: clear seaward reefs, 6 to 61 m. Common on hard bottoms of upper portion of exposed outer reef slopes (rare in Hawaii). Often paired, but also solitary or in groups. **Range:** E. Africa to Hawaiian, Marq. & Pitcairn Is., n. to s. Japan, s. to N. Cal. & Austral Is.

4 **Blackfin dartfish** *Ptereleotris evides* (Jordan & Hubbs) 14 cm
Ecology: exposed outer reef slopes, 2 to 15 m. Juveniles in aggregations, adults paired. Typically hovers 1 to 2 m above hole, often moves away when disturbed. **Range:** R. Sea to Society Is., n. to Ryuk., s. to NSW & L. Howe & Rapa Is.

5 **Spot-tail dartfish** *Ptereleotris heteroptera* (Bleeker) 12 cm
Ecology: sand and rubble bottoms of lagoon and seaward reefs, 7 to 46 m. Sometimes as high as 3 m above bottom. Juveniles may be in aggregations, adults usually paired. **Range:** R. Sea to Hawaiian, Marq. & Society Is., n. to Ryuk., s. to NSW & L. Howe Is.

6 **Flagtail dartfish** *Ptereleotris uroditaenia* Randall & Hoese >8 cm
Ecology: protected sand and rubble bottoms, 18 to 30 m. **Range:** Indonesia, Sol. Is. & GBR.

7 **Zebra dartfish** *Ptereleotris zebra* (Fowler) 11 cm
Ecology: exposed seaward reefs, 2 to 31 m, but usually less than 4 m. In aggregations over hard gently sloping surgy or current-swept bottoms. Common in Micronesia. **Range:** R. Sea to Line & Marq. Is., n. to Ryuk., s. to s. GBR.

8 **Lined dartfish** *Ptereleotris grammica* Randall & Lubbock 10 cm
Ecology: rubble or sand bottoms of seaward reefs, 36 to 50 m. **Range:** Maurit. (ssp. *melanotus*)to Sol. Is., n. to Ryuk., s. to GBR.

9 **Pearly dartfish** *Ptereleotris microlepis* Bleeker 13 cm
Ecology: over rubble and sand bottoms of lagoon and seaward reefs, 1 to 22 m. Juveniles may be in aggregations, adults usually paired. **Range:** R. Sea to Line & Tuam. Is., n. to Ryuk., s. to NSW.

10 **Filament dartfish** *Ptereleotris hanae* (Jordan & Snyder) 12 cm
Similar to *P. arabica* (R. Sea & Arab. G.). **Ecology:** over rubble and sand near reefs, 3 to 43 m. **Range:** Phil. to Line Is., n. to s Japan, s. to nw. Aust. & NSW.

Subfamily Microdesminae: single D fin; very elongate, depth 1/12 body length to tail base.

11 **Onespot wormfish** *Gunnelichthys monostigma* Smith 11 cm
Ecology: open sandy bottoms with current, 1 to 20 m. **Range:** E. Africa to Marq. & Society Is., n. to Ryuk., s. to s. GBR.

12 **Curious wormfish** *Gunnelichthys curiosus* Dawson 11.5 cm
Ecology: sand and rubble bottoms, 4 to over 25 m. Also in sea grass areas. Often in pairs. **Range:** E. Africa (common), Seychelles to Hawaiian & Society Is., s. to GBR.

13 **Yellowstripe wormfish** *Gunnelichthys viridescens* Dawson 7.2 cm
Ecology: shallow sand and rubble bottoms, to 20 m, but usually 5 m. **Range:** Seychelles, Maldives, Caroline Is., Marshall Is. & GBR.

14 **Brownstripe wormfish** *Gunnelichthys pleurotaenia* Bleeker 9 cm
Similar to *G. copleyi* (w. Indian Ocean). **Ecology:** open sandy bottoms with current, 1 to 8 m. **Range:** Java & Phil. to w. Samoa, n. to Ryuk., s. to nw. Aust. shelf reefs & s. GBR.

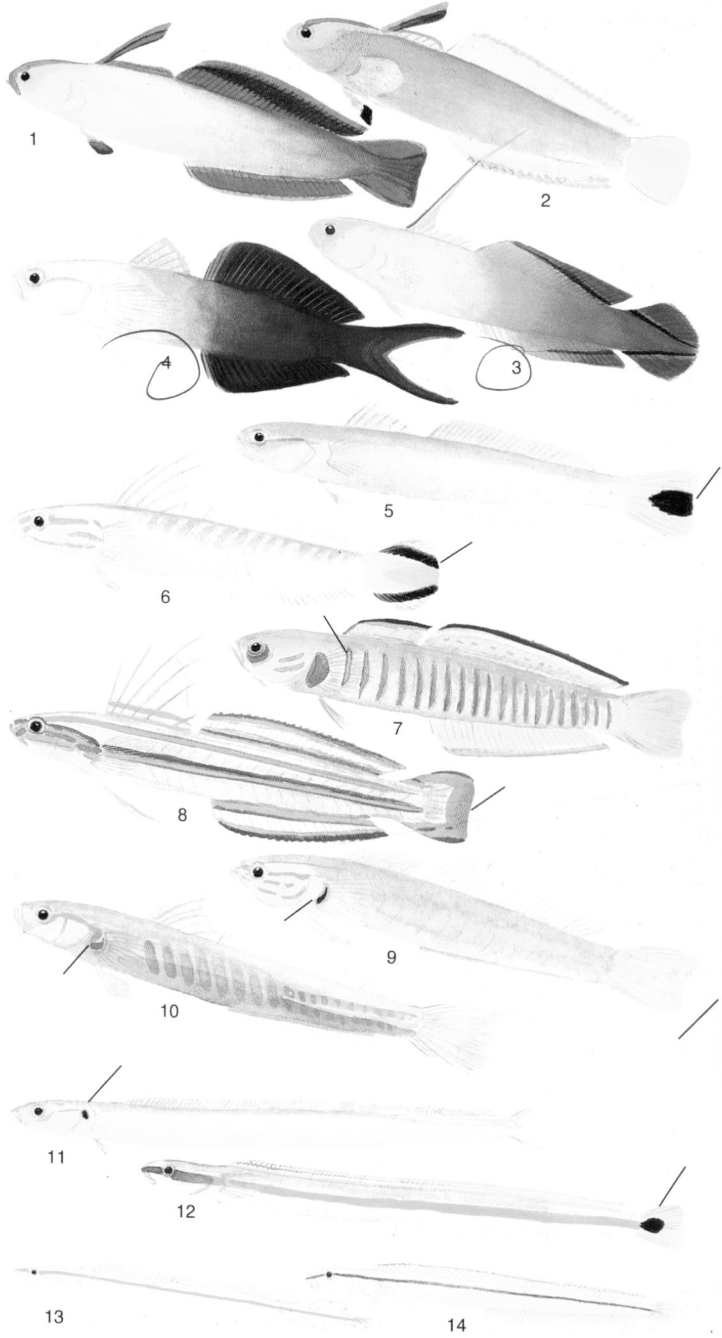
1
2
3
4
5
6
7
8
9
10
11
12
13
14

GOBIES (GOBIIDAE): small elongate blunt-headed fishes with large mouths with conical teeth, V fins close together or connected to form a disc, one or two D fins, no LL, and usually small scales. The largest family of marine fishes with about 500 Indo-Pacific species. Most are cryptic bottom-dwelling carnivores of small invetebrates, but there are many colorful species as well as planktivores that hover in the water. Gobies lay demersal eggs guarded by the male. Only a few colorful or common species are included here.
Prawn-associated gobies: the following species as well as others not included here live in a burrow in sand symbiotically with one or more species of blind or nearly blind prawns. The prawn maintains the burrow and the goby acts as a lookout. Adults are usually in pairs.

1 **Beautiful prawn-goby** *Amblyeleotris aurora* Polunin & Lubbock 9 cm
Similar to *Amblyeleotris* n. sp. from Indonesia. **Ecology:** coarse coral sand, outer reef flats to seaward reefs, 1 to 35 m. **Range:** E. Africa, Aldabra to Maldives & Andaman Is.

2 **Red-banded prawn-goby** *Amblyeleotris fasciata* (Herre) 8 cm
Ecology: outer lagoon and seaward reefs, 5 to 20 m. **Range:** Christmas Is. to Samoa, n. to Marianas, s. to GBR.

3 **Periophthalma prawn-goby** *Amblyeleotris periophthalma* (Bleeker) 11 cm
Ecology: sandy expanses of lagoon and seaward reefs, 5 to 20 m. **Range:** Andaman Sea to Samoa, n. to s. GBR.

4 **Gorgeous prawn-goby** *Amblyeleotris wheeleri* (Polunin & Lubbock) 8 cm
Ecology: clear lagoon and seaward reefs, 5 to 15 m. **Range:** s. Red Sea & E. Africa to Marshall Is., n. to Ryuk., s. to nw. Aust. & GBR.

5 **Steinitz' prawn-goby** *Amblyeleotris steinitzi* (Klausewitz) 8 cm
Ecology: outer lagoon and seaward reefs, 6 to 27 m. **Range:** R. Sea to Samoa, n. to Yaeyamas., s. to GBR.

6 **Randall 's prawn-goby** *Amblyeleotris Randall i* Hoese & Steene 9 cm
Ecology: patches of sand of clear water reefs, 25 to 48 m. **Range:** Moluccas to Fiji, n. to Ryuk., s. to GBR.

7 **Spotted prawn-goby** *Amblyeleotris guttata* (Fowler) 9 cm
Ecology: outer lagoon and seaward reefs, 10 to 34 m. **Range:** Phil. to Samoa, n. to Ryuk., s. to nw. Aust. shelf reefs & GBR.

8 **Magnus' prawn-goby** *Amblyeleotris sungami* (Klausewitz) 10 cm
Ecology: open sand bottoms of clear water reefs. **Range:** R. Sea to Seychelles; probably more widespread in Indo-w. Pacific.

9 **Banded or Yellow prawn-goby** *Cryptocentrus cinctus* (Herre) 7 cm
Also a gray ph. with thin white bars overlaying broad light and dark bands. **Ecology:** sandy expanses of shallow lagoons and protected coastal bays, 1 to 15 m. **Range:** Andaman Sea to e. Caroline Is., n. to Yaeyamas, s. to GBR.

10 **Eyebrow prawn-goby** *Amblyeleotris* sp. ca. 8 cm
Ecology: sandy slopes, 10 to 25 m. **Range:** Bali, probably more widespread in W. Pacific.

11 **Target prawn-goby** *Cryptocentrus strigilliceps* (Jordan & Seale) 6 cm
Ecology: silty bottoms of lagoon and coastal reefs to 6 m, often in areas of runoff. **Range:** E. Africa to Samoa, n. to Yaeyamas, s. to n. GBR.

12 **Ninebar prawn-goby** *Cryptocentrus cryptocentrus* (Valenciennes) 13 cm
Ecology: shallow sandy expanses in or near seagrasses. **Range:** R. Sea to Chagos, s. to Natal.

13 **Saddled prawn-goby** *Cryptocentrus leucostictus* (Günther) 7 cm
Ecology: open sand bottoms of clear seaward reefs to at least 20 m. **Range:** Andaman Sea to Samoa, n. to Phil., s. to GBR.

14 **Blue-speckled prawn-goby** *Cryptocentrus caeruleomaculatus* (Herre) 6 cm
Ecology: shallow lagoons and coastal bays to 4 m, usually in areas subject to runoff. **Range:** E. Africa to Marianas, n. to s. Japan.

15 **Barred prawn-goby** *Cryptocentrus fasciatus* (Playfair) 14 cm
Ecology: sand near patch reefs usually 5 m, but to at least 15 m. **Range:** E. Africa & Madag. to N. Britain, GBR & N. Cal.

16 **Harlequin prawn-goby** *Cryptocentrus caeruleopunctatus* (Rüppell) 13 cm
Ecology: open sand bottoms of clear water reefs. **Range:** R. Sea.

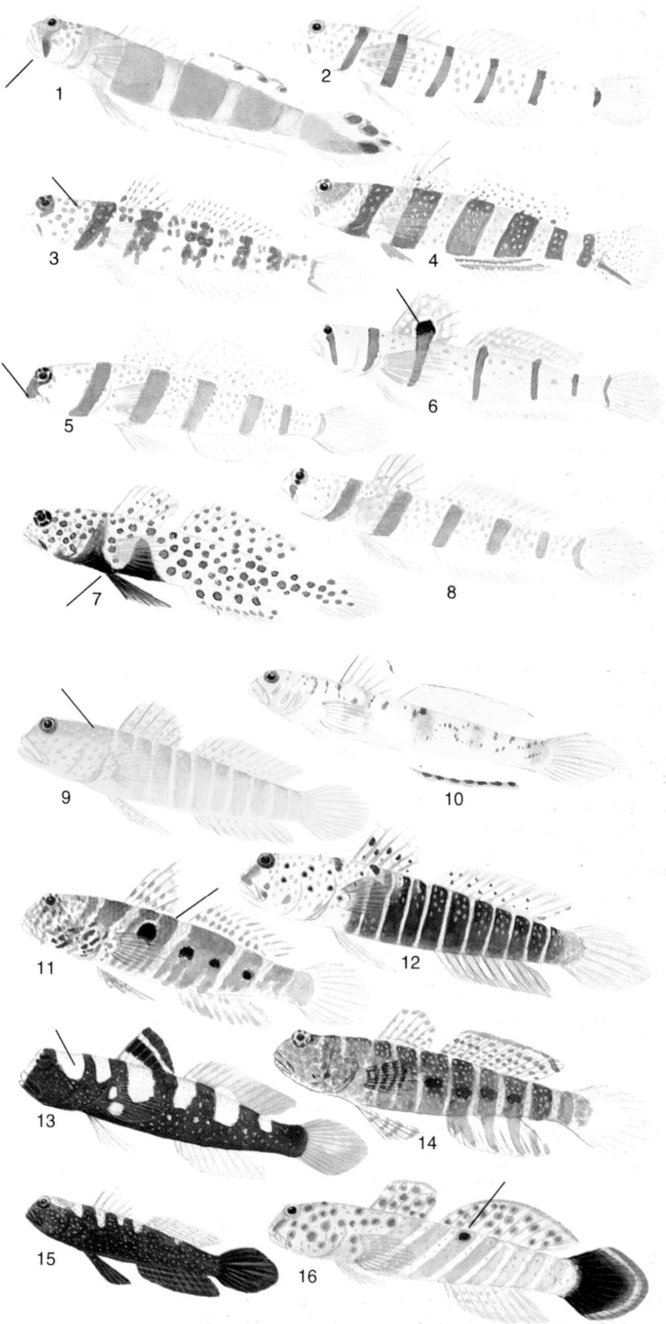
1
2
3
4
5
6
7
8
9
10
11
12
13
14
15
16

121 GOBIES

1 **Leptocephalus prawn-goby** *Cryptocentrus leptocephalus* Bleeker 10 cm **Ecology:** silty bottoms of coastal reefs and inner reef flats. **Range:** Malaysia and Indonesia to N. Cal., n. to Ryuk.

2 **Luther's prawn-goby** *Cryptocentrus lutheri* Klausewitz 11 cm **Ecology:** sand and rubble bottoms. **Range:** R. Sea, Arab. G. & E. Africa.

3 **White-rayed prawn-goby** *Stonogobiops* sp. 4 cm **Ecology:** species of *Stonogobiops* often hover above the entrance of the burrow and live with the red and white prawn *Alpheus Randall i.* Areas of fine sand to a depth of 35m. **Range:** Ryuk.

4 **Filament-finned prawn-goby** *S. nematodes* Hoese & Randall 5 cm **Ecology:** sandy slopes below 15 m. Usually in pairs or groups with *Alpheus Randall i.* **Range:** Seychelles, Andaman Sea, Phil. & Indonesia

5 **Yellownose prawn-goby** *S. xanthorhinica* Hoese & Randall 5.5 cm Similar to *S. dracula* (Seychelles to Maldives) & *S. medon* (Marq.) which looses most of its bars with growth. **Ecology:** sandy slopes, 3 to 45 m, usually below 20 m with *Alpheus Randall i.* **Range:** e. Indonesia to Sol. Is., n. to s. Japan, s. to n. GBR.

6 **Tangaroa prawn-goby** *Ctenogobiops tangaroai* Lubbock & Polunin 6 cm **Ecology:** sand patches of seaward reefs, 4 to 40 m. Uncommon. **Range:** Ryuk., GBR, Guam & Samoa.

7 **Gold-specked prawn-goby** *C. pomastictus* Lubbock & Polunin 6 cm Similar to *C. maculosus* (R. Sea) and *C. feroculus.* **Ecology:** silty sand bottoms of reef flats and lagoons to over 20 m. Common. **Range:** Andaman Sea to Marianas, n. to Ryuk., s. to nw. Australian shelf & s. GBR.

8 **Gold-streaked prawn-goby** *C. aurocingulus* Lubbock & Polunin 6 cm **Ecology:** sandy lagoon bottoms. **Range:** Phil. to Samoa, n. to Ryuk., s. to nw. Australian shelf & s. GBR.

9 **Sandy prawn-goby** *Ctenogobiops feroculus* Lubbock & Polunin 6 cm **Ecology:** shallow lagoons in areas of sand and rubble to 4 m. Common. **Range:** R. Sea to N. Cal., n. to Ryuk.

10 **Graceful prawn-goby** *Lotilia graciliosa* Klausewitz 4 cm **Ecology:** sand patches of reef flats, and lagoon and seaward reefs to 20 m. Hovers at entrance of burrow, waving its large spotted pectoral fins. Very shy. Uncommon. **Range:** R. Sea to Marshall Is. & Fiji, n. to Ryuk., s. to nw. Aust. shelf reefs & GBR.

11 **Flagfin prawn-goby** *Mahidolia mystacina* (Valenciennes) 8 cm **Ecology:** silty coastal bays to 16 m. **Range:** E. Africa to Soc. Is., n. to s. Japan (?), s. to n. Aust. & Samoa.

12 **Mertens' prawn-goby** *Vanderhorstia mertensi* Klausewitz 11 cm **Ecology:** coastal reefs, on sand or mud, 2 to 10 m. Hovers near entrance of burrow. **Range:** R. Sea to PNG, s. to GBR, n. to Ryukyus.

13 **Ornate prawn-goby** *Vanderhorstia ornatissima* Smith 8 cm **Ecology:** shallow protected sandy areas, including seagrass beds. Sits on bottom. **Range:** E. Africa to Samoa, n. to Ryuk., s. to GBR & Rapa.

14 **Ambonoro prawn-goby** *Vanderhorstia ambonoro* Fourmanoir 13 cm **Ecology:** sandy expanses of lagoons and bays, 4 to 12 m. Hovers near entrance of burrow. **Range:** E. Africa to Samoa, n. to Yaeyamas, s. to GBR.

The following two species are not associated with burrows or prawns:

15 **Spikefin goby** *Discordipinna griessingeri* Hoese & Fourmanoir 2.5 cm **Ecology:** areas with live coral, rubble, and sand, 5 to 27 m. Secretive. **Range:** R. Sea to Marq. & Gambier Is., s. to GBR.

16 **Starry goby** *Asterropteryx semipunctatus* (Bleeker) 6.5 cm **Ecology:** on algae-coated reef rock and rubble in shallow silty areas to 20 m. **Range:** R. Sea to Hawaiian, Line & Tuam. Is., n. to s. Japan, s. to L. Howe & Rapa Is.

1
2
4
3
5
6
7
8
10
9
12
11
13
14
15
16

Burrow-dwelling species not associated with prawns:

1 **Sphynx goby** *Amblygobius sphynx* (Valenciennes) 18 cm
Ecology: sandy areas of reef flats and lagoons. Behavior similar to *A. phalaena.* **Range:** E. Africa to Caroline Is. & GBR, n. to Phil.

2 **Brown-barred goby** *Amblygobius phalaena* (Valenciennes) 15 cm
Similar to *A. albimaculatus* (R. Sea) & *A. semicinctus* (Indian Ocean). **Ecology:** sandy and rubbly areas of reef flats and lagoons to 20 m. Often in pairs. Constructs a burrow under a rock or rubble. Feeds on invertebrates and algae by sifting mouthfuls of sand. Common. **Range:** Sumatra to Society Is., n. to Ryuk., s. to sw. Aust., NSW, L. Howe & Rapa Is.

3 **Hector's goby** *Amblygobius hectori* (Smith) 5.5 cm
Ecology: sand patches at the base of reefs. Stays near shelter. Uncommon. **Range:** R. Sea to e. Caroline Is. & GBR., n. to Ryuk.

4 **Old Glory; Rainford's goby** *Amblygobius rainfordi* (Whitley) 6.5 cm
Ecology: silty bases of coastal and inner lagoon reefs. Ventures out over corals and does not seem to utilize a burrow. **Range:** Phil. to Marshall Is. & Coral Sea, s. to nw. Aust. shelf reefs & GBR.

5 **Nocturn goby** *Amblygobius nocturnus* (Herre) 6 cm
Ecology: silty bottoms at the bases of inner lagoon and coastal reefs, 3 to 30 m. **Range:** Phil. to Tuam., n. to Yaeyamas, s. to nw. Aust. shelf reefs, L. Howe & Rapa Is.

6 **Crosshatch goby** *Amblygobius decussatus* (Bleeker) 8 cm
Ecology: silty bottoms of bays and lagoons, 3 to ~20 m. Lives in vertical tube-like hole. **Range:** Phil. to N. Cal., n. to Yaeyamas, s. to GBR.

7 **Blue-streak goby** *Valenciennea strigata* (Broussonet) 18 cm
Ecology: clear lagoon and seaward reefs, 1 to 20 m. On hard bottoms as well as patches of sand and rubble. Juveniles often in groups, adults usually paired. Common. **Range:** s. R. Sea to Line, Marq. & Soc. Is., n. to Ryuk., s. to s. L. Howe Is., E. Africa.

8 **Maiden goby** *Valenciennea puellaris* (Tomiyama) 17 cm
Ecology: expanses of coarse sand of clear lagoon and seaward reefs, 15 to 20 m. **Range:** R. Sea to Samoa, n. to s. Japan, s. to s. GBR & N. Cal.

9 **Longfinned goby** *Valenciennea longipinnis* (Lay & Bennett) 15 cm
Ecology: sand patches of reef flats and lagoon and seaward reefs to 20 m. Often in pairs. **Range:** e. Indian Ocean & w. Pacific to N. Cal., s. to GBR.

10 **Six-spot goby** *Valenciennea sexguttata* (Valenciennes) 14 cm
Ecology: silty or sandy bottoms of lagoons and bays. Often in pairs. **Range:** R. Sea to Samoa, n. to Yaeyamas, s. to GBR.

11 **Twostripe goby** *Valenciennea helsdingeni* (Bleeker) 16 cm
Similar *V. immaculata* (w. Pacific). **Ecology:** protected sandy areas of continental shelf coasts, 2 to ~ 30 m. Usually in pairs. Both burrow hole. Common in E. Africa. **Range:** s. Red Sea, E. Africa to Indonesia & GBR, n. to s. Japan.

12 **Mural goby** *Valenciennea muralis* (Valenciennes) 13 cm
Ecology: sandy areas of shallow lagoon reefs. **Range:** India to Fiji, n. to Ryuk., s. to nw. Aust. & S. GBR.

13 **Crab-eye goby** *Signigobius biocellatus* Hoese & Randall 6.5 cm
Ecology: sandy bottoms of lagoons and bays near coral, rubble or leaf litter, 1 to 30 m. Often in pairs that share a burrow. Feeds by sifting mouthfuls of sand. Flashes eyespots at potential predators, which make it look like a large sideways-moving crab. **Range:** Phil. & Indonesia to Sol. Is. & Vanuatu, n. to Palau, s. to s. GBR.

14 **Spinecheek goby** *Oplopomus oplopomus* (Valenciennes) 8 cm
Ecology: silty bottoms of inner lagoons and bays, 1 to 20 m. **Range:** R. Sea to Soc. Is., n. to Yaeyamas, s. to GBR.

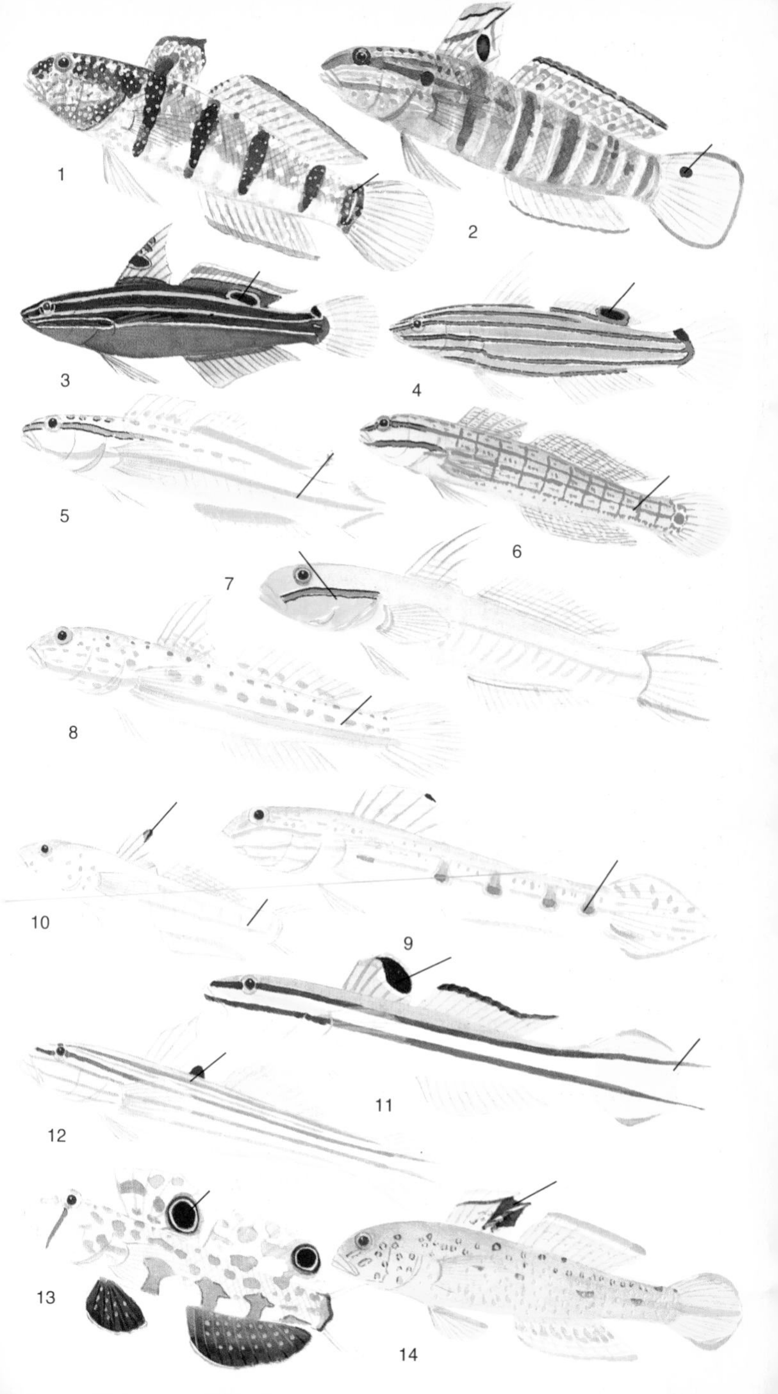
1
2
3
4
5
6
7
8
9
10
11
12
13
14

1 **Citron goby** *Gobiodon citrinus* (Rüppell) 6.6 cm
Ecology: species of *Gobiodon* produce a toxic bitter-tasting mucus and live exclusively among the branches of corals. This species lives among the branches of *Acropora* corals. **Range**: R. Sea to Samoa, n. to s. Japan, s. to s. GBR.

2 **Broad-barred goby** *Gobiodon histrio* (Valenciennes) 3.5 cm
Var. *erythrospilos* has dots instead of lines; similar to *G. rivulatus* (R.Sea to Tuam.). **Ecology**: lives among the branches of *Acropora* corals. **Range**: R. Sea to Samoa, n. to s. Japan, s. to s. GBR.

3 **Yellow coral goby** *Gobiodon okinawae* Sawada, Arai & Abe 3.5 cm
Ecology: sheltered lagoon reefs. Lives in groups among the branches of *Acropora* corals. **Range**: Indonesia to Marshalls, n. to s. Japan, s. to nw. Aust. shelf reefs & s. GBR.

4 **Five-lined coral goby** *Gobiodon quinquestrigatus* (Valenciennes) 3.5 cm
Ecology: in groups among the branches of tabletop *Acropora* corals. **Range**: Phil. to Society Is, n. to s. Japan, s. to nw. Aust. shelf reefs, s. GBR & Tonga.

5 **Redhead goby** *Paragobiodon echinocephalus* Rüppell 3.5 cm
Head & nape of genus scaleless with dense bristles. Several similar spp., all in live corals. **Ecology**: lives exclusively among the branches of *Stylophora* corals. **Range**: R. Sea to Marq. & Tuam. Is., n. to Ryuk., s. to L. Howe Is.

6 **Blackfin coral goby** *Paragobiodon lacunicolus* (Kendall & Goldsborough) 3 cm
Ecology: lives exclusively among the branches of the coral *Pocillopora damicornis*. **Range**: Seychelles to Line & Tuam. Is., n. to Ryuk. & Bonin Is., s. to L. Howe Is.

7 **Yellowskin goby** *Paragobiodon xanthosomus* (Bleeker) 4 cm
Ecology: lives exclusively among the branches of the coral *Seriatopora hystrix*. **Range**: Seychelles & Chagos Is. to Samoa, n. to Ryuk., s. to GBR.

8 **Eyebar goby** *Gnatholepis cauerensis* (Bleeker) 8 cm
Ecology: sheltered sandy areas from reef flats to seaward reefs, 0 to 46 m. Common. **Range**: R. Sea to Hawaiian, Marq. & Society Is., n. to Ryuk., s. to Rapa.

9 **Shoulder-spot goby** *Gnatholepis scapulostigma* Herre 4 cm
Ecology: sandy areas shallow sheltered reefs near pieces of rubble, rock, or coral. **Range**: E. Africa to Marshall Is., n. to Ryuk. & Bonin Is., s. to GBR.

10 **Sand goby** *Fusigobius neophytus* (Günther) 7.5 cm
Ecology: subtidal reef flats and lagoons. On sand and rubble patches. **Range**: E. Africa to Tuam., n. to Ryuk., s. to L. Howe Is.

11 **Longspine goby** *Fusigobius longipinnis* Goren 7.5 cm
Ecology: sandy floors of caves of seaward reefs, 9 to 18 m. **Range**: R. Sea to Marshall Is. (?), n. to Marianas, s. to GBR.

12 **Decorated goby** *Istigobius decoratus* (Herre) 12 cm
Ecology: sand patches of clear lagoon and seaward reefs, 1 to 18 m. Common. **Range**: R. Sea to Samoa, n. to Taiwan, s. to L. Howe Is.

13 **Ornate goby** *Istigobius ornatus* (Rüppell) 11 cm
Similar to *I. rigilius* (W. Pacific) differing in details of head pattern. **Ecology**: among mangroves and on silty inner reefs to 2 m. Common. **Range**: R. Sea to Fiji, n. to s. Taiwan, s. to GBR & N. Cal.

14 **Caesiura goby** *Trimma caesiura* Jordan & Seale 2.5 cm
Over 75 spp. of *Trimma* & *Trimmatom* many undescribed. Many similar spp. **Ecology**: clear lagoon and seaward reefs. Sits on bottom on dead coral rock and rubble. **Range**: Indonesia to Marianas & N. Brit., n. to Ryuk. & Izu Is., s. to nw. Aust. shelf reefs.

15 **Candy-cane goby** *Trimma* sp. 4.5 cm
Most similar to *T. eviotops* (Ind. Oc. to se. Polynesia). **Ecology**: Steep dropoffs, 9 to 36 m. In aggregations in caves, hovering near shelter. **Range**: Indonesia to Marianas & N. Brit., n. to Ryuk. & Izu Is., s. to nw. Aust. shelf reefs.

16 **Blue-striped cave goby** *Trimma tevegae* Cohen & Davis 4.5 cm
Ecology: steep dropoffs, 9 to 36 m. In aggregations in caves, hovers near shelter. **Range**: Indonesia to Marianas & N. Brit., n. to Ryuk. & Izu Is., s. to nw. Aust. shelf reefs.

17 **Girdled goby** *Priolepis cincta* (Regan) 6 cm
Many similar spp. including some awaiting description. **Ecology**: stays hidden in crevices and caves. **Range**: E. Africa to Marianas, n. to s. Japan, s. to GBR.

18 **Doublebar goby** *Eviota bifasciata* Lachner & Karnella 2.8 cm
Ecology: hovers in groups above branching corals of protected coastal reefs to 6 m. **Range**: Indonesia & Phil. to PNG, s. to n. Australia.

19 **Redeye goby** *Bryaninops natans* Larson 2.5 cm
Ecology: lagoon reefs, 7 to 27 m. Hovers in groups above *Acropora* corals. **Range**: R. Sea to Cook Is., n. to Ryuk., s. to n. GBR.

20 **Mud reef-goby** *Exyrias bellissimus* (Smith) 13 cm
Ecology: lagoon and sheltered reefs, 0 to 20 m. On silt under or at the base of corals. **Range**: E. Africa to Samoa, n. to Yaeyamas, s. to GBR & Fiji.

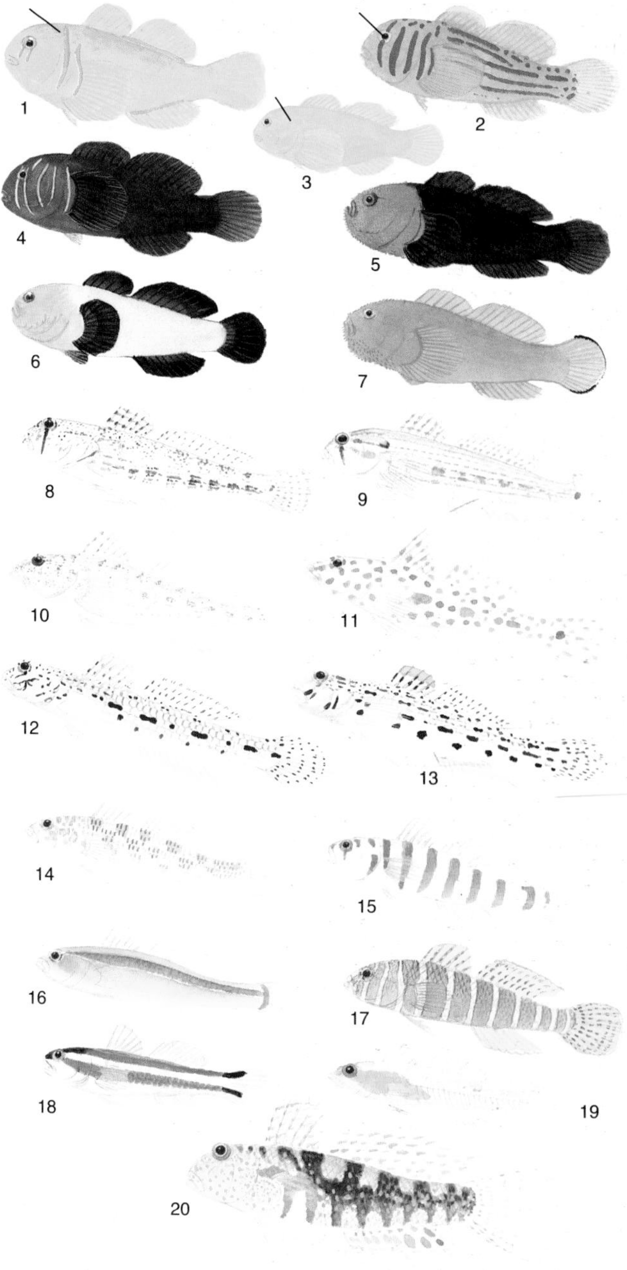
1
2
3
4
5
6
7
8
9
10
11
12
13
14
15
16
17
18
19
20

MOORISH IDOL (ZANCLIDAE): a single distinctively shaped species closely related to surgeonfishes but with a more tubular snout and without blades at the tail base.

1 **Moorish idol** *Zanclus cornutus* (Linnaeus) 16 cm
Ecology: ubiquitous around rocky and coral reefs from inner harbors and bays to seaward reefs as deep as 182 m. Usually in small groups, but occasionally in large schools. Feeds primarily on sponges. Difficult to maintain in the aquarium. **Range:** E. Africa to Mexico, n. to s. Japan & Hawaii, s. to L. Howe, Kermadec & Rapa Is.

SURGEONFISHES and UNICORNFISHES (ACANTHURIDAE): ovate to elongate compressed fishes with a small terminal mouth containing a single row of small close-set incisiform to lanceolate teeth, continuous D and A fins, complete LL, a tough skin with minute scales, and one or more pairs of sharp blades at the base of the tail. The blades may be used offensively or defensively and can inflict deep and painful wounds. Diurnal herbivores or planktivores. Most species have a long larval stage resulting in large size at settlement and broad distributions. Important foodfishes. Many colorful species popular in aquariums.

Surgeonfishes (Subfamily Acanthurinae): a single pair of scalpel-like retractible blades which fold into a groove. Many species able to change shade from pale to nearly black.

2 **Sailfin tang** *Zebrasoma veliferum* (Bloch) 40 cm
Juvs. with alternating yellow & black bars. V. similar to *Z. desjardinii*. ***Ecology:*** lagoon and seaward reefs to >30 m. Juveniles in sheltered inner reef areas. **Range:** Indonesia & Christmas Is. to Hawaiian & Tuam. Is., n. to s. Japan, s. to s. GBR, N. Cal. & Rapa.

3 **Desjardin's sailfin tang** *Zebrasoma desjardinii* (Bennett) 40 cm
Ecology: lagoon and seaward reefs to >30 m. Juveniles in sheltered inner reef areas. **Range:** R. Sea to Cocos-Keeling & Christmas Is.

4 **Brushtail tang** *Zebrasoma scopas* (Cuvier) 20 cm
Ecology: coral-rich areas of lagoon and seaward reefs, 1 to 60 m. Singly or in small groups. Hybridizes with *Z. flavescens*. **Range:** S. Africa to Tuam., n. to s. Japan, s. to L. Howe & Rapa Is.

5 **Yellow tang** *Zebrasoma flavescens* (Bennett) 20 cm
Ecology: coral-rich areas of lagoon and seaward reefs, 2 to ~46 m. Singly or in small groups. Feeds on filamentous algae. Very common in Hawaiian Is., less common elsewhere. **Range:** Ryuk., Mariana, Marshall, Marcus, Wake & Hawaiian Is.

6 **Yellowtail surgeonfish** *Zebrasoma xanthurum* (Blyth) 22 cm
Ecology: coral-rich areas, 0.5 to 20 m. Often in small groups. **Range:** R. Sea to Arab. G.

7 **Longnose surgeonfish** *Zebrasoma rostratum* (Günther) 21 cm
Ecology: lagoon and seaward reefs. **Range:** Line, Marq., Society & Tuam. Is. to Pitcairn (Ducie Is.).

8 **Gem surgeonfish** *Zebrasoma gemmatum* Valenciennes 22 cm
Ecology: coral and rocky reefs, 10 to 60 m. Juveniles shallow, adults usually 20 m. **Range:** S. Africa to Maurit. & Madagascar.

9 **Convict surgeonfish** *Acanthurus triostegus* (Linnaeus) 26.3 cm
Ecology: lagoon and seaward reefs in areas of hard substrates, 0 to 90 m. Juvs. in tidepools. Feeds on filamentous algae. Singly or in large groups. Gains access to feeding territories of other herbivores by swarming. Common in most areas. **Range:** Subsp. *triostegus*: E. Africa to Panama, n. to s. Japan, s. to Kermadec, Rapa & Ducie Is; subsp. *sandvicensis*: Hawaiian Is.

10 **Black-barred surgeonfish** *Acanthurus polyzona* (Bleeker) cm
Ecology: Unknown. **Range:** Madagascar & Réunion.

11 **Powder-blue surgeonfish** *Acanthurus leucosternon* Bennett 23 cm
Ecology: shallow, clear coastal and island reefs, 0.5 to 25 m. Generally on reef flats and along upper seaward slopes, sometimes in huge aggregations. **Range:** E. Africa to Andaman Sea, sw. Indonesia & Christmas Is.

12 **Palette surgeonfish** *Paracanthurus hepatus* (Linnaeus) 31 cm
Ecology: clear seaward reefs, 2 to 40 m, usually in current-swept areas. In loose aggregations 1 to 3 m above the bottom. Feeds on zooplankton. Shelters in groups among branches of *Pocillopora* corals or in crevices of rocks. Often highly localized. **Range:** E. Africa to Line Is., n. to s. Japan, s. to s. GBR, N. Cal. & Samoa.

13 **Whitecheek surgeonfish** *Acanthurus nigricans* (Linnaeus) 21.3 cm
Ecology: clear lagoon and seaward reefs, 1 to 67 m, usually in shallow exposed areas. **Range:** Cocos-Keeling Is. to Panama, n. to Ryuk. & Hawaiian Is., s. to s. GBR, N. Cal. & Tuam.

14 **Achilles tang** *Acanthurus achilles* Shaw 24 cm
Juvs. lack the large orange spot; hybridizes with *A. nigricans*. **Ecology:** clear seaward reefs, primarily in surge zone to 4 m. Usually in groups. Abundant in Hawaii and Fr. Polynesia, rare in w. Pacific. Hybridizes with *A. nigricans*. **Range:** W. Caroline Is. to Marq. & Ducie Is.,

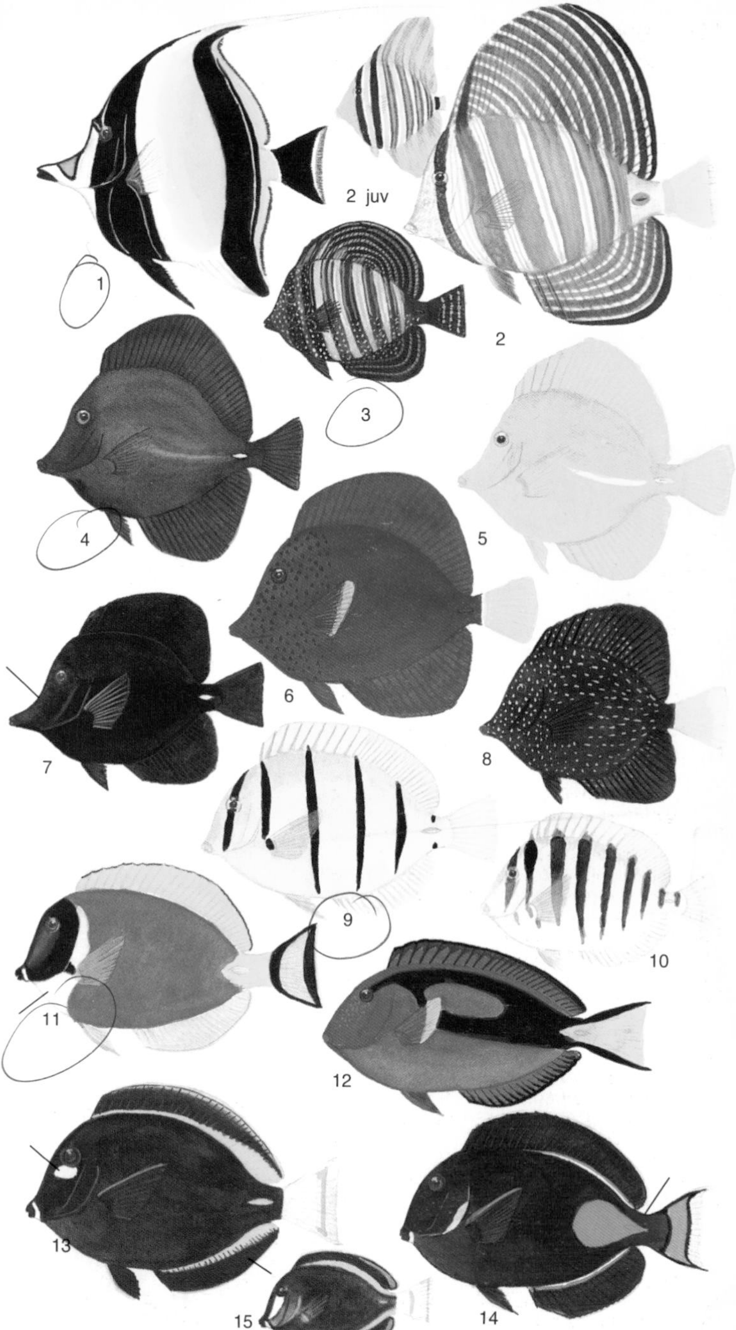

1
2 juv
2
3
4
5
6
7
8
9
10
11
12
13
14
15

n. to Marcus & Hawaiian Is., s. to N. Cal; waifs reported from n. GBR & Baja Calif.

←15 **Japan surgeonfish** *Acanthurus japonicus* 21 cm
Ecology: clear lagoon and seaward reefs, usually in shallow exposed areas. **Range**: Phil., Sulawesi & Moluccas to Ryuk.

125 SURGEONFISHES

1 **Striped surgeonfish** *Acanthurus lineatus* (Linnaeus) 38 cm
Ecology: outer reef flats and surge zone of exposed seaward reefs and patch reef tops, usually 4 m. Territorial and aggressive. Common. **Range**: E. Africa to Marq. & Tuam. Is., n. to s. Japan, s. to s. GBR & N. Cal.

2 **Sohal surgeonfish** *Acanthurus sohal* (Forsskål) 40 cm
Ecology: seaward edges of reefs exposed to surge. Aggressive and territorial. Common. **Range**: R. Sea to Arabian G.

3 **Orangeband surgeonfish** *Acanthurus olivaceus* Forster 35 cm
Juvs. 6 cm uniformly yellow, the orange bar developing early in transition to adult color. **Ecology**: lagoon and seaward reefs, 3 to ~46 m. Usually over open sandy areas, often in groups. Feeds on algal film on sand and hard bottoms. **Range**: Cocos-Keeling Is. to Hawaiian, Marq. & Tuam. Is., n. to s. Japan, s. to L. Howe Is.

4 **Eyestripe surgeonfish** *Acanthurus dussumieri* Valenciennes 54 cm
Similar to *A. mata*, but has black spots on tail; upper P rays may be yellowish. **Ecology**: seaward reefs, 4 to 131 m, usually deeper than 10 m. Feeds primarily on surface film covering sand, but occasionally browses on hard surfaces. **Range**: E. Africa to Hawaiian & Line Is., n. to s. Japan, s. to s. GBR & L. Howe Is.

5 **Elongate surgeonfish** *Acanthurus mata* Cuvier 50 cm
Body somewhat elongate; can change color from dark blueish-brown to light slaty-blue. **Ecology**: coastal and offshore reefs, enters turbid water. Often in small groups high in water; feeds on zooplankton. **Range**: R. Sea & S. Africa to Marq. & Tuam Is. n. to s. Japan, s. to s. GBR & N. Cal.

6 **Yellowfin surgeonfish** *Acanthurus xanthopterus* Valenciennes 56 cm
Similar to *A. dussumieri*, upper and outer portion on P fin yellow; yellow in front of and behind eye not as a distinct band. **Ecology**: lagoon and seaward reefs, to 91 m. Juveniles in shallow protected areas, adults usually below 20 m. Common in sandy habitats near reefs. Feeds on algal film on compacted sand as well as filamentous algae on hard surfaces. **Range**: E. Africa to Mexico, n. to s. Japan & Hawaiian Is., s. to Kermadec, Rapa & Ducie Is.

7 **Whitebar surgeonfish** *Acanthurus leucoparieus* (Jenkins) 24 cm
Ecology: outer reef flats to 85 m. Prefers surgy, boulder-strewn areas. Often in schools. **Range**: s. Japan & Marianas to Marcus & Hawaiian Is.; N. Cal. to Tuam, Rapa, Pitcairn & Easter Is.

8 **Whitespotted surgeonfish** *Acanthurus guttatus* Forster 26 cm
Ecology: surge zone of clear seaward reefs, 0.3 to 6 m. Often in large groups. Feeds on filamentous and certain calcareous red algae. The white spots help it blend in with bubbles. **Range**: Maurit. to Hawaiian, Marq. & Tuam. Is., n. to Ryuk., s. to N. Cal. & Rapa.

9 **Ringtail surgeonfish** *Acanthurus blochii* Valenciennes 42 cm
White ring around tail base not always present; P fins dark or same color as body; center of tail often with black vertical bars. **Ecology**: outer lagoon and seaward reefs, 1 to 12 m. Often in groups in open areas grazing on algal film growing on compact sand. **Range**: E. Africa to Hawaiian & Society Is., n. to Ryuk., s. to L. Howe Is.

10 **Black surgeonfish** *Acanthurus gahhm* (Forsskål) 40 cm
Similar to *A. nigricauda* which has a black line extending forward of the caudal spine. During display often with a pale tail. Regularly around 'cleaning stations'. **Ecology**: open areas near coral or rock. Often in large groups. **Range**: R. Sea & G. Aden.

11 **Fowler's surgeonfish** *Acanthurus fowleri* de Beaufort 27 cm
Ecology: clear seaward reefs and dropoffs, 10 to 45 m. Solitary and wary. **Range**: e. Indonesia & Phil.

12 **Chronixis surgeonfish** *Acanthurus chronixis* Randall >28 cm
Ecology: coral and sand bottoms of clear channels. Juveniles probably on reef flats. **Range**: Kapingamarangi Atoll (e. Caroline Is.) & possibly Ifaluk Atoll (c. Caroline Is.).

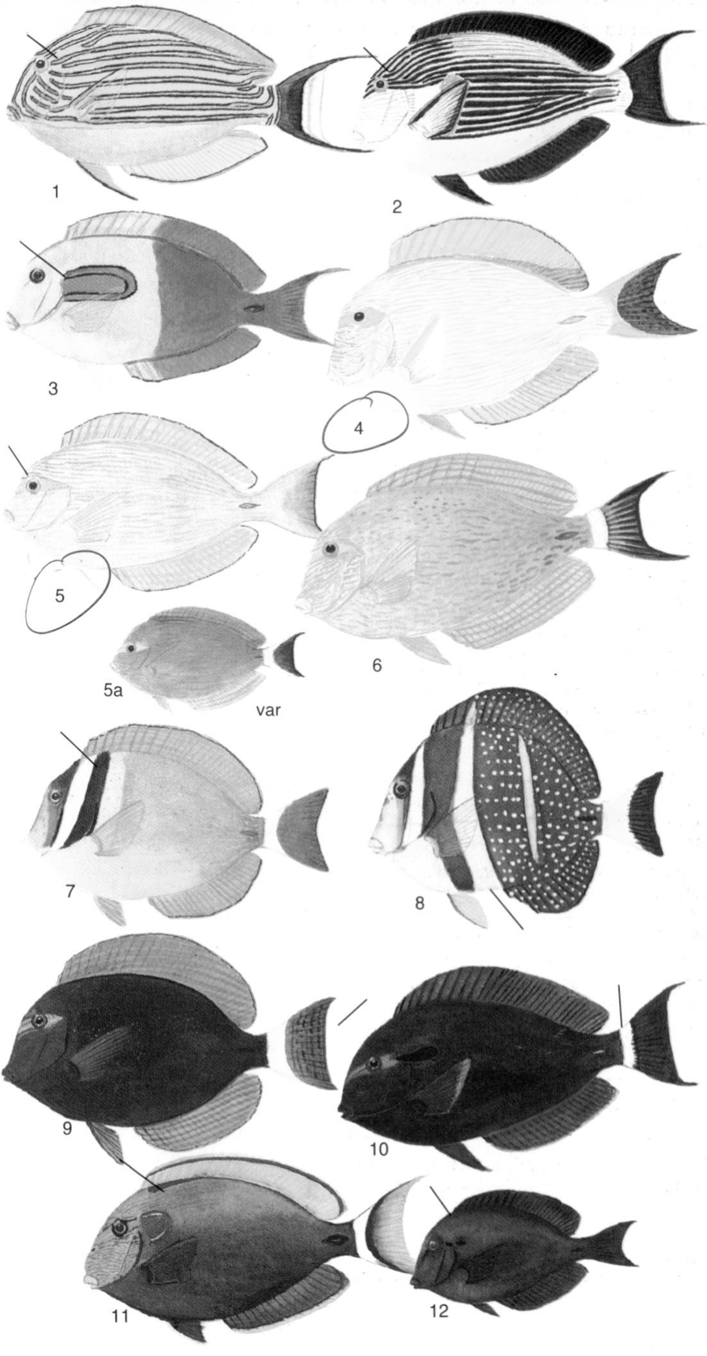
1
2
3
4
5
6
5a
var
7
8
9
10
11
12

1 **Mimic surgeonfish** *Acanthurus pyroferus* Kittlitz 25 cm
Juvs. mimic *Centropyge flavissimus* & *C. vrolikii*. (pls. 68 & 70). **Ecology:** lagoon and seaward reefs, 4 to 60 m. Solitary, prefers areas of mixed coral, rock, or sand near base of reefs. Often on silty reefs. **Range:** Indonesia & Phil. to Marq., & Tuam. Is., n. to s. Japan, s. to s. GBR & N. Cal.

2 **Indian Ocean mimic surgeonfish** *Acanthurus tristis* Tickell 25 cm
Similar to *A. pyroferus* but without red near P fin base. Juvs. mimic *Centropyge eibli* (pl.70). **Ecology:** lagoon and seaward reefs in areas of mixed coral, rock or sand, 2 to26 m. **Range:** Seychelles, Chagos, Maldives & Sri Lanka to Bali, n. to Burma.

3 **Thompson's surgeonfish** *Acanthurus thompsoni* (Fowler) 27 cm
Ecology: steep outer reef slopes and dropoffs, 4 to 75 m. Feeds on zooplankton well above the bottom. In loose aggregations. Resembles *A. nubilus* at a distance. **Range:** S. Africa to Hawaiian, Marq. & Ducie Is., n. to s. Japan, s. to Rapa.

4 **White-freckled surgeonfish** *Acanthurus maculiceps* (Ahl) 25 cm
Ecology: seaward reefs, 1 to 15 m. Solitary or in small wide-ranging groups. **Range:** Andaman Sea to Line Is., n. to Ryuk., s. to Samoa.

5 **Lietenant surgeonfish** *Acanthurus tennenti* Günther 31 cm
Ecology: lagoon and seaward reefs, 1 to over 20 m. Feeds on the algal film on compactd sand as well as rocks. Often in groups. Hybridizes with *A. olivaceus* at Bali. **Range:** E.Africa to Bali, n. to Sri Lanka & Andaman Sea.

6 **Bluelined surgeonfish** *Acanthurus nigroris* Valenciennes 25 cm
Ecology: clear lagoon and seaward refs, 1 to 90 m. Singly or in small groups, feeds on algal film of compacted sand as well filamentous algae on hard bottoms. **Range:** Aldabra & Seychelles to Hawaiian, Marq. & Tuam. Is., s. to s. GBR.

7 **Dusky surgeonfish** *Acanthurus nigrofuscus* (Forsskål) 21 cm
Ecology: lagoon and seaward reefs, 1 to over 15 m. Often in large schools, sometimes with *A. triostegus*. Swarms the territories of other surgeonfishes to feed on filamentous algae. **Range:** E. Africa to R. Sea to Hawaiian & Tuam. Is., n. to s. Japan, s. to L. Howe Is.

8 **Striped bristletooth** *Ctenochaetus striatus* (Quoy & Gaimard) 26 cm
Ecology: reef flats and lagoon and seaward reefs to over 30 m. In coral, rocky, pavement, or rubble habitats, common in most areas. Solitary or in large schools, often with other species. A key link in ciguatera food chain, occasionally toxic itself. **Range:** R. Sea & S. Africa to Tuam., n. to s. Japan, s. to s. GBR & Rapa.

9 **Twospot bristletooth** *Ctenochaetus binotatus* Randall 22 cm
Ecology: coral and rubble areas of deep lagoon and seaward reefs, 12 to 53 m. Species of *Ctenochaetus* feed on detritus and unicellular algal film of reef surfaces including the surfaces of algae and seagrasses. They are important vectors of ciguatera. **Range:** E. Africa to Tuam., n. to Ryuk., s. to s. GBR & Tonga.

10 **Tomini surgeonfish** *Ctenochaetus tominiensis* Randall 13 cm
Ecology: steep coral-rich dropoffs to 40 m. Solitary or in small groups. Uncommon. **Range:** Bali to Sol. Is., n. to Phil. & Palau.

11 **Goldring bristletooth** *Ctenochaetus strigosus* (Bennett) 18 cm
Tail emarginate in Pacific popul.; tail white in Fr. Polynesia; yellow eye ring conspicuous in Hawaiian popul., pale elsewhere. Juvs. 5 cm mostly yellow. **Ecology:** lagoon and seaward reefs, 1 to 46 m. Common in Polynesia; rare in w. Pacific. **Range:** E. Africa to Marq. & Ducie Is., n. to Mariana & Hawaiian Is., s. to s. GBR & N. Cal.

12 **Blue-spotted bristletooth** *Ctenochaetus marginatus* (Valenciennes) 27 cm
Ecology: shallow seaward reefs, 2 to 6 m. **Range:** Caroline Is. to Line, Marq. & Society Is.; Cocos Is. (e. Pacific).

13 **Hawaiian surgeonfish** *Ctenochaetus hawaiiensis* Randall 25 cm
Ecology: seaward rocky or coral reefs. Juveniles in deep coral-rich areas. Uncommon. **Range:** Palau & Marianas to Hawaiian, Marq. & Ducie Is., s. to Austral Is.

1
3
2
1juv
1 juv
5
4
7
6
9
8
7 juv
11
10
12
13 juv
13

1 **Blackstreak surgeonfish** *Acanthurus nigricauda* Duncker & Mohr 40 cm
Similar to *A. gahhm* (pl. 125-10) but has a dark streak forward of caudal spine. **Ecology:** clear lagoon and seaward reefs, 1 to 30 m. Prefers open sandy areas near coral or rocky outcrops and often occurs with *A. olivaceus* in large mixed species schools. Capable of rapidly switching between pale and dark. **Range:** E. Africa to Tuam., n. to Ryuk., s. to s. GBR.

2 **Orange-socket surgeonfish** *Acanthurus auranticavus* Randall 35 cm
Ecology: shallow lagoon and seaward reefs. Usually in small roving groups. Over sand near patch reefs. Juvs. between soft corals in only 0.2-2 m water of lagoons. **Range:** E. Africa, Maldives, Indonesia, Phil. & GBR.

3 **Roundspot surgeonfish** *Acanthurus bariene* Lesson 50 cm
Lg. indiv. with higly convex foreheads extending beyond mouth (also in *A. leucocheilus, A. maculiceps, A. nigricauda*). **Ecology:** clear seaward reef slopes below 15 m, usually below 30 m. Solitary or in pairs. Feeds on algal film of bare rock. Juvs. in shallow protected reefs between soft corals, 0.2 to 3 m. **Range:** Maldives to Sol. Is., n. to Andaman Sea & Ryuk., s. to GBR.

4 **Bluelined surgeonfish** *Acanthurus nubilus* (Fowler & Bean) 26 cm
Upper and lower head profile symmetrical; lavender spots and stripes on head & sides, resp. **Ecology:** steep current-swept dropoffs, 25 to 90 m. Feeds on zooplankton. Rare. **Range:** E. Africa to Pitcairn Is., n. to Phil. & Marianas, s. to N. Cal. & Austral Is.

5 **Palelipped surgeonfish** *Acanthurus leucocheilus* Herre ca.40 cm
Ecology: clear seaward reefs, usually near dropoffs, 4 to 30 m. In E. Africa common over deep offshore banks with little coral growth. White chin band prominent during displays. **Range:** E. Africa to Seychelles, Andaman Sea, Indonesia, Phil., Palau & Line Is.

6 **Finelined surgeonfish** *Acanthurus grammoptilus* Richardson 35 cm
Outer P rays yellowish. **Ecology:** silty coastal reefs. **Range:** Phil. to nw. Australia & inner GBR.

7 **Whitefin surgeonfish** *Acanthurus albipectoralis* Allen & Ayling 33 cm
Ecology: steep seaward reef escarpments, 5 to 20 m. Usually in small aggregations that feed on zooplankton well above the botom. **Range:** GBR and Coral Sea to Tonga.

Subfamily Prionurinae (Sawtails): three or more pairs of fixed keel-like bony plates at base of tail. Primarily warm-temperate.

8 **Yellowspotted sawtail** *Prionurus maculatus* Ogilby 45 cm
Ecology: along rocky shores. Juveniles in estuaries and bays. Feeds on benthic algae. **Range:** NSW & L. Howe Is. n. to s. Queensland & s. GBR.

9 **Sixplate sawtail** *Prionurus microlepidotus* Lacépède 70 cm
Ecology: along rocky shores. Juveniles in estuaries and bays. Feeds on benthic algae. **Range:** NSW to n. Queensland.

10 **Scalpel sawtail** *Prionurus scalprus* Valenciennes 50 cm
Ecology: shallow, surgy rocky areas. Often in groups. **Range:** Taiwan to s. Korea & c. Japan.

11 **Yellowtail sawtail** *Prionurus* sp. ca. 50 cm
Ecology: shallow surgy areas subject to upwelling (temp us. 23°C). Solitary or in small groups. **Range:** e. Bali; probably also at upwelling areas of neighbouring islands.

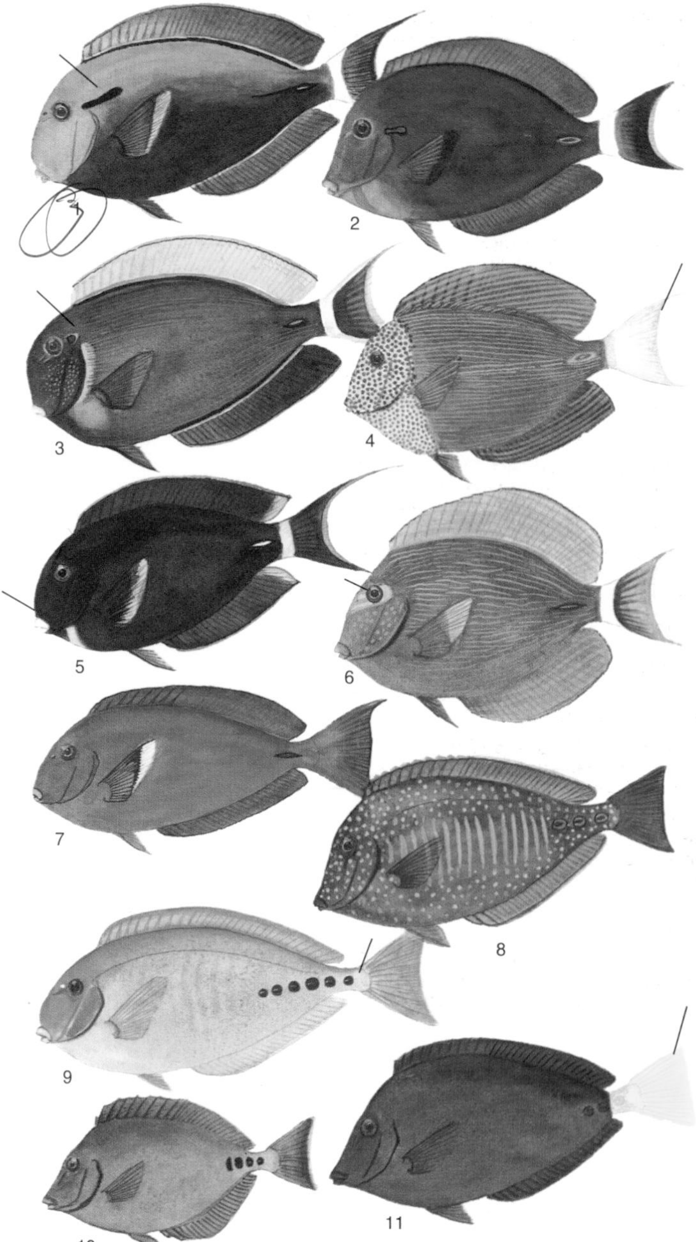
1
2
3
4
5
6
7
8
9
10
11

Subfamily Nasinae (Unicornfishes): rarely one, usually two pairs of fixed keel-like bony plates at base of tail.

1 **Orangespine unicornfish** *Naso lituratus* (Bloch & Schneider) 30 cm FL. Pacific popul. with mostly black D fin and dark gray tail with orange margin. **Ecology:** lagoon and seaward reefs, 0 to 90 m. In open sandy and rubbly areas as well as coral-rich areas. Feeds on leafy algae. Common. **Range:** R. Sea & S. Africa to Hawaiian, Marq. & Tuam. Is., n. to s. Japan, s. to s. GBR, N. Cal. & Rapa.

2 **Bignose unicornfish** *Naso vlamingi* (Valenciennes) 50 cm FL
Ecology: deep lagoon and seaward reefs, 4 to 50 m. Usually in mid-water aggregations near reef slopes where it feeds on zooplankton. Common around wrecks. Can instantly turn on or off brilliant blue markings. Males particularly colorful during courtship. **Range:** E. Africa to Line, Marq & Tuam. Is., n. to s. Japan, s. to s. GBR & N. Cal. Galapagos (rare).

3 **Bluespine unicornfish** *Naso unicornis* (Forrskål) 70 cm FL
Ecology: lagoon and seaward reefs, 1 to 80 m.Common in exposed surgy areas. Usually in groups. Feeds primarily on leafy brown algae. Common. **Range:** R. Sea to Hawaiian, Marq. & Tuam. Is., n. to s. Japan, s. to L. Howe & Rapa Is.

4 **Horseface unicornfish** *Naso fageni* Morrow 80 cm FL
Ad. ♂ may develop protruding snout; white ring around tail base not always present. **Ecology:** coral and rocky reefs, 3 to 35 m. In small groups in open water near reefs. Sometimes schools with *N. annulatus*. Probably feeds on zooplankton. Uncommon to rare. **Range:** E. Africa, Ald., Seychelles, Phil., nw. Australia, Ryuk. & s. Japan (juv.).

5 **Singlespine unicornfish** *N. thynnoides* (Valenciennes) 40 cm, us. 25 cm FL
Single pair of forward-curving caudal keels. **Ecology:** along steep outer lagoon and seaward reef slopes, 2 to 30 m. Solitary or in large schools. Common in Maldives, but generally uncommon elsewhere. **Range:** E. Africa to PNG., n. to s. Japan.

6 **Spotted unicornfish** *Naso brevirostris* (Valenciennes) 60 cm FL
Ecology: steep outer lagoon and seaward reef slopes, 4 to 46 m. Juveniles feed on benthic algae, adults feed on zooplankton. **Range:** R. Sea & S. Africa to Hawaiian, Marq. & Ducie Is., n. to s. Japan, s. to L. Howe Is. Galapagos (rare).

7 **Whitemargin unicornfish** *Naso annulatus* (Quoy & Gaimard) >100 cm FL
Ecology: juveniles in clear lagoons as shallow as 1 m, adults usually below 25 m along steep, current-swept dropoffs. Feeds on zooplankton. **Range:** E. Africa to Hawaiian, Marq. & Tuam. Is., n. to s. Japan, s. to L. Howe Is.

8 **Humpback unicornfish** *Naso brachycentron* (Valenciennes) 90 cm FL
Ecology: seaward reef slopes. Uncommon to rare. **Range:** E. Africa to Marq. & Society Is., n. to Ryuk., s. to Vanuatu.

9 **Humpnose unicornfish** *Naso tuberosus* Lacépède 60 cm FL
Ecology: clear seaward reefs, 3 to 20 m. Usually in groups, probably feeds on fleshy algae. Uncommon. **Range:** E. Africa to Gilbert & Samoan Is., n. to Ryuk., s. to s. GBR & N. Cal.

10 **Blacktongue unicornfish** *Naso hexacanthus* (Bleeker) 75 cm FL
Lg. ♂ have forward-pointing caudal blades, a black tongue & often dark opercular & preopercular margins. Very closely resembles *N. caesius* (Marianas & GBR to Hawaiian & Pitcairn Is.) which has rounded caudal blades, a white tongue & often displays light oval blotches on its sides. **Ecology:** clear lagoon and seaward reef slopes, 6 to 137 m. Feeds on larger zooplankton. Sometimes schools with *N. caesius*. **Range:** R. Sea & E. Africa to Hawaiian, Marq. & Ducie Is., n. to s. Japan, s. to L. Howe Is.

11 **Elongate unicornfish** *Naso lopezi* Herre 54 cm FL
Spotting variable, sometimes indistinct. *N. maculatus* similar but with deeper body. **Ecology:** steep outer reef dropoffs below 6 m, usually deeper. Uncommon. **Range:** Andaman Sea, w. Indonesia, Phil., Ryuk. & Palau.

12 **Spotted unicornfish** *Naso maculatus* Randall & Struhsaker 60 cm
Ecology: deep seaward reefs, 43 to 100 m. **Range:** s. Japan; Hawaiian Is.

1
2
3
4
5
6
7
8
9
10
11
12

129 RABBITFISHES

RABBITFISHES (SIGANIDAE): deep-bodied compressed fishes with venomous fin spines, a small terminal mouth with small close-set incisiform teeth, complete lateral line, and minute scales. All species have XIII, 10 D rays preceded by an embedded forward projecting spine, VII, 9 A rays, and V fins with an inner and outer spine and 3 soft rays. Wounds from the spines are extremely painful, but usually not dangerous. All are diurnal herbivores that feed on benthic algae. Some occur in schools, others as pairs. Important foodfishes, some of the colorful species popular in aquariums.

1 **Foxface rabbitfish** *Siganus vulpinus* (Schlegel & Müller) 24 cm
The similar *S. unimaculatus* (e. Phil. to Taiwan, Ryuk. & Bonins; nw. Aust. shelf) differs only by having a black spot on ea. side beneath the soft A fin and may possibly be only a variant of this species. Rare individuals may have the spot on only one side. **Ecology:** coral-rich areas of lagoon and seaward reefs to 30 m. Juveniles in schools among branching corals, adults usually paired. **Range:** Sumatra to Vanuatu & Gilbert Is., n. to Paracell Is. & Phil., s. to s. GBR & N. Cal.

2 **Uspi rabbitfish** *Siganus uspi* Gawel & Woodland 24 cm
Another sp., *S. niger* (Tonga) is entirely black. **Ecology:** coral-rich areas of lagoon and seaward reefs to 6 m. Adults in pairs among corals. Uncommon at Fiji, strays to New Caledonia. **Range:** Fiji & N. Cal.

3 **Magnificent rabbitfish** *Siganus magnificus* (Burgess) 23 cm
Ecology: protected open areas of coral reefs, 2 to 20 m. Adults paired. **Range:** Similan Is. & w. Thail.

4 **Forktail rabbitfish** *Siganus argenteus* (Quoy & Gaimard) 37 42 cm
Ecology: areas of mixed coral and rubble or bare rock of lagoon and seaward reefs to >30 m. Usually in large roving schools. **Range:** R. Sea to Marq. & Tuam. Is., n. to s. Japan, s. to GBR, N. Cal. & Rapa.

5 **Dusky rabbitfish** *Siganus fuscescens* (Houttuyn) 40 cm
Very similar to *S. canaliculatus* and *S. sutor*. **Ecology:** algal and seagrass flats and shallow lagoon and coastal reefs. Usually in schools. Juveniles feed on filamentous algae, adults feed on leafy algae and seagrasses. **Range:** Andaman Is. to Vanuatu & N. Cal., n. to s. Korea & s. Japan, s. to Perth & NSW.

6 **Rivulated rabbitfish** *Siganus rivulatus* (Forsskål) 30 cm
Ecology: inshore areas and inner reefs, particularly in weedy or seagrass areas. **Range:** R. Sea & G. Aden; recently established in e. Mediterranean Sea via Suez Canal.

7 **Whitespotted rabbitfish** *Siganus canaliculatus* (Park) 29 cm
Ecology: turbid inshore areas and inner reefs, particularly near river mouths. **Range:** Arab. G. to Irian Jaya, n. to s. China & Taiwan, s. to nw. Australia.

8 **Squaretail rabbitfish** *Siganus luridus* (Rüppell) 25 cm
Ecology: rock and rubble areas of shallow inshore reefs, 2 to 18 m. Usually in groups, occasionally solitary. **Range:** R. Sea to Mozambique, Réunion & Maurit.; recently migrated to e. Mediterranean.

9 **African Whitespotted rabbitfish** *Siganus sutor* (Valenciennes) >50 cm
Ecology: inshore areas and inner reefs, particularly in seagrass beds and weedy areas. **Range:** G. Aden & E. Africa s. to S. Africa, e. to Seychelles, Réunion & Rodriguez.

10 **Scribbled rabbitfish** *Siganus spinus* (Linnaeus) 28 cm
Ecology: reef flats and shallow lagoon reefs. Usually in schools in seagrass beds and areas of mixed coral, rubble, and sand. **Range:** s. India to Society Is, n. to s. Japan, s. to nw. Aust. & GBR.

11 **Java rabbitfish** *Siganus javus* (Linnaeus) 53 cm
Ecology: silty coastal coral and rocky reefs, 0.5 to 18 m. Enters brackish water. Solitary or in small groups. **Range:** Arab. G. to Vanuatu, n. to Hainan & Phil., s. to n. Queensland.

12 **Vermiculate rabbitfish** *Siganus vermiculatus* (Valenciennes) 45 cm
Ecology: juveniles among mangroves, adults on inner lagoon and coastal reefs. In schools. **Range:** w. India to Fiji, n. to Phil., Palau & Guam, s. to n. GBR.

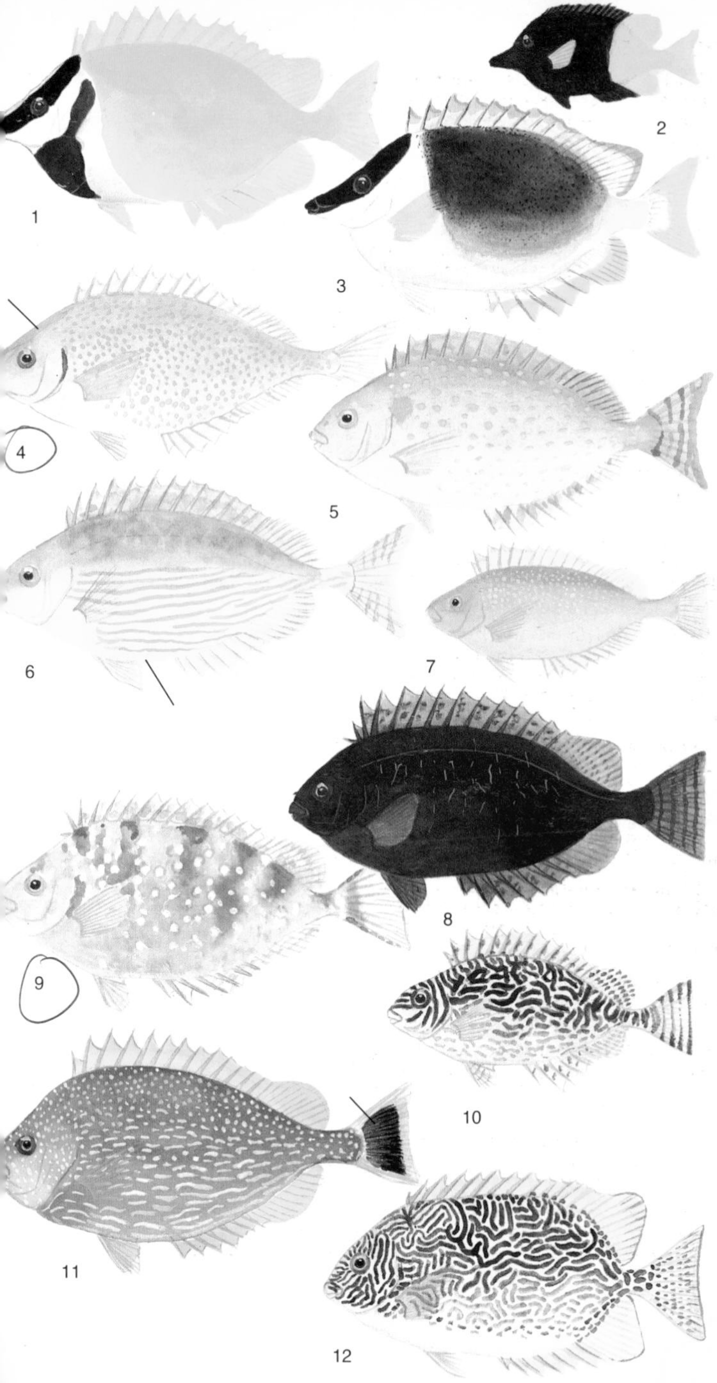
1
2
3
4
5
6
7
8
9
10
11
12

1 **Coral rabbitfish** *Siganus corallinus* Valenciennes 28 cm
Ecology: coral-rich areas of shallow lagoon and seaward reefs. Juveniles in small groups among seagrasses or corals, adults usually paired. **Range:** Seychelles to PNG, n. to Ryuk., s. to s,. GBR & N. Cal.

2 **Threeblotched rabbitfish** *Siganus trispilos* Woodland & Allen 25 cm
Ecology: coral-rich areas to 5 m. Adults usually among corals and paired. **Range:** nw. Australian coastal and offshore reefs.

3 **Goldspotted rabbitfish** *Siganus punctatus* (Forster) 40 cm
Often darker in many areas. **Ecology:** clear lagoon and seaward reefs, 1 to 40 m. Adults paired. **Range:** Cocos-Keeling & w. Sumatra to Samoa, n. to Ryuk. & Bonin Is., s. to Perth, NSW & N. Cal.

4 **Virgate rabbitfish** *Siganus virgatus* (Valenciennes) 30 cm
Similar to *S. doliatus*, but has paler sides with indistinct lines and spots. **Ecology:** coastal rocky and coral reefs, may enter fresh water. Adults usually paired. **Range:** sw. India to Irian Jaya, n. to Ryuk. s. to n. Aust.

5 **Masked rabbitfish** *Siganus puellus* (Schlegell) 38 cm
Closely related to *S. puelloides* which lacks or has an indistinct band through the eye. **Ecology:** coral-rich areas of lagoon and seaward reefs, 1 to 30 m. Adults feed on algae, tunicates, and sponges. Usually paired. **Range:** Cocos-Keeling Is. & S. China Sea to Gilbert Is., n. to Ryuk., s. to s. GBR & N. Cal.

6 **Pencil-streaked rabbitfish** *Siganus doliatus* Cuvier 24 cm
Ecology: coral-rich areas of lagoons and channels. Often in pairs. **Range:** Sulawesi to e. Caroline Is. & Tonga, n. to Yap, s. to nw. Aust., s. GBR & N. Cal.

7 **Golden rabbitfish** *Siganus guttatus* (Bloch) 42 cm
Ecology: inner lagoon and coastal reefs, among mangroves, and in brackish waters. Usually in large schools. **Range:** Andaman Is. to w. N. Guinea, n. to Ryuk., s. to Java.

8 **Lined rabbitfish** *Siganus lineatus* (Valenciennes) 43 cm
Ecology: juveniles in small schools among mangroves. Adults in groups on protected coastal and lagoon reefs. Adults feed on sponges as well as algae. **Range:** Maldives, Laccadives & Sri Lanka to Vanuatu, n. to Bonin Is., s. to GBR & N. Cal.

9 **Peppered rabbitfish** *Siganus punctatissimus* Fowler & Bean 30 cm
Ecology: lagoon and channel reefs, 12 to 30 m. Usually paired. **Range:** Phil. to PNG, n. to Yaeyamas, s. to nw. Aust. shelf reefs & GBR; Palau.

10 **Stellate rabbitfish** *Siganus stellatus* (Forsskål) 35 cm
Fish outside R. Sea are fully spotted on nape & upper back & yellow areas of fins are paler. **Ecology:** clear lagoon and seaward reefs, 1 to 27 m. Usually paired. **Range:** R. Sea (ssp. *laqueus*) s. to Mozambique, e. to Singapore & Bali, n. to Andaman Sea.

11 **Blackeye rabbitfish** *Siganus puelloides* Woodland & Randall 31 cm
Closely related to *S. puellus* which has a distinct band through the eye. **Ecology:** coral-rich areas of lagoon and seaward reefs, 1 to 30 m. Adults feed on algae, tunicates, and sponges. Usually paired. **Range:** Maldives & Similan Is. (Andaman Sea).

12 **Randall 's rabbitfish** *Siganus Randall i* Woodland 30 cm
Ecology: shallow inner lagoon and coastal reefs to over 18 m. Juveniles among mangroves, adults on coral reefs. Generally in groups. **Range:** PNG, Sol. Is., Guam & Pohnpei.

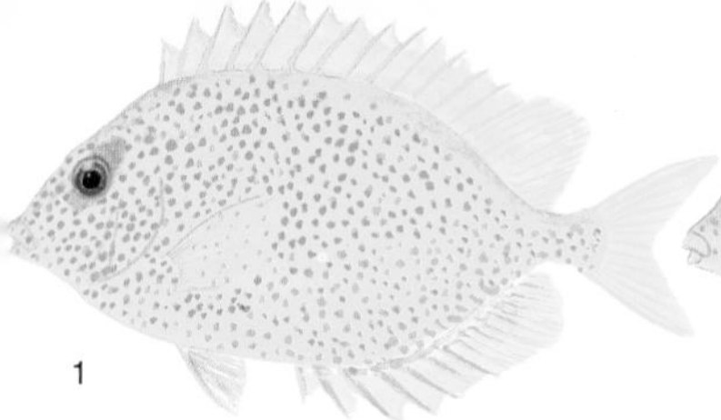

1

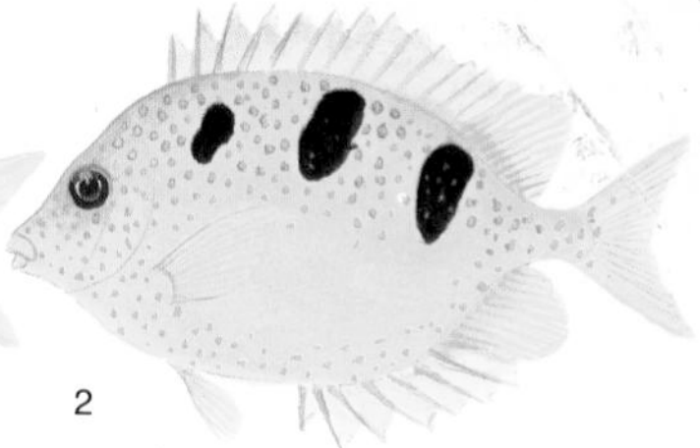

2

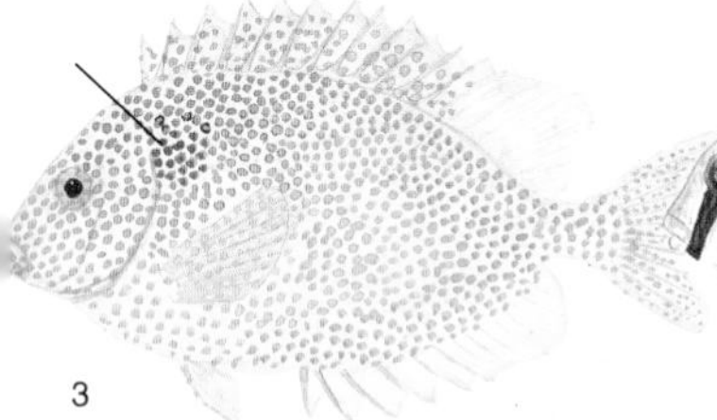

3

4

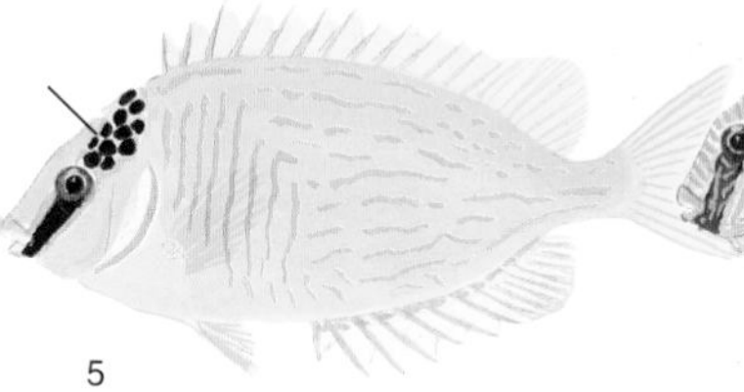

5

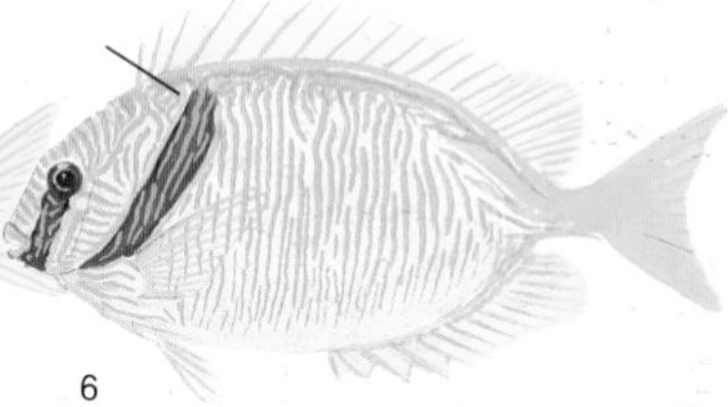

6

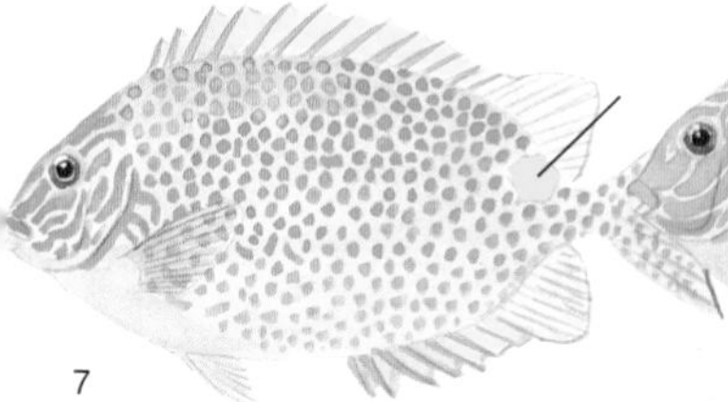

7

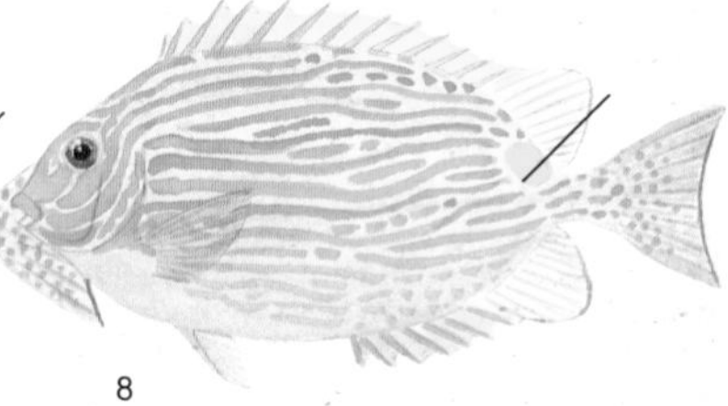

8

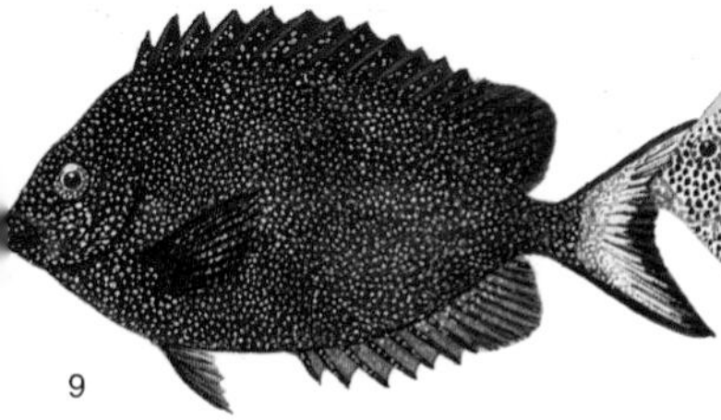

9

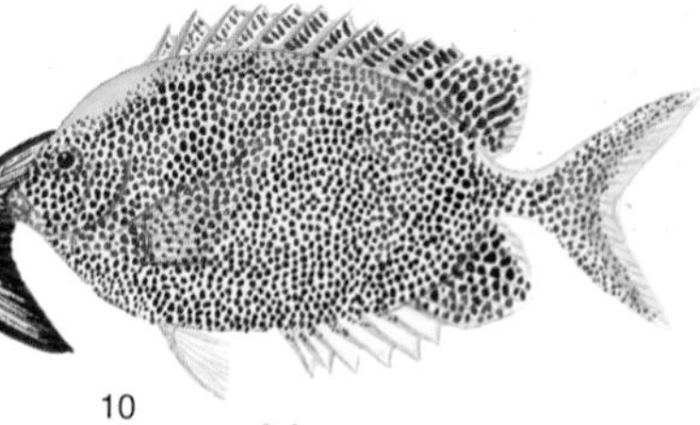

10

11

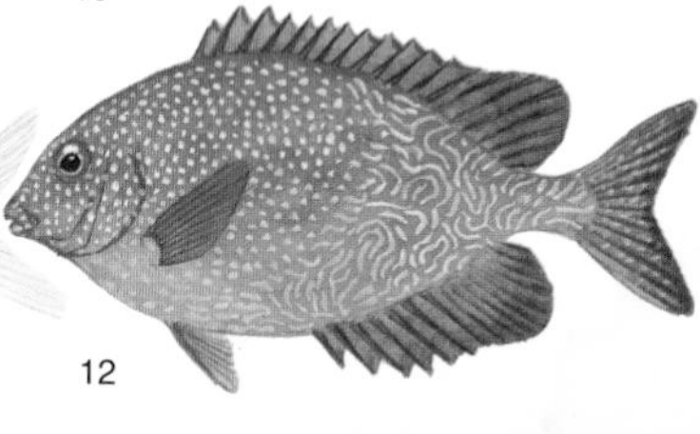

12

TUNAS, FLOUNDERS, and SOLES

TUNAS and MACKERELS (SCOMBRIDAE): medium to large silvery fusiform fishes with 2 D fins, several detached finlets behind D and A fins, deeply forked tail two or more peduncular keels and a simple lateral line. Primarily swift predators of open seas. Among the most important of commercial and recreational sport fishes. Some of the smaller species strain zooplankton through their gill rakers. Few species on coral reefs.

1 **Narrow-barred king mackerel** *Scomberomorus commerson* (Lacépède) 235 cm
Ecology: mid-water along steep lagoon and seaward reef slopes. **Range:** R. Sea to Fiji, n. to Korea & sw. Japan, s. to NSW & L. Howe Is.

2 **Dogtooth tuna** *Gymnosarda unicolor* (Rüppell) 220 cm; 131 kg; us. 190 cm
Ecology: mid-water along steep lagoon and seaward reef slopes, surface to 100 m. A voracious predator of fishes, particularly planktivores. Large ones occasionally ciguatoxic. **Range:** R. Sea to Samoa, n. to s. Korea & s. Japan, s. to N. Cal. & Rapa.

3 **Double-lined mackerel** *Grammatorcynos bilineatus* (Rüppell) 70 cm
Ecology: near surface inshore and offshore waters, occasionally over coral reefs. **Range:** R. Sea to Samoa, n. to Ryuk., s. to nw. Aust. shelf reefs, GBR & Tonga.

4 **Striped mackerel** *Rastrelliger kanagurta* (Cuvier) 38 cm
Ecology: coastal and lagoon waters In large schools. Strains plankton through gill rakers. **Range:** R. Sea to Samoa, n. to Ryuk., s. to nw. Aust. shelf reefs & GBR.

ORDER FLATFISHES (PLEURONECTIFORMES): highly compressed fishes designed for living with one side flat against the bottom. Both eyes are located on the upper pigmented side and the other side is unpigmented. The pigmented side is capable of remarkable color changes in order to match the bottom. Predators of benthic invertebrates and fishes.

LEFTEYE FLOUNDERS (BOTHIDAE): both eyes on left side. Over 200 spp., few on reefs.

5 **Peacock flounder** *Bothus mancus* (Broussonet) 42 cm
Similar to *B. pantherhines*, but eyes not vertically aligned. Males with elongate upper P rays and wider space between eyes. **Ecology:** sandy bottoms of lagoon and seaward reefs, shoreline to 84 m. **Range:** R. Sea to Mexico, n. to Ryuk. & Hawaiian Is., s. toL. Howe, Rapa & Ducie Is.

6 **Leopard flounder** *Bothus pantherhines* (Rüppell) 39 cm
Ecology: sandy bottoms of lagoon and seaward reefs, shoreline to 110 m. **Range:** R. Sea to Hawaiian, Marq. & Society Is., n. to s. Japan, s. to L. Howe Is.

RIGHTEYE FLOUNDERS (PLEURONECTIDAE): similar to Bothidae but both eyes on right side.

7 **Threespot flounder** *Samariscus triocellatus* Woods 9 cm
Ecology: lagoon and sewward reefs, 5 to 30 m. Usually in caves or under ledges, can lie flat on vertical rock surfaces. **Range:** E. Africa to Hawaiian, Marq. & Society Is., n. to Taiwan, s. to GBR.

SOLES (SOLEIDAE): eyes on right side, head rounded with inferior mouth, and tubular snout. Some species lack P fins. Over 100 species, only a few on coral reefs. Secretes a bitter toxic substance from bases of D and A fin rays that deters predation.

8 **Peacock sole** *Pardachirus pavoninus* (Lacépède) 25 cm
Ecology: secretes a bitter toxic substance from bases of D and A fin rays that deters predation, even by sharks. Sandy bottoms of lagoon and seaward reefs, 3 to 40 m. **Range:** Sri Lanka to Samoa, n. to s. Japan, s. to NSW & Tonga.

9 **Moses sole** *Pardachirus marmoratus* (Lacépède) 26 cm
Ecology: shallow sandy areas near reefs to 15 m. Secretes a toxin as does *P. pavoninus*. **Range:** R. Sea to Sri Lanka, s. to Durban.

10 **Zebra sole** *Zebrias zebra* (Schneider) 19 cm
Ecology: sand or mud bottoms to at least 100 m. **Range:** Arab. G to PNG, n. to c. Japan, s. to Queensland.

11 **Unicorn sole** *Aesopia cornuta* Kaup 22 cm
Ecology: sand or mud bottoms to at least 100 m. **Range:** R. Sea to Indonesia, n. to Arab. G. & s. Japan, s. to n. Austr.

12 **Banded sole** *Soleichthys heterorhinos* (Bleeker) 15 cm
Ecology: shallow protected sandy areas near reefs. Usually buried with only eyes & nostril exposed. More active at night. Can move extremely rapidly when disturbed. **Range:** R. Sea to Samoa, n. to s. Japan, s. to NSW.

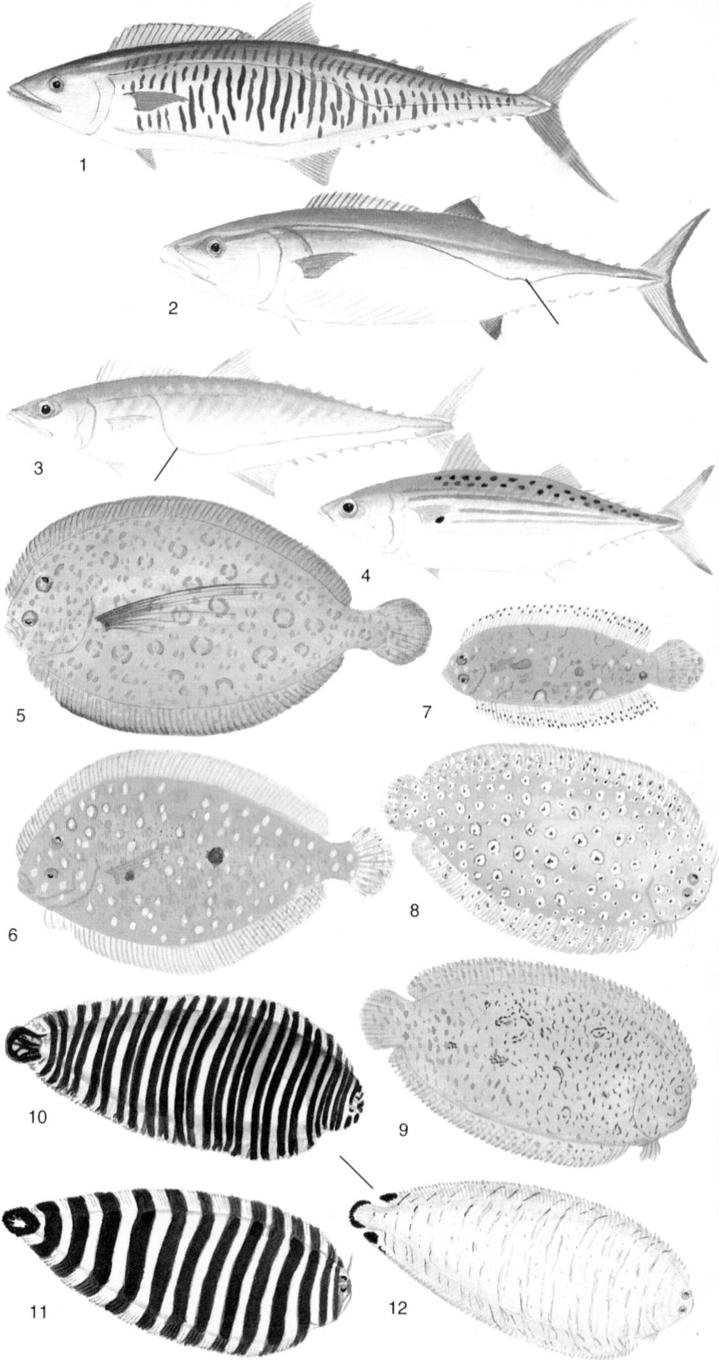
1
2
3
4
5
7
6
8
10
9
11
12

TRIGGERFISHES (BALISTIDAE): somewhat deep-bodied, compressed fishes with eyes set high on head, a small terminal mouth with large stout incisiform teeth, the first D fin with a large spike-like first spine and two smaller spines, all of which fit into a groove, second D and A fins with only rays, pelvic fin reduced to a spinous knob, and large non-overlapping armor-like scales. The first D spine locks into position and can be released only by depressing the second "trigger" spine. Most species feed on a wide variety of invertebrates, some also feed on algae or zooplankton. Triggerfishes lay demersal eggs in a sandy depression, guarded by the male. Some of the larger species will attack and bite divers during nesting. Popular in aquariums, but often ill-tempered. See pl. 173-6 for *Canthidermis maculatus*.

1 **Redtooth triggerfish** *Odonus niger* (Rüppell) 40 cm
Ecology: current-swept seaward reefs, 2 to 35 m. Usually in aggregations high in water. Feeds primarily on plankton, occasionally on sponges. When frightened they retreat into holes leaving only tail filaments visible. **Range:** R. Sea to Marq. & Soc. Is., n. to s. Japan, s. to GBR & N. Cal.

2 **Black triggerfish** *Melichthys niger* (Bloch) 35 cm
Ecology: clear seaward reefs, 0 to 75 m. Feeds on zooplankton and detached algae. Uncommon in most areas, but superabundant at certain isolated mid-oceanic islands. **Range:** all tropical seas; abundant at isolated oceanic islands.

3 **Pinktail triggerfish** *Melichthys vidua* (Solander) 35 cm
Ecology: clear seaward reefs, 4 to >60 m. Feeds on algae, invertebrates, and fishes. **Range:** E. Africa to Hawaiian, Marq. & Tuam. Is., n. to s. Japan, s. to GBR & N. Cal.

4 **Indian triggerfish** *Melichthys indicus* Randall & Klausewitz 24 cm
Ecology: coral-rich seaward reef slopes, 2 to 30 m. Solitary. **Range:** s. R. Sea, G. Aden & E. Africa to w. Thail. & Sumatra.

5 **Yellowmargin triggerfish** *Pseudobalistes flavimarginatus* (Rüppell) 60 cm
Ecology: deep lagoons, channels, and shelteR. Seaward reefs, 2 to 50 m. Feeds on corals, benthic invertebrates, and tunicates. Nests in sand channels and cuts. Common in R. Sea. **Range:** R. Sea to Tuam., n. to s. Japan, s. to GBR & Samoa.

6 **Blue or rippled triggerfish** *Pseudobalistes fuscus* (Bloch & Schneider) 55 cm
Ecology: clear lagoon and seaward reefs, 0.5 to 50 m. Prefers sandy and rubbly areas at bases of reefs. Common in R. Sea, uncommon in Pacific. **Range:** R. Sea to Society Is., n. to s. Japan, s. to GBR & N. Cal.

7 **Guilded triggerfish** *Xanthichthys auromarginatus* (Bennett) 22 cm
Females without blue throat and yellow fin margins. **Ecology:** steep seaward reefs, 8 to 147 m. Prefers upper edges of dropoffs, rarely in less than 20 m. In small aggregations. Feeds on zooplankton. **Range:** Maurit. to Hawaiian Is., n. to Ryuk., s. to N. Cal.; absent from continental shores.

8 **Lined triggerfish** *Xanthichthys lineopunctatus* (Hollard) 30 cm
Ecology: offshore reefs, often high above the bottom. Rare. **Range:** se. Africa, Maurit. & Réunion; nw. Austr; Ryuk. & Bonin Is.

9 **Crosshatch triggerfish** *Xanthichthys mento* (Jordan & Gilbert) 29 cm
Females lack the red tail of males. Similar to *X. caeruleolineatus* (Cocos-Keeling to c. America) has distinctive lateral blue line. **Ecology:** seaward reefs above dropoffs, 10 to 100 m. In aggregations. Although shallow at Wake Is. and e. Pacific, always below 39 m and normally at 90 m in Hawaii. **Range:** Primarily subtropical oceanic islands: s. Japan & Ryuk., Izu, Marcus, Wake, Hawaiian, Revillagigedo, Clipperton, Rapa, Pitcairn & Easter Is.; s. Calif.

10 **Starry triggerfish** *Abalistes stellatus* (Lacépède) 60 cm
Ecology: muddy to sandy bottoms, 4 to 120 m. Adults occasionally near reefs, juveniles on isolated patch reefs. **Range:** R. Sea to Fiji, n. to s. Japan, s. to NSW & N. Cal.

11 **Bridled triggerfish** *Sufflamen fraenatus* (Latreille) 38 cm
Ecology: seaward reefs, 8 to 186 m. Common in open areas with patches of sand and rubble below 18 m. Feeds primarily on wide variety of benthic invertebrates as well as fishes and algae. **Range:** E. Africa to Hawaiian, Marq. & Tuam. Is., n. to s. Japan, s. to L. Howe Is.

1
2
3
4
6 juv
5
6
♂
7
8
9
♂
10
11

133 TRIGGERFISHES

1 **Halfmoon triggerfish** *Sufflamen chrysopterus* (Bloch & Schneider) 30 cm
Juvs. dark brown above, white below. Similar to *S. albicaudatus* but has dark tail base. **Ecology:** shallow lagoon and seaward reefs to 30 m. Common over open bottoms with low scattered corals. **Range:** E. Africa to Samoa, n. to s. Japan, s. to L. Howe Is.

2 **Bluethroat triggerfish** *Sufflamen albicaudatus* (Rüppell) 22 cm
Similar to *S. chrysopterus* but has light zone across base of tail. **Ecology:** open bottoms with low scattered corals or rubble, 2 to 20 m. Wary. **Range:** R. Sea to G. Oman.

3 **Scythe triggerfish** *Sufflamen bursa* (Bloch & Schneider) 24 cm
Ecology: outer reef slopes below the surge zone, 3 to 90 m. Prefers areas with abundant shelter. Feeds on a wide variety of benthic invertebrates and algae. **Range:** E. Africa to Hawaiian, Marq. & Ducie Is., n. to s. Japan, s. to GBR, N. Cal. & Rapa.

4 **Clown triggerfish** *Balistoides conspicillum* (Bloch & Schneider) 50 cm
Ecology: clear seaward reefs, 1 to 75 m. Juveniles in caves below 20 m along steep dropoffs, adults often on coral-rich terraces near steep slopes. Solitary, uncommon. **Range:** E. Africa to Samoa, n. to s. Japan, s. to L. Howe Is.

5 **Orangestriped triggerfish** *Balistapus undulatus* (Park) 30 cm
Mature ♂ loose most of the orange lines on the snout. **Ecology:** coral-rich areas of lagoon and seaward reefs, 2 to 50 m. Feeds on wide variety of animals includiing corals, sponges, worms, echinoderms, crustaceans, and fishes. **Range:** R. Sea to Line, Marq. & Tuam. Is., n. to s.Japan, s. to GBR & N. Cal.

6 **Moustache triggerfish** *Balistoides viridescens* (Bloch & Schneider) 75 cm
Ecology: lagoon and seaward reefs, 1 to ~40 m. Juveniles usually in shallow sandy protected areas. Adults solitary or in pairs. Feeds on corals, benthic invertebrates, particularly hard-bodied forms, and algae. Normally wary, but will attack divers when guarding a nest. Severe bites may require medical attention. Occasionally ciguatoxic. **Range:** R. Sea to Line & Tuam. Is., n. to s. Japan, s. to NSW & N. Cal.

7 **Wedge picassofish** *Rhinecanthus rectangulus* (Bloch & Schneider) 30 cm
Ecology: outer reef flats and shallow seaward reefs subject to surge, 0.5 to 18 m. Common in areas of mixed bare rock, rubble, coral, and sand. Wary. **Range:** R. Sea to Hawaiian, Marq. & Ducie Is., n. to Izu Is., s. to L. Howe & Kermadec Is.

8 **Picassofish; Humuhumu** *Rhinecanthus aculeatus* (Linnaeus) 25 cm
Ecology: reef flats and shallow lagoons to 4 m. Abundant in sandy areas with rubble. All species in the genus feed on a wide variety of benthic invertebrates, fishes, and algae. **Range:** E. Africa to Hawaiian, Marq. & Tuam. Is., n. to s. Japan, s. to L. Howe Is.

9 **Blackbelly picassofish** *Rhinecanthus verrucosus* (Linnaeus) 23 cm
Ecology: subtidal reef flats and protected lagoon and coastal reefs, 0.3 to 20 m. Common in areas of rubble and coral among seagrasses. **Range:** Seychelles & Chagos Is. & Sri Lanka to Sol. Is. & Vanuatu, n. to s. Japan, s. to GBR.

10 **Arabian picassofish** *Rhinecanthus assasi* (Forsskål) 30 cm
Ecology: shallow sandy and rubbly areas of coral reefs. Juveniles common on reef flats where they may shelter in empty shells. **Range:** R. Sea to G. Oman & Arab. Gulf.

11 **Halfmoon picassofish** *Rhinecanthus lunula* Randall & Steene 28 cm
Similar to *R. cinereus* (Andaman Sea, Mauritius), which has a broad yellow lateral band. **Ecology:** seaward reefs below 10 m. **Range:** GBR, N. Cal., Samoa, Society & Tuam. Is. & Pitcairn Group.

1
2
3
4
4 juv
5
♀
6
6 juv
7
8
9
10
11

FILEFISHES and LEATHERJACKETS (MONACANTHIDAE): closely related to triggerfishes but have more compressed bodies, one or two D spines (the second minute), and much smaller scales, each with setae giving the skin a file-like texture. Most species feed on a wide variety of invertebrates, but some specialize on corals or zooplankton. Filefishes lay demersal eggs in a site prepared by the male.

1 **Broom filefish** *Amanses scopas* (Cuvier) 20 cm
Males with patch of long spines posteriorly on sides, females with brush-like setae. **Ecology:** areas of mixed sand, rubble, and coral on semi-protected seaward reefs, 3 to 18 m. Less approachable than most filefishes. **Range:** R. Sea to Tuam., n. to s. Japan, s. to GBR.

2 **Barred filefish** *Cantherhines dumerilii* (Hollard) 38 cm
Ecology: clear lagoon and seaward reefs, 0.5 to 35 m. Usually paired. Feeds primarily on tips of branching corals, occasionally on benthic invertebrates and algae. **Range:** E. Africa to Mexico, n. to s. Japan & Hawaiian Is., s. to L. Howe, Rapa & Ducie Is.

3 **Wire-net filefish** *Cantherhines pardalis* (Rüppell) 25 cm
Similar to *C. sandwichiensis* (Hawaiian Is.). **Ecology:** clear seaward reefs, 2 to 20 m. Solitary. Somewhat secretive. **Range:** R. Sea to Marq. & Ducie Is., n. to s. Japan, s. to L. Howe & Rapa Is.

4 **Specktacled filefish** *Cantherhines fronticintus* (Playfair & Günther) 23 cm
Similar to *C. longicaudus* (Society & Cook Is.), *C. rapanui* (Easter Is.) & *C. verecundus* (Hawaiian Is.). **Ecology:** seaward reefs, 1 to 43 m, usually below 25 m and close to shelter. Uncommon. **Range:** E. Africa to Marshall Is. & PNG, n. to s. Japan, s. to nw. Austr.

5 **Large-scaled leatherjacket** *Cantheschenia grandisquamis* Hutchins 26 cm
Ecology: sheltered coastal and offshore reefs. Uncommon. **Range:** s. GBR to n. NSW.

6 **Fantail filefish** *Pervagor spilosoma* (Lay & Bennett) 18 cm
Ecology: ubiquitous on lagoon and seaward reefs, 1 to 46 m. Feeds on algae, small benthic invertebrates, and corals. Common, in some years super abundant. **Range:** Hawaiian Is.

7 **Yelloweye filefish** *Pervagor alternans* (Ogilby) 16 cm
Ecology: coral-rich areas and rocky reefs to >15 m. Uncommon. **Range:** s. GBR to NSW, L. Howe Is. & N. Cal.; Marshall Is.

8 **Orangetail filefish** *Pervagor aspricaudus* (Hollard) 12 cm
Similar to *P. marginalis* (Line & Marq. Is.). **Ecology:** clear lagoon and seaward reefs, 1 to 25 m. Remains among corals or rubble. **Range:** Maurit.; Christmas Is.; Taiwan to s. Japan, Marcus, Marshall & Hawaiian Is.; n. GBR to N. Cal.

9 **Blackbar filefish** *Pervagor janthinosoma* (Bleeker) 14 cm
Ecology: shallow lagoon and seaward reefs to 20 m. Secretive. **Range:** E. Africa to Samoa, n. to s. Japan, s. to nw. Australia, NSW & Tonga.

10 **Blacklined filefish** *Pervagor nigrolineatus* (Herre) 10 cm
Ecology: lagoon and protected seaward reefs to 25 m. Secretive. **Range:** Sumatra to Sol. Is., n. to Phil., s. to nw. Aust. shelf reefs.

11 **Blackheaded filefish** *Pervagor melanocephalus* (Bleeker) 10 cm
Ecology: seaward reefs to 40 m. Usually below 20 m. Often in pairs. **Range:** Sumatra to Fiji & Tonga, n. to Ryuk., s. to GBR & Norfolk Is.

12 **Longnose filefish** *Oxymonacanthus longirostris* (Bloch & Schneider) 12 cm
Ecology: clear lagoon and seaward reefs, 1 to over 30 m, where *Acropora* corals are common. Feeds exclusively on *Acropora* polyps. Often in pairs or small groups. **Range:** E. Africa to Samoa, n. to Ryuk., s. to GBR, N. Cal. & Tonga.

13 **Red Sea longnose filefish** *Oxymonacanthus halli* Marshall 7 cm
Similar to *O. longirostris* but has elongate dark bar on tail instead of spot. **Ecology:** coral-rich fringing reefs. Closely associated with *Acropora* corals. Feeds exclusively on their polyps. **Range:** R. Sea.

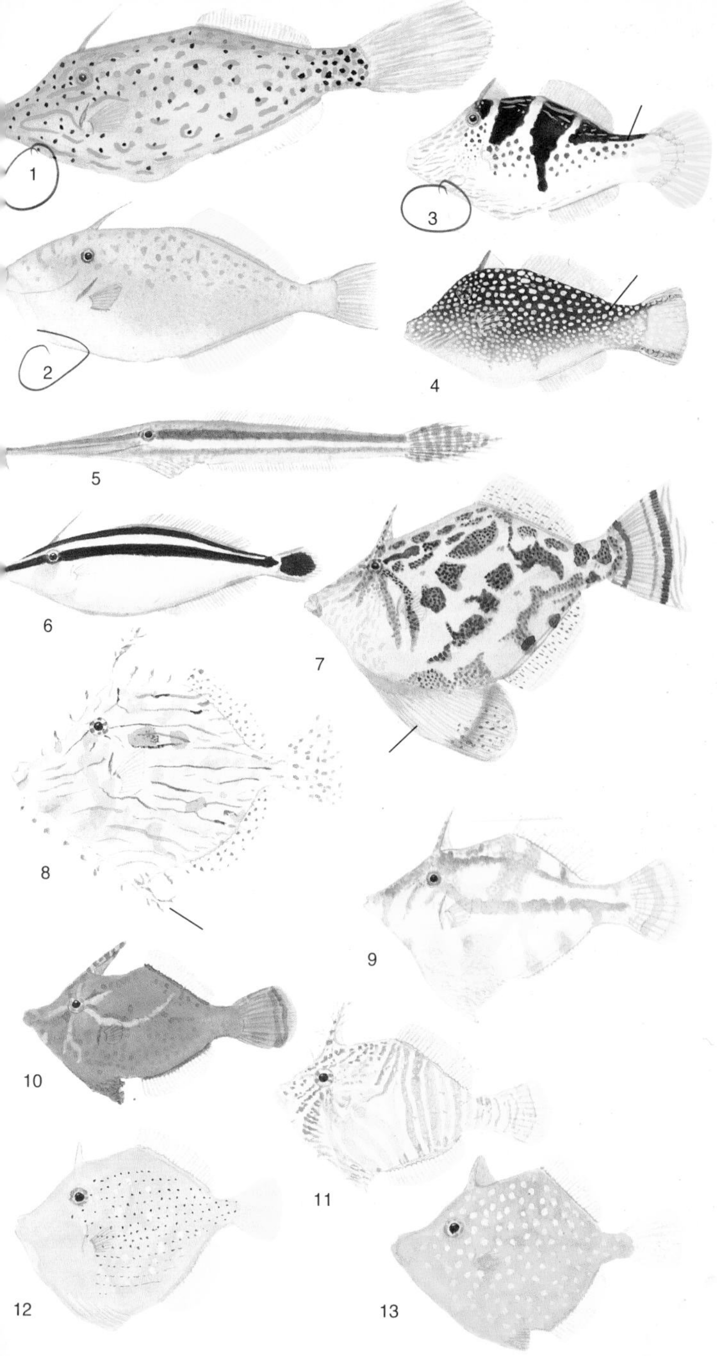
1
3
2
4
5
6
7
8
9
10
11
12
13

135 FILEFISHES

1 **Scribbled filefish** *Aluterus scriptus* (Osbeck) 110 cm
Ecology: lagoon and seaward reefs, 2 to 80 m. Solitary and uncommon in most areas. Feeds on wide variety of attached plants and animals. **Range:** All tropical and subtropical seas.

2 **Unicorn filefish** *Aluterus monoceros* (Linnaeus) 75 cm
Ecology: semi-pelagic, often around floating debris as well as around outermoast reef areas of isolated oceanic islands. Solitary and uncommon in most areas. **Range:** All tropical and subtropical seas.

3 **Blacksaddle mimic** *Paraluteres prionurus* (Bleeker) 10 cm
Ecology: clear lagoon and seaward reefs, 1 to 25 m. Solitary or in small groups. A remarkable mimic of the poisonous puffer *Canthigaster valentini.* **Range:** E. Africa to Marshall Is., n. to s. Japan, s. to GBR & N. Cal.

4 **Spotted puffer mimic** *Paraluteres* sp. 8 cm
Resembles *Canthigaster solandri* (pl. 137-7) which it mimics & *P. arquat* (R. Sea) which mimics *Canthigaster margaritata* (R. Sea). **Ecology:** coral reefs, 5 to 20 m. Mimics the poisonous puffer *Canthigaster solandri.* **Range:** Similan Is. & Phuket (Andaman Sea).

5 **Bearded filefish** *Anacanthus barbatus* Gray 35 cm
Ecology: coastal reefs in sandy weedy areas, enters mangroves. **Range:** w. India to Indonesia, s. to nw. Austr.

6 **Rhinoceros filefish** *Pseudalutarias nasicornis* (Temminck & Schlegel) 19 cm
Ecology: weedy and sandy areas of lagoon and seaward reefs, 1 to 55 m. Often paired. **Range:** E. Africa to PNG, n. to s. Japan, s. to NSW.

7 **Fan-bellied filefish** *Monacanthus chinensis* Osbeck 38 cm
Ecology: coastal rocky and coral reefs. **Range:** Malaysia & Indonesia to Samoa, n. to s. Japan, s. to nw. Austr. & NSW.

8 **Leafy filefish** *Chaetoderma penicilligera* (Cuvier) 31 cm
Ecology: weedy areas of coastal reefs. **Range:** Malaysia & Indonesia to nw. Australia & GBR, n. to s. Japan.

9 **Japanese filefish** *Paramonacanthus japonicus* (Tilesius) 10 cm
Ecology: weedy and sandy areas of coastal reefs. **Range:** E. Indies n. to s. Japan, s. to GBR.

10 **Seagrass filefish** *Acreichthys tomentosus* (Linnaeus) 10 cm
Similar to *A hajam* (E. Indies) & *A. radiatus* (w. Pacific). **Ecology:** sand and seagrass bottoms of protected reefs. **Range:** E. Africa to Fiji, n. to Ryuk., s. to NSW.

11 **Radial leatherjacket** *Acreichthys radiatus* (Popta) 7 cm
Ecology: among soft corals. **Range:** Indonesia, Phil, Ryuk., GBR & N. Cal.

12 **Japanese inflator filefish** *Brachaluteres ulvarum* Jordan & Snyder 7 cm
Brachaluteres spp. can inflate themselves like puffers. Similar to *B. fahaqa* (R. Sea), *B. taylori* (sw. Pac. & Marshall Is.) & *B. jacksonianus* (s. Austr.). **Ecology:** among bottom cover. **Range:** s. Japan (Sagami Bay to Misaki).

13 **Whitepotted pygmy filefish** *Rudarius ercodes* Jordan & Fowler 7.5 cm
Similar to *R. minutus* (Borneo, Palau, GBR) which has dark spots & an ocellus above A fin & *R. excelsus* (GBR) which is green. **Ecology:** among bottom cover. **Range:** s. Japan & s. Korea.

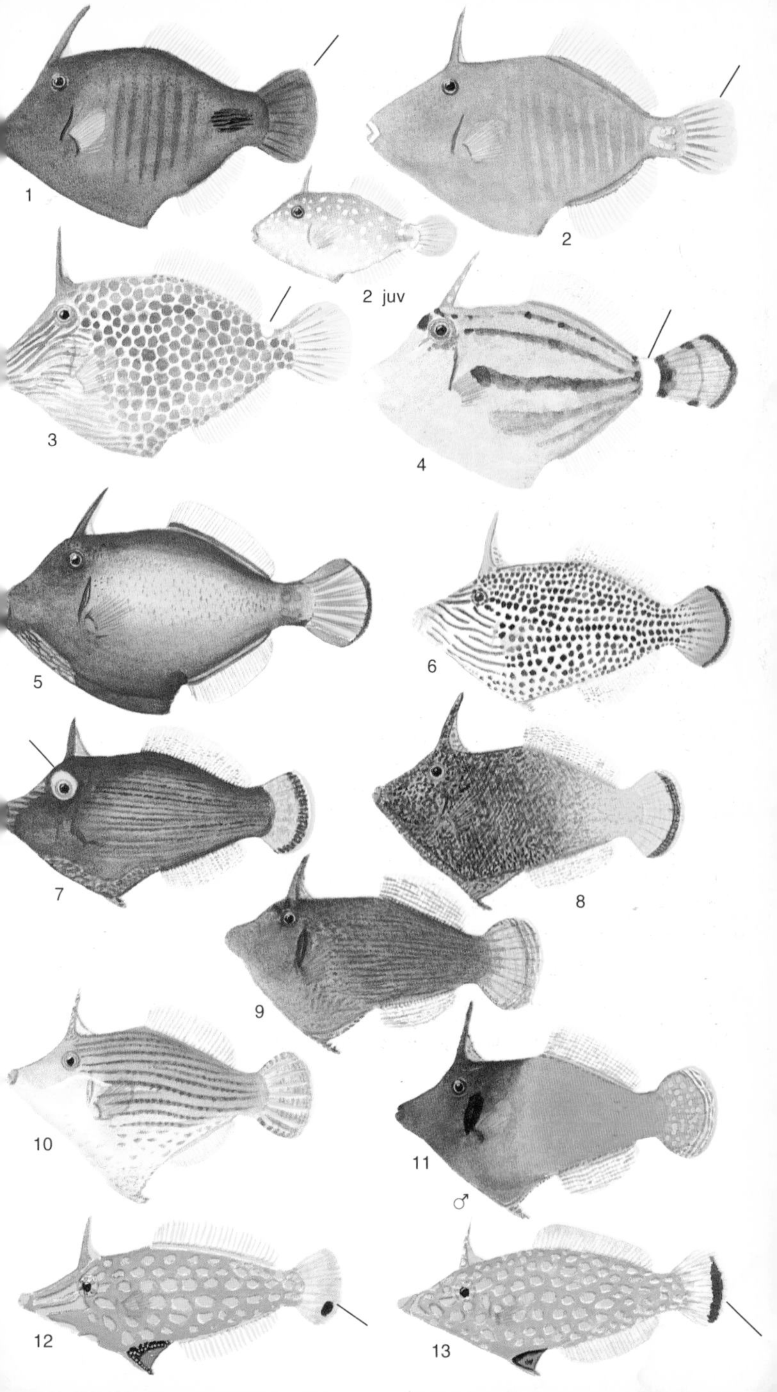

1
2
2 juv
3
4
5
6
7
8
9
10
11
♂
12
13

TRUNKFISHES (OSTRACIIDAE): boxlike fishes encased in a carapace of bony polygonal plates with gaps for the mouth, eyes, gill openings, anus, fins, and tail. Many species with angular ridges and spines. The mouth is small with stout conical to incisiform teeth used for feeding on small sessile invertebrates and algae. Trunkfishes secrete a highly toxic substance (ostracitoxin) from the skin which protects them from predation. They are territorial and haremic, spawning pelagic eggs at dusk. Swimming is ÒgondolierÓ like, soft D and A fin more ÒwaveÓ like. Not recommended for aquariums.

1 **Spotted trunkfish** *Ostracion meleagris* Shaw & Nodder 16 cm
Hawaiian subsp. without yellow inside of dark spots on sides. **Ecology:** clear lagoon and seaward reefs, 1 to 30 m. Feeds on sponges and benthic invertebrates. **Range:** E. Africa to Mexico, n. to s. Japan & Hawaiian Is., s. to GBR, N. Cal. & Rapa.

2 **Bluetail trunkfish** *Ostracion cyanurus* Rüppell 15 cm
Female similar to ♀ *O. meleagris.* **Ecology:** areas of moderate coral growth, 3 to 25 m. Solitary and close to shelter. Common in s. R. Sea. **Range:** R. Sea & G. Aden, Arab. Gulf.

3 **Roughskin trunkfish** *Ostracion trachys* Randall 11 cm
Juv. resemble juvs. of ♀ *O. meleagris* but with larger white spots. **Ecology:** rocky seaward reefs, 15 to 30 m. In holes and crevices. Solitary and uncommon. **Range:** Mauritius.

4 **Yellow boxfish** *Ostracion cubicus* Linnaeus 45 cm
R. Sea juvs. have white-centered black spots; large adults similar to *O. immaculatus* (Japan) which has larger blue dots in centers of plates & blue borders on most plates; large adults with protruberance above upper lip similar to that of *R. nasus.* **Ecology:** lagoon and seaward reefs, 1 to 35 m. Usually near shelter. Juveniles often among *Acropora* corals. **Range:** R. Sea to Tuam., n. to Ryuk., s. to n. N. Zeal, L. Howe & Rapa Is.; strays to Hawaii.

5 **Whitley's trunkfish** *Ostracion whitleyi* Fowler 15.5 cm
Ecology: clear lagoon and seaward reefs, 3 to 27 m. Rare outside of Marquesas. **Range:** Hawaiian, Johnston, Marq., Society & Tuam. Is.

6 **Striped boxfish** *Ostracion solorensis* Bleeker 11 cm
Ecology: coral-rich areas of seaward reefs, 1 to 20 m. **Range:** Indonesia to PNG, n. to Phil. & Palau, s. to Christmas Is. & n. GBR.

7 **Thornback cowfish** *Lactoria fornasini* (Bianconi) 15 cm
Ecology: clear lagoon and seaward reefs to 30 m. Close to bottom in areas of sand, rubble, and algae. Males are highly territorial. **Range:** E. Africa to Hawaiian & Rapa Is., n. to s. Japan, s. to L. Howe Is.

8 **Longhorn cowfish** *Lactoria cornuta* (Linnaeus) 46 cm
Ecology: sand and rubble bottoms of shallow protected lagoon and coastal reefs to 50 m. Solitary. Feeds on benthic invertebrates that it exposes by blowing away the sand. **Range:** s. R. Sea to Marq. & Tuam. Is., n. to s. Korea & s. Japan, s. to L. Howe Is.

9 **Spiny cowfish** *Lactoria diaphana* (Bloch & Schneider) 25 cm
Ecology: this species may spend its entire life pelagically. In s. Japan, adults settle on bottom where they feed and spawn. Weedy and rubbly areas near reefs. **Range:** E. Africa to Panama, n. to s. Japan, Hawaiian Is. & s. Calif., s. to NSW, Kermadec Is., Easter Is. & Peru.

10 **Humpback turretfish** *Tetrasomus gibbosus* (Linnaeus) 30 cm
Ecology: seagrass beds and algal flats of coastal reefs. **Range:** R. Sea to Indonesia & Phil., s. to GBR; migrated to e. Mediterrranean.

11 **Largenose boxfish** *Rhynchostracion rhinorhynchus* (Bleeker) 28 cm
Ecology: sand patches at bases of coral-rich reefs to 35 m. Uncommon. **Range:** E. Africa to Moluccas, n. to Phil., s. to n. Austr.

12 **Shortnose boxfish** *Rhynchostracion nasus* (Bloch) 30 cm
Ecology: rocky and sandy areas near reefs, 2 to 80 m. Uncommon. **Range:** E. Africa to Fiji, n. to Phil., s. to GBR.

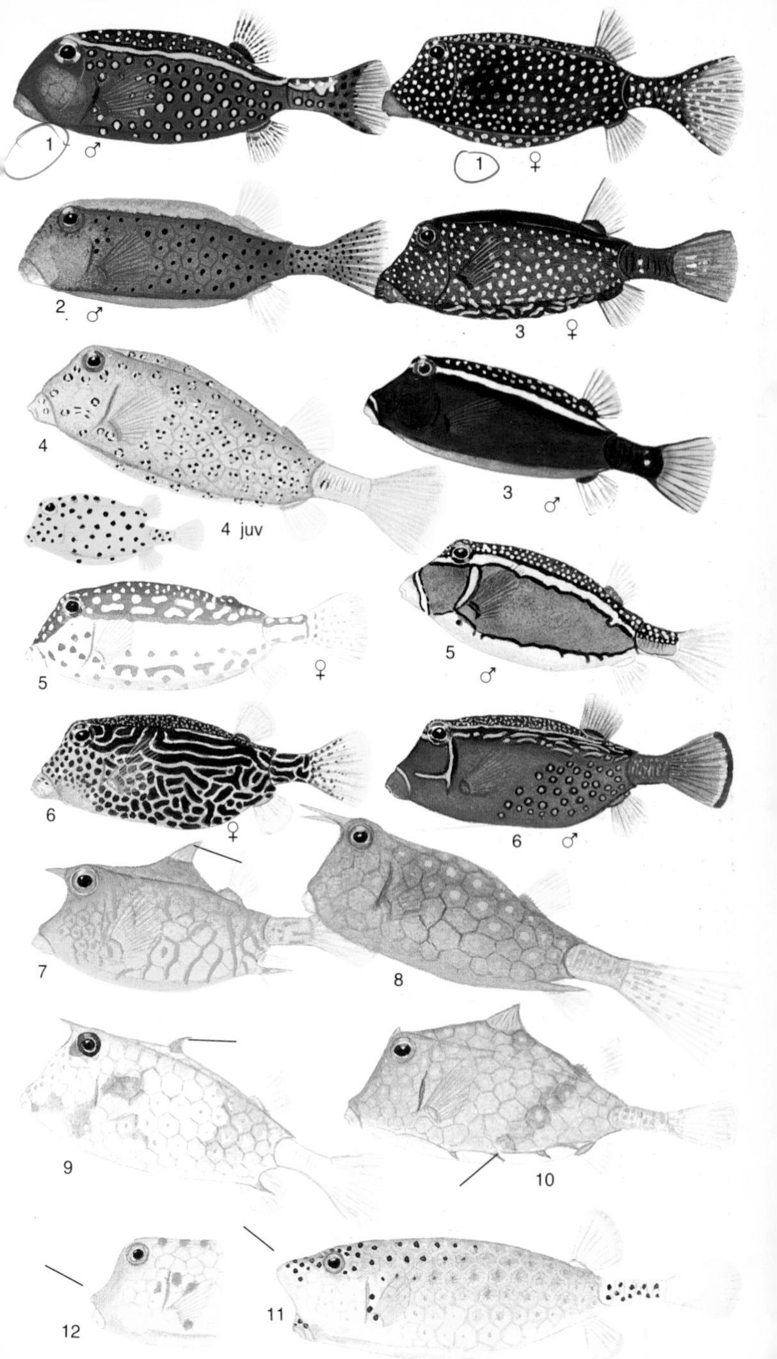
1 ♂
1 ♀
2 ♂
3 ♀
4
3 ♂
4 juv
5 ♀
5 ♂
6 ♀
6 ♂
7
8
9
10
12
11

PUFFERS (TETRAODONTIDAE): moderately elongate bulbous fishes with a tough flexible scaleless and prickly skin, small mouth with teeth fused into a beak with a median suture, a small single D fin and no fin spines, pelvic fins, or ribs. Most species without LL. Capable of greatly inflating themselves with water. Viscera, gonads, and skin of most species highly toxic. Demersal eggs laid in nest. All tropical and temperate seas, some in freshwater. Subfamily Canthigasterinae: elongate pointed snout with 1 pair of nostrils; all spp. <15 cm.

1 **Crown toby** *Canthigaster coronata* (Vaillant & Sauvage) 13.5 cm
Ecology: clear seaward reefs, 11 to 79 m, usually in open areas of sand and rubble. Feeds on algae and a wide variety of benthic invertebrates. Remains close to bottom. **Range:** R. Sea to Hawaiian Is., n. to s. Japan, s. to NSW; absent from Fr. Polynesia.

2 **Black-saddled toby** *Canthigaster valentini* (Bleeker) 10 cm
Resembles its filefish mimic, *Paraluteres prionurus* (pl. 135-3). **Ecology:** lagoon and seaward reefs, 1 to >55 m. Common in araes of mixed coral, rock, and rubble. Feeds on algae and sessile and mobile benthic invertebrates. Territorial and haremic, males spawn with a different female each day. Lays eggs in a tuft of algae. **Range:** R. Sea to Tuam., n. to s. Japan, s. to L. Howe Is.

3 **Ambon toby** *Canthigaster amboinensis* (Bleeker) 14 cm
Similar to *C. natalensis* (S. Africa). **Ecology:** surge zone of seaward reefs to 9 m. Fast swimming and wide-ranging. Feeds primarily on coralline red algae, to a lesser extent on corals and benthic invertebrates. **Range:** E. Africa to Galapagos Is., n. to s. Japan & Hawaiian Is., s. to GBR & Society Is.

4 **Honeycomb toby** *Canthigaster janthinopera* (Bleeker) 8.5 cm
Similar to *C. punctatissima* (trop. E. Pac.). **Ecology:** clear lagoon and seaward reefs, 1 to 30 m. Secretive, often in holes or under ledges. Feeds on a variety of algae, sponges, and invertebrates. **Range:** E. Africa to Line, Marq. & Oeno Is., n. to s. Japan, s. to L. Howe Is.

5 **Fingerprint toby** *Canthigaster compressa* (Procé) 11 cm
Ecology: sandy areas of shallow lagoons and channels to 16 m. **Range:** Phil. to Sol. Is. (& Fiji?), n. to Izu Is. & s. Marianas, s. to Vanuatu.

6 **Hawaiian whitespotted toby** *Canthigaster jactator* (Jenkins) 9 cm
Similar to *C. janthinoptera*, but spots larger and tail without spots. **Ecology:** ubiquitous on lagoon and seaward reefs to 30 m. Feeds on sponges, algae, detritus, and benthic invertebrates. Common. **Range:** Hawaiian Is.

7 **Spotted toby** *Canthigaster solandri* (Richardson) 10.5 cm
W. Pac. indiv. (*papua* form), with longit. lines on nape and upper C peduncle & more orange on snout and tail. The *solandri* form (7a) very similar to *S. margaritata* (R. Sea). **Ecology:** reef flats and lagoon and seaward reefs to 36 m. Feeds primarily on filamentous and coralline algae, to a lesser extent on corals, and benthic invertebrates. **Range:** E. Africa to Line & Tuam. Is., n. to Ryuk., s. to N. Cal. & Tonga.

8 **Leopard toby** *Canthigaster leoparda* Lubbock & Allen 7 cm
Ecology: in caves of steep outer reef dropoffs, 30 to 50 m. Uncommon. **Range:** Christmas Is., Phil., Moluccas & Marianas.

9 **Tyler's toby** *Canthigaster tyleri* Allen & Randall 8 cm
Ecology: rarely venturing out of caves of steep outer reef dropoffs, 8 to 40 m. **Range:** E. Africa, Comores, Seychelles, Maurit., Christmas Is. & Ambon.

10 **Bennett's toby** *Canthigaster bennetti* (Bleeker) 10 cm
Ecology: sand and rubble areas of inner reef flats and sheltered lagoons to >10 m. **Range:** E. Africa (common) to Tuam., n. to s. Taiwan, s. to n. NSW.

11 **Rivulated toby** *Canthigaster rivulata* (Schlegel) 18 cm
Ecology: rocky and coral reefs, 0 to 100 m. Abundant in s. Japan, rare in Hawaii. **Range:** E. Africa to Seychelles; s. China to s. Korea, s. Japan & Bonin Is.; Hawaiian Is.

12 **Pygmy toby** *Canthigaster pygmaea* Allen & Randall 5.6 cm
Ecology: coral reefs, 2 to 30 m. Secretive, stays hidden in holes. **Range:** R. Sea.

13 **Bicolored toby** *Canthigaster smithae* Allen & Randall 13 cm
Ecology: outer reef slopes, 20 to at least 37 m. Rare. **Range:** E. Africa (common) s. to Durban, Seychelles, Maurit., Agalega Is. & Maldives.

14 **Lantern toby** *Canthigaster epilampra* (Jenkins) 12 cm
Similar to *C. rapaensis* (Rapa) & *C. smithae*. **Ecology:** steep outer reef slopes, 9 to 60 m, usually 20 m. Feeds primarily on small benthic invertebrates. **Range:** Christmas Is. to Hawaiian & Society Is., n. to Ryuk., s. to Tonga & Rarotonga.

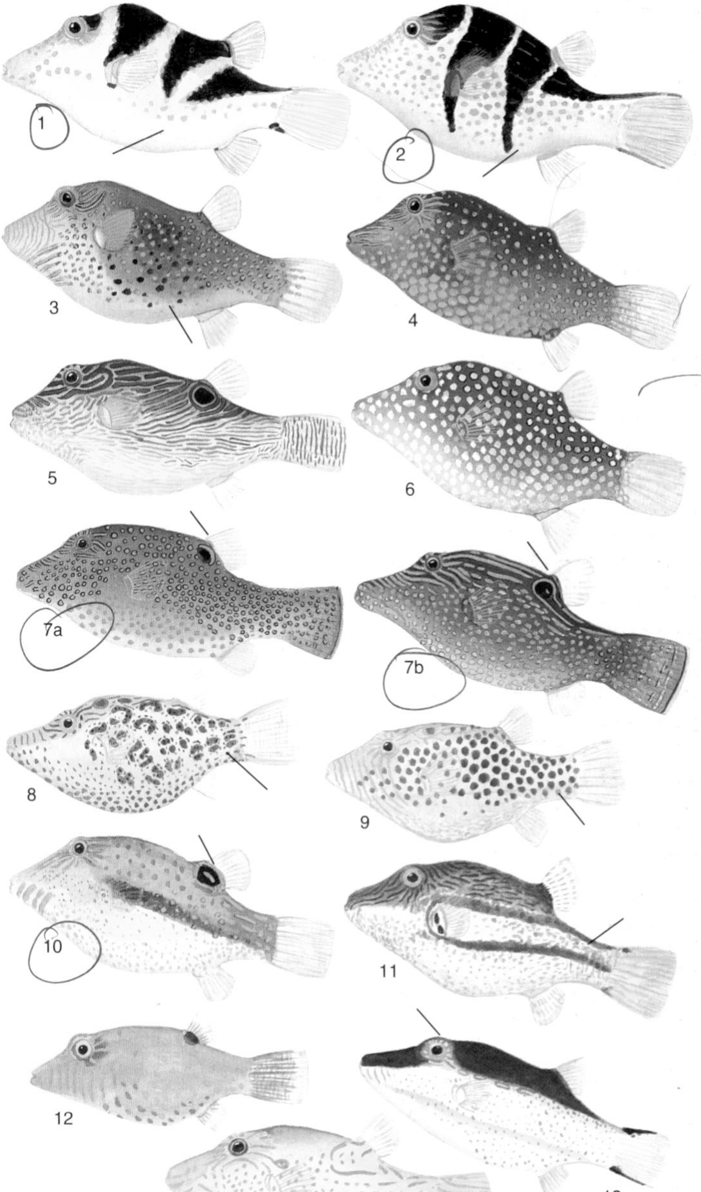
1
2
3
4
5
6
7a
7b
8
9
10
11
12
13
14

Subfamily Tetraodontinae: short blunt snout with 2 pairs of nostrils; most spp. >23 cm.

1 **Star puffer** *Arothron stellatus* (Bloch & Schneider) 120 cm
Similar *Arothron* sp. (Maldives to Indonesia & Palau) which has rings around eyes and light spots on a dark background. **Ecology:** juveniles in sandy and weedy inner reefs, adults on clear lagoon and seaward reefs, 3 to 58 m. Feeds on sponges, corals, and hard-shelled benthic invertebrates. **Range:** R. Sea to Tuam., n. to s. Japan, s. to L. Howe Is. & n. N. Zeal.

2 **Guineafowl puffer** *Arothron meleagris* (Lacépède) 50 cm
Occasionally entirely to mostly yellow. **Ecology:** coral-rich areas of clear lagoon and seaward reefs, 1 to 14 m. Feeds primarily on tips of branching corals, to a lesser extent on invertebrates and algae. **Range:** E. Africa to Panama, n. to s. Japan & Hawaii, s. to L. Howe, Rapa & Easter Is.

3 **Blackspotted puffer** *Arothron nigropunctatus* (Bloch & Schneider) 33 cm
Ecology: feeds on corals, sponges, tunicates and algae. Generally common. **Range:** E. Africa to Line Is., n. to G. Aden & Ryuk., s. to NSW & N. Cal.

4 **Masked puffer** *Arothron diadematus* (Rüppell) 30 cm
Similar to *A. nigropunctatus*, but mask more distinct. **Ecology:** common on coral-rich fringing reefs. **Range:** R. Sea.

5 **Striped puffer** *Arothron manilensis* (Procé) 31 cm
Ecology: coastal and lagoon reefs to 17 m. Common in sandy areas and seagrass beds. Juveniles among mangroves. **Range:** Borneo, Bali & Phil. to Samoa (& Society Is?), n. to Ryuk., s. to NSW & Tonga.

6 **Map puffer** *Arothron mappa* (Lesson) 65 cm
Ecology: clear lagoon and shelteR. Seaward reefs to 30 m. Feeds on algae, sponges, and benthic invertebrates. Usually close to shelter. Generally uncommon and solitary. **Range:** E. Africa to Samoa, n. to Ryuk., s. to s. Queensland & N. Cal.

7 **Immaculate puffer** *Arothron immaculatus* (Bloch & Schneider) 28 cm
Ecology: mangroves, seagrass beds, and silty weedy areas of coastal reefs, 1 to 20 m. **Range:** R. Sea to Java & Phil., n. to s. China & Ryuk.

8 **Whitespotted puffer** *Arothron hispidus* (Linnaeus) 48 cm
Similar to *A. reticularis* (India to Fiji) which has white lines encircling eye & on back. **Ecology:** sand and rubble areas of coastal, lagoon, and seaward reefs, 1 to 50 m. Feeds on wide variety of plants and animals. **Range:** R. Sea to Panama, n. to s. Japan & Hawaii, s. to L. Howe & Rapa Is.

9 **Many-striped puffer** *Feroxodon multistriatus* (Richardson) 39 cm
Ecology: shallow inshore waters and offshore soft bottoms. Feeds on fishes and invertebrates. Responsible for amputation of swimmer's toes! Highly toxic. **Range:** n. Australia from Exmouth G. to s. Queensland.

PORCUPINEFISHES (DIODONTIDAE): similar to puffers, but have prominent spines over the head and body, larger eyes, an inconspicuous lateral line, and lack the suture on the beak. When inflated, adults are nearly impossible for any predator to eat. Feed primarily on hard-shelled invertebrates crushed by the beak. Eggs are pelagic. See *Diodon hystrix* pl. 175-6 and *D. holacanthus* pl. 175-7 which also occur in the Indo-Pacific.

10 **Spottedfin burrfish** *Chilomycterus reticulatus* Linnaeus 55 cm
Ecology: rocky and coral reefs. Juveniles under 20 cm pelagic. Rare on tropical reefs. **Range:** Circumglobal; primarily subtropical and warm-temperate seas.

11 **Black blotched porcupinefish** *Diodon liturosus* Shaw 65 cm
Similar to *D. holacanthus* (circumtropical; see W. Atlantic pl. 175-7). **Ecology:** coastal and offshore reefs. Often rests under ledges by day, forages at night. **Range:** s. R. Sea & E. Africa to Society Is., n. to s. Japan, s. to NSW.

12 **Orbicular Burrfish** *Cyclichthys orbicularis* (Bloch) 30 cm
Ecology: over sand and rubble of silty inshore waters. Nocturnal. **Range:** E. Africa to GBR.

13 **Yellowspotted Burrfish** *Cyclichthys spilostylus* (Leis & Randall) 34 cm
Ecology: coastal reefs, seagrass beds, sandy areas, and wrecks, 3 to 90 m. Inactive and usually under ledges by day. **Range:** R. Sea & G. Oman to Indonesia & Phil. Galapagos (rare).

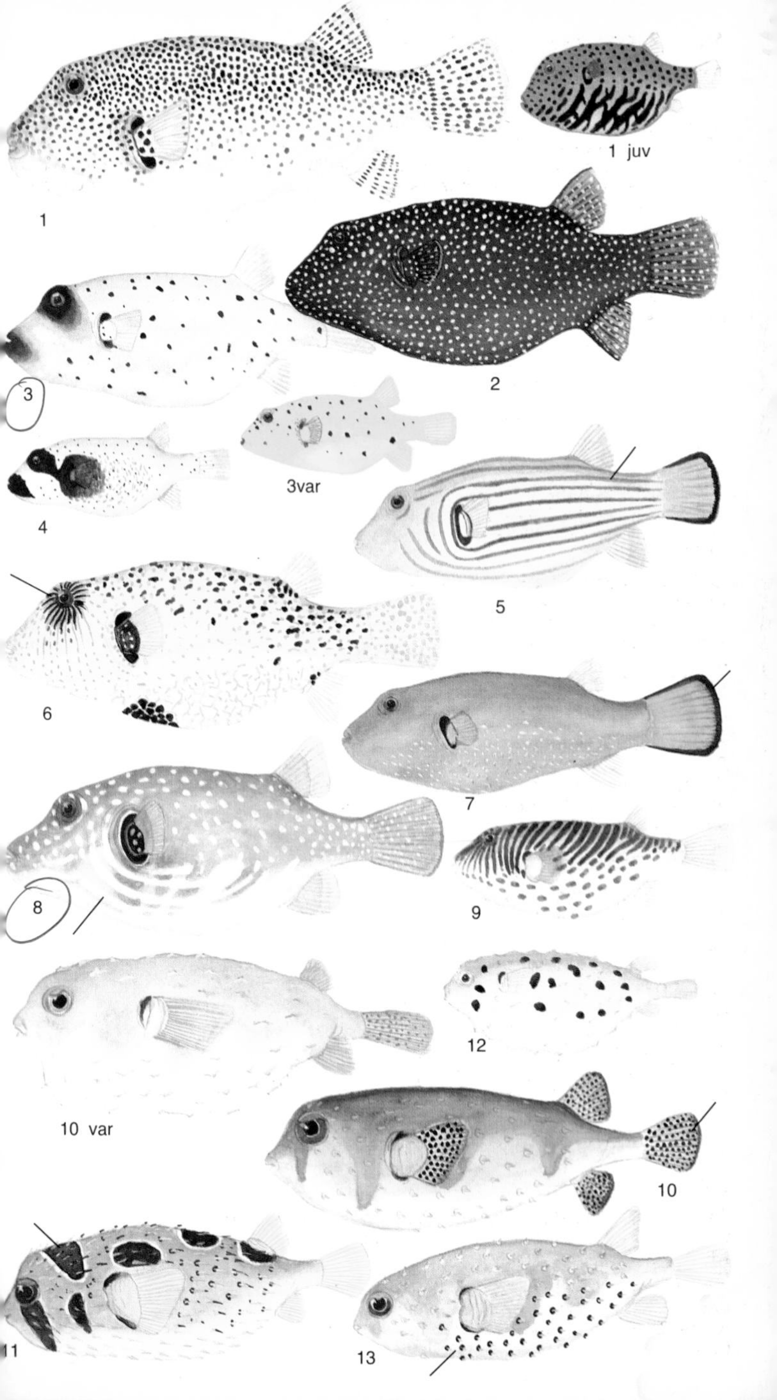
1 juv
1
2
3
3var
4
5
6
7
8
9
12
10 var
10
11
13

139 RARITIES

1 **Black-tip trevally** *Caranx sem* (Cuvier) 85 cm
Body bronzy to yellowish-green or dusky, upper tail lobe often with black tip. **Ecology:** coastal reefs, in small aggregations. **Range:** R. Sea to Fiji, n. to Ryuk.; absent from Seychelles & most oceanic islands.

2 **Diagonal-lined sweetlips** *Plectorhinchus paulayi* Steindachner 45 cm
Ecology: mangrove areas. Rare. **Range:** E. Africa, Aldabra, Maurit.

3 **Armitage angelfish** *Apolemichthys trimaculatus* x *xanthurus* (pl. 67) 21 cm
Once known as *Apolemichthys armitagei.* **Ecology:** seaward reef slopes. Rare. **Range:** Seychelles & Maldives.

4 **Bay of Bengal hogfish** *Bodianus neilli* (Day) ca. 20 cm
Ecology: shallow coastal reefs and turbid lagoon reefs. **Range:** Maldives, India & Sri Lanka to Andaman Sea coast of Thailand.

5 **Splendid hawkfish** *Cirrhitus splendens* (Ogilby) 20 cm
Ecology: seaward reefs, 5 to 30 m. At the bases of coral heads on hard bottom. **Range:** L. Howe, Norfolk & Kermadec Is. straying to NSW.

6 **Doubleheader** *Coris bulbifrons* Randall & Kuiter 60 cm
Tail truncate in lg. adult & hump on head more pronounced than in lg. *C. aygula* (pl. 97-1). **Ecology:** shallow rocky and coral reefs to 25 m. Feeds on mollusks and crabs. **Range:** se. Australia, L. Howe Is. & Middleton Reef.

7 **Purplelined wrasse** *Cirrhilabrus lineatus* Randall & Lubock 12 cm
Ecology: clear outer reef slopes, 20 to 55 m. **Range:** GBR to N. Cal & Loyalty Is.

8 **Dotted wrasse** *Cirrhilabrus punctatus* Randall & Kuiter 13 cm
Ecology: over coral or rubble of shallow protected reefs, occasioanlly in exposed areas, 2 to 32 m. **Range:** s. PNG & GBR to Fiji, s. to NSW, L. Howe & N. Cal.

9 **Rust-blotch wrasse** *Labropsis manabei* (Schmidt) 10 cm
Ecology: coral-rich reef slopes to 25 m. **Range:** Phil. to Flores, n. to Ryuk.

10 **Torpedo wrasse** *Pseudocoris heteroptera* (Bleeker) 20 cm
Juv. with light belly & broad longitudinal light stripe along back; IP dark greenish-brown. **Ecology:** current-swept seaward reefs and channels, 15 to ~24 m. Typically in groups well above open bottoms with mixed sand, rubble, and coral. Feeds on zooplankton. **Range:** E. Africa to PNG, n. to s. Japan, s. to NSW, Mauritius.

11 **Broad-banded prawn-goby** *Amblyeleotris* sp. 13 cm
Similar to *A. aurora* (pl. 120-1) but with bands instead of ocelli on tail. **Ecology:** sand patches and slopes of coastal and offshore reefs, 6 to 20 m. Inhabits burrows constructed by *Alpheus Randall i.* **Range:** Indonesia, n. to Palau.

12 **Ward's sleeper** *Valenciennea wardi* (Playfair) 13 cm
Ecology: sandy areas of shallow lagoon reefs, 5 to 20 m. **Range:** E. Africa to s. Japan.

13 **Red-lined sleeper** *Valenciennea immaculata* Ni Yong 13 cm
Ecology: sandy areas of coastal bays and harbors. **Range:** nw. Austr., Queensland to NSW & n. S. China Sea.

14 **Rayed prawn-goby** *Tomyamaichthys* sp. 7.5 cm
Ecology: coastal sand slopes. Inhabits burrows constructed by a prawn. **Range:** Indonesia

15 **Blue-barred ribbon goby** *Oxymetopon cyanoctenosum* Klausewitz & Condé 20 cm
Body highly compressed; 4-5 other similar spp. lack irridescent blue bars on the sides. **Ecology:** deep mud slopes, 12 to 40 m. Lives in pairs in burrow. **Range:** Phil. & Indonesia.

16 **Shy toby** *Canthigaster ocellicincta* Allen & Randall 6.5 cm
Ecology: steep seaward reefs, 10 to 53 m. Secretive, stays hidden in holes. **Range:** Indonesia, Phil., Ryuk., Sol. Is., GBR, N. Cal. & Fiji.

1
2
3
4
5
6
7
8
9
10
11
12
13
14
15
16

NURSE SHARKS (GINGLYMOSTOMATIDAE): bottom dwelling sharks lacking lower tail lobe and with small mouth bearing multicuspid teeth; young born fully developed at about 20 to 26 cm.

1 **Nurse shark** *Ginglymostoma cirratum* (Bonnaterre) 400 cm
Dorsal fins of nearly equal size. Small mouth with barbels. Young with spots. **Ecology:** shallow reefs, 3 to 35 m. Much of their time is spent lying on sand under ledges. Harmless but can bite when provoked. Feeds on crustaceans and mollusks. **Range:** New York to Brazil.

REQUIEM SHARKS (CARCHARHINIDAE): sleek, active swimmers with 1st D fin base located in front of V fins, single cusped teeth in a single functional row in each jaw, and tail with a distinct lower lobe. Young born fully developed. Includes several dangerous species, but most prefer to avoid divers. See pl. 2 for additional circumtropical species.

2 **Lemon shark** *Negaprion brevirostris* (Poey) 340 cm
Color variable: yellow brown to gray. Dorsal fins of nearly equal size. **Ecology:** coastal waters, including brackish and fresh water. May rest motionless on the bottom. Considered dangerous, known to attack man. In winter in Florida, this species gathers in large aggregations. **Range:** N. Carol. (rarely to NJ) to Brazil, e. to w. Africa.

3 **Reef shark** *Carcharhinus perezii* (Poey) 300 cm
Trailing edge of tail dusky; a low ridge on back between D fins; otherwise similar to 5 but with smaller gill openings. **Ecology:** coral reefs to 65 m. May rest on the bottom. The most common species of the genus around islands of the Antilles. Generally timid, but considered dangerous. **Range:** G. Mexico, Fla. & Bahamas to Brazil.

4 **Blacktip shark** *Carcharhinus limbatus* (Valenciennes) 250 cm
Long snout. Dark tips on fins fade with age. White stripe on side. **Ecology:** primarily pelagic but comes close to shore with large schools of mackerels. Occasionally in estuaries. Often taken by anglers. Pregnant females migrate to nursery areas. Young are common along beaches. Potentially dangerous. **Range:** circumtropical; Mass. to s. Brazil in W. Atlantic.

5 **Bull shark** *Carcharhinus leucas* (Valenciennes) 350 cm
Similar to 3, but trailing edge of tail not dusky & gill openings larger. **Ecology:** inshore coastal waters and shallow coastal reefs, 3 to 45 m. Occasionally in surf zone. Also commonly in fresh waters of tropical rivers and lakes connected to the sea, including Lake Nicaragua and the Zambezi River. Absent from most of the West Indies islands. A dangerous species responsible for fatal attacks on man. **Range:** circumtropical; s. N. England to Brazil in W. Atlantic.

6 **Atlantic sharpnose shark** *Rhizoprionodon porosus* (Poey) 110 cm
Slender body with pale spots & long snout. Similar to *R. terraenovae* (Yucatan to Bay of Fundy) & *R. lalandei* (Panama to Brazil) which has short P fins that don't reach as far back as mid-D fin base. ♂ mature at 60 cm, ♀ mature at 80 cm. **Ecology:** coastal waters, particularly over sandy areas, shoreline to 500 m. Feeds on squids, crabs and prawns in midwater. Not dangerous. Wary. **Range:** Bahamas & Yucatan Penin. to Uruguay.

7 **Tiger shark** *Galeocerdo cuvier* (Peron & Lesueur) >550 cm
Head wide, nearly square; dusky bars and wide, serrated teeth distinctive; ♂ mature at 290 cm, ♀ at 340 cm; up to 80 pups per litter. **Ecology:** outer reef slopes and offshore banks, usually deep during the day, but may enter shallow water at night to feed. The most dangerous tropical shark, responsible for many fatalities. Feeds on a wide range of animals, including porpoises, sea turtles, seabirds, spiny puffers, sharks, and rays. Generally solitary. **Range:** all tropical and warm-temperate seas; C. Cod to Uruguay in W. Atlantic.

HAMMERHEAD SHARKS (SPHYRNIDAE): a laterally expanded blade on either side of head; eyes located at tip of each blade. Young born fully developed. Large individuals potentially dangerous. Eight species, 6 in W. Atlantic (see pl. 3).

8 **Smooth hammerhead** *Sphyrna zygaena* (Linnaeus) 350 cm
Front of head ("hammer") smoothly convex; similar to *S. lewini* (pl. 3-4) with a scalloped leading edge of head & *S. mokarran* (pl. 3-5) with a much taller D fin. Matures at ca. 210-240 cm, 29-37 pups per litter. **Ecology:** primarily temperate coastal waters, but enters tropical waters in winter. **Range:** circumtropical-temperate; Nova Scotia & throughout Carib. to Brazil in W. Atlantic.

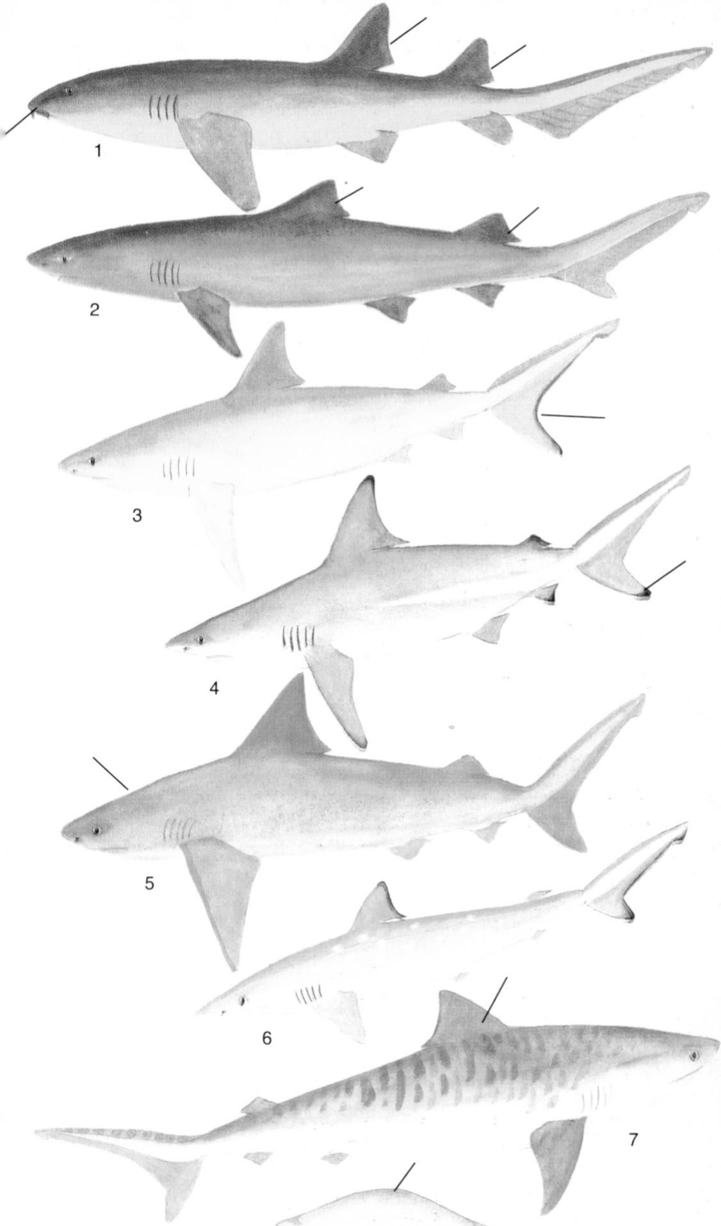
1
2
3
4
5
6
7
8

GUITARFISHES (RHINOBATIDAE): elongate rays with pointed depressed heads and sharklike bodies; teeth flattened, pavement-like. Young born fully developed.

1 **Atlantic guitarfish** *Rhinobatos lentiginosus* (Garman) 75 cm
Similar to *R. percellens* (Caribbean) which has a more pointed snout and fewer white spots. **Ecology:** sandy and weedy bottoms, sometimes near patch reefs, shoreline to >18 m. Feeds on mollusks and crustaceans. Usually buried in sand or mud. Uncommon. **Range:** Fla. and Yucatan, n. to n. G. Mexico & N. Carol.

ELECTRIC RAYS (TORPEDINIDAE): rays with 2 large kidney-shaped electric organs on either side of head. Can deliver a dangerous electric shock normally used to stun small fishes on which they feed. Young hatch inside uterus; born fully developed.

2 **Lesser electric ray** *Narcine brasiliensis* (Olfers) 46 cm
Ground color greyish or reddish to brown with rounded blotches. **Ecology:** frequents shallow sandy coastal bottoms to 36 m. Usually buried in sand with only the eyes protruding. Produces a mild electric shock of 14-37 volts. Not dangerous to man. **Range:** N. Carol. & Texas to n. Argentina; absent from W. Indies n. of Tobago.

3 **Atlantic torpedo** *Torpedo nobiliana* Bonaparte 180 cm; 90 kg
Ground colour light to dark brown; disk very broad; snout short. **Ecology:** inhabits sandy, mud, and rubble bottoms from shore to 457 m. A sluggish bottom dweller that feeds on bottom dwelling animals including flounders and small sharks. Packs a powerful electric shock of up to 220 volts. **Range:** Nova Scotia & Bay of Fundy to Fla. & Bahamas, e. to Medit. & S. Africa.

STINGRAYS (DASYATIDAE): body flattened into round or nearly round disc; small mouth with pavement-like teeth; one or more venomous barbs near base of tail. Respire by drawing water through a small hole behind the eye and expelling it through gill slits on underside of disc. Young born fully developed. All species dangerous if stepped on, the larger ones can deliver a fatal sting.

4 **Southern Stingray** *Dasyatis americana* Hildebrand & Schroeder
Olive brown to gray or even black. Disk rhomboid. width:152 cm
Ecology: seagrass beds and sand patches near coral reefs, 0 to 30 m. Easily approached by divers. Feed by creating depressions in the sand to expose invertebrates and small fishes. **Range:** N. Jersey s. to se. Brazil.

5 **Yellow stingray** *Urolophus jamaicensis* (Cuvier) 76 cm
Ecology: Brownish with numerous pale to yellow spots. Disk almost round. **Range:** sandy areas near reefs, 1-25 m. Often burried in sand. Common and easily approached. Will raise front of disc to form a tunnel to attract prey seeking shelter.
N. Carol. & Bahamas to Brazil; rare n. of Fla.; absent from P. Rico & Lesser Antilles.

EAGLE RAYS and COWNOSED RAYS (MYLIOBATIDAE): head protrudes from disc; disc wide and winglike; tail long and slender with one or more venomous barbs at its base in most species; jaws powerful with large platelike crushing teeth in several rows. Young born fully developed.

6 **Spotted eagle ray** *Aetobatus narinari* (Euphrasen) width: 229 cm; 227 kg.
White spots become ocelli in some individuals; 2-6 barbs at base of tail. Up to 4 pups per litter born at 17-35 cm. **Ecology:** seagrass flats and sandy areas of coral reefs to 80 m. Usually swims above bottom. Feeds on mollusks and crustaceans. Usually solitary but occasionally in groups. **Range:** circumtropical; N. Carol., Bermuda & n. G. Mexico to s. Brazil in w. Atlantic.

MANTAS (MOBULIDAE): large protruding flaps in front of mouth; disc wide and winglike; small D fin at base of tail; tail spine rudimentary or absent; teeth minute. Mantas feed by flitering plankton from water drawn over filter plates on the inside of gill openings. Young born fully developed. Among the largest of fishes, but harmless.

7 **Manta ray** *Manta birostris* (Donndorff)width: 670 cm; 1,820 kg.
Horn-like flaps in front of mouth; minute teeth in lower jaw only; filter plates on inside of gill openings; species of *Mobula* smaller with smaller head flaps and teeth in both jaws. **Ecology:** swims in mid-water singly or in small groups, most often in or near channels. Harmless, feeds on plankton. **Range:** circumtropical; s. N. England, Bermuda & n. G. Mexico to Brazil in w. Atlantic.

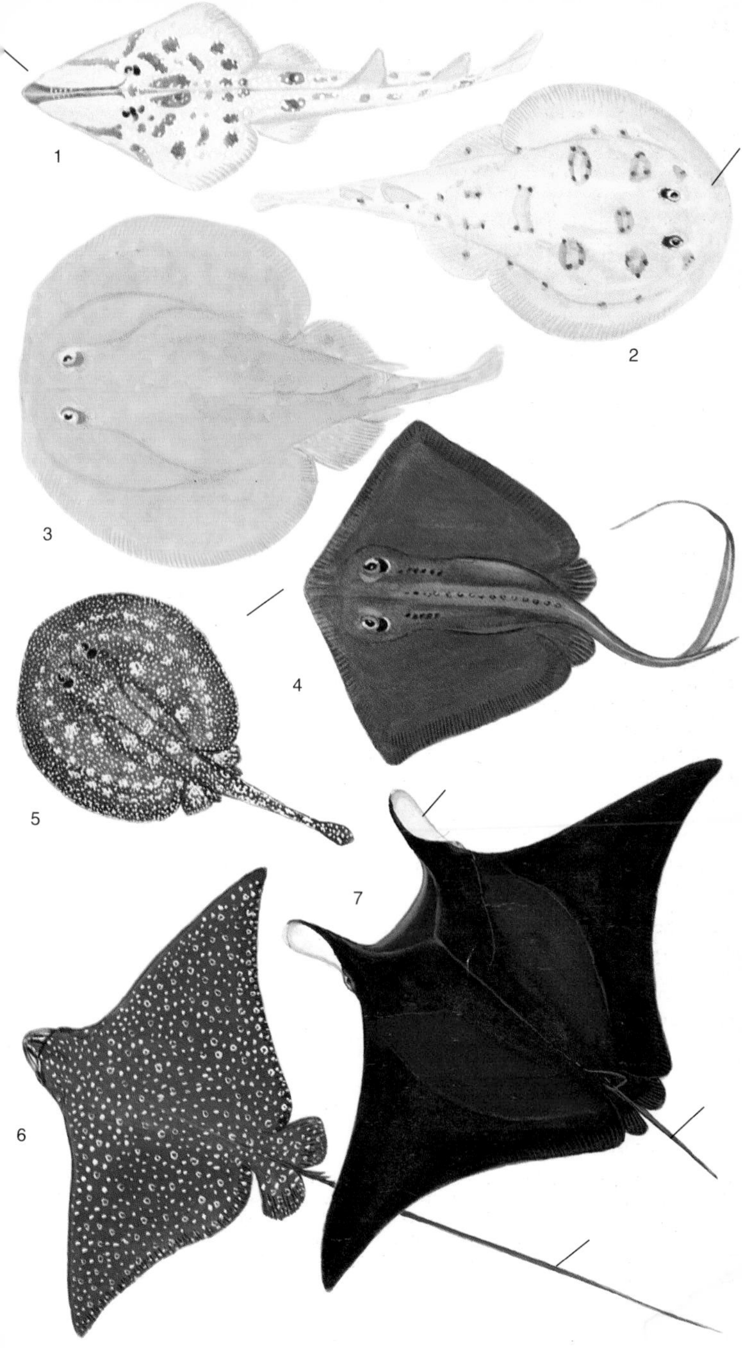

1
2
3
4
5
6
7

MORAYS (MURAENIDAE): a diverse group of extremely elongate fishes with large mouths containing numerous teeth, restricted gill openings, and no pectoral or pelvic fins. Most are secretive during the day. Widely used as food, but a few large species may be ciguatoxic. Morays are normally docile, but will bite if provoked. Bites from large morays may require medical attention and result in permanent injury. Generally hardy in captivity.

1 **Green moray** *Gymnothorax funebris* Ranzani 231 cm; 29 kg
Ecology: coral reefs incuding seagrass meadows and mangroves as well as pilings and seawalls. In caves or recesses during the day. Easily approached, but dangerous if provoked. Often ciguatoxic. The largest moray in the region. **Range:** s. Fla. & Bermuda to s. Brazil.

2 **Purplemouth moray** *Gymnothorax vicinus* (Castelnau) 100 cm
Ecology: shallow reefs with sandy patches and clear water. Most active during the night. **Range:** s. Fla. & Bermuda to s. Brazil, e. to Ascension, C. Verde & Canary Is. & w. Africa.

3 **Spotted moray** Gymnothorax moringa (Cuvier) 120 cm
Ecology: rocky and coral reefs, sometimes on grassy bottoms, to 200 m. Feeds on fishes. The most common moray in the West Indies. Attains a length of nearly 3 m at Ascension. **Range:** S. Carol., Bermuda & n. G. Mexico to s. Brazil, e. to Ascension & St. Helena.

4 **Goldentail moray** *Gymnothorax miliaris* (Kaup) 60 cm
Pattern ext. variable, us. with numerous small dots on brown underground & yellow tail; possibly belongs in genus *Siderea.* **Ecology:** shallow coral reefs in areas of rubble, 1 to 60 m. **Range:** s. Fla. & Bermuda s. to s. Brazil, e. to St. Paul's Rocks & Ascension, St. Helena & C. Verde Is.

5 **Chain moray** *Echidna catenata* (Bloch) 71 cm
Ecology: shallow clear water rocky and coral reefs and sandy areas to 12 m. **Range:** s. Fla. & Bermuda to s. Brazil, e. to St. Paul's Rocks & Ascension.

6 **Viper moray** *Enchelychore nigricans* (Bonnaterre) 87 cm
Hooked jaws with fang-like teeth. Similar to *E. carychroa* (Fla. & Bermuda to Ascension & Africa) which has jaw pores set in white spots and larger more elongate posterior nostrils set in front of eye instead of above or behind eye. **Ecology:** common on rocky coastlines and shallow coral reefs, 1 to 30 m. Secretive. **Range:** Fla. & Bermuda to e. Brazil, e. to St. Paul's Rocks & Ascension, C. Verde Is. & W. Africa.

7 **Caribbean ocellated moray** *Gymnothorax ocellatus* Agassiz 58 cm
Similar to *G. nigromarginatus* (s. Fla. to Yucatan) & *G. saxicola* (N.J. & Bermuda to Miss.). **Ecology:** common on deep soft bottom areas and banks, rarely on coral reefs, 15 to 160 m. **Range:** Cuba to s. Brazil incl. entire Caribbean.

SNAKE EELS (OPHICHTHIDAE): a large and diverse group of carnivorous snakelike eels; most with pointed snouts extending beyond the mouth and over downward pointing nostrils. Most species spend their time burried in sand and hunt small fishes and crustaceans by sense of smell. Often numerous, but seldom noticed.

8 **Goldenspotted eel** *Myrichthys ocellatus* (Lesueur) 102 cm
Ecology: sandy areas of shallow rocky or coral reefs. May move beneath sand. Forages at night on crabs. Easily approached. **Range:** s. Fla, Bahamas & Bermuda to Brazil.

9 **Sharptail eel** *Myrichthys breviceps* (Richardson) 102 cm
Ecology: clear weedy, grassy, or sandy areas of harbours and coral reefs. More common on continental shelf and in grassy areas. **Range:** s. Fla. & Bermuda to Brazil.

10 **Blackspotted snake eel** *Quassiremus ascensionis* (Studer) 70 cm
Similar to *Myrichthys ocellatus* which has black edged yellow spots. **Ecology:** shallow sandy areas, often with seagrass, to 12 m. Rare. **Range:** Bermuda, Bahamas, L. Antilles, e. Brazil & Ascension Is.

11 **Spotted snake eel** *Ophichthus ophis* (Linnaeus) 137 cm
Ecology: occupies permanent burrow in sand. Feeds at night on octopuses and small fishes. Bold and easily approached. Feared by fishermen. **Range:** s. Fla. & Bermuda to Brazil, e. to Ascension & e. Atlantic.

CONGER and GARDEN EELS (CONGRIDAE): round-bodied eels, the conger eels with large P fins and the garden eels with small to vestigial P fins and upturned mouths. Most species of conger eels occur in deep or temperate waters and are valued as food fishes. Garden eels occur in colonies in sandy areas exposed to current where they live individually in burrows from which they protrude to feed on plankton.

12 **Garden eel** *Heteroconger halis* (Böhlke) 51 cm
Ecology: in colonies on sandy patches near coral reefs. Shy, retreats into burrow instantly when frightened. **Range:** s. Fla. & Bahamas to Brazil; replaced by *H. camelopardalis* at Fernando de Noronha & Ascension.

13 See over

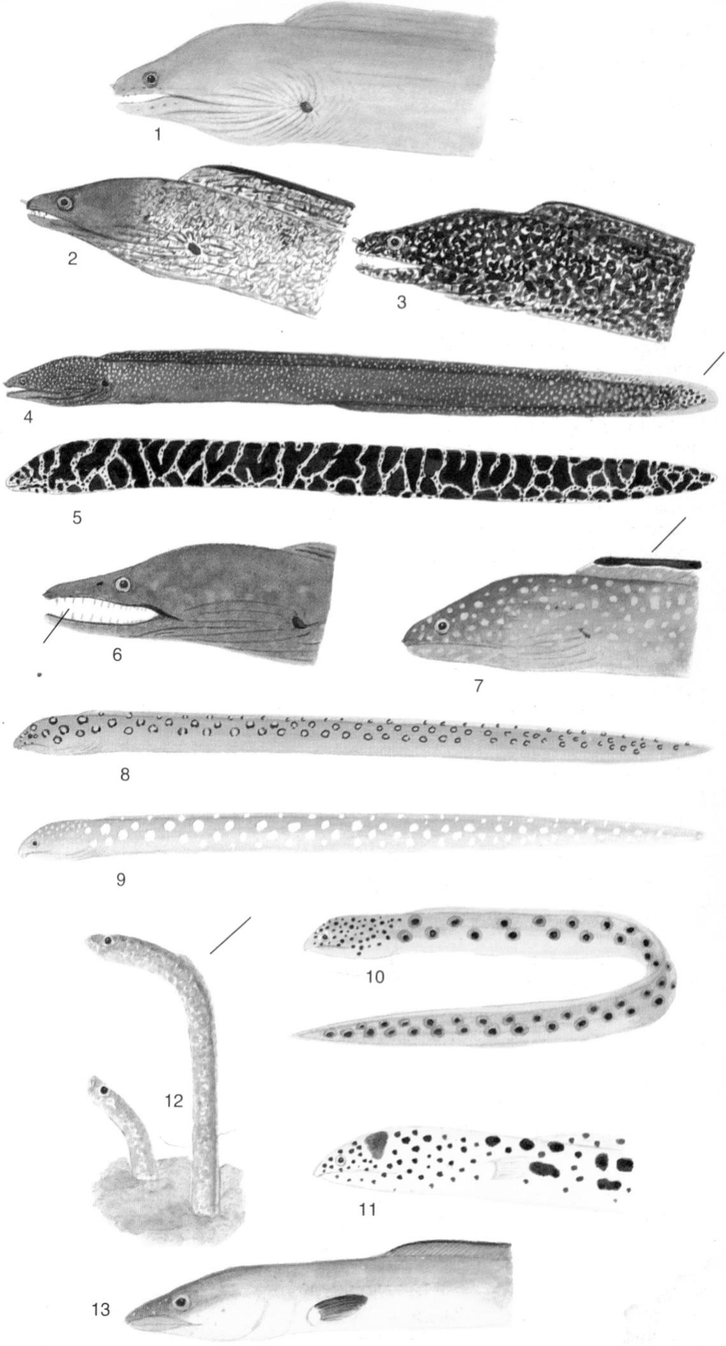
1
2
3
4
5
6
7
8
9
10
11
12
13

←13 **Manytooth conger** *Conger triporiceps* Kanazawa 92 cm
Similar to *C. esculentus* which has stouter body (length ca. 14 x depth vs. 18-22 x depth). **Ecology:** coral reefs, 3 to 54 m. More common at offshore islands. **Range:** Fla., Bermuda & Bahamas to Brazil.

143 TARPON, LADYFISH, BONEFISH, NEEDLEFISHES and HALFBEAKS

TARPONS (MEGALOPIDAE): large silvery fishes with ventral P fins, abdominal V fins, forked tail, large mouth with prominent lower jaw, and large scales. Popular gamefishes.

1 **Tarpon** *Megalops atlanticus* Valenciennes 240 cm; 159 kg
Ecology: occurs in fresh and salt water. Capable of tolerating oxygen-poor water by breathing air into a lung-like bladder. Inhabits estuaries, bays, mangrove inlets, sand and seagrass flats, and coral reefs, sometimes near steep walls. Large schools may frequent particular spots for years. Active during night and day. A spectacular gamefish. **Range:** Virginia & Bermuda to Brazil, e. to e. Atlantic.

LADYFISHES (ELOPIDAE): similar to tarpon, but scales much smaller (>103 in LL).
2 **Ladyfish** *Elops saurus* Linnaeus 91 cm
Silvery blue with a large mouth. Dorsal fin begins above pelvic fin. **Ecology:** common in lagoons and mangrove areas, rarely on coral reefs. A gamefish. **Range:** Cape Cod & Bermuda to s. Brazil.

BONEFISHES (ALBULIDAE): large silvery fishes with ventral P fins, abdominal V fins, forked tail, and mouth under snout. Five species, one in Atlantic. Highly prized sportfishes.
3 **Bonefish** *Albula vulpes* (Linnaeus) 104 cm
Ecology: coastal bays and lagoons over sand and mud flats and among mangroves, in fresh to marine waters. Can tolerate oxygen-poor water by inhaling air into a lung-like air bladder. Feeds on invertebrates by nosing in sediment. **Range:** N. Brunswick, (rare n. of s. Fla. & Bermuda) to Brazil, e. to e. Atlantic.

NEEDLEFISHES (BELONIDAE): elongate silvery fishes with greatly elongate jaws full of needle-like teeth, and abdominal V fins. Surface dwelling predators of small fishes.
4 **Timucu** *Strongylura timucu* (Walbaum) 60 cm
Similar to *S. marina* (widespread W. Atl.) which lacks the stripe behind eye & has more preD scales (210). **Ecology:** juveniles with floating algae. Adults on reef flats, in lagoons, or in freshwater. **Range:** se. G. Mexico, Fla. & Bahamas to Brazil.
5 **Redfin needlefish** *Strongylura notata* (Poey) 61 cm
Pale green on back. D fin & tail with red margin; 76-117 predorsal scales. **Ecology:** abundant in surface waters of bays and inlets, may enter fresh water. **Range:** Fla. & Bermuda to Lesser Antilles & C. America.
6 **Keeltail needlefish** *Platybelone argalus* (Le Sueur) 38 cm
Base of tail flattened, its width distinctly depth. 107-128 predorsal scales. **Ecology:** in groups at surface of clear lagoon and sheltered seaward waters. **Range:** circumtropical; N. Carol. to Brazil in W. Atlantic; subsp. *platyura* in Indo-Pacific.
7 **Houndfish** *Tylosurus crocodilus crocodilus* (Lesueur) 150 cm
Body less compressed, jaws shorter than above sp.; 240-290 predorsal scales. **Ecology:** singly or in small groups at surface of lagoon and seaward reefs. Can be dangerous when leaping into small fishing boats at night. **Range:** circumtropical; N.J. to Brazil in W. Atlantic; the subsp. *fodiator* in E. Pacific.

HALFBEAKS (HEMIRHAMPHIDAE): elongate silvery fishes with small mouth, spikelike lower jaw, and abdominal V fins. Surface dwelling omnivores of algae, zooplankton, and fishes.
8 **Balao** *Hemiramphus balao* Lesueur 38 cm
Bluish on back, upper lobe of tail bluish violet. Strongly barred. **Ecology:** prefers surface waters of offshore reefs. Feeds on small fishes and plankton. **Range:** N.Y. & Bermuda s. to Brazil, e. to e. Atlantic.
9 **Ballyhoo** *Hemiramphus brasiliensis* (Linnaeus) 38 cm
Greenish on back, upper lobe of tail and front of D fin yellow. **Ecology:** near surface of coastal waters, common. Feeds on small fishes. **Range:** N.Y. to Brazil, e. to W. Africa; replaced by *H. bermudensis* at Bermuda.
10 **Halfbeak** *Hyphoramphus unifasciatus* (Ranzani) 27 cm
Differs from *Hemirhamphus* ssp. by having scaled snout & V fin tip does not reach D fin. **Ecology:** primarily in surface waters of bays and estuaries, uncommon over reefs. **Range:** Maine & Bermuda to Argentina; throughout Carib.

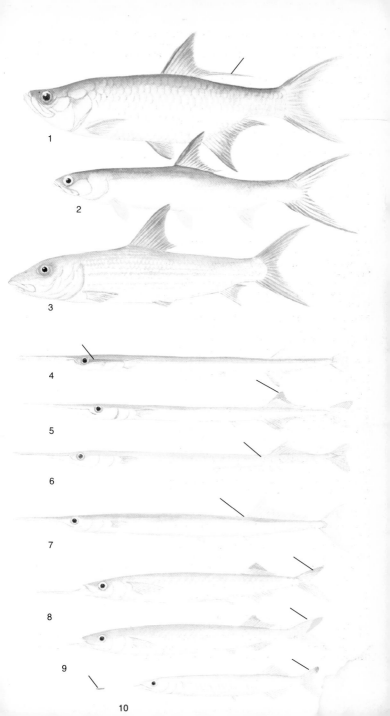

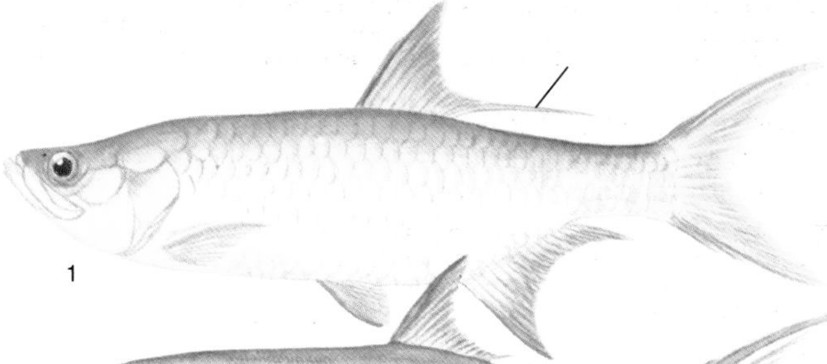

1

2

3

4

5

6

7

8

9

10

HERRINGS, SPRATS, and SARDINES (CLUPEIDAE): small silvery fishes with ventral P fins, abdominal V fins, forked tail, small mouth, and small deciduous scales. Some species migrate into fresh water to spawn.

1 **Redear sardine** *Harengula humeralis* (Cuvier) 20 cm
Reddish-orange "ear mark"; brassy stripes on back. **Ecology:** in large schools along shoreline of shallow inshore waters. Often in polluted areas. **Range:** Fla. Keys & Bermuda to Brazil.

2 **False pilchard** *Harengula clupeola* (Cuvier) 18 cm
Greenish-sivery on back, dark shoulder spot. **Ecology:** shallow coastal waters, often in schools with red-ear sardine. **Range:** s. Fla. & Bahamas to Brazil.

3 **Atlantic thread herring** *Opisthonema oglinum* (Lesueur) 30 cm
D fin prolonged. Dark margin on tail. **Ecology:** harbours and shallow coastal areas. **Range:** C. Cod & Bermuda to s. Brazil.

4 **Dwarf herring** *Jenkinsia lamprotaenia* (Gosse) 7.5 cm
Broad lateral silvery stripe. Similar to *J. majua* (s. Fla. & Bahamas to C. America) & *J. stolifera* (Fla. Keys & Bahamas to Venezuala) with narrow silvery stripe (<eye dia.). **Ecology:** abundant in clear, shallow water. In large schools. Feeds on zooplankton. **Range:** s. Fla. & Bahamas s. to Venezuela, ne. to Bermuda.

ANCHOVIES (ENGRAULIDAE): which have underslung jaw and pre-pelvic scutes and inhabit primarily coastal and brackish waters.

5 **Dusky anchovy** *Anchoa lyolepis* (Evermann & Marsh) 9 cm
Ecology: in fully saline bays and cuts, shoreline to >54 m. **Range:** n. G. Mexico to Venezuela, e. to Lesser Antilles.

SILVERSIDES (ATHERINIDAE): small schooling fishes with two D fins, forked tail, small terminal mouth, broad silver lateral band, and no lateral line. Feed on zooplankton.

6 **Hardhead silverside** *Atherinomorus stipes* (Müller & Troschel) 10 cm
Head wider than body, 2 dusky streaks on lower side. Similar to *Hypoatherina harringtonensis* which has narrow head & fewer A fin rays (11-12 vs 13-14). **Ecology:** in large schools in coastal pelagic waters. **Range:** Bahamas, s. Fla. & Yucatan to Brazil.

LIZARDFISHES (SYNODONTIDAE): small cylindrical fishes with spineless fins and large mouth full of slender sharp teeth, even on tongue. Voracious predators of small fishes.

7 **Sand diver** *Synodus intermedius* (Spix) 45 cm
Ecology: sand flats and channels, 3 to 320 m. Rests on or buried in sand. The most common lizardfish on sand in the Caribbean, but less common shallow along the continental shelf. **Range:** N. Carol., Bermuda & n. G. Mexico to Guyanas.

8 **Inshore lizardfish** *Synodus foetens* (Linneaus) 45 cm
Ecology: on mud or sand bottoms, shoreline to 200 m. Common in coastal shallows. **Range:** Mass., Bermuda & n. G. Mexico to s. Brazil.

9 **Red lizardfish** *Synodus synodus* (Linneaus) 33 cm, rarely 15 cm
Ecology: inshore rocky and coral reefs to 90 m. Rests on hard surfaces rather than on sand. **Range:** n. G. Mexico to Uraguay, e. to Madeira, Ascension & St. Helena.

10 **Snakefish** *Trachinocephalus myops* (Forster) 40 cm
Ecology: sand, shell, rock, or mud bottoms, shoreline to 400 m. **Range:** Circumglobal; Mass, Bermuda & n. G. Mexico to s. Brazil in W. Atlantic.

PEARLFISHES (CARAPODIDAE): translucent eel-like fishes which lack scales, V fins, and in some spp., P fins. Many species live commensally in the body cavities of invertebrates.

11 **Pearlfish** *Carapus bermudensis* (Jones) 20 cm
Ecology: shallow sandy areas and seagrass beds to 235 m. Inhabits the body cavities of sea cucumbers, usually *Actynopyga agassizii* and *Holuthuria mexicana*. Ventures out at night. **Range:** Fla., Bermuda, ne. G. Mexico to Venezuela.

VIVIPAROUS BROTULAS (BYTHITIDAE): elongate tapered fishes with greatly reduced thoracic V fins. Give birth to live young.

12 **Key Brotula** *Ogilbia cayorum* (Evermann & Kendall) 10 cm
Tail distinct, separate from C & A fins; several similar spp., some undescribed. **Ecology:** shallow reefs, 1 to >20 m. Deep within the reef during the day. **Range:** Fla. & Bermuda to Venezuela.

13 See over

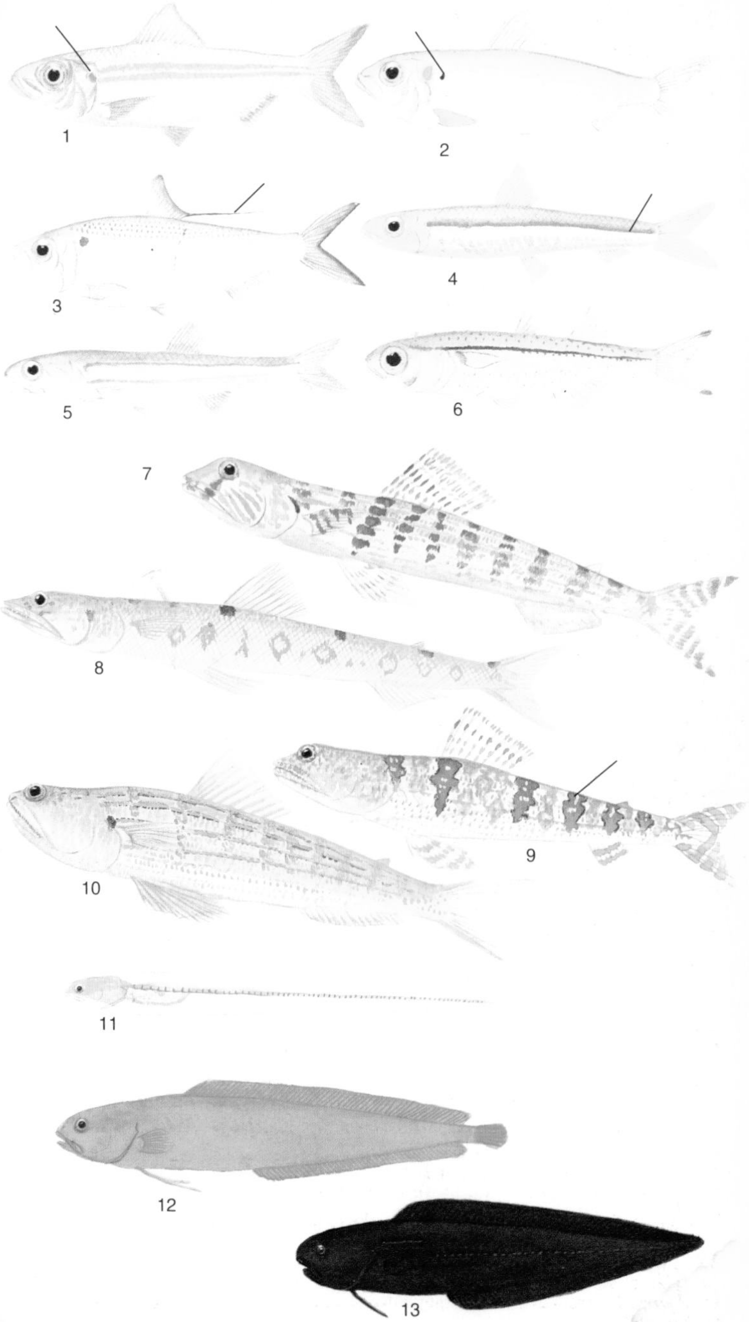
1
2
3
4
5
6
7
8
9
10
11
12
13

←13 **Black brotula** *Stygnobrotula latebricola* Böhlke 7.5 cm
Tail confluent with C & A fins. **Ecology:** shallow rocky ledges and reefs. Deep within the reef during the day. **Range:** s. Fla. & Bahamas to Venezuela.

145 TOADFISHES, FROGFISHES and BATFISHES

TOADFISHES (BATRACHOIDIDAE): bottom dwellers with large head and mouth, eyes positioned somewhat dorsally, and first D fin with III spines. West Atlantic species scaleless. Feed on invertebrates and fishes. During spawning some species migrate and make boat-whistle-like sounds. Eggs are laid in a cavity or debris and guarded by the male.
1 **Coral toadfish** *Sanopus splendidus* Collette, Stark & Phillips 20 cm
Zebra-striped head & bright yellow margins on fins; ca. 5 other less brilliant spp. in genus. **Ecology:** on sand under coral heads or in crevices in clear water, 10 to 25 m. Common. **Range:** Cozumel Is., Mexico.

2 **Sapo cano** *Thalassophryne maculosa* Günther 18 cm
D spines venomous, capable of causing severe long-lasting painful wounds; irregular blotches on head and body. Similar to *Batrachoides gilberti* (C. America). **Ecology:** sandy bottoms of reef flats, lagoons, and seaward reefs, 1 to 200 m. **Range:** Colombia to Venezuela.

FROGFISHES (ANTENNARIIDAE): small globular fishes with distensible body, loose prickly skin, limb-like P fins with an elbow-like joint, small round gill openings, very large upward directed mouth, and first D spine highly modified into a moveable fishing rod (illicium) tipped with a lure (esca). The lure is wriggled enticingly above the mouth to attract other fishes that are swallowed whole. Capable of swallowing prey as large as themselves. Extremely well-camouflaged, often adorned with fleshy or filamentous appendages. Gravid females lay thousands of eggs embedded in a large buoyant gelatinous mass.
3 **Longlure frogfish** *Antennarius multiocellatus* (Valenciennes) 14 cm
Illicium 2nd D spine length; small black ocelli on tail; often a white saddle behind last D ray and large black spot at base of soft D fin (these resemble *A. bermudensis* (s. Fla. & Bermuda to Venezuela) & *A. radiosus* (20 m deep, N.Y. to G. Mexico & Cuba)). Similar to *A. pardalis* (C. Verde Is. & W. Africa) which often has dark spots on belly. **Ecology:** shallow reefs, 0 to 66 m, usually 20 m. Mimics a sponge. Rarely seen. **Range:** s. Fla. & Bermuda to se. Brazil, e. to Ascension (& Azores?).

4 **Splitlure frogfish** *Antennarius scaber* (Cuvier) 15 cm
Esca with 2 large worm-like appendages; ground color pale to nearly black. **Ecology:** rocky and coral reefs on rocks, sand or rubble. In Bahamas, usually <2m. **Range:** N.J., Bermuda & n. G. Mexico to Uruguay; replaced by *A. striatus* in e. Atlantic & Indo-Pacific.

5 **Dwarf frogfish** *Antennarius pauciradiatus* Schultz 5 cm
Illicium short, 1st D spine length; an indistinct dark spot at base of D fin. **Ecology:** rocky or coral patch reefs, 6 to 73 m. Uncommon. **Range:** n. Fla, Bermuda & Cuba through Antilles & C. America to Columbia.

6 **Ocellated frogfish** *Antennarius ocellatus* (Bloch & Schneider) 38 cm
Illicium short, 1st D spine length, esca with fleshy filaments; 3 large black ocelli posteriorly. **Ecology:** rocky and coral reefs, 1 to 150 m, usually 20 m. **Range:** N. C. & Bermuda to Venezuela; replaced by *A. senegalensis* in W. Africa.

7 **Sargassumfish** *Histrio histrio* (Linnaeus) 14 cm (in Atlantic)
Covered with leafy and fleshy appendages, resembling floating *Sargassum* seaweed. **Ecology:** at surface, among floating *Sargassum* algae. Feeds on crustaceans and fishes. **Range:** all tropical waters except e. Pacific; Mass. & Bermuda to Argentina in W. Atlantic.

BATFISHES (OGCOCEPHALIDAE): small fishes with a flattened, often triangular head joined to stalked P fins, a rostrum with globular "lure" dangling from a short "pole" and a protrusible mouth. Bottom dwelling carnivores of small invertebrates and fishes that walk on their P and V fins. Many species on deep soft bottoms of tropical and temperate seas, 14 in W. Atlantic, only about 3 on shallow reefs.
8 **Shortnose batfish** *Ogcocephalus nasutus* (Valenciennes) 38 cm
P fins & tail with broad dark margins, tail with dark base; reddish belly. **Ecology:** open sandy, muddy or rocky bottoms, 0 to 275 m. Uncommon, often partly covered with sand. Unafraid. **Range:** s. Fla. & Bahamas to Amazon River mouth.

9 **Polka-dot batfish** *Ogcocephalus cubifrons* (Richardson) 38 cm
Tan to yellowish with numerous dark brown spots, esp. on base of P fins & tail; P fin with narrow yellow margin. Another pale species, *Haleutichthys aculeatus* (N.C. & Bahamas to n. S. America) has a round body with a reticulated network of dark lines. **Ecology:** sandy, muddy and rocky bottoms, 0 to 70 m. Rare. **Range:** N.C., Bahamas & nw. Fla. to Campeche Bank (Yucatan).

1
2
3
4 var
4
5
6
7
8
9

SOLDIERFISHES and SQUIRRELFISHES (HOLOCENTRIDAE): medium-sized fishes with bony heads, stout fin spines, large spiny scales, and large eyes; predominately red in color.

Subfamily Holocentrinae (squirrelfishes): preopercle with large spine. All spp. are primarily nocturnal. They roam the reef near the bottom to feed on invertebrates and small fishes at night and hover singly or in groups near or among corals or rocks by day.

1 **Longspine squirrelfish** *Holocentrus rufus* (Walbaum) 28cm
Red stripes sometimes blotched; tips of D spines white. **Ecology:** primarily inshore reefs, usually in groups in crevices or holes. Starts feeding at dawn on crustaceans and gastropods. Wary. **Range:** s. Fla. & Bermuda s. to Venezuela.

2 **Squirrelfish** *Holocentrus ascensionis* (Osbeck) 30 cm
Red or pinkish, sometimes blotched. Tips of D spines yellow. **Ecology:** common on patch reefs and tops of walls, 1 to 50 m. **Range:** N.Y., Bermuda & n. G. Mexico to Brazil, e. to St. Paul's Rocks, Ascension, St. Helena & e. Atlantic.

3 **Reef squirrelfish** *Sargocentron coruscum* (Poey) 13 cm
Black spot between first 2-3 D spines, the tips & base of fin white. Similar to *S. bullisi* (S.C. & Bahamas to L. Antilles) which is deeper-bodied & has a black spot only next to 1st D spine & *S. poco* (Tex., Bah. & G. Cayman) which has lg. dark blotch below 2nd D fin & on tail base. **Ecology:** shallow rocky or coral reefs, 1 to 30 m. More common on seaward reefs than on protected reefs. Retreats into recesses when alarmed. **Range:** Fla. & Bermuda to Venezuela.

4 **Dusky squirrelfish** *Sargocentron vexillarium* (Poey) 18 cm
Rusty stripes. Dark spots on axil of P fin. Dark spinous D fin. **Ecology:** inshore reefs, tidepools to 20 m. Hides in small recesses. Common, but rarely seen. Wary. **Range:** Fla. & Bermuda, s. to Venezuela.

5 **Longjaw squirrelfish** *Neoniphon marianus* (Cuvier) 17 cm
Orange stripes on body. Yellow bar on opercle. Spinous D fin yellow. **Ecology:** seaward reef slopes, 1 to 70 m. Rare shallow, becoming common below 30 m. **Range:** Fla. Keys & Bahamas, s. to Venezuela & Trinidad.

Subfamily Myripristinae (soldierfishes): preopercular spine absent, scales large, and snout short and blunt. All species are primarily nocturnal; *Myripristis* spp. swim well above the bottom to feed on large zooplankton at night. By day they hover in groups in or near caves or coral formations.

6 **Cardinal soldierfish** *Plectrypops retrospinis* (Guichenot) 13 cm
Ecology: remains in deep recesses during the day. Rarely seen. **Range:** s. Fla. & Bermuda to Venezuela.

7 **Blackbar soldierfish** *Myripristis jacobus* Cuvier 20 cm
Ecology: in crevices, holes and caves, occasionally swimming upside down, 5 to 50 m. Solitary or in groups. **Range:** N. Carol. & n. G. Mexico to Brazil, e. to e. Atlantic incl. St. Paul's Rocks, Ascension & St. Helena.

FLASHLIGHTFISHES (ANOMALOPIDAE): small uniformly black fishes with bony heads, small rough scales and a light organ beneath each eye.

8 **Atlantic flashlightfish** *Kryptophaneron alfredi* Sylvester & Fowler 12.5 cm
Ecology: vertical dropoffs, 25 to 200 m. Observed only on moonless nights. **Range:** Cayman Is., Jamaica, Curaao, P. Rico & Bahamas; probably more widspread.

CORNETFISHES (FISTULARIIDAE): body wider than deep, oval in x-sect.; tail a long filament.

9 **Bluespotted cornetfish** *Fistularia tabacaria* Linnaeus 180 cm
Ecology: hovers above the bottom in wide variety of habitats, particularly reef flats, but as deep as 200 m. Solitary or in schools, feeds on small fishes and crustaceans. **Range:** N. Scotia & Bermuda to Brazil, e. to E. Atlantic.

AULOSTOMIDAE (TRUMPETFISHES): body laterally compressed; distinct tail fin.

10 **Trumpetfish** *Aulostomus maculatus* Valenciennes 100 cm
Ecology: among rocks or corals, reef flats to 25 m. A solitary ambusher of small fishes and crustaceans that lurks among branching corals or gorgonians. Often swims behind large herbivorous fishes to sneak up on prey. Mouth opens to diameter of body to suck in prey. **Range:** s. Fla., Bermuda & n. G. Mexico to n. S. America, replaced by *A. strigosus* at Ascension, St. Helena & e. Atlantic.

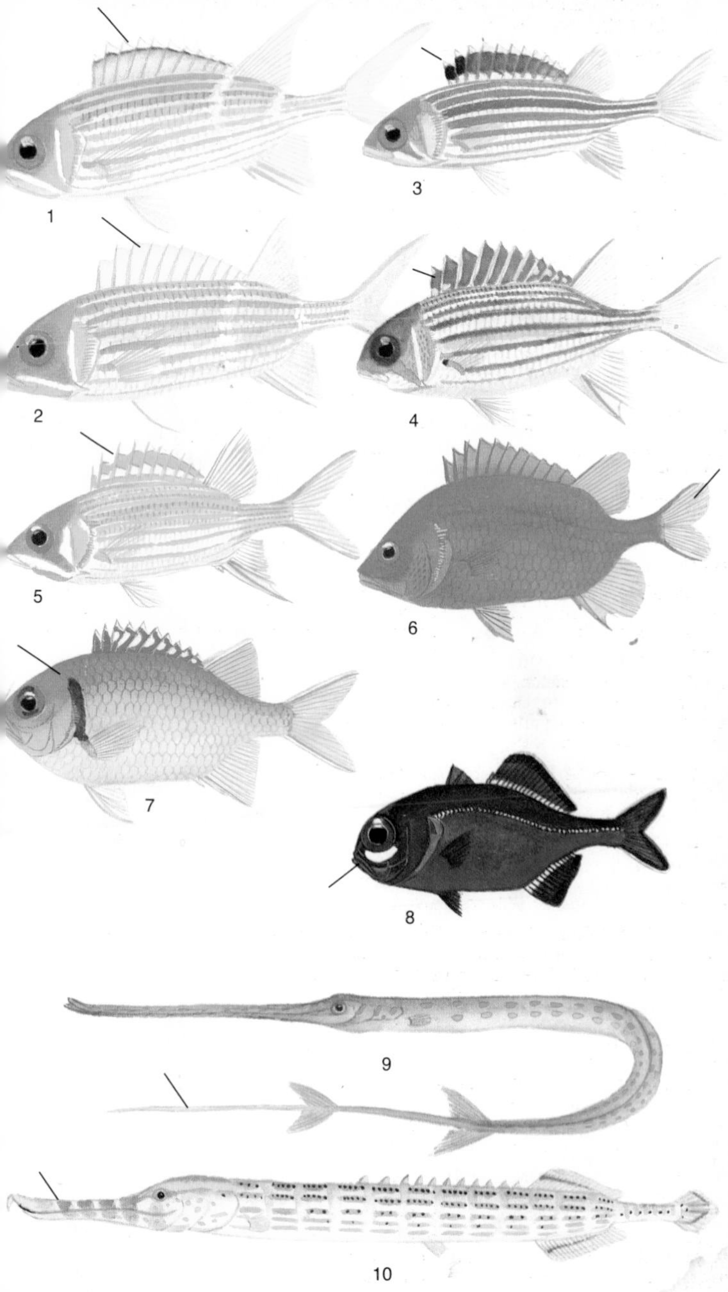
1
3
2
4
5
6
7
8
9
10

147 PIPEFISHES, SCORPIONFISHES, SEAROBINS and FLYING GURNARDS

SEAHORSES and PIPEFISHES (SYNGNATHIDAE): small elongate fishes encased in rings of bony plates. Seahorses have an angled head and prehensile tail that lacks a fin. All seahorses and pipefishes feed on minute invertebrates sucked into a tubular snout. Reproduction is highly unusual: the male has a brood pouch in which the eggs are fertilized and incubated after being deposited by the female. At least 3 species of seahorses and 20 species of pipefishes in region.

1 **Longsnout sea horse** *Hippocampus reidi* Ginsburg 10 cm (15 cm stretched)
15-18 (us. 17) D rays; *H. zosterae* has 11-14 D rays & short snout; *H. erectus* has 18-21 (us. 19-20) D rays. Color variable, but with scattered tiny black dots. **Ecology:** shoreline to >15 m. Uncommon in most areas, but may be locally common in certain places. Usually attached to gorgonians or seagrasses but may occur in floating sargassum or swim freely in midwater. **Range:** N. Carol. & Bermuda to n. S. America.

2 **Lined seahorse** *Hippocampus erectus* Perry 17.5 cm
Color highly variable, but us. with large pale blotches and dark lines on neck and back; no scattered black dots. **Ecology:** shoreline to >40 m. Rare in most areas, but may be locally abundant. Usually attached to gorgonians or seagrasses but may occur in floating sargassum or swim freely in midwater. **Range:** N. Scotia & n. G. Mexico to Argentina.

3 **Harlequin pipefish** *Micrognathus vittatus* (Kaup) 14.5 cm
All other spp. of pipefishes in region irregularly or indistinctly banded or not banded at all. Sometimes lumped with *M. crinitus* (same dist.), separable only by color. **Ecology:** in patches of rubble, usually near sea fans, tidepools to 21 m. **Range:** s. Fla. & Bermuda to Brazil, e. to Fernando de Noronha.

4 **Caribbean pipefish** *Syngnathus caribbaeus* Dawson 22.5 cm
Ecology: on weedy or sandy bottoms of shallow inshore waters. **Range:** C. & S. America, Belize to Surinam; G. & L. Antilles; replaced by *S. floridae* in Fla.

SCORPIONFISHES (SCORPAENIDAE): head large and spiny with bony ridge on cheek; D fin usually notched, fin spines venomous with groove and venom sack. Most spp. live on or near the bottom and feed on crustaceans or fishes. Most are extremely well-camouflaged and remain in or near shelter during the day. Most do well in the aquarium, but some require live food and others can be trained to take almost anything.

5 **Spotted scorpionfish** *Scorpaena plumieri* Bloch 45 cm
Three dark brown bands on tail; P axil black with white spots. **Ecology:** shallow rocky or coral reefs, 1 to 55 m. Lies motionlesss on the bottom. Diplays brightly colored inner pectoral fins when disturbed. Often on patch reefs near seagrasses. Feeds on small fishes and crustaceans. **Range:** N.Y. & Bermuda to Brazil, e. to Ascension, St. Helena & e. Atlantic.

6 **Plumed scorpionfish** *Scorpaena grandicornis* Cuvier 17 cm
Lg. tentacle above eye; P axil brown with small white spots. Similar to *S. brasiliensis*. **Ecology:** inshore habitats including seagrass beds, bays and channels, 1 to 15 m. Moves only when disturbed. Difficult to detect. **Range:** Fla. & Bermuda to s.Brazil.

7 **Barbfish** *Scorpaena brasiliensis* Cuvier 23 cm
Dark spot above P fin & 3 dark spots inside P fin. **Ecology:** inshore areas like bays and harbors, 1 to 100 m. Common on the continental shelf. **Range:** Virginia to Brazil, absent from Bermuda and Bahamas.

8 **Reef scorpionfish** *Scorpaenodes caribbaeus* Meek & Hildebrand 12 cm
Black blotch on D fin; tail spotted. Similar to *S. tredecimspinosus* which has 17 (vs. 18-19) P rays. **Ecology:** shallow inshore areas, tidepools to 15 m. Sometimes drifts above hard substratum or near ceilings of caves or ledges. Secretive but common. **Range:** Fla. & Bahamas to Panama & Venezuela.

9 **Coral scorpionfish** *Scorpaena albifimbria* Evermann & Marsh 8 cm
Lg. dark saddle above P fin; P axil without markings. **Ecology:** coral reefs, 1 to 36 m. Secretive. **Range:** s. Fla. & Bahamas to Venezuela.

SEAROBINS (TRIGLIDAE): small bony-headed fishes with winglike P fins with 2 to 3 free rays. Bottom-dwelling carnivores of benthic invertebrates. P rays used to walk on bottom. Produce sounds with swim bladder. Primarily temperate and deep tropical seas.

10 **Bandtail searobin** *Prionotus ophryas* Jordan & Swain 20 cm
Distinguished from flying gurnard by free P rays and all D fin spines bound by membranes. **Ecology:** shallow seagrass beds, sand or coral rubble, 1 to 171 m. **Range:** N.C., Bahamas & n. G. Mexico to Brazil.

HELMET GURNARDS (DACTYLOPTERIDAE): armored box-like fishes with colorful winglike P fins and rays of V fins free and used to walk on bottom. Produces sounds.

11 **Flying gurnard** *Dactylopterus volitans* (Linneus) 45 cm
1st 2 D spines form elongate detached finlet; all P rays bound by membrane. **Ecology:** seagrass beds and sandy areas near patch reefs, 1 to 12 m. Uncommon. **Range:** Mass. & Bermuda to Argentina, e. to Ascension (?) & e. Atlantic & Mediterranean.

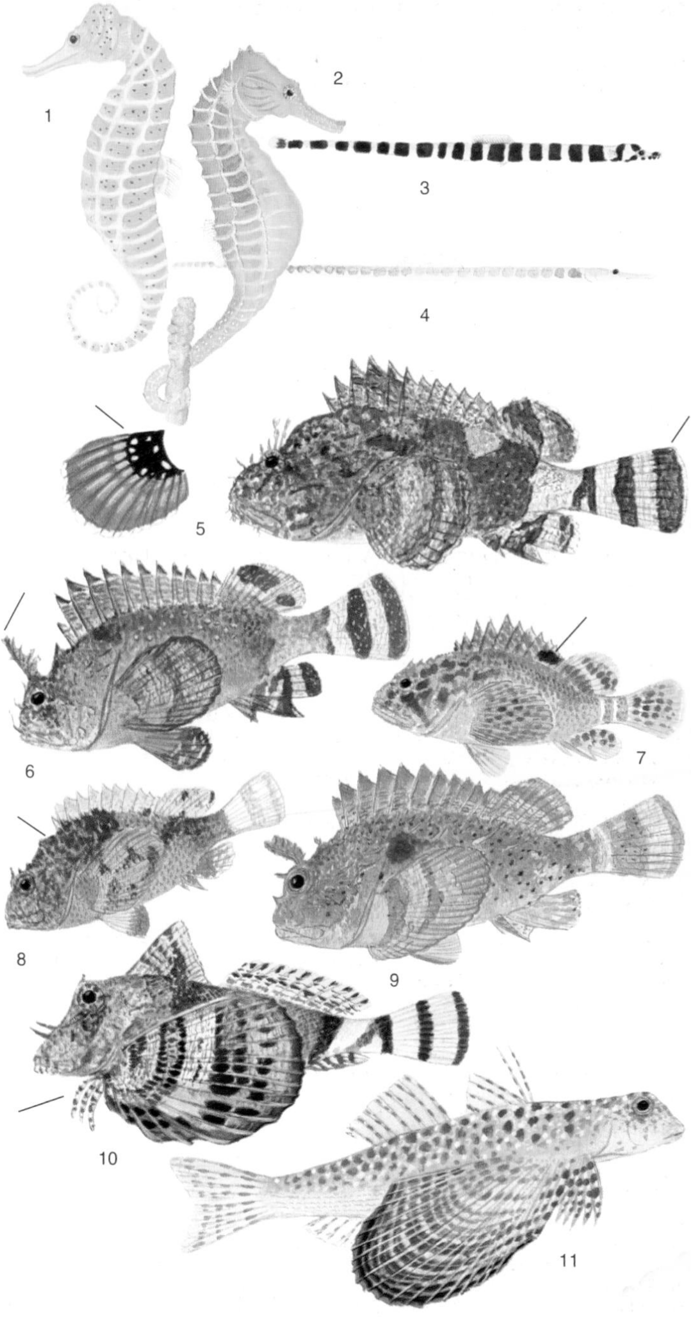
1
2
3
4
5
6
7
8
9
10
11

GROUPERS, PERCHLETS, BASSLETS, and SOAPFISHES (SERRANIDAE): a large and varied group of fishes typically with a single D fin with well-developed spines, continuous LL, 2-3 small flattened opercular spines, and small ctenoid scales. Hermaphrodites that commence maturity as females then change sex to males later in life.

Subfamily Epinephelinae (basslets, groupers, soapfishes, and podges): bottom dwelling carnivores with large mouths, robust bodies, and small ctenoid scales. Formerly divided into several families, grouped here as "tribes".

Tribe Epinephelini (groupers): medium to large robust-bodied forms with large mouths, the jaws typically containing bands of small teeth and canines in front. Typically bottom-dwelling predators of fishes and crustaceans. Important foodfishes, but some species may be ciguatoxic in certain areas. Relatively hardy in aquariums.

1 **Jewfish** *Epinephelus itajara* (Lichtenstein) 240 cm; 310, poss. 455 kg
♀ mature at 110-115 cm (4-6 yrs), ♂ at 120-135 cm (6-7 yrs); lives to 37 yrs. **Ecology**: mangrove cuts and seagrass beds to ~100 m, usually near caves or wrecks. Juveniles primarily in estuarine areas. Feeds primarily on crustaceans, particularly spiny lobsters as well as turtles and fishes, including stingrays. Territorial near its refuge cave or wreck where it may show a threat display with open mouth and quivering body. Large individuals have been known to stalk and attempt to eat divers. Overfished, particularly by spearfishing. **Range**: Fla., Bermuda & n. G. Mexico to se. Brazil; e. Atlantic, Senegal to the Congo; e. Pacific: c. Sea of Cortez to n. Peru.

2 **Nassau grouper** *Epinephelus striatus* (Bloch) 120 cm; 25 kg
Color variable depending on mood and environment. Ground colour pale with 5 irregular brown bands. Black spot on C peduncle. **Ecology**: common on shallow coral reefs and seagrass beds, 1 to 35 m. Usually close to caves. Spawns near new moon with up to 30,000 aggregating at certain spawning sites (Bimini). Heavily fished and vulnerable to overfishing, particularly when migrating or aggregating to spawn. **Range**: N. Carol. & Bermuda to Brazil.

3 **Red grouper** *Epinephelus morio* (Valenciennes) 90 cm; 23 kg
Reddish-brown with pale blotches; broad bars may be present. High D fin. **Ecology**: rocky reefs, 5 to 120 m. Usually rests on the bottom. Wary. Abundant in Florida and the Bahamas, uncommon on coral reefs. **Range**: Mass. & Bermuda s. to Brazil.

4 **Red hind** *Epinephelus guttatus* (Linnaeus) 67cm
Dark margin on posterior fins, numerous red brown spots, no dark saddle. Lives to 18 yrs but changes sex from ♀ to ♂ as young as 2 yrs with 50% ♀ mature at 3 yrs. **Ecology**: common on rocky and coral reefs, 3 to 80 m. Often drifts or lies motionless on the bottom. Easily approached by divers. An important fishery species. **Range**: N. Carol. & Bermuda to Brazil.

5 **Rock hind** *Epinephelus adscensionis* (Osbeck) 60 cm
Similar to above species but with dark saddle on C peduncle & indistinct blotches on back. **Ecology**: rocky bottoms, 1 to 50 m. Often drifts near the bottom. Difficult to approach. **Range**: Mass. (rare n. of Fla.) & Bermuda to se. Brazil, e. to Ascension & St. Helena.

6 **Graysby** *Cephalopholis cruentatus* (Lacépède) 35 cm
Reddish brown spots on pale underground, 3-5 dark spots on back. **Ecology**: abundant on shallow coral reefs with small caves or crevices, 2 to 72 m. Rests on the bottom. Easily approached and fed by divers. **Range**: n. G. Mexico, Fla. & Bermuda to se. Brazil.

7 **Coney** *Cephalopholis fulva* (Linnaeus) 41 cm
3 major color ph.: red with blue spots; reddish brown above, white below, with blue spots all over; brilliant yellow with a few blue spots on head. **Ecology**: common on rocky and coral reefs, 3 to 20 m. Usually resting on bottom where they feed on crustaceans. Wary, but approachable. **Range**: s. Fla. & Bermuda s. to se. Brazil.

8 **Marbled grouper** *Dermatolepis inermis* (Valenciennes) 91 cm
Ecology: caves and ledges on deep rocky reefs, 3 to 210 m. Secretive. Darts away when approached or frightened. **Range**: s. Fla., Bermuda & n. G. Mexico to Brazil & offshore Is.

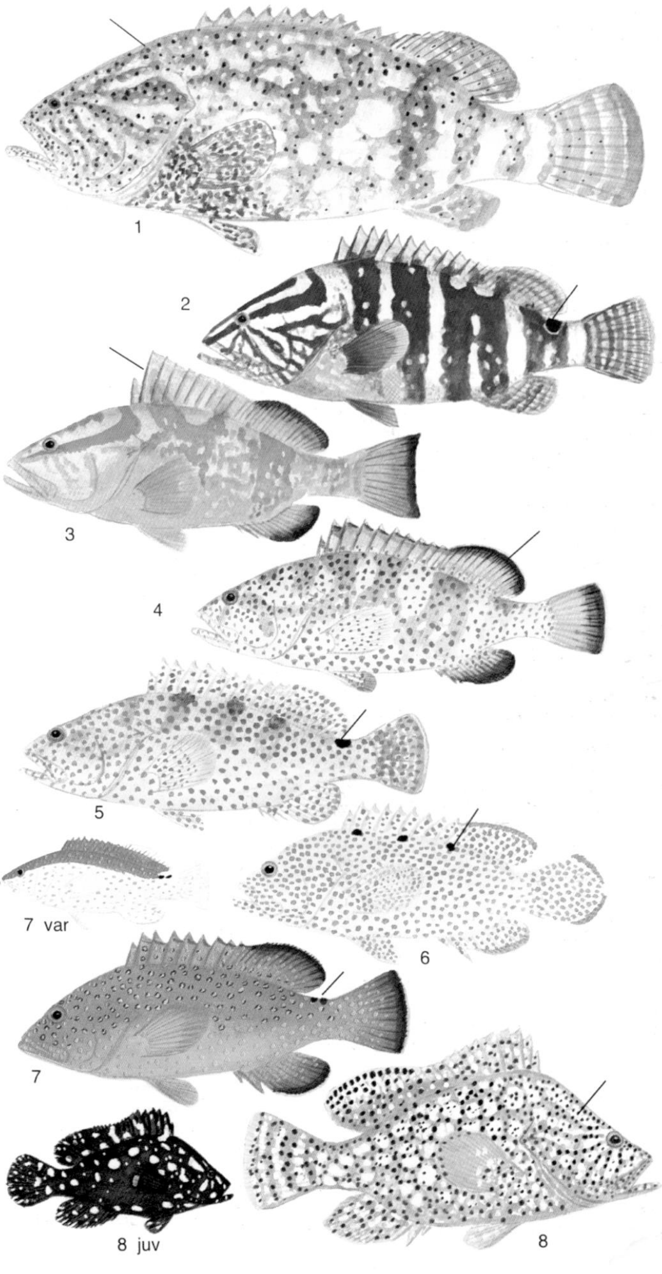
1
2
3
4
5
7 var
6
7
8 juv
8

1 **Black grouper** *Mycteroperca bonaci* (Poey) 130 cm; 82 kg
Ecology: rocky and coral reefs, 6 to 33 m. Drifts above the bottom, sometimes several meters above reef. Common, but difficult to approach. **Range:** Mass. Bermuda & G. Mexico to se. Brazil.

2 **Yellowfin grouper** *Mycteroperca venenosa* (Linnaeus) 90 cm
Color variable, blotches on pale background may be reddish, brown-olive, or even black. **Ecology:** common on shallow reefs and near walls, 3 to 30 m. Often rests on the floor of caves. Occasionally ciguatoxic. **Range:** Fla., Bermuda & s. G. Mexico to Brazil.

3 **Tiger grouper** *Mycteroperca tigris* (Valenciennes) 100 cm
About nine dark brown diagonal bars; occas. nearly entirely black. **Ecology:** coral and rocky reefs from reef flats to reef slopes below 20 m. Usually several well above the bottom. Frequents cleaning stations. Wary. **Range:** s. Fla. & Bermuda & Bay of Campeche to Brazil.

4 **Yellowmouth grouper** *Mycteroperca interstitialis* (Poey) 70 cm
Yellow mouth; sometimes blotched like the Black grouper. Juvs. with black back. **Ecology:** primarily island reefs, 3 to 25 m. Drifts over the bottom or rests in recesses. Sometimes approachable by divers. **Range:** Fla. (rare) & Bermuda s. to Brazil.

5 **Comb grouper** *Mycteroperca acutirostris* (Valenciennes) 60 cm
Brown to gray with numerous white blotches. Dark stripes from eye. **Ecology:** rocky or coral reefs, 3 to 40 m. Prefers deeper reefs where it drifts above the bottom. Juveniles in lagoons bordering mangrove swamps. **Range:** Tex., Bermuda & Gr. Antilles to Brazil; replaced in E. Atlantic by *M. fusca* (Azores, Madeira, Canary & C. Verde Is.) & *M. rubra* (Portugal to s. Angola & Medit.).

6 **Scamp** *Mycteropera phenax* Jordan & Swain 60 cm
Similar to Yellowmouth grouper but blotched and without yellow mouth. **Ecology:** primarily continental reefs. **Range:** Mass. & G. of Mexico to Venezuela.

7 **Mutton hamlet** *Alphestes afer* (Bloch) 30 cm
Mottled reddish brown to green with numerous small black spots. **Range:** various habitats inluding seagrass beds (common), coral rubble bottoms, and rocky and coral reefs, 2 to 30 m. Cryptic. **Range:** Fla. & Bermuda to Argentina; e. Pacific, n. Sea of Cortez to n. Peru incl. Galapagos Is.

8 **Sand perch** *Diplectrum formosum* (Linnaeus) 30 cm
Blue and orange lateral stripes, dark vertical stripes. Similar to *D. bivittatum* (G. Mexico to Brazil) which has two dark lateral stripes and lives on muddy bottoms. **Ecology:** inhabits burrows in grassy, sandy, or coral rubble bottoms; 1-73m. Wary. Retreats immediately into shelter when frightened. **Range:** n. G. Mexico & Virginia s. to Brazil; absent from W. Indies except Cuba & Bahamas.

Tribe Grammistinae (soapfishes): small bottom-dwelling carnivores with large mouths, robust bodies, and small ctenoid scales. Produce a bitter skin toxin called grammistin which protects them from predators and can kill other fishes in a confined space.

9 **Greater soapfish** *Rypticus saponaceus* (Bloch & Schneider) 33 cm
Gray to brown with pale spots. Concave head with an upturned mouth
Ecology: crevices and ledges of coral reefs, 1 to 55 m. Common, but secretive. **Range:** s. Fla. & Bermuda to Brazil, e. to St. Paul's Rocks, St. Helena & E. Atlantic.

10 **Spotted soapfish** *Rypticus subbifrenatus* Gill 18 cm
Ecology: clear water areas of shorelines and open reefs to 21m. Secretive. **Range:** s. Fla. & Bahamas to Venezuela, e. to E. Atlantic.

11 **Reef bass** *Pseudogramma gregoryi* (Breder) 7.5 cm
P. macrostigmus (Bahamas to Panama) has lg. round blotches on head and front of body; *P. bistrispinus* (Fla. & Bahamas to Brazil) has dark speckles all over body. **Ecology:** among living corals, shoreline to 21 m. Common in rubble but secretive. **Range:** s. Fla. & Bermuda to Venezuela, e. to Ascension.

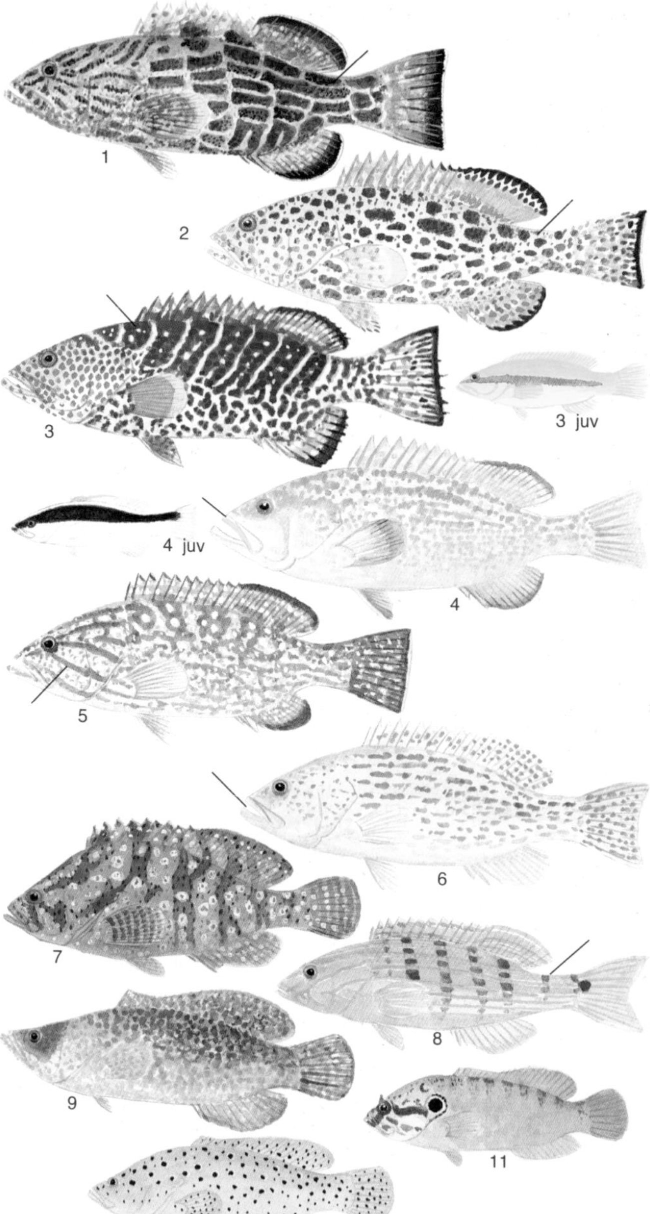
1
2
3
3 juv
4 juv
4
5
6
7
8
9
11
10

Hamlets Genus *Hypoplectrus*. A complex of 11 species which are often considered to be stable colour morphs of a single species. However, it has recently been demonstrated that these colour morphs represent recently evolved species. Some species are aggressive mimics of certain damselfishes. The distributions and habitats of the mimics may reflect that of the model damselfishes. All are simultaneous hermaphrodite species. Territorial by day, but form pairs at dusk to spawn. The 'male' wraps itself around the 'female' as the pair rise about a meter above the bottom where the gametes are released. Mixed species pairs are rare, but hybrids occasionally occur. Feeds on small fishes and crustaceans.

1 **Butter hamlet** *Hypoplectrus unicolor* (Walbaum) 13 cm
Dark spot on caudal peduncle not always present. Pale bluish. All the other seem to be color morphs of this species. **Ecology:** coral reefs, 3 to 15 m. Shy, remains close to shelter. The most common form in the Florida Keys but less common elsewhere. **Range:** Fla. Keys & Bahamas to Brazil.

2 **Masked hamlet** *Hypoplectrus* sp. 13 cm
Black wedge below eye. **Ecology:** areas of rich coral growth, 6 to 18 m. Remains near corals. **Range:** exact range unknown; Cayman Is., Belize, Honduras & Providencia Is.

3 **Black hamlet** *Hypoplectrus nigricans* (Poey) 13 cm
Uniform dark, long pelvic fins. **Ecology:** shallow reefs, 3 to 13 m. Common in localized areas throughout the West Indies. **Range:** Fla. to Bahamas & W. Indies.

4 **Blue hamlet** *Hypoplectrus gemma* Goode & Bean 13 cm
Iridescent blue. Tail with a black margin. **Ecology:** coral reefs, 3 to 13 m. Remains close to the bottom. **Range:** s. Fla. & Keys only.

5 **Golden hamlet** *Hypoplectrus gummigutta* (Poey) 13 cm
Brilliant yellow with a black blue-edged spot below eye. **Ecology:** deep reefs, 10 to 45 m, but as shallow as 2 m in the Grenadines. Maintains territories on reef tops. **Range:** s. Fla., Bahamas, Cuba, Jamaica & Domin. Rep.

6 **Yellowbelly hamlet** *Hypoplectrus abberans* (Poey) 13 cm
Bluish cast on head and on spinous dorsal fin. Dark spot on base indistinct. Melanistic forms have been observed. **Ecology:** rocky and coral reefs, 3 to 15 m. Wary. Generally uncommon. **Range:** s. Fla. to W. Indies; absent from Bahamas.

7 **Shy hamlet** *Hypoplectrus guttavarius* (Poey) 13 cm
All fins yellow. Extent of brown on back varies. **Ecology:** rocky or coral reefs, 3 to 30 m, often seen near staghorn corals. Somehow shy but curious. **Range:** Fla. Keys, Cayman Is., Bahama, Virgin Is., to W. Indies.

8 **Barred hamlet** *Hypoplectrus puella* (Cuvier) 13 cm
Front part with a broad brown bar, three small ones behind. **Ecology:** shallow rocky and coral reefs, 3 to 23 m. Always close to cover, but can be approached easily by divers. The most common form in the West Indies. **Range:** G. coast of Fla. & Bermuda to W. Indies.

9 **Yellowtail hamlet** *Hypoplectrus chlorurus* (Valenciennes) 13 cm
Black, brown or blue with a yellow tail. **Ecology:** coral-rich reefs, 3 to 23 m. Stays close to the bottom. **Range:** Texas & Bahamas to W. Indies & Venezuela; absent from Fla.

10 **Indigo hamlet** *Hypoplectrus indigo* (Poey) 13 cm
Alternating blue and white bars. **Ecology:** coral reefs, 10 to 45 m. Shy but can be approached slowly. Common in Cayman Is., occasional to rare elsewhere. **Range:** s. Fla. & Bahamas, Cayman Is., St. Lucia & Grenadines, w. to Belize.

1

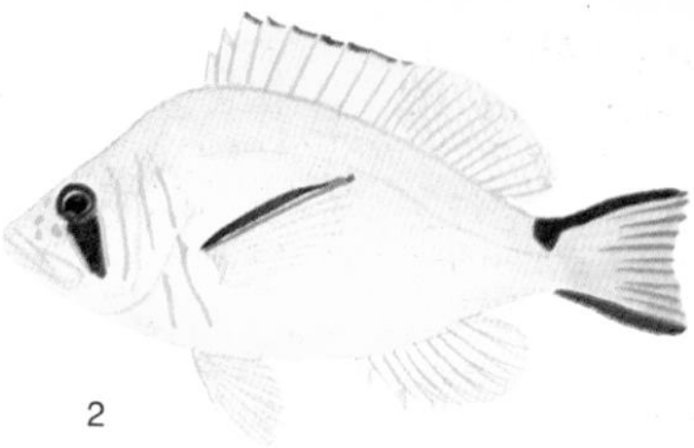
2

3

4

5

6

7

8

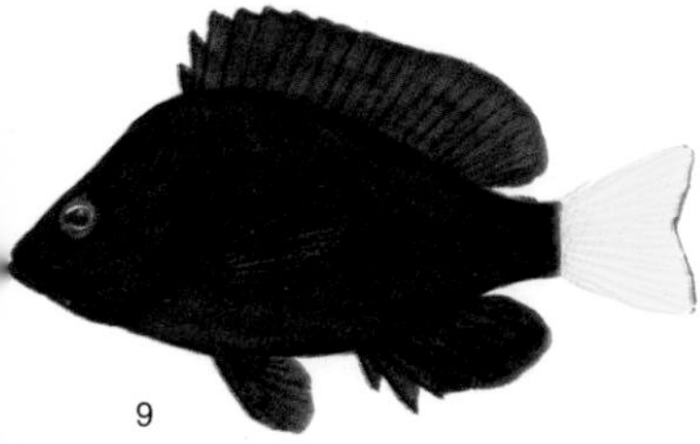
9

10

151 BASSES

1 **Tobaccofish** *Serranus tabacarius* (Cuvier) 18 cm
Ecology: common on coral reefs and coral rubble or sandy areas, 3 to 70 m. In groups on deeper reefs. **Range:** s. Fla. & Bermuda to n. Brazil.

2 **Harlequin bass** *Serranus tigrinus* (Bloch) 10 cm
Ecology: solitary or in pairs on rocky and coral reefs, seagrass, and rubble areas, 0.5 to 40 m. Feeds on crustaceans. The most common member of the genus. **Range:** n. Fla. & Bermuda to Venezuela.

3 **Lantern bass** *Serranus baldwini* (Evermann & Marsh) 7 cm
Indiv. from water 15 m have red bars below the rectangular blotches. **Ecology:** often resting on shell-rubble or corals, or in seagrass beds, 1 to 80 m. **Range:** s. Fla. & Bermuda to Venezuela.

4 **Orangeback bass** *Serranus annularis* (Günther) 9 cm
Two orange squares behind eye. Dark spots on dorsal fin. **Ecology:** in pairs close to rocky or coral rubble bottoms, 10 to 70 m, usually 30 m. **Range:** s. Fla. & Bermuda to Venezuela.

5 **Chalk bass** *Serranus tortugarum* Longley 8 cm
Ground color may be bluish, orange or brown. Dark saddles on back. **Ecology:** in small aggregations over rubble, silty or sandy bottoms, 12 to 396 m. Feeds on plankton. Difficult to approach. **Range:** s. Fla. & Bahamas to Honduras, e. to Virgin Is.

6 **Two-spot bass** *Serranus flaviventris* (Cuvier) 7.5 cm
Two distinctive spots on caudal peduncle. White belly. **Ecology:** rocky and coral reefs and seagrass beds, 2 to 402 m. **Range:** Gr. Antilles to Uruguay.

7 **Tattler** *Serranus phoebe* Poey 15 cm
Dark bars, dark stripe below eye. **Ecology:** rocky reefs, 27 to 180 m. **Range:** S. Carol., Bermuda & Yucatan to Venezuela.

8 **School bass** *Schultzea beta* (Hildebrand) 10 cm
Orange-brown above, bluish on belly. Rusty bar below eye. **Ecology:** rocky or coral reefs 15 to 110 m. Feeds in small groups on plankton. **Range:** s. Fla. to Venezuela.

Tribe Liopropomini (basslets): small elongate forms with a broad head, deeply notched or divided D fin with VIII spines (last one may be scaled over), and continuous LL arched over P region. All species are secretive, many inhabit depths below 60 m.

9 **Candy bass** *Liopropoma carmabi* (Randall) 6 cm
Ecology: recesses of coral reefs, 15 to 70 m. Secretive. **Range:** Fla. Keys, Bahamas, P.Rico, Barbados, Bonaire & Curacao.

10 **Swissguard basslet** *Liopropoma rubre* Poey 8 cm
Reddish brown and yellow stripes. Black blotches on tail are connected. **Ecology:** crevices or deep recesses, 3 to 45 m. Common, but secretive and rarely seen. **Range:** s. Fla. & Yucatan s. to Venezuela.

11 **Cave bass** *Liopropoma mowbrayi* Woods & Kanazawa 9 cm
Salmon red to red with a yellow stripe before eye. Black margin on tail. **Ecology:** rocky reefs in caves and recesses, 30 to 60 m. Secretive. **Range:** S. Fla. & Bermuda s. to Venezuela.

12 **Wrasse bass** *Liopropoma eukrines* (Starck & Courtenay) 13 cm
Ecology: rocky reefs, 30 to 150 m. **Range:** N. Carol. to Fla. Keys.

13 **Creole-fish** *Paranthias furcifer* (Valenciennes) 35 cm
Color variable from red to olive or brown. White or black spots may be present. **Ecology:** in aggregations over deep coral and rocky reefs, 8 to 100 m. Feeds in midwater on zooplankton, primarily copepods. Retreats instantly when alarmed. **Range:** N. Carol. & Bermuda to Brazil, e. to St. Helena & G. Guinea islands; replaced in E. Pacific by *P.colonus*.

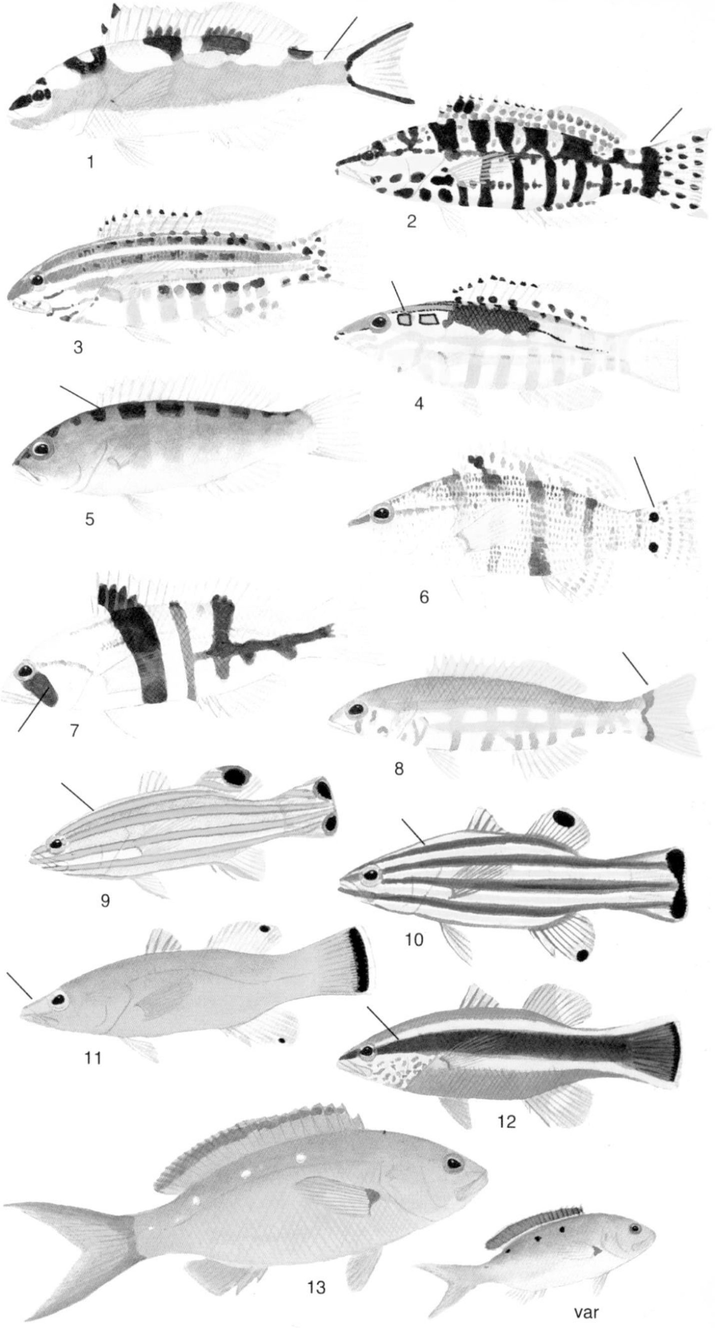
1
2
3
4
5
6
7
8
9
10
11
12
13
var

BASSLETS (GRAMMATIDAE): small colorful fishes with continuous D fin, elongate V fins, and interrupted (*Gramma*) or no LL (*Lipogramma*). Feed on copepods and small invertebrates. Males brood eggs in mouth. Several deep reef species (to 365 m). Popular with aquarists.

1 **Blackcap basslet** *Gramma melacara* Böhlke & Randall 10 cm
Ecology: steep seaward slopes and walls, 11 to 60 m, rarely solitary or in small groups near caves and recesses. Often upside-down. Retreats into recesses when alarmed. **Range:** Bahamas, Jamaica & G. Cayman, to C. America & s. Carib.

2 **Yellowcheek basslet** *Gramma linki* Starck & Colin 7 cm
Ecology: steep outer reef faces, 27 to 130 m, but below 60 m. in w. Caribbean. **Range:** Bahamas, C. America & Gr. Antilles.

3 **Fairy basslet; Royal gramma** *Gramma loreto* Poey 8 cm
Ecology: in small groups in caves, recesses, or under ledges, 1 to 60 m. Orients to substratum so upside-down near roof of caves. Retreats into recesses when alarmed. **Range:** Bermuda, Bahamas & C. America to Venezuela, e. to L. Antilles; absent from Fla.

4 **Bicolor basslet** *Lipogramma klayi* Randall 4 cm
Similar to *L. trilineatum* (s. Fla. to Venezuela) with three lines on nape & upper back. **Ecology:** steep seaward slopes and walls over 35 m. **Range:** Bahamas, P. Rico, Jamaica & C. America to Venezuela.

CARDINALFISHES (APOGONIDAE): Most species remain hidden during the day and venture out to feed on zooplankton or small benthic invertebrates at night. Males incubate eggs in mouth until hatching. They generally do well in the aquarium.

5 **Barred cardinalfish** *Apogon binotatus* (Poey) 10 cm
Ecology: ubiquitous, 1 to 50 m. In dark shelters by day, out at night. **Range:** se. Fla. & Bermuda to Venezuela.

6 **Belted cardinalfish** *Apogon townsendi* (Breder) 6 cm
Ecology: solitary or in groups in caves or holes, often near drop-offs, 3 to 55 m. **Range:** s. Fla. s. to Venezuela.

7 **Flamefish** *Apogon maculatus* (Poey) 10.5 cm
Ecology: ubiquitous near seawalls, rocks and reefs, 0.3 to 20 m. Hovers near and in holes. **Range:** Mass. (rare n. of s. Fla.), Bermuda & ne. G. Mexico to Venezuela

8 **Pale cardinalfish** *Apogon planifrons* Longley & Hildebrand 10 cm
Ecology: rocky and coral reefs, 3 to 30 m. **Range:** S. Fla. & Bahamas to Venezuela.

9 **Broadscale cardinalfish** *Apogon pillionatus* Böhlke & Randall 6.5 cm
Ecology: coral and rocky areas with little sand, 15 to 90 m. **Range:** S. Fla. & Bahamas to n. S. America.

10 **Mimic cardinalfish** *Apogon phenax* Böhlke & Randall 7.5 cm
Ecology: coral and rocky areas with little sand, 3 to 50 m. **Range:** Fla. Keys & Bahamas to Curaao.

11 **Twospot cardinalfish** *Apogon pseudomaculatus* Longley 10.5 cm
Similar to *A. maculatus*, but with black spot on upper C peduncle. **Ecology:** seaward reefs, harbours, pilings and walls, 1 to 20 m. **Range:** Mass. (uncommon n. of Fla.) & Bermuda to s. Brazil.

12 **Whitestar cardinalfish** *Apogon lachneri* Böhlke 6.5 cm
Similar to *A. evermanni* (Carib. & Indo-Pacific) which lacks the white spot on upper C peduncle. **Ecology:** clear coral reefs with caves, 5 to 70 m. **Range:** s. Fla. & Bahamas to Belize.

13 **Sawcheek cardinalfish** *Apogon quadrisquamatus* Longley 6.5 cm
Similar to *A. mosavi* (Bahamas to Haiti & Jamaica) with a dusky bar on C peduncle. **Ecology:** inhabits anemones in dark recesses, 12 to 60 m. **Range:** s. Fla. & Bahamas to Venezuela.

14 **Conchfish** *Astrapogon stellatus* (Cope) 7 cm
Similar to *A. puncticulatus* (Fla. to Brazil) with shorter V fin & lives in dead shells. **Ecology:** seagrass beds, 1 to 25 m. In mantle of the queen conch (*Strombus gigas*) by day, out at night. **Range:** s. Fla. & W. Indies to Brazil.

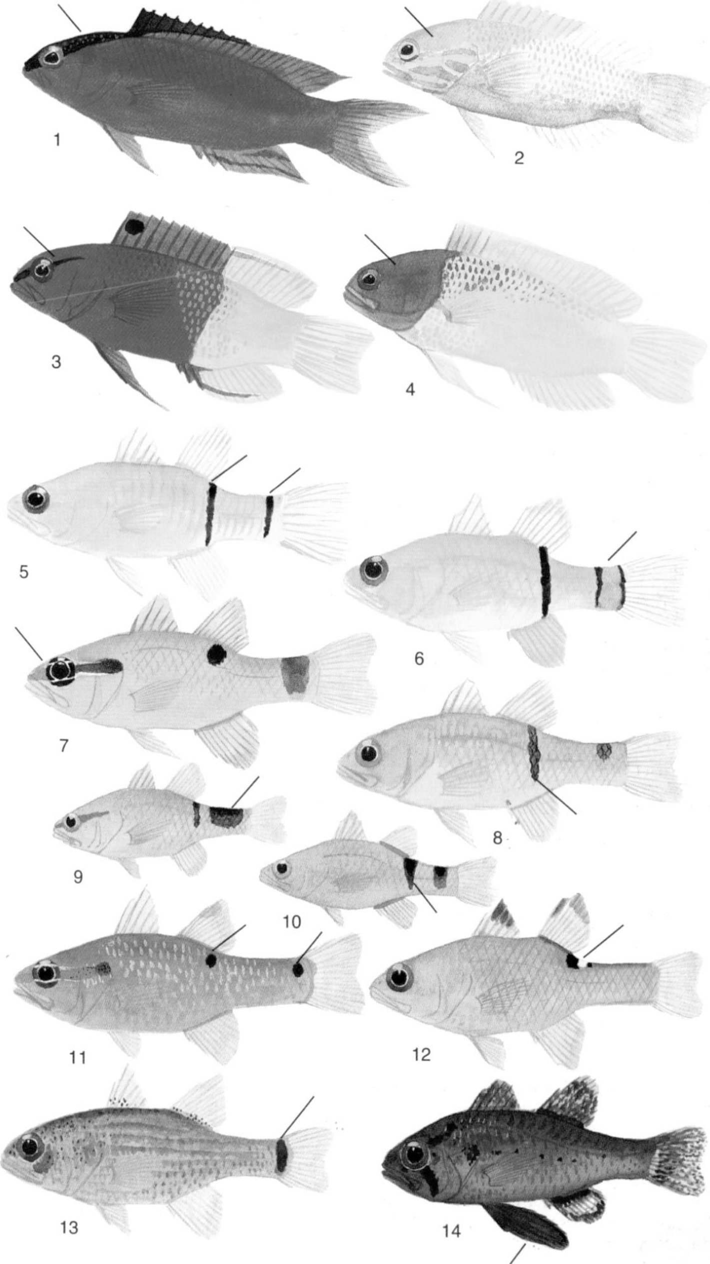
1
2
3
4
5
6
7
8
9
10
11
12
13
14

153 HAWKFISHES, BIGEYES, SAND TILEFISHES, SNOOKS, MOJARRAS, and TRIPLETAILS

1 **Freckled cardinalfish** *Phaeoptyx conklini* (Silvester) 6.5 cm
Ecology: clear shallow water. A common commensal of seastars and in empty shells. **Range:** Fla. to Venezuela.

2 **Dusky cardinalfish** *Phaeoptyx pigmentaria* (Poey) 6.5 cm
Ecology: shore to 42 m. Deep in coral or caves by day, near open basket stars at night. **Range:** Fla., Bermuda & ne. G. Mexico to Brazil, e. to E. Atlantic.

HAWKFISHES (CIRRHITIDAE): small grouper-like fishes with tuft of cirri at tip of D fin spines, thickened elongate lower P fin rays, continuous LL and single D fin. (see pls 33-34).

3 **Redspotted hawkfish** *Amblycirrhitus pinos* (Mowbray) 9.5 cm
Ecology: rocky and coral reefs, 3 to 25 m. Perches on corals or rocks. **Range:** s. Fla. to Venezuela, e. to St. Helena; replaced at Ascension by *A. earnshawi*.

BIGEYES (PRIACANTHIDAE): bigeyes have compressed bodies, large mouths, large eyes, a continuous D fin, and small scales. They remain near shelter by day and migrate away from the reef to feed on large zooplankton at night. Usually red by day, blotched or silvery at night. Foodfishes.

4 **Glasseye snapper** *Heteropriacanthus cruentatus* (Lacépède) 34 cm
Ecology: shallow coral reefs, 1 to 20 m. Hides in recesses during the day. **Range:** circumtropical; N. Jersey & n. G. Mexico to s. Brazil in W. Atlantic.

5 **Bigeye** *Priacanthus arenatus* Cuvier 30 cm
Ecology: in small groups on deep reefs, 20 to 45 m. **Range:** Mass., Bermuda & n. G. Mexico to Argentina.

SAND TILEFISHES (MALACANTHIDAE): elongate fishes with long continuous D & A fins.

6 **Sand tilefish** *Malacanthus plumieri* (Bloch) 60 cm
Ecology: sand and rubble patches, 2 to 50 m, usually below 9 m. Hovers above the bottom near a burrow of sand and rubble of its own construction. Retreats to the burrow when alarmed and at night. Feeds on invertebrates and fishes. **Range:** S. Carol. & Bermuda to s. Brazil, e. to Ascension Is.

SNOOKS (CENTROPOMIDAE): perchlike fishes with concave snout profile, separate D fins, and complete LL. Primarily estuarine. Important food and gamefishes.

7 **Snook** *Centropomus undecimalis* (Bloch) 140 cm; 23.8 kg
Body & fins olive; 3 other smaller similar spp. in region have orangish fins. **Ecology:** in small groups over muddy bottoms of mangrove areas, occasionally on seaweed flats or near shallow patch reefs. Wary. **Range:** S. Carol. to Brazil.

MOJARRAS (GERREIDAE): small silvery fishes with highly protrusible mouth, single D fin, and deeply forked tail. They feed by sorting benthic invertebrates from mouthfulls of sand. In schools over grassy and sandy areas adjacent to reefs.

8 **Yellowfin mojarra** *Gerres cinereus* (Walbaum) 41 cm
D fin continuous; silvery with indistinct bars. **Ecology:** shallow brackish to clear water areas with sand or seagrass beds adjacent to coral reefs, 1 to 15 m. Feeds on small invertebrates dug from the sand. Easily approached. **Range:** Fla., G. Mexico & Bermuda to Brazil; tropical E. Pacific, Mexico to Peru.

9 **Mottled mojarra** *Ulaema lefroyi* (Goode) 23 cm
D fin notched; diagonal bars above LL. Similar to *Eucinostomus argenteus* (N.J. to Brazil; e. Pacific) which has 3 A fin spines (vs. 2), indistinct or no mottling above LL & dusky fins. **Ecology:** along sandy shores and on sand flats. **Range:** Chesapeake Bay & Bermuda to Brazil.

LOBOTIDAE (TRIPLETAILS): grouper-like fishes with well-developed soft D & A fins.

10 **Tripletail** *Lobotes surinamensis* (Bloch) 110 cm
Ecology: pelagic, associated with drifting debris. Occasionally drifts over reefs. **Range:** circumtropical; Mass. (juvs. only n. of Fla.) & Bermuda to Argentina in W. Atlantic.

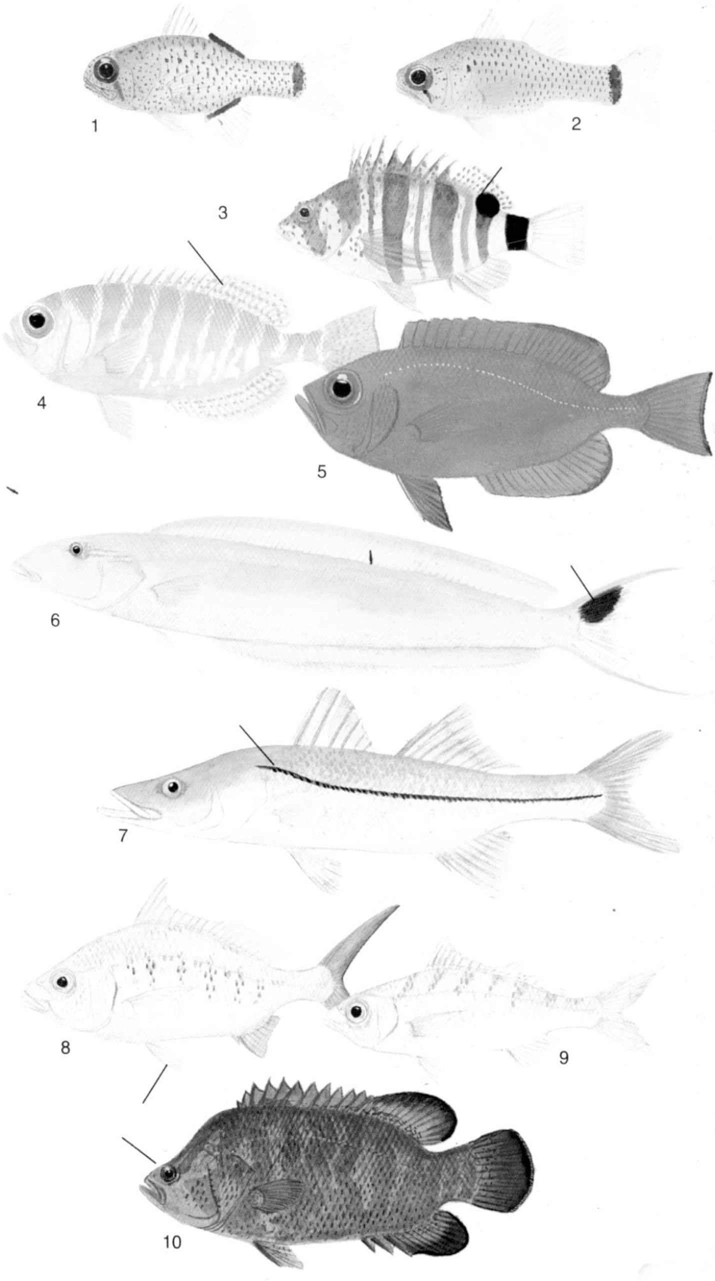
1
2
3
4
5
6
7
8
9
10

COBIA (RACHYCENTRIDAE): elongate remora-like fish with 1st 8 to 9 spines of D fin detached. A single coastal pelagic species. An excellent food and gamefish.

1 **Cobia** *Rachycentron canadum* (Linnaeus) 180 cm; 68 kg
Large ad. lose the lateral dark stripe. **Ecology:** coastal waters, 0 to 53 m. Feeds on crustaceans, fishes, and squids. **Range:** nearly circumtropical: Mass. to Argentina in W. Atlantic, rare in W. Indies.

REMORAS (ECHENEIDAE): Elongate fishes with a laminated sucking disc on top of the head which is used to attach themselves to the surfaces of larger fishes, turtles or mammals.

2 **Sharksucker** *Echeneis naucrates* Linnaeus 110 cm
Ecology: occasionally free-swimming over coral reefs. Usually associated with sharks, rays, other large fishes, or sea turtles. **Range:** circumglobal; Nova Scotia & Bermuda to Uruguay in W. Atlantic.

JACKS and TREVALLYS (CARANGIDAE): medium to large compressed silvery fishes with 2 D fins (the 1st fits into a groove), a narrow caudal peduncle usually reinforced by a series of bony scutes, and a forked tail. Fast-swimming predators of the waters above the reef and in open sea; a few root in sand. Only juveniles of a few species suitable for aquariums.

3 **Pilotfish** *Naucrates ductor* (Linnaeus) 70 cm
Has fleshy keel instead of scutes. **Ecology:** accompanies pelagic sharks, rays, turtles, or other large fishes. Juveniles with jellyfishes or in floating weed. **Range:** circumtropical; Nova Scotia to Argentina in W. Atlantic.

4 **African pompano** *Alectis ciliaris* (Bloch) 110 cm; 18 kg
Ecology: juveniles in surface waters, mimic a jellyfish. Adults in bottom waters 60 m. **Range:** circumtropical; Mass. & n. G. Mexico to se. Brazil in W. Atlantic.

5 **Permit** *Trachinotus falcatus* (Linnaeus) 114 cm; 23 kg
Similar to *T. carolinus* but head profile is not as steep. **Ecology:** over sand or reefs, 0 to 30 m. Feeds on mollusks. Curious. An important gamefish. Range: Mass. to se. Brazil; e. to Africa.

6 **Palometa** *Trachinotus goodei* Jordan & Evermann 50 cm
Front of vertical fins blackish; 4-5 narrow bars. **Ecology:** surf zone, sometimes over clear patch reefs, 0 to 12 m. Feeds on fishes and invertebrates. **Range:** Mass. to Argentina, e. to E. Atlantic.

7 **Lookdown** *Selene vomer* (Linnaeus) 30 cm
Extremely compressed with high head & indistinct bands. **Ecology:** solitary or in schools in shallow murky water, 1 to 53 m. Often over sand with head tilted down. **Range:** Maine s. to Uruguay

8 **Bigeye scad** *Selar crumenophthalmus* (Bloch) 39 cm
Large eye, brassy lateral band. **Ecology:** coastal pelagic, migrating to coastal bays, occasionally over reefs or over deep offshore waters near current lines. In large schools. Feeds on large plankton and small benthic invertebrates. An important fishery species caught by net or hook and line. **Range:** circumtropical: Nova Scotia to se. Brazil in W. Atlantic.

9 **Mackerel scad** *Decapterus macarellus* (Cuvier) 30 cm
Round x-section; silvery with a black spot behind opercle. **Ecology:** offshore reefs to 200 m. In large midwater schools. Feeds on zooplankton. **Range:** circumtropical: Nova Scotia & Bermuda to se. Brazil in W. Atlantic.

10 **Round scad** *Decapterus punctatus* (Cuvier) 23 cm
Round x-section; silvery with a black spot behind opercle and black dots on LL. **Ecology:** pelagic, but sometimes near shorelines. Feeds on zooplankton **Range:** Nova Scotia & Bermuda to se. Brazil, e. to Ascension & St. Helena.

11 **Leatherjacket** *Oligoplites saurus* (Bloch & Schneider) 30 cm
Silvery bluish on back; sinous D fin a series of 5 detached spines.
Similar to *O. saliens* (s. Carib.) which has a deeper body. **Ecology:** surface waters of bays and estuaries, often in turbid areas. May leap from the water. **Range:** Maine s. to Uruguay; e. Pacific

1
2
3
juv
4
5
6
7
8
9
10
11

1 **Black jack** *Caranx lugubris* Poey 100 cm
Color variable, from dark slate to brownish gray to light gray without much silver sheen. **Ecology:** singly or in small groups along steep outer reef slopes and offshore banks, 12 to 354 m. Large ones may be ciguatoxic. Rarely over the North American continental shelf. **Range:** circumtropical: Fla. & n. G. Mexico to se. Brazil in W. Atantic.

2 **Bar jack** *Carangoides ruber* (Bloch) 60 cm
A brilliant blue and black stripe on back; juv. with 7 black bars. **Ecology:** common on coral-rich reefs, 0 to 22 m. Usually in large aggregations, which might be spawning groups. Accompany goatfishes. Easily approached. Occasionally ciguatoxic. **Range:** N. Jersey, Bermuda & n. G. Mexico to Venezuela, e. to St. Helena.

3 **Crevalle jack** *Caranx hippos* (Linnaeus) 100 cm
Steep head; 2 dark spots, one on gill cover, the other on lower side of P fin. **Ecology:** in schools in open water above clear outer reefs, 1 to 50 m. An important foodfish. Abundant along U.S. E. coast during summer. **Range:** Nova Scotia & n. G. Mexico to Uruguay, e. to Ascension, St. Helena & E. Atlantic.

4 **Horse-eye trevally** *Caranx latus* Agassiz 75 cm
Large eye, yellow tail, black spot only on gill cover. **Ecology:** in schools on offshore reefs, 0 to 30 m. Juveniles enter fresh water. Often approaches divers. Occasionally ciguatoxic. **Range:** N. Jersey, Bermuda & n. G. Mexico to Brazil, e. to St. Paul's Rocks.

5 **Yellow jack** *Carangoides bartholomaei* Cuvier 90 cm
Bluish back and yellow fins; lower side of body yellowish. **Ecology:** common on offshore reefs, less common on inshore reefs, 0 to 50 m. **Range:** Mass. s. to Brazil.

6 **Blue runner** *Carangoides crysos* (Mitchill) 70 cm
Lobes of tail black; a black spot on upper gill cover. **Ecology:** in schools in open sea or above offshore reefs, 0 to 50 m. The best eating jack in the region. **Range:** Nova Scotia & Bermuda to Brazil, e. to Africa incl. mid-Atlantic islands.

7 **Greater amberjack** *Seriola dumerili* (Risso) 188 cm; 80 kg
Seriola spp. lack scutes. This sp. with dusky stripe through eye; bronze cast with bronze lateral band. 2nd D fin short. **Ecology:** seaward reefs, 20 to 335 m. Occasionally enters shallow inshore waters. Feeds on schooling fishes. Ciguatoxic in certain areas. **Range:** circumglobal; Mass. to se. Brazil in W. Atlantic.

8 **Almaco jack** *Seriola rivoliana* Valenciennes 110 cm
Body silvery, not bronzy; 2nd D fin longer than in *S. dumerili*. **Ecology:** outer reef slopes and offshore banks, 15 to 160 m. Feeds on fishes. **Range:** circumtropical; Mass. to Argentina in W. Atlantic.

9 **Rainbow runner** *Elagatis bipinnulata* (Quoy & Gaimard) 125 cm
Ecology: schools off clear seaward reefs and in the open sea, surface to 150 m. Occasionally in deep lagoons. Feeds on pelagic crustaceans and small fishes. **Range:** circumtropical, us. in water 21°C; Mass. & n. G. Mexico to Venez. in W. Atlantic.

1
2
3
4
5
6
7
8
9

SNAPPERS (LUTJANIDAE): medium to large perchlike fishes with a continuous D fin, large coarse scales, large canine teeth, a maxillary mostly covered by the cheek, and an emarginate to forked tail. Most species are predators of crustaceans and fishes, several are planktivores. Most Caribbean species of *Lutjanus* feed primarily on crustaceans, the largest ones feed primarily on fishes. Most species inhabit inshore and reef waters, but many occur at depths of 90 to 360 m. Important food and gamefishes. Most do well in aquaria.

1 **Yellowtail snapper** *Ocyurus chrysurus* (Bloch) 75 cm
Ecology: solitary or in groups in open water above the bottom. Feeds on small fishes and crustaceans at night. Juveniles feed primarily on plankton. **Range:** Mass. & Bermuda to Brazil, e. to C. Verde Is.

2 **Schoolmaster** *Lutjanus apodus* (Walbaum) 60 cm
Fins yellow; blue stripes below eye; eight light bars may be present on upper body. **Ecology:** mangroves and seagrass beds to rocky and coral reefs, 2 to 30 m. Often near the shelter of elkhorn corals and gorgonians. The most abundant snapper in the West Indies. **Range:** Mass. (juvs.), Bermuda & n. G. Mexico to se. Brazil, e. to e. Atlantic.

3 **Lane snapper** *Lutjanus synagris* (Linnaeus) 36 cm
Diag. yellow stripes dorsally, horiz. stripes below; dusky spot below soft D fin base. **Ecology:** shallow lagoons to deep outer reefs and shrimp grounds, 2 to 390 m. In turbid as well as clear water. Often in schools. **Range:** N. Carol., Bermuda & G. Mexico to Brazil.

4 **Dog snapper** *Lutjanus jocu* (Bloch) 90 cm; 14 kg
White triangle and blue line below eye. **Ecology:** near shelter of rocky and coral reefs or wrecks, 5 to 30 m. Juveniles enter brackish or fresh water. Feeds primarily on fishes. Often ciguatoxic. Timid. **Range:** Mass., Bermuda (introduced) & n. G. Mexico to Brazil. e. to St. Paul's Rocks & Ascension.

5 **Mahogony snapper** *Lutjanus mahogoni* (Cuvier) 38 cm
Reddish margin on D fin & tail, dark spot below soft D fin base not always present. **Ecology:** shallow coral reefs, often near gorgonians and ledges, 5 to 20 m. Solitary or in small group. Timid. **Range:** N. Carol. & Bahamas to Guianas.

6 **Mutton snapper** *Lutjanus analis* (Cuvier) 75 cm; 11 kg
Silvery to reddish with blue stripes below eye; soft D & A fins angular. **Ecology:** wide range of habitats from estuarine and mangrove areas to sand flats and coral reefs, 2 to 20 m. Young enter fresh water. Curious. **Range:** Mass., Bermuda (introduced) & n. G. Mexico to Brazil.

7 **Cubera snapper** *Lutjanus cyanopterus* (Cuvier) 150 cm; >57 kg
Steel gray to brownish on back; purplish below. The largest Atlantic snapper. **Ecology:** coral and rocky reefs, 18 to 55 m. Juveniles may enter fresh water. Adults prefer rocky ledges. Feeds primarily on fishes. Often ciguatoxic. Wary. **Range:** N. Jersey (uncommon n. of s. Fla.) & Bahamas to Brazil.

8 **Gray snapper** *Lutjanus griseus* (Linnaeus) 60 cm
Color variable from gray to coppery or reddish; often a dark stripe through eye; body occas. barred; tail with dusky margin. **Ecology:** mangrove sloughs and harbors to rocky or coral reefs, 0.5 to 25 m. Common in inshore areas. Easily approached. **Range:** Mass. (juvs.), Bermuda & n. G. Mexico to Brazil, e. to E. Atlantic.

9 **Blackfin snapper** *Lutjanus buccanella* (Cuvier) 75 cm; 14 kg
Reddish with black blotch on P fin base and black base of soft D fin. Similar to *L. campechanus* (N. Carol. & n. G. Mexico to s. Fla. & Yucatan) & *L. purpureus* (Gr. Antilles to Venez.) which have 8 soft D rays instead of 9, and lack the black areas on P & soft D fin bases. **Ecology:** rocky or coral reefs, juveniles as shallow as 9 m, adults 60 to 91 m. **Range:** Mass. (rare n.of N. Carol.), Bahamas & n. G. Mexico to Brazil.

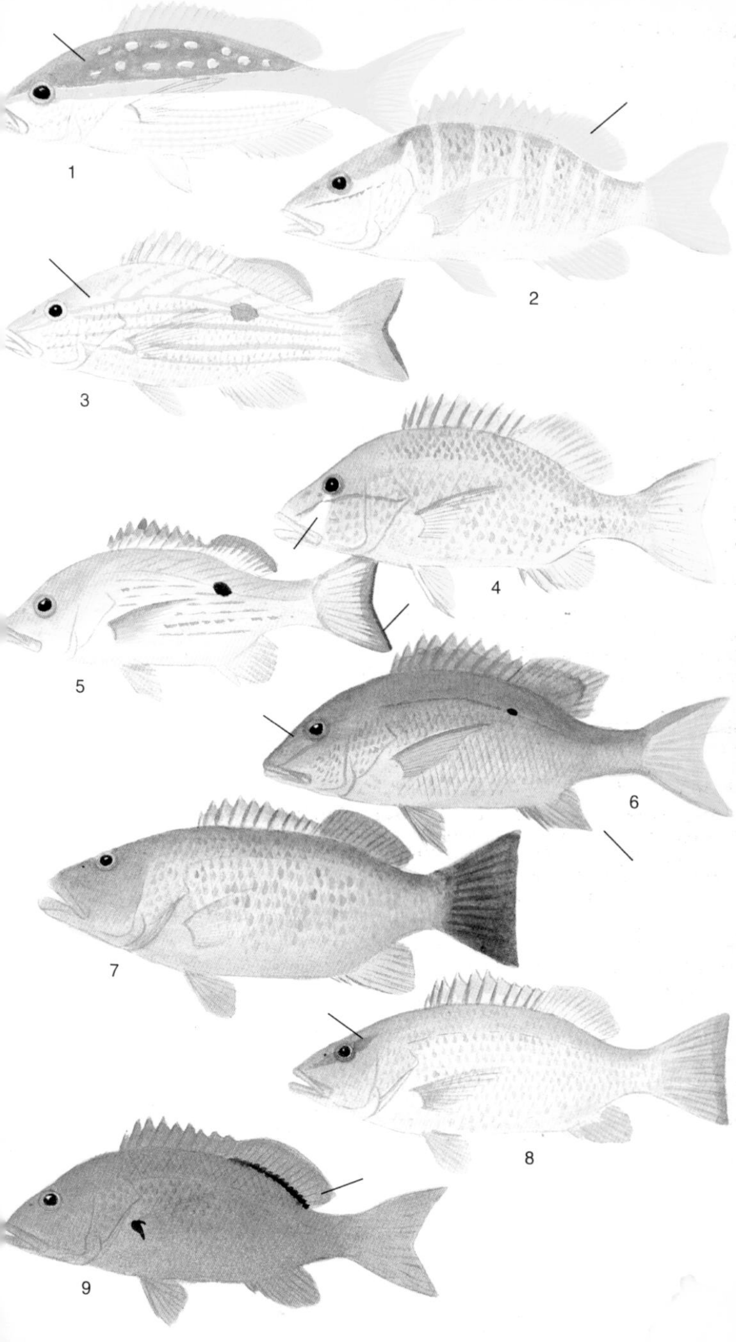
1
2
3
4
5
6
7
8
9

GRUNTS (HAEMULIDAE): medium to large fishes with small conical jaw teeth, pharyngeal teeth (in throat), medium scales, and continuous D fins. Produce grinding sounds with swimbladder and teeth. Have a territorial display consisting of a mouth-to-mouth shoving match popularly called "kissing" behaviour. Juveniles commonly occur in seagrass beds and feed on plankton near the bottom. Adults of some species also feed on plankton, but most feed on on bottom-dwelling invertebrates primarily at night. Most Caribbean species typically occur in large inactive schools near shelter during the day and disperse to feed over sand and grass flats during the night. Important foodfishes.

1 **Porkfish** *Anisotremus virginicus* (Linnaeus) 40 cm
Ecology: rocky and coral reefs, 2 to 20 m. In large aggregations during the day. Juveniles are cleaners that pick ectoparasites from larger fishes. Adults feed primarily on hard-bodied invertebrates. **Range:** Fla., Bermuda & Yucatan to Brazil.

2 **Black margate** *Anisotremus surinamensis* (Bloch) 65 cm
Ecology: reefs and rubble areas, 3 to 20 m. Solitary or in small groups, often near shelter of caves, ledges or wrecks. Feeds on fishes, crustaceans and sea urchins. **Range:** Fla., Bahamas & G. Mexico to Brazil.

3 **Black grunt** *Haemulon bonariense* Cuvier 30 sm
Juveniles of *Haemulon* spp. except *plumieri* have a black lateral stripe and black spot at the base of the tail. Adults of this sp. with dark centered scales in oblique rows; tail black. **Ecology:** variety of habitats from seagrass beds, sand or mud to coral reefs. Common along South American contininental shelf; rare in the West Indies. **Range:** s. G. Mexico & Gr. Antilles to Brazil.

4 **Sailors choice** *Haemulon parra* (Desmarest) 40 cm
Dark centered scales in oblique rows; soft D, A fins & tail dusky, but not black. **Ecology:** shallow coastal reefs, 3 to 20 m. Young on seagrass beds, adults in schools in relatively open areas of the reef. Feeds at night on mollusks and small fishes. Common on continental reefs, rare at oceanic islands. **Range:** Fla., Bahamas & n. G. Mexico to Brazil.

5 **Margate** *Haemulon album* Cuvier 60 cm
Light gray, sometimes with 3 dark lateral stripes; tail black. The largest species in genus. **Ecology:** variety of habitats from seagrass beds, sand flats to coral reefs and wrecks. Adults typically in small groups. Feeds by day and night by rooting in the sand for benthic invertebrates including peanut worms and heart urchins. **Range:** Fla. Keys & Bermuda to Brazil.

6 **Cottonwick** *Haemulon melanurum* (Linnaeus) 33 cm
Ecology: clear inshore and offshore reefs, 3 to 20 m. Juveniles usually 30 m. Uncommon. **Range:** Fla. & Bermuda to Brazil.

7 **Spanish grunt** *Haemulon macrostomum* Günther 43 cm
Ecology: clear water reefs, 5 to 25 m. Feeds on long-spined sea urchins. Wary. **Range:** Fla. & Bermuda to Brazil.

8 **Tomtate** *Haemulon aurolineatum* Cuvier 25 cm
Black spot on tail base absent in lg. adults. **Ecology:** seagrass beds, sand fats and patch reefs, 2 to 12 m. Common, but wary. **Range:** Mass., Bermuda & n. G. Mexico to Brazil.

9 **Latin grunt** *Haemulon steindachneri* (Jordan & Gilbert) 26 cm
Ecology: shallow coastal reefs. Common in the southern Caribbean. **Range:** Panama to s. Brazil; E. Pacific.

10 **Bronzestriped grunt** *Haemulon boschmae* (Metzelaar) 18 cm
Black spot on tail base persists at all sizes. The smallest species of the genus. **Ecology:** shallow coastal reefs. Absent from offshore islands. **Range:** Columbia to Fr. Guiana incl. Trinidad, Tobago & Isla de Margarita.

1
1 juv
2
3
4
5
6
7
8
8 juv
9
10

1 **Bluestriped grunt** *Haemulon sciurus* (Shaw) 45 cm
Yellow with blue stripes; dusky soft D fin & tail. **Ecology:** in small groups over rocky and coral reefs and dropoffs, 4 to 20 m. Feeds mainly on crabs, shrimps and bivalves. Common but wary. **Range:** S. Carol., Bermuda & G. Mexico to se. Brazil.

2 **French grunt** *Haemulon flavolineatum* (Desmarest) 30 cm
Oblique yellow stripes below LL; yellow fins. **Ecology:** in large schools on rocky and coral reefs, 1 to 20 m. Often seen under ledges or close to elkhorn corals. Juveniles (9 cm) abundant in nearshore seagrass beds. Wary, but approachable. The most common grunt in southern Florida and the West Indies. **Range:** S. Carol. & Bermuda to Brazil.

3 **White grunt** *Haemulon plumieri* (Lacépède) 45 cm
Blue stripes on head; scales bluish-silver and yellow. **Ecology:** in dense aggregations during the day on patch reefs, around coral formations or on sandy bottoms, 3 to 29 m. Juveniles (<13 cm) in inshore seagrass beds. Feeds on crabs, polychaetes, echinoids and fishes. Frequently exhibits a territorial "kissing" display in which two contenders push each other on the lips with their mouths wide open. **Range:** Maryland, Bermuda & n. G. Mexico to Brazil.

4 **Caesar grunt** *Haemulon carbonarium* Poey 36 cm
Bronzy stripes on body; soft A fin & tail dusky. **Ecology:** in small groups near coral or rocky reefs, 3 to 20 m. Timid. **Range:** s. Fla. & Bermuda to Brazil.

5 **Striped grunt** *Haemulon striatum* (Linnaeus) 28 cm
5 yellow stripes on upper body, the 2 lowermost the broadest; belly unstriped. **Ecology:** deep outer reefs, 10 to 97 m. Rarely on inshore reefs. Feeds on plankton. **Range:** Bermuda & G. Mexico to Brazil.

6 **Smallmouth grunt** *Haemulon chrysargyreum* Günther 23 cm
5-6 yellow stripes on body, incl. belly; fins yellow. **Ecology:** in small schools over shallow exposed rocky or coral reefs, 2 to 18 m. Often near sheltering elkhorn and staghorn corals. Feeds on plankton, crabs, shrimps and polychaetes. Timid. **Range:** s. Fla. & W. Indies to Brazil.

7 **Spotted pigfish** *Orthopristis ruber* (Cuvier) 40 cm
Similar to *O. chrysopterus* (N.Y. & Bermuda to Fla. & Mexico). **Ecology:** coastal waters over sand, mud, or hard bottoms, 1 to 70 m. **Range:** Gr. Antilles & Honduras to Brazil.

BONNETMOUTHS (INERMIIDAE): fusiform fishes with 2 keels on ea. side of C peduncle, deeply notched or separate D fins & protrusible mouth. Schooling plankton feeders of open waters.

8 **Boga** *Inermia vittata* Poey 22.5 cm
Ecology: mid waters of clear seaward reefs, 15 to 50 m. Sometimes schools with creole wrasse (pl. 164-7). **Range:** s. Fla. & Bahamas to n. S. America.

9 **Bonnetmouth** *Emmelichthyops atlanticus* Schultz 13 cm
Ecology: in open water, sometimes over coral heads, 3 to 90 m. A fast swimmer. **Range:** s. Fla. & Bahamas to n. S. America.

1
2
3
4
5
6
7
8
9

PORGIES (SPARIDAE): stocky snapper-like fishes with conical to incisiform teeth, some with molars, medium to large scales, continuous D fins, and emarginate to forked tails. Carnivores of hard-shelled benthic invertebrates. Most species from temperate waters. Important foodfishes.

1 **Pluma** *Calamus pennatula* Guichenot 35 cm
Mostly on continental shelf; 11 spp. in genus in W. Atlantic, only 4 in W. Indies. This sp. with yellow ground color with several blue lines below eye & red spot at P fin base. **Ecology:** sand bottoms and adjacent reef areas, 0.3 to 84 m. Hovers a short distance above the bottom. The commonest species of the genus in the West Indies. Curious. **Range:** Bahamas & Campeche Bank to Brazil.

2 **Saucereye porgy** *Calamus calamus* (Valenciennes) 41 cm
Bluish lines below eye; blue spot on P fin base; often mottled. **Ecology:** over sand, seagrass beds or reefs, 1 to 72 m. Easily approached. **Range:** N. Carol. & Bermuda to Brazil.

3 **Jolthead porgy** *Calamus bajonado* (Bloch & Schneider) 60 cm
White streaks below eye; yellowish area on nape and back. The largest species in the genus. **Ecology:** clear shallow water reefs and sandy expanses, 3 to 180 m. Feeds primarily on sea urchins. Occasionally ciguatoxic. Not shy. **Range:** Rhode I. & Bermuda to Brazil.

4 **Sheepshead porgy** *Calamus penna* (Valenciennes) 46 cm
Silvery with iridescent reflections; black spot at P fin base; often mottled with dark bars. **Ecology:** sandy areas adjacent to coral reefs. **Range:** G. Mexico, Fla. & Bahamas to Brazil.

5 **Roundspot porgy** *Diplodus caudimacula* (Poey) 30 cm
Large black spot on C peduncle; all fins yellowish. Similar to *D. holbrooki* (Maryland to G. Mexico), *D. bermudensis* (Bermuda) & *D. argenteus* (Brazil to Argentina). **Ecology:** surf zone of rocky coastal areas with turbulent, clear water. **Range:** Fla. & Bahamas to n. S. America.

6 **Sheepshead** *Archosargus probatocephalus* (Walbaum) 90 cm
Distinct dark bars which may fade with age. **Ecology:** bays and estuaries, around pilings and rocks in brackish to marine waters. Feeds on mollusks, barnacles, and crabs. Wary. A popular food and game fish. **Range:** N. Scotia to Brazil, absent from W. Indies & Bahamas; the subsp. *aires* from Honduras to Brazil.

7 **Sea bream** *Archosargus rhomboidalis* (Linnaeus) 33 cm
Dark spot on shoulder; brassy lateral stripes. **Ecology:** common on seagrass beds and among mangroves, occasionally on coral reefs among *Porites* corals. Feeds primarily on plant material but also takes mollusks and crustaceans. **Range:** N. J. (rare n. of Fla.) & ne. G. Mexico to Brazil, incl. W. Indies.

8 **Red porgy** *Pagrus pagrus* (Linnaeus) 91 cm
Pinkish silvery with some yellow tinge. W. Atl. popul. formerly called *P. sedicum*. **Ecology:** juveniles in coastal areas with seagrasses or sand, 9 to 70 m. Adults deeper. **Range:** N.Y. & n. G. Mexico to Argentina, e. to E. Atlantic & Medit.; absent from W. Indies.

DRUMS (SCIAENIDAE): moderatley compressed fishes with notched or separate D fins, A fin with II spines, continuous LL, rounded or lanceolate to truncate tails, and small to medium scales. Most species have large chin pores, some have barbels. Many species have an inferior mouth. First D fin of juveniles often elongate. Produce "drumming" and "croaking" noises with swimbladder. Bottom-dwelling carnivores. Many species on soft bottoms of continental shelves and in brackish or freshwater. Most species a dull silver, gray, or brown. A few colorful reef species. Typically hide during the day in crevices or under ledges. Excellent foodfishes. Juveniles popular aquarium fishes but difficult to maintain.

9 **Reef croaker** *Odontoscion dentex* (Cuvier) 20 cm
Ecology: solitary or in groups in caves or crevices, or among corals, 1 to 30 m. Feeds at night on small fishes, shrimps, and larvae. Secretive and wary. **Range:** Fla. to Brazil.

1
2
3
4
5
6
7
8
9

1 **Spotted drum** *Equetus punctatus* (Bloch & Schneider) 25 cm
Blackish fins, some with white spots. 1st D and V fins greatly produced in juvs. **Ecology:** shallow coral reefs, 3 to 30 m. Secretive and usually solitary, under ledges or near small caves. Feeds at night on crabs, shrimps and polychaetes. Easily approached. **Range:** s. Fla. & Bermuda to Brazil.

2 **Jackknife-fish** *Equetus lanceolatus* (Linnaeus) 25 cm
3 black bands; soft D & A fins light. **Ecology:** deep coral reefs, 10 to 40 m. Juveniles occasionally inshore. Uncommon. Easily approached. **Range:** S. Carol. & Bermuda to Brazil.

3 **High-hat** *Pareques acuminatus* (Schneider) 23 cm
Stripes on head horizontal, eyes connected by a dark band; fins black without white spots. **Ecology:** near caves and under ledges of coral reefs, 3 to 20 m. Secretive but approachable. **Range:** S. Carol. & Bermuda to Brazil.

4 **Cubbuyu** *Pareques umbrosus* (Jordan & Eigenmann) 25 cm
lst D fin of juvs. not elongate; stripes on top of head converge at tip of snout; another sp., *P. iwamotoi* (N. Carol. to Brazil) has a broad dark bar from 1st D fin to behind V fin. **Ecology:** shallow continental coastal waters, rarely on coral reefs, 5 to 91 m. Secretive but approachable. **Range:** N. Carol. & G. Mexico, possibly to Brazil.

GOATFISHES (MULLIDAE): medium elongate fishes with pair of barbels on chin; 2 D fins, large scales, and forked tails. The chemosensory barbels are thrust in sand or holes to detect prey. Important food fishes. Not popular for aquariums, but do well in right setting.

5 **Yellow goatfish** *Mulloidichthys martinicus* (Cuvier) 40 cm
Ecology: shallow sandy areas of lagoon and seaward reefs to 49 m. Often in large inactive aggregations by day. Feeds alone or in small groups on benthic invertebrates. Juveniles common in seagrass beds. **Range:** Fla., e. G. Mexico & Bermuda to se. Brazil, e. to C. Verde Is. & St. Helena.

6 **Spotted goatfish** *Pseudupeneus maculatus* (Bloch) 28 cm
Ecology: shallow sandy or rubbly areas of lagoon and seaward reefs to 49 m. Often rests on bottom in small groups. Juveniles common in seagrass beds. **Range:** N.J. (rare n. of Fla.) & Bermuda to s. Brazil.

SWEEPERS (PEMPHERIDAE): small compressed ovoid fishes with large eyes, small oblique mouth, single D fin, and slightly forked tail. Aggregate in caves by day and disperse to feed on zooplankton at night. Not popular for aquariums.

7 **Glassy sweeper** *Pempheris schomburgki* Müller & Troschel 15 cm
Coppery with a distinct black band at base of A fin. **Ecology:** in aggregations in dark caves or crevices, 3 to 30 m. **Range:** s. Fla. & Bahamas to Brazil.

8 **Shortfin sweeper** *Pempheris poeyi* Bean 15 cm
Ecology: in aggregations in dark caves or crevices. **Range:** Bahamas & Cuba to Tobago.

RUDDERFISHES, SEA CHUBS (KYPHOSIDAE): moderately large fishes with small heads, small terminal mouth with incisiform teeth, single D fin, small scales, and slightly forked tail. Omnivores characteristic of exposed seaward reefs.

9 **Bermuda chub** *Kyphosus sectatrix* (Linnaeus) 76 cm
Similar to *K. incisor* which has brassy instead of yellow lines & more D & A fin rays (13-15 & 12-13 vs 11-13 & 10-12); difficult to distinguish under water. **Ecology:** reefs, rocky walls, or sandy areas, shoreline to 30 m. Feeds on attached and or detached pieces of plants. Usually in aggregations. **Range:** C. Cod, Bermuda & n. G. Mexico to Brazil, e. to St. Paul's Rocks, Ascension & e. Atlantic.

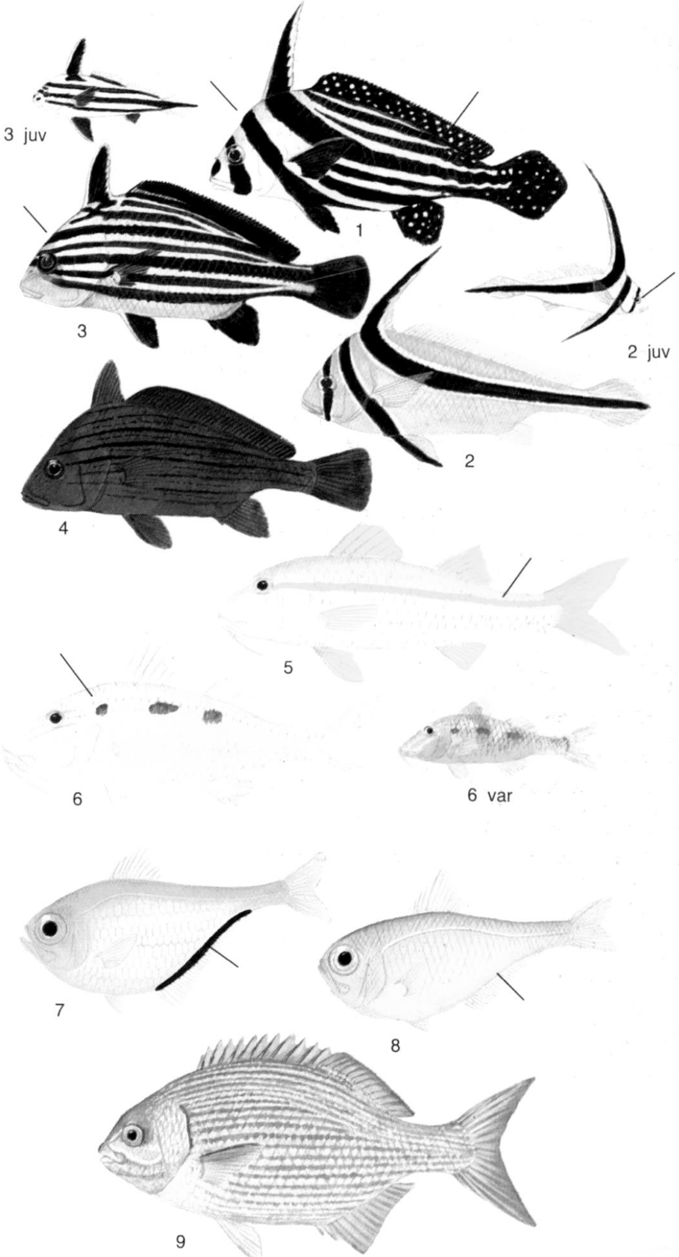
3 juv
1
3
2 juv
2
4
5
6
6 var
7
8
9

SPADEFISHES (EPHIPPIDAE): highly compressed deep-bodied fishes with small scales, a small terminal mouth and small brushlike teeth. Omnivores of algae, small sessile invertebrates, and pelagic tunicates. Juveniles popular aquarium fishes.

1 **Atlantiç spadefish** *Chaetodipterus faber* (Broussonet) 91 cm
Silvery with dark bars which may fade with age; juvs. dark brown with black bars. **Ecology:** in schools of up to 500 individuals in open water above outer reefs. Often around wrecks, piers and offshore platforms, 3 to 25 m. Will often circle divers. Juveniles inhabit shallow seagrass beds and sandy areas where they mimic dead leaves. **Range:** Mass., Bermuda (introduced) & n. G. Mexico to se. Brazil.

BUTTERFLYFISHES (CHAETODONTIDAE): small, colorfull, discoid fishes with small protractile mouths with small brush-like teeth, continuous D fins, body and head covered with small scales extending onto the median fins, and rounded to emarginate tails. Most species are diurnal and rest among corals or rocks during the night. Diet differs greatly among the species. Many feed on a variety of coelenterate polyps or tentacles, small invertebrates, fish eggs, and filamentous algae. A few feed exclusively on coral polyps and others feed primarily on zooplankton. Most species patrol a home range. Many species occur as heterosexual pairs that may remain together for years, if not life. Larval stage lengthy, from a few weeks to perhaps 2 months, and with distinctive late stage in which head and front of body are covered in bony plates. Some of the planktivores and generalists do well in the aquarium, but most species are difficult to maintain. 7 species in W. Atlantic.

2 **Foureye butterflyfish** *Chaetodon capistratus* Linnaeus 15 cm
Ocellus present at all ages; juvs. with an additional smaller ocellus on soft D fin & 2 broad dusky bars on sides. **Ecology:** reef flats to seaward reefs, 2 to 20 m. Solitary or in pairs. Prefers shallow coral-rich reefs. Feeds on zoantharians, polychaetes, gorgonians, and tunicates. The most common butterflyfish in the Caribbean. Easily approached. **Range:** Mass. (seasonal juvs. only n. of Fla.) & Bermuda to Venezuela.

3 **Banded butterflyfish** *Chaetodon striatus* Linnaeus 16 cm
Three bars at all stages; juvs. with ocellus on soft D fin. Known to hybridize with *C. ocellatus*. **Ecology:** coral and rocky reefs, 3 to 20 m. Solitary or in pairs. Feeds on coral polyps, polychaetes and crustaceans. Common. **Range:** Mass. (seasonal juvs. only n. of Fla.), Bermuda & n. G. Mexico to Brazil, e. to St. Paul's Rocks; doubtfully reported from E. Atlantic.

4 **Reef butterflyfish** *Chaetodon sedentarius* Poey 15 cm
Rectagular-shaped body with 2 dark bars; juvs. with ocellus on soft D fin. **Ecology:** coral reefs, 5 to 92 m. Often in pairs. Not shy. **Range:** N. Carol., n. G. Mexico & Bahamas to Brazil.

5 **Spotfin butterflyfish** *Chaetodon ocellatus* Bloch 20 cm
Vertical fins bright yellow; black spot on soft D fin may fade. Similar to *C. sanctaehelenae* (Ascension & St. Helena) which lacks the black D spot & has a tan eyebar. **Ecology:** shallow reefs, 3 to 28 m. Develops dusky bands during the night. Common. **Range:** N. Scotia, Mass. (seasonal juvs. only n. of Fla.), Bermuda & n. G. Mexico to Brazil.

6 **Caribbean longsnout butterflyfish** *Chaetodon aculeatus* (Poey) 10 cm
Long, pointed snout; faint eye bar and dark brown back. **Ecology:** areas of rich coral growth, 1 to 91 m. Rarely less than 12 m but the most common butterflyfish below 30 m. Feeds on small invertebrates in dark recesses. Often seen nibling on the tubefeet of sea urchins or tentacles of tubeworms. **Range:** s. Fla., w. G. Mexico & Bahamas to Venezuela.

7 **Threeband butterflyfish** *Chaetodon guyanensis* Durand 12.5 cm
Similar to *C. aya* but with a third black bar; other similar spp. in E. Atlantic (*C. marcellae*), E. Pacific (*C. falcifer*) & Indo-Pacific (*C. guezei*), all in very deep water. **Ecology:** steep rocky reefs, 60 to 230 m. Rarely seen except from submersibles at below 100 m. **Range:** se. Bahamas, Jamaica, P. Rico, Barbados, Belize & Fr. Guyana.

8 **Bank butterflyfish** *Chaetodon aya* Jordan 15 cm
Similar to *C. guyanensis* which has a 3rd black bar. **Ecology:** deep rocky slopes, 20 to 167 m. Usually below 45 m in water 16 to 22°C. Rarely seen by divers. Most specimens were trawled. **Range:** N. Carol. & ne. G. Mexico s. to Yucatan; absent from Bahamas & Antilles.

1
juv
1
2
3
juv
juv
4
5
6
7
8

ANGELFISHES (POMACANTHIDAE): small to medium-sized fishes with deep compressed bodies, small mouths with brush-like teeth, continuous D fins, small coarsely ctenoid scales extending onto the median fins, and a prominent spine at corner of the preopercle as well as smaller spines on adjacent regions of the head. The head spines, more coarsely ctenoid scales and absense of a *tholichthys* larval stage set them apart from the superficially similar butterflyfishes. All species studied to date are protogynous hermaphrodites with haremic social systems. Males typically defend a territory containing 2 to 5 females. Territory size ranges from a few square meters (*Centropyge*) to over 1,000 square meters (large *Pomacanthus*). Spawn in pairs, usually at sunset. Eggs are pelagic and larval stage lasts 3 to 4 weeks. Species of *Centropyge* feed on filamentous algae, most other Caribbean species feed primarily on sponges supplemented by soft-bodied invertebrates, fish eggs, and algae. Most *Centropyge* and a few species of *Pomacanthus* do well in aquariums, but others are generally difficult to maintain.

1 **Gray angelfish** *Pomacanthus arcuatus* (Linnaeus) 50 cm
Gray with small dark scales; inner P fin yellow. Young with a small black bar in tail. **Ecology:** coral-rich areas, 2 to 30 m. Feeds on algae, bryozoans, gorgonians, tunicates and seagrasses. Solitary or in pairs. Will approach divers. **Range:** N.Y., Bermuda (introduced) & n. G. Mexico to se. Brazil.

2 **French angelfish** *Pomacanthus paru* (Bloch) 30 cm
Black with yellow-edged scales; tail rounded. Young with a large black spot in tail. **Ecology:** coral-rich reefs, 5 to 100 m. Usually in pairs, often near sea-fans. Diet similar to diet of *P. arcuatus*. Easily approached. **Range:** Fla., Bermuda (introduced) & n. G. Mexico to Brazil, e. to e. St. Paul's Rocks & Ascension; e. Atlantic record needs confirmation.

3 **Rock beauty** *Holacanthus tricolor* (Bloch) 20 cm
Color pattern distinct. Rarely with entirely black body. Juvs. have a blue-ringed black spot & may be confused with juv. threespot damselfish (pl. 163-9). **Ecology:** common on clear seaward reefs and shallow reef flats with abundant coral growth; also on rocky and rubble bottoms, 3 to >92 m. Juveniles often associated with *Millipora* fire corals. The most common species in the genus in the West Indies. Individuals from the Caribbean islands and Bahamas are generally more colorful than those from the continental shelf. **Range:** Georgia, Bermuda & n. G. Mexico banks to Brazil.

4 **Blue angelfish** *Holacanthus bermudensis* Goode 38 cm
Ground color blue-gray with dark-centered scales; tail margin yellow. Young with yellow tail & blue bars straight in middle. *H. townsendi* is the hybrid of this and *H. ciliaris*. **Ecology:** rocky or coral reefs, 2 to >92 m. Juveniles in channels and on inshore reefs. Feeds primarily on sponges. Common in the Florida Keys, rare in the Bahamas. **Range:** Bermuda & N. Carol. (juvs. rarely to N.J.) to s. Fla. w. to n. G. Mexico offshore banks, s. to Yucatan; absent from Antilles.

5 **Queen angelfish** *Holacanthus ciliaris* (Linnaeus) 45 cm
Black-blue crown on nape; tail & P fin always yellow; blue bars of young curved. **Ecology:** offshore reefs, 2 to >70 m. Moves gracefully between seafans, seawhips and corals. Feeds primarily on sponges. Young pick ectoparasites from other fishes. Solitary or paired. Wary. Individuals from the Caribbean islands and Bahamas are generally more colorful than those from the continental shelf. **Range:** Bermuda, s. Fla., Bahamas & G. Mexico to Brazil, e. to St. Paul's Rocks.

6 **Cherubfish** *Centropyge argi* Woods & Kanazawa 8 cm
Deep blue with yellow markings on head and chest. **Ecology:** among rubble of rocky or coral reefs, 5 to >60 m. Uncommon below 30 m. Feeds on algae. Shy, retreats to holes when frightened. **Range:** Bermuda, Fla., Bahamas & n. G. Mexico banks to Venezuela.

7 **Flameback pygmy angelfish** *Centropyge aurantonotus* Burgess 6 cm
Orange extends from head to nape & mid-D fin in ad., nearly to end of D fin in juvs. Closely related to *C. acanthops* (E. Africa; pl. 68-6) & *C. resplendens* (Ascension). **Ecology:** In isolated elkhorn coral patches, 15 to 200 m, usually 25 m. **Range:** Lesser Antilles and Curaao to Brazil.

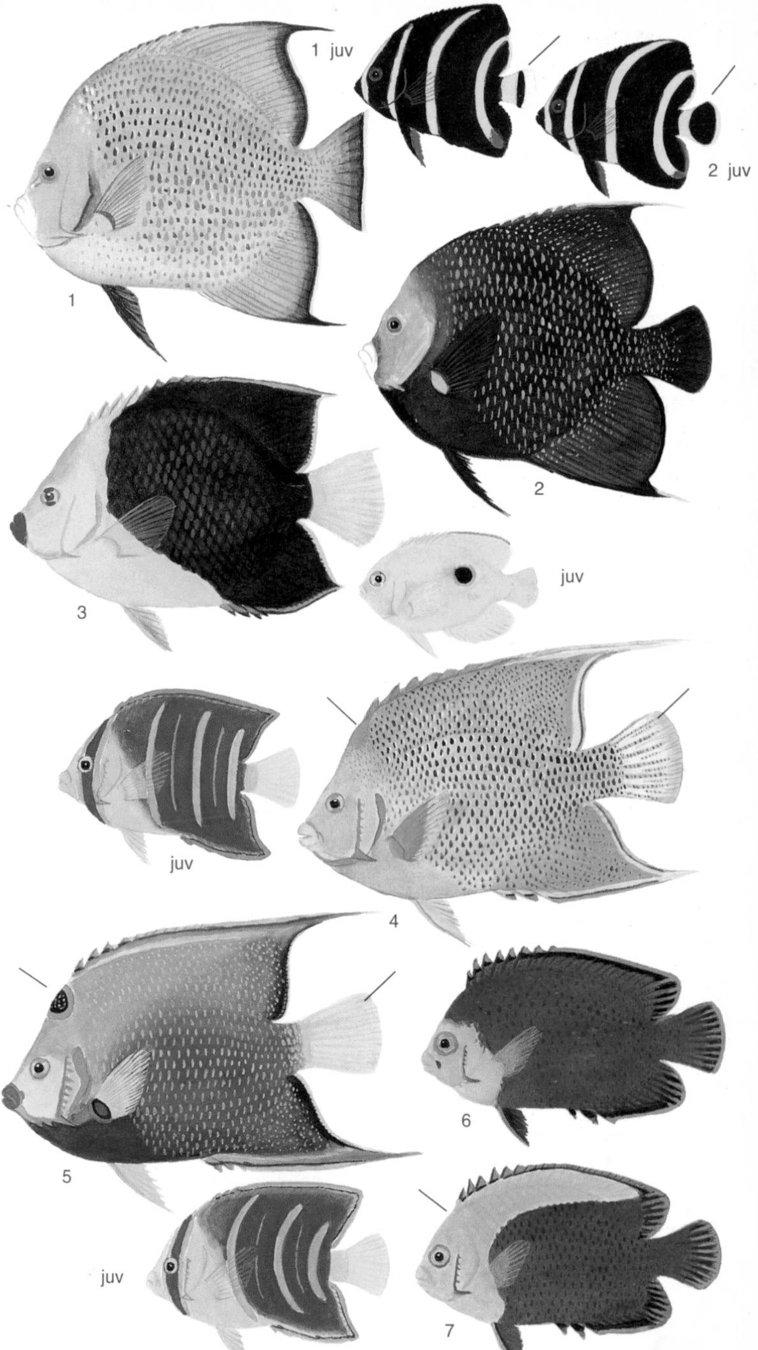
1 juv
2 juv
1
2
3
juv
juv
4
5
6
juv
7

DAMSELFISHES (POMACENTRIDAE): small, often colorful fishes with moderately deep compressed bodies, small terminal mouths with conical or incisiform teeth, moderately large scales, continuous D fins, and an interupted LL. Conspicuous and numerous on all rocky or coral reefs. Caribbean species include omnivores (*Abudefduf*, *Microspathodon* and *Stegastes*) and planktivores (*Chromis*). The omnivores are typically highly territorial; those that feed primarily on algae may be quite pugnacious. The planktivores generally aggregate above the reef. Lay demersal eggs guarded by the male. Among the hardiest of aquarium fishes, but some species extremely aggressive.

1 **Blue chromis** *Chromis cyanea* (Poey) 13 cm
Ecology: outer reef slopes and exposed patch reefs, 3 to 55 m. Form large aggregations in the water column to feed on zooplankton, primarily copepods. Often with the creole wrasse (pl. 64-7). Retreat into crevices or corals when frightened. **Range:** s. Fla., Bahamas & n. G. Mexico banks to Venezuela.

2 **Yellow-edge chromis** *Chromis multilineata* (Guichenot) 16.5 cm
Ecology: steep slopes and patch reefs, 2 to 40 m. In loose aggregations that feed on zooplankton, mainly shrimp larvae and copepods. Often with blue chromis. **Range:** Fla., Bermuda & n. G. Mexico to Brazil, e. to Ascension, St. Helena & Sao Tome Is. (W. Africa).

3 **Purple chromis** *Chromis scotti* Emery 10 cm
Juvs. blue but deeper-bodied than *C. cyanea*; adults become brownish with white belly. **Ecology:** steep seaward slopes and patch reefs, 5 to 100 m. Common from 15 to 30 m. **Range:** N. Carol., Bahamas & n. G. Mexico banks to. s. Carib.

4 **Olive chromis** *Chromis insolata* (Cuvier) 16 cm
Ads. brown with white belly. **Ecology:** seaward reefs, 20 to 100 m. **Range:** s. Fla., Bermuda & n. G. Mexico banks to Venezuela; replaced at St. Helena by *C. sanctaehelenae*.

5 **Caribbean chromis** *Chromis enchrysura* Jordan & Gilbert 10 cm
Distinctive blue oblique streak through eye which fades with age; dusky grading to pale bluish behind line from mouth to soft D fin. **Ecology:** steep seaward slopes and patch reefs, 5 to 146 m, typically 40 to 70 m. In small groups near small outcrops. **Range:** N. Carol., Bermuda & n. G. Mexico banks to Brazil, e. to St. Paul's Rocks.

6 **Yellowtail damselfish** *Microspathodon chrysurus* (Cuvier) 21 cm
Number of brilliant blue spots decreases with age. **Ecology:** shallow coral reefs, 0 to 15 m. Juveniles usually among *Millepora* fire corals where they act as cleaners by removing parasites from other fishes. Adults feed on algae and juveniles feed on coral polyps and invertebrates. Territorial and bold. Common. **Range:** s. Fla., Bermuda & n. G. Mexico banks to Venezuela.

7 **Bicolor damselfish** *Stegastes partitus* (Poey) 10 cm
Ecology: shallow coral reefs, seagrass beds or patch reefs, 0 to 45 m. Aggressively territorial but only around a small area. **Range:** s. Fla., Bermuda & n. G. Mexico banks to Brazil.

8 **Dusky damselfish** *Stegastes dorsopunicans* (Poey) 15 cm
Olive-brown with scale edges forming vertical dark bars. **Ecology:** rocky shores exposed to surge, 0 to 3 m as well as silty harbors and bays. Often in tidepools. Feed primarily on algae and detritus. Territorial and pugnacious. Common. **Range:** Fla., Bermuda & G. Mexico to n. S. America; replaced by *S. fuscus* in e. Brazil.

9 **Threespot damselfish** *Stegastes planifrons* (Cuvier) 12.5 cm
Dark spot on C peduncle and P fin base; top of eye yellowish. **Ecology:** inshore and offshore reefs, 1 to 30 m. Common in algae-rich areas. Pugnaciously guard large territories, will chase and nip intruders of all sizes, including divers. **Range:** Fla., Bermuda & n. G. Mexico to Venezula; replaced at St. Paul's Rocks by *S. sanctipauli*.

10 **Cocoa damselfish** *Stegastes variabilis* (Castelnau) 12.5 cm
Small spot on caudal peduncle; dark area above eye. **Ecology:** inshore and offshore coral reefs, 0 to 30 m. Territorial, but not particularly aggressive except when breeding. Common in s. Florida, less common elsewhere. **Range:** s. Fla., Bahamas & G. Mexico to Brazil.

11 **Longfin damselfish** *Stegastes diencaeus* (Jordan & Rutter) 12.5 cm
Ad. difficult to distinguish from *S. dorsopunicans*. **Ecology:** protected, often turbid inshore areas and shallow coral reefs, 2 to 5 m, juveniles rarely to 45 m. Territorial and pugnacious. **Range:** Fla. & Bahamas to Panama & s. Carib.

12 **Beaugregory** *Stegastes leucostictus* (Müller & Troschel) 10 cm
Similar to *S. diencaeus*, but with fewer P rays (17-19 vs. 19-21) & juvs. with more extensive blue dorsally & ads. with some yellow-centered scales dorsally. **Ecology:** various shallow habitats including sand, seagrass, rubble and coral reefs, 1 to 5m. **Range:** Maine, Bermuda & n. G. Mexico to Brazil.

1
2
3
4juv
5
juv
6
7
8
9
9 juv
8 juv
10
11 juv
10 juv
12 juv
11
12

1 **Sergeant major** *Abudefduf saxatilis* (Linnaeus) 15 cm
Similar to *A. vaigiensis* (Indo-Pacific; pl. 74-1) & *A. abdominalis* (Hawaii; pl.74-6). **Ecology:** shallow coral and rocky reefs and seagrass beds, 1 to 12 m. Feed in lose aggregations on zooplankton. Nesting males are dark blue. Juveniles are common in tide pools and in floating sargassum. Common. Attracted to divers that feed fishes. **Range:** Rhode I. & n. G. Mexico to Uruguay, e. to Africa incl. St. Paul's Rocks, Ascension & St. Helena.

2 **Night sergeant** *Abudefduf taurus* (Müller & Troschel) 25 cm
Color variable: brown, yellowish to dark blue. **Ecology:** shallow turbid rocky areas with wave action, 1 to 5 m. Feeds on benthic algae. Timid. **Range:** s. Fla., Bahamas & Texas to Venezuela.

WRASSES (LABRIDAE): a large and diverse group in both size and form. Typically with terminal mouth, somewhat thickened lips, one or more pairs of protruding canine teeth, nodular pharyngeal teeth, elongate body, continuous or interupted LL and single unnotched D fin. Most species change color with growth and sex. Typically a drab initial phase (IP) of both males and females, the latter able to change sex into a brilliant terminal male phase (TP). All species inactive at night, the smaller ones often sleep beneath the sand. Includes carnivores, planktivores, and cleaners. Most species do well in aquariums. Medium to large species are important foodfishes in many areas.

Tribe Hypsigenyini: rather large mouth with one or more pairs of canines in front of jaws and continuous LL. Carnivores of benthic invertebrates.

3 **Spanish hogfish** *Bodianus rufus* (Linnaeus) 40 cm
Color variable: with red, purplish or blue back (juvs.); blue-black in deep water. **Ecology:** rocky or coral reefs, 1 to 60 m. Moves constantly over large areas. Feeds on brittle stars, crustaceans, molluscs and sea urchins. Juveniles clean other fishes. Common. **Range:** s. Fla. & Bermuda to s. Brazil.

4 **Spotfin hogfish** *Bodianus pulchellus* (Poey) 15 cm
Red-yellow with more or less distinct lateral stripe. **Ecology:** rocky or coral reefs, 15 to 120 m, rarely >24 m. Juveniles aggregate with bluehead wrasses and serve as cleaners by picking parasites from other fishes. Bold. **Range:** s. Fla. & n. G. Mexico banks to s. Brazil.

5 **Hogfish** *Lachnolaimus maximus* (Walbaum) 91 cm; 9 kg
Color variable: pale to reddish brown; head profile distinct. **Ecology:** inshore patch reefs and seaward reefs, 3 to 30 m. Prefers open areas with abundant growth of gorgonians. Roots in sand for mollusks, crabs, and sea urchins. Highly esteemed for food, but ciguatoxic in some areas. Common. **Range:** N. Carol., Bermuda & G. Mexico to Brazil.

Tribe Cheilinini: interupted LL with posterior section along axis of tail-base.

6 **Dwarf wrasse** *Doratonotus megalepis* Günther 7.5 cm
Color variable: greenish with brown spots. May darken and become mottled. **Ecology:** shallow seagrass beds or weedy areas, 1 to 15 m. Common but seldom noticed. **Range:** s. Fla. & Bermuda to Venezuela; e. Atlantic?

Tribe Julidini: continuous LL (see also pl. 165).

7 **Creole wrasse** *Clepticus parrae* (Bloch & Schneider) 30 cm
Blue to purplish with black area above eye; changes color during display. **Ecology:** seaward reef slopes, 1 to 40 m. In large mid-water aggregations that feed on zooplankton. Common along vertical faces. Occasionally on shallow patch reefs. **Range:** N. Carol., Bermuda & n. G. Mexico banks to Venezuela.

Tribe Novaculini: interupted LL with posterior section along axis of tail-base.

8 **Pearly razorfish** *Xyrichtys novacula* (Linnaeus) 38 cm
Reddish bar on side; dark to pale greenish above. Has barred pattern when drifting. **Ecology:** clear water sandy areas, 2 to 80 m. Feeds primarily on mollusks. Builds nests with coral debris. Dives headfirst into the sand when frightened. **Range:** N. Carol. & n. G. Mexico to Brazil, e. to Africa & Medit.

9 **Rosy razorfish** *Xyrichtys martinicensis* (Valenciennes) 15 cm
Dark area at base of P fin. Females and young with a lateral orange stripe. **Ecology:** open sandy or grassy areas, 2 to 21 m. Feeds on small sand-dwelling invertebrates. Dives headfirst into the sand when frightened. Common. **Range:** s. Fla, Bahamas & Yucatan to Venezuela.

10 **Green razorfish** *Xyrichtys splendens* Castelnau 15 cm
Greenish with a small dark lateral spot & red eye. Has barred pattern when drifting. **Ecology:** seagrass beds and sandy areas, 3 to 15 m. Shy. **Range:** s. Fla., Bermuda & Yucatan to Brazil.

1
2
2 var
juv
3
juv
4
5
6
7
9 juv
8
9
10

165 WRASSES

Tribe Julidini: continuous LL; usually 1 to 2 pairs of prominent canines in front of jaws and well-developed pharyngeal teeth. Typically feed on benthic invertebrates or fishes.

1 **Bluehead** *Thalassoma bifasciatum* (Bloch) 18 cm
TP with distinctive blue head & black & white shoulder bar. IP greenish yellow, mimicked by *Hemiemblemaria simulus* (pl. 170-9). **Ecology:** ubiquitous and abundant; seagrass beds, reef flats, patch reefs, and seaward reefs, 0 to 40 m. Juveniles pick ectoparasites from other fishes. **Range:** Fla., Bermuda & s. G. Mexico to Venezuela.

2 **Pudding wife** *Halichoeres radiatus* (Linnaeus) 51 cm
Greenish to blueish with 5 pale blotches on back. TP with midbody bar. **Ecology:** shallow seaward or patch reefs, 2 to 55 m. Feeds on mollusks, sea urchins, crustaceans, and brittle stars. Common. Timid. **Range:** N. Carol., Bermuda & n. G. Mexico to Brazil, e. to St. Paul's Rocks.

3 **Yellowhead wrasse** *Halichoeres garnoti* (Valenciennes) 18 cm
IP yellowish brown; juvs. with a blue lateral stripe. **Ecology:** patch reefs in lagoons and on seaward reefs, 2 to 80 m. Feeds on various invertebrates. Constantly on the move but easily attracted by divers. Common. **Range:** s. Fla. Bermuda & n. G. Mexico banks to se. Brazil.

4 **Slippery dick** *Halichoeres bivittatus* (Bloch) 20 cm
TP with two dark lateral stripes on green ground color; IP pale with 1 to 2 stripes. **Ecology:** abundant in various habitats including sand, mud, rocks and coral reefs, 1 to 15 m. Feeds primarily on crustaceans, sea urchins, polychaetes, brittle stars and mollusks. **Range:** N. Carol. & Bermuda to Brazil.

5 **Clown wrasse** *Halichoeres maculipinna* (Müller & Tröschel) 18 cm
TP with large lateral black spot; IP with yellow back & white belly with a black stripe. **Ecology:** abundant on reef flats and shallow rocky areas, 2 to 24 m. Not shy. **Range:** N. Carol. & Bermuda to Brazil.

6 **Rainbow wrasse** *Halichoeres pictus* (Poey) 13 cm
TP green yellow above, blueish below; black spot on C peduncle; IP tan with 2 brown stripes. **Ecology:** coral reefs, normally high above the bottom. Swims with worm-like movements. Feeds on various invertebrates. Uncommon. **Range:** s. Fla. (rare) & Bahamas to Venezuela.

7 **Blackear wrasse** *Halichoeres poeyi* (Steindachner) 20 cm
TP overall purplish-brown to green on back; three red stripes on tail. **Ecology:** shallow reefs, 1 to 15 m. Common among seagrasses in clear shallow water, uncommon on reefs or in muddy areas. Easily approached. **Range:** s. Fla. & Bahamas to se. Brazil.

8 **Yellowcheek wrasse** *Halichoeres cyanocephalus* (Bloch) 30 cm
Back yellowish green, dark blue lateral band & white belly. Young bright blue with yellow back. **Ecology:** deep coral and rocky reefs, 27 to 91 m. Common in the Florida Keys, uncommon to rare elsewhere. **Range:** Fla. Keys & Antilles to Brazil.

9 **Greenband wrasse** *Halichoeres bathyphilus* (Beebe & Tee-Van) 23 cm
2 orange lateral stripes, green stripe on snout & a dark spot on C peduncle. **Ecology:** deep reefs from 28 to 155 m, usually 27 m. **Range:** Carol., Bermuda & ne. G. Mexico to Yucatan.

10 **Painted wrasse** *Halichoeres caudalis* (Poey) 23 cm
TP with bluegreen ground color & pink fins with blue stripes; IP yellowish with 2 dark orange lateral stripes. **Ecology:** deep seaward reefs, 18 to 73 m. **Range:** N. Carol. & n. G. Mexico to Venezuela.

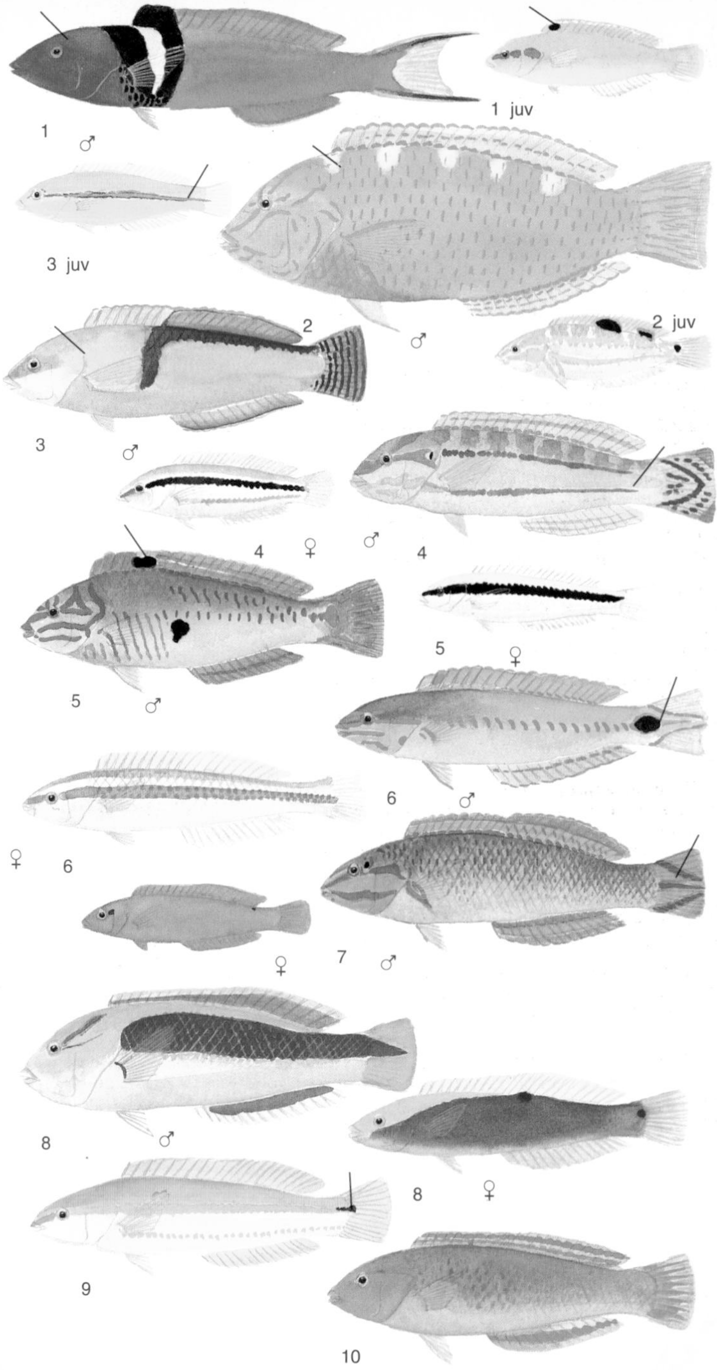

1
♂
1 juv
3 juv
2
♂
2 juv
3
♂
4
♀
♂
4
5
♀
5
♂
6
♂
♀
6
7
♀
♂
8
♂
8
♀
9
10

PARROTFISHES (SCARIDAE): medium to large wrasse-like fishes differing by having teeth fused into a beaklike plates with a median suture and unique pavement-like pharyngeal teeth. All species with large cycloid scales, continuous D fin, single LL, and herbivorous. Most species graze on the algal film growing on coral rock, a few eat leafy algae or living coral. Bits of rock eaten with the algae are crushed into sand and ground with the algae to aid in digestion, making parrotfishes among the most important producers of sand on coral reefs. Many species occur in large mixed species schools, often with surgeonfishes. At night they sleep wedged into holes or crevices. Many species secrete a mucus cocoon around themselves which may inhibit the sense of smell of predators. Like the wrasses, most parrotfishes change color with growth and sex. Typically a drab grey, brown, or reddish initial phase (IP) consisting of both females and males, the latter able to change sex into a brilliant blue to green terminal male phase (TP). Juveniles and IP of many species very similar and often very difficult to identify, TP generally more distinctive. Important foodfishes. Difficult to maintain in aquariums.

1 **Midnight parrotfish** *Scarus coelestinus* Valenciennes 76 cm; 7 kg
All phases similar: indigo blue with bright blue spots on head. **Ecology:** rocky coastal reefs to seaward reefs, 5 to 75 m. Common, often in schools feeding with surgeonfishes by scraping off algae from rocks or dead corals. Not shy. **Range:** s. Fla. & Bahamas to Brazil.

2 **Blue parrotfish** *Scarus coeruleus* (Bloch) 90 cm (rare 60 cm)
TP sky blue with a humped snout. Young & subadults with yellow nape. **Ecology:** rocky coastal reefs and offshore coral reefs, 3 to 25 m. Feeds on benthic algae. Forms large spawning aggregations. Not shy. **Range:** Maryland & Bermuda to se. Brazil; absent from n. G. Mexico.

3 **Rainbow parrotfish** *Scarus guacamaia* Cuvier 120 cm; 20 kg
IP similar to TP but paler. **Ecology:** rocky coastal areas and on offshore coral reefs, 3 to 25 m. Juveniles in mangrove areas. Not shy. **Range:** Fla. & Bermuda to Argentina, absent from n. G. Mexico.

4 **Striped parrotfish** *Scarus iserti* Bloch 35 cm
Tp with broad orange wash above P fin. **Ecology:** rocky and coral reefs, 3 to 25 m. The most common species of the genus in the W. Indies. Forages in aggregations of several hundred females and a few terminal males. Forms large spawning aggregations on outer reefs. Displays a complex social system with permanent territories of a TP "harem master", one dominant female, and several subordinate females. Immature fish have stationary territories. **Range:** s. Fla., Bermuda & ne. G. Mexico to Venezuela.

5 **Princess parrotfish** *Scarus taeniopterus* Desmarest 35 cm
TP with large orange lateral stripe; IP with three brown stripes & dark outer rays of tail. **Ecology:** rocky coastal reefs and seaward coral reefs, 2 to 25 m. IP forms large feeding aggregations. Sleeps in a mucus cocoon. **Range:** s. Fla. & Bermuda to Brazil.

6 **Queen parrotfish** *Scarus vetula* Bloch & Schneider 61 cm
IP brown with a lateral stripe.; TP with distinct markings around mouth. **Ecology:** rocky and coral reefs, 3 to 25 m. Feeds on algae scraped from rocks and dead coral. Sleeps in a mucus cocoon. Not shy. **Range:** s. Fla. & Bermuda to Argentina.

7 **Stoplight parrotfish** *Sparisoma viride* (Bonnaterre) 50 cm
TP with yellow blotch on C peduncle. Young brown with 3 rows of white dots & white bar on tail. **Ecology:** rocky and coral reefs, 3 to 49 m. Occasionally on seagrass flats. Often caught in fish traps. **Range:** Fla. Bermuda & n. G. Mexico banks to e. Brazil.

8 **Redtail parrotfish** *Sparisoma chrysopterum* (Bloch & Schneider) 46 cm
TP dark green with a blueish belly; IP mottled red with black spot at P axil. **Ecology:** lagoon and seaward reefs, 1 to 15 m. Prefers open weedy areas with rubble or seagrass. Will sit among weeds with a mottled color pattern. Not shy. **Range:** s. Fla. & Bermuda to e. Brazil.

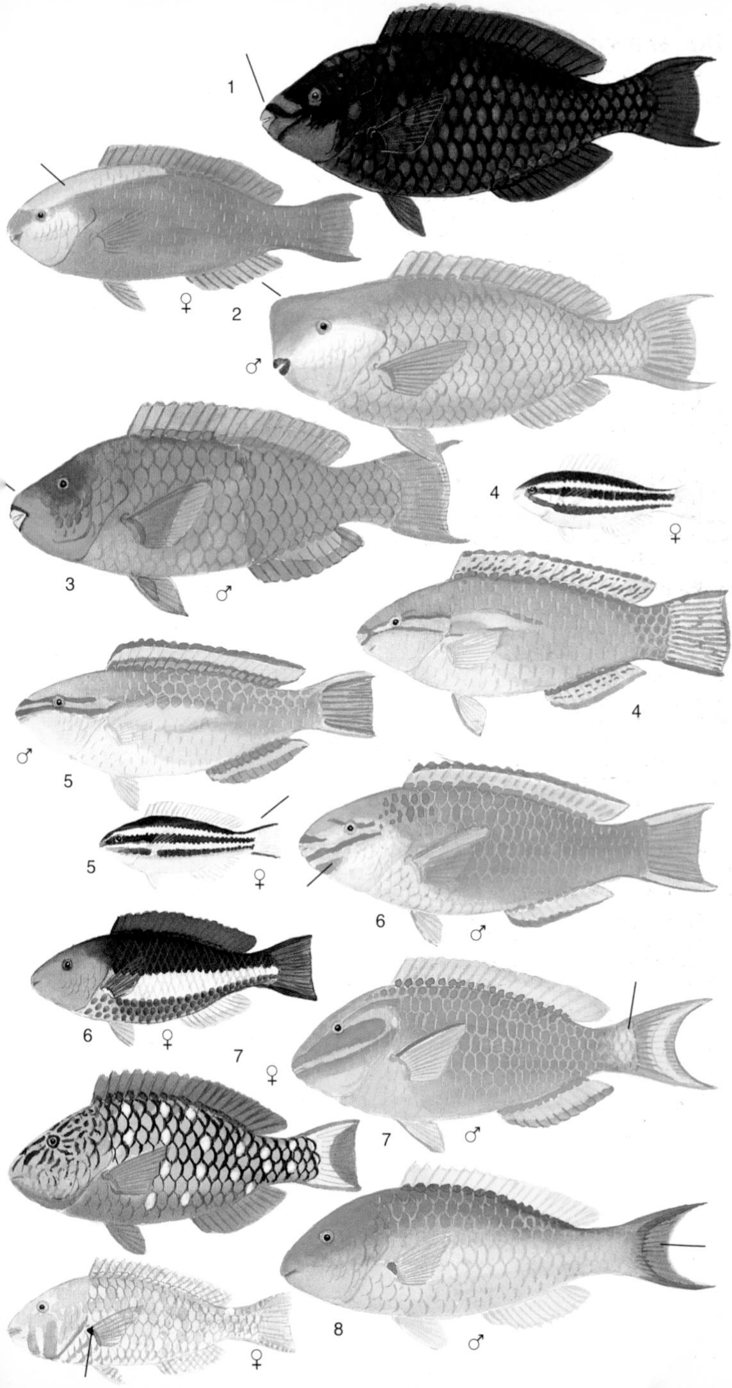
1
♀
2
♂
4
3
♂
♀
4
♂
5
5
♀
6
♂
6
♀
7
♀
7
♂
8
♀
♂

167 PARROTFISHES, JAWFISHES and STARGAZERS

1 **Redband parrotfish** *Sparisoma aurofrenatum* (Valenciennes) 28 cm
TP with red-orange band on tail; IP dull mottled red. **Ecology:** solitary or in small groups in seagrass beds and rocky and coral reefs, 2 to 20 m. Browses primarely on algae. Often rests on bottom. **Range:** Fla. & Bermuda to e. Brazil.

2 **Redfin parrotfish** *Sparisoma rubripinne* (Valenciennes) 46 cm
Ecology: shallow seagrass flats and over coral rubble, sometimes on reefs, 1 to 15 m. Spawns in groups at special sites. **Range:** Mass. & Bermuda to se. Brazil; e. to Sao Tomé (Africa).

3 **Greenblotch parrotfish** *Sparisoma atomarium* (Poey) 10 cm
TP with dark blotch above P fin. **Ecology:** deep rocky and coral reefs with steep walls, 20 to 55 m. Not shy. Rare. **Range:** s. Fla. & Bermuda to Venezuela

4 **Bucktooth parrotfish** *Sparisoma radians* (Valenciennes) 20 cm
Color variable: green to yellowish or mottled with dark spot at P base. **Ecology:** seagrass beds of protected inshore reefs, 1 to 12 m. Darts into seagrass when frightened. Feeds primarily on epiphytes and seagrass blades, leaving crescent bite marks. **Range:** Fla., Bermuda & e. G. Mexico to Venezuela.

5 **Emerald parrotfish** *Nicholsina usta* (Valenciennes) 30 cm
Head with two orange stripes; D fin with black spot. **Ecology:** seagrass beds and open sandy areas, 1 to 73 m. Adults generally deep. **Range:** N. J. to Brazil incl. continental shelf islands; absent from Bahamas & L. Antilles.

6 **Bluelip parrotfish** *Cryptotomus roseus* Cope 13 cm
Ecology: seagrass beds and weedy areas with sand. Feeds on seagrasses. Buries in sand to sleep in a mucus tube. **Range:** s. Fla. & Bermuda to e. Brazil.

OPISTOGNATHIDAE (JAWFISHES): mostly small fishes with enlarged head and mouth and narrow tapering body, and long continuous D fin. Live in burrows in sand which they enter tail-first. Feed on benthic and planktonic invertebrates and incubate their eggs orally. Many undescribed species, but few species known from any given area. Popular aquarium fishes.

7 **Swordtail jawfish** *Lonchopisthus micrognathus* (Poey) 10 cm
Ecology: in burrows on silty or muddy bottoms, sometimes in colonies. **Range:** s. Fla. & G. Mexico.

8 **Yellowhead jawfish** *Opistognathus aurifrons* (Jordan & Thompson) 10 cm
Ecology: in burrows in patches of crushed coral on sand, 3 to 40 m. Hovers vertically above the entrance of its burrow. The male courts the female by swimming in an arched position with his fins spread towards her. The male guards the eggs. **Range:** Fla. & Bahamas to Barbados & Venezuela.

9 **Banded jawfish** *Opistognathus macrognathus* Poey 20 cm
Ecology: rubble bottoms near coral reefs, 1 to 12 m. **Range:** s. Fla. & Bahamas to Venezuela.

10 **Dusky jawfish** *Opistognathus whitehurstii* (Longley) 10 cm
Ecology: seagrass flats, rubble and sandy areas with a firm limestone substratum, 1 to 12 m. Entrance of burrow not reinforced with rocks. **Range:** s. Fla. & Bahamas to Venezuela.

11 **Spotfin jawfish** *Opistognathus* sp. 15 cm
White border around D fin spot. **Ecology:** sandy bottoms, often close to reefs. **Range:** S. Carol. to Fla. Keys & Bahamas, w. to Texas.

12 **Mottled jawfish** *Opistognathus maxillosus* Poey 13 cm
Ecology: sand and rubble areas of limestone bottoms, m. **Range:** Fla. Keys & Bahamas to C. America & W. Indies.

URANOSCOPIDAE (STARGAZERS): thick bodied with massive armored head, large vertically oriented mouth with fringed lips and small teeth, a large venomous spine on shoulder girdle, 2 D fins, and no LL. *Astroscopus* with an electric organ located in a pouch behind the eyes. Lie buried in sediment with eyes and lips exposed. Feed on fishes and invertebrates. Few species near reefs.

13 **Southern stargazer** *Astroscopus y-graecum* (Cuvier) 44 cm
Ecology: silty, sandy or rubble bottoms, 2 to 40 m. **Range:** N. Carol. & n. G. Mexico to Yucatan; absent from W. Indies.

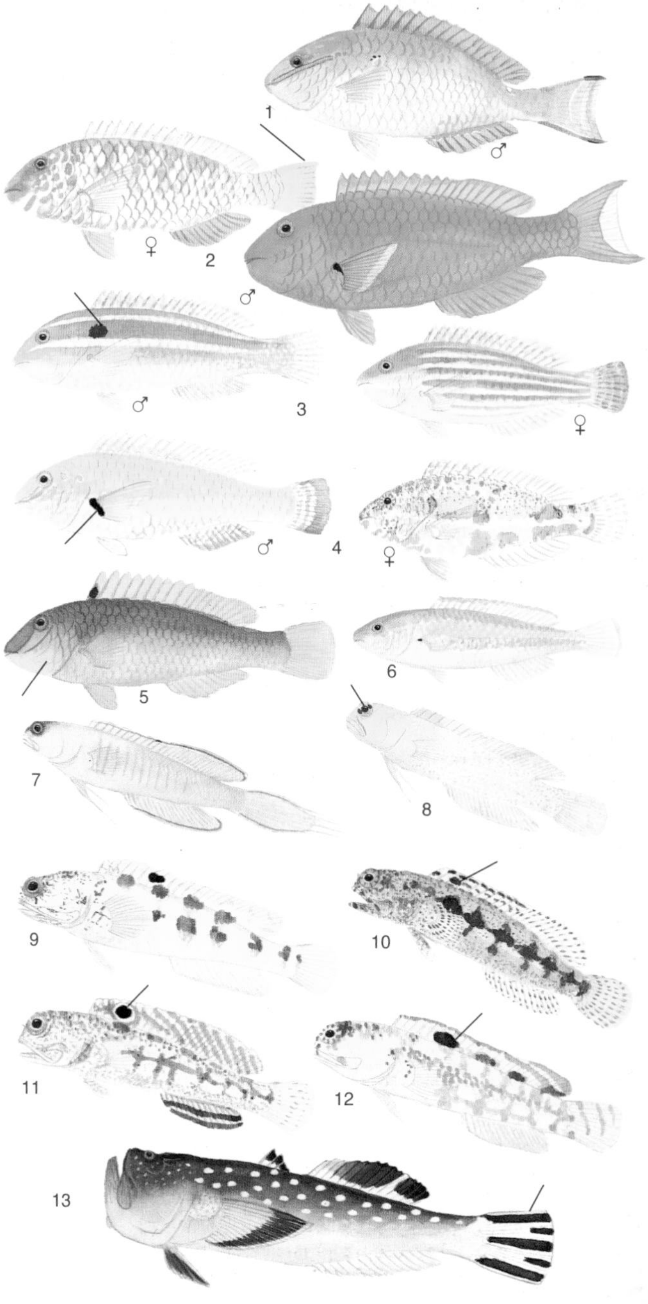
1
♂
♀
2
♂
♂
3
♀
♂
4
♀
5
6
7
8
9
10
11
12
13

MULLETS (MUGILIDAE): silvery somewhat cylindrical fishes with a short snout, small mouth with or without minute teeth, two widely spaced D fins, large scales, and no LL. Travel in schools and feed on fine algae, diatoms, and detritus of bottom sediments. Many species are estuarine or freshwater. Important food fishes.

1 **White mullet** *Mugil curema* Valenciennes 38 cm
Silvery-green with dark blue blotch at P axil and brassy opercle. **Ecology:** sandy areas, often near coral reefs. Enters fresh water. Common. **Range:** Mass. & Bermuda to Brazil, e. to e. Pacific.

THREADFINS (POLYNEMIDAE): silvery fishes with inferior mouth with minute teeth, two widely spaced D fins, forked tail, and 3 to 8 elongate free rays on lower base of P fin. Feed on benthic invertebrates of sandy to muddy bottoms. Few species near reefs. Foodfishes.

2 **Barbu** *Polydactylus virginicus* (Linnaeus) 30cm
Ecology: sand flats near reefs. Common around islands. **Range:** Virginia (rare n. of s. Fla. & Bahamas) to Brazil.

BARRACUDAS (SPHYRAENIDAE): elongate silvery fishes with two widely spaced D fins, small scales, and pointed head with large mouth and long knife-like teeth. Voracious predators of other fishes. Most species in schools by day. Juveniles often in estuaries. Food and gamefishes, but large *S. barracuda* may be ciguatoxic.

3 **Southern sennet** *Sphyraena picudilla* Poey 45 cm
Similar to *S. guachancho* which has elongate last D & A fin rays
Ecology: in large schools near rocky or coral reefs, 1 to 12 m. **Range:** Fla. & Bermuda to Uruguay.

4 **Great barracuda** *Sphyraena barracuda* (Walbaum) 190 cm; 40 kg
Ecology: wide range of habitats from turbid inshore waters to open sea. Juveniles in sheltered inner reef and estuarine waters. Solitary and diurnally active. Curious, but not dangerous in clear water unless provoked. Capable of inflicting severe wounds. Frequently ciguatoxic in tropical Atlantic. Common. **Range:** all tropical seas except E. Pacific; Mass. to s. Brazil in w. Atlantic.

TUNAS and MACKERELS (SCOMBRIDAE): medium to large silvery fusiform fishes with 2 D fins, several detached finlets behind D and A fins, deeply forked tail two or more peduncular keels and a simple LL. Primarily swift predators of open seas. Some of the smaller species strain zooplankton through their gill rakers. Few species on coral reefs.

5 **Cero** *Scomberomorus regalis* (Bloch) 86 cm; 5 kg
Brassy markings on side, 1st D fin blackish. ♂ mature at ca. 35 cm, ♀ at 41 cm. **Ecology:** mid-waters of clear seaward reefs, 1 to 20 m. Solitary or in small groups. Feeds primarily on small schooling pelagic fishes. **Range:** Mass. to n. Brazil incl. nw. G. Mexico, Bahamas & Antilles.

6 **King mackerel** *Scomberomorus cavalla* (Cuvier) 184 cm; 45 kg
Juvs. with dark spots; LL drops upruptly below 2nd D fin. ♂ mature at 77 cm, ♀ at 89 cm. **Ecology:** outer reef areas. Solitary or in small groups. Juveniles often caught from bridges. An important gamefish, but potentially ciguatoxic in certain areas. **Range:** Maine to s. Brazil incl. G. Mexico & all W. Indies; absent from Bermuda.

7 **Spanish mackerel** *Scomberomorus maculatus* (Mitchill) 83 cm; 5 kg
Similar to *S. brasiliensis* (Belize to Brazil) which has more spots and occurs on continental shelf; yellow spots more roundish than in Cero. ♂ mature at ca. 30 cm, ♀ at 27 cm. **Ecology:** mid-waters of continental shelf, sometimes in estuaries. Usually in schools. Migrates along continental shorelines. A popular gamefish. **Range:** C. Cod s. (rare n. of Cheasapeake Bay), Bermuda & G. Mexico to Cuba & Haiti; absent from Bahamas & Lesser Antilles.

8 **Little tuna** *Euthynnus alletteratus* (Rafinesque) 100 cm; 12 kg
Dark bars on back and dark spots below P fin. Matures at 35 cm off Fla. **Ecology:** mid-waters of outer bays and offshore reefs. Diving bird flocks may indicate large schools. A popular gamefish. **Range:** Maine & Bermuda s. to Brazil, e. to St. Helena, e. Atlantic & Medit.

1

2

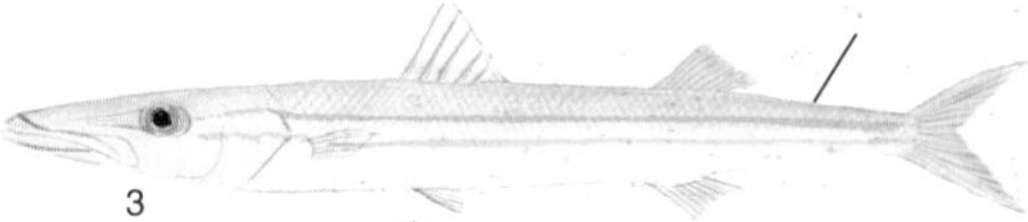

3

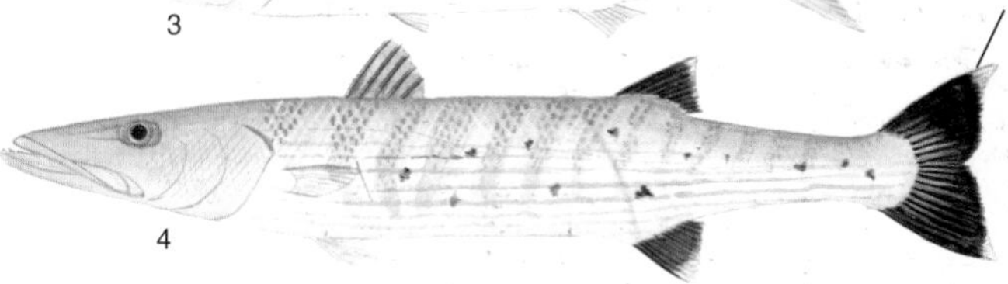

4

5

6

7

8

169 TRIPLEFINS and LABRISOMIDS

TRIPLEFINS (TRIPTERYGIIDAE): tiny moderately elongate fishes with 3 D fins and divided or continuous LL. Bottom dwellers that feed on small invertebrates. Five spp. in W. Atlantic.

1 **Redeye Triplefin** *Enneanectes pectoralis* (Fowler) 4 cm
Ecology: shallow coral-rich areas, intertidal to 6 m, usually m. **Range:** s. Fla., Bahamas & Yucatan to Venezuela.

LABRISOMIDS (LABRISOMIDAE): small elongate fishes with large mouths, conical teeth, usually scaled bodies, and more D spines than rays. Feed on small benthic invertebrates.

2 **Hairy blenny** *Labrisomus nuchipinnis* (Quoy & Gaimard) 20 cm
Similar to *L. guppy* which has 53 LS (vs. 64). **Ecology:** shoreline, rocky ledges, and patch reefs, hidden among algae or rocks. Common. **Range:** Fla., Bermuda & n. G. Mexico to Brazil, e. to Madeira & G. Guinea.

3 **Spotcheek blenny** *Labrisomus nigricinctus* Rivero 8 cm
Ecology: coral and rubble areas of clear exposed high-energy reefs, tidepools to 10 m. **Range:** s. Fla., Bahamas & Yucatan to Venezuela.

4 **Quillfin blenny** *Labrisomus filamentosus* Springer 12 cm
Ecology: usually on deeper reefs with abundant algae,12 to 35 m. Easy to approach. **Range:** s. Bahamas, Hispanola & Virgin Is., to Venezuela.

5 **Palehead blenny** *Labrisomus gobio* (Valenciennes) 6.5 cm
Ecology: shallow coral-rich areas of clear offshore reefs, 0 to 15 m. **Range:** s. Fla., Bahamas & Yucatan to Lesser Antilles.

6 **Puffcheek blenny** *Labrisomus bucciferus* (Poey) 9 cm
Ecology: exposed reef crests, seagrass beds and forereef slopes, 0 to 5 m. **Range:** s. Fla. & Bermuda to Lesser Antilles.

7 **Rosy blenny** *Malacoctenus macropus* (Poey) 5.5 cm
Has fewer LS (<45) & D soft rays (8 to 11) than *M. triangulatus* (52; 11 to 13). **Ecology:** wide variety of shoreline habitats and patch reefs to 5 m, usually 2 m. **Range:** Fla., Bermuda & Yucatan to Venezuela.

8 **Saddled blenny** *Malacoctenus triangulatus* Springer 6.5 cm
Ecology: on rubble of coral-rich fringing or patch reefs, 0 to 18 m, usually <3 m. Abundant. **Range:** s. Fla., Bahamas & Yucatan to Brazil, e. to St. Paul's Rocks.

9 **Barfin blenny** *Malacoctenus versicolor* (Poey) 7 cm
Ecology: on coral rubble of shallow sandy and rocky areas, 0 to 7 m. **Range:** Bahamas & Cuba through Antilles; absent from C. America.

10 **Diamond blenny** *Malacoctenus bohlkei* Springer 6.5 cm
Ecology: patch reefs and forereef dropoffs, 5 to 30 m. Usually associated with the anemone *Condylactis gigantea*. **Range:** Bahamas & Virgin Is. to Bonaire, w. to Belize.

11 **Dusky blenny** *Malacoctenus gilli* (Steindachner) 7.5 cm
Ecology: on coral rubble of rocky shoreline reefs, seagrass beds, and patch reefs, 1 to 5 m. **Range:** Bahamas, Gr. Antilles & Yucatan to Venezuela.

12 **Goldline blenny** *Malacoctenus aurolineatus* Smith 6 cm
Ecology: shallow clear coral-rich or rocky areas, on coral rubble near sea urchins, 0 to 5 m. **Range:** s. Fla. & Bahamas to Venezuela.

13 **Checkered blenny** *Starksia ocellata* (Steindachner) 5 cm
Ecology: rocky and coral reefs, 2 to 20 m. Often inside tube sponges. **Range:** N.C. & ne. G. Mexico to n. S. America; absent from C. America & Brazil.

14 **Key blenny** *Starksia starcki* Gilbert 4 cm
Ecology: surge channels in coral reefs with high relief, 6 to 19 m. **Range:** Fla. Keys, Belize & Honduras.

15 **Ringed blenny** *Starksia hassi* Klausewitz 4 cm
Ecology: coral-rich tops of dropoffs, 25 to 45 m. Often in the anemone *Condylactis gigantea*. **Range:** Bahamas & Gr. Antilles to n. S. America.

16 **Banded blenny** *Paraclinus fasciatus* (Steindachner) 6 cm
Ecology: protected shallow seagrass beds, 0.2 to 1.5 m. **Range:** Fla., Bahamas & ne. G. Mexico to Venezuela.

17 **Marbled blenny** *Paraclinus marmoratus* (Steindachner) 10 cm
Ecology: lagoon patch reefs, 0.3 to 6 m. **Range:** s. Fla & Bahamas to Venezuela.

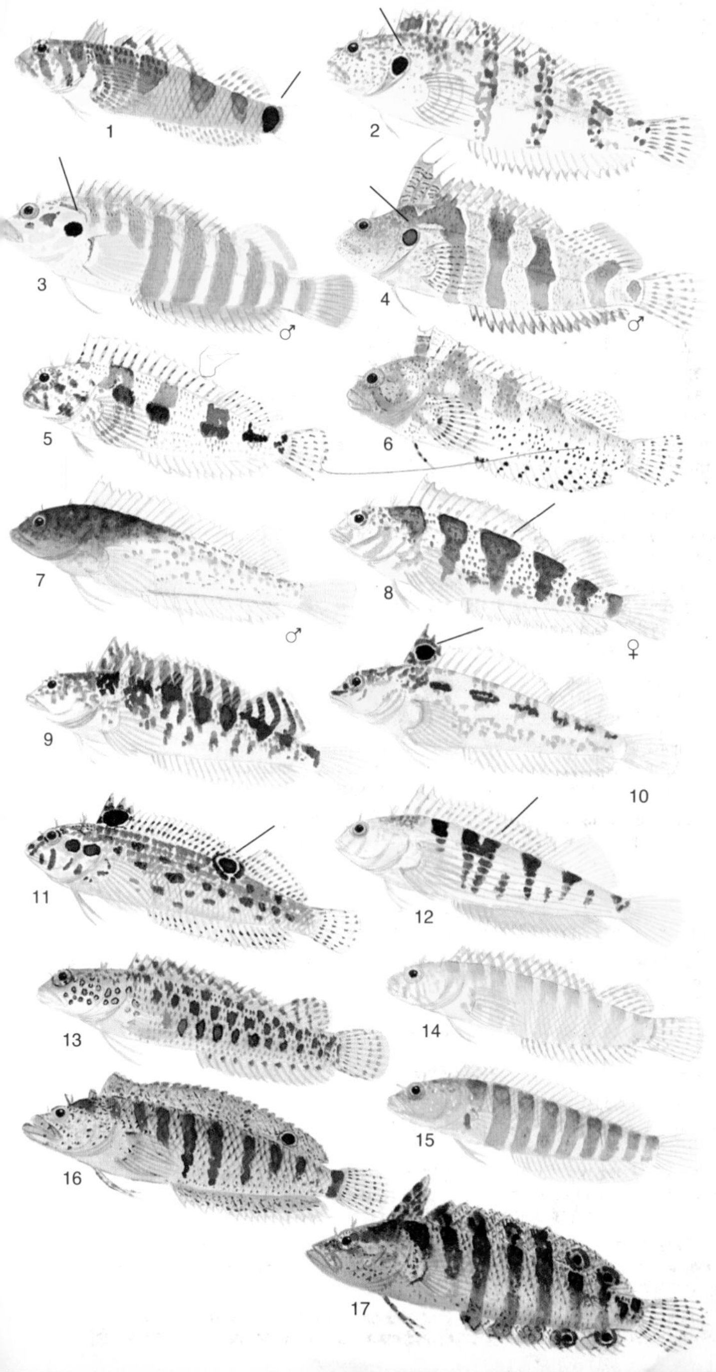
1
2
3
♂
4
♂
5
6
7
♂
8
♀
9
10
11
12
13
14
15
16
17

 BLENNIES, TUBEBLENNIES, DRAGONETS, DARTFISHES, and GOBIES

BLENNIES (BLENNIIDAE): for introduction to the family see pl. 113.

1 **Seaweed blenny** *Parablennius marmoreus* (Poey) 8.5 cm
Ecology: on mangrove roots and shallow, hard substratum covered with algae, 0.3 to 10 m. **Range:** N. Y., Bermuda & n. G. Mexico to Venezuela.

2 **Pearl blenny** *Entomacrodus nigricans* Gill 10 cm
Ecology: rocky shorelines and rock or coral rubble slopes, intertidal to 6 m, usually m. **Range:** s. Fla, Bermuda & Yucatan to Venezuela.

3 **Molly Miller** *Scartella cristata* (Linnaeus) 11 cm
Ecology: common in tidepools and shallow rocky areas, 0 to 10 m. **Range:** Fla., Bermuda & n. G. Mexico to Brazil, e. to e. Atlantic

4 **Redlip blenny** *Ophioblennius atlanticus* (Valenciennes) 12 cm
Ecology: shallow rocky and coral reefs, 1 to 40 m, usually 5 m. Territorial. Not shy. **Range:** N. C. & Bermuda to s. Brazil, e. to St. Paul's Rocks.

TUBEBLENNIES (CHAENOPSIDAE): small elongate scaleless fishes with more D spines than rays. Most dwell in abandoned invertebrate tubes and feed on small crustaceans. 32 spp. in W. Atlantic, incl. 8 *Emblemaria* and 4 *Chaenopsis*; only the most conspicous included here.

5 **Bluethroat pikeblenny** *Chaenopsis ocellata* Poey 12.5 cm
Ecology: turbid inshore areas and seagrass beds, 1 to 5 m. Inhabits worm tubes. Very territorial. Unafraid. **Range:** s. Fla. & Bahamas to Cuba.

6 **Yellowface pikeblenny** *Chaenopsis limbaughi* Robins & Randall 8.5 cm
Ecology: in groups over coral rubble, sand or limestone, 5 to 20 m. Unafraid. **Range:** s. Fla. & Bahamas to Venezuela.

7 **Pirate blenny** *Emblemaria piratula* Ginsburg & Reid 5 cm
Ecology: shorelines to deep rocky and coral reefs, intertidal to 30 m. **Range:** ne. G. Mexico.

8 **Sailfin blenny** *Emblemaria pandionis* Evermann & Marsh 5 cm
Ecology: clear water lagoon channels and channels between patch reefs, 1 to 12 m. Inhabits worm or clam holes in coral rubbble. Shy, leaves hole only for brief periods. **Range:** Fla., Bahamas & n. G. Mexico to Venezuela.

9 **Wrasse Blenny** *Hemiemblemaria simulus* Longley & Hildebrand 10 cm
Ecology: coral rubble near isolated coral heads, to 20 m. Feeds in mid-water on small fishes and shrimps. Mimics the bluehead wrasse (*Thalassoma bifasciatum*, pl.165-1). **Range:** s. Fla. & Bahamas to C. America.

10 **Arrow Blenny** *Lucayablennius zingaro* Böhlke 5 cm
Ecology: coral-rich areas of reef front dropoffs, 13 to 106 m. Drifts with bended tail to prey on small fishes. Retreats into holes or empty worm tubes. Ignores divers. **Range:** Bahamas & Jamaica to C. America & n. S. America.

DRAGONETS (CALLIONYMIDAE): small depressed broad-headed scaleless fishes with two D fins, a large serrated spine on preopercle, and gill openings restricted to a small hole. The first D fin of males is usually enlarged with a colorful and intricate pattern. Dragonets typically live on sandy bottoms and feed on small benthic invertebrates. Most species are intricately but cryptically colored, but a few are spectacular.

11 **Lancer dragonet** *Paradiplogrammus bairdi* (Jordan) 10 cm
Similar to *Diplogrammus pauciradiatus* which has fewer D & A fin soft rays (6 & 4 vs. 9 & 8) & numerous dark spots. **Ecology:** coral reefs with rubble and sand patches, 1 to 10 m. **Range:** s. Fla. & Bermuda to Venezuela.

12 **Spotted dragonet** *Diplogrammus pauciradiatus* (Gill) 5 cm
Ecology: typically occurs in seagrass beds. **Range:** N. Carol., Bermuda to Colombia.

DARTFISHES and WORMFISHES (MICRODESMIDAE): for general introduction see pl. 118

13 **Hovering goby** *Ptereleotris helenae* (Randall) 12 cm
Ecology: sandy or coral rubble bottoms, 3 to 60 m. Hovers head down near burrow. **Range:** s. Fla. & Bahamas to Antilles.

14 **Blue goby** *Ptereleotris calliurus* (Bean) 12 cm
Ecology: open sand, 5 to 50 m. Hovers over burrow. **Range:** s. Fla. to e. G. Mexico.

GOBIES (GOBIIDAE): for general intorduction see pl. 120. Over 120 W. Atlantic spp., only a few conspicuous ones included here.

15 **Frillfin Goby** *Bathygobius soprator* (Valenciennes) 15 cm
Ecology: sandy to muddy bottoms, including seagrass beds, intertidal to 3 m. Abundant. **Range:** Fla., Bermuda & n. G. Mexico to se. Brazil.

16 **Goldspot Goby** *Gnatholepis thompsoni* Jordan 6 cm
Ecology: sand and coral rubble near reefs, 0.5 to 48 m. **Range:** Fla. & Bermuda to n. S. America, e. to Ascension.

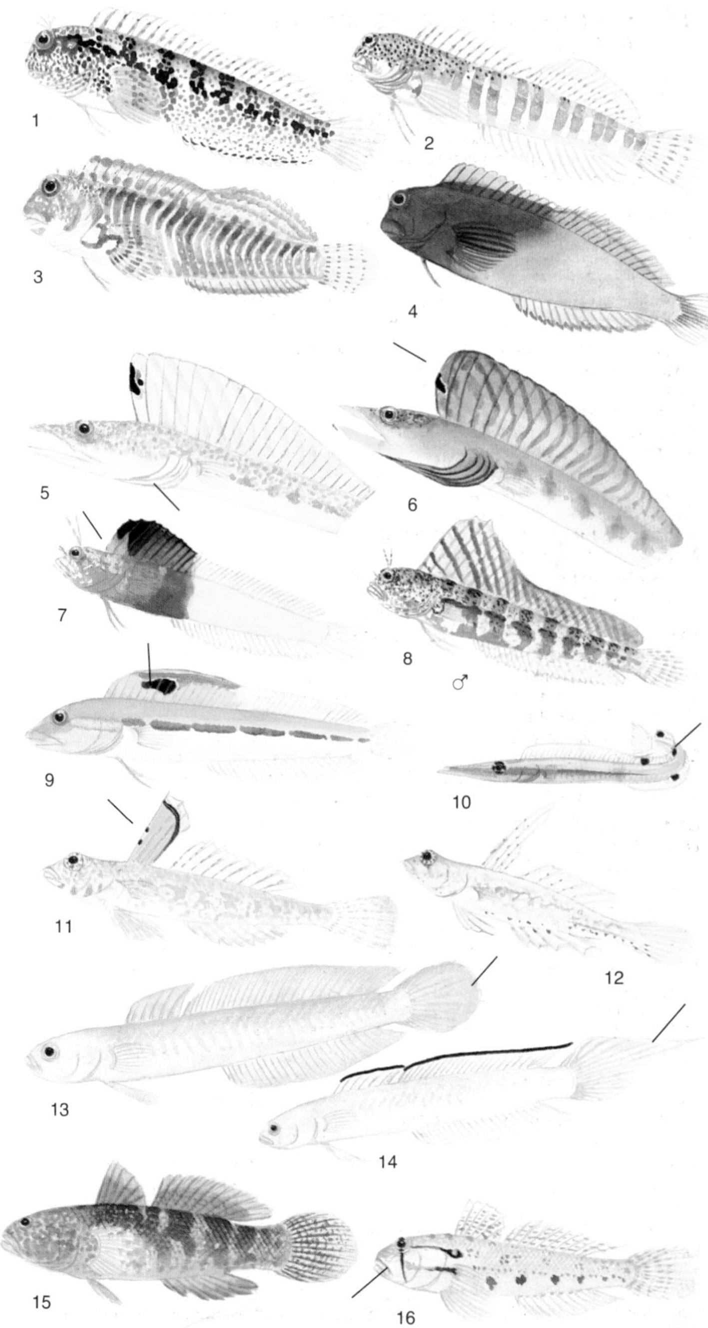
1
2
3
4
5
6
7
8
♂
9
10
11
12
13
14
15
16

171 GOBIES

1 **Nineline goby** *Ginsburgellus novemlineatus* (Fowler) 2.5 cm
Ecology: intertidal rocky shorelines, under sea urchins. **Range:** Bahamas, P. Rico & Cayman Is. to Venezuela.

2 **Sharknose goby** *Priolepis hipoliti* (Metzelaar) 4 cm
Ecology: rocky and coral bottoms, 1 to 126 m. Feeds on minute crustaceans. **Range:** Fla. to Antilles.

3 **Tiger goby** *Gobiosoma macrodon* Beebe & Tee-Van 5 cm
Ecology: on sponges, algae covered rocks and coral heads, 0.3 to 7 m. Shy. **Range:** Fla. to Haiti & Lesser Antilles.

4 **Greenbanded goby** *Gobiosoma multifasciatum* Steindachner 4 cm
Ecology: rocky shorelines and exposed shelves, intertidal to 5 m. Under rocks and among sea urchins. **Range:** Bahamas & Cuba to Venezuela.

5 **Neon goby** *Gobiosoma oceanops* (Jordan) 5 cm
Ecology: in groups near coral heads, 3 to 45 m. A cleaner that picks parasites from other fishes. Not shy. **Range:** s. Florida to Belize & Br. Honduras.

6 **Yellownose goby** *Gobiosoma randalli* Böhlke & Robins 4 cm
Ecology: in groups near coral heads, 5 to 25 m. A cleaner. **Range:** P. Rico & Lesser Antilles to Curaao & Venezuela.

7 **Barsnout goby** *Gobiosoma illecebrosum* Böhlke & Robins 4 cm
Ecology: in groups near coral heads, 10 to 30 m. A cleaner. **Range:** w. and s. Caribbean from Yucatan to Panama.

8 **Yellowprow goby** *Gobiosoma xanthiprora* Böhlke & Robins 4 cm
Ecology: on tube sponges, 7 to 26 m. Readily retreats into sponge. **Range:** N. C. to Jamaica & C. America.

9 **Sharknose goby** *Gobiosoma evelynae* Böhlke & Robins 4 cm
"V" on snout; color variable from bright to pale yellow snout with light blue to yellow stripe. Pale yellow form similar to *G. genie* (Bahamas & Gr. Cayman). **Ecology:** in pairs near coral heads, 10 to 53 m. A cleaner. **Range:** Bahamas to L. Antilles, offshore Is. of Venezuela, w. Carib. & Cuba.

10 **Spotlight goby** *Gobiosoma louisae* Böhlke & Robins 3.5 cm
Ecology: on tube sponges on deep reefs, 13 to 45 m. Shy. **Range:** Bahamas & Grand Cayman.

11 **Broadstripe goby** *Gobiosoma prochilos* Böhlke & Robins 4 cm
Ecology: in groups near coral heads, to 25 m. A cleaner. **Range:** s. Fla. & L. Antilles.

12 **Yellowline goby** *Gobiosoma horsti* Metzelaar 4 cm
Ecology: on tube and vase sponges, 7 to 27 m. Difficult to approach. **Range:** s. Fla., Bahamas to Bonaire

13 **Orangesided goby** *Gobiosoma dilepsis* (Robins & Böhlke) 2.5 cm
Ecology: on sponges and coral heads, 5 to 30 m. **Range:** Bahamas, Cayman Is., Lesser Antilles to C. America & Venezuela.

14 **Shortstripe goby** *Gobiosoma chancei* Beebe & Hollister 3 cm
Ecology: vicinity of tube sponges, 10 to 30 m. **Range:** Bahamas & Antilles to n. Venezuela; absent from C. America.

15 **Seminole goby** *Microgobius carri* Fowler 7.5 cm
Ecology: howers over burrows in open sand bottoms, 6 to 21 m. **Range:** N. C. & e. G. Mexico to Lesser Antilles.

16 **Banner goby** *Microgobius microlepis* Longley & Hildebrand 5 cm
Ecology: in schools near burrows over soft calcareous bottoms, 1 to 5 m. **Range:** s. Fla. & Bahamas to Yucatan & Belize.

17 **Spotfin goby** *Gobionellus stigmalophius* Mead & Böhlke 16 cm
Ecology: sandy and muddy bottoms, 2 to 60 m. Lives in burrows with alpheid shrimps. **Range:** Fla. & Bahamas to Surinam.

18 **Orangespotted goby** *Nes longus* (Nichols) 10 cm
Ecology: silty open bottoms. Lives in burrows with alpheid shrimps. **Range:** s. Fla. & Bermuda to Venezuela.

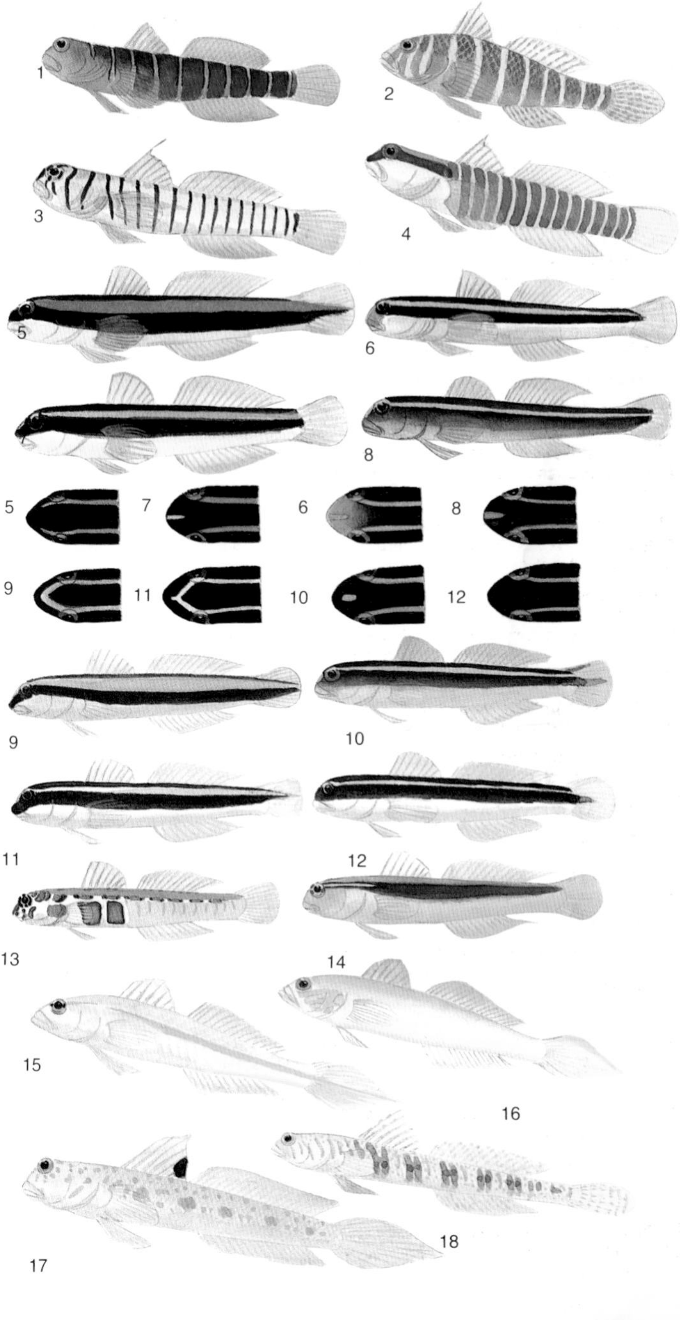
1
2
3
4
5
6
8
5
7
6
8
9
11
10
12
9
10
11
12
13
14
15
16
17
18

1 **Bridled Goby** *Coryphopterus glaucofraenum* Gill 8 cm
Similar to *C. eidolon* but with black spot above opercle & more LS (26-28 vs. 25-26). **Ecology:** rocky, sandy, or seagrass areas, 2 to 45 m. Abundant and ubiquitous. **Range:** N.C. & Bermuda to Brazil.

2 **Pallid Goby** *Coryphopterus eidolon* Böhlke & Robins 6 cm
Ecology: near coral heads, 6 to 30 m. **Range:** s. Fla. & Bahamas to Jamaica & Lesser Antilles.

3 **Colon Goby** *Coryphopterus dicrus* Böhlke & Robins 5 cm
Ecology: sand patches of coral reefs, 3 to 20 m. **Range:** s. Fla. & Bahamas to L. Antilles & C.America.

4 **Masked Goby** *Coryphopterus personatus* (Jordan & Thompson) 4 cm
P 14-16. Similar to *C. lipernes* (P 17) & *C. hyalinus* (both with black ring around anus). **Ecology:** hovers in aggregations above reefs, 3 to 30 m. **Range:** Fla. & Bermuda to Antilles.

SURGEONFISHES (ACANTHURIDAE): ovate compressed fishes with a small terminal mouth containing a single row of small close-set incisiform to lanceolate teeth, continuous D and A fins, complete LL, and a tough skin with minute scales. Atlantic spp. with a pair of sharp blades at the base of the tail which can inflict a deep and painful wound. Diurnal herbivores that scrape algae from hard surfaces and often aggregate with parrotfishes.

5 **Blue tang** *Acanthurus coeruleus* Schneider 23 cm
Juveniles yellow, subadults blue with yellow tails & adults bright blue. **Ecology:** rocky or coral reefs, 3 to 28 m. Solitary or in large aggregations. Unafraid. **Range:** N.Y. (rare n. of Fla.), Bermuda & nw. G. Mexico to Brazil, e. to Ascension

6 **Doctorfish** *Acanthurus chirurgus* (Bloch) 25 cm
Color variable: grey to dark brown but always with faint bars. **Ecology:** in loose aggregations on coral and rocky reefs, 3 to 20 m. **Range:** Mass. & Bermuda to s. Brazil, e. to e. Atlantic; strays to n. G. Mexico.

7 **Ocean surgeon** *Acanthurus bahianus* Castelnau 35 cm
Color variable: grayish blue to dark brown without bars; tail lunate. Similar to *A. randalli* which has squiggly lateral pinstripes. **Ecology:** reef flats to slopes, 3 to 20 m. Frequently associated with the doctorfish. **Range:** Mass., Bermuda & nw. G. Mexico to Brazil, e. to Ascension, St. Helena & e. Atlantic; replaced by *A. randalli* in ne. G. Mexico.

8 **Gulf surgeonfish** *Acanthurus randalli* Briggs & Caldwell 18 cm
Ecology: coral reefs, banks, and shallow rubble and hard-bottomed areas. **Range:** Miami & Fla. Keys to ne. G. Mexico.

FLATFISHES (ORDER PLEURONECTIFORMES): highly compressed fishes that live with one side flat against the bottom. Both eyes are located on the upper pigmented side and the other side is unpigmented. The pigmented side is capable of remarkable color changes in order to match the bottom. Predators of benthic invertebrates and fishes.

BOTHIDAE (LEFTEYE FLOUNDERS): both eyes on left side. 48 spp. in region, few on reefs.

9 **Eyed Flounder** *Bothus ocellatus* (Agassiz) 15 cm
Pale brown with rings and spots; 2 dark spots at base of tail. Similar to *Paralichthys* spp. which are more elongate: *P. albigutta* (N.C. & Bahamas to Texas) has three dark ocelli & *P. tropicus* (s. Carib. cont. shelf) has numerous large dark spots. **Ecology:** sandy areas with coral rubble or seagrasses, generally near patch reefs, 1 to 20 m. Common but cryptic. Lies motionless on bottom, moving only when frightened. **Range:** N.Y. & Bermuda to Brazil.

10 **Peacock Flounder** *Bothus lunatus* (Linnaeus) 45 cm
Distinctive blue rings on pale background; 2-3 dark blotches along LL. **Ecology:** common in clear sandy areas near mangroves, among seagrasses, rubble or coral, 1 to 100 m. Often partially burried in sand, occasionally on hard bottoms. **Range:** Fla. & Bermuda to Brazil, e. to Ascension & e. Atlantic.

1
2
3
4
5
6
juv
var
6 var
7
8
9
10

173 TRIGGERFISHES and FILEFISHES

TRIGGERFISHES (BALISTIDAE): somewhat deep-bodied, compressed fishes with eyes set high on head, a small terminal mouth with large stout incisiform teeth, the first D fin with a large spike-like first spine and two smaller spines, all of which fit into a groove, second D and A fins with only rays, pelvic fin reduced to a spinous knob, and large non-overlapping armor-like scales. The first D spine locks into position and can be depressed only by depressing the second "trigger" spine. Most species feed on a wide variety of invertebrates, some also feed on algae or zooplankton. Triggerfishes lay demersal eggs in a sandy depression, guarded by the male. Popular in aquariums, but often ill-tempered.

1 **Queen triggerfish** *Balistes vetula* Linnaeus 60 cm
Color variable: green, blue to yellowish. Blue lines on head and vertical fins. **Ecology:** coral reefs, in sandy and rubble areas, 2 to >53 m. Feeds on the sea urchin *Diadema antillarium* by blowing water under it to overturn it and attack where the spines are short. **Range:** Mass., Bermuda & n. G. Mexico to Brazil, e. to Ascension & e. Atlantic.

2 **Black durgeon** *Melichthys niger* (Bloch) 50 cm
Under water black with two distinctive white stripes. **Ecology:** in groups on seaward reefs, 5 to 60 m, usually m. Feeds on zooplankton (including salps, crabs and pteropods) or detached and attached benthic algae. **Range:** circumtropical; Fla., Bermuda & n. G. Mexico to Brazil in W. Atlantic; also Ascension.

3 **Sargassum triggerfish** *Xanthichthys ringens* (Linnaeus) 25 cm
Bluish gray with orange margins on tail; 3 black lines below eye. **Ecology:** seaward reef slopes, 25 to 80 m, abundant below 30 m. Solitary or in small groups. Feeds on crabs and sea urchins. Juveniles in floating *Sargassum* weed. Courtship: horizontal, cross and spiral swimming pattern. Spawns in deep water. **Range:** N. C. & Bermuda to Brazil.

4 **Gray triggerfish** *Balistes capriscus* Gmelin 30 cm
Grayish-olive with marbled brown markings; young with dark saddles. **Ecology:** bays, harbors, lagoons and seaward reefs, 5 to 30 m. Feeds on bottom dwelling invertebrates, especially mollusks. Solitary or in small groups. May drift with young at surface among dense *Sargassum* weed. Unafraid. **Range:** N. Scotia, Bermuda & n. G. Mexico to Argentina, e. to e. Atlantic. & Mediterranean.

5 **Ocean triggerfish** *Canthidermis sufflamen* (Mitchill) 65 cm
Brownish gray with a distinctive black blotch at base of P fin. **Ecology:** common near seaward reef dropoffs, 12 to 40 m. Solitary or in small groups in open water. Often associated with *Sargassum* weed. Nests in sand channels at outer edge of reef. **Range:** Fla., Bermuda & n. G. Mexico banks to Argentina, e. to St. Paul's Rocks, Ascension, St. Helena & C. Verde Is.

6 **Rough triggerfish** *Canthidermis maculatus* (Bloch) 52 cm
Olive-brown to gray with small white spots. **Ecology:** pelagic, uncommon on deep rocky reefs, 15 to 110 m. Forages in the water column in small groups near the surface. **Range:** circumtropical; N. C. to Argentina, in W. Atlantic; St. Helena.

FILEFISHES and LEATHERJACKETS (MONACANTHIDAE): closely related to triggerfishes but have more compressed bodies, one or two D spines (the second minute), and much smaller scales, each with setae giving the skin a file-like texture. Most species feed on a wide variety of invertebrates, but some specialize on corals or zooplankton. Filefishes lay demersal eggs in a site prepared by the male. See also pl. 135-2 for *A. monoceros*.

7 **Scrawled filefish** *Aluterus scriptus* (Osbeck) 110 cm
Color variable: olive, brown or gray with blue lines and spots. Similar to *A. heudeloti* (Mass. to Brazil & W. Africa but not W. Indies) which has more blue lines on head but fewer on belly. **Ecology:** lagoon and seaward reefs, 2 to 80 m. Solitary and common, often in open water. Feeds on attached organisms including algae, seagrasses, fire corals (*Millepora*) and gorgonians. Wary. **Range:** circumtropical, Nova Scotia to Brazil in W. Atlantic.

8 **Orange filefish** *Aluterus schoepfi* (Walbaum) 50 cm
Brown or gray with numerous orange dots; black mouth. **Ecology:** seagrass beds and sand or mud bottoms, occasionally on coral reefs, 3 to 15 m. Juveniles live in floating *Sargassum* weed. Solitary or in pairs. Feeds primarily on algae and seagrasses, occasionally on invertebrates. **Range:** Nova Scotia & Bermuda to Brazil.

1
2
3
4
5
6
7
8

1 **Whitespotted filefish** *Cantherhines macrocerus* (Hollard) 42 cm
White not always present; tail black, sometimes with white bars. **Ecology:** lagoon and seaward reefs, 5 to 25 m. Uncommon, generally in pairs among gorgonians. Feeds mainly on sponges, algae and gorgonians. Secretive. **Range:** Fla. & Bermuda to Brazil, e. to St. Paul's Rocks.

2 **Orangespotted filefish** *Cantherhines pullus* (Ranzani) 20 cm
Color variable; white spots on caudal peduncle always present. **Ecology:** along shoreline and on lagoon and seaward reefs, 5 to 50 m. Feeds on sponges, tunicates and algae. Usually remains near the bottom, hiding among gorgonians or branching corals. Secretive, retreats into holes or crevices when approached. Common. **Range:** Mass. & Bermuda to Brazil; e. to W. Africa.

3 **Slender filefish** *Monacanthus tuckeri* Bean 10 cm
Brownish with a reticulate pattern; dark or pale; tail base with 2 prs. of spines. **Ecology:** shallow offshore reefs, seagrass beds or coral rubble areas, 2 to 20 m. Drifts among gorgonians. Feeds on algae and small invertebrates. **Range:** N.J. & Bermuda to Lesser Antilles.

4 **Fringed filefish** *Monacanthus ciliatus* (Mitchill) 14 cm
Color variable: green, tan or brownish with irregular stripes; tail base with 2 prs. of spines. **Ecology:** seagrass beds, over coral rubble and sandy bottoms. Often seen moving head down among grass blades. Feeds mainly on crustaceans. Common. **Range:** Newfoundland & Bermuda to Argentina, e. to e. Atlantic.

5 **Pygmy filefish** *Stephanolepis setifer* (Bennett) 19 cm
Dark dashes on sides; ♂ with long D fin ray. Similar to *S. hispidus* (N. Scotia to Brazil) which lacks small dark spots on the head and belly; tail base without enlarged spines. **Ecology:** coastal lagoons with seagrass beds and coral rubble. **Range:** N. C. & Bermuda to Brazil.

TRUNKFISHES (OSTRACIIDAE): boxlike fishes encased in a carapace of bony polygonal plates with gaps for the mouth, eyes, gill openings, anus, fins, and tail. Many species with angular ridges and spines. The mouth is small with stout conical to incisiform teeth used for feeding on small sessile invertebrates and algae. Trunkfishes secrete a highly toxic substance from the skin (ostracitoxin) which protects them from predation. They are territorial and haremic, spawning pelagic eggs at dusk.

6 **Honeycomb cowfish** *Acanthostracion polygonius* Poey 48 cm
Honeycomb pattern of hexagons and pentagons; 2 spines above eyes. **Ecology:** offshore reefs, 3 to 80 m. Feeds on sponges, alcyonarians, tunicates and shrimps. Uncommon and wary, blends in with background. **Range:** N.J., Bermuda south to Brazil (absent from Gulf of Mexico); replaced by *A. notacanthus* at Ascension, St. Helena, Azores & e. Atlantic.

7 **Scrawled cowfish** *Acanthostracion quadricornis* (Linnaeus) 48 cm
Yellowish with blue lines and scrawls; 2 spines above eyes. **Ecology:** common on seagrass beds, occasionally on offshore reefs, 2 to 25 m. Feeds on sessile invertebrates such as tunicates, sea anemones or sponges. Wary. **Range:** Mass., Bermuda & n. G. Mexico to Brazil.

8 **Spotted trunkfish** *Lactophrys bicaudalis* (Linnaeus) 45 cm
Grayish with numerous dark brown spots & whitish area behind eye. **Ecology:** rocky and coral reefs, 3 to 20 m. Sometimes under ledges and near small holes. Feeds on tunicates, sea cucumbers, sea urchins and seagrasses. Uncommon and wary. **Range:** Fla. Keys, Bahamas & s. G. Mexico to Brazil.

9 **Smooth trunkfish** *Lactophrys triqueter* (Linnaeus) 30 cm
Dusky ground color with numerous white spots & yellowish midlateral area. **Ecology:** common on reefs with sandy patches, 3 to 25 m. Solitary or in small groups. Easily approached. Feeds on benthic invertebrates exposed by a jet of water ejected through the mouth. **Range:** Mass., Bermuda & n. G. Mexico banks to Brazil.

10 **Buffalo trunkfish** *Lactophrys trigonus* (Linnaeus) 45 cm
Color variable, usually olive with 2 dark blotches. **Ecology:** seagrass beds, coral rubble areas and offshore reefs, 2 to 50 m. **Range:** Mass., Bermuda to Brazil.

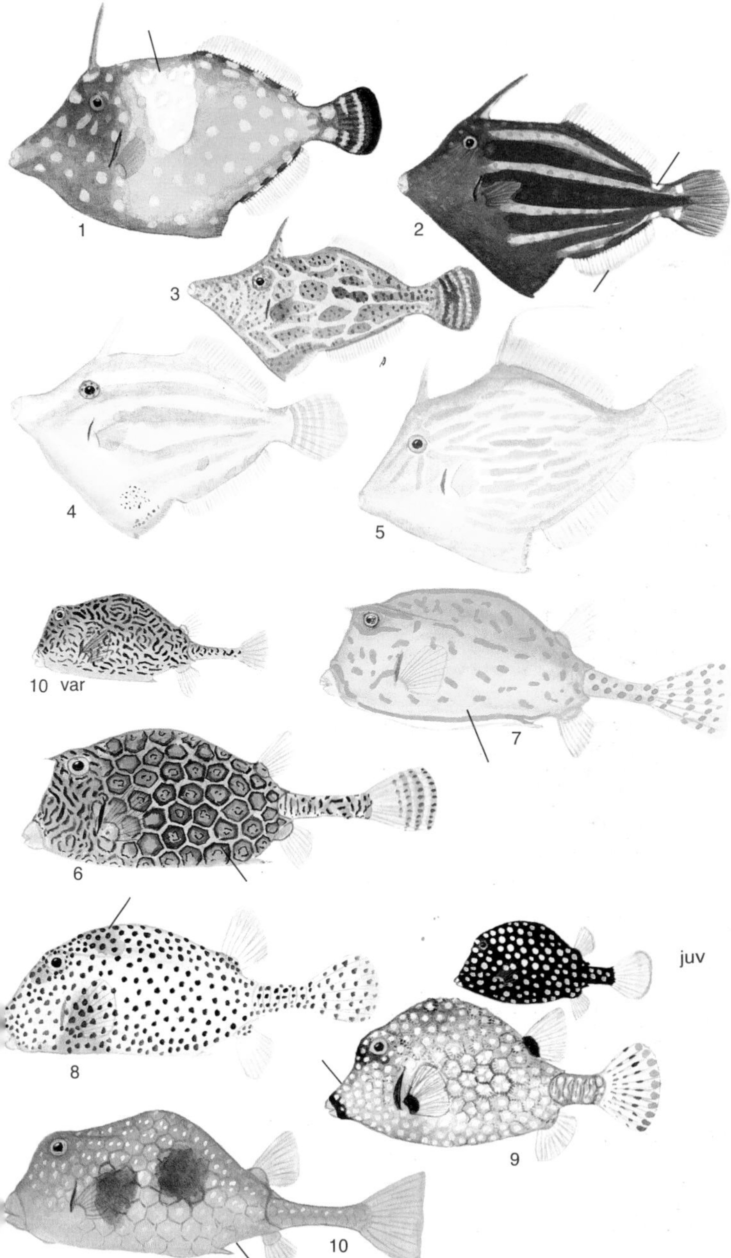
1
2
3
4
5
10 var
7
6
8
juv
9
10

175 PUFFERS and PORCUPINEFISHES

PUFFERS (TETRAODONTIDAE): moderately elongate bulbous fishes with a tough flexible scaleless and prickly skin, small mouth with teeth fused into a beak with a median suture, a small single D fin and no fin spines, pelvic fins, or ribs. Most species without LL. Capable of greatly inflating themselves with water. Viscera, gonads, and skin of most species highly cardiotoxic. Demersal eggs laid in nest. All tropical and temperate seas, some in freshwater.
Subfamily Canthigasterinae: elongate pointed snout with 1 pair of nostrils; all <15 cm.

1 **Sharpnose puffer** *Canthigaster rostrata* (Bloch) 11cm
Adults with brown back, juveniles with orange back. **Ecology:** reef flats, seagrass beds, and coral reefs, 1 to 30 m. Feeds on seagrass tips and benthic invertebrates including sponges, worms, and crustaceans. Common and unafraid. **Range:** Fla., Bermuda & n. G. Mexico banks to Venezuela; replaced by *C. sanctaehelenae* at Ascension & St. Helena.

Subfamily Tetraodontinae: short blunt snout with 2 pairs of nostrils; most spp. >23 cm.

2 **Bandtail puffer** *Sphoeroides spengleri* (Bloch) 18 cm
Dark spots from mouth to tail; 2 dark bands on tail. **Ecology:** reef flats, seagrass beds and seaward reefs, 2 to 30 m. Usually close to the bottom where they feed on benthic invertebrates. Common. **Range:** Mass., Bermuda & n. G. Mexico to Brazil;

3 **Caribbean puffer** *Sphoeroides greeleyi* Gilbert 15 cm
Numerous dark brown spots on pale background; 3 bars on tail. **Ecology:** common over muddy and sometimes sandy bottoms. Prefers turbid water. **Range:** Caribbean to Brazil.

4 **Checkered puffer** *Sphoeroides testudineus* (Linnaeus) 30 cm
Reticulated pattern with olive squares or polygons. **Ecology:** primarily in bays, tidal creeks and protected seagrass beds, including brackish water. Rarely on coral reefs to 48 m. Hides in sand when frightened. **Range:** R. Is., Bermuda & s. G. Mexico to s. Brazil.

5 **Southern puffer** *Sphoeroides nephelus* (Goode & Bean) 30 cm
Tan with dark rings or semicircles. **Ecology:** seagrass beds and tidal creeks of protected coastal waters and bays, 0 to 11 m. **Range:** ne. Fla., Bahamas & n. G. Mexico to Lesser Antilles.
PORCUPINEFISHES (DIODONTIDAE): similar to puffers, but have prominent spines over the head and body, larger eyes, an inconspicuous LL, and lack the suture on the beak. When inflated, adults are nearly impossible for any predator to eat. Feed primarily on hard-shelled invertebrates crushed by the beak. Eggs are pelagic.

6 **Porcupinefish** *Diodon histrix* Linnaeus 90 cm
Spines of *Diodon* 2-rooted and moveable; this sp. with small dark spots on body and fins. Similar to *D. eydouxi* which is exclusively pelagic. **Ecology:** shallow rocky or coral reefs, 2 to 25 m. Usually in holes and recesses during the day. Feeds in the open primarily during the night on hard-shelled invertebrates, primarily gastropods and hermit crabs. Juveniles pelagic. Common. **Range:** circumtropical; Mass. & Bermuda to Brazil in W. Atlantic.

7 **Balloonfish** *Diodon holocanthus* Linnaeus 50 cm
4 dark brown blotches on back; fins without spots. **Ecology:** shallow seaward reefs and lagoons with seagrasses and patch reefs, 2 to 25 m. A poor swimmer. Feeds on hard-shelled invertebrates. Sometimes in groups. **Range:** nearly circumtropical; Fla. & Bermuda to Brazil in W. Atlantic.

8 **Web burrfish** *Cyclichthys antillarum* (Jordan & Rutter) 25 cm
Spines of *Cyclichthys* 3-rooted and always erect. **Ecology:** coral reefs with adjacent seagreass and rubble areas, 1 to 44 m. Uncommon. **Range:** Fla. & Bahamas to Venezuela.

9 **Bridled burrfish** *Cyclichthys antennatus* (Cuvier) 23 cm
Ecology: uncommon in seagrass beds, rarely on adjacent reefs, 2 to 13 m. **Range:** s. Fla. & Bahamas to Venezuela.

10 **Striped burrfish** *Cyclichthys schoepfi* (Walbaum) 25 cm
Ecology: seagrass beds of bays and lagoons and shallow coastal reefs to 11 m. Common in Florida. **Range:** N. England (rare n. of Carolinas) to Brazil, absent from W. Indies.

1
1 juv
2
3
4
5
6
7
8
9
10

Suggested Further Reading

The following titles have been selected for their accuracy, completeness and overall usefulness for identifying coral reef fishes.

Indo-Pacific

Allen, G. R. and R. Swainston, 1988. Marine Fishes of North-western Australia. W. Australian Museum, Perth, 201 p., 1,200 col.

ditto 1992. Reef Fishes of New Guinea. Christensen Research Institute, Madang, Papua New Guinea, 120 p.

Kuiter, R. H. 1992. Tropical Reef Fishes of the Western Pacific: Indonesia and Adjacent Waters. Gramedia, Jakarta, 314 p., 1,300 col.

Masuda, H. K. Amaoka, C. Araga, T. Uyeno, and T. Yoshino. 1984. Fishes of the Japanese Archipelago. Tokai Univ. Press, Tokyo, 437 p.+ 3,700 col.

Myers, R. F. 1991. Micronesian Reef Fishes, 2nd ed. Coral Graphics, Guam USA, 298 p.+ 975 col.

Randall, J. E. 1985. Hawaiian Reef Fishes. Harrowood, Newton Square, PA, 79 p. +177 col.

ditto 1983. Red Sea Reef Fishes. IMMEL, London, 192 p., 465 col.

ditto 1992. Diver's Guide to Fishes of the Maldives. IMMEL, London, 193 p., 400+ col.

Randall, J. E., G. R. Allen, and R. C. Steene, 1990. Fishes of the Great Barrier Reef and Coral Sea. Crawford House, Australia, 507 p., 1,100 col. (Univ. of Hawaii Press in USA).

Smith, M. M., and P.C. Heemstra, eds., 1986. Smith's Sea Fishes. McMillan, Johanesburg, 1,047 p. + 2,000 col.

Tropical West Atlantic/Caribbean

Böhlke, J. E. and C. C. G. Chaplin, 1992. Fishes of the Bahamas and Adjacent Tropical Waters, 2nd ed. Univ. Texas Press, 771 p.+ 36 pls.

Humann, P. 1989. Reef Fish Identification. New World Publ., Jacksonville, FL, 272 p., 365 col.

Randall, J. E. 1968. Caribbean Reef Fishes. TFH, Neptune, NJ., 318 p., 400 col. & b/w.

Robins, C. R, G. C. Ray, J. Douglass, and R. Freund. 1986. A Field Guide to Atlantic Coast Fishes of North America. Houghton Mifflin, Boston, 354 p.+ 64 pls.

Systematic works

Allen, G. R. 1991. Damselfishes of the World. Aquarium Systems, Mentor, Ohio, 271 p., 320 col.

Allen, G. R. 1985. Butterfly and Angel Fishes of the World, vol. 2, 3rd ed. Aquarium Systems, Mentor, Ohio, 352 p., ca. 400 col.

Fautin, D. G. and G. R. Allen, 1992. Field Guide to Anemonefishes and their Host Anemones. W. Australian Museum, Perth, 160 p., ca. 130 col.

Johnson, R. H. 1978. Sharks of Polynesia. Les éditions du Pacifique, Papeete, Tahiti. 170 p.

Michael, S. W. 1993. Sharks and Rays of the World. Sea Challengers, Monterey, 107 p., ca. 165 col.

Randall, J. E. 1986. Sharks of Arabia. IMMEL, London.

Steene, R. C. 1978. Butterfly and Angel Fishes of the World, vol. 1: Australia. Aquarium Systems, Mentor, Ohio, 144 p., ca. 100 col.

Scientific Index

The initial number refers to the Plate, the second to the entry on that Plate

Common Name Index

The number refers to the Plate

INDO-PACIFIC SPECIES

ATLANTIC SPECIES